Complete Book of
Low-fat Cooking

By the Editors of Sunset Books

Sunset Publishing Corporation • Menlo Park, CA

Sunset
BOOKS

President & Publisher: Susan J. Maruyama
Director, Sales & Marketing: Richard A. Smeby
Director, New Business: Kenneth Winchester
Editorial Director: Bob Doyle
Production Director: Lory Day
Art Director: Vasken Guiragossian

EDITORIAL STAFF FOR THE COMPLETE BOOK
OF LOW-FAT COOKING

Developmental Editor: Linda J. Selden
Research & Text: Karyn I. Lipman
Copy Editors: Rebecca LaBrum, Fran Feldman
Contributing Editors: Cynthia Overbeck Bix, Sue Brownlee
Illustrations: Dick Cole
Dietary Consultant: Patricia Kearney, R.D.
Stanford University Hospital
Photo Stylists: Sandra Griswold, Susan Massey
Food Stylists: Heidi Gintner, Cynthia Scheer
Assistant Food & Photo Stylist: Elizabeth C. Davis
Photography: Keith Ovregaard—27, 30, 70, 75, 78, 83, 86,
107, 118, 126, 155, 158, 166, 187, 190, 267, 291;
Allan Rosenberg—3, 51, 54, 67, 94, 99, 102, 110, 115, 123,
131, 134, 142, 150, 163, 174, 179, 182, 195, 198, 203, 206, 211,
214, 219, 222, 227, 230, 235, 238, 243, 246, 254, 259, 262, 270,
275, 278, 283, 286, 294, 299, 302, 307, 310, 315, 318, 323, 331,
350, 355, 363, 366, 374, 379, 382, 387, 390, 398, 403, 406, 419,
422; Darrow M. Watt—43; Tom Wyatt—22;
Nikolay Zurek—6, 14, 19, 35, 38, 46, 59, 62, 91, 139,
171, 251, 334, 339, 342, 358, 371, 411, 414
Associate Photographer: Allen V. Lott
Production Coordinator: Patricia S. Williams

SUNSET PUBLISHING CORPORATION

Chairman: Jim Nelson
President & Chief Executive Officer: Stephen J. Seabolt
Chief Financial Officer: James E. Mitchell
Publisher, Sunset Magazine: Anthony P. Glaves
Director of Finance: Larry Diamond
Vice President, Manufacturing: Lorinda B. Reichert
Editor, Sunset Magazine: William R. Marken
Senior Editor, Food & Entertaining: Jerry Anne Di Vecchio

PRODUCED BY ROUNDTABLE PRESS, INC.

Directors: Susan E. Meyer, Marsha Melnick
Editor: Maryanne Bannon
Design: Laura Smyth, smythtype

Great Taste—The Low-fat Way

The benefits of a low-fat diet are daily touted in headlines, news reports, and popular television programs. While we may want to take good care of ourselves and our families, we also want to enjoy great taste and a variety of foods. Can you do both? Absolutely! Is there a one-stop cookbook that will deliver healthy, low-fat recipes and mouth-watering results? Positively!

With over 500 recipes, the *Complete Book of Low-Fat Cooking* encompasses culinary traditions from around the world, quick and easy recipes for hectic days, lavish main entrées, elegant desserts, casual snacks, vegetarian dishes, and traditional favorites. Choose from hundreds of deliciously streamlined entrées and sample exotic Kung Pao Chicken, a trim Italian Osso Bucco, or cinnamon-spiced Snapper Veracruz. Whip up a light dinner of Linguine with Yellow Tomatoes in less than 30 minutes or lavishly entertain guests with lean Beef Tenderloin with Cabernet-Cherry Sauce. A wonderful array of low-fat, full-flavored side dishes will complement everything from the simplest fare to the most exotic entrées. In our "sweets" chapters you'll find fudgy brownies, creamy cheesecakes, luscious pies, and velvety puddings—delectably "lightened" by clever ingredient choices and substitutions. A grand finale of Apricot-Amaretto Torte is worthy of any special occasion while Chocolate Cherry Brownies are wonderful lunch-box treats. Enticing appetizers, satisfying soups, crunchy salads, and fresh-baked breads complete the array of temptingly delicious foods you can enjoy as part of a low-fat lifestyle.

The recipes in this book conform to the American Heart Association's recommendations for fat intake; in each, fat accounts for no more than 30% of the total calories. Every recipe is accompanied by a nutritional analysis (see page 5) prepared by Hill Nutrition Associates, Inc., of Florida. We are grateful to Lynne Hill, R.D., for her advice and expertise.

Each recipe also lists preparation and cooking times. Keep in mind that these times are approximate and will vary, depending on your expertise in the kitchen and the cooking equipment you use.

The recipes in this book were developed in the Sunset Test Kitchens. If you have comments or suggestions, please let us hear from you. Write to us at:

Sunset Books/Cookbook Editorial
80 Willow Road
Menlo Park, CA 94025

Front cover: *Stuffed Shells with Roasted Red Pepper Sauce (page 266).
Photography by Chris Shorten. Food styling by Heidi Gintner.*

Contents

Tricolor Pepper Sauté (recipe on page 309)

Special Features

Introduction

Walk down any supermarket aisle and you can't help but notice the brightly colored labels with big letters highlighting "nonfat," "low-fat," and "reduced-fat" selections. While these labels appeal to our good intentions to reduce dietary fat, they don't give the big picture on how to do so. With over 500 recipes, this is your one-stop solution—the *Complete Book of Low-Fat Cooking*.

You want to take good care of yourself and your family but you also want to take pleasure in a diverse variety of foods deliciously prepared. Can you do both? Absolutely! Farm-fresh vegetables, lushly ripe fruits, savory legumes, and wholesome grains are all items you expect to find on a low-fat menu. With smart shopping, ingenious substitutions, and clever cooking techniques, you'll also enjoy succulent meats, creamy pastas, and lavish desserts. There are no "forbidden" foods, just healthy methods of food preparation. And you'll be assured of following the American Heart Association's recommendations for fat intake; in each recipe, fat provides no more than 30% of the total calories.

Supermarket shelves stocked with rows of pasta, salsas, chiles, soy sauce, and water chestnuts reveal just a few of the culinary traditions that have been incorporated into our everyday cooking. As you look through this book, you'll see that we've borrowed from many international cuisines. Not only are their vibrant flavors ideal for lean meals but they add interest and excitement to daily fare with tantalizingly unique and delicious taste experiences. While some dishes required a bit of adaptation to fit a low-fat cooking style, they all deliver authentic taste. And for those who would like to experiment in a different direction, our meatless main entrées offer hearty and flavorful satisfaction. Our recipes were designed for ovo-vegetarians—those who eat dairy products and eggs but no meat, poultry, and fish. You'll find that Chile Pot Pie with its flaky crust or Polenta Gnocchi with Dried Tomato Chutney flavored with robust Parmesan cheese are tempting main meals for anyone.

Smart Shopping

By developing a few new shopping habits, you'll be well on your way to a low-fat lifestyle.

Fish is naturally lean and so is poultry—with one caveat. While poultry skin is wonderful insulation for ensuring moist juicy results, it is high in fat. Before eating, discard the skin for an extra-lean entrée. When purchasing red meat, look for the leanest cuts and trim away all visible fat before cooking.

Fresh vegetables and fruits are low in fat and provide important nutrients and fiber. Their bright colors and crunchy texture add visual appeal and interest to any dish. For best results, especially in stir-frys, buy the best quality available; wrinkled, dried-out items are past their peak flavor and sure to disappoint.

When purchasing dairy products such as milk, yogurt, and sour cream, opt for the nonfat, low-fat, and reduced-fat choices so readily available. Among cheeses, there are some marvelous reduced-fat and low-fat varieties of Cheddar, Monterey Jack, mozzarella, ricotta, and cream cheese from which to choose. We also favor modest amounts of whole-milk types such as Gorgonzola, Parmesan, feta, and fontina; these are all so assertive that a small amount makes a significant contribution to a recipe's flavor.

If you would like to cut sodium as well as fat, buy reduced-sodium broths, soy sauce, and canned vegetables. And check labels. Many tomato products, for instance, have no salt added but are not specifically labeled as such.

Cutting Fat

Fat does marvelous things in cooking and baking. It carries and deepens flavor and it provides moisture for crumbly cakes and flaky pie crusts, insulation for succulent meats, and creaminess for velvety puddings. It also provides luxurious "mouth-feel" to the palate. How do we cut fat and guarantee great taste? We take advantage of naturally lean ingredients and the new assortment of nonfat, low-fat, and reduced-fat selections. And by employing a few "tricks," we reduce fat but retain full flavor and tantalizing texture.

In our baked goods, applesauce, mashed bananas, fruit purée, jelly, and/or jam is often added to intensify flavor and balance moisture when butter or another fatty ingredient is reduced or eliminated. And when eggs are called for, we use fewer whole eggs and more egg whites, so our cakes, puddings, and soufflés are just as light and fluffy as the whole-fat versions. The same substitution is also made in many savory recipes with equally delicious results.

To make up for the flavor traditionally contributed by fat, we turn to vibrant, aromatic herbs such as oregano, basil, cilantro, and thyme; piquant spices like nutmeg, cinnamon, and ginger; and zesty vinegars and intensely flavored condiments. All add excitement—but little or no fat—to lean dishes.

One easy way to cut a recipe's percentage of calories from fat is to include a healthy helping of pasta, rice, or legumes. Mild-flavored and rich in complex carbohydrates, these filling foods take well to a variety of sauces and spices.

Cooking Techniques

Baking, broiling, grilling, and steaming are the standard low-fat cooking methods, and all are represented in this book. By adapting certain recipes to these techniques, they can be enjoyed on a low-fat menu. In our deliciously streamlined Eggplant Parmesan we bake crumb-coated eggplant slices instead of frying for crispy, low-fat results.

Many of our recipes also feature braise-deglazing, a lean version of sautéing used to develop a flavorful base of cooked onions or other vegetables for a variety of dishes. To braise-deglaze, you simply omit some or all of the fat you'd typically use for pan-frying, instead adding a little water or broth to the vegetables you want to cook. Stir the mixture over medium to medium-high heat until the vegetables begin to brown and the liquid is gone; then stir in a bit more liquid, gently scraping free any browned bits sticking to the pan bottom. Repeat the process until the vegetables are as soft and browned as you like. Although braise-deglazing doesn't brown foods as quickly as sautéing does, you'll find that vegetables cooked in this way have every bit as much deep, rich flavor and color as those cooked in fat.

Although stir-frying is not synonymous with low-fat cooking, it is easily adaptable and ideal for lean meals. We use a bare minimum of fat—or sometimes none at all. Numerous recipes simply replace the fat with a little water; the liquid is fat-free but keeps foods from sticking and aids in browning, too. To keep oil to a minimal amount, we use nonstick pans—and that means we never heat the pan before adding fat, nor do we cook over high heat. Doing either can damage nonstick coatings.

Using our Recipes

When you follow our recipes, you may want to make substitutions to achieve the flavor you like. In some cases, you may decide to use products higher in fat or sodium than those we specify; perhaps you prefer part-skim ricotta cheese to the nonfat versions, or regular canned broth to the reduced-sodium type. Just be aware that such substitutions will boost the fat or sodium content of the finished dish.

Another point to consider is that low-fat does not always mean low-calorie. If you're trying to lose weight on a calorie-controlled diet, be aware of your daily limit and select foods accordingly. Many of the recipes in this book will fit right into your plan, but some are high enough in calories to qualify as occasional treats.

Remember that the preparation and cooking times given in our recipes are guides, not absolutes. Actual times will vary, depending on your level of expertise and the type of heat source and cookware you have. Even the size and freshness of the fruits and vegetables you use will affect cooking times.

A Word About Our Nutritional Data

For our recipes, we provide a nutritional analysis stating calorie count; percentage of calories from fat; grams of total fat and saturated fat; milligrams of cholesterol and sodium; grams of carbohydrates, fiber, and protein; and milligrams of calcium and iron. Generally, the analysis applies to a single serving, based on the number of servings given for each recipe and the amount of each ingredient. If a range is given for the number of servings and/or the amount of an ingredient, the analysis is based on the average of the figures given.

The nutritional analysis does not include optional ingredients or those for which no specific amount is stated. If an ingredient is listed with a substitution, the information was calculated using the first choice.

Black Bean & Fresh Corn Nachos
(recipe on page 8)

Appetizers

Appetizers are marvelously versatile foods—serving as elegant first courses at dinner parties, casual snacks at impromptu get-togethers, or satisfying accompaniments to soups and salads. Our streamlined recipes rely on lots of fresh ingredients, clever seasonings, and low-fat cooking techniques to entice the palate with vibrant flavor. Enjoy piquant White Bean & Roasted Garlic Bruschetta with soup or present tangy Chili Shrimp as an excitingly different shrimp cocktail.

Though created north of the border, this colorful entrée or appetizer was inspired by three Mexican staples: black beans, corn, and tortillas.

About 1½ cups (360 ml) Lime Salsa (page 21)

Refried Black Beans (page 148)

4 cups (660 g) cooked yellow or white corn kernels (from 4 large ears corn); or 2 packages (about 10 oz./285 g *each*) frozen corn kernels, thawed

1 cup (about 4 oz./115 g) shredded jalapeño jack cheese

About 12 cups (510 g) water-crisped corn tortilla chips (page 346) or purchased tortilla chips

Cilantro leaves

Black Bean & Fresh Corn Nachos

....
Preparation time: About 20 minutes
Cooking time: About 25 minutes
Pictured on page 6

1. Prepare Lime Salsa and refrigerate.

2. Prepare Refried Black Beans. Spoon beans onto a large, ovenproof rimmed platter; spread out evenly to make an oval. Top beans evenly with corn, then sprinkle with cheese. Bake in a 400°F (205°C) oven until hot in center (about 10 minutes).

3. Remove bean mixture from oven. Tuck some of the tortilla chips around edge of platter; serve remaining chips alongside. Garnish with cilantro.

4. To serve, spoon bean mixture onto plates; top with some of the Lime Salsa. To eat, scoop bean mixture onto chips; add more salsa to taste. Makes 12 appetizer or 8 main-dish servings.

Per serving: 423 calories (24% calories from fat), 12 g total fat, 4 g saturated fat, 22 mg cholesterol, 668 mg sodium, 67 g carbohydrates, 9 g fiber, 18 g protein, 243 mg calcium, 3 mg iron

---

Rich sharp Parmesan adds tangy flavor to this creamy artichoke gratin.

1 long, slender baguette (about 8 oz./230 g, about 25 inches/ 63 cm long), cut diagonally into 24 slices

½ cup (40 g) grated Parmesan cheese

1 large package (about 8 oz./ 230 g) Neufchâtel cheese or regular cream cheese, at room temperature

¾ cup (158 g) low-fat (2%) cottage cheese

1 cup (240 ml) nonfat sour cream

⅛ teaspoon dried dill weed (or to taste)

2 cans (about 14 oz./400 g *each*) artichoke hearts, drained and chopped

Hot Artichoke Appetizer

....
Preparation time: 10 minutes
Cooking time: 50 to 55 minutes

1. Arrange bread slices in a single layer (overlapping as little as possible) in shallow 10- by 15-inch (25- by 38-cm) baking pans. Bake in a 325°F (165°C) oven until crisp and tinged with brown (15 to 20 minutes). Transfer toast to a rack to cool.

2. In a large bowl, combine Parmesan cheese, Neufchâtel cheese, cottage cheese, sour cream, and dill weed. Beat with an electric mixer until smooth (or whirl in a food processor or blender until smooth).

3. Reserve about a fourth of the artichokes. With a spoon, stir remaining artichokes into cheese mixture until evenly distributed.

4. Transfer cheese-artichoke mixture to a shallow 4- to 5-cup (950-ml to 1.2-liter) baking dish; bake in a 325°F (165°C) oven until lightly browned (about 30 minutes).

5. Sprinkle with reserved artichokes and return to oven for about 5 minutes. Serve with toast. Makes 12 servings.

Per serving: 212 calories (30% calories from fat), 7 g total fat , 4 g saturated fat, 19 mg cholesterol, 452 mg sodium, 25 g carbohydrates, 1 g fiber, 11 g protein, 143 mg calcium, 2 mg iron

The sweet, deep flavor of roasted garlic adds robust body to this white bean spread.

White Bean & Roasted Garlic Bruschetta

Preparation time: 20 minutes
Cooking time: About 1¼ hours

1 large head garlic (about 4 oz./115 g)

½ teaspoon olive oil

8 slices crusty bread, such as Italian ciabatta or sourdough (*each* about ½ inch/1 cm thick; about 8 oz./230 g *total*)

2 cans (about 15 oz./425 g *each*) cannellini (white kidney beans)

½ cup (20 g) lightly packed fresh basil leaves

¼ cup (15 g) chopped Italian or regular parsley

¼ cup (60 ml) lemon juice

4 teaspoons (20 ml) Oriental sesame oil

½ teaspoon salt

1 pound (455 g) pear-shaped (Roma-type) tomatoes, thinly sliced

4 to 6 teaspoons drained capers (or to taste)

Fresh basil leaves

About 12 canned mild cherry peppers, drained (optional)

Pepper

1. Slice ¼ inch (6 mm) off top of garlic head. Then rub garlic with olive oil. Wrap garlic in foil and bake in a 375°F (190°C) oven until soft when pressed (about 1¼ hours). Carefully remove garlic from foil; transfer to a rack and let stand until cool enough to touch (about 10 minutes).

2. Meanwhile, arrange bread slices slightly apart in a large, shallow baking pan. Broil about 6 inches below heat, turning once, until golden on both sides (about 5 minutes). Let cool on a rack.

3. Squeeze garlic cloves from skins into a food processor or blender. Drain beans, reserving liquid. Rinse beans and add to processor along with the ½ cup (20 g) basil leaves, parsley, lemon juice, sesame oil, and salt. Whirl until coarsely puréed. If necessary, add enough of the reserved bean liquid to make mixture spreadable (do not make it too thin). Discard remaining liquid.

4. Top toast slices equally with bean mixture; arrange tomato slices, capers, and basil leaves over bean mixture. Serve with cherry peppers, if desired. Season to taste with pepper. Makes 4 servings.

Per serving: 445 calories (16% calories from fat), 8 g total fat, 1 g saturated fat, 0 mg cholesterol, 1,455 mg sodium, 77 g carbohydrates, 17 g fiber, 19 g protein, 233 mg calcium, 7 mg iron

Guacamole is offered as a condiment at many Mexican meals—and enjoyed as a snack, too. To make this creamy, reduced-fat version of the popular dip, we used a ripe avocado for flavor, but cut the fat by adding cottage cheese.

Creamy Guacamole

Preparation time: About 10 minutes

1 teaspoon grated lemon peel

2 tablespoons (30 ml) lemon juice

1 medium-size soft-ripe avocado

1 cup (210 g) low-fat (1%) cottage cheese

2 to 4 cloves garlic, peeled

⅛ teaspoon salt

2 tablespoons minced cilantro

1 fresh jalapeño or serrano chile, seeded and minced

1 tablespoon thinly sliced green onion

2 small tomatoes (about 8 oz./ 230 g *total*), finely chopped and drained well

Cilantro sprigs

About 8 cups (340 g) water-crisped corn tortilla chips (page 346), purchased tortilla chips, or bite-size pieces of raw vegetables

1. Place lemon peel and lemon juice in a blender or food processor. Pit and peel avocado; transfer avocado to blender along with cottage cheese, garlic, and salt. Whirl until smoothly puréed.

2. Spoon guacamole into a serving bowl and gently stir in minced cilantro, chile, onion, and half the tomatoes. If made ahead, cover and refrigerate for up to 2 hours; stir before serving.

3. To serve, garnish with remaining tomatoes and cilantro sprigs. To eat, scoop guacamole onto chips. Makes about 3 cups/710 ml (about 8 servings).

Per serving: 138 calories (23% calories from fat), 4 g total fat, 0.7 g saturated fat, 1 mg cholesterol, 215 mg sodium, 21 g carbohydrates, 3 g fiber, 6 g protein, 90 mg calcium, 0.9 mg iron

Grilling enhances the natural sugars in vegetables for a sweetly mellow, deep flavor.

Grilled Vegetable Appetizer

Preparation time: 25 minutes
Cooking time: About 1½ hours, including time to heat grill

2 long, slender baguettes (*each about 8 oz./230 g, about 25 inches/63 cm long*), cut diag-onally into slices about 1 inch (2.5 cm) thick

4 medium-size slender egg-plants, such as Asian or Italian (about 12 oz./340 g *total*)

3 medium-size sweet potatoes or yams (about 1¼ lbs./565 g *total*), scrubbed

1 large onion

3 tablespoons (45 ml) olive oil

2 large red bell peppers (about 1¼ lbs./565 g total), seeded

3 large heads garlic (about 12 oz./ 340 g *total*), unpeeled (leave heads whole)

1½ teaspoons chopped fresh rosemary or ½ teaspoon dried rosemary, crumbled

1½ teaspoons chopped fresh sage or ½ teaspoon dried rubbed sage

Rosemary sprigs and fresh sage leaves

Salt and pepper

1. Arrange bread slices in a single layer (overlapping as little as possible) in shallow 10- by 15-inch (25- by 38-cm) baking pans. Bake in a 325°F (165°C) oven until crisp and tinged with brown (15 to 20 minutes). Transfer toast to a rack to cool.

2. While bread is toasting, ignite 70 charcoal briquets in a large barbecue with dampers open. Spread coals out in a solid layer and let burn until medium-low to low; if fire is too hot, vegetables will scorch.

3. Cut ends from eggplants and sweet potatoes; cut unpeeled onion into quarters. Brush cut surfaces of onion with a little of the oil. Place eggplants, sweet potatoes, onion, bell peppers, and garlic on a greased grill 4 to 6 inches (10 to 15 cm) above coals. Cover barbecue. Cook until vegetables are very tender when pressed, watching carefully to prevent scorching; allow about 40 minutes for eggplant and

peppers, 50 to 60 minutes for onion and garlic, and 1 hour for sweet pota-toes. During the first 30 minutes of grilling, turn vegetables every 5 min-utes; after 30 minutes, add 10 more briquets to the fire and turn vegetables every 10 minutes. Remove vegetables from grill as they are cooked.

4. Remove peel from sweet potatoes, onion, and bell peppers. Cut heads of garlic in half horizontally. Coarsely chop eggplants, peppers, and sweet potatoes. Squeeze half the garlic cloves from skins and finely chop.

5. On a platter, arrange chopped egg-plants, peppers, and sweet potatoes; onion quarters; and whole garlic cloves. Place chopped garlic in center of platter.

6. Drizzle vegetables with remaining oil; sprinkle with chopped rosemary and sage. Garnish with rosemary sprigs and sage leaves. Place toast in a basket. Serve; or, if made ahead, cover lightly and let stand for up to 2 hours.

7. To serve, top toast with garlic (either chopped or whole cloves); then spoon other vegetables on top. Season to taste with salt and pepper. Makes 8 servings.

Per serving: 376 calories (17% calories from fat), 7 g total fat, 1 g saturated fat, 0 mg choles-terol, 365 mg sodium, 70 g carbohydrates, 7 g fiber, 10 g protein, 157 mg calcium, 3 mg iron

Mild polenta is a perfect foil for the complex flavors of assorted wild mushrooms.

- ½ cup (60 g) all-purpose flour
- ½ cup (70 g) polenta or yellow cornmeal
- ¼ cup (30 g) instant nonfat dry milk
- 1½ teaspoons baking powder
- 1 tablespoon butter or margarine
- 2 tablespoons (30 ml) olive oil or salad oil
- 1 medium-size head garlic (about 3 oz./85 g)
- 8 ounces (230 g) *each* fresh shiitake, chanterelle, and oyster mushrooms
- 1 tablespoon *each* chopped fresh rosemary and chopped fresh sage; or 1 teaspoon *each* dried rubbed sage and dried rosemary
- 2 teaspoons cornstarch mixed with ¾ cup (180 ml) fat-free reduced-sodium chicken broth
- 2 tablespoons grated Parmesan cheese
  Rosemary and sage sprigs

1. In a food processor or a medium-size bowl, whirl or stir together flour, polenta, dry milk, and baking powder. Add butter; whirl or rub with your fingers until mixture resembles coarse crumbs. Add ⅓ cup (80 ml) water;

Wild Mushroom Polenta Boards

Preparation time: 1 hour
Cooking time: About 1 hour

whirl or stir with a fork until dough begins to form a ball. Turn dough out onto a lightly floured board and pat into a ball; then knead briefly, just until dough holds together smoothly.

2. Divide dough into 6 equal portions; cover with plastic wrap. Flour board well; then, working with one piece of dough at a time, roll each piece into an irregular 6- to 7-inch (15- to 18-cm) round. As rounds are shaped, arrange them, slightly apart, on large baking sheets; cover with plastic wrap. When all rounds have been shaped, remove plastic wrap and bake polenta boards in a 350°F (175°C) oven until lightly browned (12 to 14 minutes). If made ahead, let cool completely on racks; then store airtight until next day.

3. Pour 1 tablespoon (15 ml) of the oil into a small baking pan. Cut garlic head in half crosswise (through cloves). Place garlic, cut side down, in pan; bake in a 350°F (175°C) oven until cut side is golden brown (about 45 minutes). Using a thin spatula, lift garlic from pan and transfer to a rack;

let stand until cool enough to touch (about 10 minutes). Squeeze garlic cloves from skins into a small bowl; mash garlic thoroughly.

4. While garlic is baking, trim and discard stems from shiitake mushrooms. Thinly slice shiitake mushroom caps and whole chanterelles. Place sliced shiitake and chanterelle mushrooms and whole oyster mushrooms in a 5- to 6-quart (5- to 6-liter) pan; add remaining 1 tablespoon (15 ml) oil, chopped rosemary, and chopped sage. Cover and cook over medium-high heat until mushrooms are juicy (about 8 minutes). Uncover; cook, stirring often, until almost all liquid has evaporated and mushrooms are browned (15 to 20 more minutes). Add cornstarch mixture and mashed garlic; stir until mixture boils and thickens slightly.

5. Lay polenta boards, side by side, on 2 large baking sheets. Spoon hot mushroom sauce into center of each; sprinkle evenly with cheese. Broil 4 to 6 inches (10 to 15 cm) below heat until sizzling (about 2 minutes). With a spatula, transfer to individual plates; garnish with rosemary and sage sprigs. Makes 6 servings.

Per serving: 202 calories (30% calories from fat), 7 g total fat, 2 g saturated fat, 7 mg cholesterol, 276 mg sodium, 29 g carbohydrates, 3 g fiber, 7 g protein, 160 mg calcium, 3 mg iron

Piquantly sweet tomato relish deliciously complements this smooth creamy bean pâté.

Baguette Toasts:

1 long, slender baguette (about 8 oz./230 g, about 25 inches/63 cm long), cut diagonally into 24 slices

Tomato Relish:

1 large tomato (about 8 oz./230 g), chopped and drained well

1 to 2 tablespoons chopped parsley

1 tablespoon (15 ml) balsamic vinegar

1 tablespoon drained capers

½ teaspoon sugar

Pepper

White Bean Pâté:

1 can (about 15 oz./425 g) cannellini (white kidney beans), drained and rinsed

White Bean Pâté with Tomato Relish

Preparation time: 20 minutes
Cooking time: 15 to 20 minutes

1½ teaspoons Oriental sesame oil

¾ teaspoon chopped fresh thyme or ¼ teaspoon dried thyme

¼ teaspoon grated lemon peel

4 teaspoons lemon juice

1 clove garlic, peeled

¼ teaspoon salt (or to taste)

Thyme sprigs

1. Arrange bread slices in a single layer (overlapping as little as possible) in shallow 10- by 15-inch (25- by 38-cm) baking pans. Bake in a 325°F (165°C) oven until crisp and tinged with brown (15 to 20 minutes). Transfer toast to a rack to cool.

2. In a small bowl, stir together tomato, parsley, vinegar, capers, and sugar; season to taste with pepper. Set aside; stir occasionally.

3. In a blender or food processor, combine beans, oil, chopped thyme, lemon peel, lemon juice, garlic, and salt. Whirl until almost smooth. Spoon bean pâté into a small serving bowl or crock and garnish with thyme sprigs.

4. Offer bean pâté to spread over toast. Spoon tomato relish over pâté, using a slotted spoon. Makes 8 to 12 servings.

Per serving: 86 calories (14% calories from fat), 1 g total fat, 0.2 g saturated fat, 0 mg cholesterol, 224 mg sodium, 15 g carbohydrates, 2 g fiber, 4 g protein, 25 mg calcium, 0.9 mg iron

---

Hot red chiles add extra zip to the pickling blend for these crunchy vegetables.

8 ounces (230 g) small carrots (*each* 4 to 5 inches/10 to 12.5 cm long)

1 package (about 10 oz./285 g) frozen tiny onions, thawed

1 large red bell pepper (about 8 oz./230 g), seeded and cut into strips about ½ inch (1 cm) wide

1 package (about 9 oz./255 g) frozen artichoke hearts, thawed

2 cups (470 ml) white wine vinegar

¾ cup (150 g) sugar

2 tablespoons drained capers

2 small dried hot red chiles

2 cloves garlic, peeled and crushed

Pickled Vegetables

Preparation time: 15 minutes
Cooking time: About 15 minutes
Chilling time: At least 1 day

1. In a 2- to 3-quart (1.9- to 2.8-liter) pan, bring 4 cups (950 ml) water to a boil over high heat. Add carrots and boil, uncovered, until barely tender when pierced (about 3 minutes); drain well.

2. In a clean, dry wide-mouth 1½- to 2-quart (1.4- to 1.9-liter) jar (or in two 1-quart jars), layer carrots, onions, bell pepper, and artichokes. Set aside.

3. In pan used to cook carrots, stir together vinegar, sugar, capers, chiles, and garlic. Bring to a boil over high heat, stirring until sugar is dissolved. Pour hot vinegar mixture over vegetables. Cover and refrigerate for at least 1 day or up to 2 weeks. To serve, lift vegetables from marinade. Makes about 6 cups (1.4 liters).

Per ¼ cup (60 ml): 42 calories (2% calories from fat), 0.1 g total fat, 0 g saturated fat, 0 mg cholesterol, 28 mg sodium, 10 g carbohydrates, 0.9 g fiber, 0.5 g protein, 10 mg calcium, 0.2 mg iron

Warm crab, tomatoes, and jack cheese make a great filling for quesadillas. Offer a cool fresh-chile sauce to heat up each serving.

Chile Sauce (recipe follows)

2 medium-size firm-ripe tomatoes (about 12 oz./340 g *total*), finely chopped

4 ounces (115 g) cooked crabmeat

¾ cup (86 g) shredded jack cheese

1 cup (100 g) sliced green onions

10 flour tortillas (7- to 9-inch/ 18- to 23-cm diameter)

Cilantro sprigs

1. Prepare Chile Sauce and set aside.

2. Place tomatoes in a fine wire strainer and let drain well; discard juice.

3. In a bowl, mix crab, cheese, and onions. Gently mix in tomatoes. Place 5 tortillas in a single layer on 2 lightly oiled large baking sheets. Evenly top tortillas with crab mixture, covering tortillas to within ¾ inch (2 cm) of

Tomato-Crab Quesadillas

Preparation time: About 15 minutes
Cooking time: 20 to 30 minutes

edges. Top each tortilla with one of the remaining tortillas.

4. Bake in a 450°F (230°C) oven until tortillas are lightly browned (7 to 9 minutes), switching positions of baking sheets halfway through baking.

5. Slide quesadillas onto a serving board; cut each into 6 wedges. Garnish with cilantro sprigs. Add Chile Sauce to taste. Makes 8 to 10 servings.

Chile Sauce. Place 4 medium-size **fresh green Anaheim chiles** or other large mild chiles (about 7 oz./200 g *total*) on a baking sheet. Broil 4 to 6 inches (10 to 15 cm) below heat, turning often, until charred all over (about 8 minutes). Cover with foil and let cool on baking sheet; then remove and dis-

card skins, stems, and seeds.

In a blender or food processor, whirl chiles, ¼ cup (60 ml) **dry white wine,** 2 small **shallots,** and 1 tablespoon (15 ml) **lemon juice** until smooth. Pour into a 2- to 3-quart (1.9- to 2.8-liter) pan. Bring to a boil; boil, stirring, until reduced to ⅓ cup (80 ml) (5 to 10 minutes).

Return mixture to blender or food processor. Add 1 cup (53 g) firmly packed **cilantro leaves** and ½ cup (65 g) peeled, coarsely chopped **jicama.** Whirl until smooth; scrape sides of container several times. With motor running, slowly add ¼ cup (60 ml) **low-sodium chicken broth** and 1 tablespoon (15 ml) **honey** and whirl to blend. Serve sauce cool or cold. If made ahead, cover and refrigerate for up to 4 hours. Makes about 1 cup (240 ml).

Per serving: 188 calories (26% calories from fat), 5 g total fat, 2 g saturated fat, 20 mg cholesterol, 277 mg sodium, 26 g carbohydrates, 2 g fiber, 8 g protein, 135 mg calcium, 2 mg iron

---

Beer infuses the tomato-based chili sauce with robust, tangy character.

1 bottle or can (about 12 oz./ 340 g) beer

½ cup (85 g) finely chopped onion

¾ teaspoon celery seeds

1 dried bay leaf

1 pound (455 g) large raw shrimp (31 to 35 per lb.), shelled and deveined

½ cup (120 ml) tomato-based chili sauce

1 tablespoon (15 ml) honey-flavored mustard

About 20 large fresh spinach leaves, rinsed and crisped

2 tablespoons drained capers

Chili Shrimp

Preparation time: 15 minutes
Cooking time: 15 to 20 minutes

1. In a wide frying pan, combine beer, onion, celery seeds, and bay leaf. Bring to a boil over high heat; boil for 2 minutes. Add shrimp. Reduce heat, cover, and simmer, stirring occasionally, until

shrimp are just opaque in center; cut to test (about 3 minutes). With a slotted spoon, lift shrimp from pan and transfer to a large bowl.

2. Bring shrimp cooking liquid to a boil over high heat; then boil until reduced to ⅓ cup (80 ml). Remove and discard bay leaf. Add chili sauce and mustard to reduced liquid; blend well. Serve; or cover shrimp and dressing separately and refrigerate until cool (at least 1 hour) or until next day.

3. To serve, line 4 individual plates with spinach leaves; top equally with shrimp, then with dressing. Sprinkle with capers. Makes 4 servings.

Per serving: 171 calories (10% calories from fat), 2 g total fat, 0.3 g saturated fat, 140 mg cholesterol, 731 mg sodium, 17 g carbohydrates, 1 g fiber, 21 g protein, 100 mg calcium, 4 mg iron

Garlic Chicken Bites
(recipe on facing page)

Serve these tender, garlicky chunks of skinless chicken hot from the oven, with a spicy-sweet tomato-raisin sauce.

- 3 tablespoons minced cilantro
- 2 teaspoons coarsely ground pepper
- 8 cloves garlic, minced
- 1 pound (455 g) skinless, boneless chicken thighs, cut into 1½-inch (3.5-cm) chunks
- ⅓ cup (80 ml) tomato sauce
- 1 tablespoon firmly packed brown sugar
- 1 tablespoon (15 ml) distilled white vinegar or cider vinegar
- ½ cup (73 g) raisins

Garlic Chicken Bites with Tomato-Raisin Sauce

Preparation time: About 10 minutes
Baking time: 18 to 20 minutes
Pictured on facing page

1. Mix cilantro, pepper, and 6 cloves of the garlic; rub mixture over chicken. Place chicken pieces well apart in a lightly oiled 10- by 15-inch (25- by 38-cm) rimmed baking pan.

2. Bake in a 500°F (260°C) oven until chicken is lightly browned and no longer pink in center; cut to test (18 to 20 minutes).

3. Meanwhile, in a food processor or blender, whirl remaining 2 cloves garlic, tomato sauce, sugar, vinegar, and raisins until raisins are chopped.

4. Serve chicken hot, with tomato-raisin sauce. Makes 4 servings.

Per serving: 221 calories (18% calories from fat), 5 g total fat, 1 g saturated fat, 94 mg cholesterol, 225 mg sodium, 22 g carbohydrates, 2 g fiber, 24 g protein, 42 mg calcium, 2 mg iron

---

Cool cilantro lends a refreshing note of flavor to this satisfying appetizer. Serve with a crisp green salad for a light lunch.

- Cilantro Mustard (recipe follows)
- 4 cloves garlic, minced
- 3 tablespoons minced cilantro
- ½ teaspoon coarsely ground pepper
- 1 pound (455 g) boneless, skinless chicken breast, cut into ½-inch (1-cm) pieces
- 1 teaspoon olive oil or salad oil
- 4 pita breads (*each* about 6 inches/15 cm in diameter), cut into quarters

Thai Chicken in Pitas

Preparation time: About 20 minutes, plus 1 hour for Cilantro Mustard to stand
Cooking time: 3 to 4 minutes

1. Prepare Cilantro Mustard; set aside.

2. In a large bowl, mix garlic, cilantro, pepper, and chicken. Heat oil in a wide nonstick frying pan or wok over medium-high heat. When oil is hot, add chicken mixture. Stir-fry until meat is no longer pink in center; cut to test (3 to 4 minutes). Add water, 1 tablespoon (15 ml) at a time, if pan appears dry.

3. With a slotted spoon, transfer chicken to a serving bowl. To eat, spoon chicken into pita breads; drizzle chicken with Cilantro Mustard. Makes 6 to 8 servings.

Cilantro Mustard. In a 1- to 1½-quart (950-ml to 1.4-liter) pan, stir together 3 tablespoons **dry mustard,** 3 tablespoons (45 ml) **distilled white vinegar** or white wine vinegar, and 2 tablespoons (30 ml) **water;** cover and let stand for 1 hour.

Mix 3 tablespoons **sugar** and 1 tablespoon **all-purpose flour;** add to mustard mixture along with 3 tablespoons (43 g) **butter** or margarine, cut into chunks. Bring just to a boil over medium-high heat, stirring. Remove from heat and let cool. If made ahead, cover airtight and refrigerate for up to 4 days. Just before serving, stir in 1 to 2 tablespoons chopped cilantro.

Per serving: 255 calories (27% calories from fat), 8 g total fat, 3 g saturated fat, 51 mg cholesterol, 277 mg sodium, 27 g carbohydrates, 0.6 g fiber, 19 g protein, 48 mg calcium, 2 mg iron

Serve these hearty snacks with a salad instead of sandwiches for lunch.

- 12 ounces (340 g) mild turkey Italian sausages, cut diagonally into 1-inch (2.5-cm) lengths
- 2 large onions (about 1 lb./455 g *total*), cut into wedges about ½ inch (1 cm) thick
- 5 tablespoons (75 ml) balsamic vinegar
- 12 miniature pita breads (*each about 3 inches/8 cm in diameter*), cut into halves

1. In a 9- by 13-inch (23- by 33-cm) baking pan, combine sausages, onions,

Roasted Sausage & Onion with Pita Breads

Preparation time: 15 minutes
Cooking time: About 45 minutes

and ¼ cup (60 ml) of the vinegar. Bake in a 425°F (220°C) oven until sausage is well browned and almost all liquid has evaporated (about 45 minutes); stir occasionally and add water, ¼ cup (60 ml) at a time, if drippings begin to scorch.

2. Remove pan from oven and add 1 tablespoon (15 ml) water and remaining 1 tablespoon (15 ml) vinegar. Let stand for about 3 minutes; then stir to scrape browned bits free from pan bottom.

3. Transfer sausage-onion mixture to a serving dish and keep hot. To serve, spoon mixture into pita bread halves. Makes 12 servings.

Per serving: 140 calories (22% calories from fat), 3 g total fat, 0.9 g saturated fat, 15 mg cholesterol, 339 mg sodium, 20 g carbohydrates, 1 g fiber, 8 g protein, 39 mg calcium, 2 mg iron

---

Ground beef, sweet pears, raisins, and cinnamon combine for an exotically intriguing curry.

- 1 teaspoon cornstarch
- 6 tablespoons (90 ml) cider vinegar
- 3 large firm-ripe pears (about 1½ lbs./680 g *total*)
- 12 ounces (340 g) lean ground beef
- 4 ounces (115 g) mushrooms, chopped
- ½ cup (75 g) golden raisins
- ¼ cup (55 g) firmly packed brown sugar
- 2 tablespoons *each* curry powder and tomato paste
- ½ teaspoon ground cinnamon
- ¼ cup (25 g) sliced green onions
- 2 tablespoons chopped parsley
- ½ cup (120 ml) plain nonfat yogurt
- 1 head butter lettuce (about 6 oz./170 g), separated into leaves, rinsed, and crisped
  Salt

Curry Beef in Lettuce

Preparation time: About 15 minutes
Cooking time: About 15 minutes

1. In a large bowl, blend cornstarch with 2 tablespoons (30 ml) of the vinegar. Peel, core, and finely chop pears; gently stir into vinegar mixture and set aside.

2. Crumble beef into a wide nonstick frying pan or wok; add mushrooms and raisins. Stir-fry over medium-high heat until meat is browned (about 8

minutes). Add water, 1 tablespoon (15 ml) at a time, if pan appears dry. Spoon off and discard fat from pan.

3. Stir in sugar, ¼ cup (60 ml) water, remaining ¼ cup (60 ml) vinegar, curry powder, tomato paste, and cinnamon. Bring to a boil; then stir until almost all liquid has evaporated (about 3 minutes). Add pear mixture; stir until mixture boils and thickens slightly. Transfer to a serving bowl; stir in onions and parsley.

4. To eat, spoon meat mixture and yogurt into lettuce leaves; season to taste with salt. Makes 4 to 6 servings.

Per serving: 319 calories (21% calories from fat), 8 g total fat, 3 g saturated fat, 43 mg cholesterol, 129 mg sodium, 50 g carbohydrates, 6 g fiber, 18 g protein, 101 mg calcium, 4 mg iron

For a low-fat appetizer or snack, chewy jerky made from turkey breast is a tasty choice. For the liveliest flavor, let the turkey strips marinate for the maximum time.

Turkey Jerky

Preparation time: About 10 minutes
Marinating time: At least 1 hour
Baking time: 4 to 6 hours
(in a conventional oven)

1 pound (455 g) skinless, boneless turkey breast; or 1 pound (455 g) turkey breast tenderloins
1 tablespoon salt
½ cup (120 ml) water
2 tablespoons firmly packed brown sugar
2 cloves garlic, minced or pressed; or ¼ teaspoon garlic powder
½ small onion, minced; or ¼ teaspoon onion powder
1 teaspoon pepper
½ teaspoon liquid smoke
Vegetable oil cooking spray

1. Rinse turkey and pat dry. Pull off and discard any fat and connective tissue. For easier slicing, freeze meat until it's firm but not hard. Cut into ⅛- to ¼-inch (3- to 6-mm) slices (cut breast piece with or across the grain, tenderloins lengthwise).

2. In a nonmetal bowl, stir together salt, water, sugar, garlic, onion, pepper, and liquid smoke. Add turkey and mix well. Cover and refrigerate for at least 1 hour or up to 24 hours; turkey will absorb almost all liquid.

3. You may dry turkey in a dehydrator or a conventional oven. Depending upon drying method, evenly coat dehydrator racks (you need 3, each about 10 by 13 inches/25 by 33 cm) or metal racks (to cover a 10- by 15-inch/25- by 38-cm rimmed baking pan) with cooking spray. Lift turkey strips from bowl and shake off any excess liquid; lay strips close together, but not overlapping, on racks.

4. *If using a dehydrator,* arrange trays as manufacturer directs and dry at 140°F (60°C) until jerky cracks and breaks when bent (4½ to 6 hours; remove a strip of jerky from dehydrator and let stand for about 5 minutes before testing).

If using an oven, place pan on center rack of a 150° to 200°F (66° to 95°C) oven; prop door open about 2 inches (5 cm). Dry until jerky cracks and breaks when bent (4 to 6 hours; remove a strip of jerky from oven and let stand for about 5 minutes before testing).

5. Let jerky cool on racks. Serve; or package airtight and store in a cool, dry place for up to 3 weeks, in the refrigerator for up to 4 months (freeze for longer storage). Makes about 7 ounces (200 g).

Per ounce: 93 calories (8% calories from fat), 0.8 g total fat, 0.1 g saturated fat, 40 mg cholesterol, 975 mg sodium, 5 g carbohydrates, 0.1 g fiber, 16 g protein, 19 mg calcium, 0.9 mg iron

---

Crisp watermelon wedges and jicama slices are seasoned with lemon, chili, and salt for a quick appetizer.

Watermelon, Jicama & Chili Salt

Preparation time: About 10 minutes

4 seedless or seed-in watermelon wedges (4 to 5 lbs./1.8 to 2.3 kg *total*), *each* about 3 inches (8 cm) wide and 9 inches (23 cm) long
About 1¼ pounds (565 g) jicama, peeled and rinsed
½ teaspoon *each* salt and ground red pepper (cayenne)
1 lemon, cut into quarters

1. Slide a short, sharp knife between rind and flesh of watermelon wedges to free flesh, but keep flesh in place. Then cut through melon to rind at 1½-inch (3.5-cm) intervals.

2. Cut jicama into ¼-inch (6-mm) slices, each about 2 by 3 inches (5 by 8 cm). Insert jicama slices in melon slits.

3. Mix salt and red pepper; sprinkle over melon and jicama. Serve with lemon quarters to squeeze over fruit to taste. Makes 4 servings.

Per serving: 145 calories (8% calories from fat), 2 g total fat, 0 g saturated fat, 0 mg cholesterol, 287 mg sodium, 33 g carbohydrates, 4 g fiber, 4 g protein, 59 mg calcium, 1 mg iron

Ground meat and onions simmered in a savory-sweet tomato sauce make picadillo, *a satisfying filling for bite-size turnovers. Serve these little pastries as appetizers or enjoy them as an any-time snack.*

Picadillo-stuffed Empanadas

Preparation time: About 30 minutes
Cooking time: About 1¼ hours
Pictured on facing page

Cornmeal-Cumin Pastry (recipe follows)
2 tablespoons slivered almonds
1 teaspoon salad oil
1 large onion, finely chopped
2 cloves garlic, minced or pressed
6 ounces (170 g) ground turkey or chicken breast
1 can (about 8 oz./230 g) tomato sauce
½ teaspoon ground cinnamon
⅛ teaspoon ground cloves
2 tablespoons dried currants or raisins
2 teaspoons cider vinegar
Salt

1. Prepare Cornmeal-Cumin Pastry.

2. Toast almonds in a small frying pan over medium heat until golden (5 to 7 minutes), stirring often. Transfer almonds to a bowl and let cool; then coarsely chop and set aside.

3. In a wide nonstick frying pan, combine oil, onion, garlic, and 1 tablespoon (15 ml) water. Cook over medium heat, stirring often, until mixture is deep golden (about 20 minutes); if onion sticks to pan bottom or pan appears dry, add more water, 1 tablespoon (15 ml) at a time. Crumble turkey into pan and cook over medium-high heat, stirring often, until well browned (about 10 minutes); if pan appears dry, add more water, 1 tablespoon (15 ml) at a time.

4. Stir in tomato sauce, cinnamon, cloves, and currants. Bring mixture to a boil; then reduce heat and simmer, uncovered, until almost all liquid has evaporated and mixture is slightly thickened (about 10 minutes). Remove from heat, stir in almonds and vinegar, and season to taste with salt.

5. On a floured board, roll out pastry ⅛ inch (3 mm) thick. Cut into 3½-inch (9-cm) rounds. Spoon equal amounts of turkey filling onto half of each pastry round. Moisten edges of rounds with water; fold plain half of each round over filling. Press edges together with a fork.

6. Arrange empanadas on a lightly oiled 12- by 15-inch (30- by 38-cm) baking sheet. Bake in a 400°F (205°F) oven until lightly browned (about 20 minutes). Makes about 16 empanadas.

Cornmeal-Cumin Pastry. In a food processor (or a bowl), combine 1 cup (125 g) **all-purpose flour,** ½ cup (69 g) **yellow cornmeal,** 1½ teaspoons **baking powder,** ¼ teaspoon **salt,** and 2 tablespoons **butter** or margarine. Whirl (or rub with your fingers) until mixture resembles coarse crumbs. Add ⅓ cup (80 ml) **milk,** 1 large **egg white,** and ½ teaspoon **cumin seeds;** whirl (or stir with a fork) until dough holds together (add 1 tablespoon/15 ml more milk, if needed). With lightly floured hands, pat dough into a ball. Wrap airtight and refrigerate until ready to use or for up to 1 hour.

Per serving: 96 calories (25% calories from fat), 3 g total fat, 1 g saturated fat, 11 mg cholesterol, 192 mg sodium, 13 g carbohydrates, 1 g fiber, 5 g protein, 45 mg calcium, 0.9 mg iron

Picadillo-stuffed Empanadas
(recipe on facing page)

Salsas

Salsas are much more deliciously diverse than the popular zesty tomato-based salsas with which we are all familiar. Like relishes, they can be made from a variety of ingredients and make piquant accompaniments to meats, poultry, and fish.

Spicy Pepper Relish

- 2 large red bell peppers (about 1 lb./455 g *total*)
- 2 large yellow bell peppers (about 1 lb./455 g *total*)
- 8 fresh red or green serrano chiles (about 2 oz./55 g *total*)
- 1 cup (200 g) sugar
- ⅔ cup (160 g) distilled white vinegar

1. Seed bell peppers and chiles; cut into thin strips. In a large bowl, mix peppers, chiles, sugar, and vinegar; pour into a wide frying pan.

2. Place pan over medium to medium-high heat. Cook, uncovered, stirring often, until almost all liquid has evaporated (about 30 minutes). Let cool slightly before serving. If made ahead, cover and refrigerate for up to 3 days. Makes about 1½ cups (360 ml).

Per serving: 168 calories (1% calories from fat), 0.2 g total fat, 0 g saturated fat, 0 mg cholesterol, 4 mg sodium, 43 g carbohydrates, 2 g fiber, 1 g protein, 13 mg calcium, 0.7 mg iron

Cucumber & Jicama Salsa

- 1 medium-size cucumber (about 8 oz./230 g), peeled, seeded, and diced
- About 1 pound (455 g) jicama, peeled, rinsed, and diced
- ⅓ cup (13 g) chopped fresh basil
- ⅓ cup (33 g) sliced green onions
- ¼ cup (60 ml) *each* lemon juice and plain nonfat yogurt
- 1 small fresh jalapeño chile, seeded and minced
- Salt

1. In a nonmetal bowl, mix cucumber, jicama, basil, onions, lemon juice, yogurt, and chile; season to taste with salt. If made ahead, cover and refrigerate for up to 6 hours. Makes about 6 cups (1.4 liters).

Per serving: 11 calories (2% calories from fat), 0 g total fat, 0 g saturated fat, 0 mg cholesterol, 4 mg sodium, 2 g carbohydrates, 0.4 g fiber, 0.5 g protein, 15 mg calcium, 0.2 mg iron

Cherry Tomato Salsa

- 2 cups (about 12 oz./340 g) red cherry tomatoes, cut into halves
- ⅓ cup (13 g) lightly packed cilantro leaves
- 2 fresh jalapeño chiles, seeded
- 1 clove garlic, peeled
- 2 tablespoons (30 ml) lime juice
- 2 tablespoons thinly sliced green onion
- Salt and pepper

1. Place tomatoes, cilantro, chiles, and garlic in a food processor; whirl just until coarsely chopped (or chop coarsely with a knife).

2. Turn mixture into a nonmetal bowl; stir in lime juice and onion. Season to taste with salt and pepper. If made ahead, cover and refrigerate for up to 4 hours. Makes about 2 cups (470 ml).

Per serving: 12 calories (9% calories from fat), 0.1 g total fat, 0 g saturated fat, 0 mg cholesterol, 5 mg sodium, 3 g carbohydrates, 0.7 g fiber, 0.5 g protein, 6 mg calcium, 0.3 mg iron

Corn Salsa

- 3 medium-size ears corn (about 1½ lbs./680 g *total*), *each* about 8 inches (20 cm) long, husks and silk removed
- ½ cup (73 g) finely chopped European cucumber
- ⅓ cup (80 ml) lime juice
- ¼ cup (25 g) thinly sliced green onions
- 1 tablespoon grated orange peel
- 3 tablespoons (45 g) orange juice
- 2 tablespoons chopped fresh mint or 1 teaspoon dried mint
- 1 teaspoon cumin seeds
- 1 or 2 fresh jalapeño chiles, seeded and minced
- Salt

1. In a 5- to 6-quart (4.7- to 5.7-liter) pan, bring about 3 quarts (2.8 liters) water to a boil over high heat. Add corn,

cover, and cook until hot (4 to 6 minutes). Drain; then let cool. With a sharp knife, cut kernels from cobs.

2. In a nonmetal bowl, mix corn, cucumber, lime juice, onions, orange peel, orange juice, mint, cumin seeds, and chiles; season to taste with salt. If made ahead, cover and refrigerate for up to 4 hours. Makes about 3 cups (710 ml).

Per serving: 32 calories (9% calories from fat), 0.4 g total fat, 0.1 g saturated fat, 0 mg cholesterol, 6 mg sodium, 7 g carbohydrates, 1 g fiber, 1 g protein, 7 mg calcium, 0.3 mg iron

Papaya Salsa

1 medium-size firm-ripe papaya (about 1 lb./455 g), peeled, seeded, and cut into ¼-inch (6-mm) cubes

¼ cup (10 g) chopped cilantro

3 green onions, thinly sliced

1 fresh jalapeño chile, seeded and minced

2 tablespoons (30 ml) lime juice

1. In a nonmetal bowl, gently mix papaya, cilantro, onions, chile, and lime juice. If made ahead, cover and refrigerate for up to 4 hours. Makes about 2 cups (470 ml).

Per serving: 18 calories (3% calories from fat), 0.1 g total fat, 0 g saturated fat, 0 mg cholesterol, 3 mg sodium, 5 g carbohydrates, 0.5 g fiber, 0.4 g protein, 14 mg calcium, 0.1 mg iron

Watermelon Pico de Gallo

1 medium-large orange (about 8 oz./230g)

1½ cups (240 g) seeded, diced watermelon

¾ cup (98 g) peeled, diced jicama

1 fresh jalapeño chile, seeded and minced

1 tablespoon (15 ml) lime juice

1 tablespoon minced cilantro

1. Finely grate 2 teaspoons peel (colored part only) from orange; place in a nonmetal bowl.

2. Cut off remaining peel and all white membrane from orange. Holding fruit over bowl to catch juice, cut between membranes to release orange segments; then dice segments and drop into bowl.

3. Add watermelon, jicama, chile, lime juice, and cilantro to bowl; mix gently. If made ahead, cover and refrigerate for up to 4 hours. Makes about 3 cups (710 ml).

Per serving: 17 calories (5% calories from fat), 0.1 g total fat, 0 g saturated fat, 0 mg cholesterol, 1 mg sodium, 4 g carbohydrates, 0.6 g fiber, 0.3 g protein, 10 mg calcium, 0.1 mg iron

Lime Salsa

1 large ripe red or yellow tomato (about 8 oz./230 g), finely diced

8 medium-size tomatillos (about 8 oz./230 g *total*), husked, rinsed, and chopped

¼ cup (38 g) minced red or yellow bell pepper

2 tablespoons minced red onion

1 teaspoon grated lime peel

1 tablespoon (15 ml) lime juice

1. In a nonmetal bowl, mix tomato, tomatillos, bell pepper, onion, lime peel, and lime juice. If made ahead, cover and refrigerate for up to 4 hours. Makes about 4 cups (950 ml).

Per serving: 9 calories (11% calories from fat), 0.1 g total fat, 0 g saturated fat, 0 mg cholesterol, 2 mg sodium, 2 g carbohydrates, 0.3 g fiber, 0.4 g protein, 3 mg calcium, 0.1 mg iron

Pineapple Salsa

1 cup (155 g) diced fresh or canned pineapple

½ cup (73 g) chopped peeled, seeded cucumber

1 fresh jalapeño chile, seeded and minced

1 teaspoon grated lime peel

3 tablespoons (45 ml) lime juice

2 tablespoons minced cilantro

1. In a nonmetal bowl, mix pineapple, cucumber, chile, lime peel, lime juice, and cilantro. If made ahead, cover and refrigerate for up to 4 hours. Makes about 1¾ cups (420 ml).

Per serving: 14 calories (6% calories from fat), 0.1 g total fat, 0 g saturated fat, 0 mg cholesterol, 2 mg sodium, 4 g carbohydrates, 0.4 g fiber, 0.2 g protein, 4 mg calcium, 0.1 mg iron

Italian Sausage & Bow-Tie Soup
(recipe on page 24)

Soups

Although there's nothing quite as warming on a cold winter day as hot soup, soup is delicious year-round. A bowl of chilled creamy White Gazpacho can be wonderfully refreshing on a hot summer afternoon. Plain nonfat yogurt gives our gazpacho a smooth, velvety texture without the fat of regular dairy products. Lots of fresh vegetables, legumes, lean cuts of meat, and hearty grains make our soups deliciously satisfying.

Homemade ultra-lean sausage and slow-cooked onions contribute rich flavor but very little fat to this whole-meal soup. The pasta looks like little bow ties; the Italians, though, call these noodles farfalle, *or butterflies.*

Italian Sausage & Bow-tie Soup

Preparation time: About 20 minutes
Cooking time: About 40 minutes
Pictured on page 22

Low-fat Italian Sausage (recipe follows)

2 large onions (about 1 lb./455 g *total*), chopped

2 cloves garlic, minced or pressed

5 cups (1.2 liters) beef broth

1 can (about 28 oz./795 g) pear-shaped tomatoes

1½ cups (360 ml) dry red wine

1 tablespoon *each* dried basil and sugar

1 medium-size green bell pepper (about 6 oz./170 g), seeded and chopped

2 medium-size zucchini (about 8 oz./230 g *total*), sliced ¼ inch (6 mm) thick

5 ounces/140 g (about 2½ cups) dried farfalle (about 1½-inch/3.5-cm size)

½ cup (30 g) chopped parsley
Salt and pepper

1. Prepare Low-fat Italian Sausage.

2. Combine onions, garlic, and 1 cup (240 ml) of the broth in a 5- to 6-quart (5- to 6-liter) pan. Bring to a boil over medium-high heat and cook, stirring occasionally, until liquid has evaporated and onion mixture begins to brown (about 10 minutes). To deglaze pan, add 3 tablespoons (45 ml) water, stirring to loosen browned bits. Continue to cook, stirring often, until liquid has evaporated and onion mixture begins to brown again (about 1 minute). Repeat deglazing step, adding 3 tablespoons (45 ml) more water each time, until onion mixture is richly browned.

3. Stir in sausage and ½ cup (120 ml) more water. Cook, stirring gently, until liquid has evaporated and meat begins to brown (8 to 10 minutes).

4. Add remaining 4 cups (950 ml) broth, stirring to loosen browned bits.

Stir in tomatoes (break up with a spoon) and their liquid, wine, basil, sugar, bell pepper, zucchini, and pasta. Bring to a boil over high heat; reduce heat, cover, and simmer just until pasta is tender to bite (about 15 minutes).

5. Sprinkle soup with parsley. Offer salt and pepper to add to taste. Makes 6 servings.

Low-fat Italian Sausage. Cut 1 pound (455 g) **pork tenderloin** or boned pork loin, trimmed of fat, into 1-inch (2.5-cm) chunks. Whirl in a food processor, about half at a time, until coarsely chopped (or put through a food chopper fitted with a medium blade). In a large bowl, combine **pork,** ¼ cup (60 ml) **dry white wine,** 2 tablespoons chopped **parsley,** 1½ teaspoons crushed **fennel seeds,** ½ teaspoon crushed **red pepper flakes,** and 2 cloves **garlic,** minced or pressed. Mix well. Cover and refrigerate. If made ahead, refrigerate for up to a day.

Per serving: 327 calories (13% calories from fat), 4 g total fat, 1 g saturated fat, 49 mg cholesterol, 1,632 mg sodium, 37 g carbohydrates, 4 g fiber, 23 g protein, 103 mg calcium, 5 mg iron

---

Lightening up the ingredients of the cheese mixture that's added to this soup reduces the calorie count without diminishing the soup's rich flavor.

Maritata Soup

Preparation time: About 10 minutes
Cooking time: About 15 minutes

12 cups (2.8 liters) beef broth

8 ounces (230 g) dried vermicelli, broken into short lengths

½ cup (40 g) freshly grated Parmesan cheese

⅓ cup (80 g) Neufchâtel or cream cheese

3 large egg whites

1. Bring broth to a boil in a 5- to 6-quart (5- to 6-liter) pan over high heat. Stir in pasta; reduce heat, cover, and simmer just until pasta is tender to bite (8 to 10 minutes). Meanwhile, beat Parmesan, Neufchâtel, and egg whites with an electric mixer or in a blender until well combined.

2. Slowly pour about 1 cup of the simmering broth into cheese mixture, mixing to combine. Then return cheese-broth mixture to pan, stirring constantly until hot (2 to 3 minutes). Makes 8 servings.

Per serving: 189 calories (26% calories from fat), 5 g total fat, 2 g saturated fat, 11 mg cholesterol, 2,613 mg sodium, 22 g carbohydrates, 0.7 g fiber, 9 g protein, 82 mg calcium, 2 mg iron

Lean beef contributes full flavor and heartiness to a tomato-based soup enriched with orzo.

1 teaspoon olive oil or salad oil

1 pound (455 g) lean boneless beef, cut into ¾-inch (2-cm) chunks

About 5 cups (1.2 liters) beef broth

1 small onion (about 4 oz./115 g), chopped

1½ teaspoons dried thyme

1 can (about 6 oz./170 g) tomato paste

4 ounces/115 g (about ⅔ cup) dried orzo or other rice-shaped pasta

1 large tomato (about 8 oz./230 g), chopped

2 tablespoons (30 ml) dry red wine (or to taste)

Cilantro

Salt and pepper

Tomato, Beef & Orzo Soup

Preparation time: About 25 minutes
Cooking time: About 1⅓ hours

1. Heat oil in a 4- to 5-quart (3.8- to 5-liter) pan over medium heat. Add beef and cook, stirring, until browned (about 10 minutes); if pan appears dry, stir in water, 1 tablespoon (15 ml) at a time. Add 1 cup (240 ml) of the broth; stir to loosen browned bits. Bring to a boil over high heat; reduce heat, cover, and simmer for 30 minutes.

2. Add onion and thyme. Cook, uncovered, over medium-high heat, stirring often, until liquid has evaporated and pan drippings are richly browned (about 10 minutes). Add 4 cups (950 ml) more broth and tomato paste. Bring to a boil over high heat, stirring to loosen browned bits; reduce heat, cover, and boil gently for 20 more minutes.

3. Add pasta, cover, and continue to cook, stirring often, just until pasta is tender to bite (8 to 10 minutes; or according to package directions). Stir in tomato. If soup is too thick, add a little broth or water; if too thin, continue to simmer until thickened. Remove from heat and add wine. Ladle into bowls. Garnish with cilantro. Offer salt and pepper to add to taste. Makes 4 or 5 servings.

Per serving: 300 calories (28% calories from fat), 9 g total fat, 3 g saturated fat, 59 mg cholesterol, 1,985 mg sodium, 28 g carbohydrates, 3 g fiber, 23 g protein, 40 mg calcium, 6 mg iron

---

Lamb meatballs, lentils, and couscous produce a thick, satisfying main-course soup.

1 large onion (about 8 oz./230 g), chopped

1 tablespoon minced fresh ginger

1 teaspoon cumin seeds

1 tablespoon curry powder

10 cups (2.4 liters) low-sodium chicken broth

8 ounces/230 g (about 1¼ cups) lentils, rinsed and drained

1 pound (455 g) lean ground lamb

1 teaspoon *each* ground coriander and chili powder

4 ounces/115 g (about ⅔ cup) dried couscous

¼ cup (10 g) cilantro

Plain nonfat yogurt

Lamb, Lentil & Couscous Soup

Preparation time: About 20 minutes
Cooking time: About 1 hour

1. Combine onion, ginger, cumin, and ¼ cup (60 ml) water in a 5- to 6-quart (5- to 6-liter) pan. Cook over medium-high heat, stirring often, until liquid has evaporated and onion begins to brown. To deglaze pan, add 2 tablespoons (30 ml) water, stirring to loosen browned bits. Continue to cook, stirring often, until liquid has evaporated and onion begins to brown again. Repeat deglazing step, adding 2 tablespoons (30 ml) more water each time, until onion is light golden.

2. Reduce heat to low and add curry powder; cook, stirring, until fragrant (about 1 minute). Add broth and lentils; stir to loosen browned bits. Bring to a boil over high heat; reduce heat, cover, and simmer just until lentils are almost tender to bite (20 to 30 minutes). Meanwhile, mix lamb, coriander, and chili powder in a bowl; shape into ¾-inch (2-cm) balls.

3. Drop meatballs into soup. Stir in pasta. Cover and continue to simmer just until lamb is no longer pink in center (cut to test) and pasta is tender to bite (about 5 minutes). Ladle into bowls. Sprinkle with cilantro. Offer yogurt to add to taste. Makes 6 to 8 servings.

Per serving: 322 calories (22% calories from fat), 9 g total fat, 3 g saturated fat, 43 mg cholesterol, 220 mg sodium, 38 g carbohydrates, 5 g fiber, 29 g protein, 70 mg calcium, 5 mg iron

Pozole is a pork, chicken, and hominy soup that's a favorite throughout Mexico

- 1 **pound (455 g) pork tenderloin, trimmed of fat and silvery membrane and cut into 1½-inch (3.5 cm) chunks**
- 1 **pound (455 g) skinless, boneless chicken or turkey thighs, cut into 1½-inch (3.5 cm) chunks**
- 3 **quarts (2.8 liters) low-sodium chicken broth**
- 2 **large onions (about 1 lb./455 g *total*), cut into chunks**
- 1 **teaspoon dry oregano**
- ½ **teaspoon cumin seeds**
- 2 **cans (about 14 oz./400 g *each*) yellow hominy, drained**

Pozole

Preparation time: About 15 minutes
Cooking time: About 1¾ hours

Salt and pepper
Lime slices or wedges
1½ **cups (64 g) crisp corn tortilla strips (page 346)**

1. Place pork and chicken in a 6- to 8-quart (5.7- to 7.6-liter) pan. Add broth, onions, oregano, and cumin seeds to pan. Bring to a boil over high heat; then reduce heat, cover, and simmer until meat is tender when pierced (about 1½ hours). Lift out meat with a slotted spoon; place in a bowl to cool.

2. Pour cooking broth into a strainer set over a bowl. Press residue to remove liquid; discard residue. Return broth to pan and bring to a boil over high heat.

3. Add hominy and reduce heat; simmer, uncovered, until flavors are blended (about 10 minutes). Coarsely shred meat and return to broth. Serve soup hot or warm. If made ahead, let cool; then cover and refrigerate until next day. Reheat before serving.

4. To serve, ladle into bowls. Season to taste with salt and pepper and serve with lime slices and tortilla strips. Makes 8 to 10 servings.

Per serving: 265 calories (26% calories from fat), 8 g total fat, 2 g saturated fat, 75 mg cholesterol, 429 mg sodium, 25 g carbohydrates, 4 g fiber, 27 g protein, 74 mg calcium, 2 mg iron

---

Fresh and light, this quick-to-make soup takes advantage of crunchy, sweet fresh asparagus. Each bowlful is enriched with a generous helping of seasoned shrimp.

- 8 **cups (1.9 liters) low-sodium chicken broth**
- 2 **cups (220 g) diced carrots**
- 4 **ounces/115 g (about 1 cup) dried small shell-shaped pasta**
- 2 **cups (270 g) thinly sliced asparagus**
- 1 **package (about 10 oz./285 g) frozen tiny peas**
- 1¼ **to 1½ pounds (565 to 680 g) tiny cooked shrimp**

Spring Vegetable Soup with Shells

Preparation time: About 25 minutes
Cooking time: About 15 minutes
Pictured on facing page

½ **cup (50 g) thinly sliced green onions**
¼ **cup (15 g) minced parsley**
Parsley sprigs (optional)
Salt and pepper

1. Bring broth to a boil in a 5- to 6-quart (5- to 6-liter) pan over high heat. Stir in carrots and pasta; reduce

heat, cover, and boil gently just until carrots and pasta are tender to bite (8 to 10 minutes; or according to package directions).

2. Add asparagus and peas; cook until heated through (about 2 minutes). Remove from heat and keep warm.

3. Combine shrimp, onions, and minced parsley in a small bowl. Ladle soup into bowls and spoon in shrimp mixture, dividing evenly. Garnish with parsley sprigs, if desired. Offer salt and pepper to add to taste. Makes 8 to 10 servings.

Per serving: 178 calories (16% calories from fat), 3 g total fat, 1 g saturated fat, 136 mg cholesterol, 312 mg sodium, 18 g carbohydrates, 3 g fiber, 22 g protein, 69 mg calcium, 4 mg iron

Spring Vegetable Soup with Shells
(recipe on facing page)

A full quart of buttermilk adds low-calorie nutrition, an interesting sharp flavor, and a smooth, creamy texture to this warm-weather soup. The soup takes only minutes to prepare, but it does need time to chill.

2 cups (470 ml) low-sodium chicken broth

2 large tart apples (about 1 lb./455 g *total*), peeled, cored, and chopped

1 large onion, chopped

½ teaspoon curry powder

1 large red bell pepper (about 8 oz./230 g)

4 cups (950 ml) cold buttermilk

¼ cup (60 ml) lime juice

1½ cups (248 g) cooked yellow or white corn kernels (from 2 medium-size ears corn); or 1 package (about 10 oz./285 g) frozen corn kernels, drained

Curried Corn Shrimp Soup

Preparation time: About 15 minutes
Cooking time: About 30 minutes
Chilling time: At least 3 hours

½ cup (20 g) minced cilantro

⅓ pound (150 g) tiny cooked shrimp

Cilantro sprigs

1. In a 4- to 5-quart (3.8- to 4.7-liter) pan, combine broth, apples, onion, and curry powder. Bring to a boil over high heat; then reduce heat, cover, and simmer until apples mash easily (about 30 minutes).

2. Let cool; then cover and refrigerate until cold (at least 3 hours) or until next day. Pour mixture into a blender or food processor and whirl until smoothly puréed.

3. Seed bell pepper and cut a few thin slivers from it; set slivers aside. Dice remaining pepper. Put diced pepper in a tureen and stir in apple-onion purée, buttermilk, lime juice, 1¼ cups (206 g) of the corn, and minced cilantro. (At this point, you may cover and refrigerate soup, pepper slivers, and remaining ¼ cup/42 g corn until next day.)

4. To serve, ladle soup into bowls and top equally with shrimp, remaining corn, bell pepper slivers, and cilantro sprigs. Makes 6 servings.

Per serving: 211 calories (13% calories from fat), 3 g total fat, 1 g saturated fat, 55 mg cholesterol, 277 mg sodium, 36 g carbohydrates, 4 g fiber, 14 g protein, 225 mg calcium, 2 mg iron

Steeping—cooking food in hot liquid off the heat—helps preserve delicate textures and flavors. In this easy main-dish soup, shrimp are quickly steeped in a ginger-infused broth.

6 cups (1.4 liters) low-sodium chicken broth

2 tablespoons minced fresh ginger

12 ounces (340 g) extra-large shrimp (26 to 30 per lb.), shelled and deveined

2 ounces (55 g) dried capellini, broken into 2-inch (5-cm) pieces

1 package (about 10 oz./285 g) frozen tiny peas, thawed

Gingered Shrimp & Capellini Soup

Preparation time: About 30 minutes
Cooking time: About 10 minutes

½ cup (50 g) thinly sliced green onions

Fish sauce (*nam pla* or *nuoc mam*), oyster sauce, or reduced-sodium soy sauce

1. Combine broth and ginger in a 4- to 5-quart (3.8- to 5-liter) pan. Cover and bring to a boil over high heat. Quickly stir in shrimp and pasta; cover, imme-diately remove pan from heat, and let stand for 4 minutes (do not uncover). Check shrimp for doneness (shrimp should be opaque but moist-looking in center of thickest part; cut to test). If shrimp are still translucent, cover and let stand until done, checking at 2-minute intervals.

2. Add peas, cover, and let stand until heated through (about 3 minutes).

3. Stir in onions and ladle soup into bowls. Offer fish sauce to add to taste. Makes 4 to 6 servings.

Per serving: 172 calories (20% calories from fat), 4 g total fat, 1 g saturated fat, 84 mg cholesterol, 299 mg sodium, 18 g carbohydrates, 3 g fiber, 19 g protein, 68 mg calcium, 3 mg iron

This meal-in-a-bowl features turkey meatballs, tomatoes, carrots, and spinach in a light broth.

Turkey Meatballs (recipe follows)

1 can (about 14½ oz./415 g) pear-shaped tomatoes

6 cups (1.4 liters) low-sodium chicken broth

4 cups (950 ml) beef broth

2 cups (340 g) chopped onions

6 medium-size carrots (about 1½ lbs./680 g *total*), thinly sliced

1 teaspoon dry oregano

2 teaspoons chili powder

12 ounces (340 g) stemmed spinach leaves, rinsed well and drained (about 3 cups lightly packed)

⅓ cup (13 g) chopped cilantro

1 or 2 limes, cut into wedges

Turkey Albondigas Soup

Preparation time: About 30 minutes
Cooking time: About 15 minutes

1. Prepare Turkey Meatballs; set aside.

2. Pour tomatoes and their liquid into an 8- to 10-quart (7.6- to 9.5 liter) pan; break tomatoes up with a spoon. Add chicken broth, beef broth, onions, carrots, oregano, and chili powder.

3. Bring to a boil over high heat; then reduce heat to low. Add meatballs and simmer for 10 minutes. Stir in spinach and cilantro and cook until greens are wilted (about 3 more minutes).

4. To serve, ladle soup into bowls; serve with lime wedges. Makes 6 to 8 servings.

Turkey Meatballs. In a bowl, mix 1 pound **ground turkey,** ½ cup (73 g) **cooked brown** or **white rice,** ¼ cup (30 g) **all-purpose flour,** ¼ cup (60 ml) **water,** and 1 teaspoon **ground cumin.** Shape mixture into 1- to 1½-inch (2.5- to 3.5-cm) balls and place, slightly apart, in a 10- by 15-inch (25- by 38-cm) rimmed baking pan. Bake in a 450°F (230°C) oven until well browned (about 15 minutes). Pour off fat. If made ahead, let cool; then cover and refrigerate until next day.

Per serving: 235 calories (27% calories from fat), 8 g total fat, 2 g saturated fat, 47 mg cholesterol, 341 mg sodium, 28 g carbohydrates, 6 g fiber, 19 g protein, 137 mg calcium, 4 mg iron

---

Fresh zucchini and tomato enliven not only the appearance but also the flavor of traditional chicken soup.

1 teaspoon salad oil

1 large onion (about 8 oz./230 g), chopped

8 cups (1.9 liters) fat-free reduced-sodium chicken broth

3 cloves garlic, minced or pressed

½ teaspoon dried thyme

¼ teaspoon pepper

2 large carrots (about 8 oz./230 g *total*), thinly sliced

½ cup (60 g) chopped celery

6 ounces (170 g) Egg Pasta or Food Processor Pasta (pages 284–285), cut into wide 3-inch-long (8-cm-long) noodles, or 5 ounces (140 g) dried wide egg noodles

Chicken Noodle Soup

Preparation time: About 20 minutes
Cooking time: About 25 minutes

3 cups (420 g) shredded cooked chicken

1 small zucchini (about 3 oz./ 85 g), chopped

1 medium-size tomato (about 5 oz./140 g), peeled, seeded, and chopped

2 tablespoons chopped parsley

1. Heat oil in a 5- to 6-quart (5- to 6-liter) pan over medium-high heat. Add onion and cook, stirring often, until onion is soft (about 5 minutes); if pan appears dry or onion sticks to pan bottom, stir in water, 1 tablespoon (15 ml) at a time.

2. Add broth, garlic, thyme, and pepper; bring to a boil. Stir in carrots, celery, and, if used, dried pasta; reduce heat, cover, and boil gently just until carrots are barely tender to bite (about 10 minutes). Stir homemade pasta, if used, into pan and cook just until tender to bite (1 to 3 minutes).

3. Stir in chicken, zucchini, and tomato; heat until steaming. Garnish with parsley. Makes 6 servings.

Per serving: 276 calories (23% calories from fat), 7 g total fat, 2 g saturated fat, 91 mg cholesterol, 955 mg sodium, 24 g carbohydrates, 3 g fiber, 29 g protein, 48 mg calcium, 2 mg iron

Garlic Soup with Ravioli
(recipe on facing page)

Meatballs made from ground turkey float in a peanut-flavored broth enriched with spinach and pasta.

....

Herbed Meatballs
(recipe follows)

14 cups (3.4 liters) fat-free reduced-sodium chicken broth

⅓ cup (80 ml) reduced-sodium soy sauce

⅓ cup (48 g) lightly packed brown sugar

3 tablespoons smooth peanut butter

¼ cup (60 ml) distilled white vinegar (or to taste)

10 ounces/285 g (about 4½ cups) dried ruote or other medium-size pasta shape

12 ounces (340 g) spinach (about 3 cups lightly packed), coarse stems removed, rinsed, and drained

½ cup (75 g) chopped red bell pepper

Ruote & Meatball Soup

Preparation time: About 30 minutes
Cooking time: About 30 minutes

1 teaspoon Oriental sesame oil (or to taste)

Cilantro

Crushed red pepper flakes

....

1. Prepare Herbed Meatballs.

2. Combine broth, soy sauce, sugar, peanut butter, and vinegar in a 6- to 8-quart (6- to 8-liter) pan. Bring to a boil over high heat, stirring occasionally with a whisk. Stir in meatballs and pasta; reduce heat and boil gently just until pasta is tender to bite (8 to 10 minutes; or according to package directions).

3. Add spinach and bell pepper. Cook just until heated through (about 3 minutes). Add sesame oil and ladle into bowls. Garnish with cilantro. Offer pepper flakes to add to taste. Makes 8 to 10 servings.

....

Herbed Meatballs. In a large bowl, combine 1 pound (455 g) **fresh ground turkey breast,** ½ cup (85 g) **cooked couscous,** ¼ cup (30 g) **all-purpose flour,** ¼ cup (60 ml) **water,** and ½ teaspoon **ground coriander** or dried basil. Mix well. Shape into 1- to 1½-inch (2.5- to 3.5-cm) balls. Place balls slightly apart in a lightly oiled 10- by 15-inch (25- by 38-cm) baking pan. Bake in a 450°F (230°C) oven until well browned (about 15 minutes). Pour off any fat. Keep warm.

....

Per serving: 276 calories (15% calories from fat), 5 g total fat, 0.8 g saturated fat, 29 mg cholesterol, 444 mg sodium, 40 g carbohydrates, 2 g fiber, 20 g protein, 55 mg calcium, 3 mg iron

---

Long popular as a seasoning, garlic is now showing up more and more as a principal ingredient, as in this light soup. Slow cooking modifies the garlic's assertiveness.

....

1 head garlic

1 teaspoon salad oil

6 cups (1.4 liters) low-sodium chicken broth

1 package (about 9 oz./255 g) fresh low-fat or regular cheese ravioli or tortellini

3 tablespoons *each* finely chopped red bell pepper and green onions

¼ teaspoon Oriental sesame oil (optional)

Cilantro

Garlic Soup with Ravioli

Preparation time: About 20 minutes
Cooking time: About 35 minutes
Pictured on facing page

....

1. Peel garlic; thinly slice cloves. Heat salad oil in a nonstick frying pan over medium-low heat. Add garlic and cook, stirring often, until golden brown (about 10 minutes; do not scorch); if pan appears dry or garlic sticks to pan bottom, stir in water, 1 tablespoon (15 ml) at a time. Meanwhile, bring broth to a boil in a 4- to 5-quart (3.8- to 5-liter) pan over high heat. When garlic is done, pour about ½ cup (120 ml) of the broth into frying

pan, stirring to loosen browned bits. Return garlic mixture to broth; reduce heat, cover, and simmer for 15 minutes.

2. Increase heat to high and bring to a boil. Separating any ravioli that are stuck together, add pasta to broth. Reduce heat and boil gently, stirring occasionally, just until pasta is tender to bite (4 to 6 minutes; or according to package directions).

3. Add bell pepper, onions, and, if desired, sesame oil and cook just until heated through (about 2 minutes). Garnish with cilantro. Makes 6 servings.

....

Per serving: 164 calories (28% calories from fat), 6 g total fat, 2 g saturated fat, 26 mg cholesterol, 268 mg sodium, 23 g carbohydrates, 1 g fiber, 10 g protein, 111 mg calcium, 1 mg iron

Chopped onions, fresh tomatoes, and tender homemade noodles transform this tomato soup into a chunky first-course offering.

- 1 tablespoon (15 ml) salad oil
- 2 large onions (about 1 lb./455 g *total*), chopped
- 3 pounds (1.35 kg) firm-ripe tomatoes (about 6 large), peeled, seeded, and chopped
- 3 cups (710 ml) low-sodium chicken broth
- 1 can (about 8 oz./230 g) tomato sauce
- 1 tablespoon chopped fresh oregano or 1 teaspoon dried oregano
- ½ teaspoon ground cumin
- 4 ounces (115 g) Egg Pasta or Food Processor Pasta (pages 284–285), cut for fettuccine, or purchased fresh fettuccine
- 2 tablespoons (30 ml) dry sherry (or to taste)

Fresh Tomato Soup with Homemade Pasta

Preparation time: About 30 minutes
Cooking time: About 40 minutes

Oregano sprigs
Freshly grated Parmesan cheese
Salt and pepper

1. Heat oil in a 4- to 5-quart (3.8- to 5-liter) pan over medium-high heat. Add onions and cook, stirring often, until soft (about 10 minutes); if pan appears dry or onions stick to pan bottom, stir in water, 1 tablespoon (15 ml) at a time.

2. Add tomatoes, broth, tomato sauce, chopped oregano, and cumin. Bring to a boil; reduce heat, cover, and simmer until tomatoes are soft (about 15 minutes).

3. Remove 4 cups (950 ml) of the mixture and whirl in a blender or food processor, a portion at a time, until puréed. Return to pan; bring to a boil over high heat. Meanwhile, cut pasta into 3-inch (8-cm) lengths.

4. Stir in pasta; reduce heat, cover, and boil gently just until pasta is tender to bite (1 to 3 minutes; or according to package directions).

5. Remove pan from heat and add sherry. Ladle soup into bowls. Garnish with oregano sprigs. Offer cheese, salt, and pepper to add to taste. Makes 6 servings.

Per serving: 172 calories (24% calories from fat), 5 g total fat, 1 g saturated fat, 19 mg cholesterol, 313 mg sodium, 29 g carbohydrates, 5 g fiber, 6 g protein, 49 mg calcium, 2 mg iron

Cool sour cream and sharp Cheddar complement the deep, mellow flavor of roasted vegetables.

- 2 medium-size leeks (about 1 lb./455 g *total*)
- 1 large ear corn (about 10 inches/ 25 cm long), husk and silk removed
- 1 small red onion (about 4 oz./115 g), cut in half
- 1 large red bell pepper (about 8 oz./230 g)
- 1 large yellow or green bell pepper (about 8 oz./230 g)
- 2 cloves garlic, peeled
- 4 cups (950 ml) fat-free reduced-sodium chicken broth
- 1 cup (about 4 oz./115 g) shredded reduced-fat sharp Cheddar cheese
- ¼ cup (60 ml) nonfat sour cream

Roasted Vegetable & Cheese Soup

Preparation time: 25 minutes
Cooking time: About 30 minutes

1. Trim and discard roots and tough tops from leeks; remove and discard coarse outer leaves. Split leeks lengthwise; thoroughly rinse leek halves between layers. In a large, shallow baking pan, arrange leeks, corn, onion halves, and whole bell peppers.

2. Broil 4 to 6 inches (10 to 15 cm) below heat, turning vegetables as needed to brown evenly, for 10 minutes. Add garlic. Continue to broil, turning as needed, until vegetables are

well charred (about 5 more minutes); remove vegetables from pan as they are charred. Cover vegetables loosely with foil and let stand until cool enough to handle (about 10 minutes).

3. With a sharp knife, cut corn kernels from cob. Remove and discard skins, seeds, and stems from bell peppers. Coarsely chop peppers, leeks, onion, and garlic.

4. In a 4- to 5-quart (3.8- to 5-liter) pan, combine vegetables and broth. Bring to a boil over high heat; then reduce heat, cover, and simmer for 10 minutes to blend flavors. Ladle soup into individual bowls; sprinkle with cheese, top with sour cream, and serve. Makes 4 servings.

Per serving: 231 calories (22% calories from fat), 6 g total fat, 4 g saturated fat, 30 mg cholesterol, 901 mg sodium, 30 g carbohydrates, 5 g fiber, 18 g protein, 331 mg calcium, 2 mg iron

Puréed squash and sweet potatoes give this mildly sweet-tart soup a hearty consistency.

Soup:

About 1¾ pounds (795 g) butternut or other gold-fleshed squash

3 very large sweet potatoes or yams (about 1¾ lbs./795 g *total*)

7 cups (1.6 liters) vegetable broth

¼ cup (60 ml) balsamic vinegar

2 tablespoons firmly packed brown sugar

1 tablespoon finely chopped fresh ginger

About ⅛ teaspoon crushed red pepper flakes (or to taste)

Croutons:

1 tablespoon (15 ml) olive oil

1 clove garlic, minced or pressed

3 slices French or sourdough sandwich bread

Salt and pepper

Squash & Sweet Potato Soup

Preparation time: 20 minutes
Cooking time: About 35 minutes

1. Cut peel from squash; discard seeds. Peel potatoes. Cut squash and potatoes into 1-inch (2.5-cm) pieces and place in a 5- to 6-quart (5- to 6-liter) pan. Add broth, vinegar, sugar, ginger, and red pepper flakes. Cover and bring to a boil over high heat; then reduce heat and simmer gently until squash and potatoes are soft enough to mash easily, about 30 minutes. (At this point, you may let cool, then cover and refrigerate for up to 2 days.)

2. In a small bowl, combine oil, garlic, and 1 tablespoon (15 ml) water. Spread bread cubes on a nonstick 10- by 15-inch (25- by 38-cm) baking sheet;

brush evenly with oil mixture. Season to taste with salt and pepper. Bake in a 350°F (175°C) oven until croutons are crisp and golden (10 to 12 minutes). If made ahead, let cool completely on baking sheet on a rack; then store airtight for up to 2 days.

3. In a food processor or blender, whirl squash mixture, a portion at a time, until smoothly puréed. Return purée to pan and stir often over medium-high heat until steaming. Ladle soup into bowls; top with croutons. Makes 6 to 8 servings.

Per serving: 216 calories (15% calories from fat), 4 g total fat, 0.4 g saturated fat, 0 mg cholesterol, 1,088 mg sodium, 45 g carbohydrates, 4 g fiber, 3 g protein, 76 mg calcium, 2 mg iron

---

Here's a cool no-cook soup that's perfect for hot days. Just purée cucumber and cilantro with broth and a little nonfat milk, then chill the soup to let the flavors mingle.

1 very large cucumber (about 1 lb./455 g), peeled and cut into chunks

1¼ cups (300 ml) low-sodium chicken broth

¾ cup (40 g) firmly packed cilantro leaves

Chilled Cucumber & Cilantro Soup

Preparation time: About 10 minutes
Chilling time: At least 2 hours

½ cup (120 ml) nonfat or low-fat milk

¼ cup (60 ml) lemon juice
Salt

1. In a food processor or blender, combine cucumber, broth, cilantro, milk, and lemon juice; whirl until smoothly puréed. Season purée to taste with salt.

2. Cover and refrigerate until cold (at least 2 hours) or until next day.

3. To serve, ladle into bowls. Makes 4 servings.

Per serving: 36 calories (20% calories from fat), 1 g total fat, 0.3 g saturated fat, 0.6 mg cholesterol, 62 mg sodium, 6 g carbohydrates, 0.6 g fiber, 3 g protein, 65 mg calcium, 0.4 mg iron

Yellow peppers and carrots give this soup its golden hue; potatoes lend silkiness to the texture. Complete each serving with a drizzle of olive oil, a little cotija cheese, and a few croutons.

Garlic Croutons (page 33)

2 large yellow bell peppers (about 1 lb./455 g total)

1 tablespoon (15 ml) salad oil or olive oil

1 large onion, chopped

2 large thin-skinned potatoes (about 1 lb./455 g total), peeled and cut into ½-inch (1-cm) chunks

2 large carrots (about ¾ lb./340 g total), cut into ½-inch (1-cm) slices

1 large stalk celery, thinly sliced

6 cups (1.4 liters) low-sodium chicken broth

Extra-virgin olive oil

Golden Pepper Bisque

Preparation time: About 15 minutes
Cooking time: About 50 minutes
Pictured on facing page

Salt and pepper

Shredded cotija or Parmesan cheese

1. Prepare Garlic Croutons; set aside.

2. Cut bell peppers in half lengthwise. Set halves, cut side down, in a 10- by 15-inch (25- by 38-cm) rimmed baking pan. Broil 4 to 6 inches (10 to 15 cm) below heat until charred all over (about 8 minutes). Cover with foil and let cool in pan. Remove and discard skins, stems, and seeds; cut peppers into chunks.

3. In a 5- to 6-quart (4.7- to 5.7-liter) pan, combine salad oil and onion. Cook over medium-high heat, stirring occasionally, until onion is lightly browned (about 10 minutes). Add roasted bell peppers, potatoes, carrots, celery, and broth. Bring to a boil; then reduce heat, cover, and simmer until carrots are very soft to bite (20 to 25 minutes).

4. In a blender or food processor, whirl vegetable mixture, a portion at a time, until smoothly puréed. If made ahead, let cool; then cover and refrigerate until next day. Reheat, covered, before serving.

5. To serve, ladle soup into wide bowls. Add olive oil, salt, pepper, cheese, and Garlic Croutons to taste. Makes 6 to 8 servings.

Per serving: 132 calories (26% calories from fat), 4 g total fat, 0.9 g saturated fat, 0 mg cholesterol, 126 mg sodium, 23 g carbohydrates, 4 g fiber, 5 g protein, 40 mg calcium, 0.9 mg iron

---

Once hard to find, filled pasta is now readily available in many supermarkets, as well as in pasta shops and delicatessens. In this recipe, tortellini float in chicken broth along with shredded escarole and other vegetables. Nutmeg and lemon enhance the soup's flavors.

1 tablespoon (15 ml) olive oil

1 large onion (about 8 oz./230 g), chopped

2 large carrots (about 8 oz./230 g total), chopped

1 strip lemon zest (colored part of peel), about ¼ inch by 4 inches (6 mm by 10 cm)

10 cups (2.4 liters) low-sodium chicken broth

1 package (about 9 oz./255 g) fresh cheese or meat tortellini or ravioli

Tortellini-Escarole Soup

Preparation time: About 20 minutes
Cooking time: About 25 minutes

1 package (about 10 oz./285 g) frozen tiny peas, thawed

8 ounces/230 g (about 6 cups) shredded escarole

Freshly grated or ground nutmeg

Lemon wedges

Salt

1. Heat oil in a 5- to 6-quart (5- to 6-liter) pan over medium-high heat. Add onion, carrots, and lemon zest. Cook, stirring, until onion is soft (5 to 8 minutes).

2. Add broth and bring to a boil over high heat. Add pasta; reduce heat and boil gently, stirring occasionally, just until pasta is tender to bite (4 to 6 minutes; or according to package directions).

3. Stir in peas and escarole; cook just until escarole is wilted (1 to 2 minutes). Remove and discard zest.

4. Ladle soup into bowls. Dust generously with nutmeg. Offer lemon wedges and salt to add to taste. Makes 8 servings.

Per serving: 193 calories (30% calories from fat), 7 g total fat, 2 g saturated fat, 13 mg cholesterol, 316 mg sodium, 27 g carbohydrates, 4 g fiber, 11 g protein, 92 mg calcium, 1 mg iron

Golden Pepper Bisque
(recipe on facing page)

Serve this hearty vegetable soup with crisp rolls for a satisfying winter-day lunch.

3 quarts (2.8 liters) fat-free reduced-sodium chicken broth

2 ounces (55 g) thinly sliced prosciutto or bacon, chopped

2 tablespoons salted roasted almonds

2 cups (120 g) lightly packed Italian or regular parsley sprigs

2 tablespoons (30 ml) *each* olive oil and white wine vinegar

2 teaspoons honey

1 clove garlic, peeled

1 tablespoon drained capers

⅛ to ¼ teaspoon crushed red pepper flakes

1½ cups (225 g) diced unpeeled red thin-skinned potatoes

1 cup (120 g) sliced celery

1 large zucchini (about 8 oz./ 230 g), cut into ½-inch (1-cm) slices

10 ounces (285 g) fresh Italian green beans, cut into 1-inch (2.5-cm) lengths; or 1 package (about 10 oz./285 g) frozen Italian green beans, thawed

Minestrone with Parsley Pesto

Preparation time: 25 minutes
Cooking time: About 30 minutes

1 large red or yellow bell pepper (about 8 oz./230 g), seeded and cut into ½-inch (1-cm) chunks

¾ cup (85 g) dried salad or elbow macaroni

1 cup (53 g) lightly packed shredded radicchio or red Swiss chard

½ cup (50 g) thinly sliced green onions

1. In a 5- to 6-quart (5- to 6-liter) pan, combine broth and prosciutto. Bring to a rolling boil over high heat (10 to 12 minutes).

2. Meanwhile, in a food processor or blender, combine almonds, parsley sprigs, oil, vinegar, honey, garlic, capers, red pepper flakes, and 1 tablespoon (15 ml) water. Whirl until coarsely puréed; scrape sides of container as needed and add 1 to 2 tablespoons (15 to 30 ml) more water if pesto is too thick. Transfer pesto to a small bowl and set aside.

3. Add potatoes to boiling broth; reduce heat, cover, and simmer for 10 minutes. Add celery, zucchini, beans, bell pepper, and pasta; cover and simmer until potatoes and pasta are tender to bite (about 5 more minutes).

4. Stir in radicchio and onions; simmer until radicchio is limp but still bright red (about 4 minutes). Serve immediately; offer parsley pesto to spoon into individual servings. Makes 8 servings.

Per serving: 180 calories (29% calories from fat), 6 g total fat, 0.9 g saturated fat, 6 mg cholesterol, 1,172 mg sodium, 22 g carbohydrates, 3 g fiber, 11 g protein, 66 mg calcium, 3 mg iron

This refreshing chilled soup is a wonderful summer first course or light lunch.

2 cans (about 15 oz./425 g *each*) pickled beets

About 4 cups (950 ml) plain nonfat yogurt

1 cup (240 ml) vegetable broth

Dill sprigs

Pepper

Creamy Beet Borscht

Preparation time: 10 minutes

1. Drain beets, reserving 1½ cups (360 ml) of the liquid. In a large bowl, combine beets, reserved liquid, 4 cups (950 ml) of the yogurt, and broth. In a food processor or blender, whirl beet

mixture, about a third at a time, until smoothly puréed. If made ahead, cover and refrigerate until next day.

2. Serve borscht cool or cold. To serve, ladle into wide bowls. Add yogurt to taste and garnish with dill sprigs. Season to taste with pepper. Makes 6 to 8 servings.

Per serving: 113 calories (4% calories from fat), 0.5 g total fat, 0.2 g saturated fat, 3 mg cholesterol, 582 mg sodium, 19 g carbohydrates, 1 g fiber, 8 g protein, 276 mg calcium, 1 mg iron

Couscous—granular-shaped pasta made from semolina wheat—cooks in just minutes, giving this mint-infused soup extra heartiness.

1 tablespoon (15 ml) olive oil

2 ounces (55 g) pancetta or bacon, chopped

2 cloves garlic, minced or pressed

1 large onion (about 8 oz./230 g), chopped

8 cups (1.9 liters) low-sodium chicken broth

1 large russet potato (about 8 oz./230 g), peeled and diced

2 tablespoons chopped fresh mint or 1 tablespoon dried mint

½ teaspoon dried oregano

¼ teaspoon crushed red pepper flakes (or to taste)

2 cans (about 15 oz./425 g *each*) garbanzo beans, drained

Vegetable Soup with Couscous

Preparation time: About 30 minutes
Cooking time: About 55 minutes

1½ pounds (680 g) pear-shaped (Roma-type) tomatoes (about 8 large), diced

5 ounces/140 g (about ¾ cup) dried couscous

1 pound (455 g) escarole, ends trimmed, cut into 3-inch (8-cm) slivers

Freshly grated Parmesan cheese

Salt and pepper

1. Heat oil in a 5- to 6-quart (5- to 6-liter) pan over medium-high heat (omit oil if using bacon). Add pancetta and cook, stirring often, until lightly browned (about 5 minutes). Add garlic and onion; cook, stirring, until onion is soft (about 5 more minutes). Drain off fat.

2. Add broth, potato, mint, oregano, and red pepper flakes. Bring to a boil; reduce heat, cover, and simmer for 30 minutes.

3. Add beans and tomatoes; return to a boil. Stir in pasta; reduce heat, cover, and simmer just until pasta is tender to bite (about 5 minutes).

4. Stir in escarole and cook just until wilted (about 1 minute). Serve hot or at room temperature. If made ahead, let cool and then cover and refrigerate for up to a day; bring to room temperature or reheat before serving.

5. Offer cheese, salt, and pepper to add to taste. Makes 6 to 8 servings.

Per serving: 298 calories (28% calories from fat), 10 g total fat, 3 g saturated fat, 5 mg cholesterol, 347 mg sodium, 44 g carbohydrates, 7 g fiber, 14 g protein, 92 mg calcium, 3 mg iron

---

This classic soup owes its hearty texture and full body to filling but low-fat barley.

1 tablespoon (15 ml) salad oil or olive oil

1 pound (455 g) mushrooms, thinly sliced

1 large onion (about 8 oz./230 g), chopped

2 medium-size carrots (about 8 oz./230 g *total*), thinly sliced

10 cups (2.4 liters) vegetable broth

1 cup (200 g) pearl barley, rinsed and drained

1 tablespoon finely chopped fresh oregano or 1 teaspoon dried oregano

8 ounces (230 g) red or green Swiss chard

Pepper

Mushroom Barley Soup

Preparation time: 20 minutes
Cooking time: 1 to 1¼ hours

1. Heat oil in a 5- to 6-quart (5- to 6-liter) pan over medium-high heat. Add mushrooms, onion, and carrots. Cook, stirring often, until vegetables are soft and almost all liquid has evaporated (about 25 minutes). Add broth, barley, and oregano. Bring to a boil over high heat; then reduce heat, cover, and simmer until barley is tender to bite (about 30 minutes).

2. Meanwhile, trim and discard discolored stem ends from chard. Rinse chard and drain well; then coarsely chop leaves and stems.

3. Stir chard into soup and simmer, uncovered, until leaves are limp and bright green (5 to 10 minutes). Ladle soup into bowls; season to taste with pepper. Makes 6 to 8 servings.

Per serving: 196 calories (18% calories from fat), 4 g total fat, 0.3 g saturated fat, 0 mg cholesterol, 1,512 mg sodium, 37 g carbohydrates, 7 g fiber, 5 g protein, 47 mg calcium, 2 mg iron

White Gazpacho
(recipe on facing page)

Gazpacho

When the weather sizzles, these refreshing soups are delightful for lunch or supper.

Golden Tomato-Papaya Gazpacho

2 pounds (905 g) ripe yellow regular or cherry tomatoes

1 large ripe papaya (about 1¼ lbs./565 g), peeled, seeded, and diced

1 cup (145 g) diced cucumber

¼ cup (43 g) minced onion

2 tablespoons (30 ml) white wine vinegar

2 cups (470 ml) low-sodium chicken broth

2 tablespoons minced fresh basil

⅛ teaspoon liquid hot pepper seasoning

Salt

Basil sprigs

1. Dice tomatoes; place in a large nonmetal bowl. Stir in papaya, cucumber, onion, vinegar, broth, minced basil, and hot pepper seasoning. Season to taste with salt.

2. Cover and refrigerate until cold (at least 2 hours) or until next day. Garnish with basil sprigs. Makes 10 to 12 servings.

Per serving: 37 calories (15% calories from fat), 0.7 g total fat, 0.2 g saturated fat, 0 mg cholesterol, 30 mg sodium, 8 g carbohydrates, 1 g fiber, 2 g protein, 21 mg calcium, 0.5 mg iron

White Gazpacho

Pictured on facing page

1 European cucumber (about 1 lb./455 g), peeled and coarsely chopped

2 cups (470 ml) plain nonfat yogurt

2 tablespoons (30 ml) lemon juice

1 clove garlic, peeled

2 cups (470 ml) low-sodium chicken broth

2 tablespoons minced cilantro

2 tablespoons sliced green onion

Thin cucumber slices

Thinly slivered green onion tops

1. In a blender or food processor, whirl chopped cucumber, yogurt, lemon juice, and garlic until puréed (if using a blender, add about ½ cup/120 ml of the broth). Pour into a 2-quart (1.9-liter) container and stir in broth.

2. Cover and refrigerate until cold (at least 2 hours). Then stir in cilantro and sliced onion.

3. Pour mixture into a nonmetal serving bowl or pitcher. To serve, ladle or pour into bowls or glasses; garnish with cucumber slices and slivered onion. Makes 4 servings.

Per serving: 100 calories (13% calories from fat), 2 g total fat, 0.6 g saturated fat, 2 mg cholesterol, 155 mg sodium, 15 g carbohydrates, 1 g fiber, 9 g protein, 271 mg calcium, 0.8 mg iron

Tomato & Roasted Pepper Gazpacho

3 medium-size red bell peppers (about 1¼ lbs./565 g *total*)

1½ cups (360 ml) low-sodium chicken broth

¼ cup (60 ml) lime juice

3 green onions, thinly sliced

3 medium-size firm-ripe pear-shaped (Roma-type) tomatoes (about 8 oz./230 g *total*), diced

1 *each* small yellow and green bell pepper (about ⅓ lb./150 g *each*), seeded and diced

Salt and pepper

1. Cut red bell peppers in half lengthwise. Set halves, cut side down, in a 10- by 15-inch (25- by 38-cm) rimmed baking pan. Broil 4 to 6 inches (10 to 15 cm) below heat until charred all over (about 8 minutes). Cover with foil and let cool in pan. Remove and discard skins, stems, and seeds.

2. In a food processor or blender, whirl roasted peppers, broth, and lime juice until smoothly puréed. Stir in onions, tomatoes, and yellow and green bell peppers; season to taste with salt and pepper.

3. Cover and refrigerate until cold (at least 2 hours) or until next day. Makes 4 servings.

Per serving: 75 calories (14% calories from fat), 1 g total fat, 0.4 g saturated fat, 0 mg cholesterol, 56 mg sodium, 16 g carbohydrates, 4 g fiber, 3 g protein, 35 mg calcium, 1 mg iron

Hot & Sour Tofu Soup

This soup combines the traditional flavors of Sichuan with tender strands of pasta. Season with chili oil to add heat.

Preparation time: About 35 minutes
Cooking time: About 20 minutes

8   medium-size dried shiitake mushrooms (about ¾ oz./20 g *total*)

1   teaspoons salad oil

1   clove garlic, minced or pressed

1   tablespoon minced fresh ginger

10 cups (2.4 liters) fat-free reduced-sodium chicken broth

4   ounces (115 g) dried linguine, broken into 3-inch (8-cm) pieces

1   pound (455 g) regular reduced-fat tofu, rinsed and drained, cut into ½-inch (1-cm) cubes

3   tablespoons (45 ml) seasoned rice vinegar; or 3 tablespoons (45 ml) distilled white vinegar and 2 teaspoons sugar (or to taste)

5   teaspoons (25 ml) reduced-sodium soy sauce (or to taste)

3   tablespoons cornstarch mixed with ¼ cup (60 ml) water

4   green onions, thinly sliced Chili oil

1. Soak mushrooms in boiling water to cover until soft (about 20 minutes). Drain; cut off and discard coarse stems. Cut caps into thin strips; set aside.

2. Heat salad oil in a 5- to 6-quart (5- to 6-liter) pan over medium heat. Add garlic and ginger. Cook, stirring, until garlic is light golden (about 2 minutes); if pan appears dry or garlic sticks to pan bottom, stir in water, 1 tablespoon (15 ml) at a time. Add broth and mushrooms; bring to a boil over high heat. Stir in pasta; reduce heat, cover, and boil gently just until pasta is tender to bite (8 to 10 minutes; or according to package directions).

3. Add tofu, vinegar, and soy sauce. Stir cornstarch mixture; add to soup, stirring until smooth. Cook over medium-high heat, stirring, just until soup comes to a boil and thickens slightly. Add onions; ladle into bowls. Offer chili oil to add to taste. Makes 6 to 8 servings.

Per serving: 151 calories (10% calories from fat), 2 g total fat, 0.1 g saturated fat, 0 mg cholesterol, 1,248 mg sodium, 22 g carbohydrates, 1 g fiber, 12 g protein, 11 mg calcium, 0.9 mg iron

Tomato Fava Soup

Savory, an aromatic herb, infuses the tomato purée with a piquant, minty flavor.

Preparation time: 25 minutes
Cooking time: About 30 minutes

2   tablespoons (30 ml) olive oil

1   large onion (about 8 oz./230 g), chopped

1½ pounds (680 g) ripe tomatoes, quartered

2   tablespoons finely chopped fresh savory or 1 teaspoon dried savory

¾   teaspoon sugar

¼   teaspoon pepper

2   cups shelled fava beans (about 2 lbs./905 g in the pod); see Note at right

4   cups (950 ml) fat-free reduced-sodium chicken broth

1. Heat oil in a 3- to 4-quart (2.8- to 3.8-liter) pan over medium-high heat. Add onion and cook, stirring often, until it begins to brown (5 to 10 minutes). Add tomatoes, savory, sugar, and pepper. Bring to a boil; then reduce heat and simmer, uncovered, until tomatoes are very soft when pressed (about 15 minutes).

2. Meanwhile, in a 2- to 3-quart (1.9- to 2.8-liter) pan, bring 4 cups (950 ml) water to a boil over high heat. Add beans and simmer, uncovered, until just tender when pierced (3 to 5 minutes). Drain, then let stand until cool enough to touch. With your fingers, slip skins from beans; discard skins and set beans aside.

3. In a food processor or blender, whirl tomato mixture until coarsely puréed. Return to pan and add broth; stir over high heat until hot. Ladle soup into individual bowls; sprinkle beans equally over each serving. Makes 6 servings.

Note: A few people, typically of Mediterranean descent, have a severe allergic reaction to fava beans and their pollen. If favas are new to you, check your family history before eating them.

Per serving: 261 calories (19% calories from fat), 6 g total fat, 0.8 g saturated fat, 0 mg cholesterol, 447 mg sodium, 39 g carbohydrates, 9 g fiber, 17 g protein, 70 mg calcium, 4 mg iron

Mexican cooks use nourishing, earthy-tasting black beans in a variety of dishes. To make this satisfying soup, you can use home-cooked dried beans if you like—but we suggest you speed up preparation with the canned or instant refried variety.

....

2 teaspoons salad oil

1 large onion, chopped

1¾ or 2¾ cups (420 or 650 ml) low-sodium chicken broth

1 large can (about 28 oz./795 g) tomatoes

3 cans (about 15 oz./425 g *each*) black beans, drained, rinsed, and puréed; or 1 package (about 7 oz./200 g) instant refried black bean mix

1 fresh jalapeño chile, seeded and minced

2 teaspoons cumin seeds
  Condiments
  (suggestions follow)

Black Bean Soup

....

Preparation time: About 10 minutes
Cooking time: About 30 minutes

1. In a 5- to 6-quart (4.7- to 5.7-liter) pan, combine oil and onion. Cook over medium heat, stirring often, until onion is deep golden (about 20 minutes). Add 1¾ cups (420 ml) broth (or 2¾ cups/650 g if using instant beans).

2. Add tomatoes and their liquid to pan; break tomatoes up with a spoon. Stir in beans, chile, and cumin seeds. Bring to a boil; then reduce heat and simmer, uncovered, until soup is thick and flavors are blended (7 to 10 minutes).

3. To serve, ladle soup into bowls. Add condiments to taste. Makes 4 servings.

....

Condiments. Offer in individual bowls: shredded **Cheddar cheese,** plain **nonfat yogurt, cilantro leaves, lime wedges,** and **water-crisped tortilla chips** (page 346).

....

Per serving: 327 calories (17% calories from fat), 6 g total fat, 1 g saturated fat, 0 mg cholesterol, 795 mg sodium, 51 g carbohydrates, 15 g fiber, 21 g protein, 154 mg calcium, 5 mg iron

---

Mild lentil purée is spiked with dry and cream sherries for a fruity undertone of flavor.

....

2 packages (about 12 oz./340 g *each*, about 3½ cups total) lentils

11 cups (2.6 liters) vegetable broth

3 cups (369 g) chopped celery

3 cups (390 g) chopped carrots

3 large onions, chopped

1 small red or green bell pepper (about 4 oz./115 g), seeded and finely chopped

1 medium-size zucchini (about 6 oz./170 g), finely chopped

3 tablespoons (45 ml) dry sherry

4½ teaspoons (23 ml) cream sherry

Sherried Lentil Bisque

....

Preparation time: 30 minutes
Cooking time: About 55 minutes

1 cup (240 ml) reduced-fat sour cream
  Thinly sliced green onions
  Salt and pepper

....

1. Sort through lentils, discarding any debris. Rinse and drain lentils; place in an 8- to 10-quart (8- to 10-liter) pan and add broth, celery, carrots, chopped onions, bell pepper, and zucchini.

Bring to a boil over high heat; then reduce heat, cover, and simmer until lentils are very soft to bite (about 50 minutes).

2. In a food processor or blender, whirl hot lentil mixture, a portion at a time, until smoothly puréed. Return purée to pan and stir in dry sherry and cream sherry. If made ahead, let cool; then cover and refrigerate until next day.

3. To serve, stir soup often over medium-high heat until steaming; ladle into bowls. Top with sour cream and green onions; season to taste with salt and pepper. Makes 12 servings.

....

Per serving: 293 calories (13% calories from fat), 4 g total fat, 1 g saturated fat, 7 mg cholesterol, 959 mg sodium, 47 g carbohydrates, 9 g fiber, 19 g protein, 63 mg calcium, 6 mg iron

Fresh vegetables, white kidney beans, and macaroni mingle in this colorful, hearty one-pot meal. Serve the soup hot or at room temperature.

Pesto (recipe follows)

2 **large leeks** (about 1¼ lbs./565 g *total*)

12 **cups (2.8 liters) fat-free reduced-sodium chicken broth**

2 **large carrots** (about 8 oz./230 g *total*), **thinly sliced**

2 **large stalks celery** (about 12 oz./ 230 g *total*), **thinly sliced**

2 **cans** (about 15 oz./425 g *each*) **cannellini (white kidney beans), drained**

10 **ounces/340 g** (about 2½ cups) **dried medium-size elbow macaroni**

¾ **pound (340 g) yellow crookneck squash or zucchini** (about 3 medium-size), **cut into ½-inch (1-cm) chunks**

1 **large red bell pepper** (about 8 oz./230 g), **seeded and cut into ½-inch (1-cm) pieces**

2 **packages** (about 10 oz./285 g *each*) **frozen tiny peas**

Basil sprigs

Salt and pepper

Minestrone Genovese

Preparation time: About 30 minutes
Cooking time: 25 to 30 minutes
Pictured on facing page

1. Prepare Pesto.

2. Cut off and discard root ends and green tops of leeks. Discard coarse outer leaves. Split leeks in half lengthwise and rinse well; thinly slice crosswise.

3. Combine leeks, broth, carrots, and celery in an 8- to 10-quart (8- to 10-liter) pan. Bring to a boil over high heat; reduce heat, cover, and simmer for 10 minutes.

4. Stir in beans, pasta, squash, and bell pepper; cover and simmer just until pasta is tender to bite (about 10 more minutes).

5. Add peas and bring to a boil. Stir ½ cup (120 ml) of the Pesto into soup. Serve hot or at room temperature. If made ahead, let cool and then cover and refrigerate for up to a day; bring to room temperature or reheat before serving.

6. Garnish with basil. Offer salt, pepper, and remaining Pesto to add to taste. Makes 12 servings.

Pesto. In a food processor or blender, combine 2 cups (80 g) lightly packed **fresh basil,** 1 cup (about 4 oz./115 g) freshly grated **Parmesan cheese,** ¼ cup (60 ml) **olive oil,** 2 tablespoons **pine nuts** or slivered almonds, and 1 or 2 cloves **garlic.** Whirl until smooth. Season to taste with **salt.** If made ahead, cover and refrigerate for up to a day. Makes 1 cup.

Per serving: 322 calories (23% calories from fat), 9 g total fat, 2 g saturated fat, 5 mg cholesterol, 957 mg sodium, 46 g carbohydrates, 7 g fiber, 17 g protein, 233 mg calcium, 5 mg iron

Minestrone Genovese
(recipe on facing page)

Chard Soup with Beans & Orzo

Preparation time: About 40 minutes
Cooking time: About 45 minutes

Offer this flavorful and nutritious meal-in-a-bowl with a loaf of crusty Italian bread and dry white wine.

1 pound (455 g) pear-shaped (Roma-type) tomatoes (about 5 large)

2 tablespoons (30 ml) olive oil

1 large onion (about 8 oz./230 g), chopped

1 clove garlic, minced or pressed

2 medium-size stalks celery (about 6 oz./170 g *total*), diced

2 ounces (55 g) thinly sliced pro-sciutto or cooked ham, slivered

12 cups (2.8 liters) beef broth

2 large carrots (about 8 oz./ 230 g *total*), diced

1 tablespoon minced fresh rosemary or 1 teaspoon dried rosemary

1 pound (455 g) Swiss chard, coarse stems removed

3 cans (about 15 oz./425 g *each*) pinto beans, drained and rinsed

8 ounces (230 g) green beans, cut into 1-inch (2.5-cm) lengths

1 pound (455 g) zucchini (about 3 large), cut into ¾-inch (2-cm) chunks

4 ounces/115 g (about ⅔ cup) dried orzo or other rice-shaped pasta

Freshly grated Parmesan cheese

Salt and pepper

1. Bring 4 cups (950 ml) water to a boil in an 8- to 10-quart (8- to 10-liter) pan over high heat. Drop tomatoes into water and cook for 1 minute. Lift out; peel and discard skin. Chop tomatoes and set aside. Discard water.

2. Heat oil in pan over medium-high heat. Add onion, garlic, celery, and prosciutto. Cook, stirring often, until onion is soft (5 to 8 minutes). Add broth, carrots, and rosemary. Bring to a boil; reduce heat, cover, and simmer for 10 minutes. Meanwhile, cut chard crosswise into ½-inch (1-cm) strips. Mash 1 can of the pinto beans.

3. Add mashed and whole pinto beans, green beans, zucchini, and tomatoes to pan; stir well. Cover and simmer for 5 more minutes.

4. Stir in chard and pasta; simmer, uncovered, just until pasta is tender to bite (about 10 more minutes). Serve hot or at room temperature. If made ahead, let cool and then cover and refrigerate for up to a day; bring to room temperature or reheat before serving.

5. Offer cheese, salt, and pepper to add to taste. Makes 10 to 12 servings.

Per serving: 210 calories (21% calories from fat), 5 g total fat, 0.6 g saturated fat, 4 mg cho-lesterol, 2,179 mg sodium, 30 g carbohydrates, 6 g fiber, 11 g protein, 76 mg calcium, 4 mg iron

Shell & Bean Soup

Preparation time: 20 minutes
Cooking time: About 20 minutes

Satisfying pasta and beans are a popular combination in Italian cuisine.

1 small red onion (about 8 oz./230 g), chopped

1 teaspoon olive oil

1 cup (120 g) chopped celery

4 cloves garlic, chopped

10 cups (2.4 liters) fat-free reduced-sodium chicken broth

1½ cups (173 g) dried small pasta shells

3 to 4 cups (555 to 740 g) cooked or canned white beans, drained and rinsed

1 cup (110 g) shredded carrots

1 package (about 10 oz./285 g) frozen tiny peas

½ cup (40 g) grated Parmesan cheese

1. Set aside ⅓ cup (57 g) of the chopped onion. In a 6- to 8-quart (6- to 8-liter) pan, combine remaining onion, oil, celery, and garlic. Cook over medi-um-high heat, stirring often, until onion is lightly browned (5 to 8 min-utes). Add broth and bring to a boil. Stir in pasta and beans; reduce heat, cover, and simmer until pasta is almost tender to bite (5 to 7 minutes). Add carrots and peas; bring to a boil.

2. Ladle soup into individual bowls; sprinkle equally with cheese and reserved onion. Makes 6 to 8 servings.

Per serving: 324 calories (9% calories from fat), 3 g total fat, 1 g saturated fat, 5 mg choles-terol, 1,113 mg sodium, 53 g carbohydrates, 7 g fiber, 22 g protein, 194 mg calcium, 5 mg iron

For a sophisticated presentation, smooth black bean and white bean soups are served in one bowl but not mixed.

....

- 1 large onion, chopped
- 1 clove garlic, peeled and sliced
- 3½ cups (830 ml) vegetable broth
- ⅓ cup (55 g) oil-packed dried tomatoes, drained and finely chopped
- 4 green onions, thinly sliced
- ¼ cup (60 ml) dry sherry
- 2 cans (about 15 oz./425 g *each*) black beans, drained and rinsed well
- 2 cans (about 15 oz./425 g *each*) cannellini (white kidney beans), drained and rinsed
  Slivered green onions (optional)

....

1. In a 5- to 6-quart (5- to 6-liter) pan, combine chopped onion, garlic, and ½ cup (120 ml) water. Cook over medium-high heat, stirring often, until liq-

Black & White Bean Soup

....

Preparation time: 25 minutes
Cooking time: About 20 minutes

uid evaporates and browned bits stick to pan bottom (about 10 minutes). To deglaze pan, add 2 tablespoons (30 ml) of the broth, stirring to loosen browned bits from pan; continue to cook until browned bits form again. Repeat deglazing step, using 2 tablespoons (30 ml) more broth. Then stir in ½ cup (120 ml) more broth and pour mixture into a food processor or blender.

2. In same pan, combine tomatoes and sliced green onions. Cook over high heat, stirring, until onions are wilted (about 2 minutes). Add sherry and stir until liquid has evaporated. Remove from heat.

3. To onion mixture in food processor, add black beans. Whirl, gradually adding 1¼ cups (300 ml) of the broth, until smoothly puréed. Pour into a 3- to 4-quart (2.8- to 3.8-liter) pan.

4. Rinse processor; add cannellini and whirl until smoothly puréed, gradually adding remaining 1½ cups (360 ml) broth. Stir puréed cannellini into pan with tomato mixture. Place both pans of soup over medium-high heat and cook, stirring often, until steaming.

5. To serve, pour soup into 6 wide 1½- to 2-cup (360- to 470-ml) bowls as follows. From pans (or from 2 lipped containers such as 4-cup/950-ml pitchers, which are easier to handle), pour soups simultaneously into opposite sides of each bowl so that soups flow together but do not mix. Garnish with slivered green onions, if desired. Makes 6 servings.

....

Per serving: 283 calories (25% calories from fat), 8 g total fat, 0.9 g saturated fat, 0 mg cholesterol, 996 mg sodium, 38 g carbohydrates, 11 g fiber, 14 g protein, 80 mg calcium, 4 mg iron

White Bean & Tomato Salad
(recipe on page 48)

Salads

Salads can be much more diverse and exciting than the common accompaniment of lettuce leaves with tomato slices. While our light version of Caesar Salad is a classic first course, Steak, Couscous & Greens with Raspberries makes a delightful and cool summer entrée. Grains and pasta are ideal salad ingredients offering hearty satisfaction with very little fat. And our low-fat dressings will add zip and flavor to your favorite salads.

Delicious as an accompaniment, this savory salad of warm white beans and roasted tomatoes is just as good as a lunch or supper main course.

- 1 **large red onion, cut into ¾-inch (2-cm) chunks**
- 2½ **teaspoons olive oil**
- 2 **tablespoons (30 ml) balsamic or red wine vinegar**
- 12 **to 14 medium-size firm-ripe pear-shaped (Roma-type) tomatoes (1¾ to 2 lbs./795 to 905 g *total*), cut lengthwise into halves**
  Salt
- 3 **cans (about 15 oz./425 g *each*) cannellini (white kidney beans)**
- 2 **tablespoons *each* chopped fresh thyme and chopped fresh basil; or 2 teaspoons *each* dry thyme and dry basil**
  Pepper

White Bean & Tomato Salad

Preparation time: About 15 minutes
Cooking time: About 1 hour and 10 minutes
Pictured on page 46

1. In a lightly oiled square 8- to 10-inch (20- to 25-cm) baking pan, mix onion, ½ teaspoon of the oil, and vinegar. Arrange tomatoes, cut side up, in a lightly oiled 9- by 13-inch (23- by 33-cm) baking pan; rub with remaining 2 teaspoons oil, then sprinkle with salt.

2. Bake onion and tomatoes in a 475°F (245°C) oven until edges of onion chunks and tomato halves are dark brown (40 to 50 minutes for onion, about 1 hour and 10 minutes for tomatoes); switch positions of baking pans halfway through baking.

3. Pour beans and their liquid into a 2- to 3-quart (1.9- to 2.8-liter) pan. Add fresh thyme (or both dry thyme and dry basil). Bring to a boil; reduce heat and simmer for 3 minutes, stirring. Pour beans into a fine strainer set over a bowl; reserve liquid. Place beans in a serving bowl; tap herbs from strainer into beans.

4. Chop 8 tomato halves; stir into beans along with fresh basil (if used) and onion. Add some of the reserved liquid to moisten, if desired. Season to taste with salt and pepper. Arrange remaining 16 to 20 tomato halves around edge of salad. Makes 8 side-dish or 4 main-dish servings.

Per serving: 179 calories (11% calories from fat), 2 g total fat, 0.3 g saturated fat, 0 mg cholesterol, 566 mg sodium, 32 g carbohydrates, 12 g fiber, 10 g protein, 73 mg calcium, 3 mg iron

---

Tangy sour cream, robust garlic, and tart vinegar are mellowed with honey in our refreshing pesto dressing.

- 1 **tablespoon pine nuts**
- 2 **teaspoons Oriental sesame oil**
- 1 **clove garlic, minced or pressed**
- 3 **slices Italian or sourdough sandwich bread (about 3 oz./ 85 g *total*), cut into ½-inch (1-cm) cubes**
- ¼ **cup (10 g) chopped fresh basil**
- ¼ **cup (15 g) chopped Italian or regular parsley**
- 1 **cup (240 ml) nonfat sour cream**
- 1 **tablespoon (15 ml) white wine vinegar**
- 1 **teaspoon honey**
- 1 **or 2 cloves garlic, peeled**
  Salt and pepper
- 8 **ounces/230 g (about 8 cups) mixed salad greens, rinsed and crisped**

Mixed Greens with Pesto Dressing

Preparation time: 20 minutes
Cooking time: About 15 minutes

1. Toast pine nuts in a wide nonstick frying pan over medium heat until golden (about 3 minutes), stirring often. Pour out of pan and set aside. In same pan (with pan off heat), combine 1 teaspoon of the oil, garlic, and 1 tablespoon (15 ml) water. Add bread cubes and toss gently to coat. Place

pan over medium heat; cook, stirring occasionally, until croutons are crisp and tinged with brown (about 10 minutes). Remove from pan and set aside.

2. In a food processor or blender, combine basil, parsley, sour cream, vinegar, honey, remaining 1 teaspoon oil, and garlic; whirl until smoothly puréed. Season to taste with salt and pepper; set aside.

3. Place greens in a large bowl; add dressing and mix gently but thoroughly. Add croutons and mix again. Sprinkle with pine nuts. Makes 4 servings.

Per serving: 154 calories (26% calories from fat), 4 g total fat, 0.9 g saturated fat, 0 mg cholesterol, 177 mg sodium, 20 g carbohydrates, 2 g fiber, 8 g protein, 156 mg calcium, 2 mg iron

First served many years ago in a Tijuana restaurant, the original Caesar salad calls for a dressing made from oil and a raw or coddled egg. This light version of the classic dish features a tangy nonfat sour cream dressing instead.

Garlic Croutons
(recipe follows)

⅔ cup (160 ml) nonfat or reduced-fat sour cream

1 or 2 cloves garlic, minced or pressed

2 tablespoons (30 ml) lemon juice

1 teaspoon Worcestershire (optional)

6 to 8 canned anchovy fillets, rinsed, drained, patted dry, and finely chopped

Caesar Salad

Preparation time: About 15 minutes
Baking time: 10 to 12 minutes

8 cups (440 g) lightly packed bite-size pieces of rinsed, crisped romaine lettuce

About ¼ cup (20 g) grated Parmesan cheese

1. Prepare Garlic Croutons; set aside.

2. In a large nonmetal bowl, beat sour cream, garlic, lemon juice, and Worcestershire (if desired) until blended. Stir in anchovies.

3. Add lettuce to bowl with dressing; mix gently but thoroughly to coat with dressing. Spoon salad onto individual plates and add cheese and croutons to taste. Makes 4 to 6 servings.

Garlic Croutons. In a small bowl, combine 1 tablespoon (15 ml) **olive oil,** 1 tablespoon (15 ml) **water,** and 1 clove **garlic,** minced or pressed. Cut 3 ounces/85 g (about 3 slices) **French bread** into ¾-inch (2-cm) cubes and spread in a 10- by 15-inch (25- by 38-cm) nonstick rimmed baking pan. Brush oil mixture evenly over bread cubes. Bake in a 350°F (175°C) oven until croutons are crisp and golden (10 to 12 minutes). If made ahead, let cool; then store airtight for up to 2 days. Makes about 3 cups (85 g).

Per serving: 70 calories (26% calories from fat), 2 g total fat, 0.9 g saturated fat, 6 mg cholesterol, 311 mg sodium, 5 g carbohydrates, 2 g fiber, 7 g protein, 147 mg calcium, 1 mg iron

---

Garbanzo beans, ripe tomatoes, and crisp homemade croutons team up with tart capers and olives in this zesty marinated salad. A cool, creamy dill dressing adds the finishing touch.

8 ounces (230 g) sourdough bread, cut into about ½-inch (1-cm) cubes

½ cup (120 ml) white wine vinegar

2 tablespoons (30 ml) olive oil

1 tablespoon chopped fresh oregano or 1 teaspoon dried oregano

2 teaspoons honey (or to taste)

2 cloves garlic, minced or pressed

⅛ to ¼ teaspoon pepper

2 cans (about 15 oz./425 g *each*) garbanzo beans, drained and rinsed

2 large tomatoes (about 1 lb./455 g *total*), chopped and drained well

Garbanzo Antipasto Salad

Preparation time: 30 minutes
Chilling time: At least 1 hour
Cooking time: 15 to 20 minutes

¼ cup (25 g) slivered red onion, in about 1-inch (2.5-cm) lengths

¼ cup (45 g) oil-cured olives, pitted and sliced

3 to 4 tablespoons drained capers

⅓ cup (80 ml) *each* nonfat mayonnaise and nonfat sour cream

2 tablespoons chopped fresh dill or 2 teaspoons dried dill weed

8 to 12 butter lettuce leaves, rinsed and crisped

1. Spread bread cubes in a single layer in a shallow 10- by 15-inch (25- by 38-cm) baking pan. Bake in a 325°F (165°C) oven, stirring occasionally, until crisp and tinged with brown (15 to 20 minutes). Set aside. If made ahead, let cool completely in pan on a rack, then store airtight for up to 2 days.

2. In a large bowl, combine vinegar, oil, oregano, honey, garlic, and pepper. Beat until blended. Add beans, tomatoes, onion, olives, and capers; mix gently but thoroughly. Cover and refrigerate for at least 1 hour or up to 4 hours.

3. Meanwhile, in a small bowl, beat mayonnaise, sour cream, and dill until smoothly blended; cover and refrigerate.

4. To serve, line 4 individual rimmed plates or shallow bowls with lettuce leaves. Add croutons to salad and mix gently but thoroughly, being sure to coat croutons with marinade. Then, using a slotted spoon, transfer salad to plates; top each serving with a dollop of dill dressing. Makes 4 servings.

Per serving: 466 calories (30% calories from fat), 15 g total fat, 2 g saturated fat, 0 mg cholesterol, 1,234 mg sodium, 67 g carbohydrates, 9 g fiber, 16 g protein, 144 mg calcium, 5 mg iron

Dotted with sweet green peas, this simple split pea and pasta salad is seasoned with fresh mint and lemon. Don't thaw the green peas before you stir them into the salad; they'll help to cool the freshly cooked split peas quickly.

Split Pea & Green Pea Salad

Preparation time: 15 minutes
Cooking time: About 30 minutes
Pictured on facing page

- 1 cup (200 g) green split peas
- 2 cups (470 ml) vegetable broth
- ½ teaspoon dried thyme
- 1 package (about 10 oz./285 g) frozen tiny peas (do not thaw)
- 4 ounces/115 g (about 10 tablespoons) dried orzo or other rice-shaped pasta
- ¼ cup (25 g) thinly sliced green onions
- ¼ cup (10 g) chopped fresh mint
- ¼ cup (60 ml) salad oil
- 1 teaspoon finely shredded lemon peel
- 2 tablespoons (30 ml) lemon juice

  About 24 large butter lettuce leaves, rinsed and crisped

  Mint and thyme sprigs

  Salt and pepper

1. Sort through split peas, discarding any debris; then rinse and drain peas. In a 1½- to 2-quart (1.4- to 1.9-liter) pan, bring broth to a boil over high heat. Add split peas and dried thyme. Reduce heat, cover, and simmer until split peas are tender to bite (about 25 minutes); drain and discard any remaining cooking liquid. Transfer split peas to a large bowl, add frozen peas, and mix gently but thoroughly. Let stand, stirring occasionally, until mixture is cool (about 3 minutes).

2. Meanwhile, in a 4- to 5-quart (3.8- to 5-liter) pan, bring about 8 cups (1.9 liters) water to a boil over medium-high heat; stir in pasta and cook until just tender to bite (about 5 minutes); or cook pasta according to package directions. Drain, rinse with cold water, and drain well again. Transfer pasta to bowl with peas. Add onions and chopped mint; mix gently. In a small bowl, beat oil, lemon peel, and lemon juice until blended. Add to pea mixture; mix gently but thoroughly. If made ahead, cover and refrigerate for up to 3 hours.

3. To serve, line 4 individual plates with lettuce leaves; top each plate equally with pea mixture. Garnish with mint and thyme sprigs. Season to taste with salt and pepper. Makes 4 servings.

Per serving: 458 calories (30% calories from fat), 15 g total fat, 2 g saturated fat, 0 mg cholesterol, 607 mg sodium, 62 g carbohydrates, 6 g fiber, 19 g protein, 56 mg calcium, 2 mg iron

---

Show off the season's best bell peppers in this nutritious salad. You use the peppers as edible individual bowls—so for the prettiest salad, choose bright, glossy peppers that are firm and well shaped.

Red & Yellow Pepper Salad-Salsa

Preparation time: About 15 minutes

- 5 large yellow bell peppers (about 2½ lbs./1.15 kg *total*)
- 1 large red bell pepper (about 8 oz./230 g), seeded and diced
- ⅔ cup (87 g) peeled, minced jicama
- 2 tablespoons minced cilantro
- 1½ tablespoons (23 ml) distilled white vinegar
- 1 teaspoon honey

  About ⅛ teaspoon ground red pepper (cayenne), or to taste

1. Set 4 of the yellow bell peppers upright, then cut off the top quarter of each. Remove and discard seeds from pepper shells; set shells aside. Cut out and discard stems from top pieces of peppers; then dice these pieces and transfer to a large nonmetal bowl.

2. Seed and dice remaining yellow bell pepper and add to bowl. Then add red bell pepper, jicama, cilantro, vinegar, honey, and ground red pepper; mix gently.

3. Spoon pepper mixture equally into pepper shells. If made ahead, cover and refrigerate for up to 4 hours. Makes 4 servings.

Per serving: 90 calories (5% calories from fat), 0.6 g total fat, 0.1 g saturated fat, 0 mg cholesterol, 7 mg sodium, 21 g carbohydrates, 5 g fiber, 3 g protein, 29 mg calcium, 1 mg iron

Split Pea & Green Pea Salad
(recipe on facing page)

Authentic Mexican ingredients, carefully chosen for their contrasting textures and flavors, distinguish this cold bean dish. You combine nutty-tasting black beans with roasted red peppers, cilantro, and a little onion, then enliven the mixture with a tart-sweet vinegar dressing.

Roasted Pepper & Black Bean Salad

Preparation time: About 15 minutes
Cooking time: About 8 minutes

Roasted Red Bell Peppers
(directions follow)

½ cup (120 ml) seasoned rice vinegar; or ½ cup (120 ml) distilled white vinegar plus 1 tablespoon sugar

1 tablespoon (15 ml) *each* water, olive oil, and honey

½ teaspoon chili oil

3 cans (about 15 oz./425 g *each*) black beans, drained and rinsed

¼ cup (10 g) minced cilantro

2 tablespoons thinly sliced green onion
Salt
Cilantro sprigs

1. Prepare Roasted Red Bell Peppers; set aside.

2. In a bowl, mix vinegar, water, olive oil, honey, and chili oil. Add beans and roasted peppers; mix gently but thoroughly. (At this point, you may cover and refrigerate until next day.)

3. To serve, stir minced cilantro and onion into bean mixture. Season to taste with salt and garnish with cilantro sprigs. Makes 6 servings.

Roasted Red Bell Peppers. Cut 2 large **red bell peppers** (about 1 lb./ 455 g total) in half lengthwise. Set pepper halves, cut side down, in a 10- by 15-inch (25- by 38-cm) rimmed baking pan. Broil 4 to 6 inches (10 to 15 cm) below heat until charred all over (about 8 minutes). Cover with foil and let cool in pan. Then remove and discard skins, stems, and seeds; cut peppers into strips or chunks.

Per serving: 295 calories (11% calories from fat), 4 g total fat, 0.6 g saturated fat, 0 mg cholesterol, 400 mg sodium, 52 g carbohydrates, 5 g fiber, 16 g protein, 54 mg calcium, 4 mg iron

---

Typical of the fresh salads served alongside spicy dishes in Mexico, this simple combination of sliced cucumbers and green onions offers cool relief on hot days—and provides a pleasing contrast to zesty dishes in any weather.

Cucumber & Green Onion Salad

Preparation time: About 10 minutes
Marinating time: 20 to 30 minutes

3 European cucumbers (about 3 lbs./1.35 kg *total*), thinly sliced

1 tablespoon salt

½ cup (50 g) thinly sliced green onions

⅓ cup (80 ml) seasoned rice vinegar; or ⅓ cup (80 ml) distilled white vinegar plus 2½ teaspoons sugar

1 tablespoon sugar
Pepper

1. In a bowl, lightly crush cucumbers and salt with your hands. Let stand for 20 to 30 minutes; then turn into a colander, squeeze gently, and let drain. Rinse with cool water, squeeze gently, and drain well again. (At this point, you may cover and refrigerate until next day.)

2. In a nonmetal bowl, mix cucumbers, onions, vinegar, and sugar. Season to taste with pepper. Serve in bowl or transfer with a slotted spoon to a platter. Serve cold or at room temperature. Makes 8 servings.

Per serving: 38 calories (5% calories from fat), 0.2 g total fat, 0.1 g saturated fat, 0 mg cholesterol, 337 mg sodium, 9 g carbohydrates, 2 g fiber, 1 g protein, 29 mg calcium, 0.6 mg iron

Low-fat Dressings

Light salad dressings aren't hard to make. Just base them on ingredients that are flavorful, yet virtually fat-free: vinegar, citrus juices, nonfat yogurt, or puréed chiles and herbs. The following four choices are delicous with greens, and just as good on vegetables or grilled meats.

Green Chile Dressing

- 1 small can (about 4 oz./115 g) diced green chiles
- ⅓ cup (80 ml) lime juice
- ¼ cup (60 ml) water
- ¼ cup (10 g) chopped cilantro
- 1 clove garlic, peeled
- 1 or 2 fresh jalapeño chiles, seeded and chopped
- 1½ teaspoons sugar

1. In a blender or food processor, combine green chiles, lime juice, water, cilantro, garlic, jalapeño chiles, and sugar; whirl until smoothly puréed. If made ahead, cover and refrigerate for up to 4 hours. Makes about 1 cup (240 ml).

Per tablespoon: 5 calories (2% calories from fat), 0 g total fat, 0 g saturated fat, 0 mg cholesterol, 44 mg sodium, 1 g carbohydrates, 0.1 g fiber, 0.1 g protein, 2 mg calcium, 0.1 mg iron

Red Chile Dressing

- 3 large dried red New Mexico or California chiles (about ¾ oz./ 23 g *total*)
- ¾ cup (180 ml) water

- 6 tablespoons (90 ml) cider vinegar
- 2 tablespoons sugar
- 1 tablespoon chopped fresh ginger

1. Remove and discard stems and most of seeds from chiles. Rinse chiles and cut into ½-inch (1-cm) strips with scissors. In a 1- to 1½-quart (950-ml to 1.4-liter) pan, combine chiles and water. Bring to a boil. Remove pan from heat; let chiles soak until slightly softened (about 5 minutes).

2. In a blender or food processor, combine chile mixture, vinegar, sugar, and ginger; whirl until smoothly puréed. If made ahead, let cool; then cover and refrigerate for up to 1 week. Makes about 1 cup (240 ml).

Per tablespoon: 11 calories (15% calories from fat), 0.2 g total fat, 0 g saturated fat, 0 mg cholesterol, 0.5 mg sodium, 3 g carbohydrates, 0 g fiber, 0.2 g protein, 2 mg calcium, 0.1 mg iron

Creamy Herb Dressing

- 1 cup (240 ml) plain nonfat yogurt
- 3 tablespoons (45 ml) balsamic vinegar
- 1½ teaspoons chopped fresh oregano or ¼ teaspoon dried oregano
- 1 teaspoon Dijon mustard
- 2 to 3 teaspoons sugar

1. In a nonmetal bowl, mix yogurt, vinegar, oregano,

mustard, and sugar. If made ahead, cover and refrigerate for up to 3 days. Makes 1¼ cups (300 ml).

Per tablespoon: 9 calories (2% calories from fat), 0 g total fat, 0 g saturated fat, 0.2 mg cholesterol, 15 mg sodium, 1 g carbohydrates, 0 g fiber, 0.6 g protein, 23 mg calcium, 0 mg iron

Citrus Dressing

- 2 teaspoons grated orange peel
- ½ cup (120 ml) orange juice
- 2 tablespoons (30 ml) white wine vinegar or distilled white vinegar
- 2 tablespoons minced fresh basil or 2 teaspoons dried basil
- 1 fresh jalapeño chile, seeded and minced
- 1 tablespoon (15 ml) honey
- 2 teaspoons Dijon mustard
- 1 teaspoon ground cumin
- 2 cloves garlic, pressed

1. In a nonmetal bowl, mix orange peel, orange juice, vinegar, basil, chile, honey, mustard, cumin, and garlic. If made ahead, cover and refrigerate for up to 4 hours. Makes ¾ cup (180 ml).

Per tablespoon: 14 calories (2% calories from fat), 0 g total fat, 0 g saturated fat, 0 mg cholesterol, 21 mg sodium, 3 g carbohydrates, 0 g fiber, 0.2 g protein, 8 mg calcium, 0.2 mg iron

Red Slaw
(recipe on facing page)

Crystallized ginger, pickled beets, and cherries add spicy and sweet flavors to this vibrant main-dish salad of red cabbage and kidney beans. Try it with warm buttermilk biscuits.

- 1 **medium-size head red cabbage (about 2 lbs./905 g)**
- 3 **tablespoons (45 ml)** *each* **balsamic vinegar and salad oil**
- 2 **cans (about 15 oz./425 g** *each***) red kidney beans, drained and rinsed**
- 1 **can (about 15 oz./425 g) pickled beets, drained and coarsely chopped**
- 2 **tablespoons finely chopped crystallized ginger**
- 2½ **cups (370 g) pitted sweet cherries, fresh or thawed frozen**

Red Slaw

Preparation time: 15 minutes
Pictured on facing page

- ⅓ **to ½ cup (35 to 50 g) thinly sliced green onions**
- 4 **whole green onions, ends trimmed (optional)**
  Salt and pepper

1. Remove 4 to 8 large outer cabbage leaves and set aside. Then core cabbage and finely shred enough of it to make 5 cups (350 g); set aside. Reserve any remaining cabbage for other uses.

2. In a large bowl, beat vinegar and oil until blended. Stir in beans, beets, and ginger. Gently mix in shredded cabbage and cherries. (At this point, you may cover and refrigerate slaw and whole cabbage leaves separately for up to 4 hours.)

3. To serve, stir sliced onions into slaw. Arrange 1 or 2 of the whole cabbage leaves on each of 4 individual plates. Divide slaw equally among plates; garnish with whole green onions, if desired. Season to taste with salt and pepper. Makes 4 servings.

Per serving: 468 calories (24% calories from fat), 13 g total fat, 2 g saturated fat, 0 mg cholesterol, 577 mg sodium, 78 g carbohydrates, 15 g fiber, 16 g protein, 214 mg calcium, 6 mg iron

---

Crisp green-and-red cabbage slaw, seasoned with lots of cilantro and tossed with a tart lime dressing, is a perfect companion for pork, lamb, chicken, or seafood.

- 8 **ounces (230 g) green cabbage, very finely shredded (about 3 cups)**
- 8 **ounces (230 g) red cabbage, very finely shredded (about 3 cups)**
- 1 **cup (53 g) firmly packed cilantro leaves, minced**

Cilantro Slaw

Preparation time: About 15 minutes

- ¼ **cup (60 ml) lime juice**
- 1 **tablespoon (15 ml)** *each* **water and honey**
- ½ **teaspoon cumin seeds**
  Salt and pepper

1. In a large nonmetal bowl, mix green cabbage, red cabbage, cilantro, lime juice, water, honey, and cumin seeds. Season to taste with salt and pepper. If made ahead, cover and refrigerate for up to 4 hours. Makes 6 servings.

Per serving: 33 calories (5% calories from fat), 0.2 g total fat, 0 g saturated fat, 0 mg cholesterol, 14 mg sodium, 8 g carbohydrates, 2 g fiber, 1 g protein, 44 mg calcium, 0.6 mg iron

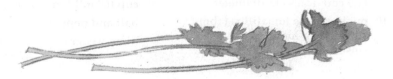

Lentils and pasta mingle in this unusual side-dish salad, enhanced by a minty, tart-sweet dressing.

- 2 cups (470 ml) beef broth
- 6 ounces/170 g (about 1 cup) lentils, rinsed and drained
- 1 teaspoon dried oregano
- 6 ounces (170 g) dried pappardelle or extra-wide egg noodles
- ⅓ cup (80 ml) lemon juice
- 3 tablespoons chopped fresh mint or 1 teaspoon dried mint
- 2 tablespoons (30 ml) olive oil
- 1 teaspoon honey (or to taste)
- 6 cups (330 g) shredded red leaf lettuce leaves
- 1 or 2 cloves garlic, minced or pressed
- ⅔ cup (85 g) crumbled feta cheese (or to taste)
  Mint sprigs

Lentil & Pappardelle Salad

Preparation time: About 20 minutes
Cooking time: About 40 minutes
Chilling time: At least 30 minutes

1. Bring broth to a boil in a 1½- to 2-quart (1.4- to 1.9-liter) pan over high heat. Add lentils and oregano; reduce heat, cover, and simmer just until lentils are tender to bite (20 to 30 minutes). Drain, if necessary. Transfer to a large nonmetal bowl and let cool. Meanwhile, bring 8 cups (1.9 liters) water to a boil in a 4- to 5-quart (3.8- to 5-liter) pan over medium-high heat. Stir in pasta and cook just until tender to bite (8 to 10 minutes); or cook according to package directions. Drain, rinse with cold water until cool, and drain well.

2. Add pasta, lemon juice, chopped mint, oil, and honey to lentils. Mix thoroughly but gently. Cover and refrigerate until cool (at least 30 minutes) or for up to 4 hours; stir occasionally.

3. Arrange lettuce on a platter. Stir garlic into pasta mixture and spoon onto lettuce. Sprinkle with cheese. Garnish with mint sprigs. Makes 6 to 8 servings.

Per serving: 273 calories (26% calories from fat), 8 g total fat, 3 g saturated fat, 34 mg cholesterol, 619 mg sodium, 37 g carbohydrates, 4 g fiber, 14 g protein, 120 mg calcium, 5 mg iron

---

Seasoned with lime and cilantro, a potpourri of tiny tomatoes—red, green, and gold—makes a refreshing salad. When buying tomatoes, purchase only those that have not been refrigerated. Keep unripe fruit at room temperature. Once it's fully ripe, refrigerate it (to slow spoilage) and use it within a day or two.

- 3 pounds/1.35 kg (about 10 cups) ripe cherry tomatoes (red, yellow, yellow-green, orange); include some that are ½ inch (1.5 cm) or less in diameter
- 10 medium-size tomatillos (about 10 oz./285 g *total*), husked, rinsed, and thinly sliced

Tomatillo & Tomato Salad

Preparation time: About 15 minutes

- 1 fresh jalapeño chile, seeded and minced
- ½ cup (20 g) lightly packed cilantro leaves
- ¼ cup (60 ml) lime juice
  Salt and pepper
  Lime wedges

1. Cut any tomatoes larger than ¾ inch (2 cm) in diameter into halves; then place tomatoes in a nonmetal bowl.

2. Add tomatillos, chile, cilantro, and lime juice; mix gently. Season to taste with salt and pepper; serve with lime wedges. Makes 8 to 10 servings.

Per serving: 39 calories (12% calories from fat), 0.6 g total fat, 0.1 g saturated fat, 0 mg cholesterol, 14 mg sodium, 8 g carbohydrates, 2 g fiber, 2 g protein, 12 mg calcium, 0.7 mg iron

Combining pasta with beans creates a complete protein.

- 4 ounces/115 g (about 2 cups) dried farfalle (about 1½-inch/3.5-cm size)
- ½ cup (120 ml) seasoned rice vinegar; or ½ cup (120 ml) distilled white vinegar and 4 teaspoons sugar
- ¼ cup (15 g) minced parsley
- 1 tablespoon (15 ml) *each* olive oil, water, and honey
- ¼ teaspoon chili oil
- 1 can (about 15 oz./425 g) kidney beans, drained and rinsed
- 1 can (about 15 oz./425 g) black beans, drained and rinsed
- 1 large pear-shaped (Roma-type) tomato (about 4 oz./115 g), diced
- ¼ cup (25 g) thinly sliced green onions

Cool Beans & Bows

Preparation time: About 15 minutes
Cooking time: About 15 minutes
Chilling time: At least 30 minutes

1. Bring 8 cups (1.9 liters) water to a boil in a 4- to 5-quart (3.8- to 5-liter) pan over medium-high heat. Stir in pasta and cook just until tender to bite (8 to 10 minutes); or cook according to package directions. Drain, rinse with cold water until cool, and drain well.

2. Combine vinegar, parsley, olive oil, water, honey, and chili oil in a large nonmetal bowl. Mix well. Add kidney and black beans, pasta, and tomato. Mix thoroughly but gently. Cover and refrigerate until cool (at least 30 minutes) or for up to 4 hours; stir occasionally.

3. Stir onions into pasta mixture just before serving. Transfer to a large serving bowl. Makes 4 to 6 servings.

Per serving: 256 calories (15% calories from fat), 4 g total fat, 0.5 g saturated fat, 0 mg cholesterol, 724 mg sodium, 44 g carbohydrates, 7 g fiber, 11 g protein, 49 mg calcium, 3 mg iron

---

Refreshing and easy to prepare, this salad is good with simple entrées such as Red Pepper Flan (page 260) or Pork in Escabeche Sauce (page 88).

- 1 can (about 15 oz./425 g) black beans, drained and rinsed
- 1 cup (130 g) peeled, finely chopped jicama
- ¼ cup (34 g) crumbled panela or feta cheese
- 3 tablespoons (45 ml) lime juice
- ⅓ cup (15 g) minced cilantro

Black Bean & Jicama Salad

Preparation time: About 15 minutes

- 2 tablespoons thinly sliced green onion
- 2 teaspoons honey
- ¼ teaspoon crushed red pepper flakes
- 4 to 8 butter lettuce leaves, rinsed and crisped

1. In a bowl, combine beans, jicama, cheese, lime juice, cilantro, onion, honey, and red pepper flakes. Mix well. If made ahead, cover and refrigerate for up to 4 hours.

2. To serve, spoon bean mixture into lettuce leaves. Makes 4 servings.

Per serving: 164 calories (13% calories from fat), 2 g total fat, 1 g saturated fat, 8 mg cholesterol, 100 mg sodium, 28 g carbohydrates, 3 g fiber, 9 g protein, 75 mg calcium, 2 mg iron

This mouthwatering blend of melon, papaya, and cool cucumber is delicious with fish, grilled meats, or tamale pie.

- **3 small cantaloupes (about 4 lbs./1.8 kg total)**
- **1 medium-size firm-ripe papaya (about 1 lb./455 g), peeled, seeded, and diced**
- **1 medium-size cucumber (about 8 oz./230 g), peeled, seeded, and diced**
- **About 2 tablespoons minced fresh mint or 1 teaspoon dried mint, or to taste**
- **3 tablespoons (45 ml) lime juice**
- **1 tablespoon (15 ml) honey**
  Mint sprigs

Melon & Cucumber Salad-Salsa

Preparation time: About 15 minutes
Pictured on facing page

1. Cut 2 of the melons in half lengthwise. Scoop out and discard seeds. If any of the melon halves does not sit steadily, cut a very thin slice from base so melon sits steadily. Set melon halves aside.

2. Peel, seed, and dice remaining melon. Transfer to a large nonmetal bowl. Add papaya, cucumber, minced mint, lime juice, and honey. Mix gently.

3. Set 1 melon half in each of 4 bowls (or on each of 4 dinner plates). Spoon a fourth of the fruit mixture into each melon half. If made ahead, cover and refrigerate for up to 4 hours. Just before serving, garnish each melon half with mint sprigs. Makes 4 servings.

Per serving: 135 calories (5% calories from fat), 0.8 g total fat, 0 g saturated fat, 0 mg cholesterol, 28 mg sodium, 33 g carbohydrates, 3 g fiber, 3 g protein, 54 mg calcium, 0.8 mg iron

---

Sweet, juicy nectarines and plums, diced and tossed with fresh basil, make a lovely summer side dish that's a cross between a fruit salad and a salsa. Be sure the fruit you use is ripe and ready to eat. You can ripen firm-ripe nectarines at room temperature, uncovered, out of direct sun; plums ripen best when grouped inside a loosely closed paper bag. Check fruit daily and refrigerate it, unwashed and packaged airtight, once it's ripe.

- **2 large firm-ripe nectarines (about 12 oz./340 g total), pitted and diced**
- **2 large firm-ripe plums (about 6 oz./170 g total), pitted and diced**

Nectarine, Plum & Basil Salad-Salsa

Preparation time: About 15 minutes

- **¼ cup (13 g) firmly packed fresh basil leaves (minced) or about 1 tablespoon dried basil, or to taste**
- **1½ tablespoons (21 ml) red wine vinegar**
- **1 tablespoon (15 ml) honey**
- **4 to 8 large butter lettuce leaves, rinsed and crisped**

1. In a large nonmetal bowl, mix nectarines, plums, basil, vinegar, and honey. If made ahead, cover and refrigerate for up to 4 hours.

2. To serve, place 1 or 2 lettuce leaves on each of 4 dinner plates. Spoon a fourth of the fruit mixture onto each plate. Makes 4 servings.

Per serving: 83 calories (7% calories from fat), 0.7 g total fat, 0 g saturated fat, 0 mg cholesterol, 2 mg sodium, 20 g carbohydrates, 2 g fiber, 1 g protein, 41 mg calcium, 0.9 mg iron

Melon & Cucumber Salad-Salsa
(recipe on facing page)

Lushly ripe red pears, dried cran-berries, and spinach leaves are a colorfully different and delicious combination for salad.

....

- ¼ cup (60 ml) red wine vinegar
- 2 tablespoons (30 ml) extra-virgin olive oil
- 1 tablespoon drained capers
- 1 tablespoon (15 ml) lemon juice
- ¼ teaspoon *each* pepper and honey
- 4 large firm-ripe red pears (about 2 lbs./905 g *total*)
- 1 package (about 10 oz./285 g) prewashed spinach leaves, coarse stems and any yellow or bruised leaves discarded, remaining leaves rinsed and crisped
- 8 ounces (230 g) mushrooms, thinly sliced

Autumn Pear Salad

....

Preparation time: 20 minutes

- ¾ cup (68 g) dried cranberries
- 4 ounces (115 g) sliced pancetta or bacon, crisply cooked, drained, and crumbled

1. In a large bowl, combine vinegar, oil, capers, lemon juice, pepper, and honey; beat until well blended. Set aside.

2. Core pears and cut each into about 16 wedges. As pears are cut, transfer them to bowl with dressing; mix gently to coat with dressing. Add spinach, mushrooms, and cranberries; mix until coated with dressing. Then divide salad among individual plates and sprinkle with pancetta. Makes 8 servings.

....

Per serving: 160 calories (29% calories from fat), 6 g total fat, 1 g saturated fat, 5 mg cholesterol, 163 mg sodium, 27 g carbohydrates, 4 g fiber, 3 g protein, 39 mg calcium, 1 mg iron

---

Pungent basil and brown sugar-baked bacon delectably complement the sweet, mellow flavor of ripe melon.

....

- 6 ounces (170 g) sliced bacon
- 1½ tablespoons firmly packed brown sugar
- 8 cups (1.4 kg) peeled, seeded melon wedges (*each* about ¾ inch by 2 inches/2 cm by 5 cm); use any soft, aromatic melon, such as honeydew, cantaloupe, and/or crenshaw
- ¼ cup (60 ml) lime juice
- ⅓ cup (15 g) finely slivered fresh basil
  Basil sprigs

Melon, Basil & Bacon Salad

....

Preparation time: 25 minutes
Cooking time: About 20 minutes

1. Line a shallow 10- by 15-inch (25- by 38-cm) baking pan with foil. Arrange bacon in pan in a single layer; bake in a 350°F (175°C) oven for 10 minutes. Spoon off and discard drippings. Evenly pat sugar onto bacon; bake until bacon is deep golden (about 10 more minutes).

2. Lift bacon to a board; let cool slightly, then cut diagonally into ½-inch (1-cm) slices. In a large, shallow bowl, combine melon, lime juice, and slivered basil. Top with bacon; garnish with basil sprigs. Makes 4 servings.

....

Per serving: 210 calories (26% calories from fat), 7 g total fat, 2 g saturated fat, 10 mg cholesterol, 226 mg sodium, 36 g carbohydrates, 3 g fiber, 6 g protein, 66 mg calcium, 1 mg iron

The sweet acidity of oranges and the delicate, licorice-like flavor of fennel combine for an intriguingly refreshing salad.

....

2 **large heads fennel (about 1½ lbs./680 g total)**

¼ **cup (60 ml) seasoned rice vinegar**

2 **tablespoons (30 ml) olive oil**

1 **tablespoon grated orange peel**

1 **teaspoon anise seeds**

4 **large oranges (about 2½ lbs./ 1.15 kg total)**

Seeds from 1 pomegranate (about 3½ inches/ 8.5 cm in diameter)

Salt

Fennel & Orange Salad

....

Preparation time: 20 minutes

1. Trim stems from fennel, reserving the feathery green leaves. Trim and discard any bruised areas from fennel; then cut each fennel head into thin slivers. Place slivered fennel in a large bowl.

2. Finely chop enough of the fennel leaves to make 1 tablespoon (reserve remaining leaves); add to bowl along with vinegar, oil, orange peel, and anise seeds. Mix well.

3. Cut off and discard peel and all white membrane from oranges. Cut fruit crosswise into slices about ¼ inch (6 mm) thick; discard seeds.

4. Divide fennel mixture among individual plates. Arrange oranges alongside fennel mixture; sprinkle salads equally with pomegranate seeds. Garnish with reserved fennel leaves. Season to taste with salt. Makes 6 servings.

....

Per serving: 147 calories (29% calories from fat), 5 g total fat, 0.6 g saturated fat, 0 mg cholesterol, 290 mg sodium, 26 g carbohydrates, 4 g fiber, 2 g protein, 110 mg calcium, 1 mg iron

---

For a red, white, and green entrée, try this salad. It's based on toasted quinoa and fresh spinach; white beans and crisp red apple lend earthy-tasting and sweet accents.

....

½ **cup (85 g) quinoa**

1 **cinnamon stick (about 3 inches/8 cm long)**

½ **teaspoon cumin seeds**

½ **cup (120 ml) *each* unsweetened apple juice and water**

3 **tablespoons dried currants**

2 **cans (about 15 oz./425 g *each*) cannellini (white kidney beans), drained and rinsed**

8 **cups (about 8 oz./230 g) bite-size pieces rinsed, crisped fresh spinach**

1 **large red-skinned apple (about 8 oz./230 g), cored and thinly sliced**

Quinoa & Spinach Salad

....

Preparation time: 20 minutes
Cooking time: About 30 minutes

....

⅓ **cup (80 ml) cider vinegar**

3 **tablespoons (45 ml) honey**

2 **tablespoons (30 ml) salad oil**

....

1. Place quinoa in a fine strainer and rinse thoroughly with cool water; drain well. Then place quinoa in a 1½- to 2-quart (1.4- to 1.9-liter) pan and cook over medium heat, stirring often, until darker in color (about 8 minutes). Add cinnamon stick, cumin seeds, apple juice, and water. Increase heat to medium-high and bring mixture to a boil; then reduce heat, cover, and simmer until almost all liquid has been absorbed and quinoa is tender to bite (about 15 minutes). Discard cinnamon stick; stir in currants and half the beans. Use quinoa mixture warm or cool.

2. In a large serving bowl, combine spinach, remaining beans, and apple. Mound quinoa mixture atop spinach mixture. In a small bowl, beat vinegar, honey, and oil until blended; pour over salad and mix gently but thoroughly. Makes 4 servings.

....

Per serving: 422 calories (20% calories from fat), 10 g total fat, 1 g saturated fat, 0 mg cholesterol, 336 mg sodium, 72 g carbohydrates, 15 g fiber, 16 g protein, 149 mg calcium, 7 mg iron

Fruited Quinoa Salad
(recipe on facing page)

Quinoa, often called the "super grain" thanks to its high protein content, is the base for this simple yet elegant salad. You'll find quinoa in well-stocked supermarkets and natural-foods stores; be sure to rinse it before cooking to remove the slightly bitter coating.

- 2 tablespoons pine nuts or slivered almonds
- 1¼ cups (about 10 oz./285 g) dried apricots
- 1½ cups (255 g) quinoa or 1 cup (170 g) bulgur
- 2 teaspoons olive oil or salad oil
- 2 or 3 cups (470 or 710 ml) low-sodium chicken broth
- 2 teaspoons grated lemon peel
- 2 tablespoons (30 ml) lemon juice
- 1 cup (145 g) dried currants
  Salt

Fruited Quinoa Salad

Preparation time: About 15 minutes
Cooking time: About 30 minutes
Pictured on facing page

1. Toast pine nuts in a small frying pan over medium heat until golden brown (3 to 5 minutes), stirring often. Transfer nuts to a bowl; set aside. Coarsely chop ½ cup (115 g) of the apricots; set aside.

2. Place quinoa in a fine strainer; rinse thoroughly with water (bulgur needs no rinsing). Heat oil in a 3- to 4-quart (2.8- to 3.8-liter) pan over medium heat. Add quinoa or bulgur; cook, stirring often, until grain turns a slightly darker brown (8 to 10 minutes).

3. To pan, add broth (3 cups/710 ml for quinoa, 2 cups/470 ml for bulgur), lemon peel, and lemon juice. Bring to a boil over high heat. Reduce heat, cover, and simmer until grain is just tender to bite (10 to 15 minutes). Drain and discard any liquid from grain. Stir chopped apricots and ½ cup (73 g) of the currants into grain. Let stand until warm; or let cool, then cover and refrigerate until next day.

4. To serve, season quinoa mixture to taste with salt. Mound mixture in center of a serving dish or large rimmed platter. Garnish with remaining ¾ cup (170 g) apricots, remaining ½ cup (73 g) currants, and pine nuts. Makes 6 servings.

Per serving: 349 calories (16% calories from fat), 7 g total fat, 1 g saturated fat, 0 mg cholesterol, 81 mg sodium, 70 g carbohydrates, 10 g fiber, 10 g protein, 70 mg calcium, 7 mg iron

---

Refreshing and easy to prepare, this sprightly salad is perfect for warm summer days. Serve it with assorted fresh fruit and a crusty loaf of bread.

- 2 cups (350 g) bulgur
- 1½ cups (60 g) firmly packed fresh mint leaves
- 1 can (about 15 oz./425 g) garbanzo beans, drained and rinsed
  About ½ cup (120 ml) lemon juice (or to taste)
- 2 tablespoons (30 ml) olive oil
  Salt and pepper
  About 8 large butter lettuce leaves, rinsed and crisped
- 2 large firm-ripe tomatoes (about 1 lb./455 g *total*), thinly sliced

Bulgur Tabbouleh Salad

Preparation time: 15 minutes, plus about 1 hour for bulgur to stand
Chilling time: At least 30 minutes

- 4 ounces (115 g) feta cheese, crumbled
  Mint sprigs and lemon slices

1. In a deep bowl, mix bulgur and 2 cups (470 ml) cold water. Let stand until grain is tender to bite and water has been absorbed (about 1 hour), stirring occasionally.

2. Finely chop mint leaves and add to bulgur along with beans, lemon juice, and oil. Mix well; season to taste with salt and pepper. Cover and refrigerate until cool (at least 30 minutes) or for up to 4 hours.

3. Line a platter with lettuce leaves. Arrange tomatoes around edge of platter; mound tabbouleh in center and sprinkle with cheese. Garnish with mint sprigs and lemon slices. Makes 4 servings.

Per serving: 486 calories (28% calories from fat), 16 g total fat, 5 g saturated fat, 25 mg cholesterol, 463 mg sodium, 74 g carbohydrates, 17 g fiber, 18 g protein, 219 mg calcium, 5 mg iron

Balsamic vinegar adds a sweet-tart accent to a warm salad of wild rice, lentils, mushrooms, and tender-crisp fresh asparagus.

Warm Wild Rice & Asparagus Salad

Preparation time: 15 minutes
Cooking time: About 1 hour and 20 minutes

1 cup (170 g) wild rice, rinsed and drained

1 cup (200 g) lentils

1 pound (455 g) mushrooms, thinly sliced

1 large onion, chopped

About 2½ cups (590 ml) vegetable broth

1 pound (455 g) slender asparagus

3 tablespoons (45 ml) balsamic vinegar

1 tablespoon (15 ml) olive oil

½ cup (40 g) grated Parmesan cheese

1. In a 5- to 6-quart (5- to 6-liter) pan, combine rice and 8 cups (1.9 liters) water. Bring to a boil over high heat; then reduce heat, cover, and simmer for 30 minutes. Meanwhile, sort through lentils, discarding any debris; rinse lentils, drain, and set aside.

2. Add lentils to rice and continue to simmer until both rice and lentils are tender to bite (about 25 more minutes). Drain and let cool.

3. In a wide nonstick frying pan, combine mushrooms, onion, and ¾ cup (180 ml) of the broth. Cook over medium-high heat, stirring often, until liquid evaporates and browned bits stick to pan bottom (about 10 minutes). To deglaze pan, add ⅓ cup (80 ml) of the broth, stirring to loosen browned bits from pan; continue to cook until browned bits form again. Repeat deglazing step about 3 more times or until vegetables are browned, using ⅓ cup (80 ml) more broth each time.

4. Snap off and discard tough ends of asparagus; thinly slice stalks. Add asparagus and ⅓ cup (80 ml) more broth to mushroom mixture; cook, stirring often, until asparagus is tender-crisp to bite (about 2 minutes).

5. Spoon rice-lentil mixture into a large bowl. Add asparagus mixture, vinegar, and oil; mix gently but thoroughly. Sprinkle with cheese. Makes 8 servings.

Per serving: 236 calories (16% calories from fat), 4 g total fat, 1 g saturated fat, 4 mg cholesterol, 413 mg sodium, 27 g carbohydrates, 6 g fiber, 15 g protein, 106 mg calcium, 4 mg iron

---

For a satisfying high-fiber salad, combine brown rice with crisp pea pods, water chestnuts and crunchy peanuts; then mix in a gingery soy-lime dresssing.

Indonesian Brown Rice Salad

Preparation time: 25 minutes
Cooking time: About 45 minutes

Brown Rice Salad:

2 cups (370 g) long-grain brown rice

2 cups (170 g) Chinese pea pods

1 medium-size red bell pepper

5 green onions

1 can (about 8 oz./230 g) water chestnuts, drained

¼ cup (10 g) cilantro leaves

1 cup (145 g) raisins

1 cup (144 g) roasted peanuts

Cilantro Sauce:

2 cups (470 ml) plain nonfat yogurt

½ cup (20 g) cilantro leaves

1 teaspoon Oriental sesame oil

½ teaspoon finely chopped garlic

¼ teaspoon salt (or to taste)

Lime Dressing:

⅔ cup (160 ml) unseasoned rice vinegar or cider vinegar

2 tablespoons (30 ml) *each* lime juice and reduced-sodium soy sauce

1 tablespoon minced fresh ginger

2 teaspoons finely chopped garlic

1 teaspoon honey

1. In a 2½- to 3-quart (2.4- to 2.8-liter) pan, bring 4½ cups (1 liter) water to a boil over medium-high heat. Stir in rice; then reduce heat, cover, and simmer until liquid has been absorbed and rice is tender to bite (about 45 minutes). Transfer to a large bowl and let cool, stirring occasionally.

2. Meanwhile, remove and discard ends and strings of pea pods; thinly slice pea pods. Seed and chop bell pepper. Thinly slice onions; chop water chestnuts.

3. To cooled rice, add pea pods, bell pepper, onions, water chestnuts, the ¼ cup cilantro, raisins, and peanuts. Mix gently but thoroughly; set aside.

4. In a small serving bowl, combine yogurt, the ½ cup cilantro, oil, the ½ teaspoon garlic, and salt. Stir until blended; set aside.

5. In another small bowl, combine vinegar, lime juice, soy sauce, ginger, the 2 teaspoons garlic, and honey. Beat until blended; pour over salad and mix gently but thoroughly. Serve salad with cilantro sauce. Makes 8 servings.

Per serving: 545 calories (24% calories from fat), 15 g total fat, 2 g saturated fat, 2 mg cholesterol, 560 mg sodium, 90 g carbohydrates, 8 g fiber, 18 g protein, 218 mg calcium, 3 mg iron

Spiked with ginger and red pepper flakes, this salad of broth-simmered wheat berries (whole, unprocessed wheat kernels) is dressed with an Indonesian-style spicy peanut sauce. Wheat berries are sold, packaged or in bulk, in health food stores and many well-stocked supermarkets.

- 2 large yellow or white onions, thinly sliced
- 2 cups (250 g) wheat berries, rinsed and drained
- 3 cups (710 ml) vegetable broth
  About ⅛ teaspoon crushed red pepper flakes (or to taste)
- 1 tablespoon finely chopped fresh ginger
- 2 tablespoons creamy peanut butter
- 2 tablespoons fruit or berry jam or jelly
- 2 tablespoons (30 ml) seasoned rice vinegar or 2 tablespoons (30 ml) distilled white vinegar plus ½ to 1 teaspoon sugar

Wheat Berry Satay Salad

Preparation time: 15 minutes, plus about 30 minutes for salad to cool
Cooking time: About 1¾ hours

About 1 tablespoon (15 ml) reduced-sodium soy sauce (or to taste)
- 1 cup (40 g) chopped cilantro
- 1 cup (100 g) sliced green onions
- ¼ cup (36 g) finely chopped salted roasted peanuts

1. In a 4- to 5-quart (3.8- to 5-liter) pan, combine yellow onions and ½ cup (120 ml) water. Cook over medium-high heat, stirring often, until liquid evaporates and browned bits stick to pan bottom (10 to 15 minutes). To deglaze pan, add ¼ cup (60 ml) more water, stirring to loosen browned bits from pan; continue to cook until browned bits form again. Repeat deglazing step 3 or 4 more times or

until onions are dark brown, using ¼ cup (60 ml) water each time.

2. Add wheat berries, broth, red pepper flakes, and ginger to pan. Bring to a boil; then reduce heat, cover, and simmer, stirring occasionally, until wheat berries are just tender to bite (50 to 60 minutes). Remove from heat; drain and reserve cooking liquid.

3. In a small bowl, beat ¼ cup (60 ml) of the reserved cooking liquid, peanut butter, and jam until smoothly blended. Stir peanut butter mixture, vinegar, and soy sauce into wheat berry mixture. Cover salad and let stand until cool (about 30 minutes).

4. Add two-thirds each of the cilantro and green onions to salad; mix gently but thoroughly. If a moister texture is desired, mix in some of the remaining cooking liquid. Transfer salad to a serving bowl; sprinkle with remaining cilantro, remaining green onions, and peanuts. Makes 4 servings.

Per serving: 517 calories (19% calories from fat), 12 g total fat, 1 g saturated fat, 0 mg cholesterol, 1,136 mg sodium, 92 g carbohydrates, 18 g fiber, 19 g protein, 96 mg calcium, 4 mg iron

---

Redolent with mint and lemon, tabbouleh, a Middle Eastern specialty, goes together quickly and is a satisfying side dish for a summertime barbecue.

- 10 ounces/285 g (about 1⅔ cups) dried couscous
- 1½ cups (55 g) firmly packed fresh mint, minced
- 2 tablespoons (30 ml) olive oil
- ½ cup (120 ml) lemon juice (or to taste)
  Salt and pepper
- 6 to 8 large butter lettuce leaves, rinsed and crisped
- 2 large tomatoes (about 1 lb./455 g *total*), thinly sliced
  Mint sprigs

Couscous Tabbouleh

Preparation time: About 15 minutes
Cooking time: About 8 minutes
Chilling time: At least 30 minutes

1. Bring 2¼ cups (530 ml) water to a boil in a 3- to 4-quart (2.8- to 3.8-liter) pan over high heat. Stir in pasta; cover, remove from heat, and let stand until liquid is absorbed (about 5 minutes). Transfer pasta to a large nonmetal bowl and let cool, fluffing occasionally with a fork.

2. Add minced mint, oil, and lemon juice to pasta. Season to taste with salt

and pepper. Mix well. Cover and refrigerate until cool (at least 30 minutes) or for up to 4 hours; fluff occasionally with a fork.

3. Line a platter with lettuce leaves. Mound tabbouleh in center; arrange tomatoes around edge. Garnish with mint sprigs. Makes 6 to 8 servings.

Per serving: 210 calories (19% calories from fat), 5 g total fat, 0.6 g saturated fat, 0 mg cholesterol, 14 mg sodium, 36 g carbohydrates, 2 g fiber, 6 g protein, 27 mg calcium, 1 mg iron

Fragrant pesto dressing flavors a good-looking pasta salad dotted with dried tomatoes.

- 1 cup (about 2 oz./55 g) dried tomatoes (not packed in oil)
- 2 tablespoons pine nuts
- 1 pound (455 g) dried medium-size pasta shells or elbow macaroni
- 1 cup (45 g) firmly packed chopped fresh spinach
- 3 tablespoons dried basil
- 1 or 2 cloves garlic, peeled
- ⅓ cup (30 g) grated Parmesan cheese
- ¼ cup (60 ml) olive oil
- 1 teaspoon Oriental sesame oil
  Salt and pepper

Pesto Pasta Salad

Preparation time: 20 minutes
Cooking time: About 15 minutes
Pictured on facing page

1. Place tomatoes in a small bowl and add boiling water to cover. Let stand until soft (about 10 minutes), stirring occasionally. Drain well; gently squeeze out excess liquid. Cut tomatoes into thin slivers and set aside.

2. While tomatoes are soaking, toast pine nuts in a small frying pan over medium heat until golden (about 3 minutes), stirring often. Pour out of pan and set aside.

3. In a 6- to 8-quart (6- to 8-liter) pan, bring 4 quarts (3.8 liters) water to a boil over medium-high heat; stir in pasta and cook until just tender to bite, 8 to 10 minutes. (Or cook pasta according to package directions.) Drain, rinse with cold water until cool, and drain well again. Pour into a large serving bowl.

4. In a food processor or blender, whirl spinach, basil, garlic, cheese, olive oil, sesame oil, and 1 teaspoon water until smoothly puréed; scrape sides of container as needed and add a little more water if pesto is too thick.

5. Add tomatoes and spinach pesto to pasta; mix well. Sprinkle with pine nuts; season to taste with salt and pepper. Makes 8 servings.

Per serving: 332 calories (28% calories from fat), 10 g total fat, 2 g saturated fat, 3 mg cholesterol, 78 mg sodium, 49 g carbohydrates, 3 g fiber, 11 g protein, 98 mg calcium, 3 mg iron

---

Literally translated as "fine hairs," capellini are lightly dressed with a soy-based dressing and tossed with green onions and bright red bell pepper.

- 3 tablespoons (45 ml) seasoned rice vinegar; or 3 tablespoons (45 ml) distilled white vinegar and 2 teaspoons sugar
- 3 tablespoons (45 ml) lime juice
- 4 teaspoons (20 ml) Oriental sesame oil (or to taste)
- 1 tablespoon (15 ml) reduced-sodium soy sauce
- ¹⁄₁₆ teaspoon ground red pepper (cayenne)
- 8 ounces (230 g) dried capellini
- ½ cup (50 g) thinly sliced green onions
- ⅓ cup (50 g) chopped red bell pepper
  Lime wedges

Capellini Chinese Style

Preparation time: About 20 minutes
Cooking time: About 15 minutes
Chilling time: At least 30 minutes

1. Combine vinegar, lime juice, oil, soy sauce, and ground red pepper in a large nonmetal serving bowl; mix until blended. Set aside.

2. Bring 8 cups (1.9 liters) water to a boil in a 4- to 5-quart (3.8- to 5-liter) pan over medium-high heat. Stir in pasta and cook just until tender to bite (about 4 minutes); or cook according to package directions. Drain, rinse with cold water until cool, and drain well.

3. Add pasta to vinegar mixture. Mix thoroughly but gently. Cover and refrigerate until cool (at least 30 minutes) or for up to 4 hours; stir occasionally.

4. Stir in onions and bell pepper just before serving. Offer lime wedges to add to taste. Makes 4 to 6 servings.

Per serving: 217 calories (18% calories from fat), 4 g total fat, 0.6 g saturated fat, 0 mg cholesterol, 305 mg sodium, 38 g carbohydrates, 1 g fiber, 6 g protein, 18 mg calcium, 2 mg iron

Pesto Pasta Salad
(recipe on facing page)

Stir-fried Salads

Ideal for chilly-weather dinners, the salads on these two pages are just as good in summer: because the cooking times are so brief, you can serve a warm entrée without overheating the kitchen (or yourself). All of our selections feature crisp greens topped with a savory stir-fry. For best results, serve stir-fried salads at once, just as soon as the greens are slightly wilted from the heat of the topping.

Warm Chinese Chicken Salad

Preparation time: About 15 minutes
Cooking time: About 5 minutes

⅓ cup (80 ml) seasoned rice vinegar; or ⅓ cup (80 ml) distilled white vinegar plus 2 teaspoons sugar

1 tablespoon (15 ml) reduced-sodium soy sauce

1½ teaspoons *each* sugar and Oriental sesame oil

7 cups (about 7 oz./200g) finely shredded iceberg lettuce

3 cups (about 3 oz./85 g) bite-size pieces of radicchio

⅓ cup (15 g) lightly packed cilantro leaves

¼ cup (25 g) sliced green onions

1 pound (455 g) boneless, skinless chicken breast, cut into thin strips

2 cloves garlic, minced or pressed

Cilantro sprigs

1. In a small bowl, stir together vinegar, 1 tablespoon (15 ml) water, soy sauce, sugar, and oil; set aside.

2. In a large serving bowl, combine lettuce, radicchio, cilantro leaves, and onions; cover and set aside.

3. In a wide nonstick frying pan or wok, combine chicken, 1 tablespoon (15 ml) water, and garlic. Stir-fry over medium-high heat until chicken is no longer pink in center; cut to test (3 to 4 minutes). Add water, 1 tablespoon (15 ml) at a time, if pan appears dry. Add vinegar mixture to pan and bring to a boil. Quickly pour chicken and sauce over greens, then mix gently but thoroughly. Garnish with cilantro sprigs and serve immediately. Makes 4 servings.

Per serving: 185 calories (17% calories from fat), 3 g total fat, 0.6 g saturated fat, 66 mg cholesterol, 626 mg sodium, 10 g carbohydrates, 1 g fiber, 28 g protein, 84 mg calcium, 2 mg iron

Warm Spinach, Pear & Sausage Salad

Preparation time: About 15 minutes
Cooking time: About 15 minutes

3 green onions

8 ounces (230 g) spinach, stems removed, leaves rinsed and crisped

1 large yellow or red bell pepper (about 8 oz./230 g), seeded and cut lengthwise into thin strips

5 medium-size firm-ripe pears (1¾ to 2 lbs./795 to 905 g *total*)

1 teaspoon olive oil or salad oil

8 to 10 ounces (230 to 285 g) mild or hot turkey Italian sausages, casings removed

⅓ cup (80 ml) balsamic vinegar

¾ teaspoon fennel seeds

1. Trim and discard ends of onions. Cut onions into 2-inch (5-cm) lengths; then cut each piece lengthwise into slivers. Tear spinach into bite-size pieces. Place onions, spinach, and bell pepper in a large serving bowl, cover, and set aside.

2. Peel and core pears; slice thinly. Heat oil in a wide nonstick frying pan or wok over medium-high heat. When oil is hot, add pears and stir-fry until almost tender to bite (about 5 minutes). Lift pears from pan with a slotted spoon; transfer to a bowl and keep warm.

3. Crumble sausage into pan and stir-fry over medium-high heat until browned (5 to 7 minutes); add water, 1 tablespoon (15 ml) at a time, if pan appears dry. Add pears, vinegar, and fennel seeds to pan. Stir gently to mix, scraping browned bits free from pan bottom. Immediately pour hot pear mixture over spinach mixture; toss gently but thoroughly until spinach is slightly wilted. Serve immediately. Makes 4 servings.

Per serving: 155 calories (11% calories from fat), 2 g total fat, 0.2 g saturated fat, 0 mg cholesterol, 36 mg sodium, 36 g carbohydrates, 7 g fiber, 3 g protein, 79 mg calcium, 2 mg iron

Warm Cioppino Salad

Preparation time: About 20 minutes
Cooking time: About 10 minutes

Lemon Dressing
(recipe follows)

3 quarts (about 12 oz./340 g) lightly packed rinsed, crisped spinach leaves, torn into bite-size pieces

1 tablespoon (15 ml) olive oil

8 ounces (230 g) extra-large raw shrimp (26 to 30 per lb.), shelled and deveined

2 cups (170 g) sliced mushrooms (¼ inch/6 mm thick)

2 cups (340 g) sliced zucchini (¼ inch/6 mm thick)

1 can (about 14½ oz./415 g) tomatoes, drained and chopped; or 1½ cups (235 g) chopped fresh tomatoes

12 pitted ripe olives

8 ounces (230 g) cooked crabmeat

1. Prepare Lemon Dressing and set aside. Place spinach in a wide serving bowl, cover, and set aside.

2. Heat oil in a wide nonstick frying pan or wok over medium-high heat. When oil is hot, add shrimp and stir-fry until just opaque in center; cut to test (3 to 4 minutes). Remove from pan with tongs or a slotted spoon and set aside.

3. Add mushrooms and zucchini to pan; stir-fry until zucchini is just tender to bite (about 3 minutes). Return shrimp to pan; add tomatoes, olives, and Lemon Dressing. Stir until mixture is heated through. Quickly pour shrimp mixture over spinach, top with crab, and mix gently but thoroughly. Serve immediately. Makes 6 servings.

Lemon Dressing. In a small bowl, stir together ¼ cup (60 ml) **lemon juice,** 1 teaspoon *each* **dried basil** and **dried oregano,** and 2 cloves **garlic,** minced or pressed.

Per serving: 149 calories (28% calories from fat), 5 g total fat, 0.7 g saturated fat, 85 mg cholesterol, 380 mg sodium, 10 g carbohydrates, 3 g fiber, 18 g protein, 159 mg calcium, 4 mg iron

Stir-fried Pork & Escarole Salad

Preparation time: About 25 minutes
Cooking time: About 5 minutes

3 quarts (about 12 oz./340 g) lightly packed rinsed, crisped escarole or spinach leaves

⅔ cup (160 ml) cider vinegar

3 tablespoons (45 ml) honey

2 large Red Delicious apples (about 1 lb./455 g *total*), cored and thinly sliced

4 teaspoons cornstarch

1 cup (240 ml) fat-free reduced-sodium chicken broth

2 teaspoons Dijon mustard

½ teaspoon dried thyme

2 teaspoons olive oil

2 large shallots, chopped

1 pound (455 g) lean boneless pork loin, loin end, or leg, trimmed of fat and cut into paper-thin ½- by 3-inch (1- by 8-cm) slices

1 cup (145 g) raisins

1. Place escarole on a wide platter. In a medium-size bowl, stir together vinegar, honey, and apples. Then remove apples with a slotted spoon and scatter over escarole. Add cornstarch, broth, mustard, and thyme to vinegar mixture in bowl; stir well and set aside.

2. Heat oil in a wide nonstick frying pan or wok over medium-high heat. When oil is hot, add shallots and pork and stir-fry until meat is lightly browned (about 3 minutes). Push meat to one side of pan. Stir vinegar mixture well, pour into pan, and stir just until boiling (about 1 minute). Stir meat into sauce; then quickly spoon meat mixture over escarole and sprinkle with raisins. Serve immediately. Makes 4 servings.

Per serving: 443 calories (18% calories from fat), 9 g total fat, 3 g saturated fat, 67 mg cholesterol, 305 mg sodium, 67 g carbohydrates, 6 g fiber, 28 g protein, 98 mg calcium, 3 mg iron

Macaroni Salad
(recipe on facing page)

Tofu lends creaminess to this lightened-up salad favorite.

....

  Tofu Mayonnaise
  (recipe follows)

8 ounces/230 g (about 2 cups)
  dried elbow macaroni

1 large hard-cooked egg,
  chopped

½ cup (60 g) thinly sliced celery

1 jar (about 2 oz./55 g) chopped
  pimentos, drained

½ cup (80 g) chopped dill pickles

¼ cup (25 g) thinly sliced green
  onions

  Green leaf lettuce leaves,
  washed and crisped

  Tomato slices

  Thyme or parsley sprigs

....

1. Prepare Tofu Mayonnaise; cover and refrigerate.

Macaroni Salad

Preparation time: About 30 minutes
Cooking time: About 15 minutes
Chilling time: At least 30 minutes
Pictured on facing page

2. Bring 8 cups (1.9 liters) water to a boil in a 4- to 5-quart (3.8- to 5-liter) pan over medium-high heat. Stir in pasta and cook just until tender to bite (8 to 10 minutes); or cook according to package directions. Drain, rinse with cold water until cool, and drain well.

3. Transfer pasta to a large nonmetal bowl. Add Tofu Mayonnaise, egg, celery, pimentos, and pickles. Mix well. Cover and refrigerate until cool (at least 30 minutes) or for up to 2 hours; stir occasionally. Just before serving, stir in onions. Arrange lettuce and tomatoes on individual plates. Top

with pasta. Garnish with thyme sprigs. Makes 8 servings.

....

Tofu Mayonnaise. Rinse 8 ounces (230 g) **soft tofu** in a colander. Coarsely mash tofu; let drain for 10 minutes. Transfer to a blender or food processor. Add ¼ cup (60 ml) **low-sodium chicken** or vegetable **broth,** 3 tablespoons (45 ml) **lemon juice,** 2 tablespoons (30 ml) **olive oil** or salad oil, 2 teaspoons *each* **prepared horseradish** and **sugar,** and 1 teaspoon *each* **dried thyme** and **Dijon mustard.** Whirl until smooth. Season to taste with salt. If made ahead, cover and refrigerate for up to an hour. Stir before using.

....

Per serving: 173 calories (28% calories from fat), 5 g total fat, 0.7 g saturated fat, 27 mg cholesterol, 165 mg sodium, 25 g carbohydrates, 1 g fiber, 6 g protein, 28 mg calcium, 2 mg iron

....

Crisp cucumbers and tender fresh tortellini produce an unusual, refreshingly cool salad.

....

1 package (about 9 oz./255 g)
  fresh cheese tortellini or ravioli

2 medium-size cucumbers (about
  1½ lbs./680 g *total*)

  About ¼ teaspoon salt

2 cups (470 ml) plain low-fat
  yogurt

3 cloves garlic, minced or
  pressed

2 tablespoons (30 ml) lemon
  juice

1 tablespoon minced fresh dill
  or 1 teaspoon dried dill weed

2 teaspoons olive oil (or to taste)

8 to 12 large butter lettuce leaves,
  rinsed and crisped

Creamy Cucumber & Tortellini Salad

Preparation time: About 20 minutes
Cooking time: About 10 minutes
Chilling time: At least 30 minutes

1 tablespoon minced fresh mint
  or 1 teaspoon dried mint

  Dill or mint sprigs

....

1. Bring 12 cups (2.8 liters) water to a boil in a 5- to 6-quart (5- to 6-liter) pan over medium-high heat. Stir in pasta and cook just until tender to bite (4 to 6 minutes); or cook according to package directions. Drain, rinse with cold water until cool, and drain well. Set aside.

2. Peel cucumbers, scrape out and discard seeds, and coarsely chop. In a colander, mix cucumbers with ¼ teaspoon of the salt; let drain for 15 minutes.

3. Transfer pasta to a large nonmetal bowl. Add cucumbers, yogurt, garlic, lemon juice, minced dill, and oil. Mix thoroughly but gently. Cover and refrigerate until cool (at least 30 minutes) or for up to 2 hours; stir occasionally.

4. Arrange lettuce on individual plates. Spoon pasta mixture onto lettuce and sprinkle with minced mint. Garnish with dill sprigs. Offer salt to add to taste. Makes 4 to 6 servings.

....

Per serving: 254 calories (24% calories from fat), 7 g total fat, 3 g saturated fat, 26 mg cholesterol, 330 mg sodium, 37 g carbohydrates, 2 g fiber, 13 g protein, 254 mg calcium, 2 mg iron

Sweet & Sour Ravioli Salad

Ravioli seasoned with a spicy sweet-sour dressing mingle with chunks of garden-fresh tomatoes.

Preparation time: About 30 minutes
Cooking time: About 10 minutes
Chilling time: At least 30 minutes

- 1 package (about 9 oz./255 g) fresh low-fat or regular cheese ravioli or tortellini
- 2 pounds (905 g) pear-shaped (Roma-type) tomatoes (about 10 large)
- ½ cup (120 ml) seasoned rice vinegar; or ½ cup (120 ml) distilled white vinegar and 4 teaspoons sugar
- 2 tablespoons firmly packed brown sugar
- ½ teaspoon *each* coriander seeds, cumin seeds, and mustard seeds
- 1/16 teaspoon ground red pepper (cayenne)
- Parsley sprigs

1. Bring 12 cups (2.8 liters) water to a boil in a 5- to 6-quart (5- to 6-liter) pan over medium-high heat. Separating any ravioli that are stuck together, add pasta. Reduce heat to medium and boil gently, stirring occasionally, just until pasta is tender to bite (4 to 6 minutes); or cook according to package directions. Lift out pasta, rinse with cold water until cool, and drain well. Transfer to a large nonmetal serving bowl and set aside.

2. Bring water in pan back to a boil. Drop in tomatoes and cook for 1 minute. Drain and let cool. Peel and discard skin; cut into bite-size pieces. Set aside.

3. Combine vinegar, brown sugar, coriander seeds, cumin seeds, mustard seeds, and ground red pepper in a 1- to 1½-quart (950-ml to 1.4-liter) pan. Bring to a simmer over low heat. Cook, stirring, just until sugar is dissolved (about 1 minute).

4. Add tomatoes and vinegar mixture to pasta. Mix thoroughly but gently. Let cool briefly; then cover and refrigerate until cool (at least 30 minutes) or for up to 4 hours; stir occasionally.

5. Garnish with parsley. Makes 6 to 8 servings.

Per serving: 153 calories (15% calories from fat), 3 g total fat, 1 g saturated fat, 22 mg cholesterol, 481 mg sodium, 27 g carbohydrates, 24 g fiber, 6 g protein, 73 mg calcium, 1 mg iron

---

Fruited Orzo

One of the reasons that pasta is so popular is that it combines easily with many different ingredients. But here's a combination that's somewhat unexpected—pasta with ripe pears and tangy cranberries. Taste the goodness of this pairing in a quick-to-make salad that complements grilled meats and poultry.

Preparation time: About 25 minutes
Cooking time: About 15 minutes
Chilling time: At least 30 minutes

- Pear Dressing (recipe follows)
- 10 ounces/285 g (about 1⅔ cups) dried orzo or other rice-shaped pasta
- 4 large red or d'Anjou pears (about 2 lbs./905 g *total*)
- 3 tablespoons (45 ml) lemon juice
- ½ cup (65 g) roasted salted almonds, coarsely chopped

1. Prepare Pear Dressing; cover and refrigerate.

2. Bring 8 cups (1.9 liters) water to a boil in a 4- to 5-quart (3.8- to 5-liter) pan over medium-high heat. Add pasta and cook just until tender to bite (8 to 10 minutes); or cook according to package directions. Drain, rinse with cold water until cool, and drain well. Transfer to a large nonmetal bowl. Add dressing. Mix thoroughly but gently. Cover and refrigerate until cool (about 30 minutes) or for up to 3 hours; stir occasionally.

3. Slice pears thinly just before serving. Coat with lemon juice. Coarsely chop a third of the fruit and stir into pasta mixture. Spoon onto individual plates. Arrange pear slices alongside. Sprinkle with nuts. Makes 6 servings.

Pear Dressing. In a small nonmetal bowl, combine ¾ cup (180 ml) canned **pear nectar** or **apple juice,** ⅓ cup (30 g) **dried cranberries,** and ¼ cup (45 g) chopped **dried pears;** let stand, stirring occasionally, until fruit is softened (about 10 minutes). Add ½ cup (120 ml) **nonfat** or **reduced-fat sour cream,** 1 tablespoon (15 ml) **lemon juice,** 2 teaspoons *each* grated **lemon peel** and **ground coriander,** and 1 teaspoon **sugar** (or to taste). Mix until blended. If made ahead, cover and refrigerate for up to an hour. Stir before using.

Per serving: 396 calories (20% calories from fat), 9 g total fat, 0.8 g saturated fat, 0 mg cholesterol, 123 mg sodium, 71 g carbohydrates, 7 g fiber, 11 g protein, 87 mg calcium, 3 mg iron

Crunchy, sweet jicama adds texture and is the surprise ingredient in the lean pesto that coats tubular-shaped ziti for this summertime salad.

Basil Pesto (recipe follows)

10 ounces/285 g (about 3 cups) dried ziti or penne

2 tablespoons pine nuts (optional)

Basil sprigs

Salt and pepper

Freshly grated Parmesan cheese

1. Prepare Basil Pesto.

2. Bring 12 cups (2.8 liters) water to a boil in a 5- to 6-quart (5- to 6-liter) pan over medium-high heat. Stir in pasta and cook just until tender to bite (8 to 10 minutes); or cook according to

Ziti with Basil Pesto

Preparation time: About 20 minutes
Cooking time: About 15 minutes
Chilling time: At least 30 minutes

package directions. Meanwhile, toast pine nuts, if desired, in a small frying pan over medium heat, shaking pan often, until golden (about 3 minutes); remove from pan and set aside.

3. Drain pasta, rinse with cold water until cool, and drain well. Transfer to a large nonmetal serving bowl. Add pesto and mix thoroughly but gently. Cover and refrigerate until cool (at least 30 minutes) or for up to 2 hours; stir occasionally.

4. Sprinkle with pine nuts, if used, and garnish with basil sprigs. Offer salt, pepper, and cheese to add to taste. Makes 6 to 8 servings.

Basil Pesto. In a blender or food processor, combine 2 cups (80 g) lightly packed **fresh basil,** 1 cup (130 g) coarsely chopped **jicama,** ½ cup (120 ml) **low-sodium chicken broth,** ¼ cup (20 g) freshly grated **Parmesan cheese,** 3 tablespoons (45 ml) **olive oil,** 2 tablespoons drained **capers,** and 2 or 3 cloves **garlic.** Whirl until smooth. If made ahead, cover and refrigerate for up to an hour. Stir before using.

Per serving: 238 calories (29% calories from fat), 8 g total fat, 1 g saturated fat, 2 mg cholesterol, 130 mg sodium, 35 g carbohydrates, 1 g fiber, 8 g protein, 161 mg calcium, 4 mg iron

---

Peppery watercress contributes sparkling color to this salad of turkey and penne ("quill pens").

⅔ pound (300 g) watercress, stems trimmed, rinsed and crisped

Watercress Dressing (recipe follows)

10 ounces/285 g (about 3 cups) dried penne

1 to 1¼ pounds (455 to 565 g) cooked turkey breast, cut into thin strips

1. Reserve ¾ cup (25 g) of the watercress for dressing. Prepare Watercress Dressing; cover and refrigerate.

2. Bring 12 cups (2.8 liters) water to a boil in a 5- to 6-quart (5- to 6-liter) pan over medium-high heat. Stir in pasta and cook just until tender to bite (8 to 10 minutes); or cook according to package directions. Drain, rinse with cold water until cool, and drain well.

Watercress, Penne & Turkey Salad

Preparation time: About 25 minutes
Cooking time: About 15 minutes
Chilling time: At least 30 minutes

3. Transfer pasta to a large nonmetal serving bowl. Add remaining watercress and about 1 cup (240 ml) of the dressing. Mix thoroughly but gently. Cover and refrigerate until cool (at least 30 minutes) or for up to 2 hours; stir occasionally.

4. Mound turkey on pasta mixture. Offer remaining dressing to add to taste. Makes 6 servings.

Per serving: 301 calories (4% calories from fat), 1 g total fat, 0.3 g saturated fat, 71 mg cholesterol, 101 mg sodium, 37 g carbohydrates, 2 g fiber, 33 g protein, 80 mg calcium, 3 mg iron

Watercress Dressing. In a blender or food processor, combine reserved ¾ cup (25 g) **watercress,** ¾ cup (180 ml) **plain nonfat** or **low-fat yogurt,** ¾ cup (180 ml) **nonfat** or **reduced-calorie mayonnaise,** 1 tablespoon (15 ml) **lemon juice,** ½ teaspoon **dried basil,** and 1 clove **garlic.** Whirl until smooth. Season to taste with **sugar** and **fish sauce** (*nam pla* or *nuoc mam*) or **reduced-sodium soy sauce.** Whirl until blended. If made ahead, cover and refrigerate for up to an hour. Stir before using. Makes 1⅔ cups (400 ml).

Per tablespoon: 9 calories (1% calories from fat), 0 g total fat, 0 g saturated fat, 0.1 mg cholesterol, 54 mg sodium, 2 g carbohydrates, 0 g fiber, 0.4 g protein, 15 mg calcium, 0 mg iron

A basil-citrus pasta salad made with corkscrew-shaped rotini accompanies naturally lean chicken breasts and sliced oranges.

2 **large oranges (about 1 lb./ 455 g** *total***)**

Citrus Pasta Salad (recipe follows)

Orange Cream (recipe follows)

¼ **cup (80 g) orange marmalade**

1 **teaspoon prepared horseradish**

6 **skinless, boneless chicken breast halves (about 1½ lbs./ 680 g** *total***)**

2 **large blood oranges (about 10 oz./285 g** *total***) or 1 small pink grapefruit (about 6 oz./ 170 g)**

2 **medium-size avocados (about 1 lb./455 g** *total***), optional**

2 **tablespoons (30 ml) lemon juice (optional)**

Basil sprigs

Finely shredded orange peel

1. Grate 4 teaspoons peel from oranges. Prepare Citrus Pasta Salad and Orange Cream, using grated peel; cover and refrigerate.

2. Mix marmalade and horseradish in a large bowl. Add chicken and stir to coat. Place chicken in a lightly oiled 10- by 15-inch (25- by 38-cm) baking pan. Bake in a 450°F (230°C) oven until meat in thickest part is no longer pink; cut to test (12 to 15 minutes). Let

Chicken & Citrus Pasta Salad

Preparation time: About 1 hour
Cooking time: About 25 minutes
Chilling time: At least 30 minutes
Pictured on facing page

cool. Meanwhile, cut peel and white membrane from oranges and blood oranges; slice fruit crosswise into rounds ¼ inch (6 mm) thick. (For grapefruit, cut segments from membrane; discard membrane.)

3. Arrange pasta salad and chicken on a platter. Place fruit around edge. If desired, pit, peel, and slice avocados; coat with lemon juice and place on platter. Garnish with basil sprigs and shredded orange peel. Offer Orange Cream to add to taste. Makes 6 servings.

Citrus Pasta Salad. Bring 12 cups (2.8 liters) **water** to a boil in a 5- to 6-quart (5- to 6-liter) pan over medium-high heat. Stir in 12 ounces/340 g (about 5 cups) **dried rotini** or other corkscrew-shaped pasta. Cook just until tender to bite (8 to 10 minutes); or cook according to package directions. Drain, rinse with cold water until cool, and drain well.

In a large nonmetal bowl, combine 1 tablespoon grated **orange peel;**

¾ cup (180 ml) **orange juice;** 1 small **orange** (about 4 oz./115 g), peeled and coarsely chopped; 3 tablespoons (45 ml) **white wine vinegar** or distilled white vinegar; 3 tablespoons chopped **fresh basil;** 1 tablespoon (15 ml) *each* **honey** and **Dijon mustard;** 1½ teaspoons **ground cumin;** and 1 fresh **jalapeño chile,** seeded and finely chopped. Mix until blended. Add pasta and mix thoroughly but gently. Cover and refrigerate until cool (at least 30 minutes) or for up to 4 hours; stir occasionally. Just before serving, stir in ¼ cup (15 g) chopped **parsley** and 2 or 3 cloves **garlic,** minced or pressed.

Per serving: 463 calories (7% calories from fat), 4 g total fat, 0.7 g saturated fat, 74 mg cholesterol, 158 mg sodium, 70 g carbohydrates, 3 g fiber, 38 g protein, 91 mg calcium, 4 mg iron

Orange Cream. In a small nonmetal bowl, combine 1 cup (240 ml) **nonfat** or **reduced-fat sour cream,** 3 tablespoons **orange marmalade,** 2 teaspoons **prepared horseradish,** and 1 teaspoon grated **orange peel.** Mix until blended. Season to taste with **ground white pepper.** If made ahead, cover and refrigerate for up to a day. Stir before serving. Makes about 1¼ cups (300 ml).

Per serving: 16 calories (0% calories from fat), 0 g total fat, 0 g saturated fat, 0 mg cholesterol, 10 mg sodium, 3 g carbohydrates, 0 g fiber, 1 g protein, 17 mg calcium, 0 mg iron

Chicken & Citrus Pasta Salad
(recipe on facing page)

Guests can help themselves to this easily prepared buffet of chicken, noodles, and vegetables, topped with a spicy dressing. Follow with a dessert of cooling fresh pineapple.

....

Chili Dressing (recipe follows)

4 **chicken breast halves (2 to 2½ lbs./905 g to 1.15 kg** *total*), skinned

1 **pound (455 g) dried capellini**

2 **teaspoons Oriental sesame oil or salad oil**

1 **large European cucumber (about 1 lb./455 g), cut into thin rounds and slivered**

8 **to 12 ounces (230 to 340 g) bean sprouts, rinsed and drained**

¾ **cup (75 g) thinly sliced green onions**

¾ **cup (30 g) chopped cilantro**

½ **cup (20 g) chopped fresh basil**

¾ **cup (110 g) finely chopped salted roasted peanuts**

Lemon wedges (optional)

Thai Chicken & Capellini Buffet

....

Preparation time: About 35 minutes
Cooking time: About 30 minutes

1. Prepare Chili Dressing; cover and refrigerate.

2. Bring 16 cups (3.8 liters) water to a boil in a 6- to 8-quart (6- to 8-liter) pan over high heat. Add chicken and return to a boil. Cover pan tightly, remove from heat, and let stand until meat in thickest part is no longer pink; cut to test (about 20 minutes). If not done, return chicken to water, cover, and let stand, checking for doneness at 2- or 3-minute intervals. Lift out chicken, reserving water, and let cool. Meanwhile, return water to a boil over medium-high heat. Stir in pasta and cook just until tender to bite (about 4 minutes); or cook according to package directions. Drain, rinse with cold water until cool, and drain well.

3. Sprinkle pasta with oil. Loosely coil small handfuls of pasta; set on a rimmed platter, stacking if necessary. Drizzle with about 1 cup (240 ml) of the dressing. Tear chicken into shreds; discard bones. Arrange chicken, cucumber, sprouts, and onions separately around pasta. Drizzle with remaining dressing (or to taste). Place cilantro, basil, nuts, and, if desired, lemon in small bowls and offer to add to taste. Makes 6 servings.

....

Chili Dressing. In a small nonmetal bowl, combine ¾ cup (180 ml) **rice vinegar** or white wine vinegar, ½ cup (120 ml) **reduced-sodium soy sauce,** 3 tablespoons **sugar,** 2 tablespoons *each* minced **fresh ginger** and **Oriental sesame oil,** 1 to 2 teaspoons **crushed red pepper flakes,** and 2 cloves **garlic,** minced or pressed. Mix until blended. If made ahead, cover and refrigerate for up to 4 hours. Stir before using. Makes about 1⅔ cups (400 ml).

....

Per serving: 638 calories (25% calories from fat), 18 g total fat, 3 g saturated fat, 64 mg cholesterol, 963 mg sodium, 77 g carbohydrates, 5 g fiber, 44 g protein, 108 mg calcium, 6 mg iron

---

Sweet litchis bring refreshing flavor to a chicken and pasta salad bathed in a lemony yogurt dressing. Look for litchis in Asian markets or in the Asian section of your supermarket.

....

5 **ounces/140 g (about 1½ cups) dried penne**

1 **can (about 11 oz./310 g) litchis**

¾ **cup (180 ml) plain low-fat or nonfat yogurt**

¾ **teaspoon grated lemon peel**

4 **teaspoons (20 ml) lemon juice**

1½ **teaspoons dried thyme**

2 **cups (280 g) bite-size pieces cooked chicken**

½ **cup (60 g) finely diced celery**

8 **large butter lettuce leaves, rinsed and crisped**

Litchi, Penne & Chicken Salad

....

Preparation time: About 20 minutes
Cooking time: About 20 minutes

....

⅓ **cup (35 g) chopped green onions**

Salt and pepper

....

1. Bring 8 cups (1.9 liters) water to a boil in a 4- to 5-quart (3.8- to 5-liter) pan over medium-high heat. Stir in pasta and cook just until tender to bite (8 to 10 minutes); or cook according to package directions. Drain, rinse with cold water until cool, and drain well.

2. Drain litchis, reserving ⅓ cup (80 ml) of the syrup; set fruit aside. In a large nonmetal bowl, mix reserved ⅓ cup (80 ml) litchi syrup, yogurt, lemon peel, lemon juice, and thyme. Add pasta, chicken, and celery. Mix thoroughly but gently. (At this point, you may cover pasta mixture and fruit separately and refrigerate for up to 4 hours; stir pasta occasionally.)

3. Arrange lettuce on individual plates. Top with pasta mixture and litchis. Sprinkle with onions. Offer salt and pepper to add to taste. Makes 4 servings.

....

Per serving: 358 calories (7% calories from fat), 7 g total fat, 2 g saturated fat, 65 mg cholesterol, 136 mg sodium, 47 g carbohydrates, 2 g fiber, 28 g protein, 120 mg calcium, 4 mg iron

Seviche Salads

Lovely as light entrées or first courses, these piquant salads taste much like classic seafood *seviche*. But there's an important difference. In authentic *seviche*, uncooked fish is marinated in citrus juice; the acid slowly firms the flesh, giving it an opaque "cooked" appearance.

Our salads, on the other hand, are made with seafood that actually is cooked. Brief simmering in a tart liquid gives fish and shellfish the characteristic *seviche* flavor, at the same time eliminating any worries one might have about eating raw seafood.

Seviche with Radishes & Peas

¾ cup (180 ml) *each* unseasoned rice vinegar and water; or 1 cup (240 ml) distilled white vinegar plus ½ cup water (120 ml)

2 tablespoons minced crystallized ginger

½ teaspoon coriander seeds

1 pound (455 g) skinless, boneless lean, firm-textured fish such as halibut, mahimahi, or swordfish, cut into ½-inch (1-cm) chunks

1 cup (227 g) frozen tiny peas, thawed

1 cup (115 g) sliced red radishes

Salt and pepper

1. In a wide nonstick frying pan, bring vinegar, water, ginger, and coriander seeds to a boil over high heat. Add fish.

Reduce heat, cover, and simmer until fish is just opaque but still moist in thickest part; cut to test (3 to 4 minutes). With a slotted spoon, transfer fish to a bowl.

2. Boil cooking liquid over high heat, uncovered, until reduced to 1 cup (240 ml); pour over fish. Cover and refrigerate until cool (at least 1½ hours) or for up to 8 hours.

3. Gently mix peas and radish slices with fish. Spoon into 4 or 6 shallow soup bowls; distribute liquid equally among bowls. Season to taste with salt and pepper. Makes 4 main-dish or 6 first-course servings.

Per serving: 196 calories (14% calories from fat), 3 g total fat, 0.4 g saturated fat, 36 mg cholesterol, 137 mg sodium, 16 g carbohydrates, 2 g fiber, 26 g protein, 87 mg calcium, 3 mg iron

Lime & Chipotle Scallop Seviche

1 pound (455 g) sea or bay scallops

1 teaspoon olive oil or salad oil

½ cup (80 g) minced shallots

½ teaspoon minced canned chipotle chiles in adobo or adobado sauce; or ½ teaspoon crushed red pepper flakes

½ cup (120 ml) *each* lime juice, distilled white vinegar, and water

8 ounces (230 g) jicama

⅓ cup (13 g) minced cilantro

Lime wedges (optional)

1. Rinse and drain scallops. If scallops are more than ½ inch (1 cm) thick, cut in half horizontally to make thinner rounds; set aside.

2. In a wide nonstick frying pan, combine oil, shallots, and chiles; cook over medium heat, stirring, until shallots are soft (about 3 minutes). Stir in lime juice, vinegar, and water; bring to a boil over high heat. Add scallops, arranging them in pan in a single layer. Reduce heat, cover, and simmer until scallops are just opaque but still moist in center; cut to test (about 2 minutes). With a slotted spoon, transfer scallops to a bowl.

3. Boil cooking liquid over high heat, uncovered, until reduced to 1 cup (240 ml); pour over scallops. Cover and refrigerate until cool (at least 1½ hours) or for up to 8 hours.

4. Meanwhile, peel jicama, rinse, and cut into matchsticks ¼ inch (6 mm) thick. Gently mix jicama with scallops and spoon into 4 or 6 shallow soup bowls; distribute liquid equally among bowls. Garnish salads with cilantro and, if desired, lime wedges. Makes 4 main-dish or 6 first-course servings.

Per serving: 158 calories (12% calories from fat), 2 g total fat, 0.2 g saturated fat, 37 mg cholesterol, 200 mg sodium, 15 g carbohydrates, 1 g fiber, 20 g protein, 49 mg calcium, 1 mg iron

Smoked Salmon Pasta Salad
(recipe on facing page)

This elegant salad features smoked salmon and fresh dill.

- 8 ounces/230 g (about 3 cups) dried radiatorre or rotini
- ¼ cup (60 ml) seasoned rice vinegar; or ¼ cup (60 ml) distilled white vinegar and 2 teaspoons sugar
- 1 tablespoon chopped fresh dill or ½ teaspoon dried dill weed
- 1 tablespoon (15 ml) olive oil
- 8 cups (440 g) bite-size pieces green leaf lettuce leaves
- ¼ cup (30 g) thinly sliced red onion
- 2 to 4 ounces (55 to 115 g) sliced smoked salmon or lox, cut into bite-size pieces

Smoked Salmon Pasta Salad

Preparation time: About 15 minutes
Cooking time: About 15 minutes
Pictured on facing page

Dill sprigs
Freshly grated Parmesan cheese

1. Bring 8 cups (1.9 liters) water to a boil in a 4- to 5-quart (3.8- to 5-liter) pan over medium-high heat. Stir in pasta and cook just until tender to bite (8 to 10 minutes); or cook according to package directions. Drain, rinse with cold water until cool, and drain well.

2. Combine vinegar, chopped dill, and oil in a large nonmetal serving bowl. Mix until blended. Add pasta, lettuce, and onion. Mix thoroughly but gently. Stir in salmon. Garnish with dill sprigs. Offer cheese to add to taste. Makes 6 servings.

Per serving: 194 calories (17% calories from fat), 4 g total fat, 0.5 g saturated fat, 3 mg cholesterol, 316 mg sodium, 32 g carbohydrates, 1 g fiber, 8 g protein, 37 mg calcium, 2 mg iron

---

Make this salad ahead of time to enjoy on a warm summer day, along with fresh fruit and crisp toast.

- Curry Dressing (recipe follows)
- 2 ounces/55 g (about ½ cup) dried small shell-shaped pasta
- 12 ounces (340 g) tiny cooked shrimp
- 1 cup (145 g) coarsely chopped cucumber
- 3 tablespoons dried tomatoes packed in oil, drained well and coarsely chopped
  Salt
- 4 to 8 large butter lettuce leaves, rinsed and crisped
  Lemon wedges

Curried Shrimp & Shell Salad

Preparation time: About 25 minutes
Cooking time: About 15 minutes
Chilling time: At least 30 minutes

1. Prepare Curry Dressing; cover and refrigerate.

2. Bring 4 cups (950 ml) water to a boil in a 3- to 4-quart (2.8- to 3.8-liter) pan over medium-high heat. Stir in pasta and cook just until tender to bite (8 to 10 minutes); or cook according to package directions. Drain, rinse with cold water until cool, and drain well.

3. Transfer pasta to a large nonmetal bowl. Add shrimp, cucumber, tomatoes, and dressing. Mix thoroughly but gently. Season to taste with salt.

Cover and refrigerate until cool (at least 30 minutes) or for up to 4 hours; stir occasionally.

4. Arrange lettuce on individual plates. Spoon pasta mixture onto lettuce. Offer lemon to add to taste. Makes 4 servings.

Curry Dressing. In a small nonmetal bowl, combine ¼ cup (60 ml) **nonfat** or **reduced-calorie mayonnaise**, 1 tablespoon (15 ml) **Dijon mustard**, ½ teaspoon grated **lemon peel**, 1 tablespoon (15 ml) **lemon juice**, 1 teaspoon *each* **dried dill weed** and **honey**, ½ teaspoon **curry powder**, and ¼ teaspoon **pepper**. Mix until blended. If made ahead, cover and refrigerate for up to an hour. Stir before using.

Per serving: 226 calories (28% calories from fat), 7 g total fat, 1 g saturated fat, 166 mg cholesterol, 395 mg sodium, 19 g carbohydrates, 2 g fiber, 21 g protein, 51 mg calcium, 4 mg iron

Fresh basil and cilantro lend flavor and color to the creamy dressing for this cooling pasta and shrimp salad, nestled in a bed of crisp shredded lettuce.

Pesto Dressing (recipe follows)

6 cups (1.4 liters) low-sodium chicken broth

8 ounces/230 g (about 1⅓ cups) dried orzo or other rice-shaped pasta

1 pound (455 g) tiny cooked shrimp

1 cup (100 g) chopped green onions

1 tablespoon grated lemon peel

½ cup (120 ml) lemon juice

1 small head iceberg lettuce (about 1 lb./455 g), rinsed and crisped

3 cups (425 g) tiny cherry tomatoes

Shrimp & Orzo with Pesto Dressing

Preparation time: About 25 minutes
Cooking time: About 10 minutes

1. Prepare Pesto Dressing; cover and refrigerate.

2. Bring broth to a boil in a 4- to 5-quart (3.8- to 5-liter) pan over medium-high heat. Stir in pasta and cook just until barely tender to bite (about 5 minutes). Drain well, reserving liquid for other uses. Let cool completely.

3. Transfer pasta to a large bowl. Add shrimp, onions, lemon peel, and lemon juice. Mix thoroughly but gently.

4. Shred lettuce and place in a shallow serving bowl. Spoon pasta mixture

into bowl. Arrange tomatoes around edge of bowl. Offer dressing to add to taste. Makes 5 or 6 servings.

Per serving: 274 calories (13% calories from fat), 4 g total fat, 1 g saturated fat, 148 mg cholesterol, 305 mg sodium, 38 g carbohydrates, 3 g fiber, 26 g protein, 122 mg calcium, 5 mg iron

Pesto Dressing. In a blender or food processor, combine ½ cup (20 g) *each* chopped **fresh basil** and chopped **cilantro,** 1 cup (240 ml) **plain nonfat yogurt,** and 1 tablespoon (15 ml) **white wine vinegar.** Whirl until smooth. If made ahead, cover and refrigerate for up to 4 hours. Stir before serving. Makes about 1¼ cups (300 ml).

Per serving: 8 calories (3% calories from fat), 0 g total fat, 0 g saturated fat, 0.2 mg cholesterol, 9 mg sodium, 1 g carbohydrates, 0 g fiber, 0.7 g protein, 32 mg calcium, 0.2 mg iron

---

A little heat can heighten flavors. Here, red onion rings and a spicy chile dressing enliven a colorful combination of lettuce, oranges, cucumber, tiny shrimp, and avocado.

Red Chile Dressing (page 53)

4 quarts (about 1 lb./455 g) rinsed, crisped leaf lettuce, torn into bite-size pieces

⅓ pound (150 g) tiny cooked shrimp

½ cup (58 g) thinly sliced red onion

1 large cucumber (10 to 12 oz./285 to 340 g), peeled (if desired) and thinly sliced

Orange-Onion Salad with Red Chile Dressing

Preparation time: About 20 minutes

3 small oranges (about 1 lb./455 g *total*)

1 medium-size firm-ripe avocado

1 tablespoon (15 ml) lemon juice

1. Prepare Red Chile Dressing; set aside.

2. Place lettuce in a large salad bowl or on a rimmed platter. Arrange shrimp, onion, and cucumber on lettuce.

3. With a sharp knife, cut peel and all white membrane from oranges; then cut oranges crosswise into ¼-inch (6 mm) slices and arrange on salad.

4. Pit and peel avocado; thinly slice lengthwise. Coat slices with lemon juice; then arrange on salad. Pour dressing over salad and mix gently. Makes 8 servings.

Per serving: 106 calories (26% calories from fat), 3 g total fat, 0.6 g saturated fat, 37 mg cholesterol, 52 mg sodium, 16 g carbohydrates, 2 g fiber, 6 g protein, 79 mg calcium, 2 mg iron

Mild butter lettuce in a creamy tofu-enriched blue cheese dressing cradles a hearty salad of marinated beef and bow-tie pasta.

- 1 **pound (455 g) lean boneless top sirloin steak (about 1 inch/2.5 cm thick), trimmed of fat**
- 2 **tablespoons (30 ml) dry sherry**
  Blue Cheese Dressing (recipe follows)
- 6 **to 8 ounces/170 to 230 g (3 to 4 cups) dried farfalle (about 1½-inch/3.5-cm size)**
- ¼ **cup (60 ml) red wine vinegar**
- 1 **tablespoon (15 ml) olive oil or salad oil**
- 1 **tablespoon chopped fresh thyme or 1 teaspoon dried thyme**
- 1 **teaspoon sugar**
  Salt and pepper
- 8 **cups (440 g) bite-size pieces butter lettuce leaves**
  Thyme sprigs

1. Slice steak across grain into strips about ⅛ inch (3 mm) thick and 3 inches (8 cm) long. Place meat and sherry in a large heavy-duty resealable plastic bag or nonmetal bowl. Seal bag and

Beef & Bow-tie Salad

Preparation time: About 30 minutes
Marinating time: At least 30 minutes
Cooking time: About 20 minutes
Chilling time: At least 30 minutes

rotate to coat meat (or stir meat in bowl and cover airtight). Refrigerate for at least 30 minutes or up to a day, turning (or stirring) occasionally.

2. Prepare Blue Cheese Dressing; cover and refrigerate.

3. Bring 8 cups (1.9 liters) water to a boil in a 4- to 5-quart (3.8- to 5-liter) pan over medium-high heat. Stir in pasta and cook just until tender to bite (8 to 10 minutes); or cook according to package directions. Drain, rinse with cold water until cool, and drain well.

4. Combine vinegar, 2 teaspoons of the oil, chopped thyme, and sugar in a large nonmetal bowl. Stir until blended. Add pasta and mix thoroughly but gently. Cover and refrigerate until cool (at least 30 minutes) or for up to 2 hours; stir occasionally. Meanwhile, heat remaining 1 teaspoon oil in a

wide nonstick frying pan over medium-high heat. Add steak and its juices and cook, stirring, until browned and done to your liking; cut to test (3 to 5 minutes). Transfer to a large nonmetal bowl and let cool. Season to taste with salt and pepper.

5. Combine lettuce and dressing in a large serving bowl; turn to coat. Add beef to pasta mixture and stir gently. Spoon onto greens. Garnish with thyme sprigs. Makes 4 to 6 servings.

Blue Cheese Dressing. In a blender or food processor, combine 4 ounces (115 g) **low-fat (1%)** or **soft tofu,** rinsed and drained; ¼ cup (60 ml) **low-fat buttermilk;** 1 tablespoon (15 ml) **white wine vinegar;** 2 teaspoons *each* **sugar** and **olive oil;** 1 teaspoon **Dijon mustard;** and 1 clove **garlic.** Whirl until smooth. Season to taste with **salt** and **pepper.** Gently stir in ¼ cup (35 g) crumbled **blue-veined cheese.** (At this point, you may cover and refrigerate for up to an hour.) Stir in 1 tablespoon chopped green onion before using.

Per serving: 376 calories (29% calories from fat), 12 g total fat, 3 g saturated fat, 61 mg cholesterol, 210 mg sodium, 36 g carbohydrates, 2 g fiber, 28 g protein, 715 mg calcium, 5 mg iron

When raspberries are in season, enjoy this quickly cooked beef and pasta salad. Fresh raspberries adorn the salad, and raspberry flavor infuses the beef, pasta, and lettuce.

1 pound (455 g) lean boneless top sirloin steak (about 1 inch/2.5 cm thick), trimmed of fat

½ cup (120 ml) dry red wine

5 tablespoons (75 ml) raspberry vinegar or red wine vinegar

¼ cup (25 g) chopped green onions

2 tablespoons (30 ml) reduced-sodium soy sauce

1 tablespoon sugar

2 teaspoons chopped fresh tarragon or ½ teaspoon dried tarragon

1 tablespoon raspberry or apple jelly

¾ cup (180 ml) low-sodium chicken broth

⅔ cup (160 ml) low-fat milk

¼ teaspoon ground coriander

6½ ounces/185 g (about 1 cup) dried couscous

1 tablespoon (15 ml) olive oil

8 cups (440 g) bite-size pieces red leaf lettuce leaves

2 cups (245 g) raspberries

Tarragon sprigs (optional)

Steak, Couscous & Greens with Raspberries

Preparation time: About 1 hour
Marinating time: At least 30 minutes
Cooking time: About 15 minutes
Chilling time: At least 30 minutes
Pictured on facing page

1. Slice steak across grain into strips about ⅛ inch (3 mm) thick and 3 inches (8 cm) long. Place meat, wine, 1 tablespoon of the vinegar, 2 tablespoons of the onions, soy sauce, 2 teaspoons of the sugar, and chopped tarragon in a large heavy-duty resealable plastic bag or large nonmetal bowl. Seal bag and rotate to coat meat (or stir meat in bowl and cover airtight). Refrigerate for at least 30 minutes or up to a day, turning (or stirring) occasionally.

2. Cook jelly in a 2- to 3-quart (1.9- to 2.8-liter) pan over low heat, stirring, until melted. Add broth, milk, and coriander; increase heat to medium-high and bring to a gentle boil. Stir in couscous. Cover, remove from heat, and let stand until liquid is absorbed (about 5 minutes).

3. Transfer couscous mixture to a large nonmetal bowl; let cool briefly, fluffing occasionally with a fork. Cover and refrigerate until cool (at least 30 minutes) or for up to 2 hours, fluffing occasionally. Meanwhile, heat 1 teaspoon of the oil in a wide nonstick frying pan over medium-high heat. Add meat and its juices and cook, stirring, until browned and done to your liking; cut to test (3 to 5 minutes). Transfer to a large nonmetal bowl and let cool.

4. Combine remaining 2 teaspoons oil, remaining 4 tablespoons (60 ml) vinegar, and remaining 1 teaspoon sugar in a large nonmetal bowl. Mix until blended. Add lettuce and turn to coat. Arrange lettuce on individual plates. Stir remaining 2 tablespoons onions into couscous mixture. Spoon onto lettuce, top with meat, and sprinkle with raspberries. Garnish with tarragon sprigs, if desired. Makes 4 servings.

Per serving: 456 calories (20% calories from fat), 10 g total fat, 3 g saturated fat, 71 mg cholesterol, 273 mg sodium, 55 g carbohydrates, 5 g fiber, 34 g protein, 151 mg calcium, 5 mg iron

Steak, Couscous & Greens with Raspberries
(recipe on facing page)

A mango and ginger dressing bastes roasted pork and tubular ziti in an appetizing, no-fuss salad.

- 6 ounces/170 g (about 2 cups) dried ziti or penne
- ⅔ cup (160 ml) mango or pear nectar
- 1 tablespoon minced fresh ginger
- 2 teaspoons olive oil
- 1 or 2 cloves garlic, minced or pressed
- 1 teaspoon Oriental sesame oil
- 1½ cups (210 g) roasted or Chinese-style barbecued pork, cut into thin ½-inch (1-cm) pieces
- ⅓ cup (50 g) chopped red bell pepper

Gingered Pork & Ziti Salad

Preparation time: About 30 minutes
Cooking time: About 15 minutes
Chilling time: At least 30 minutes

- 4 to 8 red leaf lettuce leaves, rinsed and crisped
- ¼ cup (25 g) thinly sliced green onions
- 4 whole green onions (optional)
  Salt and pepper

1. Bring 8 cups (1.9 liters) water to a boil in a 4- to 5-quart (3.8- to 5-liter) pan over medium-high heat. Stir in pasta and cook just until tender to bite (8 to 10 minutes); or cook according to package directions. Drain, rinse with cold water until cool, and drain well.

2. Combine mango nectar, ginger, olive oil, garlic, and sesame oil in a large nonmetal bowl. Mix until blended. Add pasta, pork, and bell pepper. Mix thoroughly but gently. Cover and refrigerate until cool (at least 30 minutes) or for up to 3 hours; stir occasionally.

3. Arrange lettuce on individual plates. Stir sliced onions into pasta mixture and spoon onto lettuce. Garnish with whole onions, if desired. Offer salt and pepper to add to taste. Makes 4 servings.

Per serving: 346 calories (26% calories from fat), 10 g total fat, 3 g saturated fat, 50 mg cholesterol, 51 mg sodium, 40 g carbohydrates, 2 g fiber, 24 g protein, 41 mg calcium, 3 mg iron

---

Sweet sun-dried tomatoes, salty prosciutto, and marinated artichokes combine for delicious results in this warm salad.

- ⅔ cup (about 1⅓ oz./ 38 g) dried tomatoes (not packed in oil)
- 1 jar (about 6 oz./170 g) marinated artichoke hearts
- 3 green onions
- 1 package (about 10 oz./ 285 g) prewashed spinach leaves, coarse stems and any yellow or bruised leaves discarded, remaining leaves rinsed and crisped
- ½ teaspoon olive oil
- 2 ounces (55 g) thinly sliced prosciutto, chopped
- 2 cloves garlic, minced
- ½ teaspoon dried rosemary
- 1 can (about 14 oz./400 g) artichoke hearts packed in water, drained and quartered
- ¼ cup (60 ml) balsamic vinegar
- 1 to 2 tablespoons firmly packed brown sugar

Wilted Spinach & Prosciutto Salad

Preparation time: 20 minutes
Cooking time: About 5 minutes

1. Place tomatoes in a small bowl and add boiling water to cover. Let stand until soft (about 10 minutes), stirring occasionally. Drain well; gently squeeze out excess liquid. Cut tomatoes into thin slivers; set aside.

2. While tomatoes are soaking, drain marinated artichokes, reserving marinade. Cut artichoke pieces lengthwise into halves; set aside. Cut onions into 2-inch (5-cm) lengths; then sliver each piece lengthwise. Tear spinach into bite-size pieces. Place onions and spinach in a large bowl; set aside.

3. Heat oil in a wide nonstick frying pan over medium-high heat. Add prosciutto, garlic, and rosemary. Cook, stirring often, until prosciutto is crisp and lightly browned (about 3 minutes); add water, 1 tablespoon (15 ml) at a time, if pan appears dry.

4. To pan, add tomatoes, marinated artichokes, artichoke marinade, quartered canned artichokes, vinegar, and sugar. Mix gently, stirring to scrape browned bits free from pan bottom. Pour artichoke mixture over spinach mixture; toss until spinach is slightly wilted and coated with dressing. Serve at once. Makes 4 servings.

Per serving: 170 calories (29% calories from fat), 6 g total fat, 1 g saturated fat, 11 mg cholesterol, 536 mg sodium, 22 g carbohydrates, 4 g fiber, 10 g protein, 92 mg calcium, 3 mg iron

Serve this salad on a bed of orange slices and spinach.

....

- 8 ounces/230 g (about 3½ cups) dried rotini or other corkscrew-shaped pasta

- 1 teaspoon salad oil

- 1 pound (455 g) pork tenderloin or boned pork loin, trimmed of fat, sliced into thin strips ½ inch (1 cm) wide

- 1 tablespoon minced garlic

- 1 teaspoon *each* chili powder and dried oregano

- ¾ cup (180 ml) lime juice

- 3 tablespoons sugar

- 1 teaspoon reduced-sodium soy sauce

- ⅓ cup (15 g) chopped cilantro

- 6 large oranges (about 3½ lbs./ 1.6 kg *total*)

  About 40 large spinach leaves, coarse stems removed, rinsed and crisped

Pork & Rotini Salad with Oranges

....

Preparation time: About 30 minutes
Cooking time: About 10 minutes
Chilling time: At least 30 minutes

1. Bring 8 cups (1.9 liters) water to a boil in a 4- to 5-quart (3.8- to 5-liter) pan over medium-high heat. Stir in pasta and cook just until tender to bite (8 to 10 minutes); or cook according to package directions. Drain, rinse with cold water until cool, and drain well; set aside.

2. Heat oil in a wide nonstick frying pan over medium-high heat. Add pork, garlic, chili powder, and oregano. Cook, stirring, until pork is no longer pink in center; cut to test (about 5 minutes). Remove pan from heat and add lime juice, sugar, and soy sauce; stir to loosen browned bits. Transfer to a large nonmetal bowl and let cool briefly. Add pasta and cilantro. Mix thoroughly but gently. Cover and refrigerate until cool (at least 30 minutes) or for up to 2 hours; stir occasionally.

3. Cut peel and white membrane from oranges; thinly slice fruit crosswise. Arrange spinach on individual plates. Top with orange slices and pasta mixture. Makes 6 servings.

....

Per serving: 362 calories (11% calories from fat), 5 g total fat, 1 g saturated fat, 49 mg cholesterol, 99 mg sodium, 59 g carbohydrates, 6 g fiber, 23 g protein, 121 mg calcium, 3 mg iron

Pork Tenderloin with Peanut Vermicelli
(recipe on page 88)

Meats

Flavorful and succulent—do you have to renounce red meat to eat light? Not at all. Purchasing the leanest cuts and serving modest portions will allow you to continue to offer satisfying yet healthy meals with meat. Try a new twist on an old favorite—Spiral Stuffed Meat Loaf, or for a quick yet delicious meal, stir-fry Veal with Mushrooms flavored with Marsala and serve over hot linguine.

Peanuts, plum jam, hoisin, and peas star in this dish.

- 2 **pork tenderloins (about 12 oz./340 g each), trimmed of fat and silvery membrane**
- ¼ **cup (60 ml) hoisin sauce**
- 3 **tablespoons firmly packed brown sugar**
- 2 **tablespoons (30 ml) dry sherry**
- 2 **tablespoons (30 ml) reduced-sodium soy sauce**
- 1 **tablespoon (15 ml) lemon juice**
- 12 **ounces (340 g) dried vermicelli**
- ½ **cup (160 g) plum jam or plum butter**
- ¼ **cup (60 ml) seasoned rice vinegar; or ¼ cup (60 ml) distilled white vinegar and 2 teaspoons sugar**
- ¼ **cup (65 g) creamy peanut butter**
- 3 **tablespoons Oriental sesame oil**
- 2 **cloves garlic, minced or pressed**
- ⅛ **teaspoon ground ginger**
- ¼ **teaspoon crushed red pepper flakes**
- 1 **package (about 10 oz./285 g) frozen tiny peas, thawed**

Pork Tenderloin with Peanut Vermicelli

Preparation time: About 20 minutes
Cooking time: About 35 minutes
Pictured on page 86

- ⅓ **cup (15 g) cilantro**
- 2 **tablespoons chopped peanuts (optional)**
- **Sliced kumquats (optional)**

1. Place tenderloins on a rack in a 9- by 13-inch (23- by 33-cm) baking pan. In a bowl, stir together hoisin, brown sugar, sherry, 1 tablespoon (15 ml) of the soy sauce, and lemon juice. Brush over pork, reserving remaining mixture.

2. Roast pork in a 450°F (230°C) oven, brushing with remaining marinade, until a meat thermometer inserted in thickest part registers 155°F/68°C (20 to 30 minutes; after 15 minutes, check temperature every 5 minutes); if drippings begin to burn, add 4 to 6 tablespoons (60 to 90 ml) water, stirring to loosen browned bits.

Meanwhile, bring 12 cups (2.8 liters) water to a boil in a 5- to 6-quart (5- to 6-liter) pan over medium-high heat. Stir in pasta and cook just until tender to bite (8 to 10 minutes); or cook according to package directions. Drain well and keep warm.

3. Transfer meat to a board, cover loosely, and let stand for 10 minutes. Skim and discard fat from pan drippings. Pour drippings and any juices on board into a small serving container; keep warm. Meanwhile, combine jam, vinegar, peanut butter, oil, garlic, ginger, red pepper flakes, and remaining 1 tablespoon (15 ml) soy sauce in 5- to 6-quart (5- to 6-liter) pan. Bring to a boil over medium heat and cook, whisking, just until smooth. Remove from heat and add pasta, peas, and cilantro. Lift with 2 forks to mix. Mound pasta on individual plates. Thinly slice meat across grain; arrange on pasta. Garnish with kumquats, if desired. Offer juices and, if desired, peanuts to add to taste. Makes 6 servings.

Per serving: 616 calories (26% calories from fat), 18 g total fat, 3 g saturated fat, 67 mg cholesterol, 578 mg sodium, 77 g carbohydrates, 4 g fiber, 37 g protein, 43 mg calcium, 5 mg iron

---

Escabeche, a piquant blend of spices and garlic, gives roasted pork tenderloin a wonderful flavor.

- **Escabeche Paste (recipe follows)**
- 2 **pork tenderloins (about 12 oz./340 g each), trimmed of fat and silvery membrane**
- **About 4 large oranges (about 3 lbs./1.35 kg total), peeled (if desired) and sliced crosswise**

1. Prepare Escabeche Paste; spread evenly over pork tenderloins. (At this point, you may cover and refrigerate until next day.)

2. Place tenderloins, side by side, on a

Pork in Escabeche Sauce

Preparation time: About 15 minutes
Roasting time: 20 to 30 minutes

rack in a 9- by 13-inch (23- by 33-cm) baking pan. Roast in a 450°F (230°C) oven until a meat thermometer inserted in thickest part of meat registers 155°F/68°C (20 to 30 minutes). After 15 minutes, check temperature every 5 to 10 minutes.

3. When meat is done, cover it loosely and let stand for 10 minutes. To serve,

thinly slice meat across the grain; transfer to a platter. Surround meat with orange slices. Makes 6 servings.

Escabeche Paste. Mix 4 cloves **garlic**, minced or pressed; 1 tablespoon (15 ml) *each* **orange juice** and **white wine vinegar**; 1 teaspoon **dried oregano**; ¾ teaspoon **ground cinnamon**; ½ teaspoon *each* **ground allspice, ground cloves, ground cumin,** and **ground coriander**; ¼ teaspoon **black pepper**; and ⅛ teaspoon **ground red pepper** (cayenne).

Per serving: 212 calories (16% calories from fat), 4 g total fat, 1 g saturated fat, 74 mg cholesterol, 61 mg sodium, 28 g carbohydrates, 3 g fiber, 26 g protein, 140 mg calcium, 3 mg iron

Sweet apple jelly and tart cider vinegar combine in a tempting sauce for quickly cooked pork chops. To complete the dish, poach sliced Golden Delicious apples in the pan juices; then spoon them alongside the meat.

Herbed Pork Chops with Apples

Preparation time: About 10 minutes
Cooking time: About 30 minutes

6 center-cut loin pork chops (about 2 lbs./905 g *total*), trimmed of fat

Pepper

¼ cup (60 ml) apple jelly

1 tablespoon (15 ml) *each* Dijon mustard and water

½ teaspoon ground cumin

3 large Golden Delicious apples (about 1½ lbs./680 *total*)

¼ cup (60 ml) cider vinegar

1. Sprinkle chops with pepper; then cook in a wide nonstick frying pan over medium-high heat, turning once, until well browned on both sides (about 14 minutes).

2. In a small bowl, mix jelly, mustard, water, and cumin. Spoon evenly over chops. Reduce heat to low, cover, and cook until chops look faintly pink to white in center; cut to test (about 10 minutes; meat should still be moist). With a slotted spoon or a fork, transfer chops to a platter; keep warm.

3. Peel, core, and thinly slice apples. Add apples and vinegar to pan; stir to coat apples with pan juices, scraping browned bits free. Cover and cook over medium heat until apples are barely tender when pierced (about 5 minutes).

4. With a slotted spoon, transfer apples to platter with chops. Offer hot pan juices to pour over chops and apples. Makes 6 servings.

Per serving: 236 calories (21% calories from fat), 5 g total fat, 2 g saturated fat, 64 mg cholesterol, 132 mg sodium, 24 g carbohydrates, 2 g fiber, 23 g protein, 28 mg calcium, 1 mg iron

---

Round, crisp Asian pears—sometimes called "apple pears"—make a mild, slightly sweet foil for stir-fried pork chunks. If you can't find Asian pears, use your favorite regular variety; Bartlett and Anjou are both good.

Gingered Pork with Asian Pears

Preparation time: About 15 minutes
Cooking time: About 20 minutes

3 large firm-ripe Asian or regular pears (about 1½ lbs./680 g *total*), peeled, cored, and thinly sliced

3 tablespoons (45 ml) cider vinegar

1 teaspoon salad oil

1 pound (455 g) pork tenderloin, trimmed of fat and cut into 1-inch (2.5-cm) chunks

2 tablespoons firmly packed brown sugar

⅔ cup (160 ml) *each* dry white wine and fat-free reduced-sodium chicken broth

2 teaspoons minced fresh ginger

4 teaspoons cornstarch blended with 4 teaspoons cold water

½ to ¾ cup (15 to 23 g) finely shredded spinach

1. In a large bowl, gently mix pears and 1 tablespoon (15 ml) of the vinegar. Set aside.

2. Heat oil in a wide nonstick frying pan or wok over medium-high heat. When oil is hot, add pork and stir-fry until lightly browned on outside and no longer pink in center; cut to test (about 8 minutes). Add water, 1 tablespoon (15 ml) at a time, if pan appears dry. Remove meat from pan with a slotted spoon; keep warm.

3. Add sugar and remaining 2 tablespoons (30 ml) vinegar to pan. Bring to a boil; then boil, stirring, for 1 minute. Add wine, broth, and ginger; return to a boil. Boil, stirring, for 3 minutes. Add pears and cook, gently turning pears often, until pears are heated through (about 3 minutes). Stir cornstarch mixture well and pour into pan. Cook, stirring, until sauce boils and thickens slightly (1 to 2 minutes).

4. Remove pan from heat; return meat to pan and mix gently but thoroughly. Gently stir in spinach. Makes 4 servings.

Per serving: 309 calories (18% calories from fat), 6 g total fat, 2 g saturated fat, 74 mg cholesterol, 177 mg sodium, 34 g carbohydrates, 4 g fiber, 25 g protein, 42 mg calcium, 2 mg iron

Chili verde is a pork stew that's popular throughout Mexico. We suggest serving it with rice, but it's just as good with warm tortillas.

1 pound (455 g) lean boneless pork shoulder, trimmed of fat and cut into ¾-inch (2-cm) cubes

1 large can (about 28 oz./795 g) tomatoes

2 medium-size onions, chopped

1½ cups (180 g) thinly sliced celery

1 teaspoon dry oregano

½ teaspoon rubbed sage

2 dry bay leaves

1 large green bell pepper (about 8 oz./230 g), seeded and chopped

2 medium-size fresh green Anaheim, poblano, or other large mild chiles (about 4 oz./115 g *total*), seeded and chopped

About 4 cups (820 g) hot cooked rice

Cilantro sprigs

Chili Verde

Preparation time: About 15 minutes
Cooking time: About 1½ hours
Pictured on facing page

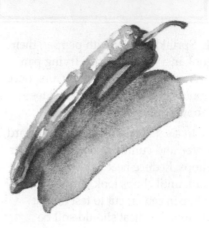

1. Place pork in a wide nonstick frying pan or 3- to 4-quart (2.8- to 3.8-liter) pan. Drain about ½ cup (120 ml) liquid from tomatoes into pan. Cover and bring to a boil over high heat; then reduce heat and simmer for 30 minutes.

2. Uncover pan; add onions, celery, oregano, and sage. Cook over high heat, stirring often, until liquid has evaporated and pan drippings are richly browned (8 to 10 minutes). Add bay leaves. Stir in tomatoes and their remaining liquid (break tomatoes up with a spoon); stir to scrape browned bits free. Reduce heat, cover, and simmer for 30 more minutes. Stir in bell pepper and chiles; cover and continue to simmer, stirring occasionally, until meat is very tender when pierced (about 15 more minutes). If chili is too thin, uncover and simmer until it's as thick as you like.

3. To serve, spoon chili over rice and garnish with cilantro sprigs. Makes 4 servings.

Per serving: 538 calories (17% calories from fat), 10 g total fat, 3 g saturated fat, 76 mg cholesterol, 469 mg sodium, 79 g carbohydrates, 5 g fiber, 31 g protein, 135 mg calcium, 6 mg iron

---

Spaetzle is often paired with sauerkraut as in this stew.

1 pound (455 g) boned pork shoulder or butt, trimmed of fat, cut into 1-inch (2.5-cm) cubes

1 can (about 1 lb./455 g) sauerkraut, drained

¼ cup (65 g) tomato paste

3 tablespoons paprika

2 tablespoons sugar

1 pound (455 g) carrots, cut diagonally ¼ inch (6 mm) thick

10½ ounces/300 g (about 2 cups) dried spaetzle or fettuccine

¼ cup (15 g) chopped parsley

½ teaspoon caraway seeds (or to taste)

Pork Stew with Spaetzle

Preparation time: About 10 minutes
Cooking time: About 2 hours

1. Place pork and ¼ cup (60 ml) water in a 5- to 6-quart (5- to 6-liter) pan. Cover and cook over medium-high heat for 10 minutes. Uncover, increase heat to high, and bring to a boil. Cook, stirring often, until liquid has evaporated and drippings are well browned.

2. Add sauerkraut, tomato paste, paprika, sugar, and 3 cups (710 ml) more water. Bring to a boil; reduce heat, cover, and simmer for 1 hour.

3. Stir in carrots. Cover and cook until pork is tender when pierced (about 30 more minutes). Meanwhile, bring 12 cups (2.8 liters) water to a boil in a 5- to 6-quart (5- to 6-liter) pan over medium-high heat. Stir in pasta and cook just until tender to bite (about 10 minutes for spaetzle, 8 to 10 minutes for fettuccine); or cook according to package directions. Drain well. Stir in 2 tablespoons of the parsley and caraway seeds. Arrange pasta and stew on individual plates. Sprinkle with remaining parsley. Makes 4 to 6 servings.

Per serving: 454 calories (21% calories from fat), 11 g total fat, 3 g saturated fat, 117 mg cholesterol, 420 mg sodium, 63 g carbohydrates, 6 g fiber, 28 g protein, 72 mg calcium, 6 mg iron

Chili Verde
(recipe on facing page)

To make couscous and rice seem richer, try cooking them in low-fat milk—or in a combination of broth and milk, as we do here. The creamy-tasting couscous, sweetened with a little shredded coconut, accompanies luscious sliced mangoes and a ginger-seasoned stir-fry of pork tenderloin and bright bell pepper.

- 2 **or 3 large mangoes (1½ to 2¼ lbs./680 g to 1.02 kg *total*)**
- 1 **to 2 tablespoons (15 to 30 ml) lime juice**

  Cooking Sauce (recipe follows)
- 1 **cup (240 ml) fat-free reduced-sodium chicken broth**
- ⅔ **cup (160 ml) low-fat milk**
- 1 **cup (185 g) couscous**
- ¼ **cup (20 g) sweetened shredded coconut**
- 2 **teaspoons olive oil**
- 1 **tablespoon minced fresh ginger**
- 2 **cloves garlic, minced or pressed**
- 1 **pound (455 g) pork tenderloin, trimmed of fat and cut into 1-inch (2.5-cm) chunks**
- 1 **large red or green bell pepper (about 8 oz./230 g), seeded and cut into thin strips**
- ¼ **cup (25 g) thinly sliced green onions**

  Lime wedges

Island Pork with Coconut Couscous

Preparation time: About 25 minutes
Cooking time: About 15 minutes

1. Peel mangoes; cut fruit from pits in thin slices and place in a large bowl. Add lime juice (use 2 tablespoons/30 ml juice if using 3 mangoes) and mix gently to coat. Arrange mangoes attractively on 4 individual plates; cover and set aside. Prepare Cooking Sauce and set aside.

2. In a 3- to 4-quart (2.8- to 3.8-liter) pan, bring broth and milk just to a boil over medium-high heat; stir in couscous. Cover, remove from heat, and let stand until liquid has been absorbed (about 5 minutes). Stir in coconut. Keep warm; fluff occasionally with a fork.

3. Heat oil in a wide nonstick frying pan or wok over medium-high heat. When oil is hot, add ginger and garlic; stir-fry just until fragrant (about 30 seconds; do not scorch). Add pork and stir-fry until lightly browned on outside and no longer pink in center; cut to test (about 8 minutes). Add water, 1 tablespoon (15 ml) at a time, if pan appears dry. Remove meat from pan with a slotted spoon; keep warm.

4. Add bell pepper and 2 tablespoons (30 ml) water to pan. Stir-fry until bell pepper is just tender-crisp to bite (about 2 minutes); add water, 1 tablespoon (15 ml) at a time, if pan appears dry.

5. Stir Cooking Sauce well and pour into pan. Cook, stirring, until sauce boils and thickens slightly (1 to 2 minutes). Remove pan from heat and add meat and onions; mix gently but thoroughly.

6. Spoon couscous alongside mango slices; spoon meat mixture alongside couscous. Serve with lime wedges. Makes 4 servings.

Cooking Sauce. Place 1 tablespoon **cornstarch** in a small bowl. Gradually add ¾ cup (180 ml) **mango** or pear nectar, stirring until cornstarch is smoothly dissolved. Stir in 1½ teaspoons **Oriental sesame oil** and ¼ teaspoon **salt**.

Per serving: 541 calories (18% calories from fat), 11 g total fat, 4 g saturated fat, 77 mg cholesterol, 398 mg sodium, 79 g carbohydrates, 5 g fiber, 33 g protein, 98 mg calcium, 3 mg iron

Ruote, wheel-shaped pasta, is enveloped in a mustard-sparked cheese sauce and served with pan-browned smoked pork chops.

- 4 smoked pork loin chops (about 1¼ lbs./565 g *total*), *each about ¾ inch (2 cm) thick, trimmed of fat*
- 8 ounces/230 g (about 4 cups) dried ruote or other medium-size pasta shape
- 1 tablespoon butter or margarine
- 1 large onion (about 8 oz./230 g), chopped
- 1 tablespoon all-purpose flour
- 1½ cups (360 ml) nonfat milk
- 1 tablespoon (15 ml) Dijon mustard
- ¼ teaspoon pepper
- 1 package (about 10 oz./285 g) frozen tiny peas

Smoked Pork Chops With Cheese Wheels

Preparation time: About 10 minutes
Cooking time: About 25 minutes

- 1 cup (about 4 oz./115 g) shredded Emmenthaler or Swiss cheese

1. Place pork chops in a wide nonstick frying pan and cook over medium-high heat, turning as needed, until browned on both sides (about 10 minutes). Transfer to a platter and keep warm. Discard any pan drippings.

2. Bring 8 cups (1.9 liters) water to a boil in a 4- to 5-quart (3.8- to 5-liter) pan over medium-high heat. Stir in pasta and cook just until tender to bite (8 to 10 minutes); or cook according to package directions. Meanwhile, melt butter in frying pan over medium-high heat. Add onion and cook, stirring often, until soft (about 5 minutes). Stir in flour and remove from heat. Add milk, mustard, and pepper; mix until blended.

3. Stir peas into pasta and water; drain and set aside. Return sauce to medium-high heat and cook, stirring, until mixture comes to a boil. Add cheese and stir until melted. Remove from heat and add pasta mixture. Mix thoroughly but gently. Spoon alongside meat. Makes 4 servings.

Per serving: 593 calories (27% calories from fat), 17 g total fat, 9 g saturated fat, 86 mg cholesterol, 1,867 mg sodium, 63 g carbohydrates, 5 g fiber, 43 g protein, 429 mg calcium, 4 mg iron

---

Shiitake mushrooms cost more than some other mushroom varieties, but their firm texture and beef-like flavor add a robust character to dishes that can't be duplicated.

- 1 package (about ½ oz./15 g) dried shiitake mushrooms
- 1 cup (185 g) long-grain white rice
- 1 medium-size head garlic (about 3 oz./85 g), separated into cloves
- 2 teaspoons salad oil
- 5 cups (325 g) broccoli flowerets
- 1 can (about 15 oz./425 g) black beans, drained and rinsed well
- 4 to 8 ounces (115 to 230 g) Chinese-style barbecued pork (or use leftover roast pork), cut into thin ½-inch (1-cm) squares
- 2 tablespoons (30 ml) reduced-sodium soy sauce
- 1 teaspoon Oriental sesame oil
- ½ teaspoon honey

Stir-fried Broccoli & Black Beans with Pork

Preparation time: 25 minutes
Cooking time: About 30 minutes

1. Place mushrooms in a small bowl and add enough boiling water to cover; let stand until mushrooms are softened (about 10 minutes). Lift mushrooms from water and squeeze dry; discard water. Trim and discard mushroom stems; then thinly slice caps. Set aside in a small bowl.

2. While mushrooms are soaking, bring 2 cups (470 ml) water to a boil in a 3- to 4-quart (2.8- to 3.8-liter) pan over high heat; stir in rice. Reduce heat, cover, and simmer until liquid has been absorbed and rice is tender to bite (about 20 minutes). Transfer to a rimmed platter and keep warm; fluff occasionally with a fork.

3. Peel and thinly slice garlic cloves. Heat salad oil in a wide nonstick frying pan over medium-high heat. Add garlic and cook, stirring, just until tinged with brown (about 2 minutes; do not scorch). Add water, 1 tablespoon (15 ml) at a time, if pan appears dry. Remove garlic from pan with a slotted spoon and place in bowl with mushrooms.

4. Add broccoli and ⅓ cup (80 ml) water to pan. Cover and cook until broccoli is almost tender-crisp to bite (about 3 minutes). Uncover and cook, stirring, until liquid has evaporated. Add beans and pork; cook, stirring often, until heated through.

5. Remove pan from heat and add mushroom mixture, soy sauce, sesame oil, and honey; mix gently but thoroughly. Spoon broccoli mixture over rice. Makes 4 servings.

Per serving: 460 calories (16% calories from fat), 9 g total fat, 2 g saturated fat, 34 mg cholesterol, 587 mg sodium, 71 g carbohydrates, 9 g fiber, 32 g protein, 149 mg calcium, 5 mg iron

Sweet & Sour Pork
(recipe on facing page)

All the classic ingredients are here—tender pork, crisp bell pepper and onion, juicy pineapple chunks, and a tart-sweet sauce—but this rendition of sweet and sour pork is far lower in fat than most traditional recipes.

Sweet-Sour Sauce (recipe follows)

1 **large egg white**

⅓ **cup (45 g) cornstarch**

1 **pound (455 g) pork tenderloin, trimmed of fat and cut into 1-inch (2.5-cm) chunks**

1 **tablespoon (15 ml) salad oil**

1 **large onion, cut into thin wedges**

1 **large green bell pepper (about 8 oz./230 g), seeded and cut into 1-inch (2.5-cm) squares**

1 **or 2 cloves garlic, minced or pressed**

1 **large tomato (about 8 oz./ 230 g), cut into wedges**

1½ **cups (235 g) fresh or canned pineapple chunks, drained**

Sweet & Sour Pork

Preparation time: About 25 minutes
Cooking time: About 15 minutes
Pictured on facing page

1. Prepare Sweet-Sour Sauce and set aside.

2. In a medium-size bowl, beat egg white to blend well. Place cornstarch in another medium-size bowl. Dip pork chunks, a portion at a time, in egg white; then coat lightly with cornstarch and shake off excess.

3. Heat oil in a wide nonstick frying pan or wok over medium-high heat. When oil is hot, add meat and stir-fry gently until golden brown on outside and no longer pink in center; cut to test (about 8 minutes). Add water, 1 tablespoon (15 ml) at a time, if pan appears dry. Remove meat from pan with a slotted spoon; keep warm.

4. Add onion, bell pepper, garlic, and 1 tablespoon (15 ml) water to pan; stir-fry for 1 minute. Add more water,

1 tablespoon (15 ml) at a time, if pan appears dry. Stir Sweet-Sour Sauce well and pour into pan. Cook, stirring, until sauce boils and thickens slightly (2 to 3 minutes).

5. Add tomato, pineapple, and meat to pan. Cook, stirring gently, just until heated through (1 to 2 minutes). Makes 4 servings.

Sweet-Sour Sauce. In a medium-size bowl, stir together 4 teaspoons **cornstarch** and ¼ cup (60 ml) **white wine vinegar** or distilled white vinegar until blended. Then stir in ¾ cup (180 ml) **water,** ¼ cup (50 g) **sugar,** 1 tablespoon (15 ml) *each* **catsup** and **reduced-sodium soy sauce,** and ⅛ teaspoon **Hot Chili Oil** (page 109) or purchased hot chili oil, or to taste.

Per serving: 355 calories (20% calories from fat), 8 g total fat, 2 g saturated fat, 74 mg cholesterol, 275 mg sodium, 45 g carbohydrates, 3 g fiber, 27 g protein, 32 mg calcium, 2 mg iron

---

A spicy tomato sauce flecked with ham enlivens penne.

1 **tablespoon (15 ml) olive oil**

6 **ounces (170 g) cooked ham, chopped**

1 **large onion (about 8 oz./230 g), finely chopped**

½ **cup (65 g) finely chopped carrot**

½ **cup (60 g) finely chopped celery**

½ **teaspoon crushed red pepper flakes**

1 **can (about 28 oz./795 g) pear-shaped (Roma-type) tomatoes**

1 **pound/455 g (about 5 cups) dried penne or ziti**

¼ **cup (20 g) freshly grated Parmesan cheese**

Penne all'Arrabbiata

Preparation time: About 10 minutes
Cooking time: About 50 minutes

1. Heat oil in a 3- to 4-quart (2.8- to 3.8-liter) pan over medium-high heat. Add ham and cook, stirring often, until lightly browned (about 5 min-

utes). Stir in onion, carrot, celery, and red pepper flakes. Reduce heat to medium and cook, stirring often, until vegetables are soft (about 15 minutes).

2. Add tomatoes and their liquid. Cook, stirring often, until sauce is reduced to about 3½ cups/830 ml (25 to 30 minutes). Meanwhile, bring 16 cups (3.8 liters) water to a boil in a 6- to 8-quart (6- to 8-liter) pan. Stir in pasta and cook just until tender to bite (8 to 10 minutes); or cook according to package directions. Drain well. Combine with sauce and cheese in a large serving bowl. Mix thoroughly but gently. Makes 4 or 5 servings.

Per serving: 500 calories (17% calories from fat), 9 g total fat, 3 g saturated fat, 24 mg cholesterol, 882 mg sodium, 80 g carbohydrates, 5 g fiber, 24 g protein, 145 mg calcium, 5 mg iron

These festive enchiladas are stuffed with pork and served in a flavorful chile sauce. The tortillas are traditionally fried, but we've omitted that step here; we simply soften them in hot water before filling them.

Red Chile Sauce
(recipe follows)

1¼ pounds (565 g) boneless pork butt or shoulder, trimmed of fat and cut into 1½-inch (3.5-cm) cubes

2 large onions, chopped

3 tablespoons chili powder

2 teaspoons dry oregano

3 cups (710 ml) beef broth

12 corn tortillas (6-inch/15 cm diameter)

⅓ cup (38 g) shredded jack cheese

1 large can (about 7 oz./200 g) diced green chiles

Cilantro sprigs

1. Prepare Red Chile Sauce and set aside.

2. Place pork, onions, and ⅓ cup (80 ml) water in a 5- to 6-quart (4.7- to 5.7-liter) pan. Cover and cook over medium-high heat for 20 minutes, stirring occasionally. Uncover; cook over high heat, stirring often, until almost all juices have evaporated and browned bits begin to stick to pan (about 20 minutes).

3. Add chili powder, oregano, and broth; stir to scrape browned bits free.

Fiesta Enchiladas

Preparation time: About 20 minutes
Cooking time: 2¾ to 3 hours

Bring mixture to a boil; then reduce heat, cover, and simmer until meat is very tender when pierced (45 minutes to 1 hour). Uncover; cook over high heat, stirring to break meat into shreds, until mixture is reduced to about 3 cups (710 ml)—about 30 minutes. (At this point, you may let cool, then cover and refrigerate until next day.)

4. To assemble enchiladas, immerse a tortilla in a bowl of very hot water until pliable (5 to 15 seconds); drain. Spoon about ¼ cup (60 ml) of the pork filling in center of tortilla; roll to enclose. Set enchilada, seam side down, in a lightly oiled 10- by 15-inch (25- by 38- cm) nonstick rimmed baking pan. Repeat to use remaining tortillas, arranging enchiladas in pan in a single layer. Cover pan with foil. (At this point, you may refrigerate for up to 2 hours.)

5. Bake, covered, in a 350°F (175°C) oven until enchiladas are hot in center (about 15 minutes; about 25 minutes if refrigerated). Uncover and sprinkle with cheese; continue to bake until cheese is melted (8 to 10 more minutes).

6. Cover a platter with green chiles; top evenly with hot Red Chile Sauce. Set enchiladas in sauce; scatter with cilantro sprigs. Makes 6 servings.

Red Chile Sauce. Lay 8 to 12 **dried red New Mexico** or California chiles (about 3 oz./85 g *total*) in a baking pan. Bake in a 300°F (150°C) oven just until fragrant (3 to 4 minutes). Remove from oven; let cool. Discard stems, seeds, and veins. Rinse and drain chiles; transfer to a 2- to 3-quart (1.9- to 2.8-liter) pan. Add 2 cups (470 ml) **beef broth,** 2 cloves **garlic** (peeled), ½ teaspoon **dry oregano,** ¼ teaspoon **ground cumin,** and ⅛ teaspoon **ground cloves.** Bring to a boil; then reduce heat, cover, and simmer until chiles are very soft (about 20 minutes).

Whirl chile mixture and 2 teaspoons **cornstarch** in a blender or food processor until smoothly puréed. Pour purée through a fine strainer into a bowl; rub with a spoon to extract liquid. Discard residue. You should have 2 cups (470 ml); if not, add water to make 2 cups (470 ml). Return purée to pan; stir over high heat until boiling (or until reduced to 2 cups (470 ml), if you have over 2 cups (470 ml) chile purée). If made ahead, let cool; then cover and refrigerate for up to 3 days. Reheat before using. Makes about 2 cups (470 ml).

Per serving: 385 calories (29% calories from fat), 13 g total fat, 4 g saturated fat, 68 mg cholesterol, 1,534 mg sodium, 44 g carbohydrates, 5 g fiber, 28 g protein, 201 mg calcium, 4 mg iron

Originating in Naples, calzone is reminiscent of a stuffed pizza. These individual calzones have a zesty sausage and cheese filling.

Sausage Calzones

Preparation time: 35 minutes
Rising time: 45 to 60 minutes
Cooking time: 25 to 30 minutes

- 1 package active dry yeast
- 1 cup (240 ml) warm water (about 110°F/43°C)
- About 2½ cups (310 g) all-purpose flour
- About ½ cup (70 g) yellow cornmeal
- 1 tablespoon sugar
- ½ teaspoon salt
- 3 tablespoons (45 ml) olive oil
- 1 pound (455 g) reduced-fat or regular mild Italian sausage, casings removed and meat crumbled
- 1 large onion, chopped
- ¼ teaspoon *each* dried marjoram, dried rubbed sage, and dried thyme
- 1 large tomato (about 8 oz./230 g), chopped
- 1 carton (about 15 oz./425 g) nonfat ricotta cheese
- ½ cup (50 g) fine dry bread crumbs
- ⅓ cup (30 g) grated Romano cheese
- ⅓ cup (20 g) chopped Italian or regular parsley
- 2 tablespoons drained capers (or to taste)

1. In a small bowl, sprinkle yeast over warm water; let stand until foamy (about 5 minutes). In a large bowl, mix 2½ cups (310 g) of the flour, ½ cup (70 g) of the cornmeal, sugar, and salt. Add yeast mixture and 2 tablespoons (30 ml) of the oil. Stir until dough is evenly moistened. To knead by hand, scrape dough onto a lightly floured board and knead until smooth and springy (about 10 minutes), adding more flour as needed to prevent sticking. To knead with a dough hook, beat dough on medium speed until it pulls cleanly from sides of bowl and is springy (5 to 7 minutes); if dough is sticky, add more flour, 1 tablespoon at a time.

2. Place dough in a greased bowl; turn over to grease top. Cover bowl with plastic wrap; let dough rise in a warm, draft-free place until almost doubled (45 to 60 minutes). Or let rise in refrigerator until next day.

3. Meanwhile, in a wide nonstick frying pan, combine sausage, onion, marjoram, sage, and thyme. Cook over medium-high heat, stirring often, until meat is tinged with brown (10 to 15 minutes); add water, 1 tablespoon (15 ml) at a time, if pan appears dry. Transfer mixture to a large bowl; let cool slightly. Stir in tomato, ricotta cheese, bread crumbs, Romano cheese, parsley, and capers; set aside.

4. Punch dough down, turn out onto a lightly floured board, and knead briefly to release air. Divide dough into 6 equal balls; roll each ball into an 8-inch (20-cm) round. Spoon a sixth of the sausage filling over half of each dough round, spreading it to within ½ inch (1 cm) of edge; fold plain half of round over filling and pinch edges firmly to seal.

5. Dust 2 greased large baking sheets with cornmeal. With a wide spatula, transfer calzones to baking sheets. Prick tops of calzones with a fork; brush lightly with remaining 1 tablespoon (15 ml) oil.

6. Bake in a 425°F (220°C) oven until richly browned (about 15 minutes), switching positions of baking sheets halfway through baking. Let cool for at least 5 minutes before serving; serve hot or warm. Makes 6 servings.

Per serving: 595 calories (30% calories from fat), 20 g total fat, 5 g saturated fat, 26 mg cholesterol, 1,062 mg sodium, 70 g carbohydrates, 4 g fiber, 33 g protein, 472 mg calcium, 5 mg iron

To make this Italian version of all-American roast beef, you baste the meat with a port marinade and serve it with poached prunes.

....

1 beef triangle tip (tri-tip) or top round roast (about 2 lbs./905 g), trimmed of fat

1¾ cups (420 ml) port

⅓ cup (73 g) firmly packed brown sugar

1 can (about 14½ oz./400 g) beef broth

2½ cups (about 1 lb./455 g) pitted prunes

2 packages (about 10 oz./285 g *each*) frozen tiny onions, thawed

1 pound (455 g) dried farfalle (pasta bow ties)

2 cloves garlic, minced

2 tablespoons chopped fresh oregano or 2 teaspoons dried oregano

Oregano sprigs

Salt and pepper

....

1. Set beef in a 9- by 13-inch (23- by 33-cm) baking pan. Set aside. In a 3- to 4-quart (2.8- to 3.8-liter) pan, combine port and sugar; stir over medium heat just until sugar is dissolved. Remove

Roast Beef with Prunes & Port

....

Preparation time: 20 minutes
Cooking time: About 50 minutes
Pictured on facing page

from heat and let cool slightly; then measure out ⅓ cup (80 ml) of the port mixture to use for basting and set it aside. Add broth, prunes, and onions to port mixture remaining in pan; set aside.

2. Roast meat in a 450°F (230°C) oven, basting 4 times with the ⅓ cup (80 ml) port mixture, until a meat thermometer inserted in thickest part registers 135°F (57°C) for rare (about 35 minutes). After 25 minutes, check temperature every 5 to 10 minutes. If pan appears dry, add water, 4 to 6 tablespoons (60 to 90 ml) at a time, stirring to scrape browned bits free from pan bottom; do not let drippings scorch.

3. While meat is roasting, bring prune mixture to a boil over high heat. Then reduce heat and boil gently, uncovered, until prunes and onions are very soft (about 30 minutes). Remove from heat; keep warm.

4. When meat is done, transfer to a carving board, cover loosely, and let stand for about 15 minutes. Meanwhile, in a 6- to 8-quart (6- to 8-liter) pan, bring about 4 quarts (3.8 liters) water to a boil over medium-high heat; stir in pasta and cook until just tender to bite, 8 to 10 minutes. (Or cook pasta according to package directions.) Drain pasta well; then transfer to a large rimmed platter, mix in garlic and chopped oregano, and keep warm.

5. Pour any meat drippings from baking pan into prune mixture; also add any meat juices that have accumulated on board. With a slotted spoon, ladle prunes and onions over and around pasta; transfer cooking liquid to a small pitcher.

6. To serve, thinly slice meat across the grain and arrange over pasta mixture. Garnish with oregano sprigs. Offer cooking liquid to pour over meat and pasta and season to taste with salt and pepper. Makes 8 servings.

....

Per serving: 581 calories (8% calories from fat), 5 g total fat, 1 g saturated fat, 65 mg cholesterol, 427 mg sodium, 99 g carbohydrates, 6 g fiber, 36 g protein, 87 mg calcium, 7 mg iron

Roast Beef with Prunes & Port
(recipe on facing page)

Served over pasta ribbons and topped with cheese, this sturdy three-meat stew is delightful for supper on a chilly day.

- 1 tablespoon (15 ml) olive oil
- 1 pound (455 g) *each* boneless pork, beef, and veal stew meat, trimmed of fat and cut into ½-inch (1-cm) cubes
- 1 large onion, chopped
- 1 large carrot (about 4 oz./115 g), chopped
- 8 ounces (230 g) mushrooms, thinly sliced
- 1 cup (120 g) thinly sliced celery
- 1 large can (about 28 oz./795 g) tomatoes
- 1 can (about 15 oz./425 g) tomato purée
- ½ cup (120 ml) dry red wine
- 1 tablespoon chopped fresh rosemary or 1 teaspoon dried rosemary
- ⅛ to ¼ teaspoon fennel seeds
- 2 pounds (905 g) dried fettuccine
- 1 cup (about 3 oz./85 g) grated Parmesan cheese
  Salt and crushed red pepper flakes

Beef, Pork & Veal Ragout with Fettuccine

Preparation time: 30 minutes
Cooking time: About 1½ hours

1. Heat oil in a 4- to 5-quart (3.8- to 5-liter) pan over medium-high heat. Add pork, beef, and veal, a portion at a time (do not crowd pan). Cook, stirring often, until meat is tinged with brown (about 5 minutes). As meat is browned, use a slotted spoon to transfer it to a large bowl; set aside.

2. Add onion, carrot, mushrooms, celery, and 1 tablespoon (15 ml) water to pan. Cook, stirring often, just until vegetables are soft (about 15 minutes). Return meat (and any juices that have accumulated in bowl) to pan; then add tomatoes (break up with a spoon) and their liquid, tomato purée, wine, rosemary, and fennel seeds. Bring to a boil over high heat, stirring often. Then reduce heat, cover, and simmer until

meat is tender when pierced (about 1 hour); stir occasionally at first, then more often near end of cooking time, watching closely to prevent scorching.

3. About 20 minutes before stew is done, bring about 6 quarts (6 liters) water to a boil in an 8- to 10-quart (8- to 10-liter) pan over medium-high heat; stir in pasta and cook until just tender to bite, 8 to 10 minutes. (Or cook pasta according to package directions.) Drain pasta well and divide among wide individual bowls; top with stew. Sprinkle with cheese. Season to taste with salt and red pepper flakes. Makes 10 servings.

Per serving: 638 calories (23% calories from fat), 16 g total fat, 5 g saturated fat, 192 mg cholesterol, 594 mg sodium, 77 g carbohydrates, 5 g fiber, 45 g protein, 198 mg calcium, 8 mg iron

This elegant-looking dish gets its wonderful sunny, fruity flavor from orange juice and raspberries.

- ½ cup (120 ml) dry red wine
- ¼ cup (60 ml) orange juice
- 2 tablespoons (30 ml) raspberry or red wine vinegar
- ¼ cup (40 g) finely chopped shallots
- 2 teaspoons chopped fresh tarragon or ½ teaspoon dried tarragon
- 1 pound (455 g) lean boneless top sirloin steak (about 1 inch/2.5 cm thick), trimmed of fat and cut across the grain into ⅛- by 2-inch (3-mm by 5-cm) strips
- 1½ pounds (680 g) asparagus
- 1 teaspoon olive oil
  About ½ cup (60 g) fresh raspberries

Stir-fried Beef & Asparagus

Preparation time: About 15 minutes
Cooking time: About 10 minutes

1. In a large bowl, stir together wine, orange juice, vinegar, shallots, and tarragon. Add steak and stir to coat. Set aside; stir occasionally.

2. Snap off and discard tough ends of asparagus; then cut spears into 3-inch (8-cm) lengths. Place asparagus and ½ cup (120 ml) water in a wide nonstick frying pan or wok. Cover; cook over medium-high heat, stirring occasionally, until asparagus is tender-crisp to bite (4 to 5 minutes). Drain asparagus, transfer to a platter, and keep warm. Wipe pan dry (be careful; pan is hot).

3. Heat oil in pan over medium-high heat. When oil is hot, lift meat from marinade and drain briefly; reserve ¼ cup (60 ml) of the marinade. Add meat to pan and stir-fry until done to your liking; cut to test (2 to 3 minutes for rare). Add the reserved ¼ cup (60 ml) marinade and bring to a boil.

4. Spoon meat mixture over asparagus and top with raspberries. Makes 4 servings.

Per serving: 213 calories (29% calories from fat), 6 g total fat, 2 g saturated fat, 69 mg cholesterol, 70 mg sodium, 8 g carbohydrates, 2 g fiber, 27 g protein, 39 mg calcium, 4 mg iron

---

Basil and fennel turn a simple pasta, beef, and tomato casserole into delicious family fare.

- 1 pound (455 g) lean ground beef
- 1 large onion (about 8 oz./230 g), chopped
- 3 cloves garlic, minced or pressed
- ¾ teaspoon fennel seeds
- 12 ounces/340 g (about 4 cups) dried mostaccioli or penne
- 2 cans (about 15 oz./425 g *each*) tomato purée
- 3 tablespoons chopped fresh basil or 1 tablespoon dried basil
- ¼ cup (60 ml) dry red wine (or to taste)
  Salt and pepper
- 2 cups (about 8 oz./230 g) shredded part-skim mozzarella cheese
  Basil sprigs (optional)

Beef Mostaccioli

Preparation time: About 15 minutes
Cooking time: About 45 minutes

1. Crumble meat into a 4- to 5-quart (3.8- to 5-liter) pan. Add onion, garlic, fennel seeds, and 2 tablespoons (30 ml) water. Cook over medium-high heat, stirring often, until meat is well browned (about 15 minutes); if pan appears dry or mixture sticks to pan bottom, add more water, 1 tablespoon (15 ml) at a time. Meanwhile, bring

12 cups (2.8 liters) water to a boil in a 5- to 6-quart (5- to 6-liter) pan over medium-high heat. Stir in pasta and cook just until tender to bite (8 to 10 minutes); or cook according to package directions. Drain well and transfer to a large nonmetal bowl; keep warm.

2. Add tomato purée and chopped basil to meat mixture; reduce heat to medium and cook, stirring, until hot. Transfer to bowl with pasta. Add wine and mix thoroughly but gently. Season to taste with salt and pepper.

3. Spoon into a 2½- to 3-quart (2.4- to 2.8-liter) casserole. Cover tightly and bake in a 350°F (175°C) oven for 15 minutes. Uncover, sprinkle with cheese, and continue to bake until mixture is bubbly (about 15 more minutes). Garnish with basil sprigs, if desired. Makes 6 to 8 servings.

Per serving: 448 calories (25% calories from fat), 13 g total fat, 6 g saturated fat, 59 mg cholesterol, 688 mg sodium, 54 g carbohydrates, 4 g fiber, 30 g protein, 275 mg calcium, 5 mg iron

Spiral Stuffed Meat Loaf
(recipe on facing page)

Each slice of this big special-occasion meat loaf sports a colorful spiral of herb-and-cheese filling.

....

1 cup (about 2 oz./55 g) dried tomatoes (not packed in oil)

2 tablespoons (30 ml) Marsala

1 teaspoon olive oil

1 large red onion (about 12 oz./ 340 g), chopped

5 slices sourdough sandwich bread (about 5 oz./140 g *total*), torn into pieces

1½ pounds (680 g) lean ground beef

4 ounces (115 g) reduced-fat or regular mild Italian sausage, casings removed and meat crumbled

1 large jar (about 4 oz./115 g) diced pimentos, drained

1 large egg

2 large egg whites

2 cloves garlic, minced or pressed

½ teaspoon dried thyme

¼ teaspoon ground sage

⅓ cup (20 g) chopped Italian or regular parsley

¼ cup (20 g) grated Parmesan cheese

¼ teaspoon pepper

1⅓ cups (193 g) dried currants

1¼ cups (50 g) lightly packed fresh basil leaves

1 ounce (28 g) thinly sliced prosciutto, coarsely chopped

Spiral Stuffed Meat Loaf

....

Preparation time: 35 minutes
Cooking time: About 1½ hours
Pictured on facing page

¼ cup (28 g) shredded fontina cheese

¼ cup (35 g) yellow cornmeal Italian or regular parsley sprigs

....

1. Place tomatoes in a small bowl and add boiling water to cover. Let stand until soft (about 10 minutes), stirring occasionally. Drain well; gently squeeze out excess liquid. Finely chop tomatoes and return to bowl. Drizzle with Marsala and set aside.

2. Heat oil in a wide nonstick frying pan over medium-high heat. Add onion and cook, stirring often, until it begins to brown (about 10 minutes); add water, ¼ cup (60 ml) at a time, if pan appears dry. Transfer onion to a large bowl and let cool slightly.

3. In a food processor or blender, whirl bread to form fine crumbs. Add crumbs to onion in bowl. Add beef, sausage, pimentos, egg, egg whites, garlic, thyme, sage, chopped parsley, Parmesan cheese, and pepper; mix until very well blended.

4. On a large sheet of parchment paper or wax paper, pat meat mixture into a 10- by 15-inch (25- by 38-cm) rectangle. Distribute chopped tomatoes, currants, basil leaves, prosciutto, and fontina cheese over meat in even layers to within 1 inch (2.5 cm) of edges. Using paper to help you, lift narrow end of rectangle nearest you over filling; then carefully roll up meat to form a cylinder. Pinch seam and ends closed. Dust a 9- by 13-inch (23- by 33-cm) baking dish with cornmeal; using 2 wide spatulas, transfer loaf to dish.

5. Bake in a 350°F (175°C) oven until loaf is well browned on top (about 1¼ hours); add water, ¼ cup (60 ml) at a time, if dish appears dry. With wide spatulas, carefully transfer loaf to a platter. Serve hot or cold. Garnish with parsley sprigs. Makes 8 to 10 servings.

....

Per serving: 369 calories (30% calories from fat), 13 g total fat, 5 g saturated fat, 82 mg cholesterol, 384 mg sodium, 39 g carbohydrates, 4 g fiber, 27 g protein, 183 mg calcium, 5 mg iron

Plump dried cherries poached in Cabernet accompany this herb-rubbed beef roast.

....

1½ teaspoons *each* whole black peppercorns, dried thyme, and grated orange peel

½ teaspoon *each* dried oregano and coriander seeds

¼ teaspoon ground cinnamon

⅛ teaspoon ground allspice

4 cloves garlic, minced or pressed

1 trimmed, tied center-cut beef tenderloin (about 5 lbs./2.3 kg)

3½ cups (830 ml) beef broth

1¾ cups (420 ml) Cabernet Sauvignon

3 cups (about 15 oz./425 g) dried pitted tart cherries

¼ cup (75 g) red currant jelly

2 tablespoons cornstarch blended with ¼ cup (60 ml) cold water

6 large oranges (about 3 lbs./1.35 kg *total*), thinly sliced

Salt and pepper

....

1. In a small bowl, mix peppercorns, thyme, orange peel, oregano, coriander

Beef Tenderloin with Cabernet-Cherry Sauce

....

Preparation time: 25 minutes
Cooking time: 35 to 50 minutes
Standing time: 15 minutes

seeds, cinnamon, allspice, and garlic. Rub mixture over beef; then set beef in a 10- by 15-inch (25- by 38-cm) roasting pan. Roast in a 450°F (230°C) oven until a meat thermometer inserted in thickest part registers 135°F (57°C) for rare (35 to 40 minutes), 140°F (60°C) for medium (about 50 minutes). Starting about 10 minutes before meat is done, check temperature every 5 to 10 minutes. If pan appears dry, add water, 4 to 6 tablespoons (60 to 90 ml) at a time, stirring to scrape browned bits free from pan bottom; do not let drippings scorch.

2. Meanwhile, in a 3- to 4-quart (2.8- to 3.8-liter) pan, combine 2 cups (470 ml) of the broth, wine, cherries, and jelly;

bring to a boil over high heat. Then reduce heat, cover, and simmer until cherries are softened (15 to 20 minutes). Remove from heat.

3. When meat is done, transfer it to a large platter. Snip and discard strings. Cover meat loosely and let stand for about 15 minutes. Meanwhile, add remaining 1½ cups (360 ml) broth to roasting pan; place over medium heat and stir to scrape browned bits free from pan bottom. Pour broth mixture into cherry mixture; bring to a boil, stirring often. Add cornstarch mixture and stir until sauce boils and thickens slightly. Pour into a bowl and keep warm.

4. Garnish meat with orange slices. To serve, slice meat across the grain and offer sauce to spoon over it; season to taste with salt and pepper. Makes about 16 servings.

....

Per serving: 362 calories (30% calories from fat), 11 g total fat, 4 g saturated fat, 88 mg cholesterol, 440 mg sodium, 30 g carbohydrates, 2 g fiber, 30 g protein, 45 mg calcium, 4 mg iron

This traditional main dish is superbly simple: you just marinate strips of skirt steak, skewer them with sweet peppers and fresh rosemary sprigs, and grill lightly.

- ⅓ cup (80 ml) dry red wine
- 1 tablespoon (15 ml) *each* lime juice and water
- 1¼ pounds (565 g) skirt steaks, trimmed of fat and cut into 6 equal pieces
- 4 large bell peppers, about 2 lbs. (905 g) *total* (use a combination of green, red, and yellow bell peppers, if desired)
- 12 rosemary sprigs (*each* about 3 inches/8 cm long)
- 12 warm corn tortillas (page 346)
  Salt and pepper

Carne Asada

Preparation time: About 10 minutes
Marinating time: At least 30 minutes
Cooking time: 10 to 15 minutes

1. In a large heavy-duty resealable plastic bag or large nonmetal bowl, combine wine, lime juice, and water. Add meat. Seal bag and rotate to coat meat (or turn meat in bowl to coat, then cover airtight). Refrigerate for at least 30 minutes or until next day, turning occasionally.

2. Seed bell peppers and cut each one lengthwise into sixths.

3. Lift meat from marinade and drain; reserve marinade. On each of six 12- to 15-inch (30- to 38-cm) metal skewers, weave 1 piece of meat and 4 bell pepper pieces, rippling meat slightly. For each skewer, tuck 2 rosemary sprigs between meat and skewer.

4. Place skewers on a grill 4 to 6 inches (10 to 15 cm) above a solid bed of hot coals. Cook, turning often and brushing with marinade, until meat is done to your liking; cut to test (6 to 10 minutes for rare).

5. Slide food off skewers. Thinly slice meat across the grain; serve with peppers and tortillas. Season to taste with salt and pepper. Makes 6 servings.

Per serving: 311 calories (30% calories from fat), 10 g total fat, 4 g saturated fat, 47 mg cholesterol, 140 mg sodium, 32 g carbohydrates, 5 g fiber, 22 g protein, 110 mg calcium, 3 mg iron

---

Complement this hearty entrée with a colorful vegetable side dish or mixed green salad.

- 12 ounces (340 g) lean boneless top sirloin steak (about 1 inch/ 2.5 cm thick), trimmed of fat and cut across the grain into ⅛- by 2-inch (3-mm by 5-cm) strips
- 1 tablespoon (15 ml) reduced-sodium soy sauce
- 1 teaspoon sugar
- ½ teaspoon lemon juice
- 1 clove garlic, minced or pressed
- ⅓ cup (50 g) hazelnuts
- 1 large onion, chopped
- 6 cups (1.4 liters) vegetable broth
- 3 cups (510 g) oat groats (uncut oats)
- 1 teaspoon salad oil
  About 6 tablespoons (90 ml) Scotch whiskey (or to taste)
- ½ cup (50 g) thinly sliced green onions

1. In a large bowl, combine beef, soy sauce, sugar, lemon juice, and garlic. Set aside; stir occasionally.

Oat Pilaf with Beef, Hazelnuts & Scotch

Preparation time: 25 minutes
Cooking time: About 1 hour

2. Spread hazelnuts in a shallow 3- to 3½-quart (2.8- to 3.3-liter) casserole, about 9 by 13 inches (23 by 33 cm). Bake in a 350°F (175°C) oven, shaking casserole occasionally, until nuts are lightly browned under skins (10 to 15 minutes). Pour nuts onto a towel; rub with towel to remove as much of the skins as possible. Lift nuts from towel; discard skins. Coarsely chop nuts and set aside.

3. In a 3- to 4-quart (2.8- to 3.8-liter) pan, combine chopped onion and ¼ cup (60 ml) water. Cook over medium-high heat, stirring often, until onion is soft (about 5 minutes); add water, 1 tablespoon (15 ml) at a time, if pan appears dry. Transfer onion to casserole used to toast nuts; set aside.

4. In pan used to cook onion, combine broth and oats. Bring just to a boil over medium-high heat. Add broth-oat mixture to casserole. Cover tightly and bake in a 350°F (175°C) oven for 15 minutes. Stir well, cover tightly again, and continue to bake until almost all liquid has been absorbed and oats are tender to bite (about 15 more minutes).

5. Meanwhile, heat oil in a wide nonstick frying pan over medium-high heat. Lift meat from marinade and drain briefly; discard marinade. Add meat to pan and cook, stirring often, until done to your liking; cut to test (2 to 3 minutes for rare). With a slotted spoon, transfer meat to a bowl and keep warm; discard pan drippings.

6. Uncover oat pilaf and stir in 6 tablespoons of the Scotch. Spoon pilaf onto a rimmed platter and top with meat (and any juices that have accumulated in bowl). Sprinkle with green onions and hazelnuts. Offer additional Scotch to add to taste. Makes 6 servings.

Per serving: 526 calories (29% calories from fat), 16 g total fat, 3 g saturated fat, 42 mg cholesterol, 1,084 mg sodium, 60 g carbohydrates, 1 g fiber, 28 g protein, 73 mg calcium, 6 mg iron

Tinged golden with saffron, couscous makes a fluffy bed for marinated beef kebabs.

1½ pounds (680 g) lean boneless top sirloin steak (about 1 inch/2.5 cm thick), trimmed of fat

½ cup (120 ml) reduced-sodium soy sauce

2 tablespoons (30 ml) *each* honey and red wine vinegar

1 clove garlic, minced or pressed

½ teaspoon ground ginger

¼ teaspoon pepper

1 teaspoon olive oil

1 large onion (about 8 oz./230 g), chopped

2 cups (470 ml) nonfat milk

¾ cup (180 ml) low-sodium chicken broth

Large pinch of saffron threads or ⅛ teaspoon saffron powder (or to taste)

10 ounces/285 g (about 1⅔ cups) dried couscous

¼ cup (20 g) freshly grated Parmesan cheese (or to taste)

Tomato wedges

Italian parsley sprigs

Beef-on-a-Stick with Saffron Couscous

Preparation time: About 15 minutes
Marinating time: At least 30 minutes
Cooking time: About 15 minutes
Pictured on facing page

1. Slice steak across grain into strips about ¼ inch (6 mm) thick and 4 inches (10 cm) long (for easier slicing, freeze steak for about 30 minutes before cutting). Place meat, soy sauce, honey, vinegar, garlic, ginger, pepper, and 2 tablespoons (30 ml) water in a large heavy-duty resealable plastic bag or large nonmetal bowl. Seal bag and rotate to coat meat (or turn meat in bowl and cover airtight). Refrigerate for at least 30 minutes or up to a day, turning (or stirring) occasionally. Meanwhile, soak 12 wooden skewers (8 to 10 inches/20 to 25 cm long) in hot water to cover for at least 30 minutes.

2. Lift meat from marinade and drain, reserving marinade. Weave 2 or 3 meat slices on each skewer so meat lies flat. Place in a lightly oiled broiler pan without a rack and set aside.

3. Heat oil in a 2- to 3-quart (1.9- to 2.8-liter) pan over medium-high heat. Add onion and cook, stirring often, until soft (about 5 minutes). Add milk, broth, and saffron; bring just to a boil. Stir in pasta; cover, remove from heat, and let stand until liquid is absorbed (about 5 minutes). Meanwhile, broil meat 3 to 4 inches (8 to 10 cm) below heat, basting with reserved marinade and turning as needed, until done to your liking; cut to test (about 5 minutes for medium-rare).

4. Fluff pasta with a fork, adding cheese. Spoon onto a platter and top with meat. Garnish with tomatoes and parsley. Makes 6 servings (2 skewers each).

Per serving: 436 calories (18% calories from fat), 9 g total fat, 3 g saturated fat, 80 mg cholesterol, 1,334 mg sodium, 49 g carbohydrates, 2 g fiber, 38 g protein, 179 mg calcium, 4 mg iron

Beef-on-a-Stick with Saffron Couscous
(recipe on facing page)

Flavored Oils

Infused with the essence of spices or herbs, flavored oils add excitement to any stir-fry. You can use a teaspoon or two in place of some of the salad or olive oil used for cooking; or, at the table, offer a cruet of oil to sprinkle over your favorite meat or vegetable combinations.

On these pages, we tell you how to make six flavored oils: curry, basil, ginger, garlic, hot chili, and thyme. As the base, use salad oil, virgin olive oil, or light olive oil. Avoid extra-virgin olive oil—it's so strong that it may overwhelm the flavors of the ingredients added to it. Heat the oil and flavoring just until warm; if the mixture gets too hot, the spices may scorch or burn.

Once the oil has been infused, simply pour it from the pan, leaving the herb or spice residue behind. Or, if you like, strain the oil. To do this, line a fine strainer with a single layer of muslin or a double layer of cheesecloth and set it over a clean, dry, deep bowl. Pour the oil mixture through; press the residue with the back of a clean, dry spoon to extract as much oil as possible, then discard the residue.

Store flavored oils in clean, dry glass bottles or jars. If you see sediment upon standing, pour off (or strain) the oil again, leaving the sediment behind. These oils keep well at room temperature, but you can refrigerate them if you prefer. Chilled olive oil will turn cloudy and thick, but will become clear and pourable again when returned to room temperature.

Note: Like any other oil, these flavored oils get almost all their calories from fat. Nonetheless, if used sparingly, they still have a place in a low-fat diet.

Curry Oil

Preparation time: About 5 minutes
Cooking time: About 5 minutes

....

¼ cup (15 g) curry powder

1 cup (240 ml) salad oil or olive oil

1 to 3 cinnamon sticks (*each about 3 inches/8 cm long*)

....

1. In a small pan, whisk together curry powder and ¼ cup (60 ml) of the oil until well blended. Gradually whisk in remaining ¾ cup (180 ml) oil. Add cinnamon stick(s). Heat over medium heat, stirring often, just until warm (not hot or boiling). Remove from heat and let cool slightly.

2. With a clean, dry slotted spoon, lift out cinnamon stick(s); set aside.

3. Carefully pour oil into a clean, dry glass bottle or jar, leaving curry sediment behind; discard sediment. (Or strain oil, if desired.) Add cinnamon stick(s) to bottle; cover airtight and store for up to 6 months. Makes about 1 cup (240 ml).

Basil Oil

Preparation time: About 10 minutes
Cooking time: About 10 minutes

....

½ cup (20 g) firmly packed fresh basil leaves

1 cup (240 ml) salad oil or olive oil

....

1. In a 4- to 5-quart (3.8- to 5-liter) pan, bring 8 cups (1.9 liters) water to a boil over high heat. Drop basil into boiling water and cook just until bright green (about 3 seconds); immediately drain, then plunge into ice water until cool. Drain basil well again; blot dry.

2. In a blender or food processor, combine basil and ¼ cup (60 ml) of the oil. Whirl until well blended. Add remaining ¾ cup (180 ml) oil and whirl until smoothly puréed.

3. Transfer oil mixture to a small pan and heat over medium heat, stirring occasionally, just until warm (not hot or boiling). Remove from heat and let cool slightly.

4. Carefully pour oil into a clean, dry glass bottle or jar, leaving basil sediment behind; discard sediment. (Or strain oil, if desired.) Cover airtight and store for up to 6 months. Makes about 1 cup (240 ml).

Ginger Oil

Preparation time: About 5 minutes
Cooking time: About 5 minutes

- ¼ cup (15 g) ground ginger
- 1 cup (240 ml) salad oil or olive oil

1. In a small pan, whisk together ginger and ¼ cup (60 ml) of the oil until well blended. Gradually whisk in remaining ¾ cup (180 ml) oil. Heat over medium heat, stirring often, just until warm (not hot or boiling). Remove from heat and let cool slightly.

2. Carefully pour oil into a clean, dry glass bottle or jar, leaving ginger sediment behind; discard sediment. (Or strain oil, if desired.) Cover airtight and store for up to 6 months. Makes about 1 cup (240 ml).

Garlic Oil

Preparation time: About 10 minutes
Cooking time: About 15 minutes

- 1 medium-size head garlic (about 3 oz./85 g)
- About 1 cup (240 ml) salad oil or olive oil

1. Separate garlic into cloves; then peel and thinly slice garlic cloves. Heat ⅓ cup (80 ml) of the oil in a wide nonstick frying pan or wok over medium-low heat. Add garlic and stir-fry until tinged with gold (about 10 minutes; do not scorch). If pan appears dry or garlic sticks to pan, add more oil, 1 tablespoon (15 ml) at a time.

2. Add ⅔ cup (160 ml) more oil to pan. Increase heat to medium and stir often just until oil is warm (not hot or boiling). Remove from heat and let cool slightly.

3. With a clean, dry slotted spoon, lift garlic from pan; discard garlic (garlic left in oil may spoil). Then carefully pour oil into a clean, dry glass bottle or jar. (Or strain oil, if desired.) Cover airtight and store for up to 6 months. Makes about 1 cup (240 ml).

Hot Chili Oil

Preparation time: About 5 minutes
Cooking time: About 5 minutes

- 6 to 12 small dried hot red chiles (use the greater number of chiles for more heat)
- 1 cup (240 ml) salad oil or olive oil

1. Place 3 whole chiles in a small pan; add oil. Split each of the remaining 3 to 9 chiles in half; add to pan. Heat over medium heat, stirring gently, just until warm (not hot or boiling). Remove from heat and let cool slightly.

2. With a clean, dry slotted spoon, remove split chiles and seeds from oil; discard. Remove whole chiles; set aside.

3. Carefully pour oil into a clean, dry glass bottle or jar. (Or strain oil, if desired.) Add whole chiles to bottle; cover airtight and store for up to 6 months. Makes about 1 cup (240 ml).

Thyme Oil

Preparation time: About 5 minutes
Cooking time: About 5 minutes

- ¼ cup (10 g) chopped fresh thyme
- 1 cup (240 ml) salad oil or olive oil

1. In a small pan, whisk together thyme and ¼ cup (60 ml) of the oil until well blended. Gradually whisk in remaining ¾ cup (180 ml) oil. Heat over medium heat, stirring often, just until warm (not hot or boiling). Remove from heat and let cool slightly.

2. Carefully pour oil into a clean, dry glass bottle or jar, leaving thyme sediment behind; discard sediment. (Or strain oil, if desired.) Cover airtight and store for up to 6 months. Makes about 1 cup (240 ml).

Garlic Beef in Pita Bread
(recipe on facing page)

Stir-fries make great hot fillings for pita breads. These sandwiches are stuffed with mixed greens and garlicky strips of sirloin; a minted yogurt sauce adds a cool, refreshing accent.

Cool Yogurt Sauce (page 172)

4 to 6 cloves garlic, minced or pressed

3 tablespoons (45 ml) reduced-sodium soy sauce

1½ teaspoons sugar

⅛ teaspoon crushed red pepper flakes

1 pound (455 g) lean boneless top sirloin steak (about 1 inch/2.5 cm thick), trimmed of fat and cut across the grain into ⅛- by 2-inch (3-mm by 5-cm) strips

3 green onions

1 teaspoon salad oil

1 teaspoon cornstarch blended with 1 teaspoon cold water

Garlic Beef in Pita Bread

Preparation time: About 15 minutes
Cooking time: About 15 minutes
Pictured on facing page

5 to 6 cups (5 to 6 oz./140 to 170 g) mixed salad greens, rinsed and crisped

4 pita breads (*each* about 6 inches/15 cm in diameter), cut crosswise into halves

1. Prepare Cool Yogurt Sauce and set aside. In a large bowl, stir together garlic, soy sauce, sugar, and red pepper flakes. Add steak and stir to coat. Set aside; stir occasionally. Trim and discard ends of onions; then cut onions into 1-inch (2.5-cm) lengths and sliver each piece lengthwise. Set aside.

2. Heat oil in a wide nonstick frying pan or wok over medium-high heat. When oil is hot, lift meat from marinade and drain briefly (reserve marinade). Add meat to pan and stir-fry until done to your liking; cut to test (2 to 3 minutes for rare). With a slotted spoon, transfer meat to a bowl; keep warm.

3. Stir cornstarch mixture well; pour into pan along with reserved marinade and any meat juices that have accumulated in bowl. Cook, stirring, until sauce boils and thickens slightly (1 to 2 minutes). Remove pan from heat and stir in meat and onions.

4. To serve, divide salad greens equally among pita bread halves; then spoon in meat mixture. Drizzle Cool Yogurt Sauce over meat. Makes 4 servings.

Per serving: 386 calories (17% calories from fat), 7 g total fat, 2 g saturated fat, 70 mg cholesterol, 886 mg sodium, 44 g carbohydrates, 2 g fiber, 34 g protein, 207 mg calcium, 6 mg iron

---

Don't let the cayenne-and-jalapeño marinade frighten you away; this dish has just the right amount of heat. If you have the time, you can marinate the beef in the refrigerator up to a day in advance.

1 fresh jalapeño or other small fresh hot chile, seeded and minced

2 cloves garlic, minced or pressed

¼ to ½ teaspoon ground red pepper (cayenne)

1 tablespoon (15 ml) reduced-sodium soy sauce

½ teaspoon sugar

1 pound (455 g) lean boneless top sirloin steak (about 1 inch/2.5 cm thick), trimmed of fat and cut across the grain into ⅛- by 2-inch (3-mm by 5-cm) strips

Chile Beef Burritos

Preparation time: About 15 minutes
Cooking time: About 15 minutes

4 to 8 low-fat flour tortillas (*each* 7 to 9 inches/18 to 23 cm in diameter)

1 large onion, thinly sliced

1 teaspoon olive oil

Condiments (suggestions follow)

1. In a large bowl, stir together chile, garlic, red pepper, soy sauce, and sugar. Add steak and stir to coat. Set aside.

2. Brush tortillas lightly with hot water; then stack, wrap in foil, and heat in a 350°F/175°C oven until warm (10 to 12 minutes).

3. Meanwhile, in a wide nonstick frying pan or wok, combine onion and ¼ cup (60 ml) water. Stir-fry over medium-high heat until onion is soft and liquid has evaporated (4 to 5 minutes). Add oil; then stir in meat and its marinade. Stir-fry until meat is done to your liking; cut to test (2 to 3 minutes for rare).

4. To serve, spoon meat mixture into tortillas; offer condiments to add to taste. Makes 4 servings.

Condiments. In individual bowls, offer 3 or more of the following: **shredded lettuce, chopped tomatoes, Tomatillo-Lime Salsa** (page 194) or purchased salsa, **nonfat sour cream, cilantro leaves,** and **lime wedges.**

Per serving: 293 calories (20% calories from fat), 7 g total fat, 2 g saturated fat, 69 mg cholesterol, 488 mg sodium, 34 g carbohydrates, 7 g fiber, 28 g protein, 114 mg calcium, 5 mg iron

Tender beef strips and onions, infused with the flavors of lime and tequila, cook together quickly for a tempting meal.

....

1 **pound (455 g) skirt or flank steak, trimmed of fat**

Fajita Marinade (recipe follows)

About 1½ cups (360 ml) Cherry Tomato Salsa (page 20) or other salsa of your choice

About 1 cup (240 ml) Creamy Guacamole (page 9)

2 **large onions**

Salad oil

4 **warm flour tortillas (page 346)**

Plain nonfat yogurt

....

1. Place steak in a large heavy-duty resealable plastic bag or large nonmetal bowl. Prepare marinade and pour over meat. Seal bag and rotate to coat meat (or turn meat in bowl to coat, then cover airtight). Refrigerate for at least 30 minutes or until next day, turning occasionally.

2. Prepare Cherry Tomato Salsa and Creamy Guacamole; refrigerate.

3. *To sauté,* lift meat from marinade and drain; discard marinade. Thinly slice meat across the grain, then thinly slice onions; set aside separately. Heat a wide cast-iron or regular frying pan or a shallow oval (about 7- by

Spicy Steak Fajitas

....

Preparation time: 40 minutes
Marinating time: At least 30 minutes
Cooking time: 13 to 20 minutes

9-inch/18- by 23-cm) cast-iron skillet over medium-high heat. When pan is hot enough to make a drop of water bounce, brush it lightly with oil. Add onions to pan and cook, stirring, until soft (about 5 minutes). Increase heat to high. Add meat to pan and cook, stirring, until lightly browned (3 to 4 minutes).

To barbecue, lift meat from marinade and drain; reserve marinade. Cut onions into quarters and brush lightly with oil. Place onions and meat on a lightly greased grill 4 to 6 inches (10 to 15 cm) above a solid bed of hot coals. Cook, basting meat and onion several times with reserved marinade and turning as needed to brown evenly, until onions are tinged with brown and meat is done to your liking; cut to test (15 to 20 minutes for rare). Slice onions or pull apart into layers; thinly slice meat across the grain.

To broil, lift meat from marinade and drain; reserve marinade. Place meat on lightly oiled rack of a broiler pan. Thinly slice onions and brush

lightly with oil; set alongside meat. Broil meat and onions 3 to 4 inches (8 to 10 cm) below heat, basting several times with reserved marinade and turning as needed to brown evenly, until onions are tinged with brown and meat is done to your liking; cut to test (15 to 20 minutes for rare). Thinly slice meat across the grain.

4. To serve, divide meat and onions among tortillas. Add salsa, guacamole, and yogurt to taste. Roll up tortillas to enclose filling; eat out of hand. Makes 4 servings.

....

Fajita Marinade. In a nonmetal bowl, stir together ½ teaspoon grated **lime peel;** ½ cup (120 ml) **lime juice;** ¼ cup (60 ml) **gold tequila** or nonalcoholic beer; 4 cloves **garlic,** minced or pressed; ½ teaspoon **pepper;** and ½ teaspoon **salt** (optional).

....

Per serving: 471 calories (30% calories from fat), 15 g total fat, 5 g saturated fat, 59 mg cholesterol, 585 mg sodium, 44 g carbohydrates, 4 g fiber, 36 g protein, 249 mg calcium, 4 mg iron

Bound to win raves from spicy-food lovers, this memorable dish is a perfect choice for cold winter nights. A complex seasoning paste flavors both the beef and the currant-dotted rice that's served alongside.

Jerk Seasoning Paste
(recipe follows)

1 **pound (455 g) lean boneless top sirloin steak (about 1 inch/2.5 cm thick), trimmed of fat and cut across the grain into ⅛- by 2-inch (3-mm by 5-cm) strips**

2 **cups (470 ml) fat-free reduced-sodium chicken broth**

¼ **cup (60 ml) half-and-half**

1 **cup (185 g) long-grain white rice**

¼ **cup (35 g) dried currants or raisins**

1 **teaspoon olive oil**
Cilantro sprigs
Lime wedges

Jamaican Jerk Beef with Spiced Rice

Preparation time: About 15 minutes, plus
Marinating time: At least 30 minutes
Cooking time: About 30 minutes

1. Prepare Jerk Seasoning Paste. Measure out 1 tablespoon of the paste; cover and set aside. Place remaining paste in a large bowl; add steak and turn or stir to coat. Cover and refrigerate for at least 30 minutes or until next day, stirring occasionally.

2. Meanwhile, in a 2- to 3-quart (1.9- to 2.8-liter) pan, combine broth, half-and-half, and the reserved 1 tablespoon seasoning paste. Bring just to a boil over medium-high heat, stirring; then stir in rice and currants. Reduce heat, cover, and simmer until liquid has been absorbed and rice is tender to bite (about 20 minutes). Spoon rice mixture onto a rimmed platter and keep warm.

3. Heat oil in a wide nonstick frying pan or wok over medium-high heat. When oil is hot, add meat and stir-fry until done to your liking; cut to test (2 to 3 minutes for rare).

4. Spoon meat over rice; garnish with cilantro sprigs. Serve with lime wedges. Makes 4 servings.

Jerk Seasoning Paste. In a blender or food processor, combine ¼ cup (10 g) firmly packed **cilantro leaves,** 3 tablespoons minced **fresh ginger,** 3 tablespoons (45 ml) **water,** 2 tablespoons **whole black peppercorns,** 1 tablespoon *each* **ground allspice** and firmly packed **brown sugar,** 2 cloves **garlic** (peeled), ½ teaspoon **crushed red pepper flakes,** and ¼ teaspoon *each* **ground coriander** and **ground nutmeg.** Whirl until smooth. If made ahead, cover and refrigerate for up to 2 days.

Per serving: 412 calories (19% calories from fat), 9 g total fat, 3 g saturated fat, 75 mg cholesterol, 403 mg sodium, 53 g carbohydrates, 2 g fiber, 31 g protein, 78 mg calcium, 7 mg iron

---

Serve these cheesy brushetta with a crisp salad and zesty dressing for a light lunch.

⅔ **cup (150 g) nonfat ricotta cheese**

¼ **cup (25 g) shredded carrot**

¼ **cup (35 g) dried currants or raisins**

2 **tablespoons thinly sliced green onion**

1 **tablespoon Dijon mustard**

½ **teaspoon dried basil**

8 **ounces (230 g) unsliced crusty bread, such as Italian ciabatta or French bread**

4 **ounces (115 g) very thinly sliced pastrami**

⅓ **cup (40 g) shredded part-skim mozzarella cheese**

North Beach Bruschetta

Preparation time: 20 minutes
Cooking time: About 7 minutes

1. In a medium-size bowl, stir together ricotta cheese, carrot, currants, onion, mustard, and basil. Set aside.

2. Cut bread in half horizontally. Set halves crust side down; if needed, cut a thin slice from cut side of halves to make each piece about 1 inch (2.5 cm) thick. Trim crust side of each piece so bread sits steadily. Then cut each piece in half crosswise.

3. Spread cut sides of bread with ricotta mixture. Loosely pleat pastrami over ricotta mixture, covering bread. Sprinkle with mozzarella cheese. Arrange bread on a 12- by 15-inch (30- by 38-cm) baking sheet and bake in a 400°F (205°C) oven until mozzarella cheese is melted (about 7 minutes). Makes 4 servings.

Per serving: 271 calories (12% calories from fat), 3 g total fat, 1 g saturated fat, 15 mg cholesterol, 880 mg sodium, 38 g carbohydrates, 3 g fiber, 19 g protein, 345 mg calcium, 3 mg iron

Start by browning veal shanks in a very hot oven, then cover and bake. When the meat is tender enough to pull apart, make risotto the easy way: stir rice into the pan juices and continue to bake, letting the grains absorb the flavorful liquid.

- 2 tablespoons (30 ml) olive oil
- 5 to 6 pounds (2.3 to 2.7 kg) meaty veal shanks (*each* about 2 inches/5 cm thick)
- 1 cup (240 ml) dry red wine
- 4 cups (950 ml) beef broth
- 2 tablespoons grated lemon peel
- 1 teaspoon *each* dried thyme and dried basil
- 2 cups (390 g) medium- or short-grain white rice
- 1 cup (130 g) chopped carrots
- ¼ cup (15 g) chopped Italian or regular parsley
- 2 cloves garlic, minced or pressed
- 1 cup (130 g) chopped zucchini
- 1 cup (150 g) chopped red bell pepper
- ½ cup (40 g) grated Parmesan cheese
  Lemon wedges
  Italian or regular parsley sprigs

Osso Buco with Risotto

Preparation time: 20 minutes
Cooking time: About 2½ hours
Pictured on facing page

1. Place oil in an 11- by 17-inch (28- by 43-cm) roasting pan. Heat in a 475°F (245°C) oven until hot (about 1 minute). Lay veal shanks in pan in a single layer. Bake, uncovered, for 30 minutes; then turn meat over and continue to bake until browned (about 10 more minutes).

2. Remove pan from oven and add wine; stir to scrape browned bits free from pan bottom. Then stir in broth, 1 tablespoon of the lemon peel, thyme, and basil; stir again, scraping browned bits free. Cover pan tightly with foil and bake until meat is tender enough to pull apart easily (about 1½ hours).

3. Uncover pan; stir 2½ cups (590 ml) water, rice, and carrots into pan juices. Bake, uncovered, stirring rice and turning meat over occasionally, until liquid has been absorbed and rice is tender to bite (20 to 25 minutes). If rice begins to dry out, add more water, about ½ cup (120 ml) at a time.

4. In a small bowl, mix remaining 1 tablespoon lemon peel, chopped parsley, and garlic. Remove meat from pan, transfer to a large platter, and sprinkle with parsley mixture. Stir zucchini and bell pepper into rice mixture; spoon rice mixture onto platter alongside meat, then sprinkle with cheese. Garnish with lemon wedges and parsley sprigs. Makes 4 to 6 servings.

Per serving: 581 calories (18% calories from fat), 11 g total fat, 3 g saturated fat, 134 mg cholesterol, 770 mg sodium, 69 g carbohydrates, 2 g fiber, 47 g protein, 155 mg calcium, 6 mg iron

Osso Buco with Risotto
(recipe on facing page)

A nontraditional warm salsa of fresh tomatoes, sautéed onion, and dried apricots soaked in lime juice makes this dish unusual. Be sure not to overcook the veal—after only a minute or two of stir-frying, it will be done just right.

- 1 **cup (185 g) long-grain white rice**
- ⅔ **cup (90 g) chopped dried apricots**
- ¼ **cup (60 ml) lime juice**
- ¾ **cup (240 g) apricot jam or preserves**
- 1 **tablespoon firmly packed brown sugar**
- ½ **teaspoon ground cinnamon**
- ¼ **teaspoon *each* salt and liquid hot pepper seasoning**
- 1 **small onion, chopped**
- 2 **large tomatoes (about 1 lb./ 455 g *total*), chopped and drained well**
- 1 **teaspoon olive oil or salad oil**
- 1 **pound (455 g) veal scaloppine, cut into ¼- by 2-inch (6-mm by 5-cm) strips**

Veal with Apricot Salsa

Preparation time: About 25 minutes
Cooking time: About 25 minutes

- 2 **cloves garlic, minced or pressed**
- 3 **tablespoons chopped cilantro Cilantro sprigs**

1. In a 3- to 4-quart (2.8- to 3.8-liter) pan, bring 2 cups (470 ml) water to a boil over high heat; stir in rice. Reduce heat, cover, and simmer until liquid has been absorbed and rice is tender to bite (about 20 minutes).

2. Meanwhile, in a small bowl, combine apricots and lime juice; let stand until apricots are softened (about 10 minutes), stirring occasionally. In another small bowl, stir together jam, ¼ cup (60 ml) water, sugar, cinnamon, salt, and hot pepper seasoning.

3. In a wide nonstick frying pan or wok, combine onion and 2 tablespoons (30 ml) water. Stir-fry over medium-high heat until onion is soft (about 4 minutes). Add more water, 1 tablespoon (15 ml) at a time, if pan appears dry.

4. Add apricot–lime juice mixture and jam mixture. Cook, stirring, until almost all liquid has evaporated (about 5 minutes). Transfer to a large bowl and add tomatoes; mix gently. Wipe pan clean (be careful; pan is hot).

5. Heat oil in pan over medium-high heat. When oil is hot, add veal, 1 tablespoon (15 ml) water, and garlic. Stir-fry just until meat is no longer pink on outside (1 to 2 minutes). Remove meat from pan with a slotted spoon; add to apricot-tomato salsa. Then add chopped cilantro; mix gently but thoroughly.

6. Spoon rice into individual bowls and top with meat mixture. Garnish with cilantro sprigs. Makes 4 servings.

Per serving: 551 calories (6% calories from fat), 4 g total fat, 0.9 g saturated fat, 89 mg cholesterol, 260 mg sodium, 102 g carbohydrates, 5 g fiber, 30 g protein, 64 mg calcium, 5 mg iron

If desired, substitute boneless veal shoulder for the roast.

- 14 to 16 ounces (400 to 455 g) Egg Pasta or Food Processor Pasta (pages 284–285), cut for thin noodles, or purchased fresh fettuccine
- 2 tablespoons (30 ml) olive oil
- 2 pounds (905 g) veal tip roast, trimmed of fat, cut into 1-inch (2.5-cm) cubes
- 2 ounces (55 g) thinly sliced prosciutto, shredded
- 1 large onion (about 8 oz./230 g), finely chopped
- 1 large carrot (about 4 oz./115 g), finely chopped
- 1 cup (240 ml) dry white wine
- 18 cups lightly packed shredded escarole (about 1½ lbs./680 g)
- 4 teaspoons cornstarch mixed with ½ cup (120 ml) water

Braised Veal with Escarole & Fresh Pasta

Preparation time: About 15 minutes
Cooking time: About 1½ hours

1. Prepare Egg Pasta. Cover and refrigerate.

2. Heat 1 tablespoon of the oil in a 5- to 6-quart (5- to 6-liter) pan (preferably nonstick) over medium-high heat. Add half the veal and cook, turning often, until browned (about 5 minutes); remove from pan. Repeat with remaining oil and veal. Set aside.

3. Add prosciutto, onion, and carrot to pan. Cook, stirring often, until soft (about 5 minutes). Return veal to pan.

Add wine and 1 cup (240 ml) water. Bring to a boil; reduce heat, cover, and simmer, stirring occasionally, until veal is tender when pierced (about 1 hour). Meanwhile, bring 16 cups (3.8 liters) water to a boil in a 6- to 8-quart (6- to 8-liter) pan. Stir in pasta and cook just until tender to bite (1 to 3 minutes; or according to package directions). Drain well and transfer to a deep platter; keep warm.

4. Add escarole to veal, a portion at a time if needed, and cook, stirring, until wilted (about 3 minutes). Stir cornstarch mixture and add to veal. Increase heat to high and cook, stirring, until mixture comes to a boil. Spoon over pasta. Makes 6 servings.

Per serving: 454 calories (24% calories from fat), 12 g total fat, 3 g saturated fat, 198 mg cholesterol, 352 mg sodium, 43 g carbohydrates, 5 g fiber, 42 g protein, 106 mg calcium, 5 mg iron

---

For a quick meal, try these sausage-topped, sautéed veal scallops, served with a lemony mustard sauce made from the pan drippings.

- 6 very thin slices capocollo (or coppa) sausage (about 1½ oz./43 g *total*)
- 6 slices veal scaloppine (about 1 lb./455 g *total*)
- 1 teaspoon olive oil
- 4 green onions, thinly sliced diagonally
- 2 cloves garlic, minced
- ¼ cup (60 ml) beef broth
- 2 tablespoons (30 ml) Dijon mustard
- 1 tablespoon (15 ml) lemon juice
- 1½ teaspoons chopped fresh basil or ½ teaspoon dried basil
  Lemon slices and basil sprigs

Veal Capocollo

Preparation time: 20 minutes
Cooking time: About 10 minutes

1. Lay a slice of sausage on each veal slice, pressing lightly so that meat and sausage stick together. Set aside.

2. Heat oil in a wide nonstick frying pan over medium heat. Add onions and garlic; stir often until onions are soft but still bright green (about 3 minutes). Push onion mixture aside; place veal in pan, overlapping slices as little as possible. Cook, turning once, just until veal is no longer pink in center; cut to test (about 3 minutes). With a slotted spatula, transfer veal slices, sausage side up, to a platter; keep warm.

3. Working quickly, add broth, mustard, lemon juice, and chopped basil to pan; stir to blend. Cook over medium-high heat, stirring, until mixture boils and thickens slightly. Drizzle sauce over meat; garnish with lemon slices and basil sprigs. Makes 4 servings.

Per serving: 172 calories (22% calories from fat), 4 g total fat, 1 g saturated fat, 94 mg cholesterol, 509 mg sodium, 6 g carbohydrates, 0.4 g fiber, 27 g protein, 45 mg calcium, 2 mg iron

Veal Chops with Noodle Pudding
(recipe on facing page)

Moist and rich noodle pudding enhances veal chops.

Veal Chops with Noodle Pudding

Preparation time: About 15 minutes
Cooking time: About 3¼ hours
Pictured on facing page

8 large veal loin chops (about 4 lbs./1.8 kg *total*), trimmed of fat

About 4 tablespoons all-purpose flour

2 teaspoons olive oil

16 sage leaves

1½ cups (360 ml) dry white wine

Noodle Pudding (page 412)

2 teaspoons brown sugar (or to taste)

2 tablespoons *each* minced parsley and finely chopped green onion

4 teaspoons (20 ml) white wine vinegar (or to taste)

Sage sprigs

1. Coat chops lightly with flour. Heat oil in a wide nonstick frying pan over medium heat. Add sage leaves. Cook, stirring, until darker in color (about 2 minutes). With a slotted spoon, remove from pan and set aside. Add chops, half at a time, and cook, turning as needed, until browned on both sides (about 6 minutes). Place in a lightly oiled 12- by 17-inch (30- by 43-cm) roasting pan, overlapping chops as little as possible. Top with sage leaves. Pour in wine. Cover tightly and bake in a 375°F (190°C) oven until tender when pierced and slightly pink in center; cut to test (about 2 hours). Meanwhile, prepare Noodle Pudding; keep warm.

2. Lift out chops and keep warm. Skim and discard fat from pan drippings and measure. If less than 1 cup (240 ml), add water and bring to a boil in a 1- to 1½-quart (950-ml to 1.4-liter) pan over high heat; if more, pour drippings into pan and boil until reduced to 1 cup (240 ml). Add sugar and cook, stirring, until melted; remove from heat. Stir in parsley, onion, and vinegar.

3. Arrange chops and pudding on individual plates. Drizzle gravy over chops. Garnish with sage sprigs. Makes 8 servings.

Per serving: 475 calories (26% calories from fat), 13 g total fat, 5 g saturated fat, 138 mg cholesterol, 313 mg sodium, 50 g carbohydrates, 1 g fiber, 33 g protein, 58 mg calcium, 3 mg iron

---

Marsala flavors a mild stir-fry of veal and sliced mushrooms to spoon over hot linguine.

Veal with Mushrooms

Preparation time: About 20 minutes
Cooking time: About 15 minutes

1 pound (455 g) veal scaloppine, cut into ¼- by 2-inch (6-mm by 5-cm) strips

⅛ teaspoon *each* salt and pepper

8 ounces (230 g) dried linguine

1 tablespoon butter or margarine

2 cloves garlic, minced or pressed

2 cups (170 g) sliced mushrooms

½ cup (120 ml) Marsala or cream sherry

3 tablespoons chopped parsley

1 large tomato (about 8 oz./230 g), chopped and drained well

¼ cup (35 g) pitted ripe olives, chopped

1. In a large bowl, mix veal, salt, and pepper; set aside.

2. In a 4- to 5-quart (3.8- to 5-liter) pan, cook linguine in 8 cups (1.9 liters) boiling water until just tender to bite (8 to 10 minutes); or cook according to package directions. Drain well, transfer to a warm rimmed platter, and keep warm.

3. While pasta is cooking, melt butter in a wide nonstick frying pan or wok over medium-high heat. Add meat and garlic; stir-fry just until meat is no longer pink on outside (1 to 2 minutes). Add water, 1 tablespoon (15 ml) at a time, if pan appears dry. Remove meat from pan with a slotted spoon; keep warm.

4. Add mushrooms and 3 tablespoons (45 ml) water to pan. Stir-fry until mushrooms are soft (about 3 minutes), gently scraping any browned bits free from pan. Add Marsala and bring to a boil; then boil, stirring, until sauce is slightly thickened (about 3 minutes). Remove pan from heat and stir in meat and parsley.

5. Spoon meat mixture over pasta; sprinkle with tomato and olives. Makes 4 servings.

Per serving: 440 calories (16% calories from fat), 7 g total fat, 3 g saturated fat, 96 mg cholesterol, 191 mg sodium, 52 g carbohydrates, 3 g fiber, 33 g protein, 39 mg calcium, 4 mg iron

To add interest to a simple lamb curry, serve it with warm home-made grape-apple chutney; while the chutney simmers, you can easily cook the meat and a pan of fluffy couscous. If you prefer, make the chutney in advance to serve cold.

Curried Lamb with Grape Chutney

Preparation time: About 25 minutes
Cooking time: About 45 minutes

Grape Chutney (page 172)

1 pound (455 g) lean boneless leg of lamb, trimmed of fat and cut into 1-inch (2.5-cm) cubes

10 ounces (285 g) tiny onions (*each* about ¾ inch/2 cm in diameter), peeled

2½ teaspoons curry powder

¼ teaspoon salt

1½ cups (360 ml) fat-free reduced-sodium chicken broth

1 cup (185 g) couscous

1 tablespoon (15 ml) olive oil

1 tablespoon chopped fresh mint, or to taste

Mint sprigs

1. Prepare Grape Chutney. When chutney is almost done, combine lamb, onions, curry powder, and salt in a large bowl; turn meat and onions to coat with seasonings. Set aside.

2. In a 3- to 4-quart (2.8- to 3.8-liter) pan, bring broth to a boil over high heat; stir in couscous. Cover, remove from heat, and let stand until liquid has been absorbed (about 5 minutes). Keep warm; fluff occasionally with a fork.

3. While couscous is standing, heat oil in a wide nonstick frying pan or wok over medium-high heat. When oil is hot, add lamb and onions. Stir-fry just until onions are heated through and meat is done to your liking; cut to test (5 to 7 minutes for medium-rare). Add water, 1 tablespoon (15 ml) at a time, if pan appears dry.

4. Spoon couscous onto a rimmed platter. Spoon meat and onions over couscous; sprinkle with chopped mint. Garnish with mint sprigs. Offer Grape Chutney to add to taste. Makes 4 servings.

Per serving: 549 calories (18% calories from fat), 11 g total fat, 3 g saturated fat, 75 mg cholesterol, 336 mg sodium, 81 g carbohydrates, 5 g fiber, 33 g protein, 80 mg calcium, 4 mg iron

---

Curry accents the lamb and onion skewers that rest atop creamy orzo studded with olives.

Lamb Kebabs with Orzo

Preparation time: About 35 minutes
Cooking time: 20 to 25 minutes

1 pound (455 g) boneless lean lamb, trimmed of fat, cut into 1-inch (2.5-cm) cubes

10 ounces (285 g) small onions (about 1-inch/2.5-cm diameter)

2½ teaspoons curry powder

2 cups (470 ml) nonfat milk

1½ cups (360 ml) low-sodium chicken broth

10 ounces/285 g (about 1⅔ cups) dried orzo or other rice-shaped pasta

1 tablespoon chopped fresh oregano or 1 teaspoon dried oregano

¼ cup (35 g) pitted black olives, cut into wedges

3 tablespoons (45 ml) dry white wine (or to taste)

2 tablespoons chopped parsley

¼ cup (20 g) freshly grated Parmesan cheese

Salt and pepper

1. Soak 8 wooden skewers (8 to 10 inches/20 to 25 cm long) in hot water to cover for at least 30 minutes.

2. Combine lamb, onions, and curry powder in a large bowl; turn to coat. Alternately thread lamb and onions onto skewers. Place on lightly oiled rack of a broiler pan. Set aside briefly.

3. Combine milk and broth in a 4- to 5-quart (3.8- to 5-liter) pan. Bring just to a boil over medium heat. Stir in pasta and oregano. Reduce heat, cover, and simmer, stirring occasionally, until most of the liquid is absorbed (15 to 20 minutes); do not scorch. Meanwhile, broil meat and onions 3 to 4 inches (8 to 10 cm) below heat, turning as needed, until meat is browned and done to your liking; cut to test (8 to 10 minutes).

4. Add olives, wine, parsley, and cheese to pasta. Stir well. Mound on individual plates and top with skewers. Offer salt and pepper to add to taste. Makes 4 servings (2 skewers each).

Per serving: 569 calories (21% calories from fat), 13 g total fat, 5 g saturated fat, 87 mg cholesterol, 354 mg sodium, 67 g carbohydrates, 3 g fiber, 43 g protein, 290 mg calcium, 6 mg iron

To temper the heat of this spicy lamb, offer rice and a crisp, cooling salad of greens, cucumbers, and fresh orange segments. Frilly green onion "brushes" make a pretty garnish; if you want to use them, be sure to allow an extra hour to soak the onion pieces in ice water.

Hunan Lamb

Preparation time: About 25 minutes, plus at least 1 hour to soak Green Onion Brushes (if used)
Cooking time: About 25 minutes

Green Onion Brushes (optional; page 216)

1 cup (185 g) long-grain white rice

1 tablespoon cornstarch

2 tablespoons (30 ml) reduced-sodium soy sauce

1 large egg white

2 tablespoons (30 ml) lemon juice

1 teaspoon honey

1 pound (455 g) lean boneless leg of lamb, trimmed of fat and cut into ⅛- by 2-inch (3-mm by 5-cm) strips

Cooking Sauce (recipe follows)

3 green onions

1 teaspoon salad oil

2 cloves garlic, minced or pressed

Hot Chili Oil (page 109) or purchased hot chili oil (optional)

1. Prepare Green Onion Brushes, if desired. Set aside.

2. In a 3- to 4-quart (2.8- to 3.8-liter) pan, bring 2 cups (470 ml) water to a boil over high heat; stir in rice. Reduce heat, cover, and simmer until liquid has been absorbed and rice is tender to bite (about 20 minutes).

3. Meanwhile, in a large bowl, stir together cornstarch and soy sauce until blended. Add egg white, lemon juice, and honey; beat until blended. Add lamb and stir to coat. Set aside; stir occasionally.

4. Prepare Cooking Sauce and set aside. Trim and discard ends of whole green onions; cut onions into 2-inch lengths, then sliver each piece lengthwise and set aside.

5. Heat salad oil in a wide nonstick frying pan or wok over medium-high heat. When oil is hot, add garlic and stir-fry just until fragrant (about 30 seconds; do not scorch). Lift meat from marinade and drain well (discard marinade). Add meat to pan and stir-fry until done to your liking; cut to test (1 to 2 minutes for medium-rare).

6. Stir Cooking Sauce well and pour into pan. Cook, stirring, until sauce boils and thickens slightly (1 to 2 minutes). Remove from heat and stir in slivered onions.

7. Spoon rice onto a rimmed platter; spoon meat mixture over rice. Garnish with Green Onion Brushes, if desired. Offer chili oil to add to taste, if desired. Makes 4 servings.

Cooking Sauce. In a small bowl, stir together 3 tablespoons (45 ml) **hoisin sauce,** 2 tablespoons (30 ml) **seasoned rice vinegar** or 2 tablespoons (30 ml) distilled white vinegar plus ¾ teaspoon sugar, 2 tablespoons **chili paste with garlic,** 2 to 3 teaspoons **sugar,** and 2 teaspoons **Oriental sesame oil.**

Per serving: 457 calories (25% calories from fat), 12 g total fat, 3 g saturated fat, 73 mg cholesterol, 807 mg sodium, 55 g carbohydrates, 0.9 g fiber, 28 g protein, 35 mg calcium, 5 mg iron

Tangy blue cheese and toasted pine nuts fill these grilled lamb chops. Serve them with hot polenta studded with corn kernels.

- 8 **small lamb rib chops** (*each about 1 inch/2.5 cm thick; about 2 lbs./905 g total*)**, trimmed of fat**
- ½ **small onion, cut into chunks**
- ¼ **cup (60 ml) reduced-sodium soy sauce**
- 2 **tablespoons firmly packed brown sugar**
- 2 **tablespoons (30 ml) lemon juice**
- 1 **large clove garlic, peeled**
- ¼ **cup (65 g) pine nuts or slivered almonds**
- ¼ **cup (62 g) packed crumbled blue-veined cheese**
  Pepper
- 2 **cups (470 ml) low-fat (1%) milk**
- ½ **cup (120 ml) beef broth**
- 1 **cup (138 g) polenta or yellow cornmeal**
- 1 **large can (about 15 oz./425 g) cream-style corn**
- 1 **teaspoon chopped fresh thyme or ¼ teaspoon dried thyme**
- ½ **teaspoon salt**
- 1 **cup (about 8 oz./230 g) nonfat ricotta cheese**
- ¼ **cup (20 g) grated Parmesan cheese**
  Thyme sprigs

Stuffed Lamb Chops with Creamy Polenta

Preparation time: 30 minutes
Marinating time: At least 30 minutes
Cooking time: About 25 minutes
Pictured on facing page

1. With a sharp knife, cut a horizontal 1½-inch-wide (3.5-cm-wide) pocket in each lamb chop, starting from meaty side and cutting through to bone. Set chops aside.

2. In a food processor or blender, combine onion, soy sauce, sugar, lemon juice, and garlic. Whirl until smoothly puréed. Pour into a heavy-duty resealable plastic food-storage bag. Add chops; seal bag and rotate to coat chops with marinade. Refrigerate for at least 30 minutes or up to 6 hours, turning bag over occasionally.

3. Toast pine nuts in a small frying pan over medium heat until golden (about 3 minutes), stirring often; then pour into a small bowl and let cool slightly. Add blue-veined cheese and mix well. Season to taste with pepper, cover, and refrigerate until ready to use.

4. When you are almost ready to grill chops, prepare polenta. In a 4- to 5-quart (3.8- to 5-liter) pan, bring milk and broth just to a boil over medium-high heat. Stir in polenta, corn, chopped thyme, and salt. Reduce heat and simmer, uncovered, stirring often and scraping pan bottom with a long-handled spoon (mixture will spatter), until polenta tastes creamy (about 15 minutes). Stir in ricotta cheese; then remove pan from heat, stir in Parmesan cheese, and keep warm.

5. Lift chops from bag; drain, reserving marinade. Using a spoon, stuff an eighth of the cheese–pine nut filling deep into pocket of each chop. Place chops on a greased grill 4 to 6 inches (10 to 15 cm) above a solid bed of hot coals. Cook, basting twice with marinade and turning once, until chops are evenly browned and done to your liking; cut in thickest part to test (6 to 8 minutes for medium-rare).

6. To serve, divide polenta among 4 individual plates; arrange 2 chops on each plate alongside polenta. Garnish with thyme sprigs. Makes 4 servings.

Per serving: 660 calories (30% calories from fat), 22 g total fat, 8 g saturated fat, 94 mg cholesterol, 1,823 mg sodium, 68 g carbohydrates, 4 g fiber, 48 g protein, 604 mg calcium, 5 mg iron

Stuffed Lamb Chops with Creamy Polenta
(recipe on facing page)

When cherries are in season, use them to make a delicious tart-sweet sauce for lamb rib chops.

Lamb Chops with Cherries & Orecchiette

Preparation time: About 15 minutes
Cooking time: About 15 minutes

8 lamb rib chops (about 2 lbs./905 g *total*), *each* about 1 inch (2.5 cm) thick, trimmed of fat

12 ounces/340 g (about 3½ cups) dried orecchiette or other medium-size pasta shape

⅓ cup (80 ml) seasoned rice vinegar; or ⅓ cup (80 ml) distilled white vinegar and 3 teaspoons sugar

1 tablespoon *each* chopped cilantro and chopped parsley

1 to 2 cloves garlic, minced or pressed

½ teaspoon ground coriander

¾ cup (225 g) currant jelly

½ cup (120 ml) raspberry vinegar

¼ cup (60 ml) orange juice

1 tablespoon chopped fresh tarragon or ¾ teaspoon dried tarragon

1½ cups (220 g) pitted dark sweet cherries

1. Place chops on lightly oiled rack of a broiler pan. Broil about 6 inches (15 cm) below heat, turning once, until done to your liking; cut to test (8 to 10 minutes). Meanwhile, bring 12 cups (2.8 liters) water to a boil in a 5- to 6-quart (5- to 6-liter) pan over medium-high heat. Stir in pasta and cook just until tender to bite (8 to 10 minutes); or cook according to package directions. Drain well. Transfer to a large non-metal bowl and add rice vinegar, cilantro, parsley, garlic, and coriander; mix thoroughly but gently. Keep warm.

2. Combine jelly, raspberry vinegar, orange juice, and tarragon in a 1½- to 2-quart (1.4- to 1.9-liter) pan. Cook over medium heat, whisking, until smoothly blended. Add cherries and cook, stirring gently, just until warm. Remove from heat.

3. Spoon pasta onto individual plates. Arrange lamb chops alongside and top with fruit sauce. Makes 4 servings.

Per serving: 709 calories (14% calories from fat), 11 g total fat, 4 g saturated fat, 66 mg cholesterol, 481 mg sodium, 120 g carbohydrates, 3 g fiber, 32 g protein, 48 mg calcium, 5 mg iron

---

Apricot wine and dried apricots flavor fluffy couscous with lamb.

Lamb with Fruited Couscous

Preparation time: About 10 minutes
Cooking time: About 2 hours

1 tablespoon (15 ml) olive oil

1 pound (455 g) boned leg of lamb, trimmed of fat, cut into 1-inch (2.5-cm) cubes

1 large onion (about 8 oz./230 g), chopped

1½ teaspoons ground coriander

1 teaspoon ground ginger

½ teaspoon ground cumin

¼ teaspoon ground allspice

1 cinnamon stick (about 3 in./8 cm long)

2 cups (470 ml) low-sodium chicken broth

¼ cup (60 ml) apricot or orange muscat dessert wine

1 cup (about 6 oz./170 g) dried apricots

10 ounces/285 g (about 1⅔ cups) dried couscous

1. Heat oil in a 5- to 6-quart (5- to 6-liter) pan over medium-high heat. Add lamb and cook, turning often, until well browned (about 8 minutes). Lift out and set aside.

2. Add onion to pan and cook, stirring often, until soft (about 5 minutes). Add coriander, ginger, cumin, allspice, cinnamon stick, broth, and lamb. Bring to a boil; reduce heat, cover, and simmer until lamb is tender when pierced (about 1½ hours). Discard cinnamon stick. (At this point, you may cool, cover, and refrigerate for up to a day; discard fat and reheat to continue.)

3. Lift out lamb and place on a platter; keep warm. Skim off and discard fat from pan drippings (if not already done). Measure drippings. If less than 2⅓ cups (550 ml), add water and return to pan; if more, boil over high heat until reduced to 2⅓ cups (550 ml). Add wine and apricots; bring to a boil. Stir in pasta; cover, remove from heat, and let stand until liquid is absorbed (about 5 minutes). Fluff with a fork.

4. Mound pasta beside lamb. Makes 4 servings.

Per serving: 603 calories (16% calories from fat), 11 g total fat, 3 g saturated fat, 73 mg cholesterol, 143 mg sodium, 89 g carbohydrates, 6 g fiber, 36 g protein, 72 mg calcium, 5 mg iron

Sliced, stir-fried Golden Delicious apples, sauced with a tart-sweet blend of apple jelly and cider vinegar, make a great partner for tender lamb. For an attractive presentation, serve the meat in red-violet radicchio cups.

- 4 **to 8 large radicchio leaves, rinsed and crisped**
- 1 **pound (455 g) lean boneless leg of lamb, trimmed of fat and cut into ¾-inch (2-cm) chunks**
- ¼ **teaspoon salt**
- ⅛ **teaspoon pepper**
- ⅓ **cup (80 ml) apple jelly**
- ⅓ **cup (80 ml) cider vinegar**
- 1 **tablespoon cornstarch blended with 1 tablespoon (15 ml) cold water**
- 1 **teaspoon Dijon mustard**
- ¾ **teaspoon chopped fresh thyme or ¼ teaspoon dried thyme**
- ⅓ **cup (50 g) dried currants or raisins**
- 3 **large Golden Delicious apples (about 1½ lbs./680 g *total*), peeled, cored, and sliced ¼ to ½ inch (6 mm to 1 cm) thick**
- 2 **teaspoons salad oil**
- 1 **to 2 tablespoons chopped parsley**
  Thyme sprigs

Sautéed Lamb with Apples

Preparation time: About 20 minutes
Cooking time: About 10 minutes

1. Arrange 1 or 2 radicchio leaves (overlapping, if necessary) on each of 4 individual plates; cover and set aside.

2. In a large bowl, mix lamb, salt, and pepper; set aside. In a small bowl, stir together jelly, 3 tablespoons (45 ml) of the vinegar, cornstarch mixture, mustard, and chopped thyme until well blended. Stir in currants and set aside. In a medium-size bowl, gently mix apples with remaining vinegar.

3. Heat 1 teaspoon of the oil in a wide nonstick frying pan or wok over medium-high heat. When oil is hot, add apples and stir-fry gently until almost tender when pierced (about 4 minutes). Add water, 1 tablespoon (15 ml) at a time, if pan appears dry.

4. Stir jelly mixture well; pour into pan and cook, stirring, just until sauce boils and thickens slightly (1 to 2 minutes). Remove apple mixture from pan and keep warm. Wipe pan clean (be careful; pan is hot).

5. Heat remaining 1 teaspoon oil in pan over medium-high heat. When oil is hot, add meat and stir-fry just until done to your liking; cut to test (about 3 minutes for medium-rare). Remove from heat and stir in parsley.

6. Spoon meat equally into radicchio leaves; spoon apple mixture alongside. Garnish with thyme sprigs. Makes 4 servings.

Per serving: 367 calories (19% calories from fat), 8 g total fat, 2 g saturated fat, 73 mg cholesterol, 114 mg sodium, 52 g carbohydrates, 4 g fiber, 25 g protein, 49 mg calcium, 3 mg iron

Roast Turkey with Apple Orzo
(recipe on page 128)

Poultry

Turkey and chicken lend themselves perfectly to a light cooking style. They are naturally lean and their unassertive flavor makes them ideal foils for seasonings and sauces. Rub sliced turkey breasts with herbs and garlic for tantalizly flavorful Oregano-rubbed Turkey. Or savor the intriguing combination of cocoa and jalapeño peppers with our streamlined Jalapeño Chicken with Mole Poblano.

Turkey and cranberries have long been traditional partners. Here they're combined in an entirely new way.

....

2 tablespoons chopped pecans

1 boned turkey breast half (3 to 3½ lbs./1.35 to 1.6 kg), trimmed of fat

⅓ cup (100 g) apple jelly

1 tablespoon (15 ml) raspberry vinegar or red wine vinegar

¼ teaspoon ground sage

2 cups (470 ml) apple juice

About 2¾ cups (650 ml) low-sodium chicken broth

10 ounces/285 g (about 1⅔ cups) dried orzo or other rice-shaped pasta

½ cup (45 g) dried cranberries or raisins

¼ teaspoon ground coriander

1 tablespoon cornstarch mixed with 3 tablespoons cold water

⅓ cup (20 g) chopped parsley or green onions

Sage sprigs

Salt and pepper

....

1. Toast nuts in a small frying pan over medium heat, shaking pan often, until golden (about 4 minutes). Remove from pan and set aside.

Roast Turkey with Apple Orzo

....

Preparation time: About 20 minutes
Cooking time: About 2¼ hours
Pictured on page 126

2. Place turkey skin side up. Fold narrow end under breast; pull skin to cover as much breast as possible. Tie snugly lengthwise and crosswise with cotton string at 1-inch (2.5-cm) intervals. Place in a nonstick or lightly oiled square 8-inch (20-cm) pan.

3. Combine jelly, vinegar, and ground sage in a 1- to 1½-quart (950-ml to 1.4-liter) pan. Cook over medium-low heat, stirring, until jelly is melted. Baste turkey with some of the mixture, reserving remaining mixture.

4. Roast turkey in a 375°F (190°C) oven, basting with pan drippings and remaining jelly mixture, until a meat thermometer inserted in thickest part registers 160°F/70°C (about 2 hours); if drippings start to scorch, add ⅓ cup (80 ml) water to pan, stirring to loosen browned bits. Meanwhile, combine apple juice and 1⅓ cups (320 ml) of the broth in a 4- to 5-quart (3.8- to 5-liter) pan. Bring to a boil over high

heat. Stir in pasta, cranberries, and coriander. Reduce heat, cover, and simmer, stirring occasionally, until almost all liquid is absorbed (about 15 minutes); do not scorch. Remove from heat and keep warm, stirring occasionally.

5. Transfer turkey to a warm platter; cover and let stand for 10 minutes. Meanwhile, pour pan drippings and accumulated juices into a 2-cup (470-ml) glass measure; skim off and discard fat. Stir cornstarch mixture and blend into drippings. Add enough of the remaining broth to make 1½ cups (360 ml). Pour into a 1- to 1½-quart (950-ml to 1.4-liter) pan and cook over medium-high heat, stirring, until boiling. Pour into a serving container.

6. Remove strings from turkey. Slice meat and arrange on individual plates. Stir parsley into pasta and mound beside turkey; sprinkle with nuts. Garnish with sage sprigs. Offer gravy, salt, and pepper to add to taste. Makes 8 to 10 servings.

....

Per serving: 436 calories (25% calories from fat), 12 g total fat, 3 g saturated fat, 93 mg cholesterol, 123 mg sodium, 40 g carbohydrates, 1 g fiber, 41 g protein, 45 mg calcium, 3 mg iron

If you're eating light but can't do without cheese, try sticking to the sharper, tangier types—the stronger the flavor, the less you'll need to use.

- 2 to 4 tablespoons (15 to 30 g) sun-dried tomatoes in olive oil
  Cooking Sauce (recipe follows)
- 1 small onion
- 8 ounces (230 g) dried penne or ziti
- 2 turkey breast tenderloins (about 1 lb./455 g *total*), cut into ½-inch (1-cm) pieces
- 1½ teaspoons chopped fresh oregano or ½ teaspoon dried oregano
- 1 large tomato (about 8 oz./230 g), chopped and drained well
- 2 tablespoons drained capers
- ½ cup (65 g) crumbled feta cheese
  Oregano sprigs

Preparation time: About 15 minutes
Cooking time: About 15 minutes

1. Drain sun-dried tomatoes well (reserve oil) and pat dry with paper towels. Then chop tomatoes and set aside. Prepare Cooking Sauce and set aside. Cut onion in half lengthwise; then cut each half crosswise into thin slices. Set aside.

2. In a 4- to 5-quart (3.8- to 5-liter) pan, cook penne in about 8 cups (1.9 liters) boiling water until just tender to bite (8 to 10 minutes); or cook according to package directions. Drain pasta well and transfer to a warm large bowl; keep warm.

3. While pasta is cooking, measure 2 teaspoons of the oil from sun-dried tomatoes. Heat oil in a wide nonstick frying pan or wok over medium-high heat. When oil is hot, add turkey and chopped oregano. Stir-fry just until meat is no longer pink in center; cut to test (2 to 3 minutes). Add water, 1 tablespoon (15 ml) at a time, if pan appears dry. Remove turkey from pan with a slotted spoon; transfer to bowl with pasta and keep warm.

4. Add sun-dried tomatoes and onion to pan; stir-fry until onion is soft (about 4 minutes). Add water, 1 tablespoon (15 ml) at a time, if pan appears dry. Stir Cooking Sauce well and pour into pan. Cook, stirring, until sauce boils and thickens slightly (1 to 2 minutes). Remove from heat and stir in fresh tomato and capers.

5. Spoon tomato mixture over pasta and turkey; mix gently but thoroughly. Divide turkey mixture among 4 warm individual rimmed plates or shallow bowls. Sprinkle with cheese and garnish with oregano sprigs. Makes 4 servings.

Cooking Sauce. In a small bowl, stir together ½ cup (120 ml) **fat-free reduced-sodium chicken broth,** 2 tablespoons (30 ml) **dry white wine,** and 1 teaspoon **cornstarch** until blended.

Per serving: 489 calories (24% calories from fat), 13 g total fat, 4 g saturated fat, 83 mg cholesterol, 464 mg sodium, 52 g carbohydrates, 3 g fiber, 39 g protein, 108 mg calcium, 4 mg iron

When time is short, try thin-sliced, sautéed turkey breast topped with cheese and aromatic fresh sage.

- 1 pound (455 g) thinly sliced turkey breast
- 2 teaspoons finely chopped fresh sage or 1 teaspoon dried sage
- 2 teaspoons olive oil
- ⅓ cup (45 g) finely shredded provolone or part-skim mozzarella cheese
  Pepper
  Sage sprigs
  Lemon wedges
  Salt

Preparation time: 15 minutes
Cooking time: About 5 minutes

1. Rinse turkey and pat dry. Sprinkle one side of each slice with chopped sage; set aside.

2. Heat 1 teaspoon of the oil in a wide nonstick frying pan over medium-high heat. Add half the turkey, sage-coated side down, and cook until golden on bottom (about 1½ minutes). Then turn pieces over and continue to cook until no longer pink in center; cut to test (30 to 60 more seconds). Transfer cooked turkey to a platter and sprinkle with half the cheese. Cover loosely with foil and keep warm.

3. Immediately cook remaining turkey, using remaining 1 teaspoon oil; add water, 1 tablespoon (15 ml) at a time, if pan appears dry. Transfer turkey to platter.

4. Sprinkle turkey with remaining cheese, then with pepper; garnish with sage sprigs. Serve at once. Season to taste with lemon and salt. Makes 4 servings.

Per serving: 184 calories (30% calories from fat), 6 g total fat, 2 g saturated fat, 78 mg cholesterol, 149 mg sodium, 0.3 g carbohydrates, 0 g fiber, 31 g protein, 94 mg calcium, 1 mg iron

Fig-stuffed Turkey Roast

Preparation time: 15 minutes
Cooking time: About 1¼ hours
Pictured on facing page

Stuffed with figs and seasoned with rosemary and mustard, this turkey roast makes a showy entrée.

- 1 turkey breast half (about 3½ lbs./1.6 kg), boned and skinned
- 3 tablespoons (45 ml) Dijon mustard
- 1 tablespoon chopped fresh rosemary or 1 teaspoon dried rosemary
- 12 dried Calimyrna or Mission figs, finely chopped
- 1 tablespoon (15 ml) honey
- 1 tablespoon (15 ml) olive oil
- 2 cloves garlic, minced
  Pepper
  Rosemary sprigs

1. Rinse turkey and pat dry. Then slice lengthwise down middle, cutting meat almost but not quite through. Push cut open and press turkey to make it lie as flat as possible. Spread turkey with mustard and sprinkle with half the chopped rosemary; set aside.

2. In a bowl, mix figs with honey. Mound fig mixture evenly down center of turkey. Starting from a long side, lift turkey and roll over filling to enclose. Tie roll snugly with cotton string at 2- to 3-inch (5- to 8-cm) intervals. Rub roll with oil, then with garlic; pat remaining chopped rosemary onto roll and sprinkle generously with pepper.

3. Place roll on a rack in a 9- by 13-inch (23- by 33-cm) baking pan; add ⅓ cup (80 ml) water to pan. Bake in a 375°F (190°C) oven until a meat thermometer inserted in thickest part of roll (insert thermometer in meat, not filling) registers 160° to 165°F (71° to 74°C), about 1¼ hours. Add water, ¼ cup (60 ml) at a time, if pan appears dry.

4. Remove roll from oven and let stand for 10 minutes; then snip and discard strings and cut roll crosswise into thick slices. Garnish with rosemary sprigs. Serve with pan juices, if desired. Makes 6 to 8 servings.

Per serving: 308 calories (10% calories from fat), 3 g total fat, 0.7 g saturated fat, 117 mg cholesterol, 232 mg sodium, 24 g carbohydrates, 3 g fiber, 44 g protein, 67 mg calcium, 3 mg iron

Oregano-rubbed Turkey

Preparation time: 15 minutes
Marinating time: At least 2 hours
Cooking time: About 5 minutes

To give tender turkey slices an intriguing flavor, "cure" them briefly in salt and sugar; then rub the meat with herbs and garlic before sautéing.

- 1 tablespoon salt
- 1½ teaspoons sugar
- 1½ pounds (680 g) thinly sliced turkey breast
- ¼ cup (25 g) sliced green onions
- 2 tablespoons finely chopped Italian or regular parsley
- 3 cloves garlic, minced
- 1 teaspoon chopped fresh oregano or ½ teaspoon dried oregano
- ½ teaspoon *each* coarsely ground pepper and grated lemon peel
- 2 teaspoons olive oil
  Italian or regular parsley sprigs
  Lemon wedges

1. In a large bowl, combine salt and sugar. Rinse turkey and pat dry; then add to bowl and turn to coat evenly with salt mixture. Cover and refrigerate for at least 2 hours or up to 3 hours. Rinse turkey well, drain, and pat dry.

2. In a small bowl, combine onions, chopped parsley, garlic, oregano, pepper, and lemon peel. Rub onion mixture evenly over both sides of each turkey slice.

3. Heat 1 teaspoon of the oil in a wide nonstick frying pan over medium-high heat. Add half the turkey and cook until golden on bottom (about 1½ minutes). Then turn pieces over and continue to cook until no longer pink in center; cut to test (30 to 60 more seconds). Transfer cooked turkey to a platter, cover loosely with foil, and keep warm.

4. Immediately cook remaining turkey, using remaining 1 teaspoon oil; add water, 1 tablespoon (15 ml) at a time, if pan appears dry. Transfer turkey to platter and garnish with parsley sprigs. Serve at once. Season to taste with lemon. Makes 6 servings.

Per serving: 148 calories (14% calories from fat), 2 g total fat, 0.4 g saturated fat, 70 mg cholesterol, 1,155 mg sodium, 2 g carbohydrates, 0.2 g fiber, 28 g protein, 29 mg calcium, 2 mg iron

Fig-stuffed Turkey Roast
(recipe on facing page)

Trim the calories and fat of classic spaghetti and meatballs by making the meatballs from lean ground turkey.

¾ cup (130 g) bulgur

12 ounces (340 g) ground turkey

1 large onion (about 8 oz./230 g), chopped

4 cloves garlic, minced or pressed

1 teaspoon dried oregano

½ teaspoon salt

¼ teaspoon pepper

8 ounces (230 g) mushrooms, sliced

1 tablespoon dried basil

¼ teaspoon crushed red pepper flakes

About 1¼ cups (300 ml) low-sodium chicken broth

1 can (about 28 oz./795 g) crushed tomatoes

1 pound (455 g) dried spaghetti

Chopped parsley

Freshly grated Parmesan cheese

Spaghetti with Turkey Meatballs

Preparation time: About 25 minutes
Cooking time: About 50 minutes

1. Mix bulgur with 1½ cups (360 ml) boiling water in a large bowl. Let stand just until bulgur is tender to bite (about 15 minutes). Drain well.

2. Combine turkey, onion, 2 cloves of the garlic, oregano, salt, pepper, and bulgur in a large bowl. Mix until blended. Shape into balls about ¼-cup (60-ml) size. Place slightly apart in a lightly oiled 10- by 15-inch (25- by 38-cm) baking pan. Bake in a 425°F (220°C) oven until well browned (25 to 30 minutes). Meanwhile, combine mushrooms, remaining 2 cloves garlic, basil, red pepper flakes, and ¼ cup (60 ml) water in a 5- to 6-quart (5- to 6-liter) pan. Cook over high heat, stirring often, until liquid has evaporated and mushrooms begin to brown (about 10 minutes). To deglaze pan, add ¼ cup (60 ml) of the broth, stirring to loosen browned bits. Continue to cook, stirring often, until liquid has evaporated and mushrooms begin to brown again. Repeat deglazing step, adding ¼ cup (60 ml) more broth each time, until mushrooms are well browned. Add tomatoes; reduce heat, cover, and simmer for 10 minutes.

3. Add meatballs to sauce mixture. Cover and simmer for 5 more minutes; add more broth if sauce sticks to pan bottom. Remove from heat and keep warm.

4. Bring 16 cups (3.8 liters) water to a boil in a 6- to 8-quart (6- to 8-liter) pan over medium-high heat. Stir in pasta and cook just until tender to bite (8 to 10 minutes); or cook according to package directions. Drain well.

5. Bring ⅓ cup (80 ml) more broth to a boil in pan. Add pasta and lift with 2 forks to mix. Pour into a wide serving bowl. Top with sauce and sprinkle with parsley. Offer cheese to add to taste. Makes 5 or 6 servings.

Per serving: 483 calories (12% calories from fat), 7 g total fat, 2 g saturated fat, 41 mg cholesterol, 487 mg sodium, 82 g carbohydrates, 7 g fiber, 25 g protein, 99 mg calcium, 6 mg iron

---

This quick and colorful stir-fry is a whole meal in itself.

8 ounces (230 g) dried vermicelli

⅓ cup (40 g) dried tomatoes packed in oil, drained (reserve oil) and slivered

2 cloves garlic, minced or pressed

1 medium-size onion (about 6 oz./170 g), chopped

1 large yellow or red bell pepper (about 8 oz./230 g), chopped

3 medium-size zucchini (about 12 oz./340 g *total*), thinly sliced

1 cup (240 ml) low-sodium chicken broth

2 cups (280 g) shredded cooked turkey breast

Vermicelli with Turkey

Preparation time: About 15 minutes
Cooking time: About 15 minutes

½ cup (20 g) chopped fresh basil or 3 tablespoons dried basil

Freshly grated Parmesan cheese

1. Bring 8 cups (1.9 liters) water to a boil in a 4- to 5-quart (3.8- to 5-liter) pan over medium-high heat. Stir in pasta and cook just until tender to bite (8 to 10 minutes); or cook according to package directions. Meanwhile, heat 1 tablespoon (15 ml) of the reserved oil from tomatoes in a wide nonstick frying pan over medium-high heat. Add tomatoes, garlic, onion, bell pepper, and zucchini. Cook, stirring often, until vegetables begin to brown (about 8 minutes).

2. Pour broth over vegetables and bring to a boil. Drain pasta well and add to vegetables with turkey and basil. Lift with 2 forks to mix. Transfer to a platter. Offer cheese to add to taste. Makes 4 servings.

Per serving: 500 calories (28% calories from fat), 16 g total fat, 2 g saturated fat, 59 mg cholesterol, 85 mg sodium, 59 g carbohydrates, 5 g fiber, 33 g protein, 130 mg calcium, 61 mg iron

Oregano, lemon, and pungent Greek olives give this dish its Mediterranean flavor. Start by cooking the couscous; then prepare a garlicky stir-fry of turkey and red bell pepper strips to serve alongside.

....

2 turkey breast tenderloins (about 1 lb./455 g *total*), cut into ½-inch (1-cm) pieces

2 cloves garlic, minced or pressed

1 teaspoon paprika

½ teaspoon grated lemon peel

⅛ teaspoon salt (optional)

⅛ teaspoon pepper
   Cooking Sauce (recipe follows)

1 cup (240 ml) fat-free reduced-sodium chicken broth

⅔ cup (160 ml) low-fat milk

1½ teaspoons chopped fresh oregano or ½ teaspoon dried oregano

1 cup (185 g) couscous

1 medium-size red bell pepper (about 6 oz./170 g), seeded and cut into thin strips

2 teaspoons olive oil

⅓ to ½ cup (45 to 70 g) chopped pitted calamata olives

¼ cup (15 g) finely chopped parsley
   Oregano sprigs

Mediterranean Turkey with Herbed Couscous

....

Preparation time: About 15 minutes
Cooking time: About 10 minutes

1. In a large bowl, mix turkey, garlic, paprika, ¼ teaspoon of the lemon peel, salt (if used), and pepper; set aside. Prepare Cooking Sauce and set aside.

2. In a 3- to 4-quart (2.8- to 3.8-liter) pan, combine broth, milk, chopped oregano, and remaining ¼ teaspoon lemon peel. Bring just to a boil over medium-high heat; stir in couscous. Cover, remove from heat, and let stand until liquid has been absorbed (about 5 minutes). Transfer to a rimmed platter and keep warm; fluff occasionally with a fork.

3. While couscous is standing, in a wide nonstick frying pan or wok, combine bell pepper and 2 tablespoons (30 ml) water. Stir-fry over medium-high heat until pepper is just tender-crisp to bite (about 2 minutes); add water, 1 tablespoon (15 ml) at a time, if pan appears dry. Remove from pan with a slotted spoon and keep warm.

4. Heat oil in pan. When oil is hot, add turkey mixture and stir-fry just until meat is no longer pink in center; cut to test (2 to 3 minutes). Stir Cooking Sauce well; pour into pan. Then add bell pepper and olives; cook, stirring, until sauce boils and thickens slightly (1 to 2 minutes).

5. Pour turkey mixture over couscous. Sprinkle with parsley and garnish with oregano sprigs. Makes 4 servings.

....

Cooking Sauce. In a bowl, smoothly blend 2 teaspoons **cornstarch** with 2 tablespoons (30 ml) **balsamic vinegar**. Stir in ½ cup (120 ml) **fat-free reduced-sodium chicken broth**.

....

Per serving: 412 calories (20% calories from fat), 9 g total fat, 1 g saturated fat, 71 mg cholesterol, 824 mg sodium, 44 g carbohydrates, 2 g fiber, 37 g protein, 101 mg calcium, 3 mg iron

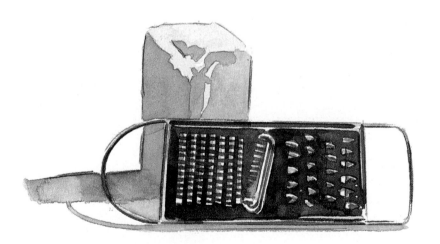

Raspberry-glazed Turkey Sauté
(recipe on facing page)

Poultry and fruit are classic partners: witness the traditional pairing of roast turkey with cranberry sauce. Here, turkey tenderloin joins up with sweet red raspberries. You toss thin strips of meat with a sauce of raspberry vinegar and jam, then top the finished dish with ripe whole berries. (When fresh raspberries are unavailable or unaffordable, use 1 cup of orange segments instead.)

3 **green onions**

⅓ **cup (100 g) seedless red raspberry jam or jelly**

3 **tablespoons (45 ml) raspberry or red wine vinegar**

1 **tablespoon Dijon mustard**

½ **teaspoon grated orange peel**

¾ **teaspoon chopped fresh tarragon or ¼ teaspoon dried tarragon**

8 **ounces (230 g) dried eggless spinach fettuccine or plain fettuccine**

1 **teaspoon olive oil or salad oil**

Raspberry-glazed Turkey Sauté

Preparation time: About 20 minutes
Cooking time: About 15 minutes
Pictured on facing page

2 **turkey breast tenderloins (about 1 lb./455 g *total*), cut into ¼- by 2-inch (6-mm by 5-cm) strips**

About 1 cup (123 g) fresh raspberries

Tarragon sprigs

1. Trim and discard ends of onions. Cut onions into 2-inch (5-cm) lengths; then cut each piece lengthwise into slivers. Set aside. In a small bowl, stir together jam, vinegar, mustard, orange peel, and chopped tarragon; set aside.

2. In a 4- to 5-quart (3.8- to 5-liter) pan, cook fettuccine in 8 cups (1.9 liters) boiling water until just tender to bite (8 to 10 minutes); or cook according to package directions.

3. Meanwhile, heat oil in a wide nonstick frying pan or wok over medium-high heat. When oil is hot, add turkey and 1 tablespoon (15 ml) water. Stir-fry just until turkey is no longer pink in center; cut to test (about 2 minutes). Add water, 1 tablespoon (15 ml) at a time, if pan appears dry. Remove turkey from pan with a slotted spoon and keep warm. Discard drippings from pan; wipe pan clean (be careful; pan is hot).

4. Add jam mixture to pan and bring to a boil over medium-high heat; then boil, stirring, just until jam is melted and sauce is smooth (about 1 minute). Remove from heat and stir in turkey and onions.

5. Drain pasta well and divide among 4 warm individual rimmed plates or shallow bowls; top with turkey mixture. Sprinkle with raspberries and garnish with tarragon sprigs. Makes 4 servings.

Per serving: 435 calories (6% calories from fat), 3 g total fat, 0.5 g saturated fat, 70 mg cholesterol, 178 mg sodium, 64 g carbohydrates, 8 g fiber, 36 g protein, 66 mg calcium, 3 mg iron

---

Orzo cooked with broth in the oven gains flavor from tomatoes and sausages.

1 **can (about 28 oz./795 g) tomatoes**

About ¾ cup (180 ml) beef broth

8 **ounces (230 g) *each* mild and hot turkey Italian sausages, casings removed, sliced ¼ inch (6 mm) thick**

2 **large onions (about 1 lb./455 g *total*), minced**

2 **tablespoons chopped fresh basil or 2 teaspoons dried basil**

12 **ounces/340 g (about 2 cups) dried orzo or other rice-shaped pasta**

¼ **cup (30 g) shredded part-skim mozzarella cheese**

One-pan Turkey Sausage & Orzo Casserole

Preparation time: About 15 minutes
Cooking time: About 1 hour and 10 minutes

1. Break up tomatoes with a spoon and drain juice into a 1-quart (950-ml) measure; reserve tomatoes. Add enough broth to juice to make 3 cups (710 ml); set aside.

2. Place sausages and onions in a shallow 2½- to 3-quart (2.4- to 2.8-liter) casserole. Bake in a 450°F (230°C) oven, stirring occasionally to loosen

browned bits, until well browned (about 45 minutes). Remove from oven. Add tomatoes, broth mixture, and basil, stirring to loosen browned bits. Return to oven and continue to bake until mixture comes to a boil (about 10 minutes).

3. Remove from oven and stir in pasta. Cover tightly with foil, return to oven, and continue to bake until liquid is absorbed and pasta is tender to bite (about 15 minutes). Sprinkle with cheese. Makes 6 servings.

Per serving: 407 calories (22% calories from fat), 10 g total fat, 3 g saturated fat, 60 mg cholesterol, 913 mg sodium, 55 g carbohydrates, 4 g fiber, 24 g protein, 101 mg calcium, 3 mg iron

White rice cooked in low-fat milk and sweetened with coconut makes a superb, rich-tasting foil for this golden turkey curry.

....

Coconut Rice
(recipe follows)

2 tablespoons (30 ml) lemon juice

1 clove garlic, minced or pressed

½ teaspoon ground cumin

¼ teaspoon chili powder

2 turkey breast tenderloins (about 1 lb./455 g *total*), cut into 1-inch (2.5-cm) pieces

½ cup (75 g) golden raisins

¼ cup (60 ml) dry white wine

2 medium-size carrots (about 8 oz./230 g *total*), cut into ¼-inch (6-mm) slanting slices

1 large onion (about 8 oz./230 g), thinly sliced

2 teaspoons olive oil or salad oil

2 to 3 teaspoons curry powder

1 to 2 tablespoons chopped fresh mint or parsley

2 tablespoons salted roasted cashews, chopped

Mint or parsley sprigs

Stir-fried Curried Turkey with Coconut Rice

....

Preparation time: About 20 minutes
Cooking time: About 25 minutes

1. Prepare Coconut Rice. Meanwhile, in a large bowl, combine 1 tablespoon (15 ml) water, lemon juice, garlic, cumin, and chili powder. Add turkey and stir to coat. Set aside; stir occasionally. In a small bowl, combine raisins and wine; let stand until raisins are softened (about 10 minutes), stirring occasionally.

2. In a wide nonstick frying pan or wok, combine carrots, onion, and ¼ cup (60 ml) water. Cover and cook over medium-high heat until carrots are tender-crisp to bite (about 5 minutes). Uncover and stir-fry until liquid has evaporated. Remove vegetables from pan with a slotted spoon and keep warm.

3. Heat oil in pan. When oil is hot, add turkey mixture. Stir-fry just until meat

is no longer pink in center; cut to test (3 to 4 minutes). Add water, 1 tablespoon (15 ml) at a time, if pan appears dry. Add curry powder and stir-fry just until fragrant (about 30 seconds; do not scorch).

4. Add raisins (and soaking liquid) to pan; return vegetables to pan. Bring to a boil; then boil, stirring, until liquid has evaporated (about 2 minutes). Remove from heat; stir in chopped mint and cashews. Spoon Coconut Rice into 4 wide bowls; top with turkey mixture and garnish with mint sprigs. Makes 4 servings.

....

Coconut Rice. In a 3- to 4-quart (2.8- to 3.8-liter) pan, combine 1 cup (240 ml) *each* **water** and **low-fat milk.** Bring just to a boil over medium-high heat. Stir in 1 cup (185 g) **long-grain white rice.** Reduce heat, cover, and simmer until liquid has been absorbed and rice is tender to bite (about 20 minutes). Stir in ¼ cup (20 g) **sweetened shredded coconut.** Keep warm until ready to serve, fluffing occasionally with a fork.

....

Per serving: 502 calories (13% calories from fat), 7 g total fat, 2 g saturated fat, 72 mg cholesterol, 158 mg sodium, 70 g carbohydrates, 5 g fiber, 36 g protein, 152 mg calcium, 5 mg iron

---

This super company dish is sure to satisfy hearty appetites at brunch or supper.

....

1 pound (455 g) turkey Italian sausages (casings removed), crumbled into ½-inch (1-cm) pieces

1 cup (185 g) long-grain white rice

1 large onion (about 8 oz./230 g), chopped

2 cloves garlic, minced or pressed

2 cups (470 ml) fat-free reduced-sodium chicken broth

1½ cups (235 g) chopped tomatoes

¼ teaspoon saffron threads

Brunch Paella

....

Preparation time: About 15 minutes
Cooking time: 35 to 40 minutes

1 package (about 9 oz./255 g) frozen artichoke hearts, thawed and drained

¼ cup (15 g) chopped parsley
Lemon wedges

....

1. In a wide nonstick frying pan or wok, stir-fry sausage over medium-high heat until browned (7 to 10 minutes). Remove sausage from pan with a slotted spoon; set aside. Pour off and discard all but 1 teaspoon fat from pan.

2. Add rice to pan; stir-fry until rice begins to turn opaque (about 3 minutes). Add onion, garlic, and 2 tablespoons (30 ml) water; stir-fry for 5 more minutes. Add more water, 1 tablespoon (15 ml) at a time, if pan appears dry.

3. Stir in broth, tomatoes, saffron, artichokes, and parsley; then return sausage to pan. Bring to a boil; reduce heat, cover, and simmer until liquid has been absorbed and rice is tender to bite (about 20 minutes). Serve with lemon wedges. Makes 4 to 6 servings.

....

Per serving: 195 calories (3% calories from fat), 0.7 g total fat, 0.1 g saturated fat, 0 mg cholesterol, 294 mg sodium, 41 g carbohydrates, 4 g fiber, 7 g protein, 39 mg calcium, 2 mg iron

Mahogany Rice, Sausage & Fennel in Squash Bowls

Preparation time: 20 minutes
Cooking time: About 1 hour and 20 minutes

Squash "bowls" make a dramatic and sophisticated presentation for this delicately flavored entrée.

- 2 **medium-size acorn squash (about 3½ lbs./1.6 kg *total*)**
- 1 **head fennel (3 to 4 inches/8 to 10 cm in diameter, about 1 lb./455 g)**
- 8 **ounces (230 g) mild turkey Italian sausage, casings removed**
- 2 **tablespoons (30 ml) balsamic vinegar**
- 4½ **cups (1.1 liters) vegetable broth**
- 1 **cup (185 g) red or black (Wehani or Black Japonica) rice (sold in natural food stores), rinsed and drained**

1. Cut squash in half lengthwise; scoop out and discard seeds and fibers. Place squash halves, cut side down, in a 9- by 13-inch (23- by 33-cm) baking pan. Pour water into pan to a depth of about ½ inch (1 cm); bake in a 400°F (205°C) oven until squash is tender when pierced (about 50 minutes). Drain liquid from pan and keep squash warm.

2. Meanwhile, trim stems from fennel; reserve feathery green leaves, then discard stems. Trim and discard discolored parts of fennel. Thinly slice fennel, place in a 5- to 6-quart (5- to 6-liter) pan, and add sausage. Cook over medium-high heat, stirring often, until mixture is well browned (about 15 minutes). Then spoon off and discard any fat from pan.

3. Add vinegar and ½ cup (120 ml) of the broth to pan. Cook, stirring often, until liquid evaporates and browned bits stick to pan bottom (about 10 minutes). To deglaze pan, add ½ cup (120 ml) more broth, stirring to loosen browned bits from pan; continue to cook until browned bits form again. Add rice and remaining 3½ cups (830 ml) broth, stirring to loosen browned bits. Bring to a boil; then reduce heat, cover, and simmer until rice is tender to bite (about 50 minutes).

4. Meanwhile, finely chop about half the reserved fennel leaves. When rice is done, remove from heat and stir in chopped fennel leaves. Place squash halves, cut side up, on a platter or individual plates. Fill squash with rice mixture; sprinkle with remaining fennel leaves. Makes 4 servings.

Per serving: 405 calories (19% calories from fat), 9 g total fat, 2 g saturated fat, 43 mg cholesterol, 1,559 mg sodium, 69 g carbohydrates, 11 g fiber, 17 g protein, 133 mg calcium, 3 mg iron

Picadillo Stew

Preparation time: About 15 minutes
Cooking time: 20 to 25 minutes

Its name comes from the word **picar** *("to mince")—and as you might expect,* **picadillo** *is made with chopped ingredients. This version of the dish is a hearty turkey stew, richly seasoned with raisins, spices, and almonds. To complete the meal, serve Blue Corn Muffins (page 336) alongside.*

- 2 **tablespoons slivered almonds**
- ¼ **cup (120 ml) dry red wine**
- 2 **tablespoons (30 ml) reduced-sodium soy sauce**
- 1 **tablespoon (15 ml) lemon juice**
- 2 **teaspoons sugar**
- 1 **teaspoon *each* ground cumin, ground coriander, and chili powder**
- ⅛ **teaspoon ground cinnamon**
- 4 **teaspoons cornstarch**
- 1 **teaspoon salad oil**
- 1 **pound (455 g) boneless turkey breast, cut into 1-inch (2.5 cm) chunks**
- 1 **large onion, chopped**
- 2 **cloves garlic, minced or pressed**
- 1 **can (about 14½ oz./415 g) tomatoes**
- ⅔ **cup (97 g) raisins**
  Pepper

1. Toast almonds in a small frying pan over medium heat until golden (5 to 7 minutes), stirring often. Transfer almonds to a bowl and set aside.

2. In a small bowl, mix wine, soy sauce, lemon juice, sugar, cumin, coriander, chili powder, cinnamon, and cornstarch until smooth. Set aside.

3. Heat oil in a wide nonstick frying pan or 5-quart (4.7-liter) pan over high heat. Add turkey, onion, and garlic. Cook, stirring, until meat is no longer pink in thickest part; cut to test (10 to 15 minutes). Add water, 1 tablespoon (15 ml) at a time, if pan appears dry. Add tomatoes and their liquid (break tomatoes up with a spoon), wine mixture, and raisins to pan. Bring to a boil; boil, stirring, just until thickened.

4. To serve, ladle stew into bowls and sprinkle with almonds. Season to taste with pepper. Makes 4 servings.

Per serving: 317 calories (13% calories from fat), 5 g total fat, 0.7 g saturated fat, 70 mg cholesterol, 538 mg sodium, 36 g carbohydrates, 3 g fiber, 32 g protein, 87 mg calcium, 3 mg iron

The single word mole *names a whole category of Mexican sauces. One popular member of the group is mellow, slightly sweet* mole poblano, *well known for its inclusion of bitter chocolate. Traditional moles are made with chiles, fruits, nuts, spices, thickeners, and—often—volumes of lard. Our streamlined* mole poblano *eliminates much of the fat and replaces the chocolate with unsweetened cocoa, yet its flavor is still as deliciously complex as that of the original.*

To accompany the chicken and sauce, you might serve warm corn tortillas (page 346), hot cooked rice, and Zesty Refried Beans (page 148) sprinkled with cotija (a Mexican cheese) or grated Parmesan. For dessert, offer a fresh fruit plate.

- 1 tablespoon sesame seeds
- 1 large onion, chopped
- 4 cloves garlic, minced or pressed
- 1 small very ripe banana, chopped
- ¼ cup (46 g) chopped pitted prunes
- 2 tablespoons raisins
- 1 tablespoon (15 ml) creamy peanut butter
- 5 tablespoons (27 g) unsweetened cocoa powder
- 3 tablespoons chili powder
- 2 teaspoons sugar
- ½ teaspoon ground cinnamon
- ⅛ teaspoon *each* ground coriander, ground cumin, ground cloves, and anise seeds, crushed

Jalapeño Chicken with Mole Poblano

Preparation time: About 25 minutes
Cooking time: About 20 minutes
Pictured on facing page

- 2 cups (470 ml) low-sodium chicken broth
- 1 small can (about 6 oz./170 g) tomato paste
- 8 skinless, boneless chicken breast halves (about 6 oz./ 170 g *each*)
- 2 tablespoons (30 ml) mild jalapeño jelly, melted; or 2 tablespoons (30 ml) apple jelly, melted and mixed with ¹⁄₁₆ teaspoon ground red pepper (cayenne)
- Salt
- Lime wedges

1. Toast sesame seeds in a wide non-stick frying pan over medium heat until golden (about 4 minutes), stirring often. Transfer to a bowl; set aside.

2. To pan, add onion, garlic, banana, prunes, raisins, peanut butter, and 3 tablespoons (45 ml) water. Cook over medium heat, stirring often, until mixture is richly browned (10 to 15 minutes); if pan appears dry, add more water, 1 tablespoon (15 ml) at a time. Stir in cocoa, chili powder, sugar, cinnamon, coriander, cumin, cloves, anise seeds, and ¾ cup (180 ml) of the broth. Bring mixture to a boil over medium-high heat.

3. Transfer hot onion mixture to a food processor or blender and add tomato paste, 2 teaspoons of the sesame seeds, and a little of the remaining broth. Whirl until smoothly puréed; then stir in remaining broth. Cover and keep warm. Or, if made ahead, let cool; then cover and refrigerate for up to 3 days (freeze for longer storage). Reheat before continuing.

4. While onion mixture is browning, rinse chicken and pat dry. Place jelly in a bowl and stir to soften; add chicken and mix to coat. Then place chicken in a lightly oiled 10- by 15-inch (25- by 38-cm) rimmed baking pan. Bake in a 450°F (230°C) oven until meat in thickest part is no longer pink; cut to test (12 to 15 minutes).

5. To serve, spoon some of the warm mole sauce onto dinner plates; top with chicken, then more mole sauce. Sprinkle with remaining 1 teaspoon sesame seeds. Season to taste with salt; serve with lime wedges. Makes 8 servings.

Per serving: 264 calories (18% calories from fat), 6 g total fat, 1 g saturated fat, 74 mg cholesterol, 322 mg sodium, 23 g carbohydrates, 4 g fiber, 34 g protein, 65 mg calcium, 3 mg iron

Jalapeño Chicken with Mole Poblano
(recipe on facing page)

Turkey Stir-fry by the Numbers

Stir-fries are generally simple dishes: bite-size pieces of meat, poultry, or fish, sliced vegetables, and a light sauce to meld all the flavors. But when you don't have a recipe to follow, figuring out the correct proportions of ingredients can be tricky. To help you, we devised the chart at right below; it lists the amounts to use for a two-, four-, or six-serving turkey stir-fry.

To make the cooking process especially fast, we start with leftover cooked turkey or other meat. You can choose from a variety of vegetables; for a good balance of flavor and texture, use three or four different kinds. If you're really short on time, you can turn to the precut fresh vegetables available at most supermarkets. Be aware, though, that these are sometimes drier than freshly cut vegetables.

Unusual and delicious combinations that go well with turkey include: Japanese eggplant, onions, Chinese pea pods, and carrots; yams, bell peppers, and button mushrooms; onions, broccoli, and mustard greens; zucchini, yellow bell peppers, onions, and enoki mushrooms; and red onions, green beans, and dried cranberries.

Our spicy cooking sauce complements whatever meat and vegetables you use. If you plan to serve the stir-fry over rice or pasta, double the sauce, since the rice or pasta will absorb much of it. (You can assemble the sauce ahead and refrigerate it for up to 2 days.)

....

Cooking Sauce. In a small bowl, combine ⅓ cup (80 ml) **fat-free reduced-sodium chicken broth;** ⅓ cup (80 ml) **mirin** or cream sherry; ¼ cup (60 ml) **reduced-sodium soy sauce;** 3 tablespoons minced **fresh ginger;** 3 cloves **garlic,** minced or pressed; 1 tablespoon **cornstarch;** and 2 teaspoons **Oriental sesame oil.** Makes 1 cup (240 ml).

....

Cooking directions. Follow the steps below, referring to the amounts shown in the chart.

1. Prepare Cooking Sauce.

2. Heat oil in a wide nonstick frying pan or wok over medium-high heat. When oil is hot, add your choice of cut-up fresh vegetables. Stir-fry until vegetables are hot and bright in color; vegetables may begin to brown (about 2 minutes).

3. Add broth (if using chicken broth, use the fat-free reduced-sodium type). Cover and cook until vegetables are just tender (2 to 6 minutes). Uncover; stir-fry until liquid has evaporated.

4. Stir Cooking Sauce well; pour into pan, then add turkey. Bring to a boil, stirring. Stir in your choice of additions and cook until all ingredients are heated through (30 seconds to 2 minutes).

5. Spoon stir-fry onto a platter; sprin-kle with a topping, if desired. Serve with rice, pasta, or napa cabbage.

Stir-fry Proportions & Choices

INGREDIENTS	SERVES 2	SERVES 4	SERVES 6
Cooking oil Olive or vegetable	2 tsp.	1 tbsp.	1½ tbsp.
Vegetables Broccoli flowerets, bell pepper wedges (green, red, or yellow), sliced carrots, green beans (cut into 1½-inch pieces), sliced Japanese eggplant, onion wedges, sliced mushrooms (button or shiitake), yams (peeled and thinly sliced), or sliced zucchini	3 cups	5 cups	7 cups
Broth or water	¼ cup	⅓ cup	⅓ cup
Cooking Sauce (above)	½ cup	¾ cup	1 cup
Cooked turkey or meat Cut into bite-size pieces	1 cup	2 cups	3 cups
Additions Anaheim or pasilla chiles (sliced and seeded), Chinese pea pods (ends and strings removed), mustard greens, or kale or red cabbage (thinly sliced)	**Vary amounts to personal taste**		
Toppings Dried cranberries, pitted calamata or green olives, crushed red pepper flakes, or enoki mushrooms	**Vary amounts to personal taste**		
On the side Cooked white or brown rice or noodles; or uncooked, thinly sliced napa cabbage	2 cups	4 cups	6 cups

Crisp bread crumbs coat these moist, lemon-seasoned chicken breasts.

....

6 **boneless, skinless chicken breast halves (about 2¼ lbs./ 1.1 kg *total*)**

1¼ **cups (38 g) soft whole wheat bread crumbs**

2 **tablespoons chopped fresh rosemary or 2 teaspoons dried rosemary**

1 **tablespoon chopped Italian or regular parsley**

1 **teaspoon grated lemon peel**

½ **teaspoon pepper**

1 **tablespoon (15 ml) lemon juice**
Lemon wedges
Salt

Lemon Rosemary Chicken

....

Preparation time: 15 minutes
Cooking time: About 25 minutes

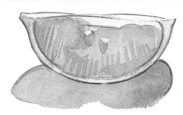

1. Rinse chicken and pat dry; then arrange, skinned side up, in an oiled shallow 10- by 15-inch (25- by 38-cm) baking pan. Set aside.

2. In a small bowl, mix bread crumbs, rosemary, parsley, lemon peel, and pepper. Moisten top of each chicken piece with lemon juice; press crumb mixture equally over each piece, covering evenly.

3. Bake in a 400°F (205°C) oven until crumb coating is browned and meat in thickest part is no longer pink; cut to test (about 25 minutes). Season chicken to taste with lemon and salt. Makes 6 servings.

....

Per serving: 185 calories (11% calories from fat), 2 g total fat, 0.5 g saturated fat, 88 mg cholesterol, 133 mg sodium, 3 g carbohydrates, 0.5 g fiber, 36 g protein, 28 mg calcium, 1 mg iron

---

The deeply mellow flavor of roasted garlic teams with mild, nutty fontina for an enticing combination of flavors.

....

1 **large head garlic (about 4 oz./115 g)**

½ **teaspoon olive oil**

4 **boneless, skinless chicken breast halves (1½ lbs./680 g *total*)**

1 **tablespoon chopped fresh thyme or 1 teaspoon dried thyme**

¼ **teaspoon coarsely ground pepper**

⅛ **teaspoon salt**

¼ **cup (28 g) shredded fontina cheese**

4 **small thyme sprigs**

Garlic Chicken

....

Preparation time: 15 minutes
Cooking time: About 1½ hours

1. Slice ¼ inch (6 mm) off top of garlic head. Then rub garlic with oil. Wrap garlic in foil and bake in a 375°F (190°C) oven until very soft when pressed (about 1¼ hours). Carefully remove garlic from foil; transfer to a rack and let stand until cool enough to touch (about 10 minutes).

2. Meanwhile, rinse chicken, pat dry, and sprinkle with chopped thyme and pepper. Place, skinned side up, in a lightly oiled 9-inch (23-cm) baking pan. Bake in a 450°F (230°C) oven until meat in thickest part is no longer

pink; cut to test (12 to 15 minutes). Meanwhile, squeeze garlic cloves from skins into a small bowl. Add salt; mash garlic thoroughly with a fork, incorporating salt.

3. Spread a fourth of the garlic mixture over each chicken piece; then sprinkle chicken with cheese. Return to oven; continue to bake just until cheese is melted and bubbly (about 3 more minutes). Press a thyme sprig into cheese on each piece of chicken. Makes 4 servings.

....

Per serving: 258 calories (18% calories from fat), 5 g total fat, 2 g saturated fat, 107 mg cholesterol, 241 mg sodium, 9 g carbohydrates, 0.5 g fiber, 43 g protein, 112 mg calcium, 2 mg iron

Chicken Curry in Pita Bread
(recipe on facing page)

Like Mu Shu Sandwiches (page 156), these chicken- and vegetable-stuffed pita breads are a satisfying choice for lunch or supper.

½ cup (75 g) raisins or dried currants

1 cup (240 ml) plain nonfat yogurt

2 tablespoons cornstarch

2 teaspoons olive oil

12 ounces (340 g) boneless, skinless chicken breast, cut into ½-inch (1-cm) pieces

1 medium-size onion, chopped

2 cloves garlic, minced or pressed

2 teaspoons curry powder

½ cup (160 g) apricot jam or preserves
 Salt and pepper

1 medium-size cucumber (about 8 oz./230 g), very thinly sliced

4 pita breads (*each* about 6 inches/15 cm in diameter), cut crosswise into halves

Chicken Curry in Pita Bread

Preparation time: About 20 minutes
Cooking time: About 20 minutes
Pictured on facing page

1. In a small bowl, combine raisins and ¼ cup (60 ml) water; let stand until raisins are softened (about 10 minutes), stirring occasionally. Meanwhile, in another small bowl, stir together yogurt and cornstarch until smoothly blended; set aside.

2. Heat oil in a wide nonstick frying pan or wok over medium-high heat. When oil is hot, add chicken and 1 tablespoon (15 ml) water. Stir-fry until meat is no longer pink in center; cut to test (3 to 4 minutes). Remove chicken from pan with a slotted spoon and keep warm. Discard drippings from pan.

3. Add onion, garlic, curry powder, and ¼ cup (60 ml) water to pan; stir-fry until onion is soft (about 4 minutes; do not scorch). Add water, 1 tablespoon (15 ml) at a time, if pan appears dry.

4. Add raisins (and soaking water) and jam. Bring to a boil; then boil, stirring, until almost all liquid has evaporated (5 to 7 minutes). Reduce heat to medium-low; stir in chicken and yogurt mixture. Simmer gently, stirring constantly, until sauce is slightly thickened (do not boil). Season to taste with salt and pepper.

5. To serve, divide cucumber slices equally among bread halves; fill equally with chicken mixture. Makes 4 servings.

Per serving: 506 calories (8% calories from fat), 5 g total fat, 0.8 g saturated fat, 51 mg cholesterol, 442 mg sodium, 88 g carbohydrates, 4 g fiber, 30 g protein, 215 mg calcium, 3 mg iron

---

Our trim rendition of this traditional French dish delivers all the satisfaction of its counterpart without the high fat content.

1 large onion, chopped

2 medium-size carrots (about 8 oz./230 g *total*), thinly sliced

1 medium-size red bell pepper (about 6 oz./170 g), seeded and thinly sliced

3 cloves garlic, minced or pressed

1 can (about 14½ oz./415 g) low-sodium stewed tomatoes

1¾ cups (420 ml) vegetable broth

⅔ cup (160 ml) dry red wine

1 teaspoon dried thyme

1 dried bay leaf

¼ teaspoon *each* pepper and liquid hot pepper seasoning

2 cans (about 15 oz./425 g *each*) cannellini (white kidney beans), drained and rinsed

Light Cassoulet

Preparation time: 30 minutes
Cooking time: About 1½ hours

1½ pounds (680 g) boneless, skinless chicken breasts, cut into 1-inch (2.5-cm) pieces

4 ounces (115 g) turkey kielbasa (Polish sausage), thinly sliced

¼ cup (15 g) finely chopped parsley

1. In a 5- to 6-quart (5- to 6-liter) pan, combine onion, carrots, bell pepper, garlic, and ½ cup (120 ml) water. Cook over medium-high heat, stirring often, until liquid evaporates and browned bits stick to pan bottom (about 10 minutes). To deglaze pan, add ⅓ cup (80 ml) water, stirring to loosen browned bits from pan; continue to cook until browned bits form again. Repeat deglazing step about 2 more times or until vegetables are browned, using ⅓ cup (80 ml) water each time.

2. Stir in tomatoes and their liquid, broth, wine, thyme, bay leaf, pepper, and hot pepper seasoning. Bring to a boil; then reduce heat, cover, and simmer for 45 minutes.

3. Stir in beans; simmer, uncovered, for 10 minutes. Stir in chicken and sausage. Continue to simmer, uncovered, until chicken is no longer pink in center; cut to test (about 10 more minutes). Just before serving, remove and discard bay leaf. To serve, ladle mixture into bowls and sprinkle with parsley. Makes 8 servings.

Per serving: 240 calories (12% calories from fat), 3 g total fat, 1 g saturated fat, 59 mg cholesterol, 557 mg sodium, 24 g carbohydrates, 7 g fiber, 29 g protein, 75 mg calcium, 3 mg iron

Fragrant Chinese five-spice stars in this entrée.

- 2 ounces (55 g) dried shiitake mushrooms
- 1 clove garlic, minced or pressed
- 1½ teaspoons Chinese five-spice; or ½ teaspoon *each* anise seeds and ground ginger and ¼ teaspoon *each* ground cinnamon and ground cloves
- 3 tablespoons (45 ml) reduced-sodium soy sauce
- 1 tablespoon sugar
- 1 tablespoon (15 ml) dry sherry
- 1 chicken (4½ to 5 lbs./2 to 2.3 kg)
- 14 ounces (400 g) dried perciatelli, bucatini, or spaghetti
- 1¼ pounds (565 g) broccoli flowerets

  Oriental Dressing (recipe follows)
- 3 tablespoons minced green onions

  Salt and pepper

1. Soak mushrooms in boiling water to cover until soft (about 20 minutes). Lift out and squeeze dry; discard liquid. Cut off and discard coarse stems. Slice in half, if desired. Place in a large bowl and set aside.

2. Combine garlic, five-spice, and 1 tablespoon (15 ml) water in a small nonstick frying pan over medium heat.

Five-Spice Chicken with Perciatelli

Preparation time: About 35 minutes
Cooking time: About 1 hour

Cook, stirring, just until fragrant and hot; do not scorch. Remove from heat and add soy sauce, sugar and sherry; stir until blended.

3. Rinse chicken and pat dry; reserve giblets for other uses. Place chicken, breast side up, on a rack in a 9- by 13-inch (23- by 33-cm) baking pan. Baste with five-spice mixture. Pour remaining mixture into cavity. Roast in a 375°F (190°C) oven until meat near thighbone is no longer pink; cut to test (about 1 hour); if drippings begin to scorch, add ⅓ cup (80 ml) water, stirring to loosen browned bits. Meanwhile bring 16 cups (3.8 liters) water to a boil in a 6- to 8-quart (6- to 8-liter) pan over medium-high heat. Stir in pasta and cook for 7 minutes. Add broccoli and cook, stirring occasionally, just until pasta is tender to bite and broccoli is tender-crisp (about 5 more minutes). Drain well and transfer to bowl with mushrooms; keep warm.

4. Prepare Oriental Dressing. Pour warm dressing over pasta; gently lift with 2 forks to mix. Keep warm.

5. Lift out chicken, draining juices into pan, and place on a platter. Stir juices to loosen browned bits. Pour into a serving container and skim off and discard fat; add onions. Mound pasta around chicken. Offer juices, salt, and pepper to add to taste. Makes 6 to 8 servings.

Oriental Dressing. In a 1- to 1½-quart (950-ml to 1.4-liter) pan, combine ½ cup (120 ml) **seasoned rice vinegar** (or ½ cup/120 ml rice vinegar and 4 teaspoons sugar); 3 tablespoons (45 ml) **reduced-sodium soy sauce;** 1 teaspoon **ground coriander;** and 1 or 2 cloves **garlic,** minced or pressed. Season to taste with **crushed red pepper flakes.** Bring just to a boil over medium heat. Use warm. Makes about ⅔ cup (160 ml).

Per serving: 615 calories (29% calories from fat), 20 g total fat, 5 g saturated fat, 119 mg cholesterol, 989 mg sodium, 60 g carbohydrates, 6 g fiber, 49 g protein, 71 mg calcium, 5 mg iron

Spiked with ginger, this specialty from the Philippines combines pasta, vegetables, chicken, and shrimp.

- 6 ounces (170 g) dried spaghetti
- 1 large onion (about 8 oz./230 g), finely chopped
- 4 cups (280 g) finely shredded cabbage
- 2 cups (280 g) diced cooked skinless chicken
- 1 cup (130 g) thinly sliced carrots
- ½ cup (120 ml) low-sodium chicken broth
- 1 tablespoon minced fresh ginger
- 4 cloves garlic, minced or pressed
- ¼ teaspoon pepper
- 3 tablespoons (45 ml) oyster sauce (or 2 tablespoons/30 ml reduced-sodium soy sauce) or to taste
- 2 tablespoons (30 ml) seasoned rice vinegar (or 2 tablespoons/ 30 ml distilled white vinegar and 1 teaspoon sugar) or to taste

Chicken & Shrimp Pansit

Preparation time: About 25 minutes
Cooking time: About 45 minutes

- 4 green onions
- 8 ounces (230 g) tiny cooked shrimp
- 2 large hard-cooked eggs, shelled, cut into wedges (optional)

1. Bring 8 cups (1.9 liters) water to a boil in a 4- to 5-quart (3.8- to 5-liter) pan over medium-high heat. Stir in pasta and cook just until tender to bite (8 to 10 minutes); or cook according to package directions. Drain well and set aside.

2. Combine chopped onion and 2 tablespoons (30 ml) water in a wide nonstick frying pan over high heat. Cook, stirring often, until liquid has evaporated and browned bits stick to bottom. To deglaze pan, add ¼ cup

(60 ml) more water, stirring to loosen browned bits. Continue to cook, stirring often, until liquid has evaporated and onion sticks to pan bottom again. Repeat deglazing step, adding ¼ cup (60 ml) more water each time, until onion is richly browned (about 15 minutes total).

3. Add pasta, cabbage, chicken, carrots, broth, ginger, garlic, and pepper to onion. Pour in oyster sauce and vinegar. Cook, stirring often, until liquid has evaporated and browned bits stick to pan bottom (about 10 minutes). Meanwhile, thinly slice 2 of the green onions; set aside.

4. Add ¼ cup (60 ml) water and remove from heat; stir to loosen browned bits. Transfer to a platter. Top with shrimp and sliced green onions. Garnish with remaining whole onions and, if desired, eggs. Makes 6 servings.

Per serving: 288 calories (15% calories from fat), 5 g total fat, 1 g saturated fat, 115 mg cholesterol, 611 mg sodium, 33 g carbohydrates, 3 g fiber, 28 g protein, 78 mg calcium, 4 mg iron

---

Dijon mustard, basil, and a touch of prosciutto flavor a hearty stir-fry to serve over spinach pasta.

- ½ cup (120 ml) fat-free reduced-sodium chicken broth or dry white wine
- ¼ cup (60 ml) Dijon mustard
- 2 tablespoons (30 ml) lemon juice
- 1 teaspoon dried basil
- 8 ounces (230 g) dried spinach spaghetti
- 2 teaspoons olive oil
- 4 green onions, thinly sliced
- 2 cloves garlic, minced or pressed
- 1 ounce (30 g) prosciutto, cut into thin strips

Pasta with Stir-fried Chicken & Prosciutto

Preparation time: About 10 minutes
Cooking time: About 15 minutes

- 1 pound (455 g) boneless, skinless chicken breast, cut into ½- by 2-inch (1- by 5-cm) strips

1. In a small bowl, stir together broth, mustard, lemon juice, and basil. Set aside.

2. In a 4- to 5-quart (3.8- to 5-liter) pan, cook spaghetti in 8 cups (1.9 liters) boiling water until just tender to bite

(8 to 10 minutes); or cook according to package directions.

3. Meanwhile, heat oil in a wide nonstick frying pan or wok over medium heat. When oil is hot, add onions, garlic, and prosciutto; stir-fry until prosciutto is lightly browned (about 3 minutes).

4. Increase heat to medium-high. Add chicken and stir-fry until no longer pink in center; cut to test (3 to 4 minutes). Add broth mixture to pan and bring to a boil. Remove from heat.

5. Drain pasta well and place in a warm wide bowl; spoon chicken mixture over pasta. Makes 4 servings.

Per serving: 399 calories (13% calories from fat), 6 g total fat, 1 g saturated fat, 72 mg cholesterol, 670 mg sodium, 45 g carbohydrates, 6 g fiber, 37 g protein, 68 mg calcium, 3 mg iron

Chicken chunks and snow peas are cloaked in a highly seasoned sauce, then lightly sprinkled with peanuts.

- 1 **cup (185 g) long-grain white rice**
  Cooking Sauce (recipe follows)
- 1½ **cups (115 g) Chinese pea pods (also called snow or sugar peas) or sugar snap peas, ends and strings removed**
- 1 **tablespoon cornstarch**
- 1 **tablespoon (15 ml) dry white wine**
- ½ **teaspoon sugar**
- 1 **pound (455 g) boneless, skinless chicken breast, cut into ¾-inch (2-cm) chunks**
- 2 **cloves garlic, minced or pressed**
- 1 **cup (130 g) peeled, shredded jicama**
- 2 **tablespoons salted roasted peanuts, chopped**

Kung Pao Chicken

Preparation time: About 25 minutes
Cooking time: About 25 minutes

1. In a 3- to 4-quart (2.8- to 3.8-liter) pan, bring 2 cups (470 ml) water to a boil over high heat; stir in rice. Reduce heat, cover, and simmer until liquid has been absorbed and rice is tender to bite (about 20 minutes). Meanwhile, prepare Cooking Sauce; set aside. Cut pea pods diagonally into ¾-inch (2-cm) pieces; set aside.

2. In a large bowl, dissolve cornstarch in wine; stir in sugar. Add chicken and stir to coat. Then turn chicken mixture into a wide nonstick frying pan or wok; add garlic and 1 tablespoon (15 ml) water. Stir-fry over medium-high heat until meat is no longer pink in center; cut to test (4 to 6 minutes). Remove from pan with a slotted spoon

and keep warm.

3. Add pea pods, jicama, and 1 tablespoon (15 ml) water to pan; stir-fry until pea pods are tender-crisp to bite (about 1 minute). Stir Cooking Sauce well; pour into pan and bring to a boil. Remove from heat and stir in chicken.

4. Spoon rice onto a rimmed platter; top with chicken mixture and sprinkle with peanuts. Makes 4 servings.

Cooking Sauce. Mix 1 tablespoon *each* **sugar** and **chili paste with garlic;** 1 tablespoon (15 ml) **unseasoned rice vinegar** or distilled white vinegar; and 1 tablespoon (15 ml) *each* **hoisin sauce** and **Oriental sesame oil.**

Per serving: 425 calories (19% calories from fat), 9 g total fat, 1 g saturated fat, 66 mg cholesterol, 122 mg sodium, 51 g carbohydrates, 3 g fiber, 33 g protein, 63 mg calcium, 4 mg iron

---

For a refreshing contrast to their slightly sweet taste, squeeze a little lemon juice over the chicken and sauce.

- 1 **cup (185 g) long-grain white rice**
- 1 **package (about 10 oz./285 g) frozen tiny peas, thawed and drained**
  Cooking Sauce (recipe follows)
- 2 **teaspoons Ginger Oil (page 109); or 2 teaspoons salad oil mixed with ¼ teaspoon ground ginger**
- 1 **pound (455 g) boneless, skinless chicken breast, cut into ¾-inch (2-cm) pieces**
- 2 **tablespoons sliced green onion**
  Lemon wedges

1. In a 3- to 4-quart (2.8- to 3.8-liter) pan, bring 2 cups (470 ml) water to a boil over high heat; stir in rice. Reduce

Peanut Chicken with Rice

Preparation time: About 15 minutes
Cooking time: About 25 minutes

heat, cover, and simmer until liquid has been absorbed and rice is tender to bite (about 20 minutes). Stir peas into rice; remove from heat and keep warm. Fluff occasionally with a fork. While rice is cooking, prepare Cooking Sauce and set aside.

2. Heat oil in a wide nonstick frying pan or wok over medium-high heat. When oil is hot, add chicken and stir-fry until no longer pink in center; cut to test (4 to 6 minutes). Remove chicken from pan with a slotted spoon and keep warm. Discard drippings from pan and wipe pan clean (be careful; pan is hot).

3. Stir Cooking Sauce well and pour into pan. Stir over medium heat just until smoothly blended and heated through. Add chicken and onion; remove pan from heat and stir to coat chicken and onion with sauce.

4. Spoon rice mixture onto a rimmed platter and top with chicken mixture. Offer lemon wedges to squeeze over stir-fry to taste. Makes 4 servings.

Cooking Sauce. In a small bowl, stir together 3 tablespoons (45 ml) crunchy or smooth **peanut butter,** 3 tablespoons (45 ml) **plum jam** or grape jelly, 2 tablespoons (30 ml) **water,** 1½ teaspoons *each* **lemon juice** and **reduced-sodium soy sauce,** and 1 teaspoon **Oriental sesame oil.**

Per serving: 481 calories (21% calories from fat), 11 g total fat, 2 g saturated fat, 66 mg cholesterol, 312 mg sodium, 58 g carbohydrates, 4 g fiber, 36 g protein, 49 mg calcium, 4 mg iron

This classic chicken-and-rice dish is perfect for a casual Mexican-style dinner.

1   can (about 14½ oz./415 g) tomatoes

    About 1½ cups (360 ml) low-sodium chicken broth

1   chicken (3 to 3½ lbs./1.35 to 1.6 kg), cut up and skinned

1   teaspoon salad oil

1   large onion, chopped

1   small green pepper (about ⅓ lb./150 g), seeded and chopped

2   cloves garlic, minced or pressed (optional)

1   cup (185 g) long-grain white rice

1   teaspoon dry oregano

¼   teaspoon *each* ground cumin and pepper

1   dry bay leaf

1   package (about 10 oz./285 g) frozen tiny peas, thawed

    Salt

¼   cup (25 g) thinly sliced green onions

Arroz con Pollo

Preparation time: About 15 minutes
Cooking time: About 1 hour and 10 minutes

1. Drain liquid from tomatoes into a glass measure; add enough broth to make 2 cups (470 ml) liquid.

2. Rinse chicken and pat dry. Heat oil in a 4- to 5-quart (3.8- to 4.7-liter) pan over medium-high heat. Add several pieces of chicken (do not crowd pan) and 2 tablespoons (30 ml) water; cook, turning as needed, until chicken is browned on all sides (about 10 minutes). Add more water, 1 tablespoon (15 ml) at a time, if pan appears dry. Repeat to brown remaining chicken, setting pieces aside as they are browned. Discard all but 1 teaspoon of the drippings.

3. Add chopped onion, bell pepper, and garlic (if desired) to pan; cook, stirring, until onion is soft (about 5 minutes). Stir in tomatoes (break them up with a spoon), broth mixture, rice, oregano, cumin, pepper, and bay leaf. Bring to a boil.

4. Return chicken to pan. Reduce heat, cover, and simmer until meat near thighbone is no longer pink; cut to test (about 45 minutes). Add more broth as needed to prevent sticking. Stir in peas; season to taste with salt. Just before serving, garnish with green onions. Makes 6 servings.

Per serving: 331 calories (15% calories from fat), 6 g total fat, 1 g saturated fat, 83 mg cholesterol, 299 mg sodium, 38 g carbohydrates, 3 g fiber, 32 g protein, 71 mg calcium, 4 mg iron

---

Complement this creamy entrée with colorful and snappy Garlic & Rosemary Green Beans (page 303).

2   teaspoons olive oil

2   boneless, skinless chicken breast halves (about 12 oz./340 g *total*), cut into ¾-inch (2-cm) pieces

⅛   teaspoon salt (or to taste)

1   large onion, chopped

1½ teaspoons chopped fresh sage or ¾ teaspoon dried rubbed sage

¼   teaspoon pepper

3½ cups (830 ml) vegetable broth

1⅓ cups (270 g) pearl barley, rinsed and drained

1   package (about 10 oz./285 g) frozen corn kernels, thawed and drained

Creamy Barley with Chicken

Preparation time: 15 minutes
Cooking time: About 40 minutes

1   can (about 15 oz./425 g) cream-style corn

¼   cup (15 g) finely chopped parsley

    Sage sprigs (optional)

1. Heat oil in a 4- to 5-quart (3.8- to 5-liter) pan over medium-high heat. Add chicken and salt. Cook, stirring often, until chicken is no longer pink in center; cut to test (2 to 3 minutes). Remove from pan with a slotted spoon and set aside.

2. Add onion, chopped sage, pepper, and ¼ cup (60 ml) water to pan. Cook, stirring often, until onion is soft (about 5 minutes). Stir in broth and barley and bring to a boil; then reduce heat, cover, and simmer until barley is tender to bite (about 30 minutes).

3. Add corn kernels, cream-style corn, and chicken. Cook, stirring, just until heated through. Spoon barley mixture onto a rimmed platter and sprinkle with parsley. Garnish with sage sprigs, if desired. Makes 6 servings.

Per serving: 352 calories (10% calories from fat), 4 g total fat, 1 g saturated fat, 33 mg cholesterol, 874 mg sodium, 62 g carbohydrates, 9 g fiber, 21 g protein, 36 mg calcium, 2 mg iron

Fillings

To add interest to tacos, burritos, tostadas, or enchiladas, simply experiment with different fillings. Though some of these fillings get more than 30 percent of their calories from fat, they still have a place in a low-fat diet; just combine them with vegetables, tortillas, and other low-fat ingredients.

Zesty Refried Beans

2　medium-size onions, chopped

2　cloves garlic, minced or pressed

2　teaspoons salad oil

2　cans (about 15 oz./425 g *each*) pinto or other beans

2　tablespoons (30 ml) cider vinegar

　About ⅛ teaspoon ground red pepper (cayenne), or to taste

　Salt (optional)

1. In a wide nonstick frying pan, combine onions, garlic, oil, and 1 tablespoon (15 ml) water. Cook over medium heat, stirring often, until mixture is deep golden (20 to 30 minutes); if onions stick to pan bottom or pan appears dry, add more water, 1 tablespoon (15 ml) at a time.

2. Drain beans, reserving ½ cup (120 ml) of the liquid from cans.

3. To pan, add beans, reserved liquid (use ½ cup/120 ml low-sodium chicken broth if using home-cooked beans), vinegar, and red pepper. Coarsely mash beans with a spoon. Season to taste with salt, if desired. Heat until steaming. If made ahead, let cool; then cover and refrigerate until next day. Reheat before serving. Makes about 3¼ cups (770 ml).

Per serving: 136 calories (13% calories from fat), 2 g total fat, 0.3 g saturated fat, 0 mg cholesterol, 591 mg sodium, 24 g carbohydrates, 6 g fiber, 7 g protein, 60 mg calcium, 2 mg iron

Refried Black Beans

4　ounces (115 g) bacon, coarsely chopped

2　medium-size onions, chopped

2　cloves garlic, minced or pressed

2　cans (about 15 oz./425 g *each*) black beans

　About 2 tablespoons (30 ml) distilled white vinegar, or to taste

　Pepper

1. In a wide nonstick frying pan, cook bacon over medium heat, stirring often, until it begins to brown and drippings form in pan (about 4 minutes). Discard all but 1 tablespoon (15 ml) of the drippings.

2. Add onions and garlic to pan; cook, stirring often, until onions are soft and bacon is browned (about 7 minutes).

3. Drain beans, reserving ½ cup (120 ml) of the liquid from cans.

4. Add beans, reserved liquid (use ½ cup/120 ml low-sodium chicken broth if using home-cooked beans), and vinegar to pan. Coarsely mash beans with a spoon. Season to taste with pepper. Heat until steaming. If made ahead, let cool; then cover and refrigerate until next day. Reheat before serving. Makes about 3¼ cups (770 ml).

Per serving: 178 calories (34% calories from fat), 7 g total fat, 2 g saturated fat, 9 mg cholesterol, 529 mg sodium, 20 g carbohydrates, 7 g fiber, 10 g protein, 49 mg calcium, 3 mg iron

Shredded Chicken Filling

6　dried ancho or pasilla chiles (about 1½ oz./45 g *total*)

1　teaspoon salad oil

2　large onions, chopped

2　cloves garlic, minced or pressed

1　can (about 14½ oz./415 g) tomatoes

2　teaspoons sugar

1　teaspoon dried oregano

½　teaspoon ground cumin

2　cups (280 g) finely shredded cooked chicken or turkey breast

　Salt and pepper

1. Place chiles on a baking sheet and toast in a 300°F (150°C) oven until fragrant (3 to 4 minutes). Remove from oven; let cool. Discard stems, seeds, and veins; then place chiles in a bowl, cover with 1½ cups (360 ml) boiling water, and let stand until pliable (about 30 minutes).

2. While chiles are soaking,

place oil, onions, garlic, and 1 tablespoon (15 ml) water in a wide nonstick frying pan. Cook over medium heat, stirring often, until mixture is deep golden (20 to 30 minutes); if onions stick to pan or pan appears dry, add more water, 1 tablespoon (15 ml) at a time.

3. Drain chiles, discarding liquid. In a blender or food processor, whirl chiles, tomatoes and their liquid, sugar, oregano, and cumin until smoothly puréed.

4. Stir chicken and chile-tomato mixture into onion mixture. Reduce heat and simmer, uncovered, stirring occasionally, until mixture is thick and flavors are blended (about 10 minutes). Season to taste with salt and pepper. Makes about 3 cups (710 ml).

Per serving: 90 calories (24% calories from fat), 3 g total fat, 0.5 g saturated fat, 20 mg cholesterol, 75 mg sodium, 10 g carbohydrates, 0.9 g fiber, 9 g protein, 34 mg calcium, 1 mg iron

Turkey Chorizo Sausage

1 large onion, chopped

2 teaspoons *each* chili powder and dried oregano

1 teaspoon *each* cumin seeds and crushed red pepper flakes

1 cup (240 ml) low-sodium chicken broth

1 pound (455 g) ground turkey or chicken breast

½ cup (120 ml) cider vinegar

1. In a wide frying pan, combine onion, chili powder, oregano, cumin seeds, red pepper flakes, and broth. Bring to a boil over high heat; boil, stirring occasionally, until liquid has

evaporated and browned bits stick to pan. Add 2 tablespoons (30 ml) water, stirring to scrape browned bits free; cook until mixture begins to brown again. Repeat this deglazing step, adding 2 tablespoons (30 ml) of water each time, until onion is a rich brown color.

2. Add 2 tablespoons (30 ml) more water, then crumble turkey into pan; cook, stirring, until browned bits stick to pan. Repeat deglazing step, adding vinegar in 2-tablespoon (30-ml) portions, until mixture is a rich brown color. If made ahead, let cool; then cover and refrigerate until next day. Makes about 3½ cups (830 ml).

Per serving: 48 calories (9% calories from fat), 0.5 g total fat, 0.1 g saturated fat, 20 mg cholesterol, 92 mg sodium, 2 g carbohydrates, 0.4 g fiber, 8 g protein, 13 mg calcium, 0.7 mg iron

Birria-style Brisket

4 dried red New Mexico or California chiles (1 to 1½ oz./ 30 to 45 g *total*); or ¼ cup (24 g) chili powder

2 small dried hot red chiles

4 cups (950 ml) water

1½ cups (360 ml) dry red wine

¼ cup (60 ml) red wine vinegar

6 cloves garlic, peeled

1½ teaspoons *each* ground cumin and dried oregano

½ teaspoon ground cinnamon

1 piece center-cut beef brisket (2½ to 3 lbs./1.15 to 1.35 kg), trimmed of fat

4 large onions, thinly sliced

1. Remove and discard stems, seeds, and veins from New Mexico and hot chiles. Rinse

chiles, place in a 2- to 3-quart (1.9- to 2.8-liter) pan, and add water. Bring to a boil over high heat. Remove from heat, cover, and let stand until pliable (about 30 minutes). Drain chiles; then place chiles (or chili powder) in a blender or food processor and add wine, vinegar, garlic, cumin, oregano, and cinnamon. Whirl until smoothly puréed.

2. Place brisket in a 12- by 15-inch (30- by 38-cm) roasting pan; top with chili purée and onions. Cover pan tightly with foil. (At this point, you may refrigerate until next day.)

3. Bake, covered, in a 350°F (175°C) oven until meat is very tender when pierced (about 4 hours). Let meat cool slightly, then shred with 2 forks; stir to mix with onions and pan juices. If made ahead, cover and refrigerate for up to 2 days. To reheat, bake, covered, in a 350° F (175°C) oven until heated through (about 45 minutes). Makes about 9 cups (2.2 liters).

Per serving: 51 calories (34% calories from fat), 2 g total fat, 0.6 g saturated fat, 14 mg cholesterol, 28 mg sodium, 3 g carbohydrates, 0.7 g fiber, 5 g protein, 12 mg calcium, 0.7 mg iron

Lemon Chicken
(recipe on facing page)

Batter-dipped, deep-fried chicken topped with a sweet lemon sauce is a popular choice at Chinese restaurants. Our stir-fried interpretation of the dish features strips of boneless chicken breast in a thin, golden crust; the light lemon sauce is deliciously tart-sweet. For a pretty presentation, serve the chicken on a bed of lemon slices.

You'll find that cooking goes most smoothly if you start heating the oil just before you drain the chicken. That way, you can transfer the chicken directly from the batter to the hot wok, with no need to set it aside.

Cooking Sauce
(recipe follows)

3 or 4 large lemons, thinly sliced

2 large egg whites

¾ cup (96 g) cornstarch

¼ cup (30 g) all-purpose flour

1 teaspoon *each* baking powder and finely minced fresh ginger

¼ teaspoon salt (optional)

⅛ teaspoon ground white pepper

1 tablespoon (15 ml) salad oil

1 pound (455 g) boneless, skinless chicken breast, cut into ½- by 3-inch (1- by 8-cm) strips
Finely shredded lemon peel
Cilantro sprigs

Lemon Chicken

Preparation time: About 20 minutes
Cooking time: About 10 minutes
Pictured on facing page

1. Prepare Cooking Sauce; set aside. Arrange lemon slices on a rimmed platter, overlapping them if necessary; cover and set aside.

2. In a large bowl, beat egg whites and ½ cup (120 ml) water to blend. Add cornstarch, flour, baking powder, ginger, salt (if used), and white pepper; stir until smoothly blended.

3. Heat oil in a wide nonstick frying pan or wok over medium-high heat. Meanwhile, dip chicken pieces in batter. Lift out and drain briefly to let excess batter drip off; discard remaining batter.

4. When oil is hot, add chicken and stir-fry gently, separating pieces, until meat is lightly browned on outside and no longer pink in center; cut to test (5 to 7 minutes; if any pieces brown too much, remove them from pan and keep warm). Arrange chicken over lemon slices on platter; keep warm. Wipe pan clean (be careful; pan is hot).

5. Stir Cooking Sauce well; pour into pan. Stir over medium-high heat until sauce boils and thickens slightly (1 to 2 minutes). Pour sauce over chicken and sprinkle with lemon peel. Garnish with cilantro sprigs. Makes 4 servings.

Cooking Sauce. Finely shred ½ teaspoon peel (colored part only) from 1 or 2 large **lemons;** set peel aside. Squeeze enough juice to measure 3 tablespoons (45 ml). In a small bowl, stir together lemon juice and 1 tablespoon **cornstarch** until blended. Then stir in lemon peel, ⅓ cup (80 ml) **fat-free reduced-sodium chicken broth,** ¼ cup (50 g) **sugar,** 2 tablespoons (30 ml) *each* **light corn syrup** and **distilled white vinegar,** 1 tablespoon (15 ml) **water,** 1 teaspoon **salad oil,** ¼ teaspoon **salt** (optional), and 2 cloves **garlic,** minced or pressed.

Per serving: 368 calories (14% calories from fat), 6 g total fat, 1 g saturated fat, 66 mg cholesterol, 245 mg sodium, 56 g carbohydrates, 0.3 g fiber, 30 g protein, 136 mg calcium, 2 mg iron

It's hard to believe that this rich-tasting entrée is low in fat. If you can't find dried chanterelles, just substitute economical button mushrooms.

- ½ ounce/15 g (about 1 cup) dried chanterelle mushrooms; or 8 ounces (230 g) fresh regular mushrooms, thinly sliced
- 1½ cups (280 g) long-grain white rice
- 2 teaspoons butter or olive oil
- 1 pound (455 g) boneless, skinless chicken breast, cut into ½- by 2-inch (1- by 5-cm) strips
- ¾ cup (180 ml) fat-free reduced-sodium chicken broth
- ¼ cup (60 ml) chardonnay
- 2 teaspoons chopped fresh tarragon or 1 teaspoon dried tarragon
- 2 tablespoons (30 ml) half-and-half

Chicken with Chanterelle-Tarragon Sauce

Preparation time: About 35 minutes, plus 30 minutes to soak mushrooms
Cooking time: About 25 minutes

1. If using chanterelles, place them in a 1½- to 2-quart (1.4- to 1.9-liter) pan and add 1½ cups (360 ml) water. Bring to a boil over high heat; then reduce heat, cover tightly, and simmer gently until mushrooms are very tender (about 30 minutes). Remove from heat and let stand for 30 minutes. Then lift chanterelles from water, squeezing liquid from them into pan; reserve water. Set chanterelles aside.

2. In a 4- to 5-quart (3.8- to 5-liter) pan, bring 3 cups (710 ml) water to a boil over high heat; stir in rice. Reduce heat, cover, and simmer until liquid has been absorbed and rice is tender to bite (about 20 minutes).

3. Meanwhile, melt butter in a wide nonstick frying pan or wok over medium-high heat. Add chicken and stir-fry until no longer pink in center; cut to test (3 to 4 minutes). Remove chicken from pan with a slotted spoon and keep warm.

4. Add chanterelles or regular mushrooms to pan; stir-fry until tinged a darker brown (about 5 minutes). Carefully pour reserved cooking water into pan, taking care not to add any grit from mushrooms. Add broth, wine, and tarragon. Bring to a boil; then boil, stirring, until liquid is reduced to ⅓ cup (80 ml). Add half-and-half; cook, stirring, until mixture returns to a boil. Remove from heat and stir in chicken.

5. Spoon rice onto a rimmed platter; spoon chicken mixture over rice. Makes 4 servings.

Per serving: 563 calories (8% calories from fat), 5 g total fat, 2 g saturated fat, 74 mg cholesterol, 226 mg sodium, 89 g carbohydrates, 2 g fiber, 36 g protein, 63 mg calcium, 5 mg iron

---

To balance the sweetness of this stir-fry's creamy sauce, choose crisp, tart apples such as Granny Smith or Newtown Pippin.

- 4 teaspoons butter or margarine
- 2 large tart apples (about 1 lb./ 455 g *total*), peeled, cored, and cut into ¼-inch-thick (6-mm-thick) slices
- 1 pound (455 g) boneless, skinless chicken breast, cut into ½- by 2-inch (1- by 5-cm) strips
- 1 large onion, finely chopped
- ⅔ cup (160 ml) dry sherry or apple juice
- ⅓ cup (80 ml) half-and-half

Chicken & Apple Stir-fry

Preparation time: About 20 minutes
Cooking time: About 15 minutes

1. Melt 1 tablespoon of the butter in a wide nonstick frying pan or wok over medium heat. Add apples and stir-fry just until tender to bite (about 2 minutes). Remove apples from pan with a slotted spoon and keep warm.

2. Increase heat to medium-high and melt remaining 1 teaspoon butter in pan. Add chicken and stir-fry until no longer pink in center; cut to test (3 to 4 minutes). Remove chicken from pan with a slotted spoon and keep warm.

3. Add onion and 2 tablespoons (30 ml) of the sherry to pan; stir-fry until onion is soft (about 3 minutes). Add remaining sherry and bring to a boil; boil, stirring, for 1 minute. Add half-and-half and boil, stirring, until sauce is slightly thickened (about 2 minutes). Return apples and chicken to pan and mix gently but thoroughly. Makes 4 servings.

Per serving: 309 calories (26% calories from fat), 8 g total fat, 4 g saturated fat, 84 mg cholesterol, 126 mg sodium, 21 g carbohydrates, 2 g fiber, 28 g protein, 52 mg calcium, 1 mg iron

Cornmeal-crusted chicken chunks, topped with warm homemade salsa and sour cream, are served on a cool, crunchy bed of shredded lettuce. On the side, you might offer low-fat tortilla chips and an orange-and-onion salad.

Tomato Salsa
(recipe follows)

About 8 cups (about 8 oz./
230 g) finely shredded iceberg
lettuce

2 large egg whites

½ cup (69 g) yellow cornmeal

1½ teaspoons chili powder

½ teaspoon ground cumin

1 pound (455 g) boneless, skinless chicken breast, cut into
1-inch (2.5-cm) pieces

2 teaspoons olive oil or salad oil

½ cup (120 ml) nonfat sour cream
Cilantro sprigs

Salsa Chicken

Preparation time: About 20 minutes
Cooking time: About 10 minutes

1. Prepare Tomato Salsa and set aside. Divide lettuce among 4 individual plates; cover and set aside.

2. In a shallow bowl, beat egg whites to blend; set aside. In a large bowl, combine cornmeal, chili powder, and cumin. Add chicken and turn to coat. Then lift chicken from bowl, shaking off excess coating. Dip chicken into egg whites, then coat again with remaining cornmeal mixture.

3. Heat oil in a wide nonstick frying pan or wok over medium-high heat. When oil is hot, add chicken and stir-fry gently until no longer pink in center; cut to test (5 to 7 minutes). Remove from pan and keep warm.

4. Pour Tomato Salsa into pan; reduce heat to medium and cook, stirring, until salsa is heated through and slightly thickened (1 to 2 minutes).

5. Arrange chicken over lettuce; top with salsa and sour cream. Garnish with cilantro sprigs. Makes 4 servings.

Tomato Salsa. In a large bowl, combine 2 medium-size **tomatoes** (about 12 oz./340 g *total*), chopped and drained well; ¼ cup (25 g) thinly sliced **green onions;** ¼ cup (60 ml) **lime juice;** 1 small fresh **jalapeño chile,** seeded and finely chopped; 1 tablespoon chopped **cilantro;** and 1 clove **garlic,** minced or pressed. If made ahead, cover and refrigerate for up to 3 hours.

Per serving: 284 calories (15% calories from fat), 5 g total fat, 0.8 g saturated fat, 66 mg cholesterol, 152 mg sodium, 26 g carbohydrates, 4 g fiber, 34 g protein, 146 mg calcium, 4 mg iron

---

Just right for special occasions, these split and roasted game hens are served on a bed of saffron-tinted orzo.

2 Rock Cornish game hens
(about 1½ lbs./680 g *each*)

¼ cup (60 ml) dry white wine or
apple juice

2 tablespoons (30 ml) *each* Dijon
mustard and honey

1 tablespoon chopped fresh
thyme or 1 teaspoon dried
thyme

3⅓ cups (790 ml) fat-free reduced-
sodium chicken broth

Large pinch of saffron threads
or ⅛ teaspoon ground saffron
(or to taste)

1¼ cups (285 g) dried orzo or other
tiny rice-shaped pasta

¼ cup (25 g) thinly sliced green
onions

Thyme sprigs

Salt and pepper

Herb-roasted Game Hens with Saffron Orzo

Preparation time: 20 minutes
Cooking time: About 25 minutes

1. Reserve game hen necks and giblets for other uses. With poultry shears or a sharp knife, split each hen in half, cutting along backbone and breastbone. Rinse hens and pat dry. In a medium-size bowl, mix wine, mustard, honey, and chopped thyme. Dip hens in marinade and turn to coat; then lift out and drain briefly, reserving marinade. Place hens, skin side up, on a rack in a foil-lined 12- by 15-inch (30- by 38-cm) broiler pan.

2. Bake hens in bottom third of a 425°F (220°C) oven until meat near thighbone is no longer pink; cut to test (about 25 minutes). Halfway through cooking, brush hens with marinade.

3. While hens are baking, bring broth and saffron to a boil in a 2- to 3-quart (1.9- to 2.8-liter) pan over high heat. Stir in pasta. Reduce heat, cover, and simmer, stirring occasionally, until almost all liquid has been absorbed (about 15 minutes); as liquid cooks down, stir more often and watch closely to prevent scorching.

4. Stir onions into pasta; then divide pasta mixture among 4 individual rimmed plates. Place one hen half on each plate; garnish with thyme sprigs. Season to taste with salt and pepper. Makes 4 servings.

Per serving: 688 calories (29% calories from fat), 21 g total fat, 6 g saturated fat, 132 mg cholesterol, 847 mg sodium, 63 g carbohydrates, 2 g fiber, 53 g protein, 48 mg calcium, 5 mg iron

While you grill the vegetables and chicken for this recipe, the capellini cooks quickly on the stovetop.

- ½ cup (20 g) *each* cilantro leaves and fresh basil
- ½ cup (40 g) freshly grated Parmesan cheese
- 3 whole chicken legs (about 1½ lbs./680 g *total*)
- 3 large red bell peppers (about 1½ lbs./680 g *total*)
- 4 slices bacon
- 12 ounces (340 g) dried capellini
- ½ cup (120 ml) seasoned rice vinegar; or ½ cup (120 ml) distilled white vinegar and 4 teaspoons sugar
- ¼ cup (30 g) capers, drained
- 1 tablespoon grated lemon peel
  Finely shredded lemon peel
  Cilantro sprigs
  Salt and pepper

1. Combine cilantro leaves, basil, and cheese in a food processor or blender. Whirl until minced.

Stuffed Chicken Legs with Capellini

Preparation time: About 25 minutes
Cooking time: About 1 hour
Pictured on facing page

2. Cut a slit just through skin at joint on outside of each chicken leg. Slide your fingers between skin and meat to separate, leaving skin in place. Tuck cilantro mixture under skin, spreading evenly. Set aside.

3. Place bell peppers on a lightly greased grill 4 to 6 inches (10 to 15 cm) above a solid bed of hot coals. Grill, turning as needed, until charred all over (about 10 minutes). Cover with foil and let cool. Pull off and discard skin, stems, and seeds. Cut into strips and set aside.

4. Lay chicken on grill when coals have cooled down to medium heat and cook, turning as needed, until meat near thighbone is no longer pink; cut to test (about 40 minutes). Meanwhile, cook bacon in a wide non-stick frying pan over medium heat until crisp (about 5 minutes). Lift out, drain well, and crumble; set aside. Discard all but 2 teaspoons of the drippings; set pan with drippings aside.

5. Bring 12 cups (2.8 liters) water to a boil in a 5- to 6-quart (5- to 6-liter) pan over medium-high heat. Stir in pasta and cook just until tender to bite (about 4 minutes); or cook according to package directions. Drain well and keep warm.

6. Add vinegar, capers, and grated lemon peel to pan with drippings. Bring just to a boil over medium heat. Add pasta and bacon. Cook, stirring, just until warm. Transfer to a platter. Cut chicken legs apart. Place chicken and bell peppers on platter. Garnish with shredded lemon peel and cilantro sprigs. Offer salt and pepper to add to taste. Makes 6 servings.

Per serving: 457 calories (30% calories from fat), 15 g total fat, 5 g saturated fat, 64 mg cholesterol, 858 mg sodium, 52 g carbohydrates, 2 g fiber, 28 g protein, 210 mg calcium, 4 mg iron

Stuffed Chicken Legs with Capellini
(recipe on facing page)

Mu Shu Sandwiches

Preparation time: About 10 minutes
Cooking time: About 10 minutes

Quick and easy! To make this dinner, fill pita bread halves with a simple stir-fry of chicken breast, onions, and bell peppers in hoisin sauce. If you like, dress up the sandwiches with pickled scallions and pickled sliced ginger; both are available in the Asian foods section of most supermarkets.

1 tablespoon (15 ml) salad oil

3 cups (345 g) thinly sliced onions

2 cups (160 g) thinly sliced green or red bell peppers

1 pound (455 g) boneless, skinless chicken breast, cut into ½- by 2-inch (1- by 5-cm) strips

¼ cup (60 ml) hoisin sauce

Whole green onions (ends trimmed)

4 pita breads (*each* about 6 inches/15 cm in diameter), cut crosswise into halves

Pickled scallions and pickled sliced ginger (optional)

1. Heat 2 teaspoons of the oil in a wide nonstick frying pan or wok over medium-high heat. When oil is hot, add onions and peppers; stir-fry until vegetables are lightly browned (2 to 3 minutes). Remove from pan with a slotted spoon; keep warm.

2. Heat remaining 1 teaspoon oil in pan. When oil is hot, add chicken and stir-fry until no longer pink in center; cut to test (3 to 4 minutes). Add hoisin sauce to pan; then return vegetables to pan and stir to mix well.

3. Pour into a bowl and garnish with green onions. Fill bread halves with chicken mixture and, if desired, pickled scallions and pickled ginger. Makes 4 servings.

Per serving: 379 calories (14% calories from fat), 6 g total fat, 0.9 g saturated fat, 66 mg cholesterol, 400 mg sodium, 45 g carbohydrates, 4 g fiber, 33 g protein, 93 mg calcium, 3 mg iron

Chicken Chimichangas

Preparation time: About 15 minutes
Cooking time: About 40 minutes

These oven-baked chimichangas offer all the authentic flavor of their traditional deep-fried counterparts, but they're lower in fat.

Shredded Chicken Filling (page 148)

About 1½ cups (360 ml) Cucumber & Jicama Salsa (page 20) or other salsa of your choice

5 cups (275 g) shredded lettuce

1½ cups (170 g) shredded carrots

8 flour tortillas (7- to 9-inch/ 18- to 23-cm diameter)

About ⅓ cup (80 ml) nonfat milk

½ cup (57 g) shredded Cheddar cheese

Plain nonfat yogurt

1. Prepare Shredded Chicken Filling; set aside. Prepare Cucumber & Jicama Salsa; refrigerate. In a small bowl, mix lettuce and carrots; set aside.

2. To assemble each chimichanga, brush both sides of a tortilla liberally with milk; let stand briefly to soften tortilla. Spoon an eighth of the filling down center of tortilla; top with 1 tablespoon of the cheese. Lap ends of tortilla over filling; then fold sides to center to make a packet. Place chimichanga, seam side down, on a lightly oiled 12- by 15-inch (30- by 38-cm) baking sheet and brush with milk. Repeat to make 7 more chimichangas.

3. Bake in a 500°F (260°C) oven, brushing with milk after 5 minutes, until golden brown (8 to 10 minutes).

4. To serve, divide lettuce mixture among 8 plates; place 1 chimichanga on each plate. Add salsa and yogurt to taste. Makes 8 servings.

Per serving: 291 calories (26% calories from fat), 9 g total fat, 3 g saturated fat, 38 mg cholesterol, 338 mg sodium, 37 g carbohydrates, 3 g fiber, 19 g protein, 184 mg calcium, 4 mg iron

Succulent chicken, steeped in a spicy-sweet broth, makes a lively tasting filling for French rolls.

....

- 1 **pound (455 g) skinless, bone-less chicken thighs**
- 4 **cups (950 ml) water**
- 2 **cups (470 ml) low-sodium chicken broth**
- ¼ **cup (24 g) chili powder**
- ¼ **cup (55 g) firmly packed brown sugar**
- 2 **teaspoons dried oregano**
- 1 **teaspoon anise seeds**
  About 1 tablespoon (15 ml) red wine vinegar, or to taste
- 2 **tablespoons *each* chopped cilantro and thinly sliced green onion**
- 4 **French rolls (*each* about 6 inches/15 cm long)**
- 8 **to 12 butter lettuce leaves, rinsed and crisped**

Chili & Anise Chicken Tortas

....

Preparation time: About 15 minutes
Cooking time: 15 to 20 minutes

Condiments: Avocado slices and asadero or string cheese

....

1. Rinse chicken and pat dry; set aside. In a 4- to 5-quart (3.8- to 4.7-liter) pan with a tight-fitting lid, combine water, broth, chili powder, sugar, oregano, and anise seeds. Bring to a rolling boil over high heat. Remove pan from heat and immediately add chicken. Cover pan and let stand until meat in thickest part is no longer pink; cut to test (15 to 20 minutes; do not uncover until ready to test). If chicken is not done, return it to hot water, cover, and let steep for 2 to 3 more minutes.

2. Drain chicken, reserving 2 cups (470 ml) of the cooking liquid. Return reserved liquid to pan. Bring to a boil over high heat; boil until reduced to ½ cup (120 ml), watching closely to prevent scorching.

3. Serve chicken and sauce warm or cold. To serve, stir vinegar, cilantro, and onion into sauce. Cut chicken across the grain into thin slanting slices; set aside. Cut rolls in half lengthwise and moisten cut surfaces evenly with sauce. Fill rolls with chicken and lettuce. Offer additional sauce and condiments to add to taste. Makes 4 servings.

....

Per serving: 464 calories (14% calories from fat), 7 g total fat, 1 g saturated fat, 94 mg cholesterol, 1,819 mg sodium, 68 g carbohydrates, 4 g fiber, 33 g protein, 71 mg calcium, 6 mg iron

---

For extra-easy (though nontraditional) enchiladas, cut corn tortillas into strips, layer them with a chicken-yogurt filling, and bake.

....

- 1 **cup (240 ml) plain nonfat yogurt**
- 1 **cup (210 g) low-fat (1%) cottage cheese**
- 2 **cloves garlic, peeled**
- 2 **teaspoons *each* chili powder, sugar, and cornstarch**
- 1 **tablespoon butter or margarine**
- ¼ **cup (30 g) all-purpose flour**
- 2 **cups (470 ml) low-sodium chicken broth**
- 1 **large can (about 7 oz./200 g) diced green chiles**
- 12 **corn tortillas (6-inch/15-cm diameter)**
- 2 **cups (280 g) bite-size pieces of cooked chicken**

Chicken-Yogurt Enchilada Casserole

....

Preparation time: About 15 minutes
Baking time: 45 to 50 minutes

- 1 **small onion, chopped**
- ½ **cup (58 g) shredded jack cheese**

....

1. In a blender or food processor, whirl yogurt, cottage cheese, garlic, chili powder, sugar, and cornstarch until smoothly puréed. Set aside.

2. Melt butter in a 1½- to 2-quart (1.4- to 1.9-liter) pan over medium-high heat. Add flour and ⅓ cup (80 ml) water; stir just until bubbly. Whisk in broth; bring to a boil, stirring. Remove from heat; let cool for 5 minutes. Whisk yogurt mixture into flour mixture; stir

in chiles. Cover bottom of a 9- by 13-inch (23- by 33-cm) baking dish with a third of the yogurt-flour mixture.

3. Dip tortillas, one at a time, in hot water. Drain briefly; cut into strips 1 inch (2.5 cm) wide. Scatter half the tortilla strips over yogurt-flour mixture in baking dish; cover with all the chicken and onion, half the jack cheese, and half the remaining yogurt-flour mixture. Top with remaining tortilla strips, yogurt-flour mixture, and jack cheese.

4. Cover dish tightly with foil and bake in a 400°F (205°C) oven for 30 minutes. Uncover; continue to bake until mixture is golden brown on top and appears firm in center when dish is gently shaken (15 to 20 more minutes). Makes 8 servings.

....

Per serving: 261 calories (27% calories from fat), 8 g total fat, 3 g saturated fat, 41 mg cholesterol, 465 mg sodium, 29 g carbohydrates, 3 g fiber, 20 g protein, 212 mg calcium, 2 mg iron

Salmon with Asian-style Capellini
(recipe on page 160)

Seafood

Seafood's delicious diversity is apparent by its prominent place in so many of the world's great cuisines. Its mildly sweet flavor and natural leanness are complemented with light citrus sauces, fruity relishes, and subtle seasonings. Delight in the sweetly piquant flavor of Salmon & Squash with Brown Sugar & Lime from the traditions of Mexico or enjoy the Mediterranean favorite of Linguine with Lemon-Basil Seafood.

The combination of rice vinegar, soy sauce, and Oriental sesame oil is popular in Asian cooking. In this easy-to-fix entrée, the sweet-tart flavors enhance tender pasta and crisp greens. Hot grilled salmon fillets complete the presentation.

- 8 ounces (230 g) dried capellini
- 5 tablespoons (75 ml) seasoned rice vinegar; or 5 tablespoons (75 ml) distilled white vinegar and 2 tablespoons sugar
- 5 tablespoons (75 ml) lime juice
- 5 teaspoons (25 ml) Oriental sesame oil
- ¼ teaspoon ground red pepper (cayenne)
- 2 teaspoons reduced-sodium soy sauce
- ½ cup (50 g) thinly sliced green onions
- 5½ to 6 ounces (155 to 170 g) mixed salad greens, rinsed and crisped
- 1 cup (40 g) *each* firmly packed cilantro and fresh basil, chopped
- 1 large cucumber (about 12 oz./ 340 g), peeled, cut in half lengthwise, seeded, and thinly sliced crosswise
- 4 thin boneless, skinless baby salmon fillets (about 6 oz./ 170 g *each*)

  Lime slices

  Basil sprigs

Salmon with Asian-style Capellini

Preparation time: About 40 minutes
Cooking time: About 10 minutes
Chilling time: At least 30 minutes
Pictured on page 158

1. Bring 8 cups (1.9 liters) water to a boil in a 4- to 5-quart (3.8- to 5-liter) pan over medium-high heat. Stir in pasta and cook just until tender to bite (about 4 minutes); or cook according to package directions. Drain, rinse with cold water, and drain well.

2. Mix 3 tablespoons (45 ml) each of the vinegar and lime juice, 4 teaspoons (20 ml) of the oil, ground red pepper, soy sauce, and onions in a large bowl. Add pasta, lifting with 2 forks to mix. Cover and refrigerate until cool (at least 30 minutes); mix occasionally.

3. Mix greens, cilantro, chopped basil, and remaining 2 tablespoons (30 ml) vinegar in a large bowl. Arrange on individual plates. Top with pasta and cucumber. Set aside.

4. Stir remaining 2 tablespoons (30 ml) lime juice with remaining 1 teaspoon oil. Brush mixture over both sides of each fish fillet.

5. Place fillets on rack of a 12- by 15-inch (30- by 38-cm) broiler pan. Broil about 4 inches (10 cm) below heat, turning once, just until opaque but still moist in thickest part; cut to test (about 4 minutes).

6. Place a hot fish fillet over pasta on each plate. Garnish with lime slices and basil sprigs. Makes 4 servings.

Per serving: 510 calories (29% calories from fat), 18 g total fat, 3 g saturated fat, 94 mg cholesterol, 568 mg sodium, 57 g carbohydrates, 3 g fiber, 44 g protein, 263 mg calcium, 8 mg iron

Fresh tuna is delicious served rare—but if you use fish that has not been previously frozen, freeze it at 0°F (-18°C) for at least 7 days to destroy any potentially harmful organisms it may contain. Thaw the fish in the refrigerator before cooking.

5½ cups (1.3 liters) fat-free reduced-sodium chicken broth

½ cup (65 g) finely chopped dried apricots

1 pound (455 g) dried orzo or other tiny rice-shaped pasta

1 can (about 6⅛ oz./174 g) tuna packed in water

1 large egg yolk or 1 tablespoon (15 ml) pasteurized egg substitute

¼ teaspoon grated lemon peel

2 tablespoons (30 ml) lemon juice

4 teaspoons (20 ml) balsamic vinegar

1 teaspoon honey

½ teaspoon Dijon mustard

½ teaspoon salt (or to taste)

¼ cup (60 ml) *each* olive oil and salad oil

3 canned anchovy fillets, drained

1 cup (240 ml) nonfat sour cream

2 tablespoons fennel seeds

1 tablespoon whole white peppercorns

1½ teaspoons coriander seeds

2 large egg whites

4 tuna (ahi) steaks (*each* about 1 inch/2.5 cm thick and about 7 oz./200 g)

Tuna Steaks with Roasted Peppers & Tuna Sauce

Preparation time: 35 minutes
Cooking time: About 20 minutes

1 teaspoon olive oil

½ cup (120 ml) bottled clam juice

1 jar roasted red peppers (about 12 oz./340 g), drained and patted dry

3 tablespoons drained capers (or to taste)

Lemon slices

Italian or regular parsley sprigs

1. In a 4- to 5-quart (3.8- to 5-liter) pan, bring broth and apricots to a boil over high heat; stir in orzo. Reduce heat, cover, and simmer, stirring occasionally, until almost all liquid has been absorbed (about 20 minutes); as liquid cooks down, stir more often and watch closely to prevent scorching. Remove from heat and keep warm.

2. While orzo is cooking, drain can of tuna, reserving ¼ cup (60 ml) of the liquid from can. Set tuna and liquid aside.

3. In a food processor or blender, combine egg yolk, lemon peel, lemon juice, vinegar, honey, mustard, and ¼ teaspoon of the salt (or to taste); whirl until blended. With motor running, slowly pour in the ¼ cup (60 ml) olive oil and salad oil in a thin, steady stream. Whirl until well blended. Add canned tuna, reserved tuna liquid, 1 tablespoon (15 ml) water, and anchovies; whirl until smoothly puréed. With a spoon or whisk, stir in sour cream; set aside.

4. Wash and dry food processor or blender; then combine fennel seeds, peppercorns, coriander seeds, and remaining ¼ teaspoon salt in processor or blender. Whirl until finely ground; transfer to a wide, shallow bowl. In another wide, shallow bowl, beat egg whites to blend. Rinse tuna steaks and pat dry; then cut each in half. Dip pieces, one at a time, in egg whites; drain briefly, then coat on both sides with seed mixture. Pat any remaining seed mixture on fish.

5. Heat the 1 teaspoon olive oil in a wide nonstick frying pan over medium-high heat. Add fish and cook, turning once, until browned on both sides. Add clam juice. Reduce heat and cook until fish is still pale pink in center; cut to test (about 5 minutes).

6. Spoon pasta onto a rimmed platter; fluff with a fork. With a slotted spoon, lift fish from pan and place atop pasta; arrange red peppers decoratively around fish. Top with half the tuna sauce and sprinkle with capers. Garnish with lemon slices and parsley sprigs. Offer remaining tuna sauce to add to taste. Makes 8 servings.

Per serving: 562 calories (29% calories from fat), 18 g total fat, 3 g saturated fat, 77 mg cholesterol, 1,201 mg sodium, 60 g carbohydrates, 2 g fiber, 39 g protein, 115 mg calcium, 5 mg iron

Pink peppercorns poached to softness add an attractive color and a delicately spicy flavor to baked swordfish steaks.

- ⅓ cup (21 g) whole pink peppercorns
- 4 swordfish or halibut steaks (*each* about 1 inch/2.5 cm thick and 5 to 6 oz./140 to 170 g)
- 8 teaspoons (40 ml) honey
- 4 large butter lettuce leaves, rinsed and crisped
- 2 jars (about 6 oz./170 g *each*) marinated artichoke hearts, drained
  Lemon wedges

Pink Peppercorn Swordfish

Preparation time: 15 minutes
Cooking time: About 15 minutes
Pictured on facing page

1. In a 1- to 1½-quart (950-ml to 1.4-liter) pan, combine peppercorns and about 2 cups (470 ml) water. Bring to a boil over high heat; then reduce heat and simmer until peppercorns are slightly softened (about 4 minutes). Drain well.

2. Rinse fish and pat dry. Arrange pieces well apart in a lightly oiled shallow 10- by 15-inch (25- by 38-cm) baking pan. Brush each piece with 2 teaspoons of the honey; then top equally with peppercorns, spreading them in a single layer.

3. Bake in a 400°F (205°C) oven until fish is just opaque but still moist in thickest part; cut to test (about 10 minutes).

4. Place one lettuce leaf on each of 4 individual plates; top lettuce with artichokes. With a wide spatula, lift fish from baking pan and arrange alongside lettuce. Season to taste with lemon. Makes 4 servings.

Per serving: 277 calories (29% calories from fat), 9 g total fat, 2 g saturated fat, 54 mg cholesterol, 361 mg sodium, 21 g carbohydrates, 3 g fiber, 30 g protein, 44 mg calcium, 3 mg iron

---

Succulent halibut fillets are quickly broiled and then served with lemony linguine.

- 1 teaspoon olive oil
- 2 cloves garlic, minced or pressed
- ⅔ cup (160 ml) dry white wine
- ⅓ cup (80 ml) lemon juice
- 2 tablespoons drained capers
- 8 ounces (230 g) dried linguine
- 1½ pounds (680 g) Pacific halibut fillets (*each* ¾ to 1 inch/2 to 2.5 cm thick)
  Pepper
- ¼ cup (20 g) freshly grated Parmesan cheese
- ½ cup (120 ml) low-sodium chicken broth
- ½ teaspoon grated lemon peel
- 2 teaspoons honey
- 1 teaspoon Dijon mustard
- 2 ounces/55 g Neufchâtel or cream cheese
- ¼ cup (15 g) minced parsley

Halibut Piccata with Lemon Linguine

Preparation time: About 15 minutes
Cooking time: About 25 minutes

1. Heat oil in a small nonstick frying pan over medium-high heat. Add garlic and cook, stirring, until fragrant and hot; do not scorch. Add ½ cup (120 ml) of the wine, 3 tablespoons (45 ml) of the lemon juice, and capers. Bring to a boil and cook until reduced to about ½ cup/120 ml (about 4 minutes). Remove from heat and keep warm.

2. Bring 8 cups (1.9 liters) water to a boil in a 4- to 5-quart (3.8- to 5-liter) pan over medium-high heat. Stir in pasta and cook just until tender to bite (8 to 10 minutes); or cook according to package directions. Drain well and keep warm.

3. Cut fish into 4 equal portions and sprinkle with pepper. Place in a single layer in a lightly oiled broiler pan without a rack. Broil about 3 inches (8 cm) below heat for 3 minutes. Turn, sprinkle with Parmesan cheese, and continue to broil until opaque but still moist in center of thickest part; cut to test (about 3 more minutes). Keep warm.

4. Combine broth, lemon peel, remaining lemon juice, honey, and mustard in a 3- to 4-quart (2.8- to 3.8-liter) pan. Bring to a boil over high heat. Remove from heat; whisk in Neufchâtel cheese just until melted. Add pasta, remaining wine, and parsley; lift with 2 forks to mix. Mound on individual plates. Arrange fish alongside; drizzle with sauce. Makes 4 servings.

Per serving: 522 calories (21% calories from fat), 11 g total fat, 4 g saturated fat, 70 mg cholesterol, 428 mg sodium, 48 g carbohydrates, 2 g fiber, 47 g protein, 201 mg calcium, 4 mg iron

Pink Peppercorn Swordfish
(recipe on facing page)

Here's an eye-catching entrée: hot, gingery fresh tuna over cool, crisp spinach leaves.

....

Soy Dressing (recipe follows)

3 quarts (about 12 oz./340 g) lightly packed rinsed, crisped spinach leaves

1 tablespoon sesame seeds

1 teaspoon salad oil

2 tablespoons finely minced fresh ginger

12 ounces (340 g) fresh tuna, cut into ½- by 2-inch (1- by 5-cm) strips

½ cup (50 g) thinly sliced green onions

1 cup (115 g) thinly sliced red radishes

Whole green onions (ends trimmed)

Stir-fried Tuna on Spinach

....

Preparation time: About 30 minutes
Cooking time: About 8 minutes

....

1. Prepare Soy Dressing; set aside. Arrange spinach on a large platter, cover, and set aside.

2. In a wide nonstick frying pan or wok, stir sesame seeds over medium heat until golden (about 3 minutes). Pour out of pan and set aside.

3. Heat oil in pan over medium-high heat. When oil is hot, add ginger and stir-fry just until lightly browned (about 30 seconds; do not scorch). Add tuna and stir-fry gently (flipping with a spatula, if needed) until just opaque

but still moist and pink in thickest part; cut to test (about 3 minutes). Stir Soy Dressing and pour into pan; stir to mix, then remove pan from heat.

4. Spoon tuna mixture over spinach on platter. Sprinkle with sliced onions, radishes, and sesame seeds. Garnish with whole onions. Makes 4 servings.

....

Soy Dressing. In a small bowl, stir together ¼ cup (60 ml) **mirin** or cream sherry, 6 tablespoons (85 ml) **unseasoned rice vinegar** or cider vinegar, 2 tablespoons (30 ml) **reduced-sodium soy sauce,** and 1 teaspoon **prepared horseradish.**

....

Per serving: 220 calories (30% calories from fat), 7 g total fat, 1 g saturated fat, 32 mg cholesterol, 411 mg sodium, 12 g carbohydrates, 3 g fiber, 24 g protein, 125 mg calcium, 4 mg iron

---

Farmed in both Mexico and the United States, tilapia is a perchlike fish with a clean, delicate flavor similar to that of petrale sole. It's appealingly lean, but remains moist and tender after cooking. For an intimate dinner for two, try baking a whole dressed tilapia on a bed of ginger-spiked onion and lemon slices.

....

1¼ pounds (565 g) red onions, cut into ⅛-inch (3 mm) slices

3 tablespoons (45 ml) lemon juice

1 tablespoon minced fresh ginger

1 whole tilapia (about 1½ lbs./ 680 g), dressed (gutted, with head and tail attached)

1 tablespoon (15 ml) extra-virgin olive oil

2 large lemons

3 tablespoons minced cilantro

Salt and pepper

Whole Tilapia with Onion & Lemon

....

Preparation time: About 15 minutes
Baking time: 20 to 25 minutes

....

1. In a large bowl, mix onions, lemon juice, and ginger. Reserve 1 or 2 onion slices; arrange remaining slices over bottom of a 9- by 13-inch (23- by 33-cm) or shallow 4- to 5-quart (3.8- to 4.7-liter) baking dish.

2. Rinse fish and pat dry. Brush both sides of fish with oil; then place fish on top of onion mixture.

3. Cut a ½-inch (1 cm) slice from each end of each lemon; stuff fish cavity with lemon ends, reserved onion slices, and half the cilantro. Thinly slice remaining piece of each lemon; tuck slices around fish. Sprinkle remaining cilantro over onion and lemon in baking dish. Bake in a 400°F (205°C) oven until a meat thermometer inserted in thickest part of fish registers 135°F (57°C) and flesh is just opaque but still moist; cut to test (20 to 25 minutes).

4. To serve, gently pull skin from fish; then spoon fish, onions, and lemon slices onto 2 dinner plates. Season to taste with salt and pepper. Makes 2 servings.

....

Per serving: 359 calories (22% calories from fat), 10 g total fat, 2 g saturated fat, 82 mg cholesterol, 177 mg sodium, 40 g carbohydrates, 5 g fiber, 38 g protein, 184 mg calcium, 3 mg iron

Named after the beautiful seacoast town where it originated, this snapper specialty features fresh fillets topped with a cinnamon-spiced sauce of bell pepper, tomatoes, and olives.

1 teaspoon salad oil or olive oil

1 small green or red bell pepper (about ⅓ lb./150 g), seeded and chopped

1 large onion, chopped

3 cloves garlic, minced or pressed (optional)

2 tablespoons (30 ml) water

1 small can (about 4 oz./115 g) diced green chiles

¼ cup (85 g) sliced pimento-stuffed green olives

3 tablespoons (45 ml) lime juice

1 teaspoon ground cinnamon

Snapper Veracruz

Preparation time: About 10 minutes
Cooking time: 20 to 25 minutes

¼ teaspoon white pepper

1 can (about 14½ oz./415 g) stewed tomatoes

4 snapper or rockfish fillets (about 2 lbs./905 g *total*)

1 tablespoon drained capers

1. Heat oil in a wide nonstick frying pan over medium-high heat. Add bell pepper, onion, garlic (if desired), and water; cook, stirring often, until vegetables are tender-crisp to bite (3 to 5 minutes).

2. Add chiles, olives, lime juice, cinnamon, and white pepper; cook for 1 more minute. Add tomatoes to pan (break tomatoes up with a spoon, if needed); then bring mixture to a boil. Boil, stirring often, until sauce is slightly thickened (about 5 minutes).

3. Rinse fish, pat dry, and arrange in a lightly greased 9- by 13-inch (23- by 33-cm) baking dish. Pour sauce over fish. Bake in a 350°F (175°C) oven until fish is just opaque but still moist in thickest part; cut to test (10 to 15 minutes).

4. With a slotted spoon, transfer fish and sauce to four dinner plates. Sprinkle with capers. Makes 4 servings.

Per serving: 310 calories (16% calories from fat), 16 g total fat, 0.9 g saturated fat, 84 mg cholesterol, 842 mg sodium, 16 g carbohydrates, 4 g fiber, 49 g protein, 135 mg calcium, 2 mg iron

---

Here's an interesting combination of sweet and savory flavors. Crunchy pea pods and chunks of mild snapper, cloaked in a sauce laced with ginger and garlic, are served over juicy fresh pineapple rings. On the side, offer a bulgur pilaf or steamed white or brown rice.

1 tablespoon finely minced fresh ginger

2 tablespoons (30 ml) *each* reduced-sodium soy sauce and unsweetened pineapple juice

2 cloves garlic, minced or pressed

1 teaspoon *each* sugar and Oriental sesame oil

⅛ teaspoon crushed red pepper flakes

1 pound (455 g) red snapper fillets (about ½ inch/1 cm thick), cut into 1-inch (2.5-cm) pieces

1 medium-size pineapple (3 to 3½ lbs./1.35 to 1.6 kg)

1 teaspoon salad oil

Red Snapper Stir-fry

Preparation time: About 20 minutes
Cooking time: About 10 minutes

1½ cups (115 g) fresh Chinese pea pods (also called snow or sugar peas) or sugar snap peas, ends and strings removed; or 1 package (about 6 oz./170 g) frozen Chinese pea pods, thawed and drained

1 tablespoon cornstarch blended with 1 tablespoon (15 ml) cold water

½ cup (50 g) thinly sliced green onions

1. In a large bowl, stir together ginger, soy sauce, pineapple juice, garlic, sugar, sesame oil, and red pepper flakes. Add fish and stir to coat. Set aside; stir occasionally.

2. Peel and core pineapple, then cut crosswise into thin slices. Arrange slices on a rimmed platter; cover and set aside.

3. Heat salad oil in a wide nonstick frying pan or wok over medium-high heat. When oil is hot, add fish mixture and stir-fry gently until fish is just opaque but still moist in thickest part; cut to test (2 to 3 minutes). Remove fish from pan with a slotted spoon; keep warm.

4. Add pea pods to pan and stir-fry for 30 seconds (15 seconds if using frozen pea pods). Stir cornstarch mixture well, then pour into pan. Cook, stirring, until sauce boils and thickens slightly (1 to 2 minutes). Return fish to pan and add onions; mix gently but thoroughly, just until fish is hot and coated with sauce. Spoon fish mixture over pineapple slices. Makes 4 servings.

Per serving: 278 calories (15% calories from fat), 5 g total fat, 0.7 g saturated fat, 42 mg cholesterol, 379 mg sodium, 34 g carbohydrates, 4 g fiber, 26 g protein, 88 mg calcium, 2 mg iron

Lingcod with Citrus Almond Couscous
(recipe on facing page)

A medley of citrus fruits accents this pasta dish.

- **5** or **6** small oranges (about 2½ lbs./1.15 kg *total*)
- **1** large pink grapefruit (about 12 oz./340 g)
- **1** medium-size lemon (about 5 oz./140 g)
- **1** medium-size lime (about 3 oz./85 g)
- **¼** cup (30 g) slivered almonds
- **2** tablespoons (30 ml) olive oil
- **¼** cup (45 g) chopped onion
- **½** teaspoon almond extract
- **10** ounces/285 g (about 1⅔ cups) dried couscous
- **2** pounds (905 g) skinless, boneless lingcod or striped bass fillets (*each* about 1 inch/2.5 cm thick)
- **¼** cup (60 ml) rice vinegar
- **2** tablespoons minced shallots

1. Shred enough peel from oranges and grapefruit to make 1½ tablespoons each. Shred enough peel from lemon and lime to make 1 teaspoon

Lingcod with Citrus Almond Couscous

Preparation time: About 30 minutes
Cooking time: About 20 minutes
Pictured on facing page

each. Combine peels in a small bowl; set aside. Remove remaining peel and white membrane from grapefruit, lemon, lime, and 2 of the oranges. Over a bowl, cut between membranes to release segments. In a separate bowl, juice remaining oranges to make 1½ cups (360 ml). Set bowls aside.

2. Toast almonds in a 2- to 3-quart (1.9- to 2.8-liter) pan over medium heat, shaking pan often, until golden (about 4 minutes). Remove from pan and set aside. Place 2 teaspoons of the oil in pan and heat over medium-high heat. Add onion and cook, stirring often, until soft (about 3 minutes). Add 1 cup (240 ml) of the orange juice,

1½ cups (360 ml) water, and almond extract. Bring to a boil. Stir in pasta; cover, remove from heat, and let stand until liquid is absorbed (about 5 minutes). Keep warm, fluffing occasionally with a fork.

3. Cut fish into 6 portions and brush with 2 teaspoons more oil. Place on rack of a 12- by 14-inch (30- by 35.5-cm) broiler pan. Broil about 4 inches (10 cm) below heat, turning once, just until opaque but still moist in thickest part; cut to test (about 10 minutes).

4. Combine remaining ½ cup (120 ml) orange juice and 2 teaspoons oil, vinegar, shallots, fruit, and accumulated juices in a wide nonstick frying pan. Cook over medium heat, stirring often, until warm (about 2 minutes).

5. Arrange pasta and fish on individual plates. Top fish with fruit sauce and sprinkle almonds over pasta. Garnish with citrus peel. Makes 6 servings.

Per serving: 455 calories (19% calories from fat), 10 g total fat, 1 g saturated fat, 79 mg cholesterol, 97 mg sodium, 57 g carbohydrates, 3 g fiber, 35 g protein, 102 mg calcium, 2 mg iron

The combination of lime and brown sugar is popular in Mexican cooking; in this easy one-pan meal, the sweet-tart flavors enhance baked salmon and winter squash. (Piloncillo is unrefined sugar shaped into hard cones; if you can't find it, regular brown sugar will do.)

- 2 pounds (905 g) banana or Hubbard squash, cut into 4 equal pieces
- 1½ cups (360 ml) low-sodium chicken broth
- 4 baby salmon fillets (about 5 oz./140 g *each*)
- ½ teaspoon salad oil
- 1 cone piloncillo (about 3 oz./ 85 g), finely chopped; or ¼ cup (55 g) firmly packed brown sugar
- ¼ cup (60 ml) lime juice
  Lime wedges
  Salt and pepper

Salmon & Squash with Brown Sugar & Lime

Preparation time: About 10 minutes
Baking time: About 1¼ hours

1. Scoop out and discard any seeds from squash. Lay squash, skin side up, in a 10- by 15-inch (25- by 38-cm) or 11- by 14-inch (28- by 35.5-cm) rimmed baking pan; pour in broth. Bake in a 350°F (175°C) oven until squash is tender when pierced (about 1 hour). Remove from oven; increase oven temperature to 450°F (230°F).

2. Rinse fish and pat dry. Turn squash over and push to one end of pan. Lift opposite end of pan so that any liquid runs down to mix with squash; then

spread oil over exposed pan bottom. Place fish fillets side by side (they can overlap slightly) in oiled part of pan. Mix piloncillo and lime juice; spoon about half the mixture over fish and squash.

3. Return pan to oven and bake until fish is just opaque but still moist in thickest part; cut to test (about 8 minutes). After fish has baked for 5 minutes, spoon remaining lime mixture over fish and squash.

4. To serve, transfer fish and squash to four dinner plates; garnish with lime wedges. Stir pan juices to blend, then pour into a small pitcher. Season fish and squash to taste with pan juices, salt, and pepper. Makes 4 servings.

Per serving: 329 calories (30% calories from fat), 11 g total fat, 2 g saturated fat, 78 mg cholesterol, 123 mg sodium, 28 g carbohydrates, 3 g fiber, 32 g protein, 57 mg calcium, 2 mg iron

---

Mild, rich-tasting Chilean sea bass, red onion, and slender green beans combine in this simple dish. Sea bass is often sold in 1-inch-thick (2.5-cm-thick) fillets; if necessary, cut the pieces horizontally to make them ½ inch (1 cm) thick.

- Sesame-Orange Sauce (recipe follows)
- 1 teaspoon sesame seeds
- 8 ounces (230 g) slender green beans (ends removed), cut diagonally into 1-inch (2.5-cm) lengths
- ½ cup (60 g) sliced red onion
- 1 teaspoon salad oil or olive oil
- 1 pound (455 g) Chilean sea bass, halibut, or orange roughy fillets (about ½ inch/1 cm thick), cut into 1-inch (2.5-cm) pieces

1. Prepare Sesame-Orange Sauce and set aside.

Sea Bass with Green Beans & Sesame-Orange Sauce

Preparation time: About 20 minutes
Cooking time: About 15 minutes

2. In a wide nonstick frying pan or wok, stir sesame seeds over medium heat until golden (about 3 minutes). Pour out of pan and set aside.

3. In pan, combine beans, onion, and ⅓ cup (80 ml) water. Increase heat to medium-high; cover and cook until beans are almost tender to bite (about 3 minutes). Uncover and stir-fry until liquid has evaporated. Transfer bean mixture to a platter and keep warm.

4. Heat oil in pan. When oil is hot, add fish and stir-fry gently until just opaque but still moist in thickest part; cut to test (3 to 4 minutes). Remove fish from pan with a slotted spoon; add to bean mixture and mix gently but thoroughly. Sprinkle with sesame seeds.

5. Stir Sesame-Orange Sauce; offer sauce to add to individual servings. Makes 4 servings.

Sesame-Orange Sauce. In a small bowl, stir together ¾ teaspoon **grated orange peel**, ¼ cup (60 ml) **orange juice**, 2 tablespoons (30 ml) **reduced-sodium soy sauce**, 1 clove **garlic** (minced or pressed), 1½ teaspoons **honey**, 1 teaspoon minced **fresh ginger**, and ½ teaspoon **Oriental sesame oil**.

Per serving: 177 calories (23% calories from fat), 4 g total fat, 0.9 g saturated fat, 47 mg cholesterol, 383 mg sodium, 11 g carbohydrates, 1 g fiber, 23 g protein, 51 mg calcium, 1 mg iron

Swordfish with Mango Relish

Preparation time: About 10 minutes, plus 30 minutes to soak onion
Cooking time: About 5 minutes

The bright colors and bold flavors of this savory-sweet fruit relish really bounce out at you! Serve it over thin strips of swordfish, quickly stir-fried to stay succulent.

Mango Relish (recipe follows)

2 teaspoons salad oil

1½ pounds (680 g) swordfish, cut into ½- by 2-inch (1- by 5-cm) strips

½ cup (20 g) lightly packed cilantro sprigs

1. Prepare Mango Relish and set aside.

2. Heat oil in a wide nonstick frying pan or wok over medium-high heat. When oil is hot, add swordfish and stir-fry gently (flipping with a spatula, if needed) until just opaque but still moist in thickest part; cut to test (about 4 minutes).

3. Spoon swordfish onto a platter; top with Mango Relish and garnish with cilantro sprigs. Makes 6 servings.

Mango Relish. Place ¼ cup (45 g) minced **white onion** in a fine strainer; rinse with cold water. Then place onion in a bowl, cover with **ice water**, and let stand for 30 minutes. Drain. Return onion to bowl; stir in 1½ cups (250 g) diced **ripe mango**, ¾ cup (115 g) diced **red bell pepper**, ¼ cup (10 g) chopped **cilantro**, 1 tablespoon minced **fresh ginger,** and 2 tablespoons (30 ml) **lemon juice.**

Per serving: 186 calories (30% calories from fat), 6 g total fat, 1 g saturated fat, 44 mg cholesterol, 106 mg sodium, 9 g carbohydrates, 0.8 g fiber, 23 g protein, 14 mg calcium, 1 mg iron

Smoked Salmon with Vodka & Bow Ties

Preparation time: About 15 minutes
Cooking time: About 25 minutes

A vodka-infused sauce enhances bow-shaped pasta and silken smoked salmon.

12 ounces/340 g (about 6 cups) dried farfalle (about 1½-inch/3.5-cm size)

1 teaspoon olive oil

1 small shallot, thinly sliced

4 small pear-shaped (Roma-type) tomatoes (about 6 oz./170 g *total*), peeled, seeded, and chopped

⅔ cup (160 ml) half-and-half

3 tablespoons (45 ml) vodka

2 tablespoons chopped fresh dill or ½ teaspoon dried dill weed (or to taste)

Pinch of ground nutmeg

4 to 6 ounces (115 to 170 g) sliced smoked salmon or lox, cut into bite-size strips

Dill sprigs

Ground white pepper

1. Bring 12 cups (2.8 liters) water to a boil in a 5- to 6-quart (5- to 6-liter) pan over medium-high heat. Stir in pasta and cook just until tender to bite (8 to 10 minutes); or cook according to package directions. Drain well and keep warm.

2. Heat oil in a wide nonstick frying pan over medium-low heat. Add shallot and cook, stirring often, until soft but not browned (about 3 minutes). Stir in tomatoes; cover and simmer for 5 minutes. Add half-and-half, vodka, chopped dill, and nutmeg. Increase heat to medium-high and bring to a boil. Cook, stirring often, for 1 minute.

3. Add pasta and mix thoroughly but gently. Remove from heat and stir in salmon. Transfer to a platter. Garnish with dill sprigs. Offer white pepper to add to taste. Makes 4 or 5 servings.

Per serving: 385 calories (24% calories from fat), 10 g total fat, 4 g saturated fat, 28 mg cholesterol, 243 mg sodium, 54 g carbohydrates, 2 g fiber, 15 g protein, 50 mg calcium, 3 mg iron

Cornmeal, one of Mexico's staple foods, is prepared like Italian polenta in this recipe: it's cooked in broth until tender and creamy. Top the chile- and cumin-seasoned cornmeal with baked white fish fillets.

4⅓ cups (1 liter) low-sodium chicken broth

1 cup (138 g) yellow cornmeal or polenta

½ teaspoon cumin seeds

1 small can (about 4 oz./115 g) diced green chiles

1 pound (455 g) skinless, boneless sea bass, orange roughy, or sole fillets, divided into 4 equal pieces

1 red bell pepper (about ⅓ lb./ 150 g), seeded and minced

1 tablespoon cilantro leaves

Salt

Lemon slices

Whitefish with Soft Cornmeal

Preparation time: About 10 minutes
Cooking time: About 20 minutes
Pictured on facing page

1. In a 3- to 4-quart (2.8- to 3.8-liter) pan, stir together broth, cornmeal, and cumin seeds until smoothly blended. Bring to a boil over high heat, stirring often with a long-handled wooden spoon (mixture will spatter). Reduce heat and simmer gently, uncovered, stirring often, until cornmeal tastes creamy (about 20 minutes). Stir in chiles.

2. When cornmeal is almost done, rinse fish, pat dry, and arrange in a single layer in a 9- by 13-inch (23- by 33-cm) baking pan. Bake in a 475°F (245°C)

oven until fish is just opaque but still moist in thickest part; cut to test (about 6 minutes).

3. To serve, spoon soft cornmeal equally onto 4 dinner plates. Top each serving with a piece of fish; sprinkle with bell pepper and cilantro. Season to taste with salt and serve with lemon slices. Makes 4 servings.

Per serving: 279 calories (17% calories from fat), 6 g total fat, 2 g saturated fat, 47 mg cholesterol, 377 mg sodium, 32 g carbohydrates, 3 g fiber, 28 g protein, 38 mg calcium, 2 mg iron

Coarsely ground dried mushrooms make an unusual coating for baked salmon fillets. Serve the fish with fresh asparagus and whimsical pasta bow ties.

¼ ounce/8 g (about ⅓ cup) dried porcini mushrooms

2 tablespoons fine dry bread crumbs

¼ teaspoon salt

8 ounces (230 g) dried farfalle (pasta bow ties)

8 ounces (230 g) asparagus, tough ends snapped off, spears cut diagonally into thin slices

1 to 1¼ pounds (455 to 565 g) boneless, skinless salmon fillet (1 inch/2.5 cm thick), cut into 4 equal pieces

2 tablespoons (30 ml) olive oil

Porcini-crusted Salmon

Preparation time: 20 minutes
Cooking time: About 15 minutes

1. In a food processor or blender, whirl mushrooms to make a coarse powder. Add bread crumbs and salt; whirl to mix, then pour into a wide, shallow bowl. Set aside.

2. In a 5- to 6-quart (5- to 6-liter) pan, bring about 3 quarts (2.8 liters) water to a boil over medium-high heat. Stir in pasta and cook for 5 minutes; then add asparagus and cook, stirring occasionally, until pasta and asparagus are just tender to bite (3 to 5 more minutes).

3. While pasta is cooking, rinse fish and pat dry; then turn fish in mushroom mixture, pressing to coat well all over. Lay fish pieces, flatter side down and well apart, in a shallow 10- by 15-inch (25- by 38-cm) baking pan. Pat any remaining mushroom mixture on fish; drizzle evenly with oil. Bake in a 400°F (205°C) oven until fish is just opaque but still moist in thickest part; cut to test (about 10 minutes).

4. When pasta mixture is done, drain it well and divide among 4 shallow individual bowls; keep warm. With a wide spatula, lift fish from baking pan; set in bowls atop pasta. Drizzle pan juices over pasta and fish. Makes 4 servings.

Per serving: 483 calories (30% calories from fat), 16 g total fat, 2 g saturated fat, 71 mg cholesterol, 226 mg sodium, 48 g carbohydrates, 2 g fiber, 35 g protein, 48 mg calcium, 4 mg iron

Whitefish with Soft Cornmeal
(recipe on facing page)

Stir-fry Sauces

The three sauces on this page offer easy ways to dress up stir-fried meats, poultry, seafood—even plain vegetables.

Grape Chutney

Preparation time: About 10 minutes
Cooking time: About 45 minutes

1 large onion, finely chopped

1 large tart apple such as Newtown Pippin or McIntosh (about 8 oz./230 g), peeled, cored, and finely chopped

2 cups (320 g) seedless red or green grapes

⅓ cup (75 g) firmly packed brown sugar

⅓ cup (80 ml) red wine vinegar

⅛ teaspoon pepper

Salt

1. In a wide nonstick frying pan or wok, combine onion and ¼ cup (60 ml) water. Cook over medium-high heat, stirring occasionally, until liquid evaporates and onion begins to brown and stick to pan bottom. To deglaze pan, add ¼ cup (60 ml) more water and stir to scrape browned bits free from pan bottom. Then continue to cook, stirring often, until liquid evaporates and browned bits stick to pan again. Deglaze with ¼ cup (60 ml) more water; then cook, stirring often, until onion is richly browned. (Total cooking time will be 10 to 15 minutes.)

2. To pan, add apple, grapes, ½ cup (120 ml) water, sugar, vinegar, and pepper. Bring to a boil; then reduce heat, cover, and simmer until grapes begin to split (about 10 minutes).

3. Uncover. Increase heat to medium-high and cook, stirring often, until mixture is thick and almost all liquid has evaporated (about 20 minutes); as mixture thickens, watch carefully and stir more often to prevent scorching. Season to taste with salt. If made ahead, let cool; then cover and refrigerate for up to 3 days. Reheat before serving, if desired. Makes about 2¼ cups (530 ml).

Per serving: 66 calories (2% calories from fat), 0.2 g total fat, 0 g saturated fat, 0 mg cholesterol, 4 mg sodium, 17 g carbohydrates, 1 g fiber, 0.4 g protein, 16 mg calcium, 0.3 mg iron

Cool Yogurt Sauce

Preparation time: About 5 minutes
Pictured on page 110

1 cup (240 ml) plain nonfat yogurt

1 tablespoon each chopped fresh mint and cilantro

Salt

Fresh mint and cilantro leaves (optional)

1. In a small bowl, stir together yogurt, chopped mint, and chopped cilantro. Season to taste with salt. If made ahead, cover and refrigerate for up to 4 hours; stir before serving. Sprinkle with mint and cilantro leaves just before serving, if desired. Makes about 1 cup (240 ml).

Per serving: 8 calories (2% calories from fat), 0 g total fat, 0 g saturated fat, 0.3 mg cholesterol, 11 mg sodium, 1 g carbohydrates, 0 g fiber, 0.8 g protein, 28 mg calcium, 0 mg iron

Citrus-Horseradish Cream

Preparation time: About 5 minutes

1 cup (240 ml) nonfat sour cream

3 tablespoons (60 g) orange marmalade

2 teaspoons prepared horseradish

About 1 teaspoon grated orange peel

Honey

Ground white pepper

1. In a small bowl, stir together sour cream, marmalade, horseradish, and 1 teaspoon of the orange peel until smoothly blended. Season to taste with honey and white pepper. If made ahead, cover and refrigerate until next day; stir before serving. Garnish with orange peel. Makes about 1¼ cups (300 ml).

Per serving: 16 calories (0% calories from fat), 0 g total fat, 0 g saturated fat, 0 mg cholesterol, 10 mg sodium, 3 g carbohydrates, 0 g fiber, 0.8 g protein, 17 mg calcium, 0 mg iron

Rich pink salmon served on a creamy, pale green tomatillo sauce makes a lovely entrée. Before using fresh tomatillos, remove the husks and rinse the fruit well to remove its sticky coating.

....

4 medium-size tomatillos (about 4 oz./115 g *total*), husked, rinsed, and chopped

1 tablespoon sliced green onion

1 clove garlic, peeled

¼ teaspoon grated lime peel

1 tablespoon (15 ml) lime juice

About ¾ teaspoon sugar, or to taste

⅛ teaspoon salt

½ cup (120 ml) plain low-fat yogurt (do not use nonfat yogurt) blended with 2 teaspoons cornstarch

8 low-fat flour tortillas (*each 7 to 9 inches/18 to 23 cm in diameter*)

1 tablespoon butter or margarine

1 pound (455 g) salmon fillets (about ½ inch/1 cm thick), skinned and cut into ¾-inch (2-cm) pieces

Stir-fried Salmon with Creamy Tomatillo Sauce

....

Preparation time: About 20 minutes
Cooking time: About 15 minutes

1 medium-size tomato (about 6 oz./170 g), chopped and drained well

2 tablespoons cilantro leaves
Lime wedges
Ground white pepper

....

1. In a blender or food processor, combine tomatillos, onion, garlic, lime peel, lime juice, sugar, and salt. Whirl until smooth. By hand, stir in yogurt mixture just until combined; do not overbeat or sauce will separate. Set aside.

2. Brush tortillas lightly with hot water; then stack, wrap in foil, and heat in a 350°F (175°C) oven until warm (10 to 12 minutes).

3. Meanwhile, melt butter in a wide nonstick frying pan or wok over medium-high heat. Add fish and stir-fry gently until just opaque but still moist in thickest part; cut to test (about 4 minutes). Remove from pan and keep warm. Wipe pan clean (be careful; pan is hot).

4. Add yogurt-tomatillo sauce to pan. Reduce heat to medium-low and simmer gently, stirring constantly, until sauce is slightly thickened (2 to 3 minutes); do not boil.

5. Divide sauce among 4 individual rimmed plates; spread sauce out evenly, then top equally with fish. Sprinkle with tomato and cilantro leaves, garnish with lime wedges, and season to taste with white pepper. Serve with tortillas. Makes 4 servings.

....

Per serving: 370 calories (27% calories from fat), 12 g total fat, 3 g saturated fat, 72 mg cholesterol, 533 mg sodium, 44 g carbohydrates, 9 g fiber, 29 g protein, 195 mg calcium, 3 mg iron

Salmon Sauté with Citrus Sauce
(recipe on facing page)

A beautiful choice for a company meal, this stir-fry combines silky salmon with a trio of citrus fruits. Fresh orange, grapefruit, and lime segments, lightly warmed in a marmalade-sweetened sauce, mingle with the moist strips of fish. Complete the menu with steamed green beans and a loaf of crusty bread for soaking up the sauce.

- 3 or 4 medium-size oranges (1½ to 2 lbs. /680 to 905 g *total*)
- 1 large pink grapefruit (about 12 oz./340 g)
- 1 large lime (about 4 oz./115 g)
- 3 green onions
- 1 tablespoon butter or margarine
- 1 pound (455 g) salmon fillets (about ½ inch/1 cm thick), skinned and cut into 1- by 2-inch (2.5- by 5-cm) strips
- ¼ cup (60 ml) dry vermouth
- ⅓ cup (100 g) orange marmalade
- 1 tablespoon chopped fresh mint
  Mint sprigs (optional)
  Salt and pepper

Salmon Sauté with Citrus Sauce

Preparation time: About 30 minutes
Cooking time: About 10 minutes
Pictured on facing page

1. Shred enough peel (colored part only) from oranges, grapefruit, and lime to make ½ teaspoon of each kind of peel. Combine peels in a small bowl; cover and set aside.

2. Cut off and discard remaining peel and all white membrane from grapefruit, lime, and 2 of the oranges. Holding fruit over a bowl to catch juice, cut between membranes to release segments; set segments aside. Pour juice from bowl into a glass measure. Squeeze juice from remaining oranges; add enough of this orange juice to juice in glass measure to make ½ cup/ 120 ml (reserve remaining orange juice for other uses). Set juice aside.

3. Trim and discard ends of onions. Cut onions into 2-inch (5-cm) lengths,

then cut each piece lengthwise into slivers; set aside.

4. Melt butter in a wide nonstick frying pan or wok over medium-high heat. Add fish. Stir-fry gently (flipping with a spatula, if needed) until fish is just opaque but still moist in thickest part; cut to test (about 4 minutes). With a slotted spoon, transfer fish to a large bowl; keep warm.

5. Add citrus juices and vermouth to pan. Bring to a boil; then boil, stirring often, until reduced to ⅓ cup/80 ml (about 3 minutes). Reduce heat to low, add marmalade, and stir until melted. Add onions and citrus segments; stir gently just until heated through. Remove from heat and stir in chopped mint.

6. Spoon fruit sauce over fish; mix gently. Divide fish mixture among 4 individual rimmed plates; garnish with citrus peels and mint sprigs, if desired. Season to taste with salt and pepper. Makes 4 servings.

Per serving: 352 calories (27% calories from fat), 10 g total fat, 3 g saturated fat, 70 mg cholesterol, 98 mg sodium, 39 g carbohydrates, 3 g fiber, 24 g protein, 89 mg calcium, 1 mg iron

---

Shrimp are plentiful along the Mexican coast. In this fragrant dish, the plump shellfish are infused with garlic and a touch of butter.

- 2 teaspoons butter or margarine
- 2 teaspoons olive oil
- 3 cloves garlic, minced or pressed
- 3 tablespoons (45 ml) water
- 1 pound (455 g) large shrimp (about 25 per lb.), shelled and deveined
  About 4 cups (820 g) hot cooked rice

Garlic Shrimp with Rice

Preparation time: About 10 minutes
Cooking time: About 5 minutes

- 3 tablespoons chopped parsley
  Salt and pepper
  Lemon wedges

1. Melt butter in a wide nonstick frying pan over medium-high heat. Add oil, garlic, water, and shrimp. Cook,

stirring, until shrimp are just opaque but still moist in center; cut to test (3 to 4 minutes).

2. To serve, spoon rice onto a platter or four dinner plates; spoon shrimp and pan juices over rice. Sprinkle with parsley. Season to taste with salt and pepper, then serve with lemon wedges. Makes 4 servings.

Per serving: 403 calories (15% calories from fat), 6 g total fat, 2 g saturated fat, 145 mg cholesterol, 161 mg sodium, 59 g carbohydrates, 0.9 g fiber, 24 g protein, 79 mg calcium, 5 mg iron

East meets West in this spicy-sweet entrée. The sauce will remind you of basic barbecue, but it's accented with ginger, soy, and sesame oil.

- 1 **cup (185 g) long-grain white rice**
- 1 **tablespoon sugar**
- 3 **tablespoons (45 ml) catsup**
- 1 **tablespoon (15 ml)** *each* **cider vinegar and reduced-sodium soy sauce**
- ½ **to 1 teaspoon crushed red pepper flakes**
- 1 **tablespoon (15 ml) salad oil**
- 1 **pound (455 g) large raw shrimp (31 to 35 per lb.), shelled (leave tails attached) and deveined**
- 1 **tablespoon minced fresh ginger**
- 3 **cloves garlic, minced or pressed**

Gingered Chili Shrimp

Preparation time: About 20 minutes
Cooking time: About 25 minutes

- ½ **teaspoon Oriental sesame oil**
  About ¼ cup (25 g) sliced green onions, or to taste

1. In a 3- to 4-quart (2.8- to 3.8-liter) pan, bring 2 cups (470 ml) water to a boil over high heat; stir in rice. Reduce heat, cover, and simmer until liquid has been absorbed and rice is tender to bite (about 20 minutes).

2. Meanwhile, in a small bowl, stir together sugar, catsup, vinegar, soy sauce, and red pepper flakes until sugar is dissolved; set aside.

3. Heat salad oil in a wide nonstick frying pan or wok over medium-high heat. When oil is hot, add shrimp. Stir-fry until just opaque in center; cut to test (3 to 4 minutes). Remove shrimp from pan with tongs or a slotted spoon; keep warm.

4. To pan, add ginger and garlic; stir-fry just until garlic is fragrant (about 30 seconds; do not scorch). Stir catsup mixture and pour into pan; bring to a boil, stirring. Remove pan from heat and add shrimp and sesame oil; mix gently but thoroughly.

5. Spoon rice onto a rimmed platter; spoon shrimp mixture over rice and sprinkle with onions. Makes 4 servings.

Per serving: 336 calories (16% calories from fat), 6 g total fat, 0.9 g saturated fat, 140 mg cholesterol, 423 mg sodium, 46 g carbohydrates, 0.8 g fiber, 23 g protein, 73 mg calcium, 5 mg iron

---

Big shrimp in a simple vegetable-wine sauce are delightful for family meals or casual company gatherings. Serve with steamed broccoli or asparagus and a crusty loaf of French bread.

- 2 **teaspoons butter or margarine**
- ½ **cup (60 g) finely chopped celery**
- ⅓ **cup (40 g) finely chopped shallots**
- 2 **cloves garlic, minced or pressed**
- 1 **medium-size red bell pepper (about 6 oz./170 g), seeded and finely chopped**
- 1¼ **cups (300 ml) fat-free reduced-sodium chicken broth**
- 1 **pound (455 g) large raw shrimp (31 to 35 per lb.), shelled and deveined**
- ⅔ **cup (160 ml) fruity white wine, such as Johannisberg Riesling**

Shrimp Sauté

Preparation time: About 15 minutes
Cooking time: About 25 minutes

1. Melt butter in a wide nonstick frying pan or wok over medium-high heat. Add celery, shallots, garlic, bell pepper, and broth. Cook, stirring often, until liquid has evaporated (about 10 minutes).

2. Add shrimp to pan and stir-fry until just opaque in center; cut to test (3 to 4 minutes). Remove shrimp from pan with tongs or a slotted spoon; place in a shallow serving bowl and keep warm.

3. Add wine to pan and bring to a boil; then boil, stirring often, until liquid is reduced by about two-thirds (about 7 minutes). Spoon sauce over shrimp. Makes 4 servings.

Per serving: 140 calories (23% calories from fat), 4 g total fat, 1 g saturated fat, 145 mg cholesterol, 374 mg sodium, 6 g carbohydrates, 0.7 g fiber, 20 g protein, 67 mg calcium, 3 mg iron

Shrimp and coconut taste delicious together—and the flavor gets even better when you add pineapple and curry. Serve this mildly spicy stir-fry over vermicelli, perhaps with a selection of tropical fruits on the side.

Coriander-Curry Shrimp

Preparation time: About 15 minutes
Cooking time: About 15 minutes

12 ounces to 1 pound (340 to 455 g) dried vermicelli or spaghetti

2 teaspoons cornstarch

⅔ cup (160 ml) pineapple-coconut juice (or ⅔ cup/160 ml unsweetened pineapple juice plus ¼ cup/20 g sweetened shredded coconut)

1 teaspoon salad oil

1 large onion, thinly sliced

1 clove garlic, minced or pressed

1 tablespoon *each* curry powder and ground coriander

¼ teaspoon ground red pepper (cayenne)

1½ pounds (680 g) large raw shrimp (31 to 35 per lb.), shelled and deveined

2 tablespoons finely chopped parsley

Lime wedges

Salt

1. In a 6- to 8-quart (6- to 8-liter) pan, cook vermicelli in about 4 quarts (3.8 liters) boiling water until just tender to bite (8 to 10 minutes); or cook according to package directions. Drain well, transfer to a warm rimmed platter, and keep warm.

2. While pasta is cooking, in a small bowl, stir together cornstarch and pineapple-coconut juice until blended; set aside.

3. Heat oil in a wide nonstick frying pan or wok over medium-high heat. When oil is hot, add onion, garlic, and 2 tablespoons (30 ml) water. Stir-fry until liquid has evaporated and onion is soft and beginning to brown (about 5 minutes).

4. Add curry powder, coriander, and red pepper to pan; stir to blend. Immediately add shrimp and stir-fry for 2 minutes. Stir cornstarch mixture well; pour into pan. Then stir until sauce is bubbly and shrimp are just opaque in center; cut to test (1 to 2 more minutes). Add parsley and mix gently but thoroughly.

5. Spoon shrimp mixture over pasta; garnish with lime wedges. Season to taste with salt. Makes 6 servings.

Per serving: 402 calories (10% calories from fat), 5 g total fat, 1 g saturated fat, 140 mg cholesterol, 152 mg sodium, 60 g carbohydrates, 3 g fiber, 28 g protein, 81 mg calcium, 5 mg iron

---

For an elegant, easy-to-fix main course, stir-fry shrimp in tequila and lime, then serve over thinly sliced red onions. Quick cooking keeps the shellfish tender and succulent.

Margarita Shrimp

Preparation time: About 15 minutes
Cooking time: About 10 minutes

¼ cup (60 ml) gold or white tequila

½ teaspoon grated lime peel

2 tablespoons (30 ml) *each* lime juice and water

2 tablespoons minced cilantro or parsley

1 tablespoon (15 ml) honey

⅛ teaspoon white pepper

1 pound (455 g) large shrimp (about 25 per lb.), shelled and deveined

About 2 teaspoons orange-flavored liqueur, or to taste (optional)

2 large red onions

Salt

Cilantro sprigs

Lime wedges

1. In a nonmetal bowl, mix tequila, lime peel, lime juice, water, minced cilantro, honey, and white pepper.

2. Pour tequila mixture into a wide nonstick frying pan. Add shrimp and cook over medium-high heat, stirring, until shrimp are just opaque but still moist in center; cut to test (3 to 4 minutes). With a slotted spoon, transfer shrimp to a bowl and keep warm.

Bring cooking liquid to a boil over high heat; boil until reduced to ⅓ cup (80 ml). Remove pan from heat; stir in liqueur, if desired.

3. While cooking liquid is boiling, thinly slice onions. Arrange onion slices in a single layer on a rimmed platter. To serve, spoon shrimp and cooking liquid over onion slices. Season to taste with salt; garnish with cilantro sprigs and lime wedges. Makes 4 servings.

Per serving: 173 calories (9% calories from fat), 2 g total fat, 0.3 g saturated fat, 140 mg cholesterol, 153 mg sodium, 19 g carbohydrates, 2 g fiber, 21 g protein, 91 mg calcium, 3 mg iron

Smoky grilled shrimp are served with a salad of crisp greens and tiny tomatoes for a quick and appealing main course.

························

1½ pounds (680 g) extra-jumbo raw shrimp (16 to 20 per lb.)

    About 2 tablespoons sea salt or kosher salt

5 to 6 ounces (140 to 170 g) Belgian endive, separated into leaves, rinsed, and crisped

8 ounces (230 g) small romaine lettuce leaves, rinsed and crisped

12 ounces (340 g) tiny red and/or yellow cherry tomatoes

    About ½ cup (120 ml) balsamic vinegar

1 tablespoon (15 ml) extra-virgin olive oil

    Pepper

Salt-grilled Shrimp

Preparation time: 25 minutes
Cooking time: About 8 minutes
Pictured on facing page

1. Insert a wooden pick under back of each shrimp between shell segments; gently pull up to remove vein. If vein breaks, repeat in another place. Rinse and drain deveined shrimp; then roll in salt to coat lightly.

2. Mix endive, lettuce, and tomatoes in a large bowl.

3. Place shrimp on a lightly greased grill 4 to 6 inches (10 to 15 cm) above a solid bed of hot coals. Cook, turning once, until shrimp are just opaque in center; cut to test (about 8 minutes). Meanwhile, divide salad among individual plates.

4. To serve, arrange shrimp atop salads. To eat, shell shrimp and season to taste with vinegar, oil, and pepper. Makes 4 servings.

························

Per serving: 213 calories (27% calories from fat), 6 g total fat, 1 g saturated fat, 210 mg cholesterol, 1,325 mg sodium, 9 g carbohydrates, 3 g fiber, 30 g protein, 104 mg calcium, 5 mg iron

---

Cook shrimp in a creamy sauce of sun-dried tomatoes and serve on hot linguine for a showy main course.

························

3 tablespoons dried tomatoes packed in oil, drained (reserve oil) and chopped

1 clove garlic, minced or pressed

1 pound (455 g) large shrimp (31 to 35 per lb.), shelled and deveined

10 ounces (285 g) dried linguine

⅔ cup (160 ml) light cream

¼ cup (25 g) thinly sliced green onions

2 tablespoons chopped fresh basil or 1 teaspoon dried basil

⅛ teaspoon ground white pepper

2 teaspoons cornstarch mixed with ¾ cup (180 ml) nonfat milk

Creamy Shrimp with Linguine

Preparation time: About 15 minutes
Cooking time: About 20 minutes

3 tablespoons (45 ml) dry vermouth (or to taste)

    Freshly grated Parmesan cheese

    Salt

························

1. Heat 1 teaspoon of the reserved oil from tomatoes in a wide nonstick frying pan over medium-high heat. Add garlic and shrimp. Cook, stirring often, just until shrimp are opaque in center; cut to test (about 6 minutes). Lift out and set aside, reserving any juices in pan.

2. Bring 12 cups (2.8 liters) water to a boil in a 5- to 6-quart (5- to 6-liter) pan over medium-high heat. Stir in pasta and cook just until tender to bite (8 to 10 minutes); or cook according to package directions. Meanwhile, combine cream, onions, basil, tomatoes, and white pepper with juices in frying pan. Bring to a boil over medium-high heat and cook, stirring, for 1 minute. Stir cornstarch mixture and add to pan. Return mixture to a boil and cook, stirring, just until slightly thickened. Remove from heat; stir in vermouth and shrimp.

3. Drain pasta well and arrange on individual plates. Top with shrimp mixture. Offer cheese and salt to add to taste. Makes 4 servings.

························

Per serving: 546 calories (29% calories from fat), 17 g total fat, 6 g saturated fat, 167 mg cholesterol, 188 mg sodium, 62 g carbohydrates, 3 g fiber, 31 g protein, 175 mg calcium, 6 mg iron

Salt-grilled Shrimp
(recipe on facing page)

Ideal for any time of year, this pretty pasta entrée features plump pink shrimp and a refreshing pesto based on parsley and toasted almonds.

- ¼ cup (35 g) whole unblanched almonds
- 2 cups (120 g) lightly packed parsley sprigs
- ¼ cup (60 ml) plus 1 teaspoon olive oil
- 3 tablespoons (45 ml) white wine vinegar
- 1 clove garlic, peeled
- 1 tablespoon drained capers
- ¼ teaspoon crushed red pepper flakes
- 1 pound (455 g) dried linguine
- 1 pound (455 g) large raw shrimp (31 to 35 per lb.), shelled and deveined

Shrimp with Parsley Pesto & Linguine

Preparation time: About 10 minutes
Cooking time: About 25 minutes

1. In a wide nonstick frying pan or wok, stir almonds over medium heat until golden beneath skins (about 8 minutes). Pour almonds into a food processor or blender; let cool. Then add parsley, ¼ cup (60 ml) of the oil, vinegar, garlic, capers, and red pepper flakes to processor. Whirl until pesto is smooth. Set aside.

2. In a 6- to 8-quart (6- to 8-liter) pan, cook linguine in about 4 quarts (3.8 liters) boiling water until just tender to bite (8 to 10 minutes); or cook accord-

ing to package directions. Drain well, transfer to a warm wide bowl, and keep warm.

3. While pasta is cooking, heat remaining 1 teaspoon oil in frying pan or wok over medium-high heat. When oil is hot, add shrimp and stir-fry until just opaque in center; cut to test (3 to 4 minutes).

4. Spoon shrimp and pesto over pasta; mix gently but thoroughly. Makes 6 servings.

Per serving: 474 calories (28% calories from fat), 15 g total fat, 2 g saturated fat, 93 mg cholesterol, 143 mg sodium, 60 g carbohydrates, 4 g fiber, 24 g protein, 93 mg calcium, 6 mg iron

---

Served cold, this light tostada features a topping of shrimp and jicama in a lemon-honey marinade. It's perfect for a hot-weather lunch or supper.

- 1 pound (455 g) tiny cooked shrimp
- 1 cup (130 g) peeled, finely minced jicama
- 3 tablespoons sliced green onions
- 1 teaspoon grated lemon peel
- 3 tablespoons (45 ml) lemon juice
- 2 teaspoons honey
  White pepper

Lemon Shrimp Tostadas

Preparation time: About 15 minutes
Chilling time: At least 20 minutes

About 1½ cups (360 ml) Cherry Tomato Salsa (page 20) or other salsa of your choice

- 6 crisp corn taco shells (page 346) or warm corn tortillas (page 346)
- 3 cups (165 g) shredded lettuce
- 1 medium-size firm-ripe tomato (about 6 oz./170 g), finely chopped

1. In a nonmetal bowl, mix shrimp, jicama, onions, lemon peel, lemon juice, and honey; season to taste with white pepper. Cover and refrigerate for at least 20 minutes or up to 3 hours.

2. Meanwhile, prepare Cherry Tomato Salsa and refrigerate.

3. To serve, place one taco shell on each of 6 dinner plates; top equally with lettuce. Scoop out shrimp mixture with a slotted spoon, drain, and divide equally among taco shells. Top equally with tomato. Add salsa to taste. Makes 6 servings.

Per serving: 156 calories (9% calories from fat), 2 g total fat, 0.3 g saturated fat, 148 mg cholesterol, 217 mg sodium, 18 g carbohydrates, 2 g fiber, 18 g protein, 94 mg calcium, 3 mg iron

Just a little Gorgonzola packs a big punch in this entrée.

Fettuccine with Shrimp & Gorgonzola

Preparation time: About 10 minutes
Cooking time: About 15 minutes

12 ounces (340 g) dried spinach or regular fettuccine

2 teaspoons butter or margarine

12 ounces (340 g) mushrooms, sliced

¾ cup (180 ml) half-and-half

3 ounces/85 g (about ⅔ cup) Gorgonzola cheese, crumbled

¾ cup (180 ml) low-sodium chicken broth

8 ounces (230 g) tiny cooked shrimp

2 tablespoons minced parsley

1. Bring 12 cups (2.8 liters) water to a boil in a 5- to 6-quart (5- to 6-liter) pan over medium-high heat. Stir in pasta and cook just until tender to bite (8 to 10 minutes); or cook according to package directions. Drain well and keep warm.

2. Melt butter in a wide nonstick frying pan over medium-high heat. Add mushrooms and cook, stirring often, until browned (about 8 minutes). Add half-and-half, cheese, and broth. Reduce heat to medium and cook, stirring, until cheese is melted (about 2 minutes); do not boil.

3. Add shrimp and pasta quickly. Lift with 2 forks to mix until most of the liquid is absorbed. Transfer to a rimmed platter. Sprinkle with minced parsley. Makes 6 servings.

Per serving: 372 calories (29% calories from fat), 12 g total fat, 6 g saturated fat, 153 mg cholesterol, 366 mg sodium, 44 g carbohydrates, 5 g fiber, 22 g protein, 160 mg calcium, 4 mg iron

---

Serve this pretty entrée with minty cool Papaya Salsa for a light summer lunch.

Shrimp & Avocado Tostadas with Papaya Salsa

Preparation time: 35 minutes
Cooking time: About 8 minutes

Crisp Taco Shells:

4 corn tortillas (*each* about 6 inches/15 cm in diameter)

Salt (optional)

Papaya Salsa:

1 medium-size firm-ripe papaya (about 1 lb./455 g), peeled, seeded, and diced

1 small cucumber (about 8 oz./230 g), peeled, seeded, and diced

1 tablespoon chopped fresh mint (or to taste)

2 tablespoons (30 ml) lime juice

1 tablespoon (15 ml) honey

Avocado & Shrimp Topping:

1 teaspoon grated lemon peel

2 tablespoons (30 ml) lemon juice

1 medium-size soft-ripe avocado

1 cup (210 g) low-fat (2%) cottage cheese

2 or 3 cloves garlic, peeled

⅛ teaspoon salt

2 tablespoons finely chopped cilantro

1 small fresh jalapeño or serrano chile, seeded and finely chopped

1 tablespoon thinly sliced green onion

1 large tomato (about 8 oz./230 g), finely chopped and drained well

4 cups (about 4 oz./115 g) shredded lettuce

6 ounces (170 g) small cooked shrimp

1. Dip tortillas, one at a time, in hot water; drain briefly. Season to taste with salt, if desired. Arrange tortillas, not overlapping, in a single layer on a large baking sheet. Bake in a 500°F (260°C) oven for 6 minutes. With a metal spatula, turn tortillas over; continue to bake until crisp and tinged with brown (about 2 more minutes). If made ahead, let cool completely; then store airtight at room temperature until next day.

2. In a medium-size bowl, stir together papaya, cucumber, mint, lime juice, and honey; set aside. If made ahead, cover and refrigerate for up to 4 hours.

3. Place lemon peel and lemon juice in a blender or food processor. Halve and pit avocado; scoop flesh from peel into blender. Add cottage cheese, garlic, and the ⅛ teaspoon salt. Whirl until smoothly puréed. With a spoon, gently stir in cilantro, chile, onion, and half the tomato.

4. To serve, place one taco shell on each of 4 individual plates. Evenly top taco shells with avocado mixture; then top shells equally with lettuce, shrimp, and remaining tomato. Offer papaya salsa to add to taste. Makes 4 servings.

Per serving: 308 calories (29% calories from fat), 10 g total fat, 2 g saturated fat, 87 mg cholesterol, 387 mg sodium, 37 g carbohydrates, 4 g fiber, 21 g protein, 179 mg calcium, 4 mg iron

Lemon Shrimp over Caper Couscous
(recipe on facing page)

Add plenty of tangy flavor, and you won't miss the fat!

....

- 1 **pound (455 g) large raw shrimp (31 to 35 per lb.), shelled and deveined**
- 2 **cloves garlic, minced or pressed (optional)**
- ¾ **teaspoon chopped fresh oregano or ¼ teaspoon dried oregano**
- ½ **teaspoon grated lemon peel**
- ⅛ **teaspoon pepper**
  Cooking Sauce (recipe follows)
- 8 **ounces (230 g) asparagus**
- 1 **medium-size red bell pepper (about 6 oz./170 g)**
- 1½ **cups (360 ml) fat-free reduced-sodium chicken broth**
- 1 **cup (185 g) couscous**
- 2 **tablespoons (30 ml) seasoned rice vinegar (or 2 tablespoons/ 30 ml distilled white vinegar plus 1 teaspoon sugar)**
- 1 **to 2 tablespoons drained capers**
- 1 **tablespoon (15 ml) olive oil**
  Lemon wedges and oregano sprigs

Lemon Shrimp over Caper Couscous

....

Preparation time: About 20 minutes
Cooking time: About 15 minutes
Pictured on facing page

1. In a large bowl, mix shrimp, garlic (if used), chopped oregano, ¼ teaspoon of the lemon peel, and pepper. Set aside; stir occasionally.

2. Prepare Cooking Sauce and set aside. Snap off and discard tough ends of asparagus; cut spears into ½-inch (1-cm) slanting slices and set aside. Seed bell pepper, cut into thin strips, and set aside.

3. In a 3- to 4-quart (2.8- to 3.8-liter) pan, combine broth and remaining ¼ teaspoon lemon peel. Bring to a boil over high heat; stir in couscous. Cover, remove from heat, and let stand until liquid has been absorbed (about 5 minutes). Stir in vinegar and capers. Keep couscous warm; fluff occasionally with a fork.

4. In a wide nonstick frying pan or wok, combine asparagus, bell pepper, and ⅓ cup (80 ml) water. Cover and cook over medium-high heat until asparagus is almost tender to bite (about 3 minutes). Uncover and stir-fry until liquid has evaporated. Remove vegetables from pan and set aside.

5. Heat oil in pan. When oil is hot, add shrimp mixture and stir-fry for 2 minutes. Stir Cooking Sauce well and pour into pan; then return asparagus and bell pepper to pan. Cook, stirring, until sauce boils and thickens slightly and shrimp are just opaque in center; cut to test (1 to 2 more minutes). Remove from heat.

6. To serve, spoon couscous onto a rimmed platter; top with shrimp mixture. Garnish with lemon wedges and oregano sprigs. Makes 4 servings.

....

Cooking Sauce. In a small bowl, stir together 1 tablespoon **cornstarch** and 2 tablespoons **dry sherry** until blended. Then stir in ½ cup **fat-free reduced-sodium chicken broth.**

....

Per serving: 355 calories (14% calories from fat), 5 g total fat, 0.8 g saturated fat, 140 mg cholesterol, 696 mg sodium, 46 g carbohydrates, 2 g fiber, 28 g protein, 71 mg calcium, 3 mg iron

---

Couscous' mild flavor lends itself to zesty dressings, robust sauces, and exotic spices.

....

- 1 **package (about 10 oz./285 g) couscous**
- 1 **small cucumber (about 8 oz./230 g)**
- 1 **cup (40 g) firmly packed fresh mint leaves**
- ½ **cup (120 ml) lemon juice**
- 2 **tablespoons (30 ml) olive oil**
  About ½ teaspoon honey (or to taste)
- 1 **cup (145 g) fresh blueberries or other fresh berries**
  Salt and pepper
- 4 **to 8 large butter lettuce leaves, rinsed and crisped**

Couscous with Berries & Shrimp

....

Preparation time: 15 minutes, plus about 10 minutes for couscous to cool
Cooking time: About 5 minutes

....

- 6 **to 8 ounces (170 to 230 g) small cooked shrimp**
  Lemon wedges and mint sprigs

....

1. In a 2½- to 3-quart (2.4- to 2.8-liter) pan, bring 2¼ cups (530 ml) water to a boil over medium-high heat. Stir in couscous; cover, remove from heat, and let stand until liquid has been absorbed (about 5 minutes). Then transfer couscous to a large bowl and let stand until cool (about 10 minutes), fluffing often with a fork.

2. Meanwhile, peel, halve, and seed cucumber; thinly slice halves and set aside. Finely chop mint leaves, place in a small bowl, and mix in lemon juice, oil, and honey. Add cucumber and blueberries to couscous; then add mint dressing and mix gently but thoroughly. Season to taste with salt and pepper.

3. Line each of 4 individual plates with 1 or 2 lettuce leaves. Mound couscous mixture in center of each plate; top with shrimp. Garnish with lemon wedges and mint sprigs. Makes 4 servings.

....

Per serving: 419 calories (18% calories from fat), 8 g total fat, 1 g saturated fat, 97 mg cholesterol, 129 mg sodium, 66 g carbohydrates, 4 g fiber, 21 g protein, 66 mg calcium, 3 mg iron

Although traditionally based on rice, this paella is made with quick-cooking couscous.

Couscous Paella

Preparation time: About 15 minutes
Cooking time: 20 to 25 minutes

4 ounces (115 g) chorizo sausages, casings removed

1 large onion (about 8 oz./230 g), chopped

1 bottle (about 8 oz./240 ml) clam juice

1¼ cups (300 ml) low-sodium chicken broth

2 teaspoons cumin seeds

9¼ ounces /260 g (about 1½ cups) dried couscous

1 medium-size red bell pepper (about 6 oz./170 g), seeded and chopped

8 ounces (230 g) tiny cooked shrimp

Lime or lemon wedges

1. Crumble chorizo into a wide non-stick frying pan; add onion. Cook over medium heat, stirring often, until well browned (15 to 20 minutes); if pan appears dry or mixture sticks to pan bottom, add water, 1 tablespoon (15 ml) at a time.

2. Add clam juice, broth, and cumin seeds. Increase heat to medium-high and bring to a boil. Stir in pasta; cover, remove from heat, and let stand until liquid is absorbed (about 5 minutes). Transfer to a wide serving bowl.

3. Stir in bell pepper and top with shrimp. Offer lime to add to taste. Makes 4 to 6 servings.

Per serving: 377 calories (25% calories from fat), 10 g total fat, 4 g saturated fat, 106 mg cholesterol, 242 mg sodium, 47 g carbohydrates, 3 g fiber, 24 g protein, 60 mg calcium, 3 mg iron

---

Try a new twist on an old favorite. Individual pizzas are topped with bean sprouts, jack cheese and Oriental-style seasonings.

Thai Pizza with Shrimp

Preparation time: 20 minutes
Cooking time: About 15 minutes

6 small Italian bread shells (*each about 5½ inches/13.5 cm in diameter and about 4 oz./ 115 g*); or 6 pita breads (*each about 5 inches/12.5 cm in diameter*); or 6 English muffins, split

½ cup (120 ml) reduced-fat creamy peanut butter

3 tablespoons (45 ml) hoisin sauce

2 tablespoons (30 ml) seasoned rice vinegar (or 2 tablespoons/ 30 ml distilled white vinegar plus 1 teaspoon sugar)

1 teaspoon Oriental sesame oil

1 cup (170 g) bean sprouts

1 cup (about 4 oz./115 g) shredded reduced-fat jack cheese

5 to 6 ounces (140 to 170 g) small cooked shrimp

¼ cup (25 g) thinly sliced green onions

Crushed red pepper flakes

1. Place bread shells, pita breads, or muffin halves (cut side up) on two 12- by 15-inch (30- by 38-cm) baking sheets.

2. In a bowl, combine peanut butter, hoisin sauce, vinegar, and sesame oil. Beat until smoothly blended; if necessary, add a little water so sauce is easy to spread. Spread equally over cupped area of bread shells or top of pita breads (or spread to edge of muffin halves). Scatter bean sprouts equally over sauce; sprinkle with cheese.

3. Bake in a 350°F (175°C) oven until cheese is melted and beginning to brown (12 to 15 minutes; if using one oven, switch positions of baking sheets after 7 minutes). Place each pizza on an individual plate; top pizzas equally with shrimp and onions. Season to taste with red pepper flakes. Makes 6 servings.

Per serving: 410 calories (29% calories from fat), 13 g total fat, 4 g saturated fat, 62 mg cholesterol, 876 mg sodium, 50 g carbohydrates, 2 g fiber, 23 g protein, 233 mg calcium, 3 mg iron

Fresh ginger and garlic add zip to this savory custard. Serve warm or cold.

8 ounces (230 g) small cooked shrimp

1 cup (240 ml) nonfat milk

1 large egg

2 large egg whites

4 teaspoons (20 ml) dry sherry

2 teaspoons *each* finely chopped fresh ginger and reduced-sodium soy sauce

1 clove garlic, minced or pressed

⅛ teaspoon Oriental sesame oil

⅛ teaspoon ground white pepper

1 teaspoon sesame seeds

Shrimp Custard

Preparation time: 15 minutes
Cooking time: About 30 minutes

1. Divide half the shrimp evenly among four ¾-cup (180-ml) custard cups or ovenproof bowls; cover and refrigerate remaining shrimp. Set custard cups in a large baking pan at least 2 inches (5 cm) deep. In a medium-size bowl, combine milk, egg, egg whites, sherry, ginger, soy sauce, garlic, oil, and white pepper; beat lightly just until blended. Pour egg mixture evenly over shrimp in custard cups.

2. Set pan on center rack of a 325°F (165°C) oven. Pour boiling water into pan around cups up to level of custard. Bake until custard jiggles only slightly in center when cups are gently shaken (about 25 minutes). Lift cups from pan. Let stand for about 5 minutes before serving. Or, if made ahead, let cool; then cover and refrigerate until next day and serve cold.

3. Meanwhile, toast sesame seeds in a small frying pan over medium heat, stirring often, until golden (about 3 minutes). Remove from pan and set aside. Just before serving, top custards with remaining shrimp; then sprinkle with sesame seeds. Makes 4 servings.

Per serving: 120 calories (20% calories from fat), 2 g total fat, 1 g saturated fat, 165 mg cholesterol, 303 mg sodium, 4 g carbohydrates, 0 g fiber, 18 g protein, 115 mg calcium, 2 mg iron

---

Big artichoke halves filled with a spicy shrimp-cilantro "salsa" make an attractive first course. Pickled scallions, available in well-stocked supermarkets and Asian markets, add a sweet crunch to the salsa.

½ cup (120 ml) seasoned rice vinegar; or ½ cup (120 ml) distilled white vinegar plus 1 tablespoon sugar

1 tablespoon mustard seeds

1 teaspoon whole black peppercorns

4 thin quarter-size slices fresh ginger

3 large artichokes (about 12 oz./ 340 g each), *each* 4 to 4½ inches(10 to 11 cm) in diameter

12 ounces(340 g) tiny cooked shrimp

⅓ cup (85 g) minced pickled scallions

¼ cup (10 g) minced cilantro

¼ cup (10 g) minced fresh mint or 1 tablespoon dried mint

2 tablespoons (30 ml) reduced-sodium soy sauce

¼ to ½ teaspoon chili oil

Mint or cilantro sprigs

Artichokes with Shrimp & Cilantro Salsa

Preparation time: About 25 minutes
Cooking time: About 35 minutes

1. In a 6- to 8-quart (7- to 8-liter) pan, combine ¼ cup (60 ml) of the vinegar, mustard seeds, peppercorns, ginger, and 4 quarts (3.8 liters) water. Cover and bring to a boil over high heat.

2. Meanwhile, remove coarse outer leaves from artichokes and trim stems flush with bases. With a sharp knife, cut off top third of each artichoke. With scissors, trim thorny tips from remaining leaves. Immerse artichokes in cold water and swish back and forth vigorously to release debris; then lift artichokes from water and shake briskly to drain.

3. Lower artichokes into boiling vinegar-water mixture. Then reduce heat and simmer, covered, until artichoke bottoms are tender when pierced (about 35 minutes). Drain, reserving cooking liquid. Let artichokes stand until they are cool enough to handle.

4. Pour artichoke cooking liquid through a fine strainer set over a bowl; discard ginger and reserve mustard seeds and peppercorns. Place shrimp in strainer. Rinse shrimp with cool water; then drain well, place in a bowl, and mix with reserved seasonings, remaining ¼ cup (60 ml) vinegar, scallions, minced cilantro, minced mint, soy sauce, and chili oil. (At this point, you may cover and refrigerate artichokes and shrimp mixture separately until next day.)

5. With a long, sharp knife, cut each artichoke in half lengthwise. Remove sharp-pointed inner leaves and scoop out fuzzy centers. Set each artichoke half on a salad plate. Spoon shrimp mixture equally into artichokes; garnish with mint sprigs. Makes 6 servings.

Per serving: 122 calories (11% calories from fat), 2 g total fat, 0.2 g saturated fat, 111 mg cholesterol, 911 mg sodium, 13 g carbohydrates, 4 g fiber, 15 g protein, 67 mg calcium, 3 mg iron

This spectacular entrée of assorted shellfish is presented on a bed of linguine. Steeping the shrimp, scallops, and mussels helps to preserve their delicate flavors and textures. To complete this very fine meal, you need add only a beverage and warm loaves of your favorite crusty bread.

Linguine with Lemon-Basil Seafood

Preparation time: About 1 hour
Cooking time: About 30 minutes
Pictured on facing page

3 **cups (710 ml) low-sodium chicken broth**

1½ **cups (360 ml) dry white wine**

2 **pounds (905 g) large shrimp (31 to 35 per lb.), shelled and deveined**

1 **pound (455 g) bay scallops, rinsed and drained**

36 **to 48 small mussels or small hard-shell clams in shell, suitable for steaming, scrubbed**
  Lemon-Basil Dressing (recipe follows)

2 **pounds (905 g) dried linguine**

3 **tablespoons chopped parsley**
  Thin lemon slices

1. Combine broth, wine, and 2 cups (470 ml) water in a 6- to 8-quart (6- to 8-liter) pan. Bring to a boil over high heat. Add shrimp. Cover tightly, remove from heat, and let stand just until shrimp are opaque in center; cut to test (about 3 minutes). With a slotted spoon, transfer shrimp to a large bowl; keep warm.

2. Return broth to a boil. Add scallops. Cover tightly, remove from heat, and let stand just until scallops are opaque in center; cut to test (about 3 minutes). With a slotted spoon, transfer scallops to bowl with shrimp; keep warm.

3. Return broth to a boil. Add mussels; reduce heat, cover, and boil gently until shells pop open (5 to 10 minutes). With a slotted spoon, transfer mussels to bowl with seafood; discard any unopened shells.

4. Pour broth from pan into a 2-quart (1.9-liter) measure, leaving sediment in pan. Measure 1¾ cups (420 ml) of the broth and reserve for dressing. Drain any liquid from cooked seafood into remaining broth; reserve for other uses.

5. Prepare Lemon-Basil Dressing. Add 1 cup (240 ml) of the dressing to seafood and stir gently. Keep warm.

6. Bring 20 cups (5 liters) water to a boil in an 8- to 10-quart (8- to 10-liter) pan over medium-high heat. Stir in pasta, half at a time, if desired, and cook just until tender to bite (8 to 10 minutes); or cook according to package directions. Drain well and transfer to a very large (15- by 21-inch/38- by 53-cm or round 16-inch/41-cm) platter or shallow bowl. Add remaining dressing and lift with 2 forks to mix.

7. Mound seafood over pasta, arranging mussel shells around edge of platter, if desired. Sprinkle with parsley and garnish with lemon. Makes 10 to 12 servings.

Lemon-Basil Dressing. In a 1- to 1½-quart (950-ml to 1.4-liter) pan, stir together 1 tablespoon finely shredded **lemon peel,** ¾ cup (180 ml) **lemon juice,** 1¾ cups (420 ml) reserved **broth from seafood,** ¼ cup (60 ml) **olive oil,** 3 tablespoons (45 ml) **honey,** and 1½ teaspoons coarsely ground **pepper.** Bring to a boil over medium heat. Remove from heat and stir in ½ cup (80 g) minced **shallots,** 2 tablespoons chopped **fresh basil** or 2 teaspoons dried basil, and 2 or 3 cloves **garlic,** minced or pressed. Keep warm.

Per serving: 518 calories (15% calories from fat), 9 g total fat, 1 g saturated fat, 124 mg cholesterol, 271 mg sodium, 71 g carbohydrates, 2 g fiber, 35 g protein, 80 mg calcium, 6 mg iron

Linguine with Lemon-Basil Seafood
(recipe on facing page)

Serve this bold seafood stew with plenty of crusty bread to soak up the flavorful broth.

Cioppino

Preparation time: 30 minutes
Cooking time: About 45 minutes

- 1 tablespoon (15 ml) olive oil
- 1 large onion, chopped
- 1 large red bell pepper (about 8 oz./230 g), seeded and chopped
- ⅓ cup (20 g) chopped Italian or regular parsley
- 2 cloves garlic, minced
- 4 or 5 large tomatoes (2 to 2½ lbs./905 g to 1.15 kg *total*), peeled and cut into chunks
- 1 large can (about 15 oz./425 g) tomato sauce
- 1 cup (240 ml) dry red wine
- 1 dried bay leaf
- 1 tablespoon chopped fresh basil or 1 teaspoon dried basil
- 2 teaspoons chopped fresh oregano or ½ teaspoon dried oregano

- 12 small hard-shell clams (suitable for steaming), scrubbed
- 1 pound (455 g) extra-jumbo raw shrimp (16 to 20 per lb.), shelled and deveined
- 1 pound (455 g) firm-textured, white-fleshed fish, such as rockfish, cut into 2-inch (5-cm) chunks
- 2 cooked whole Dungeness crabs (about 2 lbs./905 g *each*), cleaned and cracked
  Salt

1. Heat oil in an 8- to 10-quart (8- to 10-liter) pan over medium-high heat. Add onion, bell pepper, parsley, garlic, and ¼ cup (60 ml) water. Cook, stirring often, until onion is soft (about 5 minutes); add water, 1 tablespoon (15 ml) at a time, if pan appears dry.

2. Stir in tomatoes, tomato sauce, wine, bay leaf, basil, and oregano. Bring to a boil; then reduce heat, cover, and simmer until flavors are blended (about 20 minutes).

3. Gently stir in clams, shrimp, fish, and crabs. Cover tightly and bring to a boil over high heat. Reduce heat and simmer gently until clams pop open and fish is just opaque but still moist in thickest part; cut to test (10 to 15 minutes).

4. Ladle stew into large soup bowls, discarding bay leaf and any unopened clams. Season to taste with salt. Makes 8 servings.

Per serving: 264 calories (18% calories from fat), 5 g total fat, 0.8 g saturated fat, 149 mg cholesterol, 597 mg sodium, 15 g carbohydrates, 3 g fiber, 35 g protein, 126 mg calcium, 5 mg iron

---

Sliced fennel lends a refreshing anise flavor to this garlicky stew of fish and Roma tomatoes.

Fish & Fennel Stew

Preparation time: 25 minutes
Cooking time: About 40 minutes

- 1 large head fennel (about 12 oz./340 g)
- 1 tablespoon (15 ml) olive oil
- 1 large onion, chopped
- 6 cloves garlic, minced
- 1¼ pounds (565 g) pear-shaped (Roma-type) tomatoes, chopped
- 2 cups (470 ml) fat-free reduced-sodium chicken broth
- 1 bottle (about 8 oz./230 g) clam juice
- ½ cup (120 ml) dry white wine
- ¼ to ½ teaspoon ground red pepper (cayenne)

- 1½ pounds (680 g) boneless, skinless firm-textured, light-fleshed fish, such as halibut, swordfish, or sea bass, cut into 1½-inch (3.5-cm) chunks

1. Trim stems from fennel, reserving feathery green leaves. Trim and discard any bruised areas from fennel. Finely chop leaves and set aside; thinly slice fennel head.

2. Heat oil in a 5- to 6-quart (5- to 6-liter) pan over medium heat. Add sliced fennel, onion, and garlic; cook, stirring often, until onion is sweet tasting and all vegetables are browned (about 20 minutes). Add water, ¼ cup (60 ml) at a time, if pan appears dry.

3. Add tomatoes, broth, clam juice, wine, and red pepper. Bring to a boil; then reduce heat, cover, and simmer for 10 minutes. Add fish, cover, and simmer until just opaque but still moist in thickest part; cut to test (about 5 minutes). Stir in fennel leaves. Makes 4 servings.

Per serving: 317 calories (24% calories from fat), 8 g total fat, 1 g saturated fat, 54 mg cholesterol, 628 mg sodium, 16 g carbohydrates, 4 g fiber, 40 g protein, 151 mg calcium, 3 mg iron

Linguine with Tomato-Clam Sauce

Robust yet light, this traditional Italian favorite goes together in less than an hour.

....

- 2 cans (about 6½ oz./185 g *each*) chopped clams
- 1 teaspoon olive oil
- 2 cloves garlic, minced
- 1 can (about 15 oz./425 g) tomato purée
- 2 tablespoons chopped fresh basil or 1 tablespoon dried basil
- 8 ounces (230 g) dried linguine
- 1 large tomato (about 8 oz./ 230 g), finely chopped
- ¼ cup (20 g) grated Parmesan cheese

  Basil sprigs

  Crushed red pepper flakes

Preparation time: 15 minutes
Cooking time: About 25 minutes

1. Drain clams, reserving liquid; set clams and liquid aside.

2. Heat oil in a 3- to 4-quart (2.8- to 3.8-liter) pan over medium heat. Add garlic and cook, stirring, just until fragrant (about 30 seconds; do not scorch). Add clam liquid, tomato purée, and chopped basil. Bring to a boil over high heat; then reduce heat and simmer, uncovered, until reduced to 2 cups (470 ml), about 20 minutes. Stir often to prevent scorching, scraping bottom of pan as you stir.

3. While sauce is simmering, cook pasta. In a 4- to 5-quart (3.8- to 5-liter) pan, bring about 8 cups (1.9 liters) water to a boil over medium-high heat. Stir in pasta and cook until just tender to bite (8 to 10 minutes); or cook pasta according to package directions. Drain well, transfer to a large serving bowl, and keep warm.

4. Add clams and chopped tomato to sauce; stir just until heated through. Spoon sauce over pasta and sprinkle with cheese. Garnish with basil sprigs. Season to taste with red pepper flakes. Makes 4 servings.

....

Per serving: 380 calories (12% calories from fat), 5 g total fat, 2 g saturated fat, 37 mg cholesterol, 601 mg sodium, 59 g carbohydrates, 5 g fiber, 25 g protein, 189 mg calcium, 17 mg iron

---

Orecchiette with Sake-Clam Sauce

Round and rimmed, orecchiette may look like diminutive caps, but they translate as "little ears."

....

- 2 cans (about 6½ oz./185 g *each*) chopped clams
- ¾ cup (130 g) finely chopped onions
- 2 cloves garlic, minced or pressed
- 1 cup (240 ml) sake or dry vermouth
- 2 tablespoons capers, drained
- 8 ounces/230 g (about 2⅓ cups) dried orecchiette or other medium-size pasta shape
- ¼ cup (15 g) finely chopped parsley
- ¼ cup (20 g) freshly grated Parmesan cheese
- ⅛ teaspoon crushed red pepper flakes

Preparation time: About 10 minutes
Cooking time: About 20 minutes

1. Drain clams, reserving juice. Set clams aside.

2. Combine ½ cup (120 ml) of the clam juice, onions, garlic, and ¼ cup (60 ml) of the sake in a wide nonstick frying pan. Cook over high heat, stirring often, until about a quarter of the liquid remains (about 3 minutes). Add clams, capers, and remaining ¾ cup (180 ml) sake. Reduce heat and simmer, uncovered, for about 4 minutes. Remove from heat and keep warm.

3. Bring 8 cups (1.9 liters) water to a boil in a 4- to 5-quart (3.8- to 5-liter) pan over medium-high heat. Stir in pasta and cook just until tender to bite (8 to 10 minutes); or cook according to package directions. Drain well. Transfer to a wide serving bowl. Quickly add clam mixture and stir until most of the liquid is absorbed. Add parsley, cheese, and red pepper flakes. Mix thoroughly but gently. Makes 4 servings.

....

Per serving: 381 calories (10% calories from fat), 3 g total fat, 1 g saturated fat, 36 mg cholesterol, 266 mg sodium, 49 g carbohydrates, 2 g fiber, 22 g protein, 147 mg calcium, 16 mg iron

Crab with Emerald Sauce
(recipe on facing page)

A bright green sauce puréed from fresh basil and cilantro cradles delicate pasta and chunks of fresh crab.

....

- 8 ounces (230 g) basil sprigs; or 6 ounces (170 g) spinach and ¼ cup (8 g) dried basil
- 4 ounces (115 g) cilantro sprigs
- 8 ounces (230 g) dried capellini
- ¼ cup (60 ml) seasoned rice vinegar; or ¼ cup (60 ml) rice vinegar and 1 teaspoon sugar
- 1 tablespoon minced lemon peel
- 1 tablespoon (15 ml) Oriental sesame oil
- ¾ cup (180 ml) low-sodium chicken broth
- 2 tablespoons (30 ml) salad oil
- ⅓ to ½ pound (150 to 230 g) cooked crabmeat

Crab with Emerald Sauce

....

Preparation time: About 20 minutes
Cooking time: About 8 minutes
Pictured on facing page

1. Reserve 4 of the basil or cilantro sprigs for garnish.

2. Bring 8 cups (1.9 liters) water to a boil in a 4- to 5-quart (3.8- to 5-liter) pan over medium-high heat. Gather half the remaining fresh basil (or spinach) into a bunch. Holding stem ends with tongs, dip leaves into boiling water just until bright green (about 3 seconds). At once plunge into ice water. Repeat with cilantro and remaining basil.

3. Stir pasta into water and cook just until tender to bite (about 4 minutes); or cook according to package directions. Drain well. Place in a bowl. Add vinegar, lemon peel, and sesame oil; lift with 2 forks to mix. Keep warm.

4. Drain basil and cilantro; blot dry. Cut leaves from stems, discarding stems. Place leaves in a blender or food processor with dried basil (if used), broth, and salad oil. Whirl until smooth. Spread on individual plates. Top with pasta and crab. Garnish with reserved sprigs. Makes 4 servings.

....

Per serving: 382 calories (30% calories from fat), 13 g total fat, 2 g saturated fat, 43 mg cholesterol, 485 mg sodium, 49 g carbohydrates, 4 g fiber, 19 g protein, 172 mg calcium, 5 mg iron

---

Some argue that cracked crab is best with no embellishments at all—but a taste of this dish might make such purists reconsider. It's simple to make: just heat the succulent crab pieces briefly in a simple, savory blend of sherry and oyster sauce.

....

- ⅓ cup (80 ml) *each* dry sherry and water
- ¼ cup (60 ml) oyster sauce or reduced-sodium soy sauce
- 2 teaspoons cornstarch
- 14 green onions
- 1 tablespoon (15 ml) salad oil
- 3 tablespoons minced fresh ginger
- 3 large cooked Dungeness crabs (about 6 lbs./2.7 kg *total*), cleaned and cracked

Stir-fried Cracked Crab with Onion

....

Preparation time: About 15 minutes
Cooking time: About 10 minutes

1. In a small bowl, stir together sherry, water, oyster sauce, and cornstarch until blended; set aside. Trim and discard ends of onions; then cut onions into 2-inch (5-cm) lengths, keeping white and green parts separate.

2. Heat oil in a wide nonstick frying pan or wok over medium-high heat. Add ginger and white parts of onions; stir-fry until onions just begin to brown (about 2 minutes).

3. Stir sherry mixture well and pour into pan; stir until sauce boils and thickens slightly (about 1 minute). Add crab and green parts of onions; stir to coat crab with sauce. Reduce heat to low, cover, and cook, stirring occasionally, until crab is heated through (5 to 8 minutes). Makes 6 servings.

....

Per serving: 163 calories (21% calories from fat), 3 g total fat, 0.4 g saturated fat, 64 mg cholesterol, 805 mg sodium, 8 g carbohydrates, 0.8 g fiber, 21 g protein, 80 mg calcium, 1 mg iron

Try lasagne with crabmeat for an elegant casserole.

- 2¼ pounds (1.02 kg) fennel, ends trimmed
- 2 large onions (about 1 lb./455 g *total*), thinly sliced
- 12 ounces (340 g) mushrooms, sliced
- 2 cups (470 ml) low-sodium chicken broth
- 8 ounces (230 g) dried lasagne
- 2 cups (470 ml) low-fat milk
- ¼ cup (60 ml) dry sherry
- ¼ cup (32 g) cornstarch mixed with ⅓ cup (80 ml) water
- 8 ounces/230 g (about 2 cups) shredded fontina cheese
- ¾ to 1 pound (340 to 455 g) cooked crabmeat

1. Slice fennel thinly crosswise, reserving feathery tops. Mix fennel, onions, and mushrooms in a 12- by 14-inch (30- by 35.5-cm) baking pan. Bake in a

Crab Lasagne

Preparation time: About 30 minutes
Cooking time: About 1¾ hours

475°F (245°C) oven, stirring occasionally, until browned bits stick to pan bottom (about 45 minutes); do not scorch. To deglaze pan, add ½ cup (120 ml) of the broth, stirring to loosen browned bits. Continue to bake until browned bits form again (about 20 more minutes). Repeat deglazing step, adding ½ cup (120 ml) more broth, and bake until vegetables are well browned. Add ½ cup (120 ml) more broth, stirring to loosen browned bits. Keep warm.

2. Bring 12 cups (2.8 liters) water to a boil in a 5- to 6-quart (5- to 6-liter) pan over medium-high heat. Stir in pasta and cook just until tender to bite (8 to 10 minutes); or cook according to package directions. Drain well; blot dry.

3. Mince enough of the reserved fennel to make ¼ cup (60 ml). In a wide nonstick frying pan, combine minced fennel, milk, sherry, and remaining ½ cup (120 ml) broth. Bring to a boil over high heat. Stir cornstarch mixture and add to pan. Cook, stirring, until sauce comes to a boil. Remove from heat, add half the cheese, and stir until smooth. Keep hot.

4. Arrange a third of the pasta in a 9- by 13-inch (23- by 33-cm) baking pan. Spread with vegetables and half the sauce. Cover with a third more of the pasta, crab, and all but ½ cup (120 ml) of the sauce. Top with remaining pasta, sauce, and cheese. Bake in a 450°F (230°C) oven until bubbling (about 10 minutes). Broil 4 to 6 inches (10 to 15 cm) below heat until browned (4 to 5 minutes). Let stand for 5 minutes. Makes 6 to 8 servings.

Per serving: 419 calories (29% calories from fat), 13 g total fat, 7 g saturated fat, 97 mg cholesterol, 610 mg sodium, 43 g carbohydrates, 4 g fiber, 30 g protein, 407 mg calcium, 4 mg iron

---

There's a hint of heat in this quickly prepared entrée.

- 1 pound/455 g (about 7 cups) dried rotini or other corkscrew-shaped pasta
- 1½ pounds (680 g) bay scallops, rinsed and drained
- 1 teaspoon paprika
- ½ teaspoon *each* dried basil, dried thyme, dried mustard, and ground white pepper
- 2 teaspoons salad oil
- 1 cup (240 ml) low-sodium chicken broth
- 1½ tablespoons cornstarch mixed with ⅓ cup (80 ml) water
- ½ cup (120 ml) reduced-fat or regular sour cream

Scallops with Rotini

Preparation time: About 10 minutes
Cooking time: About 20 minutes

1. Bring 16 cups (3.8 liters) water to a boil in a 6- to 8-quart (6- to 8-liter) pan over medium-high heat. Stir in pasta and cook just until tender to bite (8 to 10 minutes); or cook according to package directions. Meanwhile, place scallops in a large bowl. Add paprika, basil, thyme, mustard, and white pepper. Mix until scallops are well coated. Heat oil in a wide nonstick frying pan over medium-high heat. Add scallops

and cook, stirring often, just until opaque in center; cut to test (about 3 minutes). Lift out and set aside, reserving juices in pan.

2. Drain pasta well. Transfer to a platter and keep warm.

3. Increase heat to high and cook reserved juices until reduced to about ¼ cup (60 ml). Add broth and bring to a boil. Stir cornstarch mixture and add to broth. Bring to a boil again, stirring. Remove from heat and stir in sour cream and scallops. Spoon over pasta. Makes 6 servings.

Per serving: 442 calories (14% calories from fat), 7 g total fat, 2 g saturated fat, 44 mg cholesterol, 218 mg sodium, 63 g carbohydrates, 2 g fiber, 31 g protein, 50 mg calcium, 4 mg iron

Simple, saucy, and bright—that describes this combination of green broccoli, red bell pepper, and white sea scallops. Serve the dish with fresh Chinese noodles or hot, fluffy rice.

Scallops with Broccoli & Bell Pepper

Preparation time: About 15 minutes
Cooking time: About 10 minutes

Cooking Sauce (recipe follows)
1 pound (455 g) sea scallops
2 cups (145 g) broccoli flowerets
1 medium-size red or green bell pepper (about 6 oz./170 g), seeded and cut into thin strips
1 small onion, thinly sliced
2 teaspoons salad oil
1 or 2 cloves garlic, minced or pressed

1. Prepare Cooking Sauce and set aside. Rinse scallops and pat dry; cut into bite-size pieces, if desired. Set aside.

2. In a wide nonstick frying pan or wok, combine broccoli, bell pepper, onion, and ⅓ cup (80 ml) water. Cover and cook over medium-high heat just until vegetables are tender to bite (about 4 minutes). Uncover and stir-fry until liquid has evaporated.

3. Stir Cooking Sauce well and pour into pan. Cook, stirring, until sauce boils and thickens slightly (1 to 2 minutes). Transfer vegetable mixture to a serving bowl and keep warm. Wipe pan clean (be careful; pan is hot).

4. Heat oil in pan over medium-high heat. When oil is hot, add garlic and 1 tablespoon (15 ml) water to pan. Stir-fry just until garlic is fragrant (about 30 seconds; do not scorch). Add scallops. Stir-fry until scallops are just opaque in center; cut to test (3 to 4 minutes).

5. Pour scallops and any pan juices over vegetable mixture; mix gently but thoroughly. Makes 4 servings.

Cooking Sauce. In a small bowl, stir together 4 teaspoons **cornstarch** and 2 tablespoons (30 ml) **reduced-sodium soy sauce** until blended. Stir in ¾ cup (180 ml) **fat-free reduced-sodium chicken broth,** 2 tablespoons (30 ml) **dry sherry,** 2 teaspoons finely minced **fresh ginger,** and 1½ teaspoons **sugar.**

Per serving: 196 calories (16% calories from fat), 3 g total fat, 0.4 g saturated fat, 37 mg cholesterol, 591 mg sodium, 17 g carbohydrates, 3 g fiber, 23 g protein, 68 mg calcium, 1 mg iron

---

Colorful, fragrant, and just plain delicious, this dish is a winner. Be prepared—it's likely to disappear almost as soon as you bring the platter to the table.

Scallop & Pea Pod Stir-fry with Papaya

Preparation time: About 15 minutes
Cooking time: About 8 minutes

Ginger Sauce (recipe follows)
2 medium-size papayas (about 1 lb./455 g each)
1 pound (455 g) sea scallops
1 tablespoon butter or margarine
1½ cups (115 g) fresh Chinese pea pods (also called snow or sugar peas) or sugar snap peas, ends and strings removed; or 1 package (about 6 oz./170 g) frozen Chinese pea pods, thawed and drained

1. Prepare Ginger Sauce and set aside. Cut unpeeled papayas lengthwise into halves; remove and discard seeds. Set papaya halves, cut side up, on a platter; cover and set aside.

2. Rinse scallops and pat dry; cut into bite-size pieces, if desired. Melt butter in a wide nonstick frying pan or wok over medium-high heat. Add scallops and fresh pea pods (if using frozen pea pods, add later, as directed below). Stir-fry until scallops are just opaque in center; cut to test (3 to 4 minutes).

3. Stir Ginger Sauce well, then pour into pan. Stir in frozen pea pods, if using. Cook, stirring, until sauce boils and thickens slightly (1 to 2 minutes). Spoon scallop mixture equally into papaya halves. Makes 4 servings.

Ginger Sauce. In a small bowl, stir together 2 teaspoons **cornstarch** and ¼ cup (60 ml) **water** until blended. Then stir in 1 tablespoon (15 ml) *each* **honey** and **lemon juice,** ½ teaspoon ground **ginger,** and ½ teaspoon **Chinese five-spice** (or ⅛ teaspoon *each* anise seeds, ground allspice, ground cinnamon, and ground cloves).

Per serving: 220 calories (16% calories from fat), 4 g total fat, 2 g saturated fat, 45 mg cholesterol, 219 mg sodium, 26 g carbohydrates, 2 g fiber, 21 g protein, 78 mg calcium, 1 mg iron

Start with convenient cooked crabmeat to produce a speedy meal that's definitely out of the ordinary. Warm tortillas are topped with a blend of sweet crab, chiles, and tomatoes, then garnished with sour cream and tart tomatillo salsa. Use either corn or flour tortillas, as you prefer; you can warm them in the oven while you make the filling.

Tomatillo-Lime Salsa (recipe follows)

6 to 12 corn tortillas (*each* about 6 inches/15 cm in diameter) or low-fat flour tortillas (*each* 7 to 9 inches/18 to 23 cm in diameter)

2 tablespoons (30 ml) olive oil

1 clove garlic, minced or pressed

1 small red onion, finely chopped

1 can (about 4 oz./115 g) diced green chiles

2 large firm-ripe tomatoes (about 1 lb./455 g *total*), chopped

1 pound (455 g) cooked crabmeat

3 to 6 cups (3 to 6 oz./85 to 170 g) finely shredded lettuce

¼ cup (10 g) lightly packed cilantro leaves

Lime wedges

½ cup (120 ml) nonfat sour cream

Soft Crab Tacos with Tomatillo-Lime Salsa

Preparation time: About 20 minutes
Cooking time: About 15 minutes
Pictured on facing page

1. Prepare Tomatillo-Lime Salsa; set aside. Brush tortillas lightly with hot water; then stack, wrap in foil, and heat in a 350°F (175°C) oven until warm (10 to 12 minutes).

2. Meanwhile, heat oil in a wide non-stick frying pan or wok over medium-high heat. When oil is hot, add garlic and onion; stir-fry until onion begins to brown (about 5 minutes). Add chiles and half the tomatoes; stir-fry until tomatoes are soft (about 4 minutes). Remove from heat and gently stir in crab.

3. Divide lettuce equally among tortillas; then top tortillas equally with crab mixture, remaining tomatoes, and cilantro. Garnish with lime wedges; top with Tomatillo-Lime Salsa and sour cream. Makes 6 servings.

Tomatillo-Lime Salsa. In a medium-size bowl, combine 8 medium-size **tomatillos** (about 8 oz./230 g *total*), husked, rinsed, and finely chopped; 2 tablespoons sliced **green onion;** ¼ teaspoon grated **lime peel;** 2 tablespoons (30 ml) **lime juice;** 1 teaspoon **sugar** (or to taste); and about ⅛ teaspoon **salt** (or to taste). If made ahead, cover and refrigerate for up to 4 hours; stir before serving.

Per serving: 263 calories (25% calories from fat), 7 g total fat, 0.9 g saturated fat, 76 mg cholesterol, 460 mg sodium, 29 g carbohydrates, 4 g fiber, 21 g protein, 216 mg calcium, 2 mg iron

Soft Crab Tacos with Tomatillo-Lime Salsa
(recipe on facing page)

Whimsical pasta "butterflies" are a perfect foil for stir-fried scallops seasoned with sage. Add shredded spinach and diced tomato, and you have a hearty, fresh-tasting choice for lunch or a light supper.

....

8 ounces (230 g) dried farfalle or other pasta shapes (about 1½-inch/3.5-cm size)

1 pound (455 g) sea scallops

2 tablespoons (30 g) butter or margarine

2 cloves garlic, minced or pressed

About ¾ teaspoon chopped fresh sage or ¼ teaspoon dried rubbed sage, or to taste

1 large tomato (about 8 oz./230 g), chopped and drained well

¼ cup (60 ml) dry white wine

½ to ¾ cup (15 to 23 g) finely shredded spinach

Sautéed Scallops with Spinach & Farfalle

....

Preparation time: About 20 minutes
Cooking time: About 15 minutes

About ⅓ cup (30 g) grated Parmesan cheese

Sage sprigs

Pepper

....

1. In a 4- to 5-quart (3.8- to 5-liter) pan, cook farfalle in about 8 cups (1.9 liters) boiling water until just tender to bite (8 to 10 minutes); or cook according to package directions. Drain well, transfer to a warm rimmed platter, and keep warm.

2. While pasta is cooking, rinse scallops and pat dry; cut into bite-size pieces, if desired. Melt butter in a wide nonstick frying pan or wok over medium-high heat. Add scallops and stir-fry until just opaque in center; cut to test (3 to 4 minutes). Remove scallops from pan with a slotted spoon; keep warm.

3. Add garlic and chopped sage to pan; stir-fry just until garlic is fragrant (about 30 seconds; do not scorch). Stir in tomato and wine; bring to a boil. Remove from heat, add scallops and spinach, and mix gently but thoroughly.

4. Spoon scallop mixture over pasta; sprinkle with cheese and garnish with sage sprigs. Season to taste with pepper. Makes 4 servings.

....

Per serving: 417 calories (22% calories from fat), 10 g total fat, 5 g saturated fat, 58 mg cholesterol, 381 mg sodium, 49 g carbohydrates, 2 g fiber, 30 g protein, 146 mg calcium, 3 mg iron

---

Succulent scallops and pasta seashells in a simple wine-cheese sauce are delightful for casual company gatherings or family meals.

....

2 ounces (55 g) Neufchâtel or cream cheese, at room temperature

2 teaspoons honey

1 teaspoon Dijon mustard

½ teaspoon grated lemon peel

1 pound (455 g) sea scallops

8 ounces (230 g) dried medium-size pasta shells

¾ cup (180 ml) fat-free reduced-sodium chicken broth

¼ cup (15 g) finely chopped Italian or regular parsley

2 teaspoons dry white wine (or to taste)

¼ cup (20 g) grated Parmesan cheese

Scallops & Shells with Lemon Cream

....

Preparation time: 20 minutes
Cooking time: About 15 minutes

1. In a food processor or blender, whirl Neufchâtel cheese, honey, mustard, and lemon peel until smooth; set aside. Rinse scallops and pat dry; cut into bite-size pieces, if desired. Set aside.

2. In a 4- to 5-quart (3.8- to 5-liter) pan, bring about 8 cups (1.9 liters) water to a boil over medium-high heat; stir in pasta and cook until just tender to bite (8 to 10 minutes); or cook pasta according to package directions. Drain well, transfer to a large serving bowl, and keep warm.

3. In a 3- to 4-quart (2.8- to 3.8-liter) pan, bring broth to a boil over high heat. Add scallops and cook until just opaque in center; cut to test (1 to 2 minutes).

4. With a slotted spoon, transfer scallops to bowl with pasta; keep warm. Quickly pour scallop cooking liquid from pan into Neufchâtel cheese mixture in food processor; whirl until smooth. With a spoon, stir in parsley and wine. Pour sauce over scallops and pasta; sprinkle with Parmesan cheese. Serve immediately. Makes 4 servings.

....

Per serving: 393 calories (16% calories from fat), 7 g total fat, 3 g saturated fat, 53 mg cholesterol, 509 mg sodium, 49 g carbohydrates, 2 g fiber, 31 g protein, 138 mg calcium, 3 mg iron

In Italy, scampi *just means shrimp. In America, though, the word usually refers to shrimp prepared a certain way: sautéed with plenty of oil, butter, and garlic. In making this scampi-inspired scallop dish, we've been generous with the garlic—there are three cloves in the stir-fry, another in the crisp crumb topping—but we've cut the fat to a single tablespoon. The result? A great-tasting dish that's lean, too.*

Stir-fried Crumbs (recipe follows)

1 tablespoon chopped parsley
2 tablespoons (30 ml) dry white wine
1 teaspoon lemon juice
½ teaspoon honey
1 bunch watercress (about 5 oz./140 g), coarse stems removed, sprigs rinsed and crisped
1 pound (455 g) sea scallops
1½ teaspoons butter or margarine
1½ teaspoons olive oil
3 cloves garlic, minced or pressed
Lemon wedges

Scallop Scampi

Preparation time: About 15 minutes
Cooking time: About 15 minutes

1. Prepare Stir-fried Crumbs; let cool slightly. Stir parsley into crumbs and set aside. In a small bowl, stir together wine, lemon juice, and honey; set aside. Arrange watercress on a large rimmed platter; cover and set aside.

2. Rinse scallops and pat dry; cut into bite-size pieces, if desired. Melt butter in oil in a wide nonstick frying pan or wok over medium-high heat. When butter mixture is hot, add garlic, 1 tablespoon (15 ml) water, and scallops. Stir-fry until scallops are just opaque in center; cut to test (3 to 4 minutes).

3. Stir wine mixture well and pour into pan; bring just to a boil. With a slotted spoon, lift scallops from pan; arrange over watercress. Pour pan juices into a small pitcher. Sprinkle scallops with Stir-fried Crumbs and garnish with lemon wedges. Offer pan juices to add to taste. Makes 4 servings.

Stir-fried Crumbs. Tear 1 slice (about 1 oz./30 g) **sourdough sandwich bread** into pieces; whirl in a blender or food processor to make fine crumbs. In a wide nonstick frying pan or wok, combine crumbs, 1½ teaspoons **water,** ½ teaspoon **olive oil,** and 1 clove **garlic,** minced or pressed. Stir-fry over medium heat until crumbs are crisp and golden (about 5 minutes); remove from pan and set aside. If made ahead, let cool; then cover airtight and store at room temperature until next day.

Per serving: 168 calories (27% calories from fat), 5 g total fat, 1 g saturated fat, 41 mg cholesterol, 257 mg sodium, 9 g carbohydrates, 1 g fiber, 21 g protein, 83 mg calcium, 0.7 mg iron

Eggplant Parmesan
(recipe on page 200)

Meatless Main Dishes

Vegetarian entrées can be as tempting and delectable as any meat-based menu. Hearty legumes and nutty grains are not only tasty but wonderfully satisfying. We combine them with a bit of flavorful cheese or low-fat dairy product and fresh vegetables to create nutritionally complete as well as delicious recipes. Treat your family to slimmed-down Eggplant Parmesan or entice them with Mushroom & White Bean Pizza.

Sure to become a family favorite, this layered eggplant-tomato casserole is a satisfying choice for casual company meals as well.

3 large egg whites

3 tablespoons (45 ml) Marsala

1 cup (100 g) fine dry bread crumbs

½ cup (40 g) shredded Parmesan cheese

1 tablespoon chopped fresh thyme or ½ teaspoon dried thyme

½ teaspoon salt

2 medium-size eggplants (about 2 lbs./905 g *total*)

¼ cup (35 g) yellow cornmeal

¾ cup (180 ml) nonfat sour cream

2 cloves garlic, peeled

2 teaspoons cornstarch

1 teaspoon honey

3 cans (about 14½ oz./410 g *each*) diced tomatoes, drained well

1 tablespoon chopped fresh basil or ½ teaspoon dried basil

2 large tomatoes (about 1 lb./455 g *total*), very thinly sliced

1 cup (about 4 oz./115 g) shredded mozzarella cheese

Thyme sprigs

Eggplant Parmesan

Preparation time: 30 minutes
Cooking time: About 1 hour
Pictured on page 198

1. In a wide, shallow bowl, beat egg whites and Marsala to blend. In another wide, shallow bowl, combine bread crumbs, ¼ cup (20 g) of the Parmesan cheese, chopped thyme, and salt; set aside.

2. Cut unpeeled eggplants crosswise into slices about ¼ inch (6 mm) thick. Dip slices in egg white mixture; drain briefly, then dip in crumb mixture and press to coat lightly all over. Arrange eggplant slices on 2 or 3 greased large baking sheets; pat any remaining crumb mixture on slices.

3. Bake in a 400°F (205°C) oven, turning once, until golden brown on both sides (about 30 minutes); switch positions of baking sheets halfway through baking. If any slices begin to brown excessively, remove them and set aside.

4. Meanwhile, sprinkle cornmeal over bottom of a greased 9- by 13-inch (23- by 33-cm) baking pan; set aside. In a food processor or blender, whirl sour cream, garlic, cornstarch, honey,

and two-thirds of the canned tomatoes until smoothly puréed. Stir in remaining canned tomatoes and basil.

5. Spoon a third of the tomato sauce over cornmeal in pan; top evenly with a third of the tomato slices. Arrange half the eggplant slices over tomatoes; sprinkle with half the mozzarella cheese. Top evenly with half each of the remaining tomato sauce and tomato slices, then with remaining eggplant. Top with remaining tomato sauce, tomato slices, and mozzarella cheese. Sprinkle with remaining ¼ cup (20 g) Parmesan cheese.

6. Cover and bake in a 400°F (205°C) oven for 15 minutes. Then uncover and continue to bake until sauce is bubbly and casserole is golden on top and hot in center (15 to 20 more minutes). Garnish with thyme sprigs. Makes 6 servings.

Per serving: 337 calories (27% calories from fat), 10 g total fat, 4 g saturated fat, 20 mg cholesterol, 938 mg sodium, 44 g carbohydrates, 6 g fiber, 17 g protein, 390 mg calcium, 4 mg iron

Vivid red bell peppers make bright edible containers for a sweet-spicy black bean and corn filling.

....

- 2 **very large red, yellow, or green bell peppers (about 10 oz./ 285 g each); choose wide, squarish peppers**
- ¼ **cup (30 g) slivered almonds**
- 1 **package (about 10 oz./285 g) frozen corn kernels, thawed and drained**
- 1 **can (about 15 oz./425 g) black beans, drained and rinsed well**
- 1 **can (about 8 oz./230 g) tomato sauce**
- ½ **cup (75 g) raisins or dried currants**
- ½ **cup (50 g) sliced green onions**
- 2 **teaspoons cider vinegar**
- 2 **cloves garlic, minced**
- ½ **teaspoon each ground cinnamon and chili powder**
- ¹⁄₁₆ **to ⅛ teaspoon ground cloves**
  Salt
- ½ **cup (55 g) shredded reduced-fat jack cheese**

Southwestern Stuffed Peppers

....

Preparation time: 30 minutes
Cooking time: About 45 minutes

....

- 2 **tablespoons cilantro leaves**
- 1 **cup (240 ml) plain nonfat yogurt**

....

1. Using a very sharp knife, carefully cut each pepper in half lengthwise through (and including) stem; leave stem attached and remove seeds. If any of the pepper halves does not sit flat, even out the base by trimming a thin slice from it (do not pierce wall of pepper). Set pepper halves aside.

2. Toast almonds in a 5- to 6-quart (5- to 6-liter) pan over medium heat, stirring often, until golden (about 3 minutes). Transfer almonds to a bowl and let cool; then coarsely chop and set aside.

3. In same pan, bring 3 to 4 quarts (2.8 to 3.8 liters) water to a boil over medium-high heat. Add pepper halves and cook for 2 minutes. Lift out, drain, and set aside. Discard water and dry pan. In pan (off heat) or in a large bowl, combine corn, beans, tomato sauce, raisins, onions, vinegar, garlic, cinnamon, chili powder, and cloves. Mix gently but thoroughly; season to taste with salt.

4. Spoon vegetable mixture equally into pepper halves, mounding filling at top. Set pepper halves, filled side up, in a 9- by 13-inch (23- by 33-cm) baking pan. Cover and bake in a 375°F (190°C) oven for 10 minutes. Uncover and continue to bake until filling is hot in center (about 20 more minutes; if drippings begin to scorch, carefully add about ¼ cup/60 ml water to pan). Remove from oven and sprinkle evenly with cheese; cover and let stand for 5 minutes. Garnish with cilantro; offer yogurt to add to taste. Makes 4 servings.

....

Per serving: 353 calories (20% calories from fat), 8 g total fat, 2 g saturated fat, 11 mg cholesterol, 678 mg sodium, 58 g carbohydrates, 9 g fiber, 18 g protein, 327 mg calcium, 3 mg iron

---

This pizza's crisp crust isn't made from the usual yeast dough; it's based on an herb-seasoned combination of shredded zucchini, carrots, and bread crumbs.

....

- 1 **cup (100 g) fine dry bread crumbs**
- 1 **teaspoon olive oil**
- 2 **cloves garlic, minced or pressed**
- 1 **large egg**
- 2 **large egg whites**
- 2 **tablespoons all-purpose flour**
- ¼ **teaspoon pepper**
- 1 **teaspoon dried basil**
- 1 **cup (100 g) shredded carrots**
- 1 **cup (100 g) shredded zucchini**

Zucchini-Carrot Pizza

....

Preparation time: 15 minutes
Cooking time: About 40 minutes

....

- 1 **teaspoon yellow cornmeal**
- ¾ **cup (85 g) shredded reduced-fat jack cheese**
- 1 **cup (70 g) very thinly sliced mushrooms**

....

1. In a wide nonstick frying pan, combine bread crumbs, oil, and garlic. Stir over medium-high heat until crumbs are crisp (about 6 minutes). Remove from pan and set aside.

2. In a large bowl, combine egg, egg whites, flour, pepper, basil, carrots, and zucchini. Mix until evenly blended. Add crumbs and mix well. Sprinkle a 12-inch (30-cm) nonstick or regular pizza pan with cornmeal. Spread vegetable mixture evenly in pan and bake in a 400°F (205°C) oven until browned (about 20 minutes).

3. Sprinkle crust with cheese and mushrooms and continue to bake until cheese is melted (about 10 minutes). Makes 4 servings.

....

Per serving: 261 calories (27% calories from fat), 8 g total fat, 4 g saturated fat, 68 mg cholesterol, 459 mg sodium, 32 g carbohydrates, 3 g fiber, 16 g protein, 287 mg calcium, 3 mg iron

A zesty black bean salsa accompanies savory cornmeal pancakes.

Corn Pancakes with Black Bean Salsa

Preparation time: 20 minutes
Cooking time: About 6 minutes
Pictured on facing page

Black Bean Salsa:

- 1 can (about 15 oz./425 g) black beans, drained and rinsed well
- 1 cup (115 g) peeled, finely chopped jicama
- ¾ cup (100 g) crumbled feta cheese
- 3 tablespoons (45 ml) lime juice
- ⅓ cup (15 g) chopped cilantro
- 2 tablespoons sliced green onion
- 2 teaspoons honey
- ¼ teaspoon crushed red pepper flakes

Corn Pancakes:

- 1 tablespoon butter or margarine
- 1 package (about 10 oz./285 g) frozen corn kernels, thawed and drained
- 1 large egg
- ⅓ cup (50 g) diced red bell pepper
- ⅓ cup (80 ml) nonfat milk
- 3 tablespoons yellow cornmeal
- ⅓ cup (40 g) all-purpose flour
- 1½ teaspoons *each* sugar and baking powder

Garnishes:

- Cilantro sprigs (optional)
- Lime wedges

1. To prepare salsa, in a large bowl, combine beans, jicama, cheese, lime juice, chopped cilantro, onion, honey, and red pepper flakes. Cover and set aside; stir occasionally.

2. To prepare pancakes, melt butter in a wide nonstick frying pan over low heat. Remove pan from heat. Transfer butter to a large bowl (do not wash frying pan) and add corn, egg, bell pepper, and milk; mix well. In a small bowl, stir together cornmeal, flour, sugar, and baking powder. Add cornmeal mixture to corn mixture and stir just until dry ingredients are evenly moistened.

3. Place frying pan over medium-high heat. When pan is hot, drop batter into pan in 3-tablespoon (45-ml) portions, spacing portions of batter about 3 inches (8 cm) apart. Use a spoon to spread each portion into about a 3-inch (8-cm) circle. Cook pancakes until tops look dry and bottoms are lightly browned (1 to 2 minutes); turn pancakes with a wide spatula and continue to cook until lightly browned on other side (about 1 more minute). As pancakes are cooked, transfer them to a platter and keep warm.

4. Garnish pancakes with cilantro sprigs (if desired) and lime wedges; serve with black bean salsa to add to taste. Makes 4 servings.

Per serving: 336 calories (28% calories from fat), 11 g total fat, 6 g saturated fat, 84 mg cholesterol, 700 mg sodium, 49 g carbohydrates, 6 g fiber, 14 g protein, 294 mg calcium, 3 mg iron

---

Slices of eggplant and zucchini replace the traditional wide noodles.

Eggplant-Zucchini Lasagne

Preparation time: 45 minutes
Cooking time: About 1¼ hours

- 2 medium-size eggplants (about 2½ lbs./1.15 kg *total*)
- 4 small zucchini (about 1 lb./455 g *total*)
- 1 tablespoon (15 ml) olive oil
- 10 ounces (285 g) firm reduced-fat tofu, rinsed and drained
- 1½ cups (315 g) nonfat cottage cheese
- 1½ cups (about 6 oz./170 g) shredded part-skim mozzarella cheese
- 1 cup (145 g) cooked brown rice
- ½ teaspoon fennel seeds, crushed
- ½ teaspoon crushed red pepper flakes
- 2½ cups (590 ml) purchased reduced-fat spaghetti sauce
- 2 tablespoons grated Parmesan cheese

1. Cut unpeeled eggplants crosswise into ½-inch (1-cm) slices; cut zucchini lengthwise into ¼-inch (6-mm) slices. Brush 3 shallow 10- by 15-inch (25- by 38-cm) baking pans with oil; arrange vegetable slices in a single layer in pans. Bake in a 400°F (205°C) for 15 minutes; then turn vegetables over and continue to bake until tinged with brown (about 15 more minutes).

2. Meanwhile, slice tofu; place between paper towels and press gently to release excess liquid. Place tofu in a medium-size bowl and mash well. Mix in cottage cheese, mozzarella cheese, rice, fennel seeds, and red pepper flakes.

3. Spread ½ cup (120 ml) of the spaghetti sauce in a 9- by 13-inch (23- by 33-cm) baking pan. Top evenly with half each of the eggplant, zucchini, and tofu mixture; spread with 1 cup (240 ml) more spaghetti sauce. Repeat layers. Sprinkle with Parmesan cheese. Bake in a 400°F (205°C) oven until heated through (about 45 minutes). Let stand for about 10 minutes before serving. Makes 8 servings.

Per serving: 228 calories (26% calories from fat), 7 g total fat, 3 g saturated fat, 17 mg cholesterol, 560 mg sodium, 26 g carbohydrates, 4 g fiber, 17 g protein, 282 mg calcium, 2 mg iron

Corn Pancakes with Black Bean Salsa
(recipe on facing page)

This main-dish pie of rosemary-seasoned onions and red potatoes is good as a lunch or supper entrée; or try it for a weekend brunch.

....

- 2 slices sourdough sandwich bread, torn into pieces
- 4 small red thin-skinned potatoes (about 1 lb./455 g *total*), scrubbed
- 1 large onion
- 1 tablespoon (15 ml) olive oil
- 2 teaspoons chopped fresh rosemary or ¾ teaspoon dried rosemary, crumbled
- 3 large eggs
- 6 large egg whites
- 1 cup (240 ml) smooth unsweetened applesauce
- ⅔ cup (55 g) grated Parmesan cheese

  About ¼ teaspoon salt (or to taste)

Potato-Onion Pie

....

Preparation time: 20 minutes
Cooking time: About 1 hour and 5 minutes

....

- ⅛ teaspoon pepper

  Rosemary sprigs
- 1¼ cups (300 ml) nonfat sour cream

....

1. In a blender or food processor, whirl bread to make coarse crumbs; set bread crumbs aside.

2. Cut potatoes and onion lengthwise into halves; then thinly slice potato and onion halves crosswise. Heat oil in a wide nonstick frying pan over medium-high heat. Add potatoes, onion, and chopped rosemary. Cook, stirring often, until vegetables are tinged with brown and tender when pierced (20 to 25 minutes); add water, 1 tablespoon

(15 ml) at a time, if pan appears dry.

3. Meanwhile, in a medium-size bowl, combine eggs, egg whites, applesauce, cheese, salt, and pepper. Beat until blended; set aside.

4. Spoon potato mixture into a greased deep 9-inch (23-cm) pie pan. Stir crumbs into egg mixture and pour evenly over potato mixture; stir gently so egg mixture settles to pan bottom. Center of filling will be slightly above level of pan.

5. Bake in a 350°F (175°C) oven until top of pie is tinged with brown and a knife inserted in center comes out clean (about 40 minutes). Garnish with rosemary sprigs. Offer sour cream to add to taste. Makes 6 servings.

....

Per serving: 277 calories (29% calories from fat), 9 g total fat, 3 g saturated fat, 113 mg cholesterol, 441 mg sodium, 31 g carbohydrates, 3 g fiber, 16 g protein, 219 mg calcium, 1 mg iron

---

To make this rich, layered casserole, start by baking a savory mixture of diced eggplant and olives in tomato sauce; then top with spoonfuls of ricotta cheese and a generous helping of sharp Cheddar. Bake for another 10 minutes or so and serve hot, with a salad and crunchy breadsticks.

....

- 3 small eggplants (about 3 lbs./1.35 kg *total*)
- 1 large onion, chopped
- 1 large green bell pepper (about 8 oz./230 g), seeded and chopped
- ¾ cup (75 g) fine dry bread crumbs
- 1 can (about 2¼ oz./63 g) sliced ripe olives, drained
- 1 tablespoon chopped fresh oregano or 1 teaspoon dried oregano

Eggplant & Cheese Casserole

....

Preparation time: 25 minutes
Cooking time: About 1 hour and 40 minutes

....

- 1 large can (about 15 oz./425 g) tomato sauce
- 1 cup (about 8 oz./230 g) nonfat ricotta cheese
- 1½ cups (about 6 oz./170 g) shredded reduced-fat sharp Cheddar cheese

....

1. Cut unpeeled eggplants into ¾-inch (2-cm) cubes and place in a deep 4-quart (3.8-liter) casserole. Add onion, bell pepper, bread crumbs, olives, oregano, and tomato sauce; stir well. Cover tightly and bake in a 400°F

(205°C) oven for 45 minutes. Stir vegetables thoroughly and cover tightly again. Continue to bake until vegetables are very soft when pressed (about 45 more minutes); check occasionally and add water, 1 tablespoon (15 ml) at a time, if casserole appears dry.

2. Spoon ricotta cheese in dollops over hot vegetable mixture; sprinkle with Cheddar cheese. Continue to bake, uncovered, until Cheddar cheese is melted (about 10 more minutes). Makes 8 servings.

....

Per serving: 212 calories (23% calories from fat), 5 g total fat, 3 g saturated fat, 15 mg cholesterol, 687 mg sodium, 27 g carbohydrates, 5 g fiber, 15 g protein, 447 mg calcium, 2 mg iron

Broccoli, green peas, and both russet and sweet potatoes simmer in an aromatic curry sauce to make this hearty stew. Serve it over hot brown rice; complete the meal with cooling fresh fruit.

Potato Curry

Preparation time: 30 minutes
Cooking time: About 1½ hours

Spice Mixture:

- 2 tablespoons ground coriander
- 1 tablespoon ground cumin
- ½ teaspoon ground turmeric
- ¼ to ½ teaspoon ground red pepper (cayenne), or to taste
- ¼ teaspoon ground cinnamon

Potato Curry:

- About 5 cups (1.2 liters) vegetable broth
- 2 large onions, chopped
- 4 cloves garlic, minced or pressed
- 2 tablespoons finely chopped fresh ginger
- ¼ teaspoon coconut extract
- 3 large russet potatoes (about 1½ lbs./680 g *total*)
- 2 very large sweet potatoes or yams (about 1½ lbs./680 g *total*)
- 1 pound (455 g) broccoli flowerets (about 7 cups), cut into bite-size pieces
- 1 cup (240 ml) nonfat milk
- 1 package (about 10 oz./285 g) frozen tiny peas, thawed and drained

Accompaniments:

- ¼ cup (30 g) salted roasted cashew pieces
- ½ cup (20 g) cilantro leaves
- 2 cups (470 ml) plain nonfat yogurt

1. To prepare spice mixture, combine coriander, cumin, turmeric, red pepper, and cinnamon in a 5- to 6-quart (5- to 6-liter) pan. Cook over medium-low heat, stirring, until spices are fragrant (about 5 minutes; do not scorch). Remove from pan and set aside.

2. In same pan, combine ½ cup (120 ml) of the broth, onions, garlic, and ginger. Cook over medium-high heat, stirring often, until liquid evaporates and browned bits stick to pan bottom (about 10 minutes). To deglaze pan, add ⅓ cup (80 ml) more broth, stirring to loosen browned bits from pan; continue to cook until browned bits form again. Repeat deglazing step about 2 more times or until vegetables are browned, using ⅓ cup (80 ml) more broth each time. Add spice mixture and repeat deglazing step one more time, using ⅓ cup (80 ml) more broth. Remove from heat.

3. Add coconut extract and 3 cups (710 ml) more broth to pan. Peel russet and sweet potatoes, cut into 1½- to 2-inch (4- to 5-cm) chunks, and add to broth mixture. Bring to a boil over high heat; then reduce heat, cover, and simmer until potatoes are tender when pierced (about 35 minutes). Add broccoli, cover, and continue to cook for 10 more minutes. Add milk and peas; simmer, uncovered, stirring occasionally, just until stew is hot (do not boil).

4. Pour stew into a serving bowl. Sprinkle with cashews and cilantro. Offer yogurt to add to taste. Makes 6 servings.

Per serving: 360 calories (11% calories from fat), 4 g total fat, 1 g saturated fat, 2 mg cholesterol, 1,015 mg sodium, 68 g carbohydrates, 9 g fiber, 16 g protein, 294 mg calcium, 4 mg iron

Green Potatoes with Blue Cheese
(recipe on facing page)

Sautéed sliced potatoes are tossed with slivered fresh spinach and cilantro, then topped with a cool, zesty sauce of tofu and blue cheese.

Blue Cheese Sauce (recipe follows)

3 to 4 cups (3 to 4 oz./85 to 115 g) lightly packed rinsed, crisped spinach leaves

1 tablespoon butter or margarine

1¼ pounds (565 g) small red thin-skinned potatoes, scrubbed and cut crosswise into ¼-inch (6-mm) slices

1 medium-size red bell pepper (about 6 oz./170 g), seeded and cut into thin strips

1 medium-size onion, cut into thin slivers

1 tablespoon ground cumin

1 teaspoon ground coriander

¼ teaspoon salt

⅛ teaspoon ground red pepper (cayenne)

½ to ¾ cup (20 to 30 g) lightly packed cilantro leaves

Cilantro sprigs (optional)

Green Potatoes with Blue Cheese

Preparation time: About 25 minutes
Cooking time: About 15 minutes
Pictured on facing page

1. Prepare Blue Cheese Sauce and set aside.

2. Cut 1 to 1½ cups (30 to 43 g) of the spinach into thin shreds about 2 inches (5 cm) long. Cover and set aside. Line a rimmed platter with remaining spinach leaves; cover and set aside.

3. Melt butter in a wide nonstick frying pan or wok over medium-high heat. Add potatoes, bell pepper, onion, cumin, coriander, salt, ground red pepper, and ¼ cup (60 ml) water. Stir-fry gently until potatoes are tinged with brown and tender when pierced (about 15 minutes; do not scorch). Add water, 1 tablespoon (15 ml) at a time, if pan appears dry.

4. Remove pan from heat. Sprinkle potato mixture with shredded spinach; mix gently but thoroughly. Then spoon potato mixture over spinach leaves on platter. Sprinkle with cilantro leaves; garnish with cilantro sprigs, if desired. Offer Blue Cheese Sauce to add to taste. Makes 4 servings.

Blue Cheese Sauce. In a blender or food processor, combine 4 ounces (115 g) **soft tofu**, rinsed and drained; ⅓ cup (80 ml) **low-fat buttermilk**; 1 tablespoon (15 ml) *each* **white wine vinegar** and **honey**; 1 teaspoon **Dijon mustard**; and 1 or 2 cloves **garlic** (peeled). Whirl until smoothly puréed. Gently mix in ½ cup (70 g) crumbled **blue-veined cheese.** Season to taste with **salt** and **pepper.** (At this point, you may cover and refrigerate for up to 3 hours.) Just before serving, stir in 1 tablespoon thinly sliced **green onion.**

Per serving: 279 calories (30% calories from fat), 9 g total fat, 5g saturated fat, 21 mg cholesterol, 436 mg sodium, 39 g carbohydrates, 5 g fiber, 11 g protein, 192 mg calcium, 4 mg iron

Crisp crumbs top a rich-tasting, Gorgonzola-laced spinach filling in this lean, savory crustless pie.

- 3 slices sourdough sandwich bread, torn into pieces
- 1 large onion, finely chopped
- 4 to 6 cloves garlic, minced or pressed
- ½ cup (120 ml) vegetable broth

  About ¾ cup (100 g) crumbled Gorgonzola or other blue-veined cheese
- 3 tablespoons all-purpose flour
- ⅛ teaspoon ground white pepper
- 2 packages (about 10 oz./285 g *each*) frozen chopped spinach, thawed and squeezed dry
- 1 large egg
- 6 large egg whites
- 1½ cups (360 ml) nonfat sour cream
- ¼ cup (60 ml) smooth unsweetened applesauce
- ½ teaspoon sugar
- ⅛ to ¼ teaspoon ground nutmeg

Crustless Spinach Pie

Preparation time: 15 minutes
Cooking time: About 50 minutes

1. In a blender or food processor, whirl bread to make coarse crumbs. Sprinkle ½ cup (23 g) of the crumbs evenly over bottom of a greased 1½- to 2½-quart (1.4- to 2.4-liter) baking dish or deep 9-inch (23-cm) pie pan. Set dish and remaining crumbs aside.

2. In a wide nonstick frying pan, combine onion, garlic, and ¼ cup (60 ml) water. Cook over medium-high heat, stirring often, until onion is soft (about 5 minutes); add water, 1 tablespoon (15 ml) at a time, if pan appears dry. Add broth and cheese; reduce heat to medium and cook, stirring, until cheese is melted. Sprinkle flour and white pepper over cheese mixture and

stir until blended. Remove pan from heat and stir in spinach.

3. In a medium-size bowl, whisk egg, egg whites, ½ cup (120 ml) of the sour cream, and applesauce until very well blended. Stir egg mixture into spinach mixture. Spoon into prepared dish; sprinkle with remaining crumbs. Bake in a 375°F (190°C) oven until edge of pie is browned and center feels firm when lightly pressed (about 40 minutes). Let stand for about 5 minutes before serving.

4. Meanwhile, in a small bowl, combine remaining 1 cup (240 ml) sour cream, sugar, and nutmeg. Beat until smoothly blended. To serve, offer sour cream sauce to spoon over pie. Makes 6 servings.

Per serving: 238 calories (29% calories from fat), 8 g total fat, 4 g saturated fat, 52 mg cholesterol, 606 mg sodium, 24 g carbohydrates, 3 g fiber, 18 g protein, 310 mg calcium, 3 mg iron

---

Zucchini, mushrooms, and red onion—oven-browned to develop rich, sweet flavor—are the base of this wholesome sandwich spread.

- 1 medium-size red onion (about 8 oz./230 g)
- 1¼ pounds (565 g) zucchini
- 1¼ pounds (565 g) mushrooms
- 5 teaspoons (25 ml) olive oil
- 2 tablespoons (30 ml) balsamic vinegar
- 12 slices whole wheat sandwich bread
- 6 thin slices reduced-fat Jarlsberg cheese (about 3 oz./85 g *total*)
- ¾ cup (180 ml) reduced-fat sour cream

1. Cut onion crosswise into ½-inch (1-cm) slices. Cut zucchini lengthwise

Roasted Zucchini-Mushroom Sandwiches

Preparation time: 30 minutes, plus at least 30 minutes to chill
Cooking time: About 30 minutes

into ¼-inch (6-mm) slices; cut mushrooms into ½-inch (1-cm) slices. Brush 3 shallow 10- by 15-inch (25- by 38-cm) baking pans with oil, using 1 teaspoon of the oil per pan. Lay onion and zucchini in a single layer in 2 of the pans; spread mushrooms evenly in third pan, overlapping slices as little as possible. Brush onion with all the vinegar; brush all vegetables with remaining 2 teaspoons oil.

2. Bake in a 475°F (245°C) oven for 15 minutes. Turn vegetables over and continue to bake until mushrooms are lightly browned and onion is well browned (about 15 more minutes).

3. Place onion, zucchini, and mushrooms in a food processor or blender; whirl until smoothly puréed. Before using, cover and refrigerate for at least 30 minutes or up to 3 days.

4. To make each sandwich, spread one slice of bread with about ½ cup (120 ml) of the vegetable spread; top with one slice of the cheese, 2 tablespoons (30 ml) of the sour cream, and a second slice of bread. Makes 6 servings.

Per serving: 286 calories (26% calories from fat), 9 g total fat, 2 g saturated fat, 7 mg cholesterol, 380 mg sodium, 39 g carbohydrates, 6 g fiber, 15 g protein, 108 mg calcium, 4 mg iron

This tempting casserole will remind you of a savory bread pudding. While it bakes, prepare a sweet-tart relish of dried figs, dried cranberries, and fresh pears to serve alongside.

Spinach Torta with Fig Relish

Preparation time: 30 minutes
Cooking time: About 1½ hours

1   package (about 10 oz./285 g) frozen chopped spinach, thawed and squeezed dry

3   large eggs

4   large egg whites

2   tablespoons cornstarch

2   cloves garlic, peeled

1½ teaspoons *each* chopped fresh oregano, fresh marjoram, and fresh sage; or ½ teaspoon each dried oregano, dried marjoram, and dried rubbed sage

2   cups (470 ml) half-and-half

8   slices egg or whole wheat sandwich bread (about 8 oz./230 g total), torn into large pieces

¾   cup (85 g) shredded fontina or mozzarella cheese

1   large firm-ripe pear such as Anjou or Bartlett (about 8 oz./230 g), peeled, cored, and finely chopped

⅓   cup (73 g) firmly packed brown sugar

⅓   cup (80 ml) red wine vinegar

1½ cups dried figs (about 8 oz./230 g), stems removed and fruit quartered

¾   cup (68 g) dried cranberries or raisins

¾   cup (180 ml) canned vegetable broth

⅛   teaspoon each pepper, ground cinnamon, and ground nutmeg

2   teaspoons Marsala (or to taste)

¼   cup (25 g) thinly sliced green onions

1. In a food processor or blender, combine spinach, eggs, egg whites, cornstarch, garlic, oregano, marjoram, and sage. Whirl until smoothly puréed. Transfer to a large bowl and whisk in half-and-half. Add bread and cheese; mix gently but thoroughly. Let stand until bread is softened (about 5 minutes), stirring occasionally.

2. Transfer mixture to a square 8-inch (20-cm) nonstick or greased regular baking pan. Set pan in a larger baking pan; then set on center rack of a 325°F (165°C) oven. Pour boiling water into larger pan up to level of spinach mixture. Bake until top of torta is golden brown and center no longer jiggles when pan is gently shaken (about 1 hour and 35 minutes).

3. Meanwhile, in a wide nonstick frying pan, mix pear, sugar, and vinegar. Add figs, cranberries, broth, pepper, cinnamon, and nutmeg. Bring to a boil over medium-high heat. Then cook, uncovered, stirring often, until almost all liquid has evaporated (about 20 minutes); as mixture thickens, watch carefully and stir more often to prevent scorching. Remove pan from heat and stir in Marsala and onions.

4. To serve, spoon torta from pan; offer fig relish alongside. Makes 6 servings.

Per serving: 549 calories (30% calories from fat), 19 g total fat, 10 g saturated fat, 172 mg cholesterol, 570 mg sodium, 79 g carbohydrates, 6 g fiber, 18 g protein, 338 mg calcium, 4 mg iron

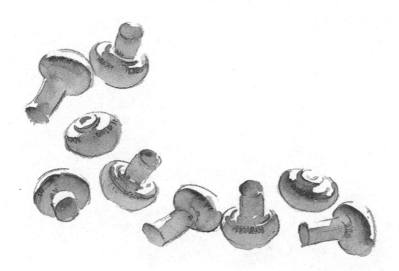

Big portabella mushrooms pan-fried in a cornmeal batter make wholesome, hearty sandwiches. Serve them in crusty rolls spread with chard-and-herb cream cheese; offer Pickled Vegetables (recipe on page 12) alongside.

- 4 **crusty rolls (about 4 oz./115 g each), split into halves**
- 1 **package (about 10 oz./285 g) frozen chopped Swiss chard, thawed and squeezed dry**
- 1 **large package (about 8 oz./ 230 g) nonfat cream cheese, at room temperature**
- ¾ **cup (85 g) shredded smoked mozzarella or smoked Gouda cheese**
- 2 **tablespoons (30 ml) nonfat mayonnaise**
- 1 **teaspoon Dijon mustard**
- ½ **teaspoon dried rubbed sage**
  About ¼ cup (60 ml) balsamic vinegar
  Pepper
- 3 **large egg whites**
- ¾ **cup (104 g) yellow cornmeal**
- ⅓ **cup (40 g) all-purpose flour**
- ¼ **teaspoon salt**
- 4 **large portabella mushrooms (about 3 oz./85 g each), stems removed**
- 2 **tablespoons (30 ml) olive oil**
- 4 **to 8 green or red leaf lettuce leaves**
- 4 **to 8 large tomato slices**

Portabella Mushroom Sandwiches

Preparation time: 25 minutes
Cooking time: About 20 minutes
Pictured on facing page

1. If needed, pull bread from base and top of each roll to make a shell about ¼ inch (6 mm) thick; reserve bread scraps for other uses, if desired. Arrange roll halves, cut side up, in a broiler pan; broil about 6 inches (15 cm) below heat until lightly toasted (1½ to 2 minutes). Set aside.

2. In a food processor or blender, combine chard, cream cheese, mozzarella cheese, mayonnaise, mustard, and sage. Whirl until chard is finely chopped, scraping sides of container as needed. Brush cut side of roll bottoms lightly with vinegar and sprinkle with pepper. Set aside about a fourth of the chard mixture; divide remaining mixture equally among roll bottoms (you need about ⅓ cup/80 ml per roll). With a spatula, spread chard mixture to fill hollows in rolls evenly.

3. In a wide, shallow bowl, beat egg whites and 2 tablespoons (30 ml) water to blend. In another wide, shallow bowl, stir together cornmeal, flour,

and salt. Dip mushrooms in egg white mixture; drain briefly, then dip in cornmeal mixture and press to coat well all over.

4. Heat 1 tablespoon (15 ml) of the oil in a wide nonstick frying pan over medium-high heat. Add 2 of the mushrooms; cook, turning once, until mushrooms are golden on both sides and tender when pierced (5 to 7 minutes). Remove from pan and keep warm. Repeat to cook remaining 2 mushrooms, using remaining 1 tablespoon (15 ml) oil.

5. Working quickly, place 1 or 2 lettuce leaves on each roll bottom; then top each with one hot mushroom and 1 or 2 tomato slices. Spoon reserved chard mixture over tomato slices. Brush cut side of roll tops lightly with vinegar and sprinkle with pepper; close sandwiches and serve immediately. Makes 4 servings.

Per serving: 709 calories (24% calories from fat), 19 g total fat, 5 g saturated fat, 36 mg cholesterol, 1,553 mg sodium, 101 g carbohydrates, 5 g fiber, 33 g protein, 436 mg calcium, 8 mg iron

Portabella Mushroom Sandwiches
(recipe on facing page)

Slow-roasted vegetables make a delicious topping for individual pizzas—and you can roast them a day ahead, then spoon them onto purchased bread shells or pita rounds and heat just minutes before mealtime.

Pizzettes:

- 1 **pound (455 g) mushrooms**
- 2 **medium-size onions**
- 1 **medium-size eggplant (about 1¼ lbs./565 g)**
- 5 **teaspoons (25 ml) olive oil**
- 12 **ounces (340 g) pear-shaped (Roma-type) tomatoes (about 4 medium-size tomatoes)**
- ½ **cup (85 g) chopped canned roasted red peppers, drained**
- 4 **small Italian bread shells (*each* about 5½ inches/13.5 cm in diameter, about 4 oz./115 g); or 4 pita breads (*each* about 5 inches/12.5 cm in diameter)**

Dressing:

- 2 **tablespoons (30 ml) balsamic vinegar**
- 1 **tablespoon (15 ml) olive oil**
- 1 **teaspoon Dijon mustard**

Accompaniments:

- 4 **cups (about 3 oz./85 g) lightly packed arugula leaves (tough stems discarded), rinsed and drained**
- ¾ **cup (60 g) shaved or shredded Parmesan cheese**

Roasted Vegetable Pizzettes

Preparation time: 25 minutes
Cooking time: About 1 hour and 10 minutes

1. Cut mushrooms into ½-inch (1-cm) slices. Cut onions into wedges about ½ inch (1 cm) thick; cut unpeeled eggplant into about ½-inch (1-cm) cubes.

2. Pour the 5 teaspoons (25 ml) oil into a shallow 10- by 15-inch (25- by 38-cm) baking pan; place in a 450°F (230°C) oven just until oil is hot. Remove pan from oven and add mushrooms, onions, and eggplant; return to oven and bake until vegetables are golden (about 45 minutes), turning vegetables every 15 minutes. Meanwhile, cut tomatoes crosswise into ¼-inch (6-mm) slices.

3. After vegetables have baked for 45 minutes, stir in tomatoes; continue to bake until almost all liquid has evaporated, about 20 more minutes. (At this point, you may let cool, then cover and refrigerate until next day.)

4. Stir red peppers into roasted vegetables. Place bread shells in a single layer on 1 or 2 baking sheets. Spread a fourth of the vegetables evenly over each bread shell (or over each whole pita bread) to within ½ inch (1 cm) of edge.

5. Bake in a 500°F (260°C) oven just until bread and vegetables are heated through (about 5 minutes). Meanwhile, in a small bowl, beat vinegar, the 1 tablespoon (15 ml) oil, and mustard until blended; set aside.

6. To serve, transfer pizzettes to individual plates and top equally with arugula (thinly slice any large arugula pieces) and cheese. Drizzle dressing over all. Makes 4 servings.

Per serving: 572 calories (30% calories from fat), 19 g total fat, 6 g saturated fat, 20 mg cholesterol, 917 mg sodium, 77 g carbohydrates, 9 g fiber, 25 g protein, 390 mg calcium, 6 mg iron

Enjoy a low-fat, no-meat version of a favorite fast food with these veggie burgers, chock-full of broccoli, red onion, and toasted almonds. Serve them with nonfat mayonnaise and a tangy homemade relish.

Red Onion Relish:

- 2 medium-size red onions (about 1 lb./455 g *total*), chopped
- 2 tablespoons firmly packed brown sugar
- 1 teaspoon olive oil
- ⅓ cup (80 ml) each balsamic vinegar and dry white wine
- 2 teaspoons prepared horseradish

Broccoli Burgers:

- 2 large eggs, lightly beaten
- 1¾ cups (125 g) chopped broccoli
- ½ cup (65 g) chopped toasted almonds

Broccoli Burgers

Preparation time: 15 minutes
Cooking time: About 45 minutes

- ¾ cup (130 g) chopped red onion
- ½ cup (50 g) seasoned fine dry bread crumbs
- Salt and pepper
- ¼ cup (60 ml) nonfat mayonnaise
- 4 hamburger buns, toasted
- 4 to 8 lettuce leaves, rinsed and crisped

1. In a wide nonstick frying pan, combine the 2 chopped onions, sugar, oil, and ½ cup (120 ml) water. Cook over medium-high heat, stirring often, until onions are soft (about 8 minutes); add more water, 1 tablespoon (15 ml) at a time, if pan appears dry. Stir in vinegar, wine, and horseradish. Cook, stir-ring often, until liquid has evaporated (about 10 minutes). Transfer relish to a small bowl and set aside; stir occasionally.

2. In a large bowl, combine eggs, broccoli, almonds, the ¾ cup onion, bread crumbs, and ¼ cup (60 ml) water. Season to taste with salt and pepper. On an oiled 12- by 15-inch (30- by 38-cm) baking sheet, shape mixture into 4 equal patties, each about ¾ inch (2 cm) thick. Bake patties in a 375°F (190°C) oven, turning halfway through baking, until golden on both sides (about 25 minutes).

3. To serve, spread mayonnaise on bun bottoms; top with patties, onion relish, and lettuce, then with bun tops. Makes 4 servings.

Per serving: 440 calories (30% calories from fat), 15 g total fat, 2 g saturated fat, 106 mg cholesterol, 808 mg sodium, 61 g carbohydrates, 7 g fiber, 16 g protein, 207 mg calcium, 4 mg iron

---

Kuchen is traditionally a sweet, fruit- or cheese-filled yeast coffee-cake served for dessert or at break-fast, but this savory version is meant to be enjoyed as a lunch or supper main dish. It's nutritious, easy to prepare—and pretty, too.

Kuchen:

- 3½ cups (about 8 oz./230 g) broccoli flowerets
- ½ cup (69 g) yellow cornmeal
- ½ cup (60 g) all-purpose flour
- 1½ teaspoons baking powder
- 1 cup (210 g) nonfat cottage cheese
- 1 large egg
- 3 large egg whites
- ½ cup (120 ml) low-fat buttermilk
- 2 tablespoons butter or margarine, melted
- 4 teaspoons sugar

Yogurt Sauce:

- 1 cup (240 ml) plain nonfat yogurt

Broccoli-Cornmeal Kuchen

Preparation time: 20 minutes
Cooking time: About 40 minutes

- ¼ cup (60 ml) white wine vinegar
- 2 tablespoons dried dill weed (or to taste)
- 1 teaspoon honey (or to taste)
- ¼ teaspoon ground cumin

1. In a 4- to 5-quart (3.8- to 5-liter) pan, bring 8 cups (1.9 liters) water to a boil over medium-high heat. Add broccoli and cook just until barely tender-crisp to bite (about 4 minutes). Drain, immerse in ice water until cool, and drain well again.

2. In a large bowl, stir together cornmeal, flour, and baking powder. In a small bowl, beat cottage cheese, egg, egg whites, buttermilk, butter, and sugar until well blended. Add cheese mixture to cornmeal mixture and stir just until dry ingredients are evenly moistened.

3. Pour batter into a greased round 8-inch (20-cm) baking pan or quiche dish. Gently press broccoli decoratively into batter. Bake in a 350°F (175°C) oven until center of kuchen feels firm when lightly pressed (about 30 minutes).

4. Meanwhile, in a small bowl, stir together yogurt, vinegar, dill weed, honey, and cumin just until blended. Set aside.

5. Let kuchen cool slightly; then cut into wedges. Offer yogurt sauce to spoon over individual portions. Makes 4 servings.

Per serving: 303 calories (27% calories from fat), 9 g total fat, 4 g saturated fat, 72 mg cholesterol, 390 mg sodium, 42 g carbohydrates, 3 g fiber, 14 g protein, 282 mg calcium, 3 mg iron

Maple-glazed Tofu in Acorn Squash
(recipe on facing page)

Tender apple slices, rosy cranberries, and mild tofu, all cloaked in a savory-sweet maple sauce, are served in edible squash bowls for a wholesome and appealing main course. For the best flavor, use pure maple syrup rather than a maple-flavored variety.

Maple-glazed Tofu in Acorn Squash

Preparation time: 20 minutes
Cooking time: About 1 hour
Pictured on facing page

2   **medium-size acorn squash (about 3½ lbs./1.6 kg *total*)**

1½ **cups (360 ml) vegetable broth**

½   **cup (73 g) dried cranberries or raisins**

¼   **cup (60 ml) pure maple syrup**

2   **large Granny Smith or Newtown Pippin apples (about 1 lb./455 g *total*)**

1   **tablespoon (15 ml) lemon juice**

¾   **teaspoon ground cinnamon**

⅛   **teaspoon ground nutmeg**

1   **tablespoon chopped walnuts**

1   **package (about 14 oz./400 g) firm tofu, rinsed, drained, and cut into ½-inch (1-cm) cubes**

1   **tablespoon (15 ml) balsamic vinegar**

1   **teaspoon cornstarch**

⅓   **cup (35 g) thinly sliced green onions**

½   **cup (120 ml) nonfat sour cream**

1. Cut each squash in half lengthwise; scoop out and discard seeds and fibers. Place squash halves, cut side down, in a 9- by 13-inch (23- by 33-cm) baking pan. Add broth. Bake in a 350°F (175°C) oven until squash is tender when pierced (about 1 hour).

2. Meanwhile, in a small bowl, combine cranberries and syrup. Let stand until cranberries are softened (about 10 minutes), stirring occasionally. Also peel, core, and thinly slice apples; place in a large bowl, add lemon juice, and gently turn apples to coat with juice. Stir in cinnamon and nutmeg; set aside.

3. Toast walnuts in a wide nonstick frying pan over medium heat, stirring often, until golden (about 3 minutes). Remove from pan and set aside.

4. In frying pan, combine apples, cranberry mixture, and ¼ cup (60 ml) water. Cook over medium-high heat, stirring gently, until apples are almost tender when pierced (about 3 minutes). Add tofu and cook just until heated through (about 2 more minutes). In a small bowl, smoothly blend vinegar and cornstarch; add to tofu mixture. Cook, stirring, until sauce boils and thickens slightly (about 2 minutes). Remove from heat and stir in onions.

5. Arrange each squash half, skin side down, in a shallow individual bowl. Fill squash halves equally with tofu mixture; top with sour cream and sprinkle with walnuts. Makes 4 servings.

Per serving: 463 calories (20% calories from fat), 11 g total fat, 1 g saturated fat, 0 mg cholesterol, 421 mg sodium, 79 g carbohydrates, 14 g fiber, 21 g protein, 371 mg calcium, 13 mg iron

Though it's based on two exceptionally mild-flavored foods—tofu and eggplant—this dish will nonetheless win favor with the fire-eaters in your family. Fresh ginger and bottled chili paste with garlic make it spicy.

Green Onion Brushes
(optional; directions follow)

Cooking Sauce (recipe follows)

About 1 pound (455 g) firm tofu, rinsed, drained, and cut into ½-inch (1-cm) cubes

10 **ounces (285 g) fresh Chinese noodles or linguine**

1 **tablespoon (15 ml) salad oil**

2 **medium-size eggplants (about 1½ lbs./680 g** *total***), peeled and cut into ½-inch (1-cm) pieces (about 8 cups)**

2 **teaspoons minced fresh ginger**

2 **green onions, thinly sliced**

½ **cup (20 g) lightly packed cilantro leaves**

1. Prepare Green Onion Brushes, if desired. Prepare Cooking Sauce. Add tofu to sauce and stir gently to coat; then set aside.

Sichuan Tofu with Eggplant

Preparation time: About 30 minutes, plus at least 1 hour to soak Green Onion Brushes (if used)
Cooking time: About 15 minutes

2. In a 5- to 6-quart (5- to 6-liter) pan, cook noodles in about 3 quarts (2.8 liters) boiling water until just tender to bite (3 to 5 minutes); or cook according to package directions. Drain well, transfer to a warm rimmed platter, and keep warm.

3. While noodles are cooking, heat oil in a wide nonstick frying pan or wok over medium-high heat. Add eggplant and ¼ cup (60 ml) water. Stir-fry until eggplant is soft and tinged with gold (8 to 10 minutes); add more water, 1 tablespoon (15 ml) at a time, if pan appears dry.

4. Add ginger and stir-fry just until fragrant (about 30 seconds; do not scorch). Add tofu mixture and cook, stirring gently, until sauce boils and

tofu is heated through (about 3 minutes). Remove from heat and stir in sliced onions.

5. Spoon tofu mixture over noodles and sprinkle with cilantro. Garnish with Green Onion Brushes, if desired. Makes 4 to 6 servings.

Green Onion Brushes. Cut the white part of 3 to 5 **green onions** into 1½-inch (3.5-cm) lengths. Using scissors or a sharp knife, slash both ends of each onion piece lengthwise 3 or 4 times, making cuts about ½ inch (1 cm) deep. Place onions in a bowl, cover with ice water, and refrigerate until ends curl (at least 1 hour) or for up to 8 hours.

Cooking Sauce. In a large bowl, stir together 3 tablespoons (45 ml) **hoisin sauce,** 2 tablespoons (30 ml) **seasoned rice vinegar** (or 2 tablespoons/30 ml distilled white vinegar plus ¾ teaspoon sugar), 1 tablespoon *each* **sugar** and **chili paste with garlic,** and 2 teaspoons **Oriental sesame oil.**

Per serving: 476 calories (30% calories from fat), 16 g total fat, 2 g saturated fat, 54 mg cholesterol, 351 mg sodium, 62 g carbohydrates, 3 g fiber, 24 g protein, 251 mg calcium, 13 mg iron

---

Spinach and tofu make a lean filling for baked manicotti.

2 **tablespoons (30 ml) olive oil**

1 **medium-size onion (about 6 oz./170 g), chopped**

3 **medium-size stalks celery (about 9 oz./255 g** *total***), chopped**

1 **clove garlic, minced or pressed**

2 **teaspoons dried oregano**

2 **cans (about 15 oz./425 g** *each***) tomato purée**

1 **cup (240 ml) dry red wine**

1 **pound (455 g) soft tofu, rinsed and drained**

1 **package (about 10 oz./285 g) thawed frozen spinach, squeezed dry**

Tofu-Spinach Manicotti

Preparation time: About 25 minutes
Cooking time: About 1½ hours

12 **dried manicotti shells (about 6 oz./170 g** *total***)**

½ **cup (60 g) shredded part-skim mozzarella cheese**

1. Heat oil in a wide nonstick frying pan over medium heat. Add onion, celery, garlic, and oregano. Cook, stirring often, until onion is soft (5 to 8 minutes). Add tomato purée, wine, and 1 cup (240 ml) water. Bring to a

boil; reduce heat, cover, and simmer, stirring often, for 25 minutes. Meanwhile, mix tofu and spinach in a bowl until well blended. Stuff dried pasta with mixture.

2. Spread 1¾ cups (420 ml) of the tomato sauce in a 9- by 13-inch (23- by 33-cm) baking pan. Arrange pasta in pan. Top with remaining sauce. Cover and bake in a 375°F (190°C) oven until tender when pierced (about 50 minutes). Sprinkle with cheese. Makes 6 servings.

Per serving: 302 calories (25% calories from fat), 9 g total fat, 2 g saturated fat, 5 mg cholesterol, 692 mg sodium, 45 g carbohydrates, 6 g fiber, 14 g protein, 195 mg calcium, 5 mg iron

Hot, fluffy rice is a must with this beautiful dish—it's essential for soaking up the sauce!

- 1 **cup (185 g) long-grain white rice**

  Sweet-Sour Sauce (recipe follows)

- 1 **pound (455 g) firm tofu, rinsed, drained, and cut into ½-inch (1-cm) cubes**
- 1 **teaspoon paprika**
- 1 **or 2 cloves garlic, minced or pressed**
- ¼ **teaspoon salt**
- 1 **teaspoon salad oil**
- 1 **small red onion, cut into thin wedges**
- 1 **large green, red, or yellow bell pepper (about 8 oz./230 g), seeded and cut into 1-inch (2.5-cm) squares**
- 1 **medium-size tomato (about 6 oz./170 g), cut into thin wedges**
- 1½ **cups (235 g) fresh or canned pineapple chunks, drained**

Sweet & Sour Tofu

Preparation time: About 15 minutes
Cooking time: About 25 minutes

1. In a 3- to 4-quart (2.8- to 3.8-liter) pan, bring 2 cups (470 ml) water to a boil over high heat; stir in rice. Reduce heat, cover, and simmer until liquid has been absorbed and rice is tender to bite (about 20 minutes).

2. Meanwhile, prepare Sweet-Sour Sauce and set aside. In a large bowl, gently mix tofu, paprika, garlic, and salt; set aside.

3. Heat oil in a wide nonstick frying pan or wok over medium-high heat. When oil is hot, add tofu and stir-fry gently until heated through (3 to 4 minutes). Add water, 1 tablespoon (15 ml) at a time, if pan appears dry. Remove tofu from pan with a slotted spoon; keep warm.

4. Add onion, bell pepper, and 2 tablespoons (30 ml) water to pan. Stir-fry

for 1 minute; add water, 1 tablespoon (15 ml) at a time, if pan appears dry.

5. Stir Sweet-Sour Sauce well; pour into pan. Cook, stirring, until sauce boils and thickens slightly (2 to 3 minutes). Stir in tomato, pineapple, and tofu; stir gently just until heated through (about 2 minutes).

6. To serve, spoon rice onto a rimmed platter; top with tofu mixture. Makes 4 servings.

Sweet-Sour Sauce. In a medium-size bowl, stir together 4 teaspoons **cornstarch** and ¼ cup (60 ml) **white wine vinegar** or distilled white vinegar until blended. Then stir in ¾ cup (180 ml) **water,** ¼ cup (50 g) **sugar,** 1 tablespoon (15 ml) *each* **catsup** and **reduced-sodium soy sauce,** and ⅛ teaspoon **Hot Chili Oil** (page 109) or purchased hot chili oil, or to taste.

Per serving: 482 calories (22% calories from fat), 12 g total fat, 2 g saturated fat, 0 mg cholesterol, 223 mg sodium, 75 g carbohydrates, 3 g fiber, 23 g protein, 273 mg calcium, 15 mg iron

---

Tofu is mild by nature—but it doesn't stay that way here!

- 1⅓ **cups (247 g) long-grain white rice**
- 1 **package (about 1 lb./455 g) firm reduced-fat tofu, rinsed and drained**
- 1½ **pounds (680 g) baby bok choy**
- 1 **tablespoon (15 ml) salad oil**
- 3 **cloves garlic, minced or pressed**
- 8 **green onions, thinly sliced**
- 2 **large red bell peppers (about 1 lb./455 g *total*), seeded and thinly sliced**
- 6 **tablespoons (90 ml) reduced-sodium soy sauce**
- 4 **teaspoons sugar**
- 1 **teaspoon liquid hot pepper seasoning (or to taste)**

Spicy Tofu Bok Choy

Preparation time: 25 minutes
Cooking time: About 25 minutes

- 2 **teaspoons cornstarch blended with 2 tablespoons (30 ml) cold water**

1. Cook rice as directed for Mabu Tofu on page 220. Meanwhile, cut tofu into 1-inch (2.5-cm) slices. Place slices on paper towels and cover with more paper towels. Then set a flat pan on top layer of towels; set a 1-pound (455-g) can on pan. Let tofu drain for 10 minutes. While tofu is draining, cut each bok choy in half lengthwise; if any bok choy half is thicker than 1 inch (2.5 cm) at the base, cut it in half lengthwise. Set aside.

2. Cut tofu into 1-inch (2.5-cm) cubes. Heat oil in a wide nonstick frying pan over medium-high heat. Add tofu and cook, turning gently, until golden brown (about 5 minutes). With a slotted spoon, transfer tofu to paper towels to drain.

3. Add bok choy, garlic, onions, bell peppers, and ¼ cup (60 ml) water to pan. Cover and cook, stirring often, until bok choy stems are just tender when pierced (about 3 minutes). Uncover pan and add tofu, soy sauce, sugar, hot pepper seasoning, and cornstarch mixture; bring to a boil, stirring gently.

4. To serve, spoon rice onto a platter or individual plates; spoon tofu mixture over rice. Makes 4 servings.

Per serving: 438 calories (12% calories from fat), 6 g total fat, 1 g saturated fat, 0 mg cholesterol, 1,149 mg sodium, 79 g carbohydrates, 5 g fiber, 18 g protein, 281 mg calcium, 6 mg iron

Definitely not your standard tacos, these tofu-topped soft tortillas are sure to appeal to the vegetarian crowd. The filling is a colorful combination of bell pepper, corn kernels, and teriyaki-seasoned tofu; a crunchy pineapple-jicama salsa adds a refreshing accent. You can make the flavored oils used in the marinade yourself (see pages 108 and 109) or use purchased equivalents.

- **3 tablespoons (45 ml) reduced-sodium soy sauce**
- **2 tablespoons (30 ml) honey**
- **1 tablespoon (15 ml) Basil Oil (page 108) or purchased basil oil (or 1 tablespoon salad oil plus ½ teaspoon dried basil)**
- **1 teaspoon Hot Chili Oil (page 109) or purchased hot chili oil**
- **2 cloves garlic, minced or pressed**
- **12 ounces (340 g) firm tofu, rinsed, drained, and cut into ½-inch (1-cm) cubes**

Tofu Tacos with Pineapple Salsa

Preparation time: About 15 minutes
Cooking time: About 20 minutes
Pictured on facing page

- **Pineapple Salsa (recipe follows)**
- **4 low-fat flour tortillas (*each* 7 to 9 inches/18 to 23 cm in diameter)**
- **1 large red bell pepper (about 8 oz./230 g), seeded and finely chopped**
- **1 large onion, finely chopped**
- **1 package (about 10 oz./285 g) frozen corn kernels, thawed and drained**

1. In a medium-size bowl, stir together soy sauce, honey, Basil Oil, Hot Chili Oil, and garlic. Add tofu and stir gently to coat. Set aside; stir occasionally. Prepare Pineapple Salsa and set aside.

2. Brush tortillas lightly with hot water; then stack tortillas, wrap in foil, and heat in a 350°F (175°C) oven until warm (10 to 12 minutes).

3. Meanwhile, in a wide nonstick frying pan or wok, combine tofu (and any marinade), bell pepper, and onion. Stir-fry gently over medium-high heat until tofu is browned (about 15 minutes). Add water, 1 tablespoon (15 ml) at a time, if pan appears dry. Add corn and stir-fry until heated through.

4. Top tortillas equally with tofu mixture and Pineapple Salsa; roll up and eat out of hand. Makes 4 servings.

Pineapple Salsa. In a large bowl, mix 1 cup (155 g) diced **fresh or canned pineapple**; ½ cup (65 g) peeled, shredded **jicama**; 1 teaspoon grated **lime peel**; 3 tablespoons (45 ml) **lime juice**; and 2 tablespoons minced **fresh basil.**

Per serving: 411 calories (30% calories from fat), 15 g total fat, 2 g saturated fat, 0 mg cholesterol, 761 mg sodium, 57 g carbohydrates, 5 g fiber, 20 g protein, 317 mg calcium, 11 mg iron

---

Meatless but surprisingly hearty, these burritos are stuffed with fresh corn, cucumber, and beans.

- **Lime Marinade (recipe follows)**
- **1½ cups (255 g) fresh-cut yellow or white corn kernels (from 2 medium-size ears corn); or 1 package (about 10 oz./285 g) frozen corn kernels, thawed**
- **1 can (about 15 oz./425 g) red kidney beans, drained and rinsed**
- **1 medium-size cucumber (about 8 oz./230 g), peeled, seeded, and finely chopped**
- **½ cup (50 g) sliced green onions**
- **2 tablespoons minced cilantro**
- **8 warm flour tortillas (page 346)**

1. Prepare Lime Marinade and pour into a large heavy-duty resealable plastic bag or large nonmetal bowl. Add corn, beans, cucumber, onions, and cilantro. Seal bag; rotate to mix vegetables (or mix vegetables in bowl, then cover airtight). Refrigerate for at least 20 minutes or up to 4 hours; rotate bag (or stir vegetables in bowl) occasionally.

2. To eat, scoop out corn mixture with a slotted spoon; drain (discard marinade), then divide equally among tortillas. Roll up tortillas to enclose filling; eat out of hand. Makes 8 servings.

Lime Marinade. In a nonmetal bowl, stir together 1 teaspoon grated **lime peel**; ⅓ cup (80 ml) **lime juice**; 2 tablespoons (30 ml) **distilled white vinegar**; 1 tablespoon (15 ml) **honey**; 2 teaspoons **Dijon mustard**; 1 teaspoon **ground cumin**; 2 cloves **garlic**, minced or pressed; and 1 fresh **jalapeño chile,** seeded and minced.

Per serving: 189 calories (15% calories from fat), 3 g total fat, 0.4 g saturated fat, 0 mg cholesterol, 256 mg sodium, 34 g carbohydrates, 4 g fiber, 7 g protein, 68 mg calcium, 2 mg iron

Tofu Tacos with Pineapple Salsa
(recipe on facing page)

Besides its delicious tangy-spicy-sweet flavor, this dish offers great contrasts of color and texture.

....

- 1 **pound (455 g) firm tofu, rinsed, drained, and cut into ½-inch (1-cm) cubes**
- 1 **teaspoon chili powder**
- ¼ **teaspoon salt**
- ½ **teaspoon grated lime peel**
- 2 **tablespoons (30 ml) lime juice**
- 2 **teaspoons honey**
- ¾ **teaspoon ground cumin**
- 1 **large onion, chopped**
- 1 **medium-size red bell pepper (about 6 oz./170 g), seeded and chopped**
- 1 **can (about 15 oz./430 g) black beans, drained and rinsed**
- 1 **package (about 10 oz./285 g) frozen corn kernels, thawed and drained**
- 1 **teaspoon olive oil**

Sautéed Tofu with Black Bean & Corn Salsa

....

Preparation time: About 20 minutes
Cooking time: About 15 minutes

- 1 **or 2 cloves garlic, minced or pressed**
- ¼ **cup (10 g) lightly packed cilantro leaves**
  Lime wedges

....

1. In a large bowl, gently mix tofu, chili powder, and salt; set aside. In a small bowl, stir together lime peel, lime juice, honey, and cumin; set aside.

2. In a wide nonstick frying pan or wok, combine onion, bell pepper, and

¼ cup (60 ml) water. Stir-fry over medium-high heat until onion is soft (about 5 minutes). Add beans, corn, and lime juice mixture; stir-fry gently until beans and corn are heated through (about 3 minutes). Remove bean mixture from pan and keep warm. Wipe pan clean (be careful; pan is hot).

3. Heat oil in pan over medium-high heat. When oil is hot, add tofu and garlic. Stir-fry gently until tofu is heated through (3 to 4 minutes); add water, 1 tablespoon (15 ml) at a time, if pan appears dry.

4. Divide bean mixture among 4 individual plates; top equally with tofu. Sprinkle with cilantro and garnish with lime wedges. Makes 4 servings.

....

Per serving: 365 calories (28% calories from fat), 12 g total fat, 2 g saturated fat, 0 mg cholesterol, 220 mg sodium, 43 g carbohydrates, 6 g fiber, 27 g protein, 318 mg calcium, 14 mg iron

---

Meaty shiitake mushrooms add interest to a sake-sauced stir-fry.

....

- 1⅓ **cups (247 g) long-grain white rice**
- 1 **package (about 1 lb./455 g) firm reduced-fat tofu, rinsed and drained**
- 6 **medium-size dried shiitake mushrooms (about ⅓ oz./10 g total)**
- 8 **green onions**
- 2 **teaspoons salad oil**
- 1 **pound (455 g) broccoli flowerets (about 7 cups)**
- ½ **cup (120 ml) sake**
- ¼ **cup (60 ml) reduced-sodium soy sauce**
- 1 **tablespoon sugar**
- 1 **teaspoon finely chopped fresh ginger**
- ½ **teaspoon pepper**
- 2 **teaspoons cornstarch blended with 1 tablespoon (15 ml) cold water**

Mabu Tofu

....

Preparation time: 25 minutes
Cooking time: About 25 minutes

....

1. In a 3½- to 4-quart (3.3- to 3.8-liter) pan, bring 3 cups (710 ml) water to a boil over high heat; stir in rice. Reduce heat, cover, and simmer until liquid has been absorbed and rice is tender to bite (about 20 minutes).

2. Meanwhile, cut tofu into ½-inch (1-cm) chunks; place on paper towels and let drain for 10 minutes. Also, in a small bowl, combine mushrooms and 1 cup (240 ml) boiling water; let stand until mushrooms are softened (about 10 minutes). Lift mushrooms from water (reserve water); holding mushrooms over bowl, squeeze dry. Cut off and discard mushroom stems; then thinly slice caps and return to soaking water.

3. Thinly slice onions, keeping white and green parts separate. Heat oil in a wide nonstick frying pan over medium-high heat. Add broccoli and white part of onions; cook, stirring, for 1 minute. Add mushrooms and their soaking water; cover and cook, stirring occasionally, for 3 minutes. Add sake, soy sauce, sugar, ginger, pepper, and cornstarch mixture; bring to a boil, stirring. Add tofu, reduce heat, and simmer, stirring occasionally, until heated through (about 3 minutes).

4. To serve, spoon rice onto a platter or individual plates; top with tofu mixture and green part of onions. Makes 4 servings.

....

Per serving: 446 calories (14% calories from fat), 7 g total fat, 1 g saturated fat, 0 mg cholesterol, 676 mg sodium, 76 g carbohydrates, 5 g fiber, 19 g protein, 132 mg calcium, 5 mg iron

Here's a delicious meatless version of fajitas. Beans, sweet fresh corn, and red bell pepper are marinated in a lively citrus sauce, then warmed and rolled in soft flour tortillas.

- ¼ cup (60 ml) lime juice
- 1 tablespoon salad oil
- 1 teaspoon ground coriander
- ½ teaspoon ground cumin
- 2 cans (about 15 oz./425 g *each*) black beans, drained and rinsed;

  About 1½ cups (248 g) cooked yellow or white corn kernels (from 2 medium-size ears corn); or 1 package (about 10 oz./285 g) frozen corn kernels, thawed
- 1 medium-size red bell pepper (about 6 oz./170 g), seeded and diced

Black Bean, Corn & Pepper Fajitas

Preparation time: 25 minutes
Marinating time: At least 20 minutes
Cooking time: 10 to 12 minutes

- 1 fresh jalapeño chile, seeded and minced

  About 1½ cups (360 ml) Lime Salsa (page 21) or other salsa of your choice
- 8 warm flour tortillas (page 346)
- ½ cup (20 g) lightly packed chopped cilantro

  Salt and pepper

1. In a large heavy-duty resealable plastic bag or large nonmetal bowl, combine lime juice, oil, coriander, and cumin. Seal bag and rotate to mix (or stir well). Add beans, corn, bell pepper, and chile. Seal bag and rotate to coat vegetables (or mix vegetables in bowl, then cover airtight). Refrigerate for at least 20 minutes or until next day.

2. Prepare Lime Salsa; refrigerate.

3. Transfer bean mixture and marinade to a 1½- to 2-quart (1.4- to 1.9-liter) pan. Heat over medium-high heat just until hot.

4. To eat, scoop out bean mixture with a slotted spoon; drain (discard marinade), then divide among tortillas. Sprinkle evenly with cilantro; add salsa, salt, and pepper to taste. Roll up tortillas to enclose filling; eat out of hand. Makes 8 servings.

Per serving: 335 calories (14% calories from fat), 5 g total fat, 0.8 g saturated fat, 0 mg cholesterol, 177 mg sodium, 59 g carbohydrates, 9 g fiber, 15 g protein, 110 mg calcium, 4 mg iron

---

Like traditional shepherd's pie, this vegetarian rendition is topped with spoonfuls of mashed potato. The filling, though, omits the usual beef or lamb; instead, it's a combination of herb-seasoned lentils, walnuts, and whole wheat bread crumbs.

- 1½ cups (300 g) lentils
- 2 cloves garlic, minced or pressed
- 1½ teaspoons *each* dried thyme and dried savory
- ½ teaspoon dried rubbed sage
- 5½ cups (1.3 liters) vegetable broth
- ½ cup (65 g) chopped walnuts
- 2 cups (90 g) soft whole wheat bread crumbs
- 2 pounds (905 g) thin-skinned potatoes, peeled and cut into 2-inch (5-cm) chunks
- 1 cup (about 4 oz./115 g) shredded reduced-fat sharp Cheddar cheese

Lentil-Nut Shepherd's Pie

Preparation time: 15 minutes
Cooking time: About 1 hour and 10 minutes

1. Sort through lentils, discarding any debris. Rinse lentils, drain, and place in a 3- to 4-quart (2.8- to 3.8-liter) pan. Add garlic, thyme, savory, sage, and 3½ cups (830 ml) of the broth. Bring to a boil over high heat; then reduce heat, cover, and simmer until lentils are tender to bite (about 25 minutes). Remove from heat and stir in walnuts and bread crumbs.

2. While lentils are simmering, combine potatoes and remaining 2 cups (470 ml) broth in a 2- to 3-quart (1.9- to 2.8-liter) pan. Bring to a boil over high heat; then reduce heat, cover, and simmer until potatoes mash easily when pressed (15 to 20 minutes). Drain, reserving liquid. Leaving potatoes in pan, beat or mash them until smooth. Mix in ½ cup (120 ml) of the reserved liquid; then stir in cheese.

3. Stir remaining potato-cooking liquid into lentil mixture; spoon into a 9- by 13-inch (23- by 33-cm) baking pan. Drop potatoes in spoonfuls onto lentil mixture. Bake in a 375°F (190°C) oven until potatoes are golden brown (about 35 minutes). Makes 8 servings.

Per serving: 340 calories (23% calories from fat), 9 g total fat, 2 g saturated fat, 10 mg cholesterol, 874 mg sodium, 49 g carbohydrates, 7 g fiber, 19 g protein, 172 mg calcium, 5 mg iron

Stir-fried Broccoli, Garlic & Beans
(recipe on facing page)

Broccoli, earthy-tasting black beans, and plenty of garlic go into this Asian-inspired stir-fry.

1 **package (about ½ oz./15 g) dried shiitake mushrooms**

1 **cup (185 g) long-grain white rice**

1 **medium-size head garlic (about 3 oz./85 g)**

2 **teaspoons salad oil**

5 **cups (355 g) broccoli flowerets**

1 **can (about 15 oz./430 g) black beans, drained and rinsed**

2 **tablespoons (30 ml) reduced-sodium soy sauce**

1 **teaspoon Oriental sesame oil**

½ **teaspoon honey**

1. Soak mushrooms in hot water to cover until soft and pliable (about 20 minutes). Rub mushrooms gently to release any grit; then lift mushrooms from water. Discard water. Squeeze

Stir-fried Broccoli, Garlic & Beans

Preparation time: About 25 minutes
Cooking time: About 30 minutes
Pictured on facing page

mushrooms gently to remove moisture; trim and discard tough stems. Thinly slice caps, place in a small bowl, and set aside.

2. While mushrooms are soaking, in a 3- to 4-quart (2.8- to 3.8-liter) pan, bring 2 cups (470 ml) water to a boil over high heat; stir in rice. Reduce heat, cover, and simmer until liquid has been absorbed and rice is tender to bite (about 20 minutes). Transfer to a rimmed platter and keep warm. Fluff occasionally with a fork.

3. Separate garlic into cloves; then peel and thinly slice garlic cloves. Heat

salad oil in a wide nonstick frying pan or wok over medium-high heat. When oil is hot, add garlic and stir-fry gently just until tinged with brown (about 2 minutes; do not scorch). Add water, 1 tablespoon (15 ml) at a time, if pan appears dry. Remove garlic from pan with a slotted spoon; place in bowl with mushrooms.

4. Add broccoli and ⅓ cup (80 ml) water to pan. Cover and cook until broccoli is almost tender-crisp to bite (about 3 minutes). Uncover and stir-fry until liquid has evaporated. Add beans and stir-fry gently until heated through. Remove from heat and add mushroom mixture, soy sauce, sesame oil, and honey; mix gently but thoroughly. Spoon broccoli mixture over rice. Makes 4 servings.

Per serving: 352 calories (12% calories from fat), 5 g total fat, 0.6 g saturated fat, 0 mg cholesterol, 516 mg sodium, 66 g carbohydrates, 10 g fiber, 15 g protein, 139 mg calcium, 5 mg iron

---

Jalapeño jack cheese adds just the right amount of heat to these bean- and corn-filled burritos.

Cooking Sauce (recipe follows)

8 **low-fat flour tortillas (each 7 to 9 inches/18 to 23 cm in diameter)**

1 **teaspoon salad oil**

1 **large onion, chopped**

1 **medium-size red or green bell pepper (about 6 oz./170 g), seeded and diced**

1 **can (about 15 oz./430 g) pinto or kidney beans, drained and rinsed**

About 1½ cups (250 g) cooked fresh corn kernels (from 2 small ears yellow or white corn); or 1 package (about 10 oz./285 g) frozen corn kernels, thawed and drained

1 **cup (about 4 oz./115 g) shredded jalapeño or regular jack cheese**

Sautéed Bean Burritos

Preparation time: About 20 minutes
Cooking time: About 15 minutes

½ **cup (20 g) lightly packed cilantro leaves**

½ **to 1 cup (120 to 240 ml) nonfat sour cream**

1. Prepare Cooking Sauce and set aside. Brush tortillas lightly with hot water; then stack, wrap in foil, and heat in a 350°F (175°C) oven until warm (10 to 12 minutes).

2. Meanwhile, heat oil in a wide nonstick frying pan or wok over medium-high heat. When oil is hot, add onion, bell pepper, and 2 tablespoons (30 ml) water; stir-fry until onion is soft (about 5 minutes). Add more water, 1 table-

spoon (15 ml) at a time, if pan appears dry. Add beans and corn; stir-fry gently until heated through (about 3 minutes). Stir Cooking Sauce well and pour into pan. Cook, stirring gently, until sauce boils and thickens slightly (1 to 2 minutes).

3. Top tortillas equally with bean mixture. Sprinkle with cheese and cilantro, top with sour cream, and roll to enclose; eat out of hand. Makes 4 servings.

Cooking Sauce. In a small bowl, stir together 1 teaspoon **water** and ½ teaspoon **cornstarch** until blended. Stir in ½ teaspoon grated **lime peel**, 2 tablespoons (30 ml) **lime juice**, 1 teaspoon **honey**, ½ teaspoon **ground coriander**, and ¼ teaspoon **ground cumin**.

Per serving: 456 calories (23% calories from fat), 13 g total fat, 5 g saturated fat, 30 mg cholesterol, 766 mg sodium, 75 g carbohydrates, 15 g fiber, 21 g protein, 419 mg calcium, 4 mg iron

A spinach-flecked cheese spread and a zesty bean filling are wrapped inside flour tortillas to make these cool sandwiches. Try them for lunch on a warm summer day, perhaps with a fresh fruit salad alongside.

- 1 package (about 10 oz./285 g) frozen chopped spinach, thawed and squeezed dry
- 1 large package (about 8 oz./ 230 g) nonfat cream cheese or Neufchâtel cheese, at room temperature
- ½ cup (40 g) grated Parmesan cheese
- 2 tablespoons (30 ml) nonfat mayonnaise
- 1 teaspoon prepared horseradish (or to taste)
- 1/16 teaspoon ground allspice (or to taste)
- 1 can (about 15 oz./425 g) cannellini (white kidney beans)
- 1 tablespoon (15 ml) seasoned rice vinegar; or 1 tablespoon (15 ml) distilled white vinegar plus ½ teaspoon sugar
- 2 teaspoons honey

Bean Roll-ups

Preparation time: 25 minutes

- ¾ teaspoon chopped fresh thyme or ¼ teaspoon dried thyme
- ⅓ cup (35 g) thinly sliced green onions
- ⅓ cup (20 g) finely chopped parsley
- 6 reduced-fat flour tortillas (*each* about 7 inches/18 cm in diameter)

    About 48 whole fresh spinach leaves, rinsed and crisped

    Thyme sprigs (optional)

1. In a medium-size bowl, combine chopped spinach, cream cheese, Parmesan cheese, mayonnaise, horseradish, and allspice. Mix well; set aside.

2. Drain beans, reserving liquid. Rinse beans well, place in another medium-size bowl, and add vinegar, honey, and chopped thyme. Coarsely mash beans with a spoon; add enough of the reserved bean liquid to give mixture a spreadable consistency (do not make it too thin). Set aside. In a small bowl, combine onions and parsley; set aside.

3. To assemble sandwiches, divide spinach mixture equally among tortillas. With a spatula, spread spinach mixture to cover tortillas evenly. Then top tortillas equally with bean filling; carefully spread to cover spinach mixture. Sprinkle with onion mixture. Roll up each tortilla tightly to enclose filling. (At this point, you may cover tightly and refrigerate for up to 3 hours.)

4. Line 6 individual plates with spinach leaves. With a serrated knife, carefully cut each tortilla diagonally into 4 equal slices (wipe knife clean between cuts, if desired); arrange on spinach-lined plates. Garnish with thyme sprigs, if desired. Makes 6 servings.

Per serving: 230 calories (17% calories from fat), 4 g total fat, 1 g saturated fat, 9 mg cholesterol, 964 mg sodium, 33 g carbohydrates, 7 g fiber, 15 g protein, 388 mg calcium, 3 mg iron

This hearty main dish resembles the classic Cobb Salad in that the ingredients are arranged spoke-fashion on the serving platter—but that's where the similarity ends. We've replaced the traditional chicken, bacon, avocado, and blue cheese with beans, green peas, golden bell pepper, and tangy feta. Serve with chilled mineral water or iced tea, if you like.

Kidney Cobb Salad

Preparation time: 20 minutes

Dressing:

- ⅓ cup (80 ml) *each* nonfat mayonnaise and nonfat sour cream
- 2 tablespoons (30 ml) *each* balsamic vinegar and smooth unsweetened applesauce
- 1 tablespoon (15 ml) *each* olive oil and Dijon mustard
- 1 tablespoon chopped fresh dill or 1 teaspoon dried dill weed
- 1 teaspoon sugar (or to taste)
    Dill sprigs (optional)

Salad:

- 2 cans (about 15 oz./425 g *each*) red kidney beans
- 1 large yellow or red bell pepper (about 8 oz./230 g)
- 6 ounces (170 g) feta cheese
- 1 very small red onion (about 4 oz./115 g)
- 1 large head red leaf lettuce (1½ lbs./680 g), separated into leaves, rinsed, and crisped
- 1 package (about 10 oz./285 g) frozen tiny peas, thawed and drained

1. In a small bowl, combine mayonnaise, sour cream, vinegar, applesauce, oil, mustard, chopped dill, and sugar. Beat until smoothly blended. If a thinner dressing is desired, add water, 1 tablespoon (15 ml) at a time, until dressing has the desired consistency. Spoon into a small serving bowl; garnish with dill sprigs, if desired. Cover lightly and refrigerate while you prepare salad.

2. Drain beans and rinse well. Seed and finely chop bell pepper. Crumble cheese. Thinly slice onion; separate slices into rings.

3. To assemble salad, line a rimmed platter or a wide salad bowl with large lettuce leaves, then break remaining leaves into bite-size pieces and arrange atop whole leaves. Mound peas, beans, bell pepper, and cheese separately on lettuce; place onion in center. Offer dressing to add to taste. Makes 6 servings.

Per serving: 256 calories (26% calories from fat), 7 g total fat, 4 g saturated fat, 25 mg cholesterol, 718 mg sodium, 32 g carbohydrates, 9 g fiber, 16 g protein, 279 mg calcium, 4 mg iron

Looking for a warming dish for winter days? Serve aromatic black bean chili laced with orange juice and peel, then topped with refreshing orange slices.

Black Bean Chili with Oranges

Preparation time: 25 minutes
Cooking time: About 40 minutes

- 2 large onions, chopped
- 2 cloves garlic, minced or pressed
- 1 tablespoon (15 ml) salad oil
- 3 cans (about 15 oz./425 g *each*) black beans, drained and rinsed well
- 1 cup (240 ml) vegetable broth
- 1 tablespoon coriander seeds
- 1 teaspoon dried oregano
- ¼ teaspoon ground allspice
    About ⅛ teaspoon crushed red pepper flakes (or to taste)
- ⅛ teaspoon ground cardamom
- 4 large navel oranges (2 to 2½ lbs./905 g to 1.15 kg *total*)
- 1 cup (240 ml) nonfat sour cream
    Salt

1. In a 5- to 6-quart (5- to 6-liter) pan, combine onions, garlic, oil, and ¼ cup (60 ml) water. Cook over medium-high heat, stirring often, until onions are tinged with brown (about 10 minutes); add water, 1 tablespoon (15 ml) at a time, if pan appears dry. Add beans, broth, coriander seeds, oregano, allspice, red pepper flakes, and cardamom. Bring to a boil; then reduce heat, cover, and simmer until flavors are blended (about 10 minutes).

2. Meanwhile, finely shred enough peel (colored part only) from oranges to make 2 teaspoons. Squeeze juice from enough oranges to make ½ cup (120 ml). Set shredded peel and juice aside. Cut peel and all white membrane from remaining oranges; thinly slice fruit crosswise. Cover sliced oranges and set aside.

3. Uncover chili; bring to a boil over medium heat. Then boil, stirring occasionally, until thickened (15 to 20 minutes; as chili thickens, reduce heat and stir more often). Stir 1 teaspoon of the orange peel and the ½ cup (120 ml) orange juice into chili. Ladle chili into bowls; top with orange slices and sour cream. Garnish with remaining 1 teaspoon orange peel. Season to taste with salt. Makes 4 servings.

Per serving: 383 calories (13% calories from fat), 6 g total fat, 0.6 g saturated fat, 0 mg cholesterol, 810 mg sodium, 66 g carbohydrates, 15 g fiber, 19 g protein, 251 mg calcium, 4 mg iron

This savory pot pie is filled with a colorful chili made from pinto beans, bell pepper strips, and tiny sweet onions. You might serve it with a crisp green salad and a platter of juicy orange wedges. We call for Worcestershire as a seasoning, but since it's made with anchovies (or other fish), strict vegetarians will want to use soy sauce instead.

Chili Pot Pie

Preparation time: 30 minutes
Cooking time: About 1 hour
Pictured on facing page

Chili:

- 1 tablespoon chili powder (or to taste)
- 2 tablespoons (30 ml) pure maple syrup
- 1½ teaspoons dry mustard
- 1½ teaspoons Worcestershire or reduced-sodium soy sauce
- 2 cloves garlic, minced or pressed
- 1 can (about 15 oz./425 g) pinto beans, drained and rinsed
- 1 package (about 1 lb./455 g) frozen mixed bell pepper strips, thawed and drained; or about 4 cups fresh yellow, red, and green bell pepper strips (or use all of one color)
- 1 package (about 10 oz./285 g) frozen tiny onions, thawed and drained
- 1 large tomato (about 8 oz./ 230 g), chopped
- ¼ cup (35 g) yellow cornmeal

Pastry:

- ⅔ cup (140 g) low-fat (2%) cottage cheese
- ⅓ cup (76 g) butter or margarine, cut into chunks
- 1 large egg
- ¼ cup (60 ml) smooth unsweetened applesauce
- ¼ teaspoon *each* ground cumin and salt
- 1⅔ cups (210 g) bread flour or all-purpose flour
- 2 tablespoons (30 ml) nonfat milk

1. In a large bowl, combine chili powder, syrup, mustard, Worcestershire, and garlic. Add beans, bell peppers, onions, and tomato. Mix gently but thoroughly. Sprinkle cornmeal over bottom of a 9-inch (23-cm) pie pan or dish. Spoon bean mixture over cornmeal in pan; set aside.

2. In a food processor or a large bowl, combine cottage cheese, butter, egg, apple-sauce, cumin, and salt. Whirl or beat with an electric mixer until smoothly puréed. Add flour; whirl or stir with a fork until dough holds together (dough will be sticky and soft). Scrape dough out onto a heavily floured board; with floured fingers, pat into a ball. Then, still using floured fingers, pat pastry into a 10-inch (25-cm) round. With a floured cookie cutter, cut one or more shapes (each 1 to 2 inches/2.5 to 5 cm in diameter) from center of pastry. Set cutouts aside.

3. Carefully lift pastry and place over filling in pie pan. Fold edge under to make it flush with pan rim; flute firmly against rim. Arrange cutouts decoratively atop pastry. Set pie in a shallow 10- by 15-inch (25- by 38-cm) baking pan. Brush pastry (including cutouts) with milk.

4. Bake on lowest rack of a 400°F (205°C) oven until pastry is well browned and filling is hot in center (about 1 hour). If pastry rim or cutouts begin to darken excessively before center of pastry is brown, drape rim and cover cutouts with foil. To serve, spoon filling and crust from dish. Makes 6 servings.

Per serving: 405 calories (29% calories from fat), 13 g total fat, 7 g saturated fat, 65 mg cholesterol, 463 mg sodium, 58 g carbohydrates, 4 g fiber, 15 g protein, 89 mg calcium, 4 mg iron

Chili Pot Pie
(recipe on facing page)

Garlic and chili powder add spice to this mellow vegetable stew. Serve it with warm, soft flour tortillas; present the tortillas as "lids" for individual bowls of stew.

Pueblo Stew

Preparation time: 20 to 30 minutes
Cooking time: About 45 minutes

1 teaspoon olive oil or salad oil

1 large onion, chopped

2 cloves garlic, minced or pressed

1½ tablespoons chili powder

2 teaspoons cumin seeds

1 teaspoon dry oregano

1 *each* medium-size zucchini, pattypan, and crookneck squash (about 6 oz./170 g *each*), cut into 1-inch (2.5-cm) chunks

1 can (about 14 oz./400 g) yellow hominy, drained

1 pound (455 g) firm-ripe tomatoes, chopped

4 ounces (115 g) green beans, cut into 1-inch (2.5-cm) lengths

2 cans (about 15 oz./425 g *each*) pinto beans, drained and rinsed

4 vegetable or chicken bouillon cubes

2 cups (470 ml) water

1 tablespoon minced cilantro

4 warm flour tortillas (page 346)
  Cilantro sprigs
  Reduced-fat sour cream (optional)
  Shredded jack cheese (optional)

1. Heat oil in a 4- to 5-quart (3.8- to 4.7-liter) pan over medium-high heat. Add onion, garlic, chili powder, cumin seeds, and oregano. Cook, stirring often, until onion begins to brown (about 8 minutes); add water, 1 tablespoon (15 ml) at a time, if pan appears dry. Stir in squash, hominy, and tomatoes; cook until tomatoes begin to fall apart (about 5 minutes).

2. Stir in green beans, pinto beans, bouillon cubes, and 2 cups (470 ml) water; bring to a boil. Then reduce heat and simmer, uncovered, stirring occasionally, until green beans and squash are tender when pierced and mixture has the consistency of a thick stew (about 30 minutes). If mixture is too thick, add a little water; if it's too thin, continue to simmer, uncovered, until it's as thick as you like.

3. To serve, stir in minced cilantro; then ladle stew into 4 straight-sided 2-cup (470 ml) bowls. Lay a warm tortilla over each bowl; if desired, tie tortilla in place with raffia or string. Garnish with cilantro sprigs. Eat tortillas with stew; add sour cream and cheese to taste, if desired. Makes 4 servings.

Per serving: 411 calories (15% calories from fat), 7 g total fat, 0.8 g saturated fat, 6 mg cholesterol, 1,686 mg sodium, 73 g carbohydrates, 14 g fiber, 17 g protein, 172 mg calcium, 7 mg iron

---

Creamy cannellini beans are the base of this easy vegetable stew.

Tuscan Bean Stew

Preparation time: 25 minutes
Cooking time: About 45 minutes

6 slices Italian sandwich bread (about 6 oz./ 170 g *total*), cut into ½-inch (1-cm) cubes

2 teaspoons olive oil

2 large onions, chopped

4 cloves garlic, minced

½ teaspoon *each* dried rubbed sage, dried thyme, and dried marjoram

¼ cup (10 g) chopped fresh basil

4 large tomatoes (about 2 lbs./ 905 g total), chopped

3 cans (about 15 oz./425 g *each*) cannellini (white kidney beans), drained and rinsed

1 cup (240 ml) canned vegetable broth

1 tablespoon (15 ml) red wine vinegar

¼ cup (20 g) grated Parmesan cheese

1. Toast bread cubes as directed for Garbanzo Beans with Olive Pesto (page 329). Set aside.

2. Heat oil in a 4- to 5-quart (3.8- to 5-liter) pan over medium-high heat. Add onions, garlic, sage, thyme, marjoram, and ¼ cup (60 ml) water. Cook, stirring often, until onions are soft (about 5 minutes). Add water, 1 tablespoon (15 ml) at a time, if pan appears dry. Stir in basil and half the tomatoes. Cook, stirring often, just until tomatoes are soft (about 3 minutes). Remove from heat and let cool slightly.

3. Transfer onion mixture to a food processor or blender; whirl until smoothly puréed. Return purée to pan and add beans, broth, and vinegar. Bring to a boil over medium-high heat; then reduce heat, cover, and simmer for 15 minutes.

4. Stir croutons into bean stew; spoon stew into individual bowls. Sprinkle remaining tomatoes around edge of each bowl. Sprinkle with cheese and serve at once. Makes 4 servings.

Per serving: 505 calories (12% calories from fat), 7 g total fat, 2 g saturated fat, 4 mg cholesterol, 1,716 mg sodium, 89 g carbohydrates, 25 g fiber, 25 g protein, 260 mg calcium, 7 mg iron

It's every bit as hearty as traditional chili—but this sturdy dish is made entirely without meat. Try it with Blue Corn Muffins (page 336) alongside.

All-vegetable Chili

Preparation time: About 15 minutes
Cooking time: About 30 minutes

2 medium-size carrots (about 8 oz./230 g *total*), chopped

1 large onion, coarsely chopped

¼ cup (60 ml) water

1 can (about 14½ oz./ 415 g) tomatoes

1 can (about 15 oz./425 g) pinto beans

1 can (about 15 oz./425 g) red kidney beans

2 tablespoons chili powder

About ½ cup (120 ml) plain nonfat yogurt

Salt and crushed red pepper flakes

1. In a 4- to 5-quart (3.8- to 4.7-liter) pan, combine carrots, onion, and water. Cook over high heat, stirring often, until liquid has evaporated and vegetables begin to brown and stick to pan (about 10 minutes).

2. Add tomatoes and their liquid to pan; break tomatoes up with a spoon. Stir in all beans and their liquid (if using home-cooked beans, add 1 cup (120 ml) low-sodium chicken broth mixed with 1 teaspoon cornstarch). Add chili powder; stir to scrape browned bits free. Bring to a boil; then reduce heat and simmer, uncovered, until flavors are blended (about 15 minutes). If chili is too thick, add a little water; if it's too thin, continue to simmer until it's as thick as you like.

3. Ladle chili into bowls. Add yogurt, salt, and red pepper flakes to taste. Makes 4 servings.

Per serving: 260 calories (6% calories from fat), 2 g total fat, 0.2 g saturated fat, 0.6 mg cholesterol, 1,057 mg sodium, 50 g carbohydrates, 16 g fiber, 15 g protein, 187 mg calcium, 5 mg iron

---

Pineapple, ripe banana, and a hearty helping of peanut butter give this fruit-and-vegetable stew its rich, slightly sweet flavor. Serve the dish over creamy couscous simmered in a fragrant blend of milk and banana nectar.

Peanut Stew with Banana Couscous

Preparation time: 20 minutes
Cooking time: About 20 minutes

1 can (about 12 oz./360 ml) banana nectar

About 1¼ cups (300 ml) low-fat (2%) milk

1 medium-size red onion (about 8 oz./230 g), finely chopped

1 can (about 20 oz./570 g) crushed pineapple packed in its own juice

1 medium-size very ripe banana (about 6 oz./170 g), mashed

1 package (about 10 oz./285 g) frozen chopped spinach, thawed and squeezed dry

½ cup (120 ml) crunchy peanut butter

About ⅛ teaspoon crushed red pepper flakes

1 package (about 10 oz./285 g) couscous

¼ cup (10 g) *each* coarsely chopped fresh mint and cilantro

Lime wedges

1. Pour banana nectar into a 4-cup (950-ml) glass measure. Add enough milk to make 2¾ cups (650 ml); set aside.

2. In a wide nonstick frying pan, combine onion and ¼ cup (60 ml) water. Cook over medium-high heat, stirring often, until onion is soft (about 5 minutes); add water, 1 tablespoon (15 ml) at a time, if pan appears dry.

3. Add undrained pineapple and mashed banana to onion mixture; bring to a boil. Stir in spinach; then reduce heat, cover, and simmer for 5 minutes. Add peanut butter and red pepper flakes. Simmer, uncovered, for 5 minutes, stirring until peanut butter is melted and smoothly blended into sauce.

4. Meanwhile, pour milk mixture into a 2- to 3-quart (1.9- to 2.8-liter) pan and bring just to a boil over medium-high heat. Stir in couscous. Cover, remove from heat, and let stand until liquid has been absorbed (5 to 6 minutes).

5. Spoon couscous into 4 wide individual bowls and top with spinach mixture. Sprinkle with mint and cilantro; garnish with lime wedges. Makes 4 servings.

Per serving: 696 calories (23% calories from fat), 19 g total fat, 4 g saturated fat, 6 mg cholesterol, 271 mg sodium, 115 g carbohydrates, 8 g fiber, 23 g protein, 243 mg calcium, 4 mg iron

Mushroom & White Bean Pizza
(recipe on facing page)

Our tender no-yeast pizza dough gets a pleasantly moist texture—and extra protein—from cottage cheese. The topping offers some delicious surprises: smoked Gouda cheese and mild, creamy-textured white beans join the familiar mushrooms and tomatoes.

Mushroom & White Bean Pizza

Preparation time: 30 minutes
Cooking time: About 20 minutes
Pictured on facing page

- 1 jar (about 6 oz./170 g) marinated quartered artichoke hearts
- 8 ounces (230 g) mushrooms, thinly sliced
- 4 cloves garlic, minced or pressed
- 3 tablespoons yellow cornmeal
- 2 cups (250 g) all-purpose flour
- 1 tablespoon baking powder
- ¼ teaspoon salt
- ¾ cup (158 g) low-fat (2%) cottage cheese
- 1 tablespoon sugar
- 2 tablespoons (30 ml) *each* nonfat milk and olive oil
- ¾ cup (85 g) *each* shredded smoked Gouda and part-skim mozzarella cheese (or use all of one kind)
- 1 tablespoon chopped fresh oregano or 1 teaspoon dried oregano
- 1 can (about 15 oz./425 g) cannellini (white kidney beans), drained and rinsed
- 1 large firm-ripe pear-shaped (Roma-type) tomato (about 4 oz./115 g), very thinly sliced lengthwise
- ¼ cup (25 g) very thinly sliced red onion
  About ⅛ teaspoon crushed red pepper flakes (or to taste)
  Oregano sprigs (optional)

1. Drain artichokes well, reserving marinade; you should have ¼ cup (60 ml) marinade. (If necessary, add equal parts water and olive oil to marinade to make ¼ cup/60 ml liquid.) Set artichokes and marinade aside.

2. In a medium-size nonstick frying pan, combine mushrooms, garlic, and ¼ cup (60 ml) water. Cook over medium-high heat, stirring occasionally, until mushrooms are soft and almost all liquid has evaporated (about 7 minutes; do not scorch). Remove from pan and set aside.

3. Sprinkle cornmeal over bottom of a lightly greased 12-inch (30-cm) deep-dish pizza pan; set aside. In a medium-size bowl, stir together flour, baking powder, and salt; set aside.

4. In a food processor or a large bowl, combine cottage cheese, the reserved ¼ cup (60 ml) artichoke marinade, sugar, milk, and oil. Whirl or beat with an electric mixer until smoothly puréed. Add flour mixture; whirl or beat just until dough holds together. Turn dough out onto a lightly floured board and knead several times, or until dough holds together (dough will be soft). Then place dough in pizza pan. Flour your hands thoroughly; then flatten dough with the heels of your hands and your fingertips to cover pan bottom evenly. (Or roll dough on board into a 12½-inch/31-cm round and carefully fit into pan.)

5. Gently stretch edge of dough up sides of pan to form about a ½-inch (1-cm) rim. Prick dough all over with a fork; then sprinkle evenly with Gouda cheese, mozzarella cheese, and chopped oregano.

6. Arrange mushrooms, beans, artichokes, tomato, and onion over cheese. Bake pizza on middle rack of a 500°F (260°C) oven until crust is golden and cheese is melted (about 10 minutes). Sprinkle with red pepper flakes and garnish with oregano sprigs, if desired. Serve immediately. Makes 6 servings.

Per serving: 420 calories (29% calories from fat), 14 g total fat, 5 g saturated fat, 24 mg cholesterol, 855 mg sodium, 54 g carbohydrates, 5 g fiber, 21 g protein, 390 mg calcium, 4 mg iron

Juicy fresh apricots add a tart and surprising accent to this vegetarian version of a sweet-spiced Moroccan-style stew.

....

- 1 **teaspoon sesame seeds**
- 1 **large onion, chopped**
- 1½ **cups (360 ml) low-fat (2%) milk**
- 1 **package (about 10 oz./285 g) couscous**
- 2 **cans (about 15 oz./425 g *each*) cannellini (white kidney beans), drained and rinsed**
- ½ **cup (120 ml) vegetable broth**
- 3 **tablespoons (45 ml) honey**
- ¼ **teaspoon *each* ground ginger and ground cinnamon**
- ⅛ **teaspoon ground saffron or a large pinch of saffron threads**
- ⅛ **teaspoon ground white pepper**
- 6 **apricots (about 12 oz./340 g *total*), pitted and quartered**
- ⅓ **cup (15 g) cilantro leaves**
  Salt

White Bean Tagine

....

Preparation time: 15 minutes
Cooking time: About 20 minutes

1. Toast sesame seeds in a wide nonstick frying pan over medium heat, stirring often, until golden (about 3 minutes). Remove from pan and set aside.

2. In same pan, combine onion and ¼ cup (60 ml) water. Cook over medium-high heat, stirring often, until onion is soft (about 5 minutes); add water, 1 tablespoon (15 ml) at a time, if pan appears dry. Remove from heat.

3. In a 2- to 3-quart (1.9- to 2.8-liter) pan, bring milk and 1 cup (240 ml) water just to a boil over medium-high heat. Stir in couscous; cover, remove from heat, and let stand until liquid has been absorbed (about 5 minutes). Keep warm; fluff occasionally with a fork.

4. Meanwhile, to onion mixture, add beans, broth, honey, ginger, cinnamon, saffron, and white pepper. Bring to a boil over medium-high heat. Then reduce heat so mixture boils gently; cook, stirring occasionally, for 5 minutes. Add apricots; cook, stirring gently, just until heated through (about 3 minutes).

5. To serve, spoon couscous onto a rimmed platter; top with bean mixture. Sprinkle with cilantro and sesame seeds; season to taste with salt. Makes 4 servings.

....

Per serving: 578 calories (7% calories from fat), 4 g total fat, 1 g saturated fat, 7 mg cholesterol, 445 mg sodium, 111 g carbohydrates, 13 g fiber, 25 g protein, 210 mg calcium, 4 mg iron

---

This mild, distinctive curry goes together quickly. Fresh tomatoes enrich the aromatic sauce and garnish the finished dish.

....

- 1 **teaspoon olive oil**
- 1 **large onion, chopped**
- 4 **cloves garlic, minced**
- ½ **teaspoon ground coriander**
- ¼ **teaspoon ground ginger**
- ⅛ **teaspoon ground red pepper (cayenne), or to taste**
- ¼ **cup (10 g) cilantro leaves**
- 2 **large tomatoes (about 1 lb./ 455 g *total*), chopped**
- 2 **teaspoons butter or margarine**
- ⅛ **teaspoon ground turmeric**
- 2 **cans (about 15 oz./425 g *each*) garbanzo beans, drained and rinsed**
- ½ **cup (120 ml) vegetable broth**

Curried Garbanzo Beans

....

Preparation time: 20 minutes
Cooking time: About 30 minutes

- 2 **teaspoons lime juice**
  Salt
- 1½ **cups (360 ml) plain nonfat yogurt**
  Lime wedges

....

1. Heat oil in a 3- to 4-quart (2.8- to 3.8-liter) pan over medium-high heat. Add onion, garlic, coriander, ginger, red pepper, and ¼ cup (60 ml) water. Cook, stirring often, until onion is soft (about 5 minutes; do not scorch). Add water, 1 tablespoon (15 ml) at a time, if pan appears dry. Stir in cilantro and half the tomatoes. Cook, stirring often, just until tomatoes are soft (about 3 minutes).

2. Carefully transfer onion mixture to a food processor or blender. Whirl until smoothly puréed. Return to pan; add butter and turmeric. Bring just to a boil over medium-high heat (2 to 3 minutes). Add beans, broth, and lime juice. Return to a boil; then reduce heat, cover, and simmer for 15 minutes.

3. Spoon curry into wide individual bowls; sprinkle remaining tomatoes evenly around edge of each bowl. Season to taste with salt; offer yogurt and lime to add to taste. Makes 4 servings.

....

Per serving: 275 calories (23% calories from fat), 7 g total fat, 2 g saturated fat, 7 mg cholesterol, 457 mg sodium, 40 g carbohydrates, 8 g fiber, 14 g protein, 238 mg calcium, 3 mg iron

How to Cook Legumes

The recipes in this book call for only a few kinds of legumes, but you should feel free to experiment with other choices. On this page, we provide a guide for cooking some of the most widely available types. If you'd like to substitute home-cooked beans for canned ones, keep in mind that a 15-ounce can (425 g) holds about 2 cups cooked (about 1 cup dried) beans.

To ensure good texture and digestibility, always prepare legumes properly. Rinse them in a colander; as you rinse, remove and discard any debris and imperfect legumes. Drain. Then soak (if necessary) and cook as directed at right. If you wish to add salt, do so after cooking; otherwise, the legumes may become tough.

Soaking legumes. All legumes except black-eyed peas, lentils, and split peas should be soaked. Use the quick-soak method if you're in a hurry; otherwise, soak overnight.

Quick soaking. For each pound of dried legumes, bring 2 quarts (1.9-liters) water to a boil in a 4- to 5-quart (3.8- to 5-liter) pan over high heat. Add rinsed legumes; boil for 10 minutes. Remove from heat, cover, and let stand for 1 hour. Drain, discarding water; rinse well.

Overnight soaking. For each pound of dried legumes, pour 2 quarts (1.9 liters) of water into a large bowl. Add rinsed legumes; let soak at room temperature until next day. Drain, discarding water; rinse well.

Cooking legumes. Cooking times vary depending on the type of legume and the length of time it has been stored. The older the legume, the longer it takes to cook—so don't combine newly purchased legumes with those already on your shelf.

For each pound (455 g) of dried legumes (unsoaked weight), pour 2 quarts (1.9 liters) cold water into a 3- to 4-quart (2.8- to 3.8-liter) pan. Add legumes (soaked, if necessary) and bring to a boil over high heat. Then reduce heat, cover, and simmer until tender to bite (see our times; or follow package directions). If needed, add water to keep legumes moist. Start tasting when the minimum recommended time is up; when they're done, legumes should be tender but not mushy.

Black beans (turtle beans). Popular in Latin American and Caribbean cuisine, black beans have a rich, mellow flavor. Soak first. Cook for 1½ to 2 hours.

Black-eyed peas. Beige ovals with distinctive black spots, black-eyed peas have an earthy taste. Do not soak. Cook for about 50 minutes.

Garbanzo beans (chick peas, ceci beans). Rich, nutty flavor and toothsome texture make garbanzos a natural for soups and salads. Soak first. Cook for 2 to 2½ hours.

Great Northern beans. These mild-flavored, medium-size white beans are similar in shape to kidney beans. You can use them in place of cannellini (white kidney beans). Soak first. Cook for 1 to 1½ hours.

Kidney beans. Kidney beans have a firm texture and a meaty flavor. The red variety is more widely sold than the white type; if you can't find the white beans (cannellini), substitute Great Northerns. Soak first. Cook for 1 to 1½ hours.

Lentils. Mild and earthy in flavor, disk-shaped lentils come in many varieties, including brown, green, and pink types. Decorticated (skinless) lentils turn mushy if overcooked. Do not soak. Cook for about 40 minutes.

Lima beans. Limas cook up softer than other legumes. Serve as a side dish or in casseroles and soups. Soak first. Cook for about 1 hour.

Pinto, pink, red, cranberry, and other speckled beans. These beans may be mottled or solid in color; all work well in chilis, casseroles, and soups. Soak first. Cook for about 1½ hours.

Split peas. These green or yellow halved peas have a distinctive flavor and a soft texture; use them in soups and side dishes. Do not soak. Cook for 35 to 45 minutes.

White navy beans. Small, creamy white navy beans are the classic choice for baked beans. Soak first. Cook for about 1 hour.

Mention bread pudding, and most people think of an old-fashioned dessert. But this pudding is a savory main course: squares of whole-grain bread baked in an herbed custard that's flavored with dried porcini and fresh button mushrooms. Serve the dish atop a bed of sautéed spinach.

Mushroom Bread Pudding with Wilted Spinach

Preparation time: 20 minutes
Cooking time: About 1¾ hours
Pictured on facing page

Mushroom Bread Pudding:

- 1 package (about 1 oz./30 g) dried porcini
- 4 ounces (115 g) small button mushrooms
- 1 teaspoon butter or margarine
- 4 cloves garlic, minced or pressed
- 1½ teaspoons chopped fresh thyme or ¾ teaspoon dried thyme
- 1 large onion, chopped
- 2 large eggs
- 2 large egg whites
- 1 tablespoon cornstarch
- 1½ cups (360 ml) buttermilk
- 1¼ cups (300 ml) nonfat milk
- 2 teaspoons sugar
- ¼ teaspoon salt
- ⅛ teaspoon ground white pepper
- 8 slices whole wheat sandwich bread or egg sandwich bread (crusts removed), cut into 1-inch (2.5-cm) squares

Wilted Spinach:

- 1 pound (455 g) fresh spinach
- 1 tablespoon butter or margarine
- ⅛ teaspoon ground nutmeg (or to taste)
  Salt and black pepper

Garnish:

  Thyme sprigs (optional)

1. Place porcini in a small bowl and add ½ cup (120 ml) boiling water. Let stand, stirring occasionally, until porcini are soft (about 10 minutes). Lift out porcini and, holding them over bowl, squeeze very dry; then coarsely chop and set aside. Without disturbing sediment at bottom of bowl, pour soaking liquid into a measuring cup; you should have about ¼ cup (60 ml). Set liquid aside; discard sediment.

2. While porcini are soaking, slice button mushrooms ¼ to ½ inch (6 mm to 1 cm) thick; set aside. Melt the 1 teaspoon butter in a wide nonstick frying pan over medium-high heat. Add garlic and chopped thyme; cook, stirring, until fragrant (about 30 seconds; do not scorch). Add button mushrooms, onion, and ¼ cup (60 ml) water; cook, stirring, until mushrooms are soft and browned bits stick to pan bottom (6 to 8 minutes). Add 2 tablespoons (30 ml) more water and remove pan from heat; stir to loosen any browned bits from pan. Transfer onion mixture to a small bowl and set aside.

3. In a large bowl, beat eggs and egg whites until well blended. Smoothly blend cornstarch with porcini soaking liquid; add cornstarch mixture, buttermilk, milk, sugar, the ¼ teaspoon salt,

and white pepper to eggs and whisk until blended. Stir in onion mixture and chopped porcini. Add bread and mix gently but thoroughly; let stand until softened (about 5 minutes), stirring occasionally.

4. Transfer mixture to a square 8-inch (20-cm) nonstick or greased regular baking pan. Set pan of pudding in a larger baking pan; then set on center rack of a 325°F (165°C) oven. Pour boiling water into larger pan up to level of pudding. Bake until top of pudding is golden brown and center no longer jiggles when pan is gently shaken (about 1 hour and 35 minutes).

5. When pudding is almost done, discard stems and any yellow or wilted leaves from spinach; rinse remaining leaves. Place half the spinach in a 4- to 5-quart (3.8- to 5-liter) pan. Cook over medium-high heat, stirring often, until wilted (2 to 4 minutes). Pour into a colander and drain well, then transfer to a bowl; keep warm. Repeat to cook remaining spinach. To cooked spinach, add the 1 tablespoon butter and nutmeg; season to taste with salt and black pepper and mix gently.

6. Divide spinach among 4 individual rimmed plates. Spoon pudding over spinach (or cut pudding into wedges and place atop spinach). Garnish with thyme sprigs, if desired. Makes 4 servings.

Per serving: 385 calories (25% calories from fat), 11 g total fat, 5 g saturated fat, 148 mg cholesterol, 716 mg sodium, 53 g carbohydrates, 4 g fiber, 21 g protein, 405 mg calcium, 7 mg iron

Mushroom Bread Pudding with Wilted Spinach
(recipe on facing page)

Dal is a spicy Indian dish based on dried legumes; this one features yellow split peas, curry seasonings, and an abundance of fresh vegetables. It does take several hours to cook, so plan to serve it on a day when you can afford to spend some time in the kitchen.

- 1 **cup (200 g) yellow split peas**
  About 5½ cups (1.3 liters) vegetable broth
- 2 **large onions, chopped**
- 2 **medium-size carrots (about 8 oz./230 g *total*), diced**
- 2 **tablespoons finely chopped fresh ginger**
- 2 **large cloves garlic, minced or pressed**
- 2 **teaspoons *each* ground turmeric and chili powder**
- 1 **large can (about 28 oz./795 g) crushed tomatoes**
- 1 **pound (455 g) butternut or other gold-fleshed squash, peeled and cut into ¾-inch (2-cm) cubes**
- 2 **cups (370 g) long-grain brown rice**
- 3 **cups (200 g) broccoli flowerets**
- ½ **cup (20 g) cilantro leaves**
  About 1½ cups (240 ml) plain nonfat yogurt
  Lime wedges
  Crushed red pepper flakes
  Salt

Yellow Split Pea Dal with Brown Rice & Broccoli

Preparation time: 30 minutes
Cooking time: About 2½ hours

1. Sort through peas, discarding any debris; then rinse peas, drain, and set aside.

2. In a 6- to 8-quart (6- to 8-liter) pan, combine 1 cup (240 ml) of the broth, onions, carrots, ginger, and garlic. Cook over medium-high heat, stirring often, until liquid evaporates and browned bits stick to pan bottom (about 15 minutes). To deglaze pan, add ⅓ cup (80 ml) more broth, stirring to loosen browned bits from pan; continue to cook until browned bits form again. Repeat deglazing step about 3 more times or until vegetables are browned, using about ⅓ cup (80 ml) broth each time.

3. To vegetable mixture, add peas, turmeric, chili powder, tomatoes and their liquid, and 3 cups (710 ml) more broth. Bring to a boil; then reduce heat, cover, and simmer for 1 hour. Add squash; cover and simmer, stirring often, until squash is tender to bite (40 to 50 more minutes).

4. Meanwhile, in a 5- to 6-quart (5- to 6-liter) pan, bring 4 cups (950 ml) water to a boil over high heat; stir in rice. Reduce heat, cover, and simmer until liquid has been absorbed and rice is tender to bite (about 45 minutes). Remove from pan and keep warm; fluff occasionally with a fork.

5. Wash pan and add broccoli and ⅓ cup (80 ml) water. Cover and cook over medium-high heat until broccoli is almost tender-crisp to bite (about 3 minutes). Uncover and continue to cook, stirring, until all liquid has evaporated.

6. To serve, spoon rice, broccoli, and split pea mixture onto individual plates. Offer cilantro, yogurt, lime, red pepper flakes, and salt to season each serving to taste. Makes 6 servings.

Per serving: 516 calories (7% calories from fat), 4 g total fat, 0.6 g saturated fat, 1 mg cholesterol, 1,445 mg sodium, 102 g carbohydrates, 10 g fiber, 22 g protein, 253 mg calcium, 5 mg iron

Flavored with basil and thyme, this garden-fresh specialty features popular ratatouille—a Provençal vegetable stew of eggplant, zucchini, and bell peppers—served with couscous and tangy feta cheese.

Ratatouille:

- 1 **small onion, cut into thin slivers**
- 1 **small red bell pepper (about 4 oz./115 g), seeded and thinly sliced**
- 1 **small eggplant (about 1 lb./ 455 g), peeled and cut into ½-inch (1-cm) cubes**
- 1 **tablespoon chopped fresh basil or ¾ teaspoon dried basil (or to taste)**
- 1½ **teaspoons chopped fresh thyme or ½ teaspoon dried thyme (or to taste)**
   About ¼ teaspoon *each* salt and pepper (or to taste)
- 1 **small zucchini (about 4 oz./ 115 g), cut into ¼-inch (6-mm) slices**
- 1 **can (about 15 oz./425 g) garbanzo beans, drained and rinsed**
- 1 **large tomato (about 8 oz./ 230 g), coarsely chopped**

Couscous with Ratatouille & Feta Cheese

Preparation time: 20 minutes
Cooking time: About 15 minutes

Couscous:

- 2¼ **cups (530 ml) low-fat (1%) milk**
- 1 **package (about 10 oz./285 g) couscous**
- 1 **cup (about 4½ oz./130 g) crumbled feta cheese**

Garnish:

   Basil or thyme sprigs

1. In a wide nonstick frying pan, combine onion, bell pepper, eggplant, chopped basil, chopped thyme, salt, pepper, and ½ cup (120 ml) water. Cover and cook over medium-high heat until vegetables are almost tender when pierced (about 5 minutes). Uncover and add zucchini. Cook, stirring gently, until almost all liquid has evaporated. Add beans and tomato; stir gently just until heated through (about 3 minutes).

2. Meanwhile, in a 2½- to 3-quart (2.4- to 2.8-liter) pan, bring milk just to a boil over medium-high heat. Stir in couscous and ¾ cup (100 g) of the cheese; cover, remove from heat, and let stand until liquid has been absorbed (about 5 minutes).

3. Divide couscous equally among 4 shallow individual bowls. Top with vegetable mixture and sprinkle with remaining ¼ cup (33 g) cheese. Garnish with basil sprigs. Makes 4 servings.

Per serving: 537 calories (19% calories from fat), 11 g total fat, 6 g saturated fat, 36 mg cholesterol, 714 mg sodium, 85 g carbohydrates, 8 g fiber, 24 g protein, 430 mg calcium, 4 mg iron

Polenta Pepper Torte
(recipe on facing page)

Brilliant red peppers accent this golden combination of polenta, eggs, and cream-style corn in a mildly sweet polenta crust.

Polenta Pepper Torte

Preparation time: 25 minutes
Cooking time: About 1 hour
Pictured on facing page

⅔ cup (85 g) all-purpose flour

1⅓ cups (183 g) polenta or yellow cornmeal

¼ cup (50 g) sugar

½ teaspoon salt

5 tablespoons (71 g) butter or margarine, cut into chunks

1 jar (about 7 oz./200 g) roasted red peppers, rinsed and patted dry

1 large can (about 15 oz./425 g) cream-style corn

½ cup (120 ml) nonfat sour cream

1 large egg

5 large egg whites

2 tablespoons cornstarch

¼ cup (28 g) shredded fontina or mozzarella cheese

1 tablespoon chopped fresh oregano or 1 teaspoon dried oregano

Oregano sprigs

1. In a food processor or a large bowl, whirl or stir together flour, ⅔ cup (92 g) of the polenta, sugar, and ¼ teaspoon of the salt. Add butter and 1 tablespoon (15 ml) water; whirl or rub together with your fingers until mixture resembles coarse crumbs. If pastry is too dry, add a little more water.

2. Press pastry firmly over bottom and about 1 inch (2.5 cm) up sides of a 9-inch (23-cm) nonstick or well-greased regular cheesecake pan with a removable rim. Prick all over with a fork to prevent puffing. Bake in a 350°F (175°C) oven until crust is tinged with gold and feels slightly firmer when pressed (about 15 minutes). Let cool on a rack for 5 minutes.

3. Cut any very large pieces of red peppers into smaller pieces. Arrange peppers in baked crust. In food processor, whirl remaining ⅔ cup (92 g) polenta, corn, sour cream, egg, egg whites, cornstarch, and remaining ¼ teaspoon salt until smooth. Pour egg mixture over peppers in crust. Sprinkle with cheese.

4. Return torte to oven and bake until filling is golden and a knife inserted in center comes out clean (about 45 minutes). Let cool on a rack for about 10 minutes. To serve, sprinkle with chopped oregano and garnish with oregano sprigs. Remove pan rim; then cut torte into wedges with a very sharp knife. Makes 6 servings.

Per serving: 498 calories (28% calories from fat), 15 g total fat, 9 g saturated fat, 80 mg cholesterol, 809 mg sodium, 76 g carbohydrates, 3 g fiber, 14 g protein, 65 mg calcium, 3 mg iron

---

Like many traditional paellas, this meatless version calls for sweet peppers, green peas, artichokes, and saffron—but it's made with quick-cooking couscous, not rice, and the protein comes from black beans rather than chicken and shellfish. Serve it with a warm sourdough loaf and crisp greens tossed with a light vinaigrette.

Couscous Bean Paella

Preparation time: About 15 minutes
Cooking time: About 15 minutes

2 teaspoons olive oil

1 large onion, chopped

1 medium-size red bell pepper (about 6 oz./170 g), seeded and cut into ½-inch (1-cm) squares

2¼ cups (590 ml) canned vegetable broth

⅛ teaspoon saffron threads, or to taste

1 package (about 9 oz./255 g) frozen artichoke hearts, thawed and drained

1 cup (145 g) frozen peas, thawed and drained

1½ cups (275 g) couscous

1 can (about 15 oz./430 g) black beans, drained and rinsed

Lime or lemon wedges

1. Heat oil in a wide nonstick frying pan or wok over medium-high heat. When oil is hot, add onion, bell pepper, and ¼ cup (60 ml) water. Stir-fry until onion is soft (about 5 minutes); add water, 1 tablespoon (15 ml) at a time, if pan appears dry.

2. Add broth, saffron, artichokes, and peas to pan. Bring to a rolling boil. Stir in couscous. Cover pan, remove from heat, and let stand until liquid has been absorbed (about 5 minutes). Gently stir in beans; cover and let stand for 2 to 3 minutes to heat beans. Serve with lime wedges. Makes 4 servings.

Per serving: 435 calories (9% calories from fat), 4 g total fat, 0.5 g saturated fat, 0 mg cholesterol, 816 mg sodium, 82 g carbohydrates, 11 g fiber, 17 g protein, 73 mg calcium, 3 mg iron

A creamy cheese topping covers rice dotted with onion and brilliant bell peppers in this colorful casserole.

....

1⅓ cups (247 g) long-grain white rice

4 large red or green bell peppers (about 2 lbs./905 g *total*)

1 large onion, chopped

2 cloves garlic, minced or pressed

1 cup (240 ml) vegetable broth

4 large eggs

About 2 cups (about 15 oz./425 g) part-skim ricotta cheese

¾ cup (60 g) grated Parmesan cheese

....

1. In a 3½- to 4-quart (3.3- to 3.8-liter) pan, bring 3 cups (710 ml) water to a boil over high heat. Stir in rice; then reduce heat, cover, and simmer until

Pepper, Rice & Cheese Casserole

....

Preparation time: 15 minutes
Cooking time: About 1½ hours

liquid has been absorbed and rice is tender to bite (about 20 minutes).

2. Meanwhile, seed bell peppers; then slice or chop them. Place peppers in a 5- to 6-quart (5- to 6-liter) pan and add onion, garlic, and ¼ cup (60 ml) of the broth. Cook over medium-high heat, stirring often, until liquid evaporates and browned bits stick to pan bottom (about 10 minutes). To deglaze pan, add water, 1 tablespoon (15 ml) at a time, if pan appears dry. Add ¼ cup (60 ml) more broth, stirring to loosen browned bits from pan. Remove pan from heat.

3. Stir cooked rice into pepper mixture; then spread mixture in a deep 3-quart (2.8-liter) casserole.

4. In a bowl, combine remaining ½ cup (120 ml) broth, eggs, ricotta cheese, and half the Parmesan cheese; beat until blended. Spread cheese mixture over rice mixture; sprinkle with remaining Parmesan cheese. Bake in a 375°F (190°C) oven until topping is golden brown (about 45 minutes). Makes 6 servings.

....

Per serving: 437 calories (28% calories from fat), 14 g total fat, 7 g saturated fat, 175 mg cholesterol, 503 mg sodium, 55 g carbohydrates, 3 g fiber, 23 g protein, 413 mg calcium, 3 mg iron

....

Wholesome, chewy barley seasoned with garlic, rosemary, and fennel mingles with tender lima beans and sweet bell pepper in this one-pan entrée. Garnish the dish with crunchy roasted almonds and aromatic rosemary sprigs.

....

3½ cups (830 ml) vegetable broth

4 cloves garlic, minced or pressed

½ teaspoon dried rosemary, crumbled

¼ teaspoon fennel seeds, crushed

1 cup (200 g) pearl barley, rinsed and drained

1 package (about 10 oz./285 g) frozen baby lima beans, thawed and drained

1 large red or yellow bell pepper (about 8 oz./230 g), seeded and finely chopped

⅓ cup (35 g) thinly sliced green onions

Barley Casserole

....

Preparation time: 20 minutes
Cooking time: About 50 minutes

1 tablespoon (15 ml) balsamic vinegar

½ cup (65 g) salted roasted almonds

Rosemary sprigs (optional)

....

1. In a shallow 1½- to 2-quart (1.4- to 1.9-liter) casserole, combine 3 cups (710 ml) of the broth, garlic, dried rosemary, and fennel seeds. Bake, uncovered, in a 450°F (230°C) oven until mixture comes to a rolling boil (about 20 minutes). Remove from oven and carefully stir in barley. Cover tightly, return to oven, and bake for 10 more minutes. Stir well, cover again, and continue to bake until barley is tender to bite (about 15 more minutes).

2. Stir remaining ½ cup (120 ml) broth, beans, and bell pepper into barley mixture. Bake, uncovered, for 5 more minutes. Remove from oven and stir in onions and vinegar. Spoon barley mixture onto a platter and sprinkle with almonds. Garnish with rosemary sprigs, if desired. Makes 4 servings.

....

Per serving: 423 calories (27% calories from fat), 13 g total fat, 1 g saturated fat, 0 mg cholesterol, 1,070 mg sodium, 66 g carbohydrates, 14 g fiber, 15 g protein, 102 mg calcium, 4 mg iron

Wheat Germ Burgers

Toasted wheat germ, shredded zucchini, and fresh herbs come together in these winning meatless burgers. Serve them with low-fat embellishments, such as catsup, Dijon mustard, and spoonfuls of plain yogurt.

Preparation time: 20 minutes
Cooking time: About 10 minutes

2 large eggs

¾ cup (72 g) toasted wheat germ

½ cup (55 g) shredded reduced-fat jack cheese

¼ cup (20 g) chopped mushrooms

3 tablespoons finely chopped onion

½ teaspoon *each* dried thyme and dried rosemary, crumbled

1½ cups (150 g) long zucchini shreds

Salt and pepper

1 to 2 teaspoons salad oil

4 kaiser rolls or hamburger buns

½ cup (120 ml) plain nonfat yogurt

About ¼ cup (60 ml) catsup

About 2 tablespoons (30 ml) Dijon mustard

4 to 8 butter lettuce leaves, rinsed and crisped

1 large tomato (about 8 oz./ 230 g), thinly sliced

1. In a large bowl, beat eggs to blend. Stir in wheat germ, cheese, mushrooms, onion, thyme, rosemary, and zucchini. Season to taste with salt and pepper.

2. On plastic wrap, shape wheat germ mixture into 4 equal patties, each about ¾ inch (2 cm) thick.

3. Heat 1 teaspoon of the oil in a wide nonstick frying pan over medium heat. Add patties and cook until deep golden on bottom (4 to 5 minutes). Turn patties over; add 1 teaspoon more oil to pan, if needed. Cook until deep golden on other side (about 4 more minutes).

4. To serve, place patties on bottoms of buns. Top with yogurt, catsup, mustard, lettuce leaves, and tomato, then with tops of buns. Makes 4 servings.

Per serving: 416 calories (27% calories from fat), 13 g total fat, 4 g saturated fat, 117 mg cholesterol, 885 mg sodium, 54 g carbohydrates, 5 g fiber, 22 g protein, 311 mg calcium, 5 mg iron

Double Wheat Burgers

Herbed wheat germ and walnut patties served on whole wheat buns make a filling lunch or dinner. Dress up the burgers with lettuce, slices of tomato and onion, and creamy Thousand Island dressing.

Preparation time: 15 minutes
Cooking time: About 7 minutes

2 large eggs

1 cup (45 g) soft whole wheat bread crumbs

½ cup (48 g) toasted wheat germ

¼ cup (30 g) chopped walnuts

½ cup (50 g) sliced green onions

½ cup (105 g) small-curd low-fat (1%) cottage cheese

2 tablespoons chopped parsley

1 teaspoon dried basil

½ teaspoon *each* dried oregano and paprika

Salt

4 thin slices reduced-fat jack cheese (about 2 oz./55 g *total*)

4 whole wheat hamburger buns, toasted

¼ cup (60 ml) nonfat Thousand Island dressing or mayonnaise

1 very large tomato (about 10 oz./285 g), thinly sliced

1 small white onion, thinly sliced

4 to 8 red leaf lettuce leaves, rinsed and crisped

1. In a large bowl, beat eggs to blend. Stir in bread crumbs, wheat germ, walnuts, green onions, cottage cheese, parsley, basil, oregano, and paprika. Season to taste with salt.

2. On an oiled 12- by 15-inch (30- by 38-cm) baking sheet, shape mixture into 4 equal patties, each about ½ inch (1 cm) thick. Broil patties about 3 inches (8 cm) below heat, turning once, until deep golden on both sides (about 6 minutes). Top each patty with a slice of jack cheese and continue to broil just until cheese is melted (about 30 more seconds).

3. To serve, place patties on bottoms of buns. Top with dressing, tomato, onion slices, and lettuce, then with tops of buns. Makes 4 servings.

Per serving: 424 calories (30% calories from fat), 15 g total fat, 4 g saturated fat, 117 mg cholesterol, 784 mg sodium, 54 g carbohydrates, 9 g fiber, 24 g protein, 259 mg calcium, 5 mg iron

Crunchy on the outside and creamy-textured within, these baked polenta cutouts are enhanced with an unusual chutney based on sweet, richly flavored dried tomatoes, capers, and pimentos.

....

Polenta Gnocchi:

   2 **cups (470 ml) low-fat (1%) milk**

   ½ **cup (120 ml) vegetable broth**

   1 **cup (138 g) polenta or yellow cornmeal**

   ½ **teaspoon salt**

   1 **teaspoon chopped fresh sage or ¼ teaspoon ground sage**

   1 **large egg**

   1 **tablespoon butter or margarine**

   ¼ **cup (20 g) finely shredded Parmesan cheese**

Dried Tomato Chutney:

   1 **cup (about 2½ oz./70 g) dried tomatoes (not oil-packed)**

   1 **large jar (about 4 oz./115 g) diced pimentos**

   ½ **cup (85 g) drained capers**

   4 **cloves garlic, peeled**

   2 **tablespoons chopped fresh basil or 2 teaspoons dried basil**

   1 **tablespoon (15 ml) olive oil**

   4 **teaspoons (20 ml) Marsala or port (or to taste)**

   1 **teaspoon Dijon mustard**

Garnish:

   Sage sprigs

Polenta Gnocchi with Dried Tomato Chutney

....

Preparation time: 30 minutes, plus 15 minutes for polenta to stand
Cooking time: About 45 minutes
Pictured on facing page

1. In a 4- to 5-quart (3.8- to 5-liter) pan, bring milk and broth just to a boil over medium-high heat. Stir in polenta, salt, and chopped sage. Reduce heat and simmer, uncovered, stirring often and scraping pan bottom with a long-handled spoon (mixture will spatter), until polenta tastes creamy (about 15 minutes). Remove from heat and stir in egg and butter.

2. Working quickly, brush a 9- by 13-inch (23- by 33-cm) baking pan liberally with water; then spoon polenta into pan and spread to make level. Let stand in pan on a rack for 15 minutes. Then cut polenta diagonally into diamonds, making cuts about 1½ inches (3.5 cm) apart. Carefully arrange polenta pieces, overlapping slightly, in a greased shallow 1½- to 2-quart (1.4- to 1.9-liter) casserole. (At this

point, you may let cool, then cover and refrigerate until next day.) Sprinkle with cheese and bake, uncovered, in a 350°F (175°C) oven until hot and tinged with brown (about 20 minutes; about 35 minutes if refrigerated).

3. Meanwhile, place tomatoes in a small bowl and add boiling water to cover. Let stand until soft (about 10 minutes). Drain well; squeeze out excess liquid. Transfer tomatoes to a food processor or blender. Add ⅓ cup (80 ml) water, pimentos, capers, garlic, basil, oil, Marsala, and mustard. Whirl until mixture is puréed and has a spoonable consistency. If chutney is too thick, add a little more water. Transfer to a small bowl.

4. Divide gnocchi among 4 individual plates; garnish with sage sprigs. Offer chutney to add to taste. Makes 4 servings.

....

Per serving: 361 calories (29% calories from fat), 12 g total fat, 5 g saturated fat, 70 mg cholesterol, 1,100 mg sodium, 51 g carbohydrates, 6 g fiber, 14 g protein, 277 mg calcium, 4 mg iron

Polenta Gnocchi with Dried Tomato Chutney
(recipe on facing page)

Pizza en casserole? It may sound a bit strange, but it's delicious! Layers of favorite pizza toppings—mushrooms, onions, red peppers, tomatoes, and cheese—are topped with a cornmeal batter, then baked. Accompany the dish with a crisp green salad.

Filling:

- 1 cup (210 g) low-fat (2%) cottage cheese
- ¼ cup (10 g) fresh basil leaves
- 1 tablespoon grated Parmesan cheese
- 2 or 3 cloves garlic, minced or pressed
- 1 teaspoon Oriental sesame oil
- ½ cup (69 g) yellow cornmeal
- 1 teaspoon olive oil
- 8 ounces (230 g) mushrooms, thinly sliced
- 1 large onion, chopped
- ½ teaspoon dried thyme
- 1 large jar (about 14 oz./400 g) roasted red peppers, drained and rinsed
- 1 cup (about 4 oz./115 g) shredded part-skim mozzarella cheese
- ¼ teaspoon *each* dried rubbed sage and dried marjoram
- 1 large tomato (about 8 oz./230 g), very thinly sliced

Upside-down Pizza Pie

Preparation time: 30 minutes
Cooking time: About 45 minutes

Batter Topping:

- 1⅓ cups (165 g) all-purpose flour
- ⅓ cup (45 g) yellow cornmeal
- 1 tablespoon sugar
- 1½ teaspoons baking powder
- ¼ to ½ teaspoon dried oregano
- ¼ teaspoon salt
- ½ cup (120 ml) nonfat milk
- 2 tablespoons (30 ml) olive oil
- 2 large egg whites

1. In a blender or food processor, combine cottage cheese, basil, Parmesan cheese, garlic, and sesame oil. Whirl until smoothly puréed; set aside. Sprinkle the ½ cup (69 g) cornmeal evenly over bottom of a greased deep 2½- to 3-quart (2.4- to 2.8-liter) casserole; set aside.

2. Heat the 1 teaspoon olive oil in a wide nonstick frying pan over medium-high heat. Add mushrooms, onion, thyme, and ¼ cup (60 ml) water. Cook, stirring occasionally, until vegetables

are soft and almost all liquid has evaporated (about 10 minutes).

3. Spoon vegetable mixture over cornmeal in casserole. Top evenly with cottage cheese mixture, spreading to smooth top. Cover cottage cheese layer with red peppers, overlapping if necessary; sprinkle peppers evenly with mozzarella cheese, sage, and marjoram. Top with tomato slices, overlapping if necessary. Press gently to compact; set aside while you prepare batter.

4. In a large bowl, stir together flour, the ⅓ cup (45 g) cornmeal, sugar, baking powder, oregano, and salt. In a small bowl, combine milk, the 2 tablespoons (30 ml) olive oil, 2 tablespoons (30 ml) water, and egg whites; beat until blended. Add egg mixture to flour mixture and stir just until dry ingredients are evenly moistened.

5. Working quickly, spoon batter over tomatoes, spreading to smooth top. Bake in a 375°F (190°C) oven until topping is lightly browned and firm to the touch (about 35 minutes). Makes 6 servings.

Per serving: 392 calories (25% calories from fat), 11 g total fat, 3 g saturated fat, 15 mg cholesterol, 645 mg sodium, 54 g carbohydrates, 3 g fiber, 18 g protein, 308 mg calcium, 5 mg iron

Swiss chard tastes something like spinach—and like spinach, it's leafy, deep green, and rich in vitamin A and iron. Here, the slivered leaves are sautéed with onions and a little lemon peel, then topped with nutty garbanzo beans and tomatoes for a satisfying supper dish. Serve with a crusty whole wheat loaf and a fresh fruit salad.

Swiss Chard with Garbanzos & Parmesan

Preparation time: About 20 minutes
Cooking time: About 20 minutes

3 tablespoons (45 ml) molasses

1½ teaspoons dry mustard

1½ teaspoons Worcestershire or reduced-sodium soy sauce

¾ teaspoon chopped fresh oregano or ¼ teaspoon dried oregano

1 pound (455 g) Swiss chard

1 teaspoon olive oil

2 large onions, thinly sliced

½ teaspoon grated lemon peel
 Salt

2 large tomatoes (about 1 lb./ 455 g *total*), chopped

1 can (about 15 oz./430 g) garbanzo beans, drained and rinsed

1 teaspoon cornstarch blended with 1 teaspoon cold water

½ cup (43 g) shredded Parmesan cheese
 Oregano sprigs

1. In a small bowl, stir together molasses, mustard, Worcestershire, and chopped oregano. Set aside.

2. Trim and discard discolored stem ends from chard; then rinse chard, drain, and cut crosswise into ½-inch (1-cm) strips. Set aside.

3. Heat oil in a wide nonstick frying pan or wok over medium-high heat. When oil is hot, add onions, lemon peel, and 2 tablespoons (30 ml) water. Stir-fry until onions are soft (about 7 minutes). Add water, 1 tablespoon (15 ml) at a time, if pan appears dry.

4. Add half the chard and 1 tablespoon (15 ml) more water to pan; stir-fry until chard just begins to wilt. Then add remaining chard and 1 tablespoon (15 ml) more water; stir-fry until all chard is wilted and bright green (3 to 4 more minutes). Season to taste with salt. Spoon chard mixture around edge of a rimmed platter and keep warm.

5. Stir molasses mixture and pour into pan; add tomatoes and beans. Stir-fry gently until beans are heated through and tomatoes are soft (about 3 minutes). Stir cornstarch mixture well and pour into pan. Cook, stirring gently, until mixture boils and thickens slightly (1 to 2 minutes).

6. Spoon bean mixture into center of platter; sprinkle cheese over all. Garnish with oregano sprigs. Makes 4 servings.

Per serving: 264 calories (22% calories from fat), 7 g total fat, 2 g saturated fat, 8 mg cholesterol, 566 mg sodium, 42 g carbohydrates, 8 g fiber, 12 g protein, 275 mg calcium, 5 mg iron

Squash Strata with Cranberry Chutney
(recipe on page 248)

Eggs & Cheese

Eggs and cheese are not just for breakfast—they're versatile additions to the luncheon or dinner table. To make them part of a healthy, low-fat diet, we use more egg whites than whole eggs in our recipes. And just a bit of a robust cheese adds lots of flavor while keeping fat to a minimum. Whip up our oregano and feta cheese-flavored Vegetable Scramble Pockets—perfect for a quick lunch—or prepare a light supper of Chicken Frittata.

Deep orange pumpkin contributes flavor and color to this tempting layered casserole. While the dish bakes, you can easily prepare a sweet-tart chutney made with both fresh and dried cranberries to serve alongside.

Squash Strata:

- 1 large onion, very thinly sliced
- 1½ cups (268 g) canned pumpkin
- 2 large eggs
- 4 large egg whites
- ¾ cup (180 ml) half-and-half
- ½ cup (120 ml) nonfat milk
- 1 tablespoon cornstarch
- 1½ teaspoons chopped fresh thyme or ½ teaspoon dried thyme
- 1 cup (about 3 oz./85 g) grated Parmesan cheese
- 9 slices egg sandwich bread or whole wheat sandwich bread, torn into large pieces

Cranberry Chutney:

- ½ cup (120 ml) currant or raspberry jelly
- ½ cup (120 ml) orange marmalade
- 1 cup (95 g) fresh cranberries
- ¼ cup (23 g) dried cranberries or raisins
- 1 teaspoon balsamic vinegar (or to taste)

Garnish:

- 1 to 2 tablespoons finely chopped parsley

Squash Strata with Cranberry Chutney

•••••••••••••••••••••••••••••••
Preparation time: 25 minutes
Cooking time:
About 1 hour and 20 minutes
Pictured on page 246

1. In a wide nonstick frying pan, combine onion and 2 tablespoons (30 ml) water. Cook over medium-high heat, stirring often, until liquid evaporates and browned bits stick to pan bottom (about 10 minutes). To deglaze pan, add ¼ cup (60 ml) more water, stirring to loosen browned bits from pan. Continue to cook until onion is lightly browned (about 10 more minutes); add water, 1 tablespoon (15 ml) at a time, if pan appears dry. Remove onion from pan and set aside.

2. In a food processor or a large bowl, combine pumpkin, eggs, egg whites, half-and-half, milk, cornstarch, and thyme. Whirl or beat with an electric mixer until smoothly puréed. Stir in three-fourths of the cheese; set aside.

3. Arrange 3 slices of bread (overlapping, if necessary) over bottom of a greased deep 2½- to 3-quart (2.4- to 2.8-liter) casserole. Top evenly with a third each of the onion and pumpkin mixture. Repeat layers twice, ending with pumpkin mixture. Sprinkle with remaining cheese.

4. Cover tightly and bake in a 350°F (175°C) oven for 30 minutes. Then uncover and continue to bake until top is tinged with brown and a knife inserted in center comes out clean (about 30 more minutes).

5. Meanwhile, in a 1½- to 2-quart (1.4- to 1.9-liter) pan, combine ¼ cup (60 ml) water, jelly, marmalade, fresh cranberries, and dried cranberries. Bring to a boil over medium-high heat, stirring. Reduce heat and boil gently, stirring occasionally, until fresh cranberries split and are soft (about 8 minutes). Remove from heat and stir in vinegar; set aside.

6. Let casserole cool for about 5 minutes before serving. Garnish with parsley. Offer chutney to spoon over individual servings. Makes 6 servings.

Per serving: 462 calories (22% calories from fat), 12 g total fat, 6 g saturated fat, 93 mg cholesterol, 586 mg sodium, 75 g carbohydrates, 4 g fiber, 16 g protein, 336 mg calcium, 3 mg iron

Though light and airy in texture, typical soufflés are rich in butter and eggs. With a few modifications, however, you can still enjoy these luxurious dishes—and feel virtuous while doing so! To trim down our spinach soufflé, we cut back on the egg yolks and butter and used cornstarch to thicken the mixture.

Soufflé:

About 1 teaspoon salad oil

4½ teaspoons cornstarch

1 cup (240 ml) nonfat milk

3 tablespoons chopped fresh marjoram or 1 tablespoon dried marjoram

1 tablespoon instant minced onion

½ teaspoon pepper

⅛ teaspoon ground nutmeg

½ cup (100 g) frozen chopped spinach, thawed and very well drained

¼ cup (20 g) shredded Parmesan cheese

Spinach Soufflé

....

Preparation time: 20 minutes
Cooking time: About 30 minutes

2 large egg yolks

6 large egg whites

¼ teaspoon cream of tartar

Sour Cream Sauce:

1 cup (240 ml) nonfat sour cream

1 teaspoon sugar

⅛ teaspoon ground nutmeg

1. Lightly coat bottom and sides of a 1½- to 1¾-quart (1.4- to 1.5-liter) soufflé dish or other straight-sided baking dish with oil.

2. Place cornstarch in a 2- to 3-quart (1.9- to 2.8-liter) pan; smoothly stir in milk. Add marjoram, onion, pepper, and nutmeg. Bring to a boil over medium-high heat, stirring. Pour mixture into a blender; add spinach

and whirl until smoothly puréed. Add 2 tablespoons of the cheese and the egg yolks; whirl again until smoothly puréed.

3. In a large bowl, beat egg whites and cream of tartar with an electric mixer on high speed until whites hold soft peaks. Gently fold spinach mixture into whites; then scrape mixture into oiled dish. Sprinkle with remaining 2 tablespoons cheese. With the tip of a knife, draw a circle on top of soufflé about 1 inch (2.5 cm) in from edge of dish. Bake in a 375°F (190°C) oven until soufflé is richly browned and center jiggles only slightly when dish is gently shaken (about 25 minutes).

4. Meanwhile, in a small bowl, beat sour cream, sugar, and nutmeg until smoothly blended. Set aside.

5. Serve soufflé immediately; offer sour cream sauce to add to taste. Makes 4 servings.

Per serving: 180 calories (29% calories from fat), 5 g total fat, 2 g saturated fat, 111 mg cholesterol, 281 mg sodium, 14 g carbohydrates, 1 g fiber, 16 g protein, 291 mg calcium, 2 mg iron

---

Quick and easy! To make this light dinner or lunch, fill tortillas with seasoned black beans, jack cheese, tomatoes, and red onion. Serve with tall glasses of lemonade and a selection of fresh fruit.

1 can (about 15 oz./425 g) black beans, drained and rinsed well

¼ cup (60 ml) nonfat mayonnaise

2 teaspoons wine vinegar

1 teaspoon chili powder

4 nonfat flour tortillas (*each about 7 inches/18 cm in diameter*)

1 cup (about 4 oz./115 g) shredded reduced-fat jack or sharp Cheddar cheese

Baked Quesadillas

....

Preparation time: 15 minutes
Cooking time: About 7 minutes

2 small firm-ripe pear-shaped (Roma-type) tomatoes (about 4 oz./115 g *total*), chopped

½ cup (85 g) chopped red onion

⅓ cup (15 g) cilantro leaves

½ cup (120 ml) purchased or homemade green tomatillo salsa

1. In a medium-size bowl, coarsely mash beans. Add mayonnaise, vinegar, and chili powder; stir until well blended.

2. Lightly brush both sides of each tortilla with water. Spoon a fourth of the bean mixture over half of each tortilla; evenly sprinkle a fourth each of the cheese, tomatoes, onion, and cilantro over bean mixture on each tortilla. Fold plain half of tortilla over to cover filling.

3. Set quesadillas slightly apart on a lightly greased 12- by 15-inch (30- by 38-cm) baking sheet. Bake in a 500°F (260°C) oven until crisp and golden (about 7 minutes). Serve with salsa. Makes 4 servings.

Per serving: 250 calories (27% calories from fat), 8 g total fat, 4 g saturated fat, 20 mg cholesterol, 998 mg sodium, 30 g carbohydrates, 5 g fiber, 16 g protein, 381 mg calcium, 2 mg iron

For a leaner twist on a classic favorite, these chiles are roasted, not battered and fried—and they're stuffed with thyme-accented eggs instead of cheese. You can use stubby poblanos, slender Anaheims, or any other large chile suitable for stuffing.

Roasted Chiles with Eggs

Preparation time: About 20 minutes
Cooking time: About 10 minutes
Pictured on facing page

Roasted Chiles
(directions follow)

1 cup (240 ml) Lime Salsa
(page 21)

2 large eggs

4 large egg whites

½ cup (105 g) nonfat cottage
cheese

½ cup (30 g) finely chopped
spinach leaves

1 tablespoon thinly sliced green
onion

2 teaspoons cornstarch blended
with 1 tablespoon (15 ml) cold
water

1½ teaspoons fresh thyme leaves
or ¼ teaspoon dried thyme

⅛ teaspoon *each* salt and white
pepper

1 teaspoon salad oil

Sliced fresh hot red chiles
(seeded, if desired)

Thyme sprigs

About ¾ cup (180 ml) plain
nonfat yogurt

Thinly sliced green onion

1. Prepare Roasted Chiles; set aside. Prepare Lime Salsa; refrigerate.

2. In a food processor, whirl eggs, egg whites, cottage cheese, spinach, the 1 tablespoon onion, cornstarch mixture, thyme leaves, salt, and white pepper until smoothly puréed. (Or place ingredients in a bowl and beat with a spoon until well blended.) Set aside.

3. Heat oil in a medium-size nonstick frying pan over medium heat. Add egg mixture to pan; stir to combine. Cook until mixture is softly set and looks like scrambled eggs (3 to 5 minutes).

4. Spoon hot egg mixture equally into chiles. Place filled chiles on a platter and garnish with red chile slices and thyme sprigs. Add yogurt, thinly sliced onion, and Lime Salsa to taste. Makes 4 servings.

Roasted Chiles. Place 4 **fresh green poblano** or **Anaheim chiles** (or other large mild chiles) on a 12- by 15-inch (30- by 38-cm) baking sheet. Broil 4 to 6 inches (10 to 15 cm) below heat, turning often, until charred all over (5 to 8 minutes). Cover with foil and let cool on baking sheet; then remove and discard skins. Cut a slit down one side of each chile, but do not cut all the way to stem end and tip; be careful not to puncture opposite side of chile. Remove and discard seeds and veins from chiles.

Per serving: 138 calories (26% calories from fat), 4 g total fat, 1 g saturated fat, 110 mg cholesterol, 298 mg sodium, 11 g carbohydrates, 0.7 g fiber, 14 g protein, 132 mg calcium, 1 mg iron

---

Get your day off to a hearty start with these high-protein burritos. Refried beans and scrambled eggs seasoned with salsa, chiles, and cilantro make a delicious filling for flour tortillas.

Egg & Bean Burritos

Preparation time: About 25 minutes
Cooking time: About 40 minutes

¾ cup (180 ml) Cherry Tomato
Salsa (page 258) or other salsa

1½ cups (360 ml) (about half a
recipe) Zesty Refried Beans
(page 148); or 1½ cups (360 ml)
purchased nonfat refried beans

1 small can (about 4 oz./115)
diced green chiles

4 large eggs

4 large egg whites

1 teaspoon cornstarch

⅓ cup (15 g) chopped cilantro

6 warm flour tortillas (page 346)

½ cup (58 g) shredded jack
cheese

1 cup (240 ml) plain nonfat
yogurt

Lime wedges

1. Prepare Cherry Tomato Salsa; refrigerate.

2. Prepare Zesty Refried Beans. Place beans in a wide nonstick frying pan and add chiles; cook over medium heat, stirring often, until bubbly (3 to 4 minutes). Meanwhile, in a large bowl, beat eggs, egg whites, and cornstarch until well blended. Stir in cilantro and 3 tablespoons (45 ml) of the salsa.

3. Push beans to one side of pan. Pour egg mixture into cleared area and cook over medium to medium-high heat, stirring often, until eggs are softly set (about 4 minutes).

4. For each burrito, spoon a sixth each of the beans and eggs in center of a tortilla; sprinkle with a sixth of the cheese, then roll to enclose. Serve each burrito, seam side down, on a warm plate. Add yogurt and remaining salsa to taste; garnish with lime wedges. Makes 6 servings.

Per serving: 312 calories (28% calories from fat), 10 g total fat, 3 g saturated fat, 152 mg cholesterol, 739 mg sodium, 38 g carbohydrates, 5 g fiber, 18 g protein, 242 mg calcium, 3 mg iron

Roasted Chiles with Eggs
(recipe on facing page)

This version of the familiar oven strata—a layered make-ahead casserole of bread, cheese, and eggs—gets a fiery kick from chiles and hot pepper seasoning. Serve it with a homemade tomato salsa.

Oven Strata:

- 12 slices firm-textured whole wheat sandwich bread
- 2 cups (140 g) thinly sliced mushrooms
- 1 cup (100 g) sliced green onions
- 1 large can (about 7 oz./200 g) diced green chiles
- 3 cups (about 12 oz./340 g) shredded reduced-fat sharp Cheddar cheese
- 3 large eggs
- 4 large egg whites
- 2½ cups (590 ml) nonfat milk
- 1 tablespoon dry mustard
  About 1 teaspoon liquid hot pepper seasoning (or to taste)
- 1 cup (115 g) coarsely crushed low-fat baked tortilla chips

Overnight Fiery Oven Strata

Preparation time: 20 minutes, plus at least 8 hours to chill
Cooking time: About 55 minutes

Salsa:

- 2 medium-size tomatoes (about 12 oz./340 g *total*), chopped
- ½ small onion, finely chopped
- 1 can (about 4 oz./115 g) diced green chiles
- 4 teaspoons (20 ml) distilled white vinegar
- 1 tablespoon chopped cilantro
  Sugar

1. Line bottom of a 9- by 13-inch (23- by 33-cm) baking pan with a single layer of bread; use about half the bread slices, trimming them to fit and reserving scraps. Top bread with half each of the mushrooms and green onions, half the large can of chiles, and

half the cheese. Repeat layers, starting with remaining bread (and any reserved scraps) and ending with cheese.

2. In a large bowl, beat eggs and egg whites until blended. Add milk, mustard, and hot pepper seasoning; beat to blend well. Pour egg mixture slowly over ingredients in pan; cover and refrigerate for at least 8 hours or up to 24 hours. Then uncover, sprinkle with tortilla chips, and bake in a 350°F (175°C) oven until golden (about 55 minutes). Let stand for about 15 minutes before serving.

3. Meanwhile, in a medium-size bowl, stir together tomatoes, chopped onion, the 4-ounce (115-g) can of chiles, vinegar, and cilantro. Season to taste with sugar.

4. To serve, cut strata into squares or spoon it from pan. Offer salsa to add to taste. Makes 10 servings.

Per serving: 297 calories (29% calories from fat), 10 g total fat, 5 g saturated fat, 89 mg cholesterol, 759 mg sodium, 32 g carbohydrates, 5 g fiber, 22 g protein, 439 mg calcium, 2 mg iron

---

Serve this hearty entrée as you would any other egg dish, at brunch or for a light lunch or dinner.

- 2 cups (470 ml) vegetable broth
- 1 cup (175 g) bulgur
- 2 teaspoons butter or margarine
- 1 medium-size onion, thinly sliced
- 1 medium-size red bell pepper (about 6 oz./170 g), seeded and thinly sliced
- 2 large eggs
- 4 large egg whites
- ¼ cup (20 g) grated Parmesan cheese

Scrambled Eggs & Bulgur

Preparation time: 10 minutes, plus 10 minutes for bulgur to stand
Cooking time: About 15 minutes

1. In a 1- to 1½-quart (950-ml to 1.4-liter) pan, bring broth to a boil over high heat. Stir in bulgur; cover, remove from heat, and let stand until liquid has been absorbed (about 10 minutes).

2. Meanwhile, melt 1 teaspoon of the butter in a wide nonstick frying pan over medium heat. Add onion and bell pepper; cook, stirring often, until onion is lightly browned (about

10 minutes). Add water, 1 tablespoon (15 ml) at a time, if pan appears dry. Meanwhile, in a small bowl, beat eggs, egg whites, and ¼ cup (60 ml) water until blended.

3. Add remaining 1 teaspoon butter to onion mixture in pan and reduce heat to medium-low. Add egg mixture; cook until eggs are softly set, gently lifting cooked portion with a wide spatula to allow uncooked eggs to flow underneath.

4. Divide bulgur and egg mixture equally among 4 individual plates. Sprinkle with cheese. Makes 4 servings.

Per serving: 254 calories (25% calories from fat), 7 g total fat, 3 g saturated fat, 116 mg cholesterol, 726 mg sodium, 35 g carbohydrates, 8 g fiber, 14 g protein, 123 mg calcium, 2 mg iron

Great at any time of day, this mild hash of diced potatoes and red kidney beans is topped with gently cooked eggs. You can serve it straight out of the cooking pan—there's no need for a serving bowl.

Egg, Bean & Potato Hash

Preparation time: About 10 minutes
Cooking time: About 35 minutes

- 1 tablespoon butter or margarine
- 1 pound (455 g) small thin-skinned potatoes, scrubbed and cut into ¼-inch (6-mm) cubes
- 1 small red onion, cut into thin slivers
- 1 teaspoon chili powder
- 1 can (about 15 oz./430 g) red kidney beans, drained and rinsed
- 1 large tomato (about 8 oz./230 g), chopped
- ¾ teaspoon chopped fresh sage or ¼ teaspoon dried rubbed sage, or to taste

- 4 large eggs
- ⅓ cup (15 g) lightly packed cilantro leaves
- ¾ cup (180 ml) nonfat sour cream

1. Melt butter in a wide nonstick frying pan or wok over medium-high heat. Add potatoes, onion, chili powder, and ¼ cup (60 ml) water. Stir-fry until potatoes are tinged with brown and tender when pierced (about 15 minutes; do not scorch). Add water, 1 tablespoon (15 ml) at a time, if pan appears dry.

2. Add beans, tomato, sage, and 2 tablespoons (30 ml) water to pan. Stir-fry gently until heated through, scraping any browned bits free from pan bottom.

3. With a spoon, make 4 depressions in potato mixture; carefully break an egg into each depression. Reduce heat to low, cover, and cook until egg yolks are set to your liking (about 15 minutes for firm but moist yolks). Sprinkle with cilantro and top with sour cream. Makes 4 servings.

Per serving: 328 calories (25% calories from fat), 9 g total fat, 3 g saturated fat, 220 mg cholesterol, 280 mg sodium, 43 g carbohydrates, 8 g fiber, 18 g protein, 125 mg calcium, 3 mg iron

---

This light casserole-style version of popular chiles rellenos is lacking in fat and calories—but not in flavor. The chiles are filled with high-protein tofu and just a small amount of cheese.

Chiles Rellenos Casserole

Preparation time: About 25 minutes
Cooking time: 1 to 1¼ hours

- 2 cups (470 ml) Red Chile Sauce (page 96) or Cherry Tomato Salsa (page 258)
  About 1 pound (455 g) soft tofu, rinsed
- 1 cup (about 4 oz./155g) shredded reduced-fat jack cheese
- 2 large cans (about 7 oz./200 g *each*) whole green chiles
- 2 large eggs
- 6 large egg whites
- ⅔ cup (160 ml) nonfat milk
- 1 cup (125 g) all-purpose flour
- 1 teaspoon baking powder
- ¾ cup (85 g) shredded reduced-fat Cheddar cheese
  Sliced ripe olives (optional)

1. Prepare Red Chile Sauce; set aside.

2. Coarsely mash tofu with a fork or your fingers; place in a colander and

let drain for 10 minutes. Transfer to a bowl and mix in jack cheese. Cut a slit down one side of each chile; fill chiles equally with tofu mixture and arrange side by side in a lightly oiled shallow 2½- to 3-quart (2.4- to 2.8-liter) casserole.

3. In a large bowl, beat eggs and egg whites with an electric mixer on high speed until thick and foamy. Add milk, flour, and baking powder; beat until smooth. Fold in a third of the Cheddar cheese. Pour egg mixture over chiles; sprinkle with remaining Cheddar cheese.

4. Bake in a 375°F (190°C) oven until top is a rich golden brown (30 to 40 minutes). Scatter olives over casserole, if desired. Spoon onto plates and accompany with warm Red Chile Sauce. Makes 8 servings.

Per serving: 252 calories (32% calories from fat), 9 g total fat, 4 g saturated fat, 71 mg cholesterol, 838 mg sodium, 25 g carbohydrates, 1 g fiber, 19 g protein, 326 mg calcium, 2 mg iron

Bruschetta with Tomato, Basil & Yogurt Cheese
(recipe on facing page)

In Italy, bruschetta is thick-sliced bread that's grilled over charcoal and brushed with olive oil and garlic—and sometimes topped with tomatoes and seasonings. Here's a lean version to enjoy for lunch or a light dinner. Start by preparing a tangy, basil-seasoned yogurt cheese; then spread it thickly on toasted crusty bread and top with more fresh basil, tomatoes, and pine nuts.

Bruschetta with Tomato, Basil & Yogurt Cheese

Preparation time: 20 minutes, plus at least 12 hours to chill
Cooking time: About 8 minutes
Pictured on facing page

Yogurt Cheese:

- 4 cups (950 ml) plain nonfat yogurt
- ¼ cup (10 g) finely chopped fresh basil

Bruschetta:

- ½ cup (55 g) pine nuts
- 8 slices crusty bread (*each* about ½ inch/1 cm thick; about 1 lb./ 455 g *total*), such as Italian ciabatta or French bread
- 1 cup (40 g) lightly packed fresh basil leaves
- 1 pound (455 g) pear-shaped (Roma-type) tomatoes, finely chopped
- ½ cup (40 g) grated Parmesan cheese

Garnish:

- Basil sprigs (optional)

1. To prepare yogurt cheese, line a fine strainer with a double layer of cheesecloth. Set strainer over a deep bowl (bottom of strainer should sit at least 2 inches/5 cm above bottom of bowl). In a large bowl, stir together yogurt and chopped basil; then scrape mixture into cloth-lined strainer. Cover airtight and refrigerate until yogurt has the consistency of whipped cream cheese (at least 12 hours) or for up to 2 days; occasionally drain and discard liquid as it accumulates.

2. Toast pine nuts in a medium-size frying pan over medium heat, stirring often, until golden (about 3 minutes). Remove from pan and set aside.

3. Arrange bread slices slightly apart in a shallow 10- by 15-inch (25- by 38-cm) baking pan. Broil about 6 inches below heat, turning once, until golden on both sides (about 5 minutes). Let toast cool on a rack.

4. Top each toast slice with equal portions of yogurt cheese, basil leaves, tomatoes, pine nuts, and Parmesan cheese. Garnish with basil sprigs, if desired. Makes 8 servings.

Per serving: 279 calories (25% calories from fat), 8 g total fat, 2 g saturated fat, 5 mg cholesterol, 491 mg sodium, 39 g carbohydrates, 3 g fiber, 15 g protein, 347 mg calcium, 4 mg iron

---

For breakfast, lunch, or supper, try these warm and filling sandwiches. Pita breads overflow with a colorful scramble of eggs, fresh vegetables, and feta cheese.

Vegetable Scramble Pockets

Preparation time: About 10 minutes
Cooking time: About 15 minutes

- 1 large egg
- 6 large egg whites
- 1 teaspoon ground oregano
- 1 cup (about 4½ oz./130 g) crumbled feta cheese
- 1 tablespoon (15 ml) olive oil
- 1 large onion, thinly sliced
- 2 large red bell peppers (about 1 lb./455 g *total*), seeded and thinly sliced
- 8 ounces (230 g) mushrooms, thinly sliced
- 1 package (about 10 oz./285 g) frozen chopped spinach, thawed and squeezed dry
  Pepper
- 4 whole wheat pita breads (*each* about 6 inches/15 cm in diameter), cut crosswise into halves

1. In a large bowl, lightly beat whole egg, egg whites, oregano, and cheese until blended. Set aside.

2. Heat oil in a wide nonstick frying pan or wok over medium-high heat. When oil is hot, add onion, bell peppers, and mushrooms; stir-fry until liquid has evaporated and mushrooms are tinged with brown (about 7 minutes). Add spinach to pan and stir-fry until heated through (about 3 minutes).

3. Pour egg mixture over vegetables in pan; stir-fry until eggs are softly set and look scrambled (3 to 5 minutes). Season to taste with pepper. Fill pita halves equally with egg mixture. Makes 4 servings.

Per serving: 398 calories (28% calories from fat), 13 g total fat, 5 g saturated fat, 78 mg cholesterol, 813 mg sodium, 54 g carbohydrates, 9 g fiber, 22 g protein, 265 mg calcium, 3 mg iron

Eggs poached in a tomato sauce enriched with fiery serrano chiles, onions, and spices make a great one-pan meal.

1 can (about 14½ oz./415 g) tomatoes

2 cloves garlic, peeled

¾ cup (180 ml) water

2 teaspoons chili powder

1½ teaspoons *each* dried oregano and sugar

4 large eggs

¼ cup (25 g) thinly sliced green onions

4 fresh serrano chiles, halved and seeded

Drowned Eggs

Preparation time: About 10 minutes
Cooking time: About 25 minutes

2 tablespoons cilantro leaves

Salt and pepper

8 warm corn tortillas (page 346)

1. Pour tomatoes and their liquid into a blender or food processor. Add garlic, then whirl until smoothly puréed.

2. Transfer tomato purée to a wide frying pan. Stir in water, chili powder, oregano, and sugar; bring to a boil over medium-high heat. Reduce heat

so sauce is simmering. Carefully crack eggs, one at a time, into sauce. Distribute onions and chile halves over sauce, disturbing eggs as little as possible. Cook, carefully basting eggs occasionally with sauce, until yolks are set to your liking (about 20 minutes for firm but moist yolks).

3. Divide eggs, onions, chile halves, and sauce equally among 4 shallow (about 1½-cup/360-ml size) casseroles. Sprinkle with cilantro; season to taste with salt and pepper. Serve with tortillas. Makes 4 servings.

Per serving: 225 calories (26% calories from fat), 7 g total fat, 2 g saturated fat, 213 mg cholesterol, 326 mg sodium, 33 g carbohydrates, 4 g fiber, 11 g protein, 160 mg calcium, 3 mg iron

---

Individual egg, bean, and sausage casseroles are a colorful choice for brunch or supper. Alongside, serve Tomatillo & Tomato Salad (page 56) or a selection of ripe fresh fruit.

1 cup (240 ml) Cucumber & Jicama Salsa (page 20)

2 cans (about 15 oz./425 g *each*) pinto beans

4 ounces (115 g) ground turkey sausage, crumbled

3 medium-size thin-skinned potatoes (about 1 lb./455 g *total*), cooked, peeled, and diced

2 teaspoons minced fresh basil or ½ teaspoon dried basil

About ⅛ teaspoon pepper

4 large eggs

⅓ cup (38 g) shredded Cheddar cheese

4 green onions, ends trimmed

8 warm flour tortillas (page 346)

Fiesta Brunch Casseroles

Preparation time: About 10 minutes
Baking time: About 30 minutes

1. Prepare Cucumber & Jicama Salsa; refrigerate.

2. Drain beans, reserving ½ cup (120 ml) of the liquid from cans. Pour half the beans into a bowl; add reserved liquid (if using home-cooked beans, add ½ cup/120 ml low-sodium chicken broth mixed with 1 teaspoon cornstarch). Mash beans until fairly smooth. Stir in remaining beans,

sausage, potatoes, basil, and ⅛ teaspoon of the pepper.

3. Divide bean mixture equally among 4 shallow 2-cup (470-ml) casseroles. Set casseroles in one or two 10- by 15-inch (25- by 38-cm) rimmed baking pans. Bake in a 400°F (305°C) oven for about 10 minutes. Stir; bake for 5 more minutes, then remove from oven.

4. With the back of a spoon, impress an egg-size hollow in center of bean mixture in each casserole. Break an egg into each hollow. Sprinkle cheese equally over bean mixture. Return casseroles in pan(s) to oven and continue to bake until egg yolks are set to your liking (about 15 more minutes for firm but moist yolks). Garnish each casserole with an onion. Serve with tortillas; add salsa and pepper to taste. Makes 4 servings.

Per serving: 511 calories (23% calories from fat), 13 g total fat, 5 g saturated fat, 244 mg cholesterol, 1,004 mg sodium, 71 g carbohydrates, 12 g fiber, 28 g protein, 270 mg calcium, 6 mg iron

Serve this streamlined classic "Sunday" breakfast specialty with a citrus fruit salad or fresh-squeezed pink grapefruit juice.

- ¼ cup (60 ml) lemon juice
- 3 tablespoons cornstarch
- 1½ cups (360 ml) vegetable broth
- 1 cup (240 ml) low-fat (2%) milk
- 1 tablespoon butter or margarine, cut into chunks
- 2 teaspoons finely chopped fresh thyme or ½ teaspoon dried thyme
- 1 teaspoon *each* Dijon mustard and honey
- ⅛ teaspoon ground white pepper
- 8 very thin slices Canadian bacon (about 4 oz./115 g *total*)
- 4 English muffins, split
- 3 tablespoons (45 ml) distilled white vinegar
- 8 large eggs
  Thyme sprigs and lemon wedges

Eggs Benedict

Preparation time: 25 minutes
Cooking time: About 20 minutes

1. In a small bowl, smoothly blend lemon juice and cornstarch; set aside.

2. In a 2- to 3-quart (1.9- to 2.8-liter) pan, combine broth, milk, butter, chopped thyme, mustard, honey, and white pepper. Set pan over medium-high heat and, stirring with a wire whisk, slowly add cornstarch mixture. Cook, whisking constantly, until sauce comes to a boil and thickens slightly. Remove from heat and keep warm; stir occasionally.

3. Cook bacon in a wide nonstick frying pan over medium heat, turning as needed, just until hot and tinged with brown. Meanwhile, toast muffin halves. Arrange 2 muffin halves, cut side up, on each of 4 individual rimmed plates. Top each muffin half with a slice of bacon; set aside.

4. In a 5- to 6-quart (5- to 6-liter) pan, bring vinegar and 3 quarts (2.8 liters) water to a gentle boil over high heat. Reduce heat, maintaining a temperature that causes bubbles to form on pan bottom (a bubble may pop up to the top occasionally).

5. Cook eggs 4 at a time. To cook, hold each egg as close to water as possible; then carefully break directly into water. Cook until eggs are done to your liking; lift one egg from pan with a slotted spoon and cut into it to test (about 4 minutes for soft yolks and firm whites). Lift out cooked eggs, drain well, and keep hot until all eggs have been cooked.

6. To serve, arrange hot eggs on bacon-topped muffins; ladle about ½ cup (120 ml) warm sauce over each serving. Garnish with thyme sprigs and lemon wedges; serve immediately. Makes 4 servings.

Per serving: 554 calories (30% calories from fat), 18 g total fat, 7 g saturated fat, 452 mg cholesterol, 1,522 mg sodium, 65 g carbohydrates, 2 g fiber, 29 g protein, 330 mg calcium, 5 mg iron

---

Fresh fruit and ricotta cheese are wrapped in flour tortillas for an extra-easy morning meal.

- 2 flour tortillas (7- to 9-inch/18- to 23-cm diameter)
- ¼ cup (115 g) part-skim ricotta cheese or ¼ cup (58 g) Neufchâtel cheese
- 1 cup (198 g) sliced hulled strawberries or 1 cup (123 g) whole raspberries
  Sugar

1. Spread tortillas equally with ricotta cheese, then top equally with berries. Sprinkle with sugar to taste. Fold

Berry Ricotta Breakfast Burritos

Preparation time: About 5 minutes
Baking time: 5 to 8 minutes

opposite sides of each tortilla over filling, then roll each from one end to enclose.

2. You may bake or microwave burritos.

To bake, arrange burritos, seam side down, on a nonstick baking sheet; brush lightly with water. Bake in a

350°F (175°C) oven until filling is hot in center (5 to 8 minutes).

To microwave, heat one burrito at a time: set a burrito, seam side down, on a microwave-safe plate and brush lightly with water. Microwave, uncovered, on HIGH (100%) for 1 to 2 minutes or until tortilla is hot to touch; check after 1 minute. Repeat to heat remaining burrito.

3. Let burritos cool slightly before eating. Makes 2 servings.

Per serving: 179 calories (26% calories from fat), 5 g total fat, 2 g saturated fat, 10 mg cholesterol, 206 mg sodium, 26 g carbohydrates, 3 g fiber, 7 g protein, 138 mg calcium, 2 mg iron

Stuffed with scrambled eggs and a spicy tomato sauce, these pita bread sandwiches make a satisfying brunch or lunch.

- 1 teaspoon olive oil
- 1 small onion, chopped
- 2 cloves garlic, minced or pressed
- 3 large pear-shaped (Roma-type) tomatoes (about 12 oz./340 g total), chopped
- 1½ teaspoons chili powder
- ½ teaspoon ground turmeric
- 3 tablespoons chopped cilantro
- 4 large eggs
- 8 large egg whites
- 2 teaspoons butter or margarine

Indian-spiced Scrambled Eggs

Preparation time: 20 minutes
Cooking time: About 20 minutes
Pictured on facing page

- 4 pita breads (*each* about 5 inches/12.5 cm in diameter), cut crosswise into halves

1. Heat oil in a wide nonstick frying pan over medium-high heat. Add onion and garlic; cook, stirring, until onion is soft (about 5 minutes). Add tomatoes, chili powder, turmeric, and 1 tablespoon of the cilantro; cook, stir-ring occasionally, until almost all liquid has evaporated (about 8 minutes). Transfer sauce to a bowl and keep warm. Wash and dry pan.

2. In a large bowl, beat eggs, egg whites, and ¼ cup (60 ml) water until blended. Melt butter in frying pan over medium-low heat. Add eggs and cook until softly set, gently lifting cooked portion with a wide spatula to allow uncooked eggs to flow underneath. Fill pita bread halves equally with eggs; top with sauce and remaining 2 tablespoons cilantro. Makes 4 servings.

Per serving: 335 calories (25% calories from fat), 9 g total fat, 3 g saturated fat, 218 mg cholesterol, 532 mg sodium, 42 g carbohydrates, 3 g fiber, 20 g protein, 97 mg calcium, 3 mg iron

---

French toast needn't be limited to breakfast time, nor must it be sweet. This version—batter-dipped sandwiches filled with chiles and cheese—is a savory supper or lunch entrée. To save fat, we've made the batter with extra egg whites, then oven-baked the toast rather than frying it in butter.

French Toast:

- 1 large egg
- 4 large egg whites
- 1 cup (240 ml) nonfat milk
- 8 diagonal slices French bread (*each* about 3 by 6 inches/8 by 15 cm and about ⅓ inch/1 cm thick)
- 1 cup (about 4 oz./115 g) shredded reduced-fat jack cheese
- 1 can (about 4 oz./115 g) diced green chiles
- ¼ cup (10 g) finely chopped cilantro

Cherry Tomato Salsa:

- 2 cups (285 g) red cherry tomatoes, cut into halves

Chile-Cheese French Toast with Cherry Tomato Salsa

Preparation time: 20 minutes
Cooking time: About 25 minutes

- ⅓ cup (15 g) cilantro leaves
- 2 small fresh jalapeño chiles, seeded
- 1 clove garlic, peeled
- 2 tablespoons (30 ml) lime juice
- 2 tablespoons thinly sliced green onion

1. In a large bowl, beat egg, egg whites, and milk until well blended. Dip 4 slices of bread into egg mixture; turn to saturate both sides. Arrange slices in a shallow 10- by 15-inch (25- by 38-cm) nonstick baking pan.

2. Top bread in baking pan evenly with cheese, green chiles, and chopped cilantro. Dip remaining 4 bread slices into egg mixture, turning to coat both sides; place atop cheese-covered bread to form 4 sandwiches. Bake sandwiches in a 400°F (205°C) oven until bread begins to brown (about 12 minutes). Then carefully turn sandwiches over with a wide spatula; continue to bake until golden brown (about 10 more minutes).

3. Meanwhile, in a food processor, combine tomatoes, cilantro leaves, jalapeño chiles, and garlic; whirl just until tomatoes are coarsely chopped (or chop ingredients with a knife). Spoon mixture into a small bowl. Add lime juice and onion; stir to mix well.

4. To serve, transfer French toast sandwiches to individual plates. Offer salsa to add to taste. Makes 4 servings.

Per serving: 306 calories (24% calories from fat), 8 g total fat, 4 g saturated fat, 74 mg cholesterol, 811 mg sodium, 37 g carbohydrates, 3 g fiber, 22 g protein, 385 mg calcium, 2 mg iron

Indian-spiced Scrambled Eggs
(recipe on facing page)

For a satisfying lunch, choose savory flan instead of a sandwich. Infused with the subtle flavor of roasted red peppers, the delicate custard is enhanced by zesty Black Bean & Jicama Salad.

- 2 **jars (about 7 oz./200 g *each*) roasted red peppers, drained and patted dry (about 1 cup peppers *total*)**
- 3 **large eggs**
- ⅓ **cup (80 ml) low-sodium chicken broth**
  Black Bean & Jicama Salad (page 57)
  Cilantro sprigs
  Salt and pepper

Red Pepper Flan

Preparation time: About 20 minutes
Baking time: 25 to 35 minutes

1. In a blender or food processor, combine red peppers, eggs, and broth; whirl until smoothly puréed. Pour purée equally into four ¾-cup (180-ml) ramekins or baking dishes (about 2 inches/5 cm deep). Set ramekins, side by side, in a larger pan (at least 2 inches/5 cm deep). Set pan on middle rack of a 325°F (165°C) oven.

2. Pour boiling water into larger pan up to level of pepper mixture. Bake until center of flan no longer jiggles when ramekins are gently shaken (25 to 35 minutes). Lift ramekins from water. Serve hot or cool. If made ahead, let cool completely; then cover and refrigerate until next day.

3. Prepare Black Bean & Jicama Salad; refrigerate until ready to serve or for up to 4 hours. To serve, set each ramekin on a plate; serve salad alongside. Garnish with cilantro sprigs; season to taste with salt and pepper. Makes 4 servings.

Per serving: 257 calories (22% calories from fat), 6 g total fat, 3 g saturated fat, 167 mg cholesterol, 367 mg sodium, 35 g carbohydrates, 3 g fiber, 14 g protein, 94 mg calcium, 4 mg iron

---

Easy Corn-Cheese Bread (page 336) and a crisp salad make wonderful accompaniments to this hearty frittata.

- 2 **large eggs**
- 4 **large egg whites**
- 1 **tablespoon cornstarch blended with 2 tablespoons (30 ml) cold water**
- 1 **pound (455 g) small red thin-skinned potatoes, scrubbed and thinly sliced**
- 1 **large onion, thinly sliced**
- 1 **tablespoon butter or margarine**
- 1½ **teaspoons chopped fresh rosemary or ¾ teaspoon dried rosemary, crumbled**
- ⅓ **cup (80 ml) Marsala or port**
- 1 **jar (about 2 oz./55 g) diced pimentos**
- 8 **ounces (230 g) boneless, skinless chicken breast, cut into ½- by 2-inch (1- by 5-cm) strips**
- 2 **cloves garlic, minced or pressed**
- ½ **cup (55 g) shredded reduced-fat sharp Cheddar cheese**
  Rosemary sprigs

Chicken Frittata

Preparation time: 20 minutes
Cooking time: About 30 minutes

1. In a small bowl, whisk eggs, egg whites, and cornstarch mixture until blended; set aside.

2. In a wide nonstick frying pan with an ovenproof handle, combine potatoes, onion, and 2 teaspoons of the butter. Add ¾ cup (180 ml) water. Cover and cook over medium-high heat, stirring occasionally, until potatoes are tender when pierced (10 to 15 minutes); add more water, ¼ cup (60 ml) at a time, if pan appears dry.

3. Uncover pan and add chopped rosemary, Marsala, and pimentos. Bring to a boil; then boil, stirring, until almost all liquid has evaporated (about 4 minutes).

4. Whisk egg mixture and pour over potato mixture. Reduce heat to low and cook until eggs begin to set at pan rim (about 5 minutes). Then broil about 6 inches (15 cm) below heat until top of egg mixture feels set when lightly touched (about 5 minutes).

5. Meanwhile, melt remaining 1 teaspoon butter in a small nonstick frying pan over medium-high heat. Add chicken and garlic. Cook, stirring, just until chicken is no longer pink in center; cut to test (3 to 4 minutes).

6. With a slotted spoon, lift chicken from pan and arrange over frittata. Sprinkle with cheese; broil until cheese is melted (about 30 seconds). Serve hot or warm. To serve, garnish with rosemary sprigs; then spoon from pan. Makes 4 servings.

Per serving: 339 calories (26% calories from fat), 9 g total fat, 4 g saturated fat, 157 mg cholesterol, 277 mg sodium, 31 g carbohydrates, 3 g fiber, 27 g protein, 166 mg calcium, 2 mg iron

Great any time of day, this attractive frittata can be served straight from the pan—there's no need for a serving dish.

- 1 teaspoon olive oil
- ½ teaspoon dried rosemary
- 1 pound (455 g) red thin-skinned potatoes, scrubbed and cut into ¼-inch (6-mm) cubes
- 1 small red onion (about 8 oz./230 g), thinly sliced and cut into 1-inch (2.5-cm) slivers
- 4 ounces (115 g) green beans (ends trimmed), cut into 1-inch (2.5-cm) pieces
- ⅓ cup (80 ml) canned vegetable broth
- 1 tablespoon cornstarch
- ¼ teaspoon salt
- 4 large eggs
- 4 large egg whites
- ⅔ cup (60 g) dried cranberries
- ½ cup (55 g) shredded part-skim mozzarella cheese
- 1 large red bell pepper (about 8 oz./230 g), seeded and chopped
- ⅛ teaspoon crushed red pepper flakes (or to taste)

Potato, Green Bean & Bell Pepper Frittata

Preparation time: 25 minutes
Cooking time: About 30 minutes

1. Pour oil into a wide frying pan with an ovenproof handle. Heat oil over medium-high heat; then add rosemary and cook, stirring, just until fragrant (about 30 seconds; do not scorch). Add potatoes, onion, beans, and ½ cup (120 ml) water. Cover, reduce heat to medium, and cook, stirring occasionally, just until potatoes are tender when pierced (about 12 minutes). Add water, about ¼ cup (60 ml) at a time, if pan appears dry.

2. Meanwhile, whisk broth, cornstarch, and salt in a large bowl until smoothly blended. Add eggs and egg whites; whisk until blended. Stir in cranberries and cheese. Set aside.

3. Uncover pan and add half the bell pepper. Cook, stirring, until all liquid has evaporated from vegetable mixture. Whisk egg mixture and pour over vegetables; stir gently to combine. Reduce heat to low; cook until eggs begin to set at pan rim (about 6 minutes). Then broil about 6 inches (15 cm) below heat until frittata feels set when lightly pressed (4 to 6 minutes). Sprinkle with remaining bell pepper and red pepper flakes. Spoon from pan to serve. Makes 4 servings.

Per serving: 329 calories (23% calories from fat), 8 g total fat, 3 g saturated fat, 217 mg cholesterol, 426 mg sodium, 47 g carbohydrates, 5 g fiber, 17 g protein, 170 mg calcium, 2 mg iron

Fettuccine Alfredo
(recipe on page 264)

Pasta

Pasta is a simple food, low in fat but high in satisfaction. It's mild taste and firm texture make it an ideal foundation for all types of sauces and foods. While pasta is identified with Italian cooking, noodles have a place in many culinary traditions. We've borrowed fresh ginger and soy sauce from the Orient for our Asparagus & Pasta Stir-fry and offer a streamlined Italian Fettuccine Alfredo.

Alfredo aficionados will enjoy this variation on an Italian classic. Artichoke hearts enhance the tender pasta and its creamy two-cheese sauce.

- 2 cans (about 14 oz./400 g *each*) artichoke hearts packed in water, drained and quartered
- 3 tablespoons chopped Italian or regular parsley
- 3 tablespoons thinly sliced green onions
- 12 ounces (340 g) dried fettuccine
- 1 tablespoon butter or olive oil
- 3 cloves garlic, minced
- 1 tablespoon all-purpose flour
- 1½ cups (360 ml) low-fat (2%) milk
- 1 large package (about 8 oz./ 230 g) nonfat cream cheese, cut into small chunks
- 1½ cups (about 4½ oz./130 g) shredded Parmesan cheese
- ⅛ teaspoon ground nutmeg (optional)

  Pepper

Fettuccine Alfredo

Preparation time: 15 minutes
Cooking time: About 25 minutes
Pictured on page 262

1. In a medium-size bowl, combine artichokes, parsley, and onions. Set aside.

2. In a 5- to 6-quart (5- to 6-liter) pan, bring about 3 quarts (2.8 liters) water to a boil over medium-high heat; stir in pasta and cook until just tender to bite, 8 to 10 minutes. (Or cook pasta according to package directions.) Drain well, return to pan, and keep hot.

3. Melt butter in a wide nonstick frying pan over medium heat. Add garlic and cook, stirring, until fragrant (about 30 seconds; do not scorch). Whisk in flour until well blended, then gradually whisk in milk. Cook, whisking constantly, until mixture boils and thickens slightly (about 5 minutes). Whisk in cream cheese, 1 cup

(3 oz./85 g) of the Parmesan cheese, and nutmeg (if desired). Continue to cook, whisking constantly, until cheese is melted and evenly blended into sauce.

4. Working quickly, pour hot sauce over pasta and lift with 2 forks to mix. Spoon pasta into center of 4 shallow individual bowls. Then quickly arrange artichoke mixture around pasta. Sprinkle with remaining ½ cup (40 g) Parmesan cheese, then with pepper. Serve immediately (sauce thickens rapidly and is absorbed quickly by pasta). Makes 4 servings.

Per serving: 641 calories (24% calories from fat), 17 g total fat, 9 g saturated fat, 126 mg cholesterol, 924 mg sodium, 82 g carbohydrates, 4 g fiber, 39 g protein, 753 mg calcium, 6 mg iron

---

Broccoli adds crunch to this wholesome meatless entrée.

- 12 ounces/340 g (about 5 cups) dried rotini or other corkscrew-shaped pasta
- 2 tablespoons (30 ml) olive oil
- 5 green onions, thinly sliced
- 1 pound (455 g) broccoli flowerets, cut into bite-size pieces
- 1½ cups (345 g) part-skim ricotta cheese

  Freshly grated Parmesan cheese

  Coarsely ground pepper

Rotini with Broccoli & Ricotta

Preparation time: About 10 minutes
Cooking time: About 10 minutes

1. Bring 12 cups (2.8 liters) water to a boil in a 5- to 6-quart (5- to 6-liter) pan over medium-high heat. Stir in pasta and cook just until tender to bite (8 to 10 minutes); or cook according to package directions. Meanwhile, heat oil in a wide nonstick frying pan over medium-high heat. Add onions and cook, stirring, for 1 minute. Add broc-

coli and continue to cook, stirring, until bright green (about 3 minutes). Pour in ¼ cup (60 ml) water and bring to a boil; reduce heat, cover, and simmer until broccoli is tender-crisp (about 5 minutes).

2. Drain pasta well, reserving ¼ cup (60 ml) of the water. Place in a large serving bowl. Add vegetables and ricotta. Mix thoroughly but gently; if too dry, stir in enough of the reserved water to moisten. Offer Parmesan and pepper to add to taste. Makes 4 servings.

Per serving: 540 calories (26% calories from fat), 16 g total fat, 6 g saturated fat, 29 mg cholesterol, 149 mg sodium, 75 g carbohydrates, 6 g fiber, 25 g protein, 324 mg calcium, 5 mg iron

Spaghetti and its vegetable name-sake star in this svelte pasta dish. Lima beans add protein.

1 spaghetti squash (about 2½ lbs./1.15 kg)

1½ cups (360 ml) vegetable broth

1 package (about 10 oz./285 g) frozen baby lima beans

2 tablespoons fresh thyme or 2 teaspoons dried thyme

1½ teaspoons grated lemon peel

8 cups (440 g) lightly packed spinach leaves, cut into narrow strips

12 ounces (340 g) dried spaghetti
Salt and pepper

1. Pierce squash shell in several places. Place in a shallow pan slightly larger

Spaghetti with Beans & Spaghetti Squash

Preparation time: About 15 minutes
Cooking time: About 1¾ hours

than squash. Bake in a 350°F (175°C) oven until shell gives readily when pressed (1¼ to 1½ hours).

2. Halve squash lengthwise; remove seeds. Scrape squash from shell, using a fork to loosen strands, and place in a 3- to 4-quart (2.8- to 3.8-liter) pan. Add broth, beans, thyme, and lemon peel. Bring to a boil over high heat; reduce

heat, cover, and simmer, stirring often, just until beans are tender to bite (about 5 minutes). Add spinach. Cover and cook until spinach is wilted (1 to 2 more minutes). Remove from heat and keep warm.

3. Bring 12 cups (2.8 liters) water to a boil in a 5- to 6-quart (5- to 6-liter) pan over medium-high heat. Stir in pasta and cook just until tender to bite (8 to 10 minutes); or cook according to package directions. Drain well; return to pan. Add squash mixture and lift with 2 forks to mix. Transfer to a serving bowl. Offer salt and pepper to add to taste. Makes 8 servings.

Per serving: 259 calories (6% calories from fat), 2 g total fat, 0.3 g saturated fat, 0 mg cholesterol, 301 mg sodium, 51 g carbohydrates, 6 g fiber, 11 g protein, 120 mg calcium, 5 mg iron

---

Artichokes rather than basil star in the nontraditional pesto for this pasta dish.

¼ cup (35 g) pine nuts

1 can (about 10 oz./285 g) artichoke hearts in water, drained

½ cup (40 g) freshly grated Parmesan cheese

3 ounces (85 g) Neufchâtel or cream cheese

¼ cup (45 g) diced onion

1 tablespoon (15 ml) Dijon mustard

1 clove garlic, minced or pressed

⅛ teaspoon ground nutmeg

¾ cup (180 ml) vegetable broth

1 pound (455 g) dried fettuccine

¼ cup (15 g) minced parsley

¼ teaspoon crushed red pepper flakes

Artichoke Pesto Pasta

Preparation time: About 15 minutes
Cooking time: About 15 minutes

1. Toast pine nuts in a small frying pan over medium heat, shaking pan often, until golden (about 3 minutes). Remove from pan and set aside.

2. Combine artichokes, Parmesan,

Neufchâtel, onion, mustard, garlic, nutmeg, and ½ cup (120 ml) of the broth in a food processor or blender. Whirl until blended. Set aside.

3. Bring 16 cups (3.8 liters) water to a boil in a 6- to 8-quart (6- to 8-liter) pan over medium-high heat. Stir in pasta and cook just until tender to bite (8 to 10 minutes); or cook according to package directions. Drain well and return to pan. Reduce heat to medium, add remaining ¼ cup (60 ml) broth, and cook, lifting pasta with 2 forks, until broth is hot (about 30 seconds).

4. Transfer to a large serving bowl. Quickly add artichoke mixture, parsley, red pepper flakes, and nuts; lift with 2 forks to mix. Makes 8 servings.

Per serving: 307 calories (26% calories from fat), 9 g total fat, 3 g saturated fat, 66 mg cholesterol, 309 mg sodium, 44 g carbohydrates, 3 g fiber, 13 g protein, 105 mg calcium, 3 mg iron

A zesty bean mixture fills jumbo pasta shells.

··

Roasted Red Pepper Sauce (page 268)

1 to 2 tablespoons pine nuts

20 jumbo shell-shaped pasta (about 6⅔ oz./190 g *total*)

1 can (about 15 oz./425 g) garbanzo beans

¼ cup (10 g) lightly packed fresh basil

2 tablespoons chopped parsley

2 tablespoons (30 ml) lemon juice

2 teaspoons Oriental sesame oil

2 cloves garlic

¼ teaspoon ground cumin

Salt and pepper

Parsley sprigs

Stuffed Shells with Roasted Red Pepper Sauce

··

Preparation time: About 20 minutes
Cooking time: About 1 hour
Pictured on facing page

1. Prepare Roasted Red Pepper Sauce; set aside. Toast pine nuts in a small frying pan over medium heat, shaking pan often, until golden (about 3 minutes). Remove from pan and set aside.

2. Bring 12 cups (2.8 liters) water to a boil in a 5- to 6-quart (5- to 6-liter) pan over medium-high heat. Stir in pasta and cook just until almost tender (about 8 minutes; do not overcook).

Meanwhile, drain beans, reserving liquid. Combine beans, basil, chopped parsley, lemon juice, oil, garlic, and cumin in a blender or food processor. Whirl, adding reserved liquid as necessary, until smooth but thick. Season to taste with salt and pepper.

3. Drain pasta, rinse with cold water, and drain well. Spoon half the red pepper sauce into a shallow 2- to 2½-quart (1.9- to 2.4-liter) casserole. Fill shells with bean mixture and arrange, filled sides up, in sauce. Top with remaining sauce. Cover tightly and bake in a 350°F (175°C) oven until hot (about 40 minutes). Sprinkle with nuts. Garnish with parsley sprigs. Makes 4 servings.

··

Per serving: 467 calories (17% calories from fat), 9 g total fat, 2 g saturated fat, 4 mg cholesterol, 424 mg sodium, 80 g carbohydrates, 8 g fiber, 17 g protein, 176 mg calcium, 5 mg iron

---

Roma tomatoes, mushrooms, and plenty of leafy chard go into this fresh and hearty supper dish. For the pasta, choose the whimsical little corkscrews called rotini, *or opt for elbow macaroni or another favorite shape.*

··

12 ounces (340 g) Swiss chard

1 pound (455 g) dried rotini or elbow macaroni

3 tablespoons (45 ml) olive oil or salad oil

1 pound (455 g) mushrooms, sliced

1 medium-size onion, chopped

3 cloves garlic, minced or pressed

½ cup (120 ml) canned vegetable broth

½ cup (43 g) grated Parmesan cheese

1½ pounds (680 g) pear-shaped (Roma-type) tomatoes, chopped and drained well

Italian Garden Pasta

··

Preparation time: About 25 minutes
Cooking time: About 15 minutes

1. Trim and discard discolored stem ends from chard; then rinse and drain chard. Cut stems from leaves; finely chop stems and leaves, keeping them in separate piles.

2. In a 6- to 8-quart (6- to 8-liter) pan, cook rotini in about 4 quarts (3.8 liters) boiling water until just tender to bite (8 to 10 minutes); or cook according to package directions. Drain well, transfer to a warm wide bowl, and keep warm.

3. While pasta is cooking, heat oil in a wide nonstick frying pan or wok over medium-high heat. When oil is hot, add chard stems, mushrooms, onion, and garlic. Cover and cook until

mushrooms release their liquid and onion is soft (about 6 minutes). Then uncover and stir-fry until liquid has evaporated and mushrooms are tinged with brown. Add broth and chard leaves; stir until chard is just wilted (1 to 2 more minutes).

4. Pour chard-mushroom mixture over pasta, sprinkle with half the cheese, and top with tomatoes. Mix gently but thoroughly. Sprinkle with remaining cheese. Makes 4 to 6 servings.

··

Per serving: 531 calories (22% calories from fat), 13 g total fat, 3 g saturated fat, 8 mg cholesterol, 402 mg sodium, 84 g carbohydrates, 7 g fiber, 21 g protein, 203 mg calcium, 7 mg iron

Stuffed Shells with Roasted Red Pepper Sauce
(recipe on facing page)

Pasta Sauces

Nowhere is the versatility of pasta more evident than when you consider the variety of sauces that can accompany it. Here's a selection of four light sauces. All can be made ahead and refrigerated or frozen; simply reheat (thaw first, if necessary) and serve with hot pasta for a delicious meal that takes only minutes to make.

Although some of these sauces get more than 30 percent of their calories from fat, they still have a place in a nutritious, low-fat diet when paired with pasta and other low-fat ingredients.

Sweet Spice Meat Sauce

Preparation time: About 20 minutes
Cooking time: About 1⅔ hours

....

Spice Blend (recipe follows)

4 slices bacon, chopped

1 pound (455 g) lean ground beef

4 medium-size onions (about 1½ lbs./680 g *total*), chopped

1 cup (120 g) finely chopped celery

2 cloves garlic, minced or pressed

2 tablespoons minced parsley

3 cans (about 15 oz./425 g *each*) tomato sauce

1 can (about 6 oz./170 g) tomato paste

2 tablespoons (30 ml) red wine vinegar

1. Prepare Spice Blend.

2. Combine bacon and beef in a 5- to 6-quart (5- to 6-liter) pan. Cook over medium-high heat, stirring often, until well browned (about 15 minutes).

3. Pour off fat. Add onions, celery, garlic, parsley, and Spice Blend. Cook, stirring often, until onions are soft (about 20 minutes).

4. Add tomato sauce, tomato paste, and vinegar; stir well. Bring to a boil; reduce heat and simmer until reduced to about 8 cups/1.9 liters (about 1 hour). If made ahead, let cool and then cover and refrigerate for up to 2 days; reheat before using. Makes about 8 cups (1.9 liters).

....

Spice Blend. In small bowl, combine 1 tablespoon firmly packed **brown sugar;** ½ teaspoon *each* **ground cinnamon, dried oregano, pepper, rubbed sage,** and **dried thyme;** and ¼ teaspoon *each* **ground cloves** and **ground nutmeg.** Mix until blended.

....

Per serving: 121 calories (35% calories from fat), 5 g total fat, 2 g saturated fat, 19 mg cholesterol, 616 mg sodium, 13 g carbohydrates, 2 g fiber, 7 g protein, 34 mg calcium, 2 mg iron

Roasted Red Pepper Sauce

Preparation time: About 10 minutes
Cooking time: About 20 minutes

....

Roasted Red Bell Peppers (directions follow)

1 teaspoon olive oil

1 large onion (about 8 oz./230 g), chopped

3 cloves garlic, minced or pressed

2 tablespoons (30 ml) dry sherry (or to taste)

1 tablespoon (15 ml) white wine vinegar (or to taste)

⅛ teaspoon ground white pepper

¼ cup (20 g) freshly grated Parmesan cheese

Salt

....

1. Prepare Roasted Red Bell Peppers. Set aside with any drippings in a blender or food processor.

2. Heat oil in a wide nonstick frying pan over medium-high heat. Add onion and garlic. Cook, stirring often, until onion is soft (about 5 minutes); if pan appears dry or onion mixture sticks to pan bottom, add water, 1 tablespoon (15 ml) at a time.

3. Transfer onion mixture to blender with peppers. Whirl until smooth. Add sherry, vinegar, and pepper. Whirl until of desired consistency. (At this point, you may cover and refrigerate for up to 2 days; reheat before continuing.)

4. Add cheese. Season to taste with salt. Makes about 3 cups (710 ml).

....

Roasted Red Bell Peppers. Cut 4 large **red bell peppers** (about 2 lbs./905 g *total*) in half lengthwise. Place, cut sides down, in a 10- by 15-inch (25- by 38-cm) baking pan. Broil 4 to 6 inches (10 to 15 cm) below heat, turning as needed, until charred all over (about 8 minutes). Cover with foil and let cool in pan. Pull off and discard skins, stems, and seeds. Cut into chunks.

....

Per serving: 40 calories (23% calories from fat), 1 g total fat, 0.4 g saturated fat, 1 mg cholesterol, 33 mg sodium, 6 g carbohydrates, 1 g fiber, 1 g protein, 34 mg calcium, 0.3 mg iron

Turkey Italian Sausage Sauce

Preparation time: About 10 minutes
Cooking time: About 40 minutes

....

1 **pound (455 g) mild or hot turkey Italian sausages, casings removed, or Low-fat Italian Sausage (page 24)**

1 **large onion (about 8 oz./230 g), chopped**

3 **cloves garlic, minced or pressed**

1 **can (about 29 oz./820 g) tomato purée**

3 **tablespoons chopped fresh basil or 1 tablespoon dried basil**

½ **teaspoon fennel seeds**

2 **tablespoons (30 ml) dry red wine (or to taste)**

   Salt and pepper

....

1. Chop or crumble sausages. Place in a 4- to 5-quart (3.8- to 5-liter) pan with onion, garlic,

and 2 tablespoons (30 ml) water. Cook over medium heat, stirring often, until sausage mixture is well browned (about 15 minutes); if pan appears dry or sausage mixture sticks to pan bottom, add water, 1 tablespoon (15 ml) at a time.

2. Stir in tomato purée, basil, and fennel seeds. Increase heat to medium-high and bring to a boil; reduce heat and simmer until reduced to about 4½ cups/ 1 liter (about 20 minutes).

3. Remove from heat and add wine. Season to taste with salt and pepper. If made ahead, let cool and then cover and refrigerate for up to 2 days; reheat before using. Makes about 4½ cups (1 liter).

....

Per serving: 54 calories (3% calories from fat), 0.2 g total fat, 0 g saturated fat, 0 mg cholesterol, 366 mg sodium, 12 g carbohydrates, 3 g fiber, 2 g protein, 43 mg calcium, 1 mg iron

Porcini-Tomato Sauce

Preparation time: About 35 minutes
Cooking time: About 1½ hours

....

⅔ **ounce (20 g) dried porcini mushrooms (about ⅔ cup)**

8 **ounces (230 g) pancetta or bacon, finely chopped**

1 **large onion (about 8 oz./230 g), finely chopped**

2 **small carrots (about 4 oz./115 g *total*), finely chopped**

2 **large stalks celery (about 8 oz./230 g *total*), finely chopped**

2 **cloves garlic, minced or pressed**

¼ **cup (15 g) finely chopped parsley**

1 **can (about 15 oz./425 g) chopped or puréed tomatoes**

2 **cups (470 ml) beef broth**

1 **can (about 6 oz./170 g) tomato paste**

   Salt

....

1. Soak mushrooms in 1½ cups (360 ml) boiling water until soft (about 20 minutes). Lift out and squeeze dry. Chop finely and set aside. Without disturbing sediment at bottom, pour soaking liquid into a measuring cup and set aside. Discard sediment.

2. Cook pancetta in a 5- to 6-quart (5- to 6-liter) pan over medium-high heat, stirring often, until browned and crisp (7 to 10 minutes). Add onion, carrots, celery, garlic, and parsley. Cook, stirring often, until vegetables begin to brown and stick to pan bottom (7 to 10 more minutes).

3. Stir in tomatoes and their liquid, broth, tomato paste, mushrooms, and reserved soaking liquid. Bring to a boil; reduce heat and simmer until reduced to about 6 cups/1.4 liters (about 1 hour).

4. Season to taste with salt. If made ahead, let cool and then cover and refrigerate for up to 2 days; reheat before using. Makes about 6 cups (1.4 liters).

....

Per serving: 205 calories (73% calories from fat), 17 g total fat, 6 g saturated fat, 19 mg cholesterol, 715 mg sodium, 9 g carbohydrates, 2 g fiber, 4 g protein, 38 mg calcium, 1 mg iron

Oven-baked Mediterranean Orzo
(recipe on facing page)

This combination of tiny pasta, artichokes, and two kinds of beans is an easy one-dish entrée. Raisins and dried apricots add sweet, sunny flavor.

- 1 large can (about 28 oz./795 g) tomatoes

  About 2 cups (470 ml) vegetable broth
- 1 teaspoon olive oil
- 1 large onion, cut into very thin slivers
- 1 can (about 15 oz./425 g) *each* black beans and cannellini (white kidney beans), drained and rinsed well
- 1 package (about 9 oz./255 g) frozen artichoke hearts, thawed and drained
- ½ cup (65 g) dried apricots, cut into halves
- ⅓ cup (50 g) raisins

  About 1 tablespoon drained capers (or to taste)
- 4 teaspoons chopped fresh basil or 1½ teaspoons dried basil
- ½ teaspoon fennel seeds, crushed

Oven-baked Mediterranean Orzo

Preparation time: 20 minutes
Cooking time: About 50 minutes
Pictured on facing page

- 1½ cups (about 10 oz./285 g) dried orzo or other rice-shaped pasta
- ½ cup (65 g) crumbled feta cheese
  Pepper

1. Break up tomatoes with a spoon and drain liquid into a 4-cup (950-ml) measure; set tomatoes aside. Add enough of the broth to tomato liquid to make 3 cups (710 ml); set aside.

2. Place oil and onion in an oval 3- to 3½-quart (2.8- to 3.3-liter) casserole, about 9 by 13 inches (23 by 33 cm) and at least 2½ inches (6 cm) deep. Bake in a 450°F (230°C) oven until onion is soft and tinged with brown (about 10 minutes). During baking, stir occasionally to loosen browned bits from casserole bottom; add water,

1 tablespoon (15 ml) at a time, if casserole appears dry.

3. Remove casserole from oven and carefully add tomatoes, broth mixture, black beans, cannellini, artichokes, apricots, raisins, capers, basil, and fennel seeds. Stir to loosen any browned bits from casserole. Return to oven and continue to bake until mixture comes to a rolling boil (about 20 minutes).

4. Remove casserole from oven and carefully stir in pasta, scraping casserole bottom to loosen any browned bits. Cover tightly, return to oven, and bake for 10 more minutes; then stir pasta mixture well, scraping casserole bottom. Cover tightly again and continue to bake until pasta is just tender to bite and almost all liquid has been absorbed (about 10 more minutes). Sprinkle with cheese, cover, and let stand for about 5 minutes before serving. Season to taste with pepper. Makes 6 to 8 servings.

Per serving: 358 calories (12% calories from fat), 5 g total fat, 2 g saturated fat, 9 mg cholesterol, 807 mg sodium, 66 g carbohydrates, 9 g fiber, 15 g protein, 140 mg calcium, 5 mg iron

---

Made from pure white goat's milk, goat cheese (often marketed under its French name, chèvre) is distinguished by its unique, delightfully tart flavor. In this recipe, it's melted into a smooth sauce to serve over pasta and spinach.

- 12 ounces (340 g) dried spinach fettuccine
- 3 quarts (about 12 oz./340 g) lightly packed rinsed, drained fresh spinach leaves, cut or torn into 2-inch (5-cm) pieces
- ⅔ cup (160 ml) vegetable broth
- 8 ounces (230 g) unsweetened soft fresh goat cheese (plain or flavored), broken into chunks, if possible (some types may be too soft to break)

Goat Cheese-Spinach Pasta

Preparation time: 15 to 20 minutes
Cooking time: About 15 minutes

- 2 cups (285 g) ripe cherry tomatoes (at room temperature), cut into ⅓-inch (1-cm) slices
  Salt and pepper

1. In a 5- to 6-quart (5- to 6-liter) pan, bring about 3 quarts water to a boil over medium-high heat; stir in pasta and cook until just tender to bite, 8 to 10 minutes. (Or cook pasta according to package directions.) Stir spinach

into boiling water with pasta; continue to boil until spinach is wilted (30 to 45 more seconds). Drain pasta-spinach mixture well and return to pan.

2. While pasta is cooking, bring broth to a boil in a 1- to 2-quart (950-ml to 1.9-liter) pan over medium-high heat. Add cheese and stir until melted; remove from heat.

3. Spoon cheese mixture over pasta and spinach; mix gently but thoroughly. Spoon onto a platter; scatter tomatoes over top. Season to taste with salt and pepper. Makes 4 servings.

Per serving: 537 calories (28% calories from fat), 17 g total fat, 9 g saturated fat, 107 mg cholesterol, 617 mg sodium, 70 g carbohydrates, 12 g fiber, 30 g protein, 351 mg calcium, 11 mg iron

Piquant Gorgonzola cheese and a hint of sherry give this creamy ravioli its sprightly character.

Ravioli with Gorgonzola

Preparation time: 15 minutes
Cooking time: About 25 minutes

2 packages (about 9 oz./255 g *each*) fresh low-fat or regular cheese-filled ravioli

¼ cup (45 g) finely chopped onion

2 cloves garlic, minced or pressed

4 teaspoons cornstarch

1 cup (240 ml) nonfat milk

½ cup (120 ml) *each* half-and-half and vegetable broth

2 ounces (55 g) Gorgonzola or other blue-veined cheese, crumbled

¼ teaspoon *each* dried thyme, marjoram, and rubbed sage

⅛ teaspoon ground nutmeg

1 teaspoon dry sherry (or to taste)

Finely shredded lemon peel

Salt and pepper

1. In a 6- to 8-quart (6- to 8-liter) pan, bring about 4 quarts (3.8 liters) water to a boil over medium-high heat. Stir in ravioli, separating any that are stuck together; reduce heat and boil gently, stirring occasionally, until pasta is just tender to bite (4 to 6 minutes); or cook pasta according to package directions. Drain well, return to pan, and keep warm.

2. While pasta is cooking, combine onion, garlic, and 1 tablespoon (15 ml) water in a wide nonstick frying pan. Cook over medium-high heat, stirring often, until onion is soft (3 to 4 minutes); add water, 1 tablespoon (15 ml) at a time, if pan appears dry. Remove from heat.

3. Smoothly blend cornstarch with 2 tablespoons (30 ml) of the milk. Add corn-starch mixture, remaining milk, half-and-half, and broth to pan. Return to medium-high heat and bring to a boil, stirring. Reduce heat to low and add cheese, thyme, marjoram, sage, and nutmeg; stir until cheese is melted. Remove pan from heat and stir in sherry.

4. Spoon sauce over pasta; mix gently. Spoon pasta onto individual plates; sprinkle with lemon peel. Season to taste with salt and pepper. Makes 6 servings.

Per serving: 315 calories (29% calories from fat), 10 g total fat, 6 g saturated fat, 69 mg cholesterol, 545 mg sodium, 40 g carbohydrates, 2 g fiber, 15 g protein, 270 mg calcium, 2 mg iron

---

Bell peppers, fresh herbs, and garbanzo beans produce a richly flavored pasta sauce that's very low in fat.

Linguine with Red & Green Sauce

Preparation time: About 25 minutes
Cooking time: About 35 minutes

8 medium-size red bell peppers (about 3 lbs./1.35 kg *total*)

1 pound (455 g) dried linguine

1 cup (100 g) thinly sliced green onions

1 can (about 15 oz./425 g) garbanzo beans, drained

¾ cup (30 g) chopped fresh basil or ¼ cup (8 g) dried basil

1½ tablespoons chopped fresh tarragon or 1½ teaspoons dried tarragon

3 tablespoons capers, drained

Salt and pepper

1. Place bell peppers in a 10- by 15-inch (25- by 38-cm) baking pan. Broil about 3 inches (8 cm) below heat, turning as needed, until charred all over (about 15 minutes). Cover with foil and let cool in pan. Pull off and discard skins, stems, and seeds. Chop finely in a food processor or with a knife. Set aside.

2. Bring 16 cups (3.8 liters) water to a boil in a 6- to 8-quart (6- to 8-liter) pan over medium-high heat. Stir in pasta and cook just until tender to bite (8 to 10 minutes); or cook according to package directions. Meanwhile, combine bell peppers, onions, beans, basil, tarragon, and capers in a 3- to 4-quart (2.8- to 3.8-liter) pan. Cook over medium-high heat, stirring often, until steaming (5 to 7 minutes).

3. Drain pasta well and transfer to a wide, shallow serving bowl. Add vegetable mixture and lift with 2 forks to mix. Offer salt and pepper to add to taste. Makes 8 servings.

Per serving: 295 calories (6% calories from fat), 12 g total fat, 0.2 g saturated fat, 0 mg cholesterol, 151 mg sodium, 59 g carbohydrates, 5 g fiber, 11 g protein, 93 mg calcium, 5 mg iron

This dish says "summer." Plain and perfect for warm-weather meals, it's a simple combination of tender pasta ribbons, juicy-ripe cherry tomatoes, and fragrant fresh basil leaves.

- 1 pound (455 g) dried linguine
  About 2 tablespoons (30 ml) Hot Chili Oil (page 109) or purchased hot chili oil
- 1 clove garlic, minced or pressed
- 1 large onion, chopped
- 6 cups (905 g) yellow or red cherry or other tiny tomatoes (or use some of *each* color), cut into halves
- 2 cups (80 g) firmly packed fresh basil leaves

Linguine with Yellow Tomatoes

Preparation time: About 15 minutes
Cooking time: About 15 minutes

Basil sprigs (optional)
Grated Parmesan cheese
Salt

1. In a 6- to 8-quart (6- to 8-liter) pan, cook linguine in 4 quarts (3.8 liters) boiling water until just tender to bite (8 to 10 minutes); or cook according to package directions. Drain well, transfer to a wide bowl, and keep warm.

2. While pasta is cooking, heat 2 tablespoons of the chili oil in a wide nonstick frying pan or wok over medium-high heat. When oil is hot, add garlic and onion; stir-fry until onion is soft (about 5 minutes). Add tomatoes and basil leaves; stir gently until tomatoes are heated through (about 2 minutes).

3. Pour hot tomato mixture over pasta. Garnish with basil sprigs, if desired. Offer cheese to add to taste; season to taste with more chili oil and salt. Makes 6 to 8 servings.

Per serving: 322 calories (15% calories from fat), 5 g total fat, 0.7 g saturated fat, 0 mg cholesterol, 18 mg sodium, 59 g carbohydrates, 4 g fiber, 10 g protein, 80 mg calcium, 4 mg iron

---

Offer this spicy entrée with a cooling cucumber salad.

- 1 cup (240 ml) vegetable broth
- 1 cup (200 g) sugar
- ¼ cup (60 ml) reduced-sodium soy sauce
- 2 tablespoons (30 ml) cider vinegar
- 1 tablespoon cornstarch
- 2 teaspoons paprika
- 1 teaspoon crushed red pepper flakes
- 1 teaspoon salad oil
- ⅓ cup minced garlic
- 8 to 10 ounces (230 to 285 g) dried tagliatelle or fettuccine
- 1 pound (455 g) regular tofu, rinsed and drained, cut into ½-inch (1-cm) cubes
- 1 large red bell pepper (about 8 oz./230 g), cut into ½-inch (1-cm) pieces
- 1 package (about 10 oz./285 g) frozen tiny peas, thawed

Thai Tofu & Tagliatelle

Preparation time: About 15 minutes
Cooking time: 20 to 25 minutes

1. Combine broth, sugar, soy sauce, vinegar, cornstarch, paprika, and red pepper flakes in a small bowl; mix until well blended. Set aside.

2. Heat oil in a wide nonstick frying pan over medium-high heat. Add garlic and cook, stirring often, until tinged with gold (about 4 minutes; do not scorch); if pan appears dry, stir in water, 1 tablespoon (15 ml) at a time.

3. Add broth mixture. Cook, stirring often, until sauce comes to a boil. Continue to cook until reduced to about 1¼ cups/300 ml (10 to 15 minutes). Meanwhile, bring 12 cups (2.8 liters) water to a boil in a 5- to 6-

quart (5- to 6-liter) pan over medium-high heat. Stir in pasta and cook just until tender to bite (8 to 10 minutes); or cook according to package directions. Drain well and transfer to a wide, shallow serving bowl.

4. Combine tofu, bell pepper, peas, and half the sauce in a large bowl. Mix thoroughly but gently. Spoon over pasta. Offer remaining sauce to add to taste. Makes 4 servings.

Per serving: 634 calories (12% calories from fat), 8 g total fat, 1 g saturated fat, 0 mg cholesterol, 987 mg sodium, 121 g carbohydrates, 6 g fiber, 23 g protein, 178 mg calcium, 11 mg iron

Pasta lovers will enjoy this light and savory pie, made from cooked spaghetti, eggs, and two kinds of cheese. A creamy tomato sauce enhances the dish.

Pasta Pie

Preparation time: 15 minutes
Cooking time: About 30 minutes
Pictured on facing page

Pasta Pie:

- ½ cup (120 ml) nonfat milk
- 1 teaspoon cornstarch
- 2 large eggs
- 6 large egg whites
- ¾ cup (85 g) shredded part-skim mozzarella cheese
- ¼ cup (20 g) grated Parmesan cheese
- 2 tablespoons chopped fresh oregano or 1½ teaspoons dried oregano
- 2 cloves garlic, minced or pressed
- ¼ teaspoon salt
- ⅛ teaspoon crushed red pepper flakes
- 3 cups (390 g) cold cooked spaghetti
- 1 teaspoon salad oil

Tomato Cream Sauce:

- 1 large can (about 28 oz./795 g) diced tomatoes
- ½ cup (120 ml) reduced-fat sour cream
- 2 or 3 cloves garlic, peeled
- 2 teaspoons chopped fresh thyme or ½ teaspoon dried thyme
- 1 teaspoon sugar (or to taste)
  Salt and pepper

Garnish:

  Oregano sprigs and fresh oregano leaves

1. In a large bowl, combine milk and cornstarch; beat until smoothly blended. Add eggs and egg whites and beat well. Stir in mozzarella cheese, Parmesan cheese, chopped oregano, minced garlic, the ¼ teaspoon salt, and red pepper flakes. Add pasta to egg mixture; lift with 2 forks to mix well. Set aside.

2. Place a round 9-inch (23-cm) baking pan (do not use a nonstick pan) in oven while it heats to 500°F (260°C). When pan is hot (after about 5 minutes), carefully remove it from oven and pour in oil, tilting pan to coat. Mix pasta mixture again; then transfer to pan. Bake on lowest rack of oven until top of pie is golden and center feels firm when lightly pressed (about 25 minutes).

3. Meanwhile, pour tomatoes and their liquid into a food processor or blender. Add sour cream, peeled garlic, thyme, and sugar; whirl until smoothly puréed. Season to taste with salt and pepper; set aside. Use at room temperature.

4. When pie is done, spread about ¾ cup (180 ml) of the sauce on each of 4 individual plates. Cut pie into 4 wedges; place one wedge atop sauce on each plate. Garnish with oregano sprigs and leaves. Offer remaining sauce to drizzle over pie. Makes 4 servings.

Per serving: 411 calories (30% calories from fat), 14 g total fat, 6 g saturated fat, 133 mg cholesterol, 782 mg sodium, 47 g carbohydrates, 3 g fiber, 26 g protein, 340 mg calcium, 4 mg iron

Pasta Pie
(recipe on facing page)

Originating in Genoa, pesto is an uncooked sauce featuring a variety of crushed or chopped ingredients. Pesto tends to derive over 30% of its calories from fat but it still fits into lean menus. Just use it sparingly.

Mixed Herb Pesto

Preparation time: 15 minutes

2 **cups (80 g) lightly packed fresh basil leaves**

½ **cup (50 g) thinly sliced green onions**

⅓ **cup (15 g) lightly packed fresh oregano leaves**

¼ **cup (20 g) grated Parmesan cheese**

¼ **cup (60 ml) red wine vinegar**

2 **tablespoons fresh rosemary leaves**

2 **tablespoons (30 ml) olive oil**

¼ **to ½ teaspoon pepper**

1. In a food processor or blender, whirl basil, onions, oregano, cheese, vinegar, rosemary, oil, and pepper until smoothly puréed. Makes about 1 cup (240 ml).

Per tablespoon: 29 calories (62% calories from fat), 2 g total fat, 0.5 g saturated fat, 1 mg cholesterol, 25 mg sodium, 2 g carbohydrates, 0.1 g fiber, 0.9 g protein, 74 mg calcium, 1 mg iron

Red Pepper Pesto

Preparation time: 10 minutes

1 **jar (12 oz./340 g) roasted red peppers, drained, patted dry**

1 **cup (40 g) lightly packed fresh basil leaves**

1 **clove garlic, peeled**

⅓ **cup (30 g) grated Parmesan cheese**

Salt and pepper

1. In a food processor or blender, whirl peppers, basil, garlic, and cheese until basil is finely chopped. Season to taste with salt and pepper. Makes about 1½ cups (360 ml).

Per tablespoon: 14 calories (25% calories from fat), 0.4 g total fat, 0.2 g saturated fat, 0.9 mg cholesterol, 51 mg sodium, 2 g carbohydrates, 0 g fiber, 0.7 g protein, 47 mg calcium, 0.8 mg iron

Basil Pesto

Preparation time: 10 minutes

2 **cups (80 g) lightly packed fresh basil leaves**

½ **cup (40 g) grated Parmesan cheese**

⅓ **cup (80 ml) olive oil**

¼ **cup (31 g) walnut pieces**

2 **cloves garlic, peeled**

1. In a food processor or blender, whirl basil, cheese, oil, walnuts, and garlic until smoothly puréed. Makes about 1 cup (240 ml).

Per tablespoon: 69 calories (80% calories from fat), 6 g total fat, 1 g saturated fat, 2 mg cholesterol, 48 mg sodium, 2 g carbohydrates, 0.1 g fiber, 2 g protein, 84 mg calcium, 1 mg iron

Mint Pesto

Preparation time: 10 minutes
Cooking time: About 3 minutes

½ **cup (65 g) pine nuts**

1 **cup (40 g) lightly packed fresh mint leaves**

3 **cloves garlic, peeled**

3 **tablespoons (45 ml) olive oil**

¼ **cup (20 g) grated Parmesan cheese**

1. Stir pine nuts in a wide frying pan over medium heat until golden (about 3 minutes). Pour into a food processor or blender; let cool slightly.

2. To pine nuts, add mint, garlic, oil, and cheese. Whirl until smoothly puréed. Makes about ¾ cup (180 ml).

Per tablespoon: 71 calories (81% calories from fat), 7 g total fat, 1 g saturated fat, 1 mg cholesterol, 31 mg sodium, 1 g carbohydrates, 0.7 g fiber, 2 g protein, 29 mg calcium, 0.8 mg iron

Pistachio Pesto

Preparation time: 15 minutes

¼ **cup (30 g) shelled salted roasted pistachio nuts**

1 **cup (60 g) firmly packed Italian or regular parsley sprigs**

¼ **cup (60 ml) white wine vinegar**

¼ **cup (60 ml) canned vegetable broth**

2 **tablespoons (30 ml) olive oil**

1. In a food processor or blender, whirl pistachios, parsley, vinegar, broth, and oil until smoothly puréed. Makes about ¾ cup (180 ml).

Per tablespoon: 40 calories (77% calories from fat), 4 g total fat, 0.5 g saturated fat, 0 mg cholesterol, 36 mg sodium, 2 g carbohydrates, 0.4 g fiber, 0.8 g protein, 17 mg calcium, 0.8 mg iron

If you like sharp, savory flavors, this dish is for you. Hot linguine is tossed with a sauce of marinated artichoke hearts, ripe olives, anchovy paste, and a little grated Parmesan cheese.

Pasta with Artichokes & Anchovies

Preparation time: About 10 minutes
Cooking time: About 15 minutes

8 ounces (230 g) dried linguine

1 jar (about 6 oz./170 g) marinated artichoke hearts

2 cloves garlic, minced or pressed

1 tablespoon anchovy paste

1 can (about 2¼ oz./65 g) sliced ripe olives, drained

½ cup (30 g) chopped parsley

¼ cup (20 g) grated Parmesan cheese

Parsley sprigs

Pepper

1. In a 4- to 5-quart (3.8- to 5-liter) pan, cook linguine in 8 cups (1.9 liters) boiling water until just tender to bite (8 to 10 minutes); or cook according to package directions. Drain well, transfer to a warm wide bowl, and keep warm.

2. While pasta is cooking, carefully drain marinade from artichokes into a wide nonstick frying pan or wok. Cut artichokes into bite-size pieces and set aside. Heat marinade over medium heat; add garlic and stir-fry until pale gold (about 3 minutes). Add anchovy paste, olives, and artichokes; stir-fry until heated through (about 2 minutes).

3. Pour artichoke mixture over pasta. Add chopped parsley and cheese; mix gently but thoroughly. Garnish with parsley sprigs; season to taste with pepper. Makes 4 to 6 servings.

Per serving: 245 calories (23% calories from fat), 6 g total fat, 1 g saturated fat, 5 mg cholesterol, 499 mg sodium, 38 g carbohydrates, 3 g fiber, 10 g protein, 100 mg calcium, 3 mg iron

---

On busy days, try this Oriental-style pasta entrée for a quick, satisfying meal.

Pasta with Shrimp & Shiitake Mushrooms

Preparation time: 20 minutes
Cooking time: About 15 minutes

2 cups (about 2 oz./55 g) dried shiitake mushrooms

8 ounces (230 g) dried capellini

2 teaspoons Oriental sesame oil

6 tablespoons (90 ml) oyster sauce or reduced-sodium soy sauce

1 tablespoon (15 ml) salad oil

12 ounces (340 g) medium-size raw shrimp (31 to 35 per lb.), shelled and deveined

1 tablespoon finely chopped fresh ginger

3 green onions, thinly sliced

1. Place mushrooms in a medium-size bowl and add enough boiling water to cover; let stand until mushrooms are softened (about 10 minutes). Squeeze mushrooms dry. Cut off and discard stems. Slice caps into strips about ¼ inch (6 mm) thick.

2. In a 4- to 5-quart (3.8- to 5-liter) pan, bring about 8 cups (1.9 liters) water to a boil over medium-high heat; stir in pasta and cook until just tender to bite (about 3 minutes); or cook according to package directions. Drain pasta, rinse with hot water, and drain well again. Then return to pan, add sesame oil and 3 tablespoons (45 ml) of the oyster sauce, and lift with 2 forks to mix. Keep warm.

3. Heat salad oil in a wide nonstick frying pan over medium-high heat. Add mushrooms, shrimp, and ginger. Cook, stirring often, until shrimp are just opaque in center; cut to test (about 5 minutes). Add onions and remaining 3 tablespoons (45 ml) oyster sauce; mix gently but thoroughly. Pour noodles into a wide bowl; pour shrimp mixture over noodles. Makes 4 servings.

Per serving: 409 calories (17% calories from fat), 8 g total fat, 1 g saturated fat, 105 mg cholesterol, 1,181 mg sodium, 64 g carbohydrates, 2 g fiber, 25 g protein, 59 mg calcium, 5 mg iron

Southwestern Fettuccine
(recipe on facing page)

This satisfying Tex-Mex pasta sauce is based on bell pepper, corn kernels, and nippy jalapeño jack cheese. To thicken it, we've used rich-tasting cream-style corn, puréed in the blender until smooth.

- 12 ounces (340 g) dried fettuccine
- 1 can (about 15 oz./425 g) cream-style corn
- ⅔ cup (160 ml) nonfat milk
- 1 teaspoon salad oil
- ½ teaspoon cumin seeds
- 1 small onion, chopped
- 1 large red or yellow bell pepper (about 8 oz./230 g), seeded and cut into thin strips
- 1 package (about 10 oz./285 g) frozen corn kernels, thawed and drained
- 1 cup (about 4 oz./115 g) shredded jalapeño jack cheese
- ¼ cup (10 g) cilantro leaves

Southwestern Fettuccine

Preparation time: 15 minutes
Cooking time: About 20 minutes
Pictured on facing page

- 1½ to 2 cups (210 to 285 g) yellow or red cherry tomatoes, cut into halves
- Cilantro sprigs
- Lime wedges
- Salt

1. In a 5- to 6-quart (5- to 6-liter) pan, bring about 3 quarts (2.8 liters) water to boil over medium-high heat; stir in pasta and cook until just tender to bite (8 to 10 minutes); or cook pasta according to package directions. Drain pasta well and return to pan; keep warm. While pasta is cooking, whirl cream-style corn and milk in a blender or food processor until smoothly puréed; set aside.

2. Heat oil in a wide nonstick frying pan over medium-high heat. Add cumin seeds, onion, and bell pepper. Cook, stirring often, until onion is soft (about 5 minutes); add water, 1 tablespoon (15 ml) at a time, if pan appears dry. Stir in cream-style corn mixture, corn kernels, and cheese. Reduce heat to medium and cook, stirring, just until cheese is melted.

3. Pour corn-cheese sauce over pasta. Add cilantro leaves; mix gently but thoroughly. Divide pasta among 4 shallow individual bowls; sprinkle with tomatoes. Garnish with cilantro sprigs. Season to taste with lime and salt. Makes 4 servings.

Per serving: 627 calories (21% calories from fat), 15 g total fat, 6 g saturated fat, 112 mg cholesterol, 540 mg sodium, 104 g carbohydrates, 7 g fiber, 25 g protein, 298 mg calcium, 5 mg iron

---

Offer this piquant pasta dish with chunks of bread to dunk into any leftover sauce.

- 10 ounces (285 g) dried bucatini, perciatelli, or spaghetti
- ⅔ cup (160 ml) seasoned rice vinegar; or ⅔ cup (160 ml) distilled white vinegar and 2 tablespoons sugar
- 2 tablespoons (30 ml) honey
- 1 tablespoon (15 ml) olive oil
- ½ teaspoon chili oil
- 2 cans (about 15 oz./425 g *each*) black beans, drained and rinsed
- 4 large pear-shaped (Roma-type) tomatoes (about 12 oz./340 g *total*), diced
- ⅓ cup (20 g) finely chopped parsley

Bucatini & Black Beans

Preparation time: About 15 minutes
Cooking time: About 20 minutes

- ¼ cup (25 g) thinly sliced green onions
- ¾ cup (100 g) crumbled feta cheese (or to taste)
- Parsley sprigs

1. Bring 12 cups (2.8 liters) water to a boil in a 5- to 6-quart (5- to 6-liter) pan over medium-high heat. Stir in pasta and cook just until tender to bite (10 to 12 minutes); or cook according to package directions. Drain well and keep warm.

2. Combine vinegar, honey, olive oil, and chili oil in pan. Bring just to a boil over medium-high heat. Add pasta, beans, and tomatoes. Cook, stirring, until hot. Remove from heat; stir in chopped parsley and onions.

3. Spoon pasta mixture into bowls. Sprinkle with cheese. Garnish with parsley sprigs. Makes 4 servings.

Per serving: 564 calories (18% calories from fat), 11 g total fat, 5 g saturated fat, 23 mg cholesterol, 1,095 mg sodium, 96 g carbohydrates, 5 g fiber, 21 g protein, 176 mg calcium, 6 mg iron

Served in wedges, this hearty timbale is a grand meatless main dish. To make it, you layer roasted eggplant slices with a savory mixture of cooked macaroni, marinara sauce, herbs, and cheese; then bake.

Sicilian Pasta Timbale

Preparation time: 20 minutes, plus 15 minutes for eggplant to stand
Cooking time: About 1 hour

Marinara Sauce:

- 1 teaspoon olive oil
- 3 cloves garlic, minced or pressed
- 1 large can (about 28 oz./795 g) tomato purée
- ¼ cup (10 g) chopped fresh basil or 2 tablespoons dried basil
  Salt

Pasta Timbale:

- 2 small eggplants (about 1 lb./455 g *each*)
- 2 teaspoons salt
- 4 to 6 teaspoons (20 to 30 ml) olive oil
- 1 pound (455 g) dried salad macaroni
- 2 cups (about 8 oz./230 g) shredded provolone cheese
- ½ cup (40 g) grated Romano cheese
  About 1 teaspoon butter or margarine, at room temperature
- 2 tablespoons fine dry bread crumbs

Garnish:

  Basil sprigs

1. Heat the 1 teaspoon oil in a 3- to 4-quart (2.8- to 3.8-liter) pan over medium heat. Add garlic and cook, stirring, just until fragrant (about 30 seconds; do not scorch). Add tomato purée and chopped basil. Bring to a boil; then reduce heat and simmer, uncovered, stirring occasionally, until sauce is reduced to about 3 cups/710 ml (about 20 minutes). Season to taste with salt; set aside.

2. While sauce is simmering, cut eggplants lengthwise into ¼-inch (6-mm) slices; sprinkle with the 2 teaspoons salt. Let stand for 15 minutes; then rinse well and pat dry. Coat 2 or 3 shallow 10- by 15-inch (25- by 38-cm) baking pans with oil, using 2 teaspoons oil per pan. Turn eggplant slices in oil to coat both sides; arrange in a single layer. Bake in a 425°F (220°C) oven until eggplant is browned and soft when pressed (about 25 minutes; remove pieces as they brown).

3. In a 6- to 8-quart (6- to 8-liter) pan, bring about 4 quarts (3.8 liters) water to a boil over medium-high heat; stir in pasta and cook until just barely tender to bite (6 to 8 minutes); or cook pasta according to package directions, cooking slightly less than time recommended. Drain pasta well and mix with provolone cheese, 2 cups (470 ml) of the marinara sauce, and 6 tablespoons (30 g) of the Romano cheese.

4. Butter sides and bottom of a 9-inch (23-cm) cheesecake pan with a removable rim. Dust pan with bread crumbs. Arrange a third of the eggplant slices in pan, overlapping them to cover bottom of pan. Cover with half the pasta mixture. Add a layer of half the remaining eggplant, then evenly top with remaining pasta mixture. Top evenly with remaining eggplant. Press down gently to compact layers and to make timbale level. Sprinkle with remaining 2 tablespoons Romano cheese. (At this point, you may cover and refrigerate until next day.)

5. Bake, uncovered, in a 350°F (175°C) oven until hot in center, about 30 minutes. (If refrigerated, bake, covered, for 30 minutes; then uncover and continue to bake until hot in center, about 30 more minutes.) Let stand for about 5 minutes before serving.

6. Meanwhile, pour remaining marinara sauce into a 1- to 1½-quart (950-ml to 1.4-liter) pan; stir over medium heat until steaming. Transfer to a small pitcher or sauce boat. With a knife, cut around edge of timbale to release; remove pan rim. Garnish timbale with basil sprigs. Cut into wedges; serve with hot marinara sauce. Makes 6 to 8 servings.

Per serving: 503 calories (27% calories from fat), 15 g total fat, 7 g saturated fat, 30 mg cholesterol, 994 mg sodium, 71 g carbohydrates, 6 g fiber, 22 g protein, 416 mg calcium, 5 mg iron

Tortellini with Roasted Eggplant, Garlic & Pepper

Preparation time: About 25 minutes
Cooking time: 20 to 30 minutes

Garlic lovers will enjoy this light and delicious tortellini entrée.

- ½ recipe Roasted Red Bell Peppers (page 269)
  Balsamic Vinegar Dressing (recipe follows)
- 3 large heads garlic (about 8 oz./230 g *total*), cloves peeled
- 2 teaspoons olive oil
- 1 pound (455 g) slender Oriental eggplants, halved lengthwise and cut into thirds
- 1 package (about 9 oz./255 g) fresh cheese tortellini or ravioli
- 2 tablespoons chopped parsley
- 24 to 32 spinach leaves, coarse stems removed, rinsed and crisped
  Salt and pepper

1. Prepare Roasted Red Bell Peppers and Balsamic Vinegar Dressing; set aside.

2. Mix garlic and 1 teaspoon of the oil in a lightly oiled square 8-inch (20-cm) baking pan. Rub eggplant skins with remaining 1 teaspoon oil and arrange, skin sides down, in a lightly oiled 10- by 15-inch (25- by 38-cm) baking pan.

3. Bake garlic and eggplants in a 475°F (245°C) oven, switching pan positions halfway through baking, until garlic is tinged with brown (remove cloves as they brown) and eggplants are richly browned and soft when pressed (20 to 30 minutes); if drippings begin to burn, add 4 to 6 tablespoons (60 to 90 ml) water, stirring to loosen browned bits. Meanwhile, bring 12 cups (2.8 liters) water to a boil in a 5- to 6-quart (5- to 6-liter) pan over medium-high heat. Stir in pasta and cook just until tender to bite (4 to 6 minutes); or cook according to package directions.

4. Drain pasta well and transfer to a large nonmetal bowl. Add bell peppers, garlic, eggplants, parsley, and dressing. Mix thoroughly but gently. Arrange spinach on 4 individual plates. Spoon on pasta mixture. Offer salt and pepper to add to taste. Makes 4 servings.

Balsamic Vinegar Dressing. In a small bowl, combine 2 tablespoons (30 ml) **reduced-sodium soy sauce,** 2 teaspoons **balsamic vinegar,** 1 teaspoon **Oriental sesame oil,** and ½ teaspoon **honey.** Beat until blended.

Per serving: 445 calories (19% calories from fat), 10 g total fat, 3 g saturated fat, 28 mg cholesterol, 844 mg sodium, 75 g carbohydrates, 7 g fiber, 19 g protein, 360 mg calcium, 5 mg iron

Penne, Tofu & Asparagus

Preparation time: About 15 minutes
Marinating time: 15 minutes
Cooking time: About 20 minutes

Tofu marinated in a light and refreshing basil-scented vinaigrette gives this pasta entrée a protein boost.

- ½ cup (120 ml) seasoned rice vinegar; or ½ cup (120 ml) distilled white vinegar and 4 teaspoons sugar
- ¼ cup (20 g) freshly grated Parmesan cheese
- 3 tablespoons finely chopped fresh basil or 1 tablespoon dried basil
- 2 tablespoons (30 ml) olive oil
- 1 tablespoon (15 ml) Dijon mustard
- 1 clove garlic, minced or pressed
- 8 ounces (230 g) regular tofu, rinsed and drained, cut into ½-inch (1-cm) cubes
- 1 pound (455 g) asparagus, tough ends removed, cut diagonally into 1½-inch (3.5-cm) pieces
- 8 ounces/230 g (about 2½ cups) dried penne

1. Combine vinegar, cheese, basil, oil, mustard, and garlic in a large serving bowl. Mix well. Add tofu and stir to coat. Cover and let stand for 15 minutes.

2. Bring 12 cups (2.8 liters) water to a boil in a 5- to 6-quart (5- to 6-liter) pan over medium-high heat. Add asparagus and cook until tender when pierced (about 4 minutes). Lift out with a slotted spoon, add to tofu mixture, and keep warm.

3. Stir pasta into boiling water and cook just until tender to bite (8 to 10 minutes); or cook according to package directions. Drain well. Add pasta to tofu and asparagus. Mix thoroughly but gently. Makes 6 servings.

Per serving: 254 calories (28% calories from fat), 8 g total fat, 2 g saturated fat, 3 mg cholesterol, 524 mg sodium, 35 g carbohydrates, 2 g fiber, 11 g protein, 118 mg calcium, 4 mg iron

Classic pesto sauce is made with fresh basil, but this version is based on bright broccoli flowerets instead. Accented with sesame oil and rice vinegar, the smooth green sauce is delicious over any kind of pasta; we use bow ties here.

1 pound (455 g) broccoli flowerets (about 7 cups)

2 or 3 cloves garlic, minced or pressed

½ cup (40 g) grated Parmesan cheese

3 tablespoons (45 ml) olive oil

1½ teaspoons Oriental sesame oil

½ teaspoon salt

12 ounces (340 g) dried pasta bow ties (farfalle)

1 to 2 tablespoons (15 to 30 ml) seasoned rice vinegar; or 1 to 2 tablespoons (15 to 30 ml) distilled white vinegar plus ½ to 1 teaspoon sugar

1 small tomato (about 4 oz./ 115 g), chopped

Bow Ties with Broccoli Pesto

Preparation time: 15 minutes
Cooking time: About 20 minutes
Pictured on facing page

1. In a 4- to 5-quart (3.8- to 5-liter) pan, bring 8 cups (1.9 liters) water to a boil over medium-high heat. Stir in broccoli and cook until just tender to bite (about 7 minutes). Immediately drain broccoli, immerse in ice water until cool, and drain again. In a food processor or blender, combine a third of the broccoli with garlic, cheese, olive oil, sesame oil, salt, and 3 tablespoons (45 ml) water. Whirl until smooth. Scrape down sides of container, add half the remaining broccoli, and whirl until smooth again. Add remaining broccoli; whirl until smooth. Set aside.

2. In a 5- to 6-quart (5- to 6-liter) pan, bring about 3 quarts (2.8 liters) water to a boil over medium-high heat; stir in pasta and cook until just tender to bite (8 to 10 minutes); or cook pasta according to package directions.

3. Drain pasta well. Transfer to a large serving bowl and stir in vinegar. Add pesto and mix gently but thoroughly. Garnish with tomato and serve immediately. Makes 4 servings.

Per serving: 510 calories (29% calories from fat), 17 g total fat, 4 g saturated fat, 8 mg cholesterol, 604 mg sodium, 73 g carbohydrates, 6 g fiber, 19 g protein, 204 mg calcium, 4 mg iron

---

Here's an interesting presentation for fresh asparagus—and a way to make it go a little farther, too.

6 ounces (170 g) dried vermicelli

1 pound (455 g) asparagus

2 teaspoons salad oil

1 clove garlic, minced or pressed

1 teaspoon minced fresh ginger

½ cup (50 g) diagonally sliced green onions

2 tablespoons (30 ml) reduced-sodium soy sauce

⅛ teaspoon crushed red pepper flakes

Asparagus & Pasta Stir-fry

Preparation time: About 10 minutes
Cooking time: About 15 minutes

1. In a 4- to 5-quart (3.8- to 5-liter) pan, cook pasta in about 8 cups (1.9 liters) boiling water until just tender to bite (8 to 10 minutes); or cook according to package directions.

2. Meanwhile, snap off and discard tough ends of asparagus; then cut asparagus into 1½-inch (3.5-cm) slant-

ing slices and set aside. Heat oil in a wide nonstick frying pan or wok over medium-high heat. When oil is hot, add garlic, ginger, asparagus, and onions. Stir-fry until asparagus is tender-crisp to bite (about 3 minutes). Add soy sauce and red pepper flakes; stir-fry for 1 more minute.

3. Drain pasta well, add to asparagus mixture, and stir-fry until heated through. Makes 4 to 6 servings.

Per serving: 167 calories (13% calories from fat), 3 g total fat, 0.3 g saturated fat, 0 mg cholesterol, 246 mg sodium, 30 g carbohydrates, 2 g fiber, 7 g protein, 32 mg calcium, 2 mg iron

Bow Ties with Broccoli Pesto
(recipe on facing page)

Homemade Egg Pasta

Tender, springy fresh pasta dough is perfect for noodles of all sizes. To alter the flavor and texture, you can use whole wheat or semolina flour for up to half the all-purpose flour.

Remember that the amount of liquid any flour can absorb varies with the flour's natural moisture content and with the air temperature and humidity. In fact, you won't know just how much water you need until you start working with the dough, so add water gradually, always paying close attention to the dough's texture.

Here are two recipes for making egg pasta. In the first, the dough is mixed and kneaded by hand. The second recipe utilizes the food processor, which reduces mixing time to seconds and kneading time from 10 minutes to 2 or 3 minutes. With either recipe, the dough can be rolled and cut by hand or with a pasta machine.

It's best to cook homemade pasta right away, but if you make more than you need, let it stand until dried but still pliable (30 minutes to 1 hour). Then enclose it in a plastic bag; refrigerate for up to 2 days or freeze for up to 2 months. Do not thaw the pasta before you cook it.

Egg Pasta

About 2 cups (250 g) all-purpose flour

2 large eggs

3 to 6 tablespoons (45 to 90 ml) water

....

1. Mound 2 cups (250 g) of the flour on a work surface or in a large bowl and make a deep well in center. Break eggs into well. With a fork, beat eggs lightly; stir in 2 tablespoons of the water. Using a circular motion, draw in flour from sides of well. Add 1 tablespoon (15 ml) more water and continue to mix until flour is evenly moistened. If necessary, add more water, 1 tablespoon (15 ml) at a time. When dough becomes too stiff to stir easily, use your hands to finish mixing.

2. Pat dough into a ball and knead a few times to help flour absorb liquid. To knead, flatten dough ball slightly and fold farthest edge toward you. With heel of your hand, push dough away from you, sealing fold. Rotate dough a quarter turn and continue folding-pushing motion, making a turn each time.

3. Clean and lightly flour work surface.

If you plan to use a rolling pin, knead dough until smooth and elastic (about 10 minutes), adding flour if needed to prevent sticking. Cover and let rest for 20 minutes.

If you plan to use a pasta machine (manual or electric), knead dough until no longer sticky (3 to 4 minutes), adding flour if needed to prevent sticking.

4. Use a rolling pin or pasta machine to roll out and cut dough as directed on facing page. Makes 14 to 16 ounces (400 to 455 g) uncooked pasta (machine-rolled dough makes about 32 pieces lasagne or about 4 cups/640 g cooked medium-wide noodles; yield of hand-rolled pasta varies).

....

Per ounce: 71 calories (11% calories from fat), 0.8 g total fat, 0 g saturated fat, 28 mg cholesterol, 9 mg sodium, 13 g carbohydrates, 0.5 g fiber, 3 g protein, 6 mg calcium, 1 mg iron

Food-Processor Pasta

About 2 cups (250 g) all-purpose flour

2 large eggs

About ¼ cup (60 ml) water

....

1. Combine 2 cups (250 g) of the flour and eggs in a food processor; whirl until mixture resembles cornmeal (about 5 seconds). With motor running, pour ¼ cup (60 ml) of the water through feed tube and whirl until dough forms a ball. Dough should be well blended but not sticky. If dough feels sticky, add a little flour and whirl to blend; if it looks crumbly, add 1 or 2 teaspoons more water. If processor begins to slow down or stop (an indication that dough is properly mixed), turn off motor and proceed to next step.

2. Turn dough out onto a floured board and knead a few times just until smooth.

If you plan to use a rolling pin, cover and let rest for 20 minutes.

If you plan to use a pasta machine (manual or electric), roll out at once.

3. Use a rolling pin or pasta machine to roll out and cut dough (see below). Makes 14 to 16 ounces (400 to 455 g) uncooked pasta (machine-rolled dough makes about 32 pieces lasagne or about 4 cups/640 g cooked medium-wide noodles; yield of hand-rolled pasta varies).

Per ounce: 71 calories (11% calories from fat), 0.8 g total fat, 0 g saturated fat, 28 mg cholesterol, 9 mg sodium, 13 g carbohydrates, 0.5 g fiber, 3 g protein, 6 mg calcium, 1 mg iron

....

Pasta by Hand. Here's how to roll out pasta with a rolling pin and cut pasta by hand.

Rolling. Keeping unrolled portions of dough covered, use a rolling pin to roll a fourth of the dough into a rectangle about 1/16 inch (1.5 mm) thick (if dough is sticky, turn and flour both sides as you roll). Transfer rolled strip to a lightly floured board or cloth. Let dry, uncovered, until dough feels leathery but still pliable (5 to 10 minutes); then cover airtight with plastic wrap. Meanwhile, roll out remaining portions.

Cutting. Sprinkle one of the strips of rolled dough with flour. Starting at narrow end, roll up jelly-roll fashion and cut crosswise into slices of desired width (tagliarini is about 1/8 inch/3 mm wide, fettuccine about 1/4 inch/6 mm wide, lasagne about 2 inches/5 cm wide). Repeat to cut remaining portions.

Pasta by Machine. These directions apply to both manual and electric pasta machines. But because machines differ slightly in size and function, you'll also want to consult the manufacturer's directions.

Kneading and rolling. Keeping unrolled dough covered, flatten a fourth of the dough slightly; flour dough and feed through widest roller setting. Fold dough into thirds and feed through rollers again. Repeat folding and rolling process 8 to 10 more times or until dough is smooth and pliable. If it feels damp or sticky, flour both sides each time dough is rolled.

Set rollers one notch closer together and feed dough through. Flour dough if it is damp or sticky. Continue to roll, setting rollers closer each time, until dough is a long strip of desired thinness. Cut strip in half crosswise for easy handling; place pieces on a lightly floured board or cloth. Let dry, uncovered, until dough feels leathery but still pliable (5 to 10 minutes); then cover airtight with plastic wrap. Meanwhile, roll out remaining portions.

Cutting. Feed each strip through medium-wide blades for fettuccine or through narrow blades for thin noodles or tagliarini. Some machines have attachments for wide and narrow lasagne; if yours doesn't, cut by hand.

Lightly flour cut pasta to keep strands separate. Toss in a loose pile or gather strands and lay in rows.

....

Cooking Homemade Pasta. These homemade pastas cook quickly; the time depends on the thinness of the pasta. Cook in a generous quantity of boiling water just until tender to bite (1 to 3 minutes).

Capellini with Cilantro Pesto & White Beans
(recipe on facing page)

Because the pesto is based on water rather than oil, it may weep a bit on standing—so be sure to stir it well before using it.

Cilantro Pesto (recipe follows)

8 ounces (230 g) dried capellini

2 tablespoons (30 ml) seasoned rice vinegar; or 2 tablespoons (30 ml) distilled white vinegar plus ¾ teaspoon sugar

1 medium-size red onion, cut into thin slivers

1 tablespoon (15 ml) balsamic vinegar

1 can (about 15 oz./430 g) cannellini (white kidney beans), drained and rinsed

7 medium-size firm-ripe pear-shaped (Roma-type) tomatoes (about 1 lb./455 g *total*), chopped

1½ teaspoons chopped fresh thyme or ½ teaspoon dried thyme

Thyme and cilantro sprigs

Pepper

1. Prepare Cilantro Pesto and set aside.

Capellini with Cilantro Pesto & White Beans

Preparation time: About 20 minutes
Cooking time: About 15 minutes
Pictured on facing page

2. In a 4- to 5-quart (3.8- to 5-liter) pan, cook capellini in 8 cups (1.9 liters) boiling water until just tender to bite (about 3 minutes); or cook according to package directions. Drain well, rinse with hot water, and drain well again. Quickly return pasta to pan; add rice vinegar and lift with 2 forks to mix. Keep warm.

3. While pasta is cooking, combine onion and ⅓ cup (80 ml) water in a wide nonstick frying pan or wok. Cover and cook over medium-high heat until onion is almost soft (about 3 minutes). Uncover, add balsamic vinegar, and stir-fry until liquid has evaporated. Add beans, tomatoes, and chopped thyme to pan; stir-fry gently until beans are heated through and tomatoes are soft (about 3 minutes). Remove pan from heat.

4. Stir Cilantro Pesto well; spread evenly on 4 individual plates. Top with pasta, then with bean mixture. Garnish with thyme and cilantro sprigs; serve immediately. Season to taste with pepper. Makes 4 servings.

Cilantro Pesto. In a blender or food processor, combine 3 cups (120 g) firmly packed **cilantro leaves**, 1 cup (about 3 oz./85 g) grated **Parmesan cheese**, ½ cup (120 ml) **water**, 1 tablespoon grated **lemon peel**, 1 tablespoon (15 ml) **Oriental sesame oil**, 3 cloves **garlic** (peeled), and 2 teaspoons **honey**. Whirl until smoothly puréed. If pesto is too thick, add a little more water. If made ahead, cover and refrigerate for up to 3 hours; bring to room temperature before using.

Per serving: 473 calories (21% calories from fat), 11 g total fat, 4 g saturated fat, 16 mg cholesterol, 786 mg sodium, 73 g carbohydrates, 9 g fiber, 20 g protein, 340 mg calcium, 4 mg iron

---

Simmered in herb-seasoned broth, nutritious lentils make a great topping for linguine.

1 cup (190 g) lentils

2 cups (470 ml) canned vegetable broth

1 teaspoon dried thyme

⅓ cup (80 ml) lemon juice

3 tablespoons chopped fresh basil

2 tablespoons (30 ml) olive oil

1 teaspoon honey (or to taste)

2 cloves garlic, minced

12 ounces (340 g) dried linguine

1 large tomato (about 8 oz./230 g), chopped and drained

¾ cup (60 g) grated Parmesan cheese

Linguine with Lentils

Preparation time: 20 minutes
Cooking time: About 35 minutes

1. Rinse and sort lentils, discarding any debris; drain lentils. In a 1½- to 2-quart (1.4- to 1.9-liter) pan, bring broth to a boil over high heat; add lentils and thyme. Reduce heat, cover, and simmer just until lentils are tender to bite (25 to 30 minutes). Drain and discard any remaining cooking liquid; keep lentils warm.

2. While lentils are cooking, combine lemon juice, chopped basil, oil, honey, and garlic in a small bowl; set aside. Also bring about 3 quarts (2.8 liters) water to a boil in a 5- to 6-quart (5- to 6-liter) pan over medium-high heat; stir in pasta and cook until just tender to bite, 8 to 10 minutes. (Or cook pasta according to package directions.)

3. Working quickly, drain pasta well and transfer to a large serving bowl. Add basil mixture, lentils, and tomato. Lift with 2 forks to mix. Sprinkle with cheese and serve immediately. Makes 6 servings.

Per serving: 426 calories (19% calories from fat), 9 g total fat, 3 g saturated fat, 8 mg cholesterol, 531 mg sodium, 66 g carbohydrates, 5 g fiber, 21 g protein, 185 mg calcium, 6 mg iron

Refreshing oranges lend flavor and color to this combination of tender lentils and fanciful pasta shapes. To complete the presentation, serve the dish atop a bed of butter lettuce leaves and orange slices.

- 4 or 5 large oranges (2 to 2½ lbs./905 g to 1.15 kg *total*)
- 8 large butter lettuce leaves, rinsed and crisped
- 1 tablespoon grated orange peel
- ¾ cup (180 ml) fresh orange juice
- 3 tablespoons chopped fresh basil or 1 tablespoon dried basil
- 3 tablespoons (45 ml) white wine vinegar
- 1 tablespoon (15 ml) *each* honey and Dijon mustard
- 2 to 3 cloves garlic, minced or pressed
- 1½ teaspoons ground cumin
- ⅛ teaspoon crushed red pepper flakes (or to taste)
- 2 cups (470 ml) vegetable broth
- ¾ cup (150 g) lentils

Pasta with Lentils & Oranges

Preparation time: 20 minutes
Cooking time: About 30 minutes

- 12 ounces (340 g) dried radiatorre or fusilli
- Basil sprigs

1. Cut peel and all white membrane from oranges. Coarsely chop one of the oranges and set aside. Thinly slice remaining 3 or 4 oranges crosswise. Arrange lettuce leaves in a wide, shallow bowl or on a rimmed platter. Top with orange slices; cover and set aside.

2. In a small bowl, stir together chopped orange, orange peel, orange juice, 2 tablespoons of the chopped basil (or 2 teaspoons of the dried basil), vinegar, honey, mustard, garlic, cumin, and red pepper flakes. Beat until blended; set aside.

3. In a 1½- to 2-quart (1.4- to 1.9-liter) pan, bring broth to a boil over medium-high heat. Sort through lentils, discarding any debris; rinse, drain, and add to pan along with remaining 1 tablespoon chopped basil (or 1 teaspoon dried basil). Reduce heat, cover, and simmer until lentils are tender to bite (about 25 minutes).

4. Meanwhile, in a 5- to 6-quart (5- to 6-liter) pan, bring about 3 quarts (2.8 liters) water to a boil over medium-high heat; stir in pasta and cook until just until tender to bite (8 to 10 minutes); or cook pasta according to package directions.

5. Drain pasta well; if necessary, drain lentils well. Transfer pasta and lentils to a large bowl. Add orange dressing and mix gently but thoroughly. Spoon pasta over orange slices. Garnish with basil sprigs. Makes 4 servings.

Per serving: 563 calories (4% calories from fat), 3 g total fat, 0.3 g saturated fat, 0 mg cholesterol, 601 mg sodium, 115 g carbohydrates, 10 g fiber, 21 g protein, 145 mg calcium, 7 mg iron

---

Because it isn't layered like the traditional dish, this lasagne goes together quickly.

- 12 ounces (340 g) dried lasagne
- 2½ cups (590 ml) low-fat (2%) milk
- ¼ cup (32 g) cornstarch
- 1½ teaspoons dried basil
- ½ teaspoon *each* dried rosemary and salt
- ¼ teaspoon ground nutmeg
- 1 cup (about 8 oz./230 g) nonfat ricotta cheese
- 2 packages (about 10 oz./285 g *each*) frozen chopped Swiss chard, thawed and squeezed dry
- 2 large ripe tomatoes (about 1 lb./ 455 g *total*), chopped

Three-cheese Lasagne with Chard

Preparation time: 20 minutes
Cooking time: About 1 hour

- 2 cups (about 8 oz./230 g) shredded mozzarella cheese
- ⅓ cup (30 g) grated Parmesan cheese

1. In a 5- to 6-quart (5- to 6-liter) pan, bring about 3 quarts (2.8 liters) water to a boil over medium-high heat; stir in pasta and cook until just barely tender to bite, about 8 minutes. Drain pasta well and lay out flat; cover lightly.

2. In pasta-cooking pan, smoothly blend milk, cornstarch, basil, rosemary, salt, and nutmeg. Stir over medium-high heat until mixture boils and thickens slightly (about 5 minutes). Stir in ricotta cheese, chard, tomatoes, and half the mozzarella cheese. Gently stir in pasta.

3. Transfer mixture to a 9- by 13-inch (23- by 33-cm) baking pan; gently push pasta down to cover it with sauce. Sprinkle with remaining mozzarella cheese, then with Parmesan cheese. Bake in a 375°F (190°C) oven until lasagne is bubbly in center (about 40 minutes). Let stand for about 5 minutes before serving. Makes 8 servings.

Per serving: 362 calories (24% calories from fat), 10 g total fat, 5 g saturated fat, 33 mg cholesterol, 531 mg sodium, 48 g carbohydrates, 3 g fiber, 22 g protein, 499 mg calcium, 3 mg iron

Tangy goat cheese transforms a savory pasta-lentil mixture into a sprightly main-course offering.

....

- 2 cups (470 ml) vegetable broth
- 6 ounces/170 g (about 1 cup) lentils, rinsed and drained
- 1 tablespoon chopped fresh thyme or 1 teaspoon dried thyme
- 8 ounces/230 g (about 2⅓ cups) dried orecchiette or other medium-size pasta shape
- ⅓ cup (80 ml) white wine vinegar
- 3 tablespoons chopped parsley
- 2 tablespoons (30 ml) olive oil
- 1 teaspoon honey (or to taste)
- 1 clove garlic, minced or pressed
- ½ cup (65 g) crumbled goat or feta cheese

Orecchiette with Lentils & Goat Cheese

....

Preparation time: About 10 minutes
Cooking time: About 35 minutes

Thyme sprigs
Salt and pepper

....

1. Bring broth to a boil in a 1½- to 2-quart (1.4- to 1.9-liter) pan over high heat. Add lentils and chopped thyme; reduce heat, cover, and simmer until lentils are tender to bite (20 to 30 minutes). Meanwhile, bring about 8 cups

(1.9 liters) water to a boil in a 4- to 5-quart (3.8- to 5-liter) pan over medium-high heat. Stir in pasta and cook just until tender to bite (8 to 10 minutes); or cook according to package directions. Drain pasta and, if necessary, lentils well. Transfer pasta and lentils to a large serving bowl; keep warm.

2. Combine vinegar, parsley, oil, honey, and garlic in a small bowl. Beat until blended. Add to pasta mixture and mix thoroughly but gently. Sprinkle with cheese. Garnish with thyme sprigs. Offer salt and pepper to add to taste. Makes 4 servings.

....

Per serving: 515 calories (24% calories from fat), 14 g total fat, 5 g saturated fat, 13 mg cholesterol, 648 mg sodium, 75 g carbohydrates, 7 g fiber, 25 g protein, 91 mg calcium, 7 mg iron

---

Asian-style peanut sauce is great with all sorts of foods, from pork and beef to chicken and noodles. Here, it's tossed with chunky pasta tubes and marinated tofu.

....

- ¼ cup (60 ml) seasoned rice vinegar; or ¼ cup (60 ml) distilled white vinegar plus 2 teaspoons sugar
- 3 tablespoons (45 ml) Oriental sesame oil
- 1 tablespoon (15 ml) reduced-sodium soy sauce
- 1 teaspoon sugar
- 1 package (about 14 oz./400 g) regular tofu, rinsed, drained, and cut into ½-inch (1-cm) cubes
- 12 ounces (340 g) dried penne
- 2 cups (170 g) Chinese pea pods (also called snow or sugar peas), ends and strings removed
- 2 cloves garlic, minced
- ½ cup (120 ml) plum jam
- ¼ cup (60 ml) crunchy peanut butter

Peanut Pasta & Tofu

....

Preparation time: 20 minutes
Cooking time: About 20 minutes

⅛ teaspoon ground ginger
⅓ cup (15 g) cilantro leaves
¼ cup (25 g) sliced green onions
Cilantro sprigs
Crushed red pepper flakes

....

1. In a shallow bowl, beat vinegar, 1 tablespoon (15 ml) of the oil, soy sauce, and sugar until blended. Add tofu and mix gently. Set aside; stir occasionally.

2. In a 5- to 6-quart (5- to 6-liter) pan, bring about 3 quarts (2.8 liters) water to a boil over medium-high heat; stir in pasta and cook until almost tender to bite (7 to 9 minutes); or cook according to package directions, cooking for a little less than the recommended time.

Add pea pods to boiling water with pasta and cook for 1 more minute. Drain pasta mixture, rinse with hot water, and drain well again; keep warm.

3. With a slotted spoon, transfer tofu to a large, shallow serving bowl; reserve marinade from tofu.

4. In pan used to cook pasta, heat remaining 2 tablespoons (30 ml) oil over medium heat. Add garlic and cook, stirring, just until fragrant (about 30 seconds; do not scorch). Add jam, peanut butter, marinade from tofu, and ginger. Cook, whisking, just until sauce is smooth and well blended. Remove pan from heat and add pasta mixture, cilantro leaves, and onions. Mix gently but thoroughly. Transfer pasta to bowl with tofu and mix very gently. Garnish with cilantro sprigs. Serve at once; season to taste with red pepper flakes. Makes 4 servings.

....

Per serving: 714 calories (30% calories from fat), 25 g total fat, 4 g saturated fat, 0 mg cholesterol, 558 mg sodium, 103 g carbohydrates, 6 g fiber, 25 g protein, 162 mg calcium, 10 mg iron

As the vegetables for this pasta dish brown slowly in the oven, they caramelize, giving a rich, sweet flavor.

....

1 **medium-size red onion, cut into ¾-inch (2-cm) chunks**

1 **tablespoon (15 ml) olive oil**

6 **tablespoons (90 ml) balsamic vinegar**

14 **medium-size pear-shaped (Roma-type) tomatoes (about 1¾ lbs./795 g total), halved lengthwise**

Salt

8 **ounces (230 g) dried capellini**

2 **cans (about 15 oz./425 g *each*) cannellini (white kidney beans)**

3 **tablespoons chopped fresh thyme or 1 tablespoon dried thyme**

3 **tablespoons chopped fresh basil or 1 tablespoon dried basil**

Thyme sprigs

Capellini with Roasted Tomatoes & White Beans

....

Preparation time: About 15 minutes
Cooking time: About 1¼ hours
Pictured on facing page

1. Mix onion, 1 teaspoon of the oil, and 2 tablespoons (30 ml) of the vinegar in a lightly oiled square 8-inch (20-cm) baking pan. Arrange tomatoes, cut sides up, in a lightly oiled 9- by 13-inch (23- by 33-cm) baking pan; rub with remaining 2 teaspoons oil and season to taste with salt.

2. Bake onion and tomatoes in a 475°F (245°C) oven, switching pan positions halfway through baking, until edges are well browned (40 to 50 minutes for onion, about 1 hour and 10 minutes for tomatoes); if drippings begin to burn, add 4 to 6 tablespoons (60 to 90 ml) water to each pan, stirring to

loosen browned bits. Meanwhile, bring 8 cups (1.9 liters) water to a boil in a 4- to 5-quart (3.8- to 5-liter) pan over medium-high heat. Stir in pasta and cook just until tender to bite (about 4 minutes); or cook according to package directions.

3. Drain pasta well and keep warm. Pour beans and their liquid into pan. Add chopped thyme (or dried thyme and dried basil, if used). Bring to a boil; reduce heat and simmer, stirring often, for 3 minutes. Add pasta; lift with 2 forks to mix. Remove from heat; keep warm.

4. Chop 10 of the tomato halves. Add to pasta with chopped basil (if used), onion, and remaining ¼ cup (60 ml) vinegar. Transfer pasta to a wide, shallow serving bowl. Arrange remaining tomato halves around edge. Garnish with thyme sprigs. Makes 4 to 6 servings.

....

Per serving: 401 calories (12% calories from fat), 6 g total fat, 0.8 g saturated fat, 0 mg cholesterol, 616 mg sodium, 73 g carbohydrates, 15 g fiber, 17 g protein, 111 mg calcium, 6 mg iron

Capellini with Roasted Tomatoes & White Beans
(recipe on facing page)

Because this slimmed-down lasagne is not layered like traditional lasagne, it goes together quickly.

....

Low-fat Italian Sausage (page 24)

3 large onions (about 1½ lbs./ 680 g *total*), chopped

2 large stalks celery (about 8 oz./230 g *total*), chopped

2 medium-size carrots (about 6 oz./170 g *total*), chopped

5 cups (1.2 liters) beef broth

1 can (about 6 oz./170 g) tomato paste

1½ teaspoons dried basil

½ teaspoon dried rosemary

¼ teaspoon ground nutmeg

12 ounces (340 g) dried lasagne

3 tablespoons cornstarch

1½ cups (360 ml) nonfat milk

2 cups (about 8 oz./230 g) shredded fontina cheese

½ cup (40 g) freshly grated Parmesan cheese

....

1. Prepare Low-fat Italian Sausage; refrigerate, covered.

2. Combine onions, celery, carrots, and 1½ cups (360 ml) of the broth in a 5- to 6-quart (5- to 6-liter) pan (preferably nonstick). Bring to a boil over high heat and cook, stirring occasionally, until liquid has evaporated and vegetables begin to brown (12 to 15 minutes).

Italian Sausage Lasagne

....

Preparation time: About 25 minutes
Cooking time: About 2 hours

To deglaze pan, add ¼ cup (60 ml) water, stirring to loosen browned bits. Continue to cook, stirring often, until mixture begins to brown again. Repeat deglazing step, adding ¼ cup (60 ml) more water each time, until mixture is richly browned.

3. Crumble sausage into pan; add ½ cup (120 ml) more water. Cook, stirring occasionally, until liquid has evaporated and meat begins to brown (about 10 minutes). Add ⅓ cup (80 ml) more water and cook, stirring, until meat is browned (2 to 4 more minutes). Reduce heat to medium-low and add 2½ cups (590 ml) more broth, stirring to loosen browned bits. Add tomato paste, basil, rosemary, and nutmeg. Bring to a boil; reduce heat, cover, and simmer, stirring occasionally, until flavors have blended (about 20 minutes). Meanwhile, bring 12 cups (2.8 liters) water to a boil in a 5- to 6-quart (5- to 6-liter) pan over medium-high heat. Stir in pasta and cook just until barely tender to bite (about 8 minutes). Drain well and keep warm.

4. Blend remaining 1 cup (240 ml) broth with cornstarch and milk until smooth. Add to meat mixture. Cook over medium-high heat, stirring, until bubbling and thickened. Stir in 1 cup (115 g) of the fontina; remove from heat. Gently stir in pasta. Transfer to a shallow 3-quart (2.8-liter) baking dish; swirl pasta. Sprinkle with Parmesan and remaining 1 cup (115 g) fontina. (At this point, you may cool, cover, and refrigerate for up to a day.)

5. Bake in a 375°F (190°C) oven until bubbling (about 30 minutes; 35 to 40 minutes if chilled). Makes 8 servings.

....

Per serving: 480 calories (27% calories from fat), 14 g total fat, 7 g saturated fat, 76 mg cholesterol, 1,625 mg sodium, 53 g carbohydrates, 4 g fiber, 32 g protein, 376 mg calcium, 4 mg iron

When you don't have the time to make your own homemade pasta, purchased egg roll (spring roll), potsticker (gyoza), and won ton wrappers can help you turn out pasta specialties that are still impressive and delicious. In general, the purchased wrappers are thinner than freshly made pasta, so be sure to handle them gently when working with them.

Because these Asian wrappers are generous in size, they hold more filling than their classic counterparts, making rather large versions of each pasta specialty. To cut the skins into rounds for tortellini, use a 3- to 3¼-inch (8- to 8.25-cm) cookie cutter.

Look for the wrappers in the produce or refrigerated dairy section of your supermarket or in an Asian market.

....

    Chicken-Prosciutto Filling
    (recipe follows)
6   **dozen (12 to 14 oz./340 to 400 g)**
    potsticker (gyoza) or won ton
    skins, cut into 3- to 3¼-inch
    (8- to 8.25-cm) rounds
1   **large egg white**
    Lean Cream Sauce
    (recipe follows)
½   **cup (40 g) freshly grated**
    Parmesan cheese

....

1. Prepare Chicken-Prosciutto Filling. Lay a wrapper flat, keeping remaining wrappers covered, and place about 1 teaspoon of the filling in center. Moisten edges with egg white, fold over filling, and press to seal. Bring pointed ends together, overlapping; moisten ends with egg white and press to seal. Lay on a lightly floured large baking sheet and cover with

Chicken Tortellini with Cream Sauce

....

Preparation time: About 1 hour
Cooking time: About 1¼ hours

plastic wrap. Repeat to use all filling, arranging pasta in a single layer; use 2 baking sheets, if necessary. (At this point, you may refrigerate for up to 4 hours.)

2. Prepare Lean Cream Sauce.

3. Bring 12 cups (2.8 liters) water to a boil in each of two 5- to 6-quart (5- to 6-liter) pans over medium-high heat. Reduce heat to a gentle boil. Carefully lower half the pasta into each pan and cook just until tender to bite (4 to 5 minutes); if tortellini stick to each other or to pan bottom, stir gently to loosen. Drain well.

4. Pour a third of the sauce into a large serving bowl. Add pasta and top with remaining sauce. Sprinkle with cheese. Makes 6 to 8 servings.

....

Chicken-Prosciutto Filling. Finely chop 4 ounces (115 g) thinly sliced **prosciutto**. Bone and skin a 1-pound (455-g) **chicken breast**; cut meat into ½-inch (1-cm) pieces. Set aside.

Combine 1 extra-large **onion** (about 10 oz./285 g), chopped, and 1 cup (240 ml) **low-sodium chicken broth** in a wide nonstick frying pan. Bring to a boil over high heat and cook, stirring occasionally, until liquid has evaporated and onion begins to brown (about 12 minutes). To deglaze pan, add ⅓ cup (80 ml) **water,** stirring to loosen browned bits. Continue to cook, stirring often, until liquid has evaporated

and onion begins to brown again. Repeat deglazing step, adding ⅓ cup (80 ml) more water each time, until onion is richly browned.

Add chicken and prosciutto. Cook, stirring often, until chicken is no longer pink in center; cut to test (about 3 minutes).

Whirl mixture in a food processor until coarsely ground; or finely chop. Mix with 1 large **egg white,** ¼ cup (20 g) freshly grated **Parmesan cheese,** 2 tablespoons **all-purpose flour,** 2 tablespoons (30 ml) **low-sodium chicken broth,** and ¼ teaspoon **ground nutmeg.** Season to taste with **salt** and **pepper.**

....

Lean Cream Sauce. Combine 1 extra-large **onion** (about 10 oz./285 g), finely chopped, and 1 cup (240 ml) **low-sodium chicken broth** in a wide nonstick frying pan. Bring to a boil over high heat and cook, stirring occasionally, until liquid has evaporated and onion begins to brown (about 12 minutes). To deglaze pan, add ⅓ cup (80 ml) **water,** stirring to loosen browned bits. Continue to cook, stirring often, until liquid has evaporated and onion begins to brown again. Repeat deglazing step, adding ⅓ cup (80 ml) more water each time, until onion is richly browned.

Add 1 tablespoon **cornstarch,** ¼ teaspoon **ground nutmeg,** 2 cups (470 ml) **low-fat milk,** and ½ cup (120 ml) more **low-sodium chicken broth.** Bring just to a boil, stirring. Remove from heat and keep warm.

....

Per serving: 344 calories (19% calories from fat), 7 g total fat, 3 g saturated fat, 51 mg cholesterol, 844 mg sodium, 43 g carbohydrates, 2 g fiber, 27 g protein, 234 mg calcium, 3 mg iron

Roasted Artichokes with Vinaigrette
(recipe on page 296)

Side Dishes

Add color and excitement to the simplest low-fat fare with cleverly seasoned vegetables, savory beans, and subtly flavored rice and grain dishes. Delicious side dishes not only enhance the main entrée but provide essential nutrients and fiber. Entice meat and potato fans with our bold, creamy Risotto with Mushrooms laced with sherry and Gorgonzola cheese or enjoy the mellow, complex flavors of Cocoa-glazed Carrots & Onions.

A zesty vinaigrette dresses up these tender whole artichokes.

- 4 **large artichokes** (*each 4 to 4½ inches/10 to 11 cm in diameter*)
- 2 **cups (470 ml) fat-free reduced-sodium chicken broth**
- 1 **teaspoon** *each* **dried rosemary, dried oregano, dried thyme, and mustard seeds**
- ¼ **cup (60 ml) balsamic vinegar**
- 1 **pound (455 g) pear-shaped (Roma-type) tomatoes, seeded and chopped**
- ⅓ **cup (35 g) sliced green onions**
- 2 **tablespoons chopped Italian or regular parsley**

1. Break small, coarse outer leaves from artichokes. With a sharp knife, cut off thorny tops; with scissors, snip any remaining thorny tips from leaves. With knife, peel stems and trim bases. Immerse artichokes in water and swish up and down to rinse well; lift

Roasted Artichokes with Vinaigrette

Preparation time: 30 minutes
Cooking time: About 1¼ hours
Chilling time: At least 2 hours
Pictured on page 294

out and, holding by stem end, shake to remove water.

2. Place artichokes in a 9- by 13-inch (23- by 33-cm) baking pan. Mix broth, 1 cup (240 ml) water, rosemary, oregano, thyme, and mustard seeds; pour into pan. Cover very tightly with foil and bake in a 450°F (230°C) oven until artichoke bottoms are tender when pierced (about 50 minutes). Uncover and continue to bake until artichokes are just tinged with brown (about 8 more minutes).

3. With a slotted spoon, lift artichokes from pan. Hold briefly above pan to drain; transfer to a rimmed dish. Reserve juices in pan. When artichokes are cool enough to touch, ease center of each open; using a spoon, scoop out a few of the tiny center leaves and the choke.

4. Boil pan juices over high heat until reduced to ½ cup (120 ml), about 10 minutes. Remove from heat, stir in vinegar, and pour over artichokes. Cover; refrigerate for at least 2 hours or until next day, spooning marinade over artichokes occasionally.

5. With a slotted spoon, transfer artichokes to individual plates. Stir tomatoes, onions, and parsley into artichoke marinade; spoon mixture around artichokes and into their centers. Makes 4 servings.

Per serving: 96 calories (7% calories from fat), 0.9 g total fat, 0.1 g saturated fat, 0 mg cholesterol, 441 mg sodium, 19 g carbohydrates, 8 g fiber, 7 g protein, 85 mg calcium, 3 mg iron

---

To add interest to familiar vegetables, try using unexpected seasonings. Here, we've spiced up slivered carrots and zucchini with chili powder and aromatic cumin and mustard seeds.

- 1 **small onion, thinly sliced**
- 2 **teaspoons chili powder**
- 1 **teaspoon** *each* **cumin seeds and mustard seeds**
- 1 **large carrot (about 6 oz./170 g), cut into matchstick strips**
- 1¼ **pounds (565 g) zucchini, cut into matchstick strips**
  Salt and pepper

Zucchini & Carrot Sauté

Preparation time: About 10 minutes
Cooking time: About 10 minutes

1. In a wide nonstick frying pan or wok, combine onion and 3 tablespoons (45 ml) water. Stir-fry over medium-high heat until onion is soft (about 5 minutes). Stir in chili powder, cumin seeds, and mustard seeds.

2. Add carrot and zucchini to pan; stir-fry until carrot is tender-crisp to bite (about 5 minutes). Season to taste with salt and pepper. Makes 6 servings.

Per serving: 39 calories (12% calories from fat), 0.6 g total fat, 0 g saturated fat, 0 mg cholesterol, 22 mg sodium, 8 g carbohydrates, 2 g fiber, 2 g protein, 34 mg calcium, 1 mg iron

Fresh dill brings a pleasant, mildly tart flavor to this attractive side dish. Garnishes of feta cheese and capers add that all-important zing—without a lot of fat.

- ½ cup (50 g) thinly sliced green onions
- 1 clove garlic, minced or pressed
- 1½ teaspoons chopped fresh dill or ½ teaspoon dried dill weed
- 2 medium-size firm-ripe pear-shaped (Roma-type) tomatoes (about 6 oz./170 g *total*), chopped
- 1¼ pounds (565 g) spinach, stems removed, leaves rinsed and drained
- 3 to 4 tablespoons (25 to 35 g) crumbled feta cheese
- 1 tablespoon drained capers, or to taste

  Pepper

Mediterranean Spinach

....

Preparation time: About 15 minutes
Cooking time: About 10 minutes

1. In a wide nonstick frying pan or wok, combine onions, garlic, dill, and ¼ cup (60 ml) water. Stir-fry over medium-high heat until onions are soft and almost all liquid has evaporat-

ed (about 3 minutes). Transfer mixture to a bowl and stir in tomatoes. Keep warm.

2. Add half the spinach and 1 tablespoon (15 ml) water to pan; stir-fry over medium heat until spinach is just beginning to wilt. Then add remaining spinach; stir-fry just until all spinach is wilted (about 2 more minutes).

3. With a slotted spoon, transfer spinach to a rimmed platter and spread out slightly; discard liquid from pan. Top spinach with tomato mixture, then sprinkle with cheese and capers. Season to taste with pepper. Makes 4 to 6 servings.

....

Per serving: 44 calories (29% calories from fat), 2 g total fat, 0.9 g saturated fat, 5 mg cholesterol, 179 mg sodium, 5 g carbohydrates, 3 g fiber, 4 g protein, 122 mg calcium, 3 mg iron

---

Crisp pine nuts top this colorful combination of chard, red bell pepper, and currants.

- 1½ pounds (680 g) Swiss chard
- 1 tablespoon pine nuts
- 1 teaspoon olive oil
- 2 cloves garlic, minced or pressed
- 1 large red bell pepper (about 8 oz./230 g), seeded and cut into slivers about 2 inches (5 cm) long
- ⅓ cup (50 g) dried currants

....

1. Cut off and discard coarse stem ends of chard. Rinse and drain chard.

Sautéed Chard with Pine Nuts

....

Preparation time: 15 minutes
Cooking time: About 10 minutes

Then thinly slice stems crosswise up to base of leaves; set sliced stems aside. Use a few whole leaves to line a large rimmed serving dish; coarsely chop remaining leaves. Set aside serving dish and all chard.

2. Toast pine nuts in a wide nonstick frying pan over medium heat until golden (about 3 minutes), stirring

often. Pour out of pan and set aside. Heat oil in pan over medium-high heat. Add garlic, chard stems, and 1 tablespoon (15 ml) water; cook, stirring, until stems are softened (about 2 minutes). Stir in chopped leaves, bell pepper, and currants. Cover and cook until leaves are wilted (about 5 minutes), stirring occasionally.

3. With a slotted spoon, lift chard mixture from pan and arrange in serving dish. Sprinkle with pine nuts. Makes 4 servings.

....

Per serving: 105 calories (20% calories from fat), 3 g total fat, 0.3 g saturated fat, 0 mg cholesterol, 336 mg sodium, 20 g carbohydrates, 2 g fiber, 4 g protein, 99 mg calcium, 4 mg iron

For a colorful side dish, present this quintet of richly browned roasted vegetables.

- 1 large beet (about 8 oz./230 g), peeled
- 2 small red thin-skinned potatoes (about 8 oz./230 g *total*)
- 1 medium-size sweet potato or yam (about 8 oz./230 g), peeled
- 2 large carrots (about 8 oz./230 g *total*)
- 1 small red onion (about 8 oz./230 g)
- 5 teaspoons (25 ml) olive oil
- 2 tablespoons *each* chopped fresh oregano and chopped fresh basil; or 2 teaspoons *each* dried oregano and dried basil
- 1 or 2 cloves garlic, minced or pressed

Roasted Vegetable Medley

Preparation time: 30 minutes
Cooking time: About 45 minutes
Pictured on facing page

- ¼ cup (20 g) grated Parmesan cheese
- Oregano and basil sprigs
- Salt

1. Cut beet, unpeeled thin-skinned potatoes, and sweet potato into ¾-inch (2-cm) chunks. Cut carrots diagonally into ½-inch (1-cm) pieces; cut onion into ¾-inch (2-cm) wedges. Combine all vegetables in a shallow 10- by 15-inch (25- by 38-cm) baking pan; drizzle with oil and toss to coat vegetables evenly with oil.

2. Bake in a 475°F (245°C) oven until vegetables are richly browned and tender when pierced (35 to 45 minutes), stirring occasionally. Watch carefully to prevent scorching. As pieces brown, remove them and keep warm; add water, ¼ cup (60 ml) at a time, if pan appears dry.

3. Transfer vegetables to a platter or serving dish and sprinkle with chopped oregano, chopped basil, garlic, and a little of the cheese. Garnish with oregano and basil sprigs. Season to taste with salt and remaining cheese. Makes 6 servings.

Per serving: 162 calories (28% calories from fat), 5 g total fat, 1 g saturated fat, 3 mg cholesterol, 104 mg sodium, 26 g carbohydrates, 4 g fiber, 4 g protein, 87 mg calcium, 1 mg iron

---

Crisp, garlicky bread crumbs enhance cooked, cooled spring asparagus in this easy dish.

- 3 slices sourdough sandwich bread (about 3 oz./85 g *total*), torn into pieces
- 2 teaspoons olive oil
- 2 cloves garlic, minced or pressed
- 36 thick asparagus spears (about 3 lbs./1.35 kg *total*), tough ends snapped off
- Salt and pepper

1. In a blender or food processor, whirl bread to form fine crumbs. Pour crumbs into a wide nonstick frying pan; add oil and garlic. Cook over

Asparagus with Garlic Crumbs

Preparation time: 15 minutes
Cooking time: About 25 minutes

medium-high heat, stirring often, until crumbs are lightly browned (5 to 7 minutes). Remove from pan and set aside.

2. Trim ends of asparagus spears so that spears are all the same length (reserve scraps for soups or salads). For the sweetest flavor and most tender texture, peel spears with a vegetable peeler.

3. In frying pan, bring about 1 inch (2.5 cm) water to a boil over medium-high heat. Add a third of the asparagus and cook, uncovered, until just tender when pierced (about 4 minutes). Lift from pan with a slotted spoon and place in a bowl of ice water to cool. Repeat with remaining asparagus, cooking it in 2 batches.

4. Drain cooled asparagus well; then arrange on a large platter. Sprinkle with crumb mixture; season to taste with salt and pepper. Makes 8 servings.

Per serving: 70 calories (20% calories from fat), 2 g total fat, 0.3 g saturated fat, 0 mg cholesterol, 68 mg sodium, 11 g carbohydrates, 2 g fiber, 5 g protein, 39 mg calcium, 1 mg iron

Roasted Vegetable Medley
(recipe on facing page)

For a lovely complement to Carne Asada (page 105), serve this combination of tender-crisp broccoli and sweet roasted garlic in a light sesame dressing.

· ·

3 **large heads garlic (about 12 oz./340 g *total*)**

2 **teaspoons olive oil**

About 1¼ pounds/565 g (about 9 cups) broccoli flowerets

2 **tablespoons (30 ml) reduced-sodium soy sauce**

1 **teaspoon Oriental sesame oil**

Roasted Garlic & Broccoli

· ·

Preparation time: About 15 minutes
Cooking time: About 20 minutes

1. Separate garlic heads into cloves; then peel cloves and place in a lightly oiled square 8- to 10-inch (20- to 25-cm) baking pan. Mix in olive oil. Bake in a 475°F (245°C) oven just until garlic is tinged with brown; do not scorch (about 20 minutes; remove smaller cloves as they brown, if needed). Set aside.

2. While garlic is roasting, in a 5- to 6-quart (4.7- to 5.7-liter) pan, bring 3 to 4 quarts (2.8 to 3.8 liters) water to a boil over high heat. Add broccoli and cook until tender-crisp to bite (about 5 minutes). Drain, immerse in ice water until cool, and drain again.

3. In a shallow bowl, mix soy sauce and sesame oil. Add garlic cloves and broccoli; toss gently to mix. Makes 6 servings.

· ·

Per serving: 123 calories (18% calories from fat), 3 g total fat, 0.3 g saturated fat, 0 mg cholesterol, 229 mg sodium, 22 g carbohydrates, 4 g fiber, 6 g protein, 127 mg calcium, 2 mg iron

---

Served at room temperature, this easy-to-assemble side dish is appealingly simple: just roasted eggplant, bell peppers, and garlic, dressed with a splash of balsamic vinegar.

· ·

2 **large red bell peppers (about 1 lb./455 g *total*)**

3 **large heads garlic (about 12 oz./340 g *total*)**

1 **medium-size eggplant (about 1 lb./ 455 g), unpeeled, cut into 2-inch (5-cm) pieces**

2 **teaspoons olive oil**

3 **tablespoons (45 ml) balsamic vinegar**

2 **tablespoons chopped Italian or regular parsley**

Salt and pepper

Roasted Eggplant with Bell Peppers

· ·

Preparation time: 25 minutes
Cooking time: 30 to 40 minutes

1. Cut bell peppers lengthwise into halves and arrange, cut side down, in a shallow baking pan. Broil 4 to 6 inches (10 to 15 cm) below heat until skins are charred (about 8 minutes). Cover loosely with foil and let stand until cool enough to handle (about 10 minutes).

2. Meanwhile, separate garlic heads into cloves; peel garlic cloves. Place garlic in a shallow 10- by 15-inch (25- by 38-cm) baking pan; add eggplant and oil. Mix to coat vegetables with oil. Bake in a 475°F (245°C)

oven until eggplant is richly browned and soft when pressed, and garlic is tinged with brown (20 to 30 minutes). Watch carefully to prevent scorching; remove pieces as they brown and add water, ¼ cup (60 ml) at a time, if pan appears dry.

3. While eggplant is cooking, remove and discard skins, seeds, and stems from bell peppers. Cut peppers into chunks, place in a large serving bowl, and set aside.

4. Add eggplant, garlic, and vinegar to bowl with peppers; mix gently but thoroughly. Sprinkle with parsley; season to taste with salt and pepper. Serve at room temperature. Makes 4 to 6 servings.

· ·

Per serving: 149 calories (13% calories from fat), 2 g total fat, 0.3 g saturated fat, 0 mg cholesterol, 16 mg sodium, 30 g carbohydrates, 4 g fiber, 5 g protein, 148 mg calcium, 2 mg iron

Toasted hazelnuts and crisp, hazelnut-seasoned crumbs flavor these simple poached leeks.

- ¼ **cup (34 g) hazelnuts**
- 3 **slices sourdough sandwich bread (about 3 oz./85 g** *total*)**, torn into pieces**
- 2 **cloves garlic, minced or pressed**
- ¼ **teaspoon dried thyme**
- 1 **teaspoon hazelnut oil or olive oil**
- 8 **medium-size leeks (about 4 lbs./ 1.8 kg** *total*)**
  Balsamic vinegar

1. Spread hazelnuts in a single layer in a shallow baking pan. Bake in a 375°F (190°C) oven until nuts are golden beneath skins (about 10 minutes). Let nuts cool slightly; then pour into a

Poached Leeks with Hazelnuts

Preparation time: 25 minutes
Cooking time: 20 to 25 minutes

towel, fold to enclose, and rub to remove as much of loose skins as possible. Let cool; then coarsely chop and set aside.

2. While nuts are toasting, in a food processor or blender, whirl bread to form fine crumbs. Pour crumbs into a medium-size nonstick frying pan and add garlic and thyme. Drizzle with oil and 1 tablespoon (15 ml) water. Then stir over medium-high heat until crumbs are lightly browned (5 to 7 minutes). Remove from pan and set aside.

3. Trim and discard roots and tough tops from leeks; remove and discard coarse outer leaves. Split leeks lengthwise. Thoroughly rinse leek halves between layers; tie each half with string to hold it together.

4. In a 5- to 6-quart (5- to 6-liter) pan, bring 8 cups (1.9 liters) water to a boil over high heat. Add leeks; reduce heat, cover, and simmer until tender when pierced (5 to 7 minutes). Carefully transfer leeks to a strainer; let drain. Snip and discard strings; arrange leeks on a platter. Sprinkle with crumb mixture, then hazelnuts; offer vinegar to add to taste. Makes 4 to 6 servings.

Per serving: 185 calories (25% calories from fat), 5 g total fat, 0.5 g saturated fat, 0 mg cholesterol, 134 mg sodium, 31 g carbohydrates, 3 g fiber, 5 g protein, 115 mg calcium, 4 mg iron

---

Delicious with roast pork, this hearty casserole will remind you of an oven-baked frittata.

- 1 **pound (455 g) mushrooms, thinly sliced**
- 1 **medium-size onion, chopped About 1⅓ cups (320 ml) canned vegetable broth**
- 3 **large eggs**
- 4 **large zucchini (about 2 lbs./ 905 g** *total*)**, shredded**
- ½ **cup (50 g) fine dry bread crumbs**
- ¼ **cup (20 g) grated Parmesan cheese**
- ¼ **teaspoon** *each* **pepper and dried oregano**
- 2 **tablespoons thinly sliced green onion**

Baked Zucchini with Mushrooms

Preparation time: 20 minutes
Cooking time: About 1 hour

1. In a wide nonstick frying pan, combine mushrooms, chopped onion, and ½ cup (120 ml) water. Cook over medium-high heat, stirring often, until liquid has evaporated and vegetables are beginning to brown. To deglaze, add ⅓ cup (80 ml) of the broth and stir to scrape browned bits free from pan bottom. Then continue to cook, stirring occasionally, until vegetables begin to brown again. Repeat deglazing and browning steps 2 or 3 more times,

using ⅓ cup (80 ml) broth each time; onion should be golden brown (about 15 minutes total). Remove pan from heat.

2. In a large bowl, beat eggs to blend; stir in mushroom mixture, zucchini, bread crumbs, cheese, pepper, and oregano.

3. Pour egg mixture into a greased 9- by 13-inch (23- by 33-cm) baking dish; spread out evenly. Bake in a 325°F (165°C) oven until casserole appears set in center when dish is gently shaken (about 45 minutes). Let stand for 5 to 10 minutes; then sprinkle with green onion and serve. Makes 8 servings.

Per serving: 112 calories (30% calories from fat), 4 g total fat, 1 g saturated fat, 82 mg cholesterol, 306 mg sodium, 14 g carbohydrates, 2 g fiber, 7 g protein, 85 mg calcium, 2 mg iron

Baked Fennel with Gorgonzola
(recipe on facing page)

Braised fresh fennel with a baked-on blue cheese topping is a nice accompaniment for your favorite fish fillets or steaks.

½ cup (50 g) fine dry bread crumbs

4 large heads fennel (about 3 lbs./1.35 kg *total*)

1¾ cups (420 ml) fat-free reduced-sodium chicken broth

3 tablespoons packed crumbled Gorgonzola, cambozola, or other blue-veined cheese

Salt and pepper

1. Sprinkle three-fourths of the bread crumbs over bottom of a rectangular baking dish (about 8 by 12 inches/ 20 by 30 cm). Set aside.

Baked Fennel with Gorgonzola

Preparation time: 15 minutes
Cooking time: About 50 minutes
Pictured on facing page

2. Trim stems from fennel, reserving about 1 cup (30 g) of the feathery green leaves. Trim and discard any bruised areas from fennel; then cut each fennel head in half lengthwise. Lay fennel halves in a wide frying pan. Pour broth into pan and bring to a boil over high heat; then reduce heat, cover, and simmer until fennel is tender when pierced (about 25 minutes). With a slotted spoon, transfer fennel

halves to baking dish, arranging them in a single layer with cut side up.

3. Bring cooking broth to a boil over high heat; boil until reduced to ½ cup (120 ml), about 10 minutes. Stir in half the reserved fennel leaves. Spoon mixture over fennel halves in baking dish.

4. In a small bowl, mash cheese with remaining bread crumbs and 1 teaspoon water; dot mixture evenly over fennel. Bake in a 375°F (190°C) oven until topping begins to brown and fennel is heated through (about 15 minutes). Tuck remaining fennel leaves around fennel halves. Season to taste with salt and pepper. Makes 8 servings.

Per serving: 74 calories (28% calories from fat), 2 g total fat, 1 g saturated fat, 5 mg cholesterol, 416 mg sodium, 9 g carbohydrates, 2 g fiber, 4 g protein, 113 mg calcium, 2 mg iron

---

Great-tasting, pretty to look at, very easy to make . . . this dish is a winner. Use the slimmest, most tender green beans you can find.

¼ to ½ ounce (8 to 15 g) prosciutto or bacon, chopped

1 or 2 cloves garlic, minced or pressed

1½ teaspoons chopped fresh rosemary or ½ teaspoon dried rosemary

1 pound (455 g) slender green beans, ends removed

About ⅛ teaspoon salt, or to taste

Garlic & Rosemary Green Beans

Preparation time: About 10 minutes
Cooking time: About 7 minutes

Rosemary sprigs
Pepper

1. In a wide nonstick frying pan or wok, stir-fry prosciutto over medium-high heat just until crisp (about 1 minute). Remove from pan with a slotted spoon and set aside.

2. Add garlic, chopped rosemary, and 2 tablespoons (30 ml) water to pan. Stir-fry just until garlic is fragrant (about 30 seconds; do not scorch). Add beans, ⅓ cup (80 ml) water, and salt. Cover and cook just until beans are tender to bite (about 3 minutes). Uncover and stir-fry until liquid has evaporated. Arrange beans on a rimmed platter, sprinkle with prosciutto, and garnish with rosemary sprigs. Season to taste with pepper. Makes 4 servings.

Per serving: 39 calories (10% calories from fat), 0.5 g total fat, 0.1 g saturated fat, 2 mg cholesterol, 125 mg sodium, 8 g carbohydrates, 2 g fiber, 3 g protein, 40 mg calcium, 1 mg iron

Juicy mandarin oranges add a sweet and surprising accent to this springtime special.

1½   pounds (680 g) asparagus

2   teaspoons olive oil

8   ounces (230 g) mushrooms, thinly sliced

1   clove garlic, minced or pressed

⅓   cup (80 ml) dry white wine

1   tablespoon grated orange peel

⅛   teaspoon crushed red pepper flakes

¼   teaspoon dried tarragon

½   cup (75 g) drained canned mandarin oranges or fresh orange segments

Asparagus Sauté

Preparation time: About 15 minutes
Cooking time: About 10 minutes

1. Snap off and discard tough ends of asparagus. Cut spears into 1-inch (2.5-cm) slanting slices.

2. Heat oil in a wide nonstick frying pan or wok over medium-high heat. When oil is hot, add asparagus, mushrooms, and garlic; stir-fry until asparagus is hot and bright green (about 3 minutes).

3. Add wine, orange peel, red pepper flakes, and tarragon. Cover and cook until asparagus is just tender-crisp to bite (about 3 minutes). Uncover and continue to cook until liquid has evaporated (1 to 2 more minutes). Stir in oranges. Makes 4 servings.

Per serving: 90 calories (27% calories from fat), 3 g total fat, 0.4 g saturated fat, 0 mg cholesterol, 7 mg sodium, 12 g carbohydrates, 2 g fiber, 4 g protein, 32 mg calcium, 2 mg iron

---

If you have a vegetable garden, you probably plant zucchini. And if you plant zucchini, there's a time—usually at the height of summer—when you're longing for new ways to serve this prolific squash. Here's one delicious choice: a satisfying combination of rice and julienned zucchini, seasoned with soy and topped with almonds.

1   cup (185 g) long-grain white rice

½   cup (60 g) slivered almonds

6   large zucchini (about 2 lbs./ 905 g *total*), cut into ¼- by 2-inch (6-mm by 5-cm) sticks

2   cloves garlic, minced or pressed

About 2 tablespoons (30 ml) reduced-sodium soy sauce

Almond & Zucchini Stir-fry

Preparation time: About 10 minutes
Cooking time: About 25 minutes

1. In a 3- to 4-quart (2.8- to 3.8-liter) pan, bring 2 cups (470 ml) water to a boil over high heat; stir in rice. Reduce heat, cover, and simmer until liquid

has been absorbed and rice is tender to bite (about 20 minutes).

2. Meanwhile, in a wide nonstick frying pan or wok, stir almonds over medium heat until golden (4 to 5 minutes). Pour out of pan and set aside.

3. To pan, add zucchini, garlic, and 2 tablespoons (30 ml) water. Increase heat to medium-high; stir-fry until zucchini is tender-crisp to bite and liquid has evaporated (about 9 minutes). Add 2 tablespoons (30 ml) of the soy sauce; mix gently.

4. To serve, spoon rice into a bowl and pour zucchini over it; sprinkle with almonds. Offer more soy sauce to add to taste. Makes 6 servings.

Per serving: 205 calories (27% calories from fat), 6 g total fat, 0.6 g saturated fat, 0 mg cholesterol, 207 mg sodium, 32 g carbohydrates, 2 g fiber, 7 g protein, 64 mg calcium, 2 mg iron

Stir-frying Fresh Vegetables

To stir-fry fresh vegetables:

1. Cut vegetables into uniform slices or small pieces, as directed in the chart below.

2. Heat 2 teaspoons of oil in a wide (12-inch/30 cm) nonstick frying pan or wok over medium-high heat. When oil is hot, add vegetables all at once and stir-fry, uncovered, for time noted in chart.

3. Add designated amount of liquid (fat-free reduced-sodium chicken broth, vegetable broth, or water). Cover tightly and cook for remaining time noted in chart. As vegetables cook, all or almost all liquid will evaporate. If any liquid remains, uncover pan and stir-fry, uncovered, until all or almost all liquid has evaporated.

Remember that the times noted below should be used as guides. Actual times may vary, depending on the freshness and maturity of the vegetables and on the degree of doneness you prefer. Taste vegetables after the minimum cooking time; if you prefer a softer texture, continue to cook, tasting often, until vegetables are done to your liking.

VEGETABLE (4 cups, cut up)	WEIGHT (untrimmed / trimmed)	SALAD OIL (teaspoons)	STIR-FRY (minutes uncovered)	LIQUID (tablespoons)	COOK (minutes covered)
Asparagus Cut into 1-inch (2.5-cm) slanting slices	1½ lbs. (680 g) / 1 lb. (455 g)	2	1	1 (15 ml)	2
Beans, green Cut into 1-inch (2.5-cm) pieces	1 lb. (455 g) / 15½ oz. (440 g)	2	1	4 (60 ml)	4
Bok choy Cut into ¼-inch (6-mm) slices; shred leaves and add during last 2 minutes of cooking time	14 oz. (400 g) / 13 oz. (370 g)	2	1	1 (15 ml)	3½
Broccoli Cut into 1-inch (2.5-cm) flowerets	1¼ lbs. (565 g) / 12 oz. (340 g)	2	1	4 (60 ml)	3
Cabbage Green or red. Shredded	1⅛ lbs. (510 g) / 14 oz. (400 g)	2	1	2 (30 ml)	3
Cabbage Napa. Cut white part into 1-inch (2.5-cm) slices; shred leaves and add during last 2 minutes of cooking time	1 lb. (455 g) / 14 oz. (400 g)	2	1	2 (30 ml)	4
Carrots Cut into ¼-inch (6-mm) slices	1¾ lbs. (795 g) / 1¼ lbs. (565 g)	2	1	2 (30 ml)	4
Cauliflower Cut into 1-inch (2.5-cm) flowerets	2 lbs. (905 g) / 1 lb. (455 g)	2	1	4 (60 ml)	4
Celery Cut into ¼-inch (6-mm) slices	1¼ lbs. (565 g) / 1 lb. (455 g)	2	1	1 (15 ml)	3
Eggplant Cut into ½-inch (1-cm) cubes	12 oz. (340 g) / 10 oz. (285 g)	2	1	4 (60 ml)	3½
Fennel Cut into ¼-inch (6-mm) slices	2 lbs. (905 g) / 1 lb. (455 g)	2	4	none	none
Mushrooms Cut into ¼-inch (6-mm) slices	12 oz. (340 g) / 11½ oz. (325 g)	2	4	none	none
Onions Cut into ¼-inch (6-mm) slices	1 lb. (455 g) / 14 oz. (400 g)	2	1	2 (30 ml)	4
Pea pods, Chinese	1 lb. (455 g) / 15 oz. (430 g)	2	1	1 (15 ml)	½
Peppers, bell Cut into 1-inch (2.5-cm) slices	1 lb. 5oz. (600 g) / 1⅛ lbs. (510 g)	2	1	2 (30 ml)	5
Potatoes Russet. Cut into ¼-inch (6-mm) cubes	1⅜ lbs. (625 g) / 1¼ lbs. (565 g)	2	1	6 (90 ml)	6
Spinach Whole leaves	12 oz. (340 g) / 4 oz. (115 g)	2	½	none	2
Sprouts, bean	1 lb. (455 g) / 1 lb. (455 g)	2	1	none	½
Squash, summer Cut into ¼-inch (6-mm) slices	1 lb. (455 g) / 15½ oz. (440 g)	2	1	2 (30 ml)	3
Swiss chard Cut stems into ¼-inch (6-mm) slices; shred leaves and add during last 2 minutes of cooking time	8 oz. (230 g) / 8 oz. (230 g)	2	1	1 (15 ml)	3½

Looking for a side dish to serve with poached fish or chicken? These thin-sliced carrots are a marvelous choice; their natural sweetness is intensified both by quick stir-frying and by a fresh-tasting glaze of orange juice, maple syrup, and curry.

- 1 tablespoon grated orange peel
- ¾ cup (180 ml) orange juice
- 2 tablespoons (30 ml) maple syrup
- 2 teaspoons cornstarch blended with 2 tablespoons (30 ml) cold water
- 1 teaspoon curry powder
- 1¼ pounds (565 g) carrots, cut diagonally into ¼-inch (6-mm) slices
- 2 tablespoons minced parsley
  Salt and pepper

Curry-glazed Carrots

Preparation time: About 20 minutes
Cooking time: About 10 minutes
Pictured on facing page

1. In a bowl, stir together orange peel, orange juice, syrup, and cornstarch mixture; set aside.

2. In a wide nonstick frying pan or wok, stir curry powder over medium-high heat just until fragrant (about 30 seconds; do not scorch). Add carrots and ⅓ cup (80 ml) water. Cover and cook just until carrots are tender when pierced (about 4 minutes). Uncover and stir-fry until liquid has evaporated.

3. Stir orange juice mixture well; then pour into pan and cook, stirring, until sauce boils and thickens slightly. Pour carrots and sauce into a serving bowl and sprinkle with parsley. Season to taste with salt and pepper. Makes 4 servings.

Per serving: 117 calories (3% calories from fat), 0.4 g total fat, 0 g saturated fat, 0 mg cholesterol, 52 mg sodium, 28 g carbohydrates, 5 g fiber, 2 g protein, 56 mg calcium, 1 mg iron

---

If you like cauliflower, garlic, and basil, you'll enjoy this robust stir-fry; it's a good addition to a late-summer menu. Sliced zucchini and diced tomatoes offer a nice color contrast to the creamy-pale cauliflower.

- 2 teaspoons olive oil
- 1 large cauliflower (about 2 lbs./905 g), cut into bite-size flowerets
- 2 cloves garlic, minced or pressed
- 1 large onion, chopped
- 8 ounces (230 g) small zucchini, cut crosswise into ¼-inch (6-mm) slices

Stir-fried Herbed Cauliflower

Preparation time: About 15 minutes
Cooking time: About 10 minutes

- ⅓ cup (80 ml) dry white wine
- 3 medium-size firm-ripe pear-shaped (Roma-type) tomatoes (about 8 oz./230 g *total*), chopped
- 1 tablespoon chopped fresh basil

1. Heat oil in a wide nonstick frying pan or wok over medium-high heat.

When oil is hot, add cauliflower, garlic, onion, and zucchini; stir-fry until zucchini is hot and bright in color (2 to 3 minutes).

2. Add wine, tomatoes, and basil to pan. Cover and cook until cauliflower is just tender to bite (about 4 minutes). Uncover and continue to cook until liquid has evaporated (2 to 3 more minutes). Makes 4 servings.

Per serving: 93 calories (27% calories from fat), 3 g total fat, 0.4 g saturated fat, 0 mg cholesterol, 23 mg sodium, 58 g carbohydrates, 4 g fiber, 4 g protein, 56 mg calcium, 1 mg iron

Curry-glazed Carrots
(recipe on facing page)

A tablespoon of apple eau de vie (or more, if you like) adds a subtle accent to this woodsy-tasting sauté of chanterelles and button mushrooms.

....

8   ounces (230 g) *each* fresh chanterelle mushrooms and large regular mushrooms

1   teaspoon butter or margarine

4   cloves garlic, minced or pressed

1½ teaspoons chopped fresh thyme or ½ teaspoon dried thyme

    About ⅛ teaspoon salt, or to taste

1   tablespoon (15 ml) apple eau de vie or apple brandy, or to taste

1   tablespoon (15 ml) cream sherry, or to taste

    Thyme sprigs

    Pepper

Sautéed Mushrooms with Apple Eau de Vie

....

Preparation time: About 15 minutes
Cooking time: About 10 minutes

1. Rinse mushrooms and scrub gently, if needed; pat dry. Cut into ¼- to ½-inch-thick (6-mm- to 1-cm-thick) slices; set aside.

2. Melt butter in a wide nonstick frying pan or wok over medium-high heat. Add garlic and chopped thyme; stir-fry just until fragrant (about 30 seconds; do not scorch). Add mushrooms and ¼ cup (60 ml) water; stir-fry until mushrooms are soft and almost all liquid has evaporated (about 8 minutes). Then add salt and ¼ cup (60 ml) more water; stir-fry until liquid has evaporated (about 2 minutes). Add eau de vie and sherry; stir-fry until liquid has evaporated.

3. Spoon into a serving bowl and garnish with thyme sprigs. Season to taste with pepper. Makes 4 servings.

....

Per serving: 58 calories (23% calories from fat), 1 g total fat, 0.7 g saturated fat, 3 mg cholesterol, 84 mg sodium, 8 g carbohydrates, 2 g fiber, 3 g protein, 17 mg calcium, 2 mg iron

---

A lovely and refreshing choice for a family meal, this emerald-green dish features sweet snow peas accented with a light, tart vinegar sauce and a sprinkling of smoky bacon. Be sure to serve at once; upon standing, the pea pods will lose their bright color.

....

¼   cup (60 ml) *each* fat-free reduced-sodium chicken broth and distilled white vinegar

2   teaspoons sugar

1   teaspoon cornstarch

2   thick slices bacon, finely chopped

1   pound (455 g) fresh Chinese pea pods (also called snow or sugar peas), ends and strings removed; or 3 packages (about 6 oz./170 g *each*) frozen Chinese pea pods, thawed and drained

1   tablespoon chopped fresh mint

    Mint sprigs

Snow Peas with Bacon & Mint

....

Preparation time: About 15 minutes
Cooking time: About 10 minutes

1. In a small bowl, stir together broth, vinegar, sugar, and cornstarch; set aside.

2. In a wide nonstick frying pan or wok, stir-fry bacon over medium-high heat until browned and crisp (about 3 minutes). Remove bacon from pan with a slotted spoon and set aside. Pour off and discard drippings from pan. Wipe pan clean (be careful; pan is hot).

3. Add pea pods and ⅓ cup (80 ml) water to pan. Cover and cook over medium-high heat until pea pods are tender-crisp to bite (about 1 minute for fresh pea pods, about 30 seconds for frozen). Uncover and stir-fry until liquid has evaporated. Transfer to a rimmed platter and keep warm.

4. Stir broth mixture well; pour into pan. Bring to a boil over high heat; boil, stirring, until slightly thickened. Remove from heat and stir in chopped mint. Pour sauce over pea pods, sprinkle with bacon, and garnish with mint sprigs. Serve immediately. Makes 4 to 6 servings.

....

Per serving: 73 calories (27% calories from fat), 2 g total fat, 0.8 g saturated fat, 4 mg cholesterol, 104 mg sodium, 10 g carbohydrates, 2 g fiber, 4 g protein, 40 mg calcium, 2 mg iron

This warm, crunchy offering is nice for winter days.

....

- 6 cups (about 6 oz./170 g) lightly packed rinsed, crisped spinach leaves
- ¼ cup (60 ml) unseasoned rice vinegar or white wine vinegar
- 2 tablespoons (30 ml) reduced-sodium soy sauce
- 2 teaspoons honey
- 1 teaspoon Oriental sesame oil
- 2 teaspoons sesame seeds
- 2 teaspoons salad oil
- 5 cups (355 g) broccoli flowerets
- 1 pound (455 g) carrots, cut into ¼-inch (6-mm) slanting slices
- 1½ cups (180 g) thinly sliced celery
- 1 medium-size onion, thinly sliced

Oriental Winter Salad

....

Preparation time: About 15 minutes
Cooking time: About 25 minutes

1. Arrange spinach leaves on a large platter; cover and set aside. In a small bowl, stir together vinegar, soy sauce, honey, and sesame oil; set aside.

2. In a wide nonstick frying pan or wok, stir sesame seeds over medium heat until golden (about 3 minutes). Pour out of pan and set aside.

3. Heat 1 teaspoon of the salad oil in pan over medium-high heat. When oil is hot, add half each of the broccoli, carrots, celery, and onion. Stir-fry until vegetables are hot and bright in color

(about 3 minutes). Add ⅓ cup (80 ml) water to pan, cover, and cook until vegetables are just tender to bite (about 3 minutes). Uncover and continue to cook, stirring, until liquid has evaporated (1 to 2 more minutes). Remove vegetables from pan and set aside.

4. Repeat to cook remaining broccoli, carrots, celery, and onion, using remaining 1 teaspoon salad oil and adding ⅓ cup (80 ml) water after the first 3 minutes of cooking.

5. Return all cooked vegetables to pan and stir in vinegar mixture. Spoon vegetables onto spinach-lined platter and sprinkle with sesame seeds. Makes 6 servings.

....

Per serving: 118 calories (22% calories from fat), 3 g total fat, 0.4 g saturated fat, 0 mg cholesterol, 297 mg sodium, 20 g carbohydrates, 7 g fiber, 6 g protein, 114 mg calcium, 2 mg iron

---

This colorful side dish is guaranteed to brighten up any menu. Simply spoon stir-fried, ginger-seasoned yellow, red, and green bell peppers over hot rice; you can make the topping while the rice is cooking.

....

- 1 cup (185 g) long-grain white rice
- 1 to 2 teaspoons sesame seeds
- 3 medium-size bell peppers (1 to 1¼ lbs./455 to 565 g *total*); use 1 *each* red, yellow, and green bell pepper
- 1 teaspoon salad oil
- 1 small onion, cut into thin slivers
- 1 tablespoon minced fresh ginger
- 1 clove garlic, minced or pressed

Tricolor Pepper Sauté

....

Preparation time: About 15 minutes
Cooking time: About 25 minutes

- 1 cup (85 g) bean sprouts
- 2 teaspoons Oriental sesame oil
  Reduced-sodium soy sauce or salt

....

1. In a 3- to 4-quart (2.8- to 3.8-liter) pan, bring 2 cups (470 ml) water to a boil over high heat; stir in rice. Reduce heat, cover, and simmer until liquid has been absorbed and rice is tender to bite (about 20 minutes).

2. Meanwhile, in a wide nonstick frying pan or wok, stir sesame seeds

over medium heat until golden (about 3 minutes). Pour out of pan and set aside.

3. Seed bell peppers and cut into thin slivers, 2 to 3 inches (5 to 8 cm) long. Heat salad oil in pan over medium-high heat. When oil is hot, add onion, ginger, and garlic; stir-fry for 1 minute. Add peppers; stir-fry until tender-crisp to bite (about 3 minutes). Add bean sprouts and stir-fry until barely wilted (about 1 minute). Remove from heat and stir in sesame oil.

4. Spoon rice onto a rimmed platter; pour vegetable mixture over rice and sprinkle with sesame seeds. Offer soy sauce to add to taste. Makes 4 servings.

....

Per serving: 253 calories (16% calories from fat), 5 g total fat, 0.7 g saturated fat, 0 mg cholesterol, 7 mg sodium, 48 g carbohydrates, 3 g fiber, 5 g protein, 43 mg calcium, 3 mg iron

Mediterranean Squash
(recipe on facing page)

Bright, cheery, and as bountiful as a summer garden, this pretty dish offers a tempting taste of the Mediterranean. It's seasoned with thyme and plenty of lemon juice; chopped black olives and feta cheese make tangy garnishes.

Mediterranean Squash

Preparation time: About 25 minutes
Cooking time: About 20 minutes
Pictured on facing page

2 teaspoons olive oil

1 large onion, chopped

1 pound (455 g) mushrooms, thinly sliced

1½ pounds (680 g) yellow crookneck squash or yellow zucchini, cut crosswise into ¼-inch (6-mm) slices

1½ tablespoons fresh thyme leaves or 1½ teaspoons dried thyme

3 tablespoons (45 ml) lemon juice

6 medium-size firm-ripe pear-shaped (Roma-type) tomatoes (about 1 lb./455 g *total*), cut crosswise into ¼-inch (6-mm) slices

½ cup (50 g) thinly sliced green onions

1 ounce (30 g) feta cheese, crumbled

2 oil-cured black olives, pitted and chopped

1. Heat 1 teaspoon of the oil in a wide nonstick frying pan or wok over medium-high heat. When oil is hot, add half each of the chopped onion, mushrooms, squash, and thyme. Stir-fry until squash is hot and bright in color (about 3 minutes).

2. Add ¼ cup (60 ml) water and 1½ tablespoons (23 ml) of the lemon juice to pan; cover and cook until vegetables are just tender to bite (about 3 minutes). Uncover and continue to cook, stirring, until liquid has evaporated (about 3 more minutes). Remove vegetables from pan and set aside.

3. Repeat to cook remaining chopped onion, mushrooms, squash, and thyme, using remaining 1 teaspoon oil; add ¼ cup (60 ml) water and remaining 1½ tablespoons (23 ml) lemon juice after the first 3 minutes of cooking.

4. Return all cooked vegetables to pan; gently stir in tomatoes. Transfer vegetables to a serving dish; sprinkle with green onions, cheese, and olives. Makes 8 servings.

Per serving: 78 calories (28% calories from fat), 3 g total fat, 0.8 g saturated fat, 3 mg cholesterol, 72 mg sodium, 12 g carbohydrates, 3 g fiber, 3 g protein, 57 mg calcium, 2 mg iron

Sautéed mushrooms laced with sherry and balsamic vinegar embellish these tender-crisp green beans.

Green Beans with Sautéed Mushrooms

Preparation time: 20 minutes
Cooking time: About 30 minutes

1 tablespoon butter or margarine

1 small onion, finely chopped

1 pound (455 g) mushrooms, finely chopped

½ cup (120 ml) dry sherry

1 tablespoon (15 ml) reduced-sodium soy sauce

2 tablespoons (30 ml) balsamic vinegar

1 teaspoon *each* cornstarch and Oriental sesame oil

3 pounds (1.35 kg) green beans, ends trimmed

1. Melt butter in a wide nonstick frying pan over medium-high heat. Add onion and cook, stirring often, until soft. Add mushrooms, ¼ cup (60 ml) of the sherry, and ¼ cup (60 ml) water; cook, stirring often, until almost all liquid has evaporated and mushrooms are lightly browned (about 15 minutes).

2. In a small bowl, stir together remaining ¼ cup (60 ml) sherry, ½ cup (120 ml) water, soy sauce, vinegar, cornstarch, and oil. Add to mushroom mixture and cook, stirring, until sauce boils and thickens slightly. Remove from heat and keep warm.

3. In a 5- to 6-quart (5- to 6-liter) pan, bring 3 quarts (2.8 liters) water to a boil over high heat. Add beans; cook, uncovered, until just tender to bite (4 to 6 minutes). Drain well, arrange on a platter, and top with mushroom-onion mixture. Makes 12 servings.

Per serving: 70 calories (21% calories from fat), 2 g total fat, 0.7 g saturated fat, 3 mg cholesterol, 69 mg sodium, 10 g carbohydrates, 2 g fiber, 3 g protein, 42 mg calcium, 2 mg iron

Fresh corn flavored with a tart marinade has the natural goodness so typical of Mexican food. Easily assembled in just a few minutes, the dish is both nutritious and flavorful.

6 **medium-size ears corn (about 3 lbs/1.35 kg. *total*), *each* about 8 inches (20 cm) long, husks and silk removed**

Vinegar Marinade (recipe follows)

Salt and pepper

1. With a sharp, heavy knife, cut corn crosswise into 1-inch (2.5cm) rounds. In a large pan, bring 4 quarts

Seasoned Sweet Corn

Preparation time: About 10 minutes
Cooking time: About 5 minutes

(3.8 liters) water to a boil over high heat. Add corn, cover, and cook until hot (3 to 4 minutes). Drain corn well and pour into a shallow rimmed dish (about 9 by 13 inches/23 by 33 cm).

2. Prepare Vinegar Marinade. Pour marinade over corn; let stand, frequently spooning marinade over corn, until corn is cool enough to eat

out of hand. Season to taste with salt and pepper. Makes 6 servings.

Vinegar Marinade. In a small pan, combine ½ cup (120 ml) **distilled white vinegar;** ¼ cup (60 ml) **lime juice;** 1 cup (170 g) minced **onion;** 3 tablespoons **sugar;** 1 small jar (about 2 oz./55 g) diced **pimentos;** 1 teaspoon **mustard seeds;** and ¼ to ½ teaspoon crushed **red pepper flakes.** Bring to a boil over high heat; then boil, stirring, just until sugar is dissolved. Use hot.

Per serving: 115 calories (9% calories from fat), 1 g total fat, 0.1 g saturated fat, 0 mg cholesterol, 17 mg sodium, 27 g carbohydrates, 3 g fiber, 3 g protein, 12 mg calcium, 0.7 mg iron

---

In Mexico, chocolate isn't just for desserts—it's used in savory dishes, too. Here, a small amount of unsweetened cocoa brings mellow, complex flavor to a sauce for baby carrots and pearl onions.

10 **ounces (285 g) fresh pearl onions (*each* about 1 inch / 2.5 cm in diameter); or 1 package (about 10 oz./285 g) frozen pearl onions**

1½ **pounds (680 g) baby or small carrots, peeled**

1 **tablespoon butter or margarine**

2 **tablespoons (30 ml) lemon juice**

1 **tablespoon (15 ml) *each* water and honey**

1 **tablespoon unsweetened cocoa powder**

1 **teaspoon grated fresh ginger**

Cocoa-glazed Carrots & Onions

Preparation time: About 15 minutes
Cooking time: 20 to 30 minutes

1. If using fresh onions, place them in a bowl and cover with boiling water. Let stand for 2 to 3 minutes. Drain; then pull or slip off skins and discard them. Also trim root and stem ends of onions.

2. Place peeled fresh onions or frozen onions in a wide nonstick frying pan. Barely cover with water and bring to a boil over high heat. Reduce heat, cover, and simmer gently until onions are tender when pierced (10 to 15 minutes). Drain onions, pour out of pan, and set aside.

3. If using baby carrots, leave whole; if using small carrots, cut diagonally into ¼-inch (6 mm) slices. Place carrots in pan used for onions, barely cover with water, and bring to a boil over high heat. Reduce heat, cover, and simmer gently until carrots are just tender when pierced (7 to 10 minutes). Drain carrots and set aside.

4. In pan, combine butter, lemon juice, the 1 tablespoon (15 ml) water, honey, cocoa, and ginger. Stir over medium-high heat until smoothly blended. Add carrots and onions. Stir gently over high heat until sauce is thick enough to cling to vegetables (2 to 3 minutes). Makes 6 servings.

Per serving: 91 calories (20% calories from fat), 2 g total fat, 1 g saturated fat, 5 mg cholesterol, 61 mg sodium, 18 g carbohydrates, 4 g fiber, 2 g protein, 47 mg calcium, 0.8 mg iron

Sweet Potato-Fennel Gratin

Preparation time: 45 minutes
Cooking time: About 2¼ hours

This unusual gratin is made with layers of sweet potato slices, buttery-rich Jarlsberg cheese, and braised fennel. A seasoning of fennel seeds brings out the fresh vegetable's mild licorice flavor.

- 3 **heads fennel (each 3 to 4 inches/8 to 10 cm in diameter; about 2 lbs./905 g *total*)**
- 2 **large onions, chopped**
- 1 **teaspoon fennel seeds, crushed**
  About 4 cups (950 ml) vegetable broth
- ¼ **cup (30 g) all-purpose flour**
- ¼ **teaspoon ground nutmeg**
- ½ **cup (120 ml) half-and-half**
- 4 **very large sweet potatoes or yams (about 3 lbs./1.35 kg *total*)**
- 3 **cups (about 12 oz./340 g) shredded reduced-fat Jarlsberg cheese**

1. Trim stems from fennel; reserve some of the feathery leaves for garnish. Discard stems. Trim and discard discolored parts of fennel. Finely chop fennel.

2. In a 5- to 6-quart (5- to 6-liter) pan, combine chopped fennel, onions, fennel seeds, and ½ cup (120 ml) of the broth. Cook over medium-high heat, stirring often, until liquid evaporates and browned bits stick to pan bottom (about 10 minutes). To deglaze pan, add ⅓ cup (80 ml) more broth, stirring to loosen browned bits from pan; continue to cook until browned bits form again. Repeat deglazing step about 3 more times or until vegetables are browned, using ⅓ cup (80 ml) more broth each time. Add flour and nutmeg to vegetables; mix well. Add half-and-half and 2 cups (470 ml) more broth; stir over medium heat until mixture comes to a boil (about 5 minutes). Remove from heat.

3. Peel sweet potatoes and thinly slice crosswise. Arrange a fourth of the fennel mixture in a 9- by 13-inch (23- by 33-cm) baking pan. Cover with a fourth of the sweet potatoes and ¾ cup (85 g) of the cheese. Repeat layers 2 more times. Add remaining fennel mixture in an even layer; top evenly with remaining sweet potatoes. Reserve remaining ¾ cup (85 g) cheese.

4. Cover tightly and bake in a 350°F (175°C) oven for 45 minutes; then uncover and sprinkle with remaining ¾ cup (85 g) cheese. Continue to bake, uncovered, until potatoes are tender when pierced and top of casserole is golden brown (about 1 more hour). Garnish with reserved fennel leaves. Makes 8 to 10 servings.

Per serving: 294 calories (25% calories from fat), 8 g total fat, 4 g saturated fat, 25 mg cholesterol, 679 mg sodium, 39 g carbohydrates, 5 g fiber, 15 g protein, 91 mg calcium, 2 mg iron

Orange & Rum Sweet Potatoes

Preparation time: About 10 minutes
Cooking time: About 20 minutes

Simmered sweet potato slices in an orange-rum sauce make an easy, interesting side dish that's especially tasty with roast pork or chicken.

- 1 **teaspoon salad oil**
- 3 **medium-size sweet potatoes (about 1¼ lbs./565 g *total*), peeled and cut into ¼-inch (6-mm) slices**
- ¾ **cup (180 ml) low-sodium chicken broth**
- ½ **cup (120 ml) orange juice**
- 1 **tablespoon (15 ml) rum**
  About 2 teaspoons honey, or to taste
- 2 **teaspoons cornstarch**
- ⅛ **teaspoon white pepper**
  Salt
- 1 **tablespoon minced parsley**

1. Heat oil in a wide nonstick frying pan over medium-high heat. Add potatoes and ½ cup (120 ml) of the broth. Bring to a boil over medium-high heat; then reduce heat, cover, and simmer until potatoes are tender when pierced (about 10 minutes). Uncover and continue to cook, stirring occasionally, until liquid has evaporated and potatoes are tinged with brown (about 5 more minutes).

2. In a bowl, mix remaining ¼ cup (60 ml) broth, orange juice, rum, honey, cornstarch, and white pepper. Add cornstarch mixture to pan and bring to a boil over medium heat; boil, stirring, just until thickened. Season to taste with salt and sprinkle with parsley. Makes 4 servings.

Per serving: 155 calories (11% calories from fat), 2 g total fat, 0.3 g saturated fat, 0 mg cholesterol, 35 mg sodium, 32 g carbohydrates, 3 g fiber, 2 g protein, 29 mg calcium, 0.7 mg iron

When you're choosing recipes for your holiday table, don't pass up this one. Diced sweet potatoes are stir-fried and sweetened with golden raisins, spices, and coconut; pomegranate seeds, stirred in at the last minute, are a gleaming, jewel-bright accent.

Sweet Potato Stir-fry

Preparation time: About 15 minutes
Cooking time: About 15 minutes
Pictured on facing page

3   large oranges (about 1¾ lbs./795 g *total*)

About 24 large spinach leaves (about 2 oz./55 g *total*), rinsed and crisped

½   cup (120 ml) fat-free reduced-sodium chicken broth (or use canned vegetable broth)

½   cup (75 g) golden raisins

¼   cup (60 ml) orange juice

2   teaspoons honey

⅛   teaspoon *each* ground cloves and ground nutmeg

2   teaspoons salad oil

2   large sweet potatoes or yams (about 1 lb./455 g *total*), peeled and cut into ¼-inch (6-mm) cubes

¼   cup (20 g) sweetened shredded coconut

⅓   cup (55 g) pomegranate seeds

1. Cut off and discard peel and all white membrane from oranges; then cut fruit crosswise into thin slices. Cover and set aside. Arrange spinach leaves on a rimmed platter; cover and set aside. In a bowl, stir together broth, raisins, orange juice, honey, cloves, and nutmeg; set aside.

2. Heat oil in a wide nonstick frying pan or wok over medium-high heat. When oil is hot, add sweet potatoes and 2 tablespoons (30 ml) water; stir-fry until potatoes begin to brown and are just tender-crisp to bite (about 7 minutes). Add water, 1 tablespoon (15 ml) at a time, if pan appears dry.

3. Add broth mixture to pan; cover and cook until potatoes are just tender to bite (about 5 minutes). Uncover and stir-fry until liquid has evaporated. Remove pan from heat and stir in coconut and ¼ cup (40 g) of the pomegranate seeds.

4. Arrange orange slices over spinach leaves on platter. Spoon potato mixture over oranges; sprinkle with remaining pomegranate seeds. Makes 4 servings.

Per serving: 284 calories (13% calories from fat), 4 g total fat, 2 g saturated fat, 0 mg cholesterol, 117 mg sodium, 61 g carbohydrates, 8 g fiber, 4 g protein, 108 mg calcium, 1 mg iron

Roasting does wonderful things for vegetables. Carrots taste intensely sweet; potatoes take on a mellower flavor. Here, the richly browned vegetables are tossed with a light citrus-chile dressing for a zesty Mexican touch. Serve the colorful combination with any main dish.

Roasted Potatoes & Carrots with Citrus Dressing

Preparation time: About 15 minutes
Baking time: 35 to 45 minutes

Citrus Dressing (page 53)

2   pounds (905 g) small red thin-skinned potatoes (*each* about 1½ inches/3.5 cm in diameter), scrubbed and cut into 1-inch (2.5 cm) chunks

4   teaspoons (20 ml) olive oil or salad oil

4   medium-size carrots (about 1 lb./455 g *total*), cut into 1-inch (2.5 cm) chunks

Salt and pepper
Basil sprigs

1. Prepare Citrus Dressing; refrigerate.

2. In a lightly oiled 10- by 15-inch (25- by 38-cm) rimmed baking pan, mix potatoes with 2 teaspoons of the oil. In another lightly oiled 10- by 15-inch (25- by 38-cm) rimmed baking pan, mix carrots with remaining 2 teaspoons oil. Bake potatoes and carrots in a 475°F (245°C) oven, stirring occasionally, until richly browned (35 to 45 minutes); switch positions of baking pans halfway through baking.

3. In a shallow bowl, combine potatoes, carrots, and Citrus Dressing. Serve hot or warm. Before serving, season to taste with salt and pepper; garnish with basil sprigs. Makes 6 to 8 servings.

Per serving: 176 calories (15% calories from fat), 3 g total fat, 0.4 g saturated fat, 0 mg cholesterol, 66 mg sodium, 35 g carbohydrates, 4 g fiber, 3 g protein, 30 mg calcium, 2 mg iron

Sweet Potato Stir-fry
(recipe on facing page)

Garlic Mashed Potatoes

Preparation time: 20 minutes
Cooking time: About 35 minutes

These robust, creamy mashed potatoes are an ideal accompaniment to simply prepared red meats or poultry.

- 1 tablespoon (15 ml) olive oil
- 3 or 4 medium-size heads garlic (9 to 12 oz./ 255 to 340 g *total*)
- 4 pounds (1.8 kg) russet potatoes
- 1 large package (about 8 oz./ 230 g) Neufchâtel cheese, at room temperature
- ¾ to 1 cup (180 to 240 ml) fat-free reduced-sodium chicken broth
  Salt

1. Pour oil into a shallow baking pan. Cut garlic heads in half crosswise through cloves; place, cut side down, in pan. Bake in a 375°F (190°C) oven until cut side is golden brown (about 35 minutes). Using a thin spatula, lift garlic from pan and transfer to a rack; let stand until cool enough to touch (about 10 minutes).

2. While garlic is baking, peel potatoes and cut into 2-inch (5-cm) chunks; place in a 5- to 6-quart (5- to 6-liter) pan and add enough water to cover. Bring to a boil over medium-high heat; reduce heat, cover, and boil gently until potatoes mash very easily when pressed (25 to 30 minutes). Drain potatoes well; transfer to a large bowl and keep warm.

3. Reserve 1 or 2 half-heads of garlic. Squeeze cloves from remaining garlic; add to potatoes along with Neufchâtel cheese. Mash potatoes with a potato masher or an electric mixer, adding broth as needed to make potatoes as soft and creamy as desired. Season to taste with salt and swirl into a shallow serving dish. Garnish with reserved roasted garlic. Makes 8 servings.

Per serving: 304 calories (26% calories from fat), 9 g total fat, 4 g saturated fat, 22 mg cholesterol, 205 mg sodium, 48 g carbohydrates, 4 g fiber, 9 g protein, 80 mg calcium, 2 mg iron

Roasted Potatoes, Fennel & Green Beans with Sherry Dressing

Preparation time: 25 minutes
Cooking time: 50 to 60 minutes

A lemon-sherry vinaigrette flavors fennel, green beans, and chunks of russet potato in a dish that's just right for a buffet.

- 2 large heads fennel (about 1½ lbs./680 g *total*)
- 1 pound (455 g) slender green beans, ends trimmed
- 2 tablespoons (30 ml) olive oil
- 2 very large russet potatoes (about 1½ lbs./680 g *total*), peeled and cut into 1-inch (2.5-cm) chunks
- 1 teaspoon *each* mustard seeds, cumin seeds, and fennel seeds
- ⅓ cup (80 ml) sherry vinegar
- ⅓ cup (80 ml) Gewürztraminer or orange juice
- 1 tablespoon grated lemon peel

1. Trim stems from fennel, reserving some of the feathery green leaves for garnish. Trim and discard any bruised areas from fennel; then cut fennel into ¾-inch (2-cm) chunks. Transfer to a large, shallow baking pan. Add beans and 4 teaspoons (20 ml) of the oil; stir to coat vegetables. In a square 9-inch (23-cm) baking pan, mix potatoes and remaining 2 teaspoons oil.

2. Bake all vegetables in a 475°F (245°C) oven, stirring occasionally, until richly browned (about 45 minutes for fennel and beans, 50 to 60 minutes for potatoes). Watch carefully to prevent scorching. As pieces brown, remove them and keep warm; add water, ¼ cup (60 ml) at a time, if pans appear dry.

3. While vegetables are baking, stir mustard seeds, cumin seeds, and fennel seeds in a small frying pan over medium heat until fragrant (2 to 5 minutes). Remove pan from heat and stir in vinegar, Gewürztraminer, and lemon peel; set aside.

4. Transfer fennel, beans, and potatoes to a large rimmed serving bowl; add dressing and mix gently to coat vegetables. Garnish with reserved fennel leaves. Makes 4 to 6 servings.

Per serving: 210 calories (27% calories from fat), 6 g total fat, 0.7 g saturated fat, 0 mg cholesterol, 126 mg sodium, 33 g carbohydrates, 5 g fiber, 5 g protein, 99 mg calcium, 3 mg iron

Potato lovers are sure to delight in this dish. To make it, you cook potato slices and sweet red pepper with Indian-style seasonings of cumin, chili, and coriander, then top the combination with fresh cilantro and a big spoonful of cool, tart sour cream.

- 1¼ pounds (565 g) small red thin-skinned potatoes, scrubbed
- 2 tablespoons (30 g) butter or margarine
- 1 medium-size red bell pepper (about 6 oz./170 g), seeded and cut into thin slivers
- 1 medium-size onion, cut into thin slivers
- 1 tablespoon ground cumin

Indian Potatoes

Preparation time: About 10 minutes
Cooking time: About 15 minutes

- 1 teaspoon ground coriander
- ¼ teaspoon Hot Chili Oil (page 109) or purchased hot chili oil, or to taste
- ⅓ cup (15 g) chopped cilantro
- ½ cup (120 ml) nonfat sour cream
  Cilantro sprigs
  Salt

1. Cut potatoes crosswise into ¼-inch (6-mm) slices. Melt butter in a wide nonstick frying pan or wok over medi-um-high heat. Add potatoes, bell pepper, onion, cumin, coriander, chili oil, and 3 tablespoons (45 ml) water. Stir-fry gently until potatoes are tinged with brown and tender when pierced (about 15 minutes; do not scorch). Add water, 1 tablespoon (15 ml) at a time, if pan appears dry.

2. Remove pan from heat. Sprinkle potato mixture with chopped cilantro and mix gently but thoroughly. Spoon into a serving bowl, top with sour cream, and garnish with cilantro sprigs. Season to taste with salt. Makes 4 servings.

Per serving: 220 calories (27% calories from fat), 7 g total fat, 4 g saturated fat, 16 mg cholesterol, 94 mg sodium, 34 g carbohydrates, 4 g fiber, 6 g protein, 67 mg calcium, 2 mg iron

---

Hash browns? Yes, but not the standard kind. True, the potatoes are there—but so are Golden Delicious apples, red bell pepper, and aromatic cumin seeds. Sprinkled with Cheddar cheese, the dish is good alongside grilled Canadian bacon or any other favorite partner for hash browns.

- 2 large Golden Delicious apples (about 1 lb./455 g *total*), peeled, cored, and finely chopped
- 1 tablespoon (15 ml) lemon juice
- 2 teaspoons butter or margarine
- 2 large russet potatoes (about 1 lb./455 g *total*), peeled and cut into ¼-inch (6-mm) cubes
- 1 medium-size onion, chopped
- 1 medium-size red bell pepper (about 6 oz./170 g), seeded and diced

Cheese & Apple Hash Browns

Preparation time: About 25 minutes
Cooking time: About 20 minutes

- ½ teaspoon cumin seeds
- ¼ cup (15 g) chopped parsley
- ½ cup (55 g) shredded reduced-fat sharp Cheddar cheese
  Salt and pepper

1. In a medium-size bowl, mix apples and lemon juice. Set aside; stir occasionally.

2. Melt butter in a wide nonstick frying pan or wok over medium heat. Add potatoes, onion, and bell pepper. Stir-fry until potatoes are tinged with brown and tender when pierced (about 15 minutes). Add water, 1 tablespoon (15 ml) at a time, if pan appears dry.

3. Stir in apples and cumin seeds; stir-fry until apples are tender to bite (about 5 minutes). Remove pan from heat and stir in parsley; then spoon potato mixture into a serving bowl. Sprinkle with cheese. Season to taste with salt and pepper. Makes 4 to 6 servings.

Per serving: 178 calories (20% calories from fat), 4 g total fat, 2 g saturated fat, 12 mg cholesterol, 114 mg sodium, 31 g carbohydrates, 4 g fiber, 6 g protein, 119 mg calcium, 1 mg iron

Italian Greens Risotto
(recipe on facing page)

Broccoli rabe (also called rapini) is a pungent, bitter green that's very popular in Italy. In this recipe, it combines with fresh asparagus in a satisfying risotto.

- 12 ounces (340 g) broccoli rabe (rapini)
- 12 ounces (340 g) asparagus, tough ends snapped off
- 4 teaspoons (20 ml) olive oil
- 1 large onion, finely chopped
- 1 cup (200 g) short- or medium-grain white rice
- 3 cups (710 ml) fat-free reduced-sodium chicken broth
- ½ cup (120 ml) dry white wine
- ½ cup (40 g) grated Parmesan cheese

1. Cut off and discard any coarse stem ends from broccoli rabe; discard any bruised or yellow leaves. If any stems are thicker than ⅜ inch (1 cm), cut them in half lengthwise. Rinse and drain broccoli rabe.

Italian Greens Risotto

Preparation time: 15 minutes
Cooking time: About 45 minutes
Pictured on facing page

2. Chop or thinly slice half each of the broccoli rabe and asparagus. Leave remaining asparagus spears and broccoli rabe leaves and flowerets whole.

3. In a wide nonstick frying pan, combine chopped broccoli rabe, chopped asparagus, and 1 tablespoon (15 ml) of the oil. Cook over medium-high heat, stirring, until vegetables are just tender to bite (about 4 minutes). Remove from pan and set aside. To pan, add ½ cup (120 ml) water, whole asparagus spears, and whole broccoli rabe leaves and flowerets. Cover and cook, turning vegetables often with a wide spatula, until vegetables are just

tender to bite (about 4 minutes). Lift from pan; set aside.

4. In same pan, combine remaining 1 teaspoon oil and onion; cook over medium-high heat, stirring often, until onion is tinged with brown (5 to 8 minutes). Add rice and stir until opaque (3 to 4 minutes). Stir in broth and wine. Bring to a boil, stirring often. Then reduce heat and simmer, uncovered, until rice is tender to bite and almost all liquid has been absorbed (about 25 minutes); stir occasionally at first, more often as mixture thickens. Stir in sautéed chopped vegetables and cheese. Spoon onto a platter; surround with whole vegetables and serve immediately. Makes 6 servings.

Per serving: 237 calories (22% calories from fat), 5 g total fat, 2 g saturated fat, 5 mg cholesterol, 480 mg sodium, 35 g carbohydrates, 3 g fiber, 10 g protein, 154 mg calcium, 3 mg iron

---

Tangy dried tomatoes and sliced mushrooms dot this lively pilaf.

- 1 tablespoon (15 ml) olive oil
- 8 ounces (230 g) portabella or button mushrooms, sliced
- 1 medium-size onion, chopped
- 1 cup (185 g) long-grain white rice
- 2½ cups (590 ml) fat-free reduced-sodium chicken broth
- ¾ cup (about 1½ oz./43 g) dried tomatoes (not packed in oil), chopped
- ¼ cup (10 g) chopped cilantro
  Salt and pepper

Dried Tomato Pilaf

Preparation time: 15 minutes
Cooking time: 35 to 45 minutes

1. Heat oil in a 3- to 4-quart (2.8- to 3.8-liter) pan over medium-high heat. Add mushrooms and onion; cook, stirring often, until almost all liquid has evaporated and vegetables are lightly browned (10 to 12 minutes).

2. Add rice and stir until opaque (3 to 4 minutes). Add broth and tomatoes.

Bring to a boil; then reduce heat, cover, and simmer until rice is tender to bite (20 to 25 minutes). Stir in cilantro. Season to taste with salt and pepper. Makes 6 servings.

Per serving: 181 calories (13% calories from fat), 3 g total fat, 0.4 g saturated fat, 0 mg cholesterol, 280 mg sodium, 34 g carbohydrates, 3 g fiber, 6 g protein, 17 mg calcium, 2 mg iron

Delicate risotto studded with sweet corn kernels is ideal for a summer evening. Serve it with a platter of sliced red-ripe tomatoes.

....

4 **medium-size ears corn (***each about 8 inches/20 cm long***)**

4 **cups (680 g) finely chopped onions**

1 **tablespoon butter or margarine**

2 **cups (400 g) arborio or short-grain white rice**

8 **cups (1.9 liters) vegetable broth**

   About ½ cup (120 ml) lime juice

2 **to 4 tablespoons thinly sliced green onion tops or snipped chives**

½ **cup (40 g) finely shaved or shredded Parmesan cheese**

   Salt and pepper

Sweet Corn Risotto

....

Preparation time: 20 minutes
Cooking time: About 40 minutes

1. Remove and discard husks and silk from corn. In a shallow pan, hold one ear of corn upright and, with a sharp knife, cut kernels from cob. Then, using blunt edge of knife, scrape juice from cob into pan. Repeat with remaining ears of corn. Discard cobs.

2. In a wide nonstick frying pan, combine 2 cups (340 g) of the chopped onions, butter, and ¼ cup (60 ml) water. Cook over medium-high heat, stirring often, until onions are soft (5 to 10 minutes); add water, 1 tablespoon (15 ml) at a time, if pan appears dry. Add rice and cook, stirring often,

until opaque (about 3 minutes). Meanwhile, bring broth to a simmer in a 3- to 4-quart (2.8- to 3.8-liter) pan; keep broth warm.

3. Add ¼ cup (60 ml) of the lime juice and 6 cups (1.4 liters) of the broth to rice mixture. Cook, stirring often, until liquid has been absorbed (about 15 minutes). Add remaining 2 cups (470 ml) broth, corn kernels and juice, and remaining 2 cups (340 g) chopped onions. Cook, stirring often, until rice is tender to bite and mixture is creamy (about 10 minutes).

4. Spoon risotto into wide individual bowls; top with green onions and cheese. Season to taste with salt, pepper, and remaining lime juice. Makes 4 servings.

....

Per serving: 628 calories (15% calories from fat), 10 g total fat, 4 g saturated fat, 17 mg cholesterol, 2,289 mg sodium, 120 g carbohydrates, 7 g fiber, 17 g protein, 225 mg calcium, 6 mg iron

---

Tangy with lemon and vinegar, this easy-to-make side dish is delicious with any simply cooked main course. You might serve it with Carne Asada (page 105) or Whole Tilapia with Onion & Lemon (page 164).

....

6 **slices bacon**

1 **cup (200 g) short- or medium-grain rice**

1 **tablespoon grated lemon peel**

2½ **cups (590 ml) water**

3 **tablespoons drained capers**

¼ **cup (60 ml) seasoned rice vinegar; or ¼ cup (60 ml) distilled white vinegar plus 1½ teaspoons sugar**

Lemon-Caper Rice

....

Preparation time: About 5 minutes
Cooking time: About 25 minutes

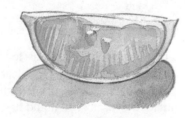

1. Cook bacon in a 2- to 3-quart (1.9- to 2.8-liter) pan over medium heat until crisp (about 5 minutes). Lift out,

drain, crumble, and set aside. Discard all but 2 teaspoons of the drippings.

2. To pan, add rice, lemon peel, and water. Bring to a boil over high heat. Stir; then reduce heat, cover, and simmer until liquid has been absorbed and rice is tender to bite (about 20 minutes). Uncover; stir in crumbled bacon, capers, and vinegar. Makes 6 to 8 servings.

....

Per serving: 150 calories (23% calories from fat), 4 g total fat, 1 g saturated fat, 5 mg cholesterol, 357 mg sodium, 24 g carbohydrates, 0.3 g fiber, 4 g protein, 3 mg calcium, 1 mg iron

Here's risotto in a new guise: it's formed into patties, pan-fried until crisp, and served with a tomato-basil purée.

2 tablespoons (30 ml) olive oil; or 2 tablespoons butter

1¼ cups (244 g) short- or medium-grain white rice

1¾ cups (420 ml) fat-free reduced-sodium chicken broth

5 to 6 ounces (140 to 170 g) mozzarella cheese, shredded

¼ cup (20 g) grated Parmesan cheese

4 green onions, finely chopped

1 can (about 14½ oz./415 g) diced tomatoes

¼ cup (60 ml) plain nonfat yogurt

¼ cup (10 g) coarsely chopped fresh basil
  Basil sprigs

1. Heat 1 tablespoon (15 ml) of the oil in a 3- to 4-quart (2.8- to 3.8-liter) pan over medium-high heat. Add rice and

Risotto Cakes with Tomato Purée

Preparation time: 25 minutes
Cooking time: About 1¼ hours

stir until opaque (3 to 4 minutes). Stir in broth and 1½ cups (360 ml) water. Bring to a boil, stirring often. Then reduce heat and simmer, uncovered, until rice is tender to bite and almost all liquid has been absorbed (25 to 30 minutes); stir occasionally at first, more often as mixture thickens. Remove from heat and stir in mozzarella cheese, Parmesan cheese, and onions. Let cool uncovered. (At this point, you may cover and refrigerate until next day.)

2. In a food processor or blender, com-

bine tomatoes and their liquid, yogurt, and chopped basil. Whirl until smoothly puréed; set aside.

3. Divide rice mixture into 12 equal portions; shape each portion into a cake about ¾ inch (2 cm) thick. Heat 1 teaspoon of the oil in a wide non-stick frying pan over medium-high heat. Add risotto cakes to pan, a portion at a time (do not crowd pan); cook, turning once, until golden on both sides (about 20 minutes). Add remaining 2 teaspoons oil to pan as needed. As cakes are cooked, arrange them in a single layer in a large, shallow baking pan; cover loosely with foil and keep warm in a 300°F (150°C) oven until all cakes have been cooked.

4. To serve, arrange cakes on individual plates; top with tomato purée and garnish with basil sprigs. Makes 6 servings.

Per serving: 286 calories (28% calories from fat), 9 g total fat, 3 g saturated fat, 12 mg cholesterol, 507 mg sodium, 38 g carbohydrates, 1 g fiber, 13 g protein, 313 mg calcium, 3 mg iron

---

Bold with onions and Gorgonzola cheese, this mushroom risotto is good with juicy steaks or chops.

1 teaspoon olive oil

8 ounces (230 g) mushrooms, thinly sliced

1 large onion, chopped

1 clove garlic, minced

1 cup (200 g) short- or medium-grain white rice

¼ teaspoon each dried thyme, dried marjoram, and dried rubbed sage

3 cups (790 ml) fat-free reduced-sodium chicken broth

½ cup (125 g) packed crumbled Gorgonzola or other blue-veined cheese

1 teaspoon dry sherry (or to taste)

Risotto with Mushrooms

Preparation time: 15 minutes
Cooking time: About 45 minutes

1. Heat oil in a wide nonstick frying pan over medium heat. Add mushrooms, onion, and garlic. Cook, stirring often, until vegetables are soft and are beginning to stick to pan bottom (about 15 minutes); add water, 1 tablespoon (15 ml) at a time, if pan drippings begin to scorch.

2. Add rice, thyme, marjoram, and sage; stir until rice is opaque (3 to 4 minutes). Stir in broth. Bring to a boil, stirring often. Then reduce heat

and simmer, uncovered, until rice is tender to bite and almost all liquid has been absorbed (about 25 minutes); stir occasionally at first, more often as mixture thickens.

3. Remove rice mixture from heat and stir in cheese and sherry. Makes 4 to 6 servings.

Per serving: 230 calories (19% calories from fat), 5 g total fat, 3 g saturated fat, 10 mg cholesterol, 450 mg sodium, 38 g carbohydrates, 2 g fiber, 8 g protein, 76 mg calcium, 2 mg iron

Aromatic basmati rice simmers in mango nectar for an especially fragrant pilaf. The dish is pretty to look at, too—it's dotted with dried apricots, currants, and bright orange lentils. Look for orange lentils in Indian markets; if you can't find them, use the familiar brown, yellow, or green variety.

Fruited Basmati Pilaf

Preparation time: 20 minutes
Cooking time: About 35 minutes
Pictured on facing page

- 1 cup (200 g) orange lentils
- 2 teaspoons butter or margarine
- 1 cup (185 g) basmati or long-grain white rice
- 4¼ cups (1 liter) vegetable broth
- 1 can (about 12 oz./360 ml) mango or apricot nectar
- ⅛ teaspoon ground coriander
- ¼ cup (35 g) coarsely chopped dried apricots
- 4 large mangoes (about 3 lbs./1.35 kg *total*)
- 3 tablespoons (45 ml) lime juice
- ½ cup (75 g) dried currants or raisins
- ⅓ cup (35 g) thinly sliced green onion tops
- ¾ cup (108 g) coarsely chopped salted roasted macadamia nuts or peanuts
  Lime wedges or slices

1. Sort through lentils, discarding any debris. Rinse and drain lentils; then set aside.

2. Melt butter in a 4- to 5-quart (3.8- to 5-liter) pan over medium heat. Add rice and cook, stirring often, until opaque (about 3 minutes). Add broth, mango nectar, and coriander. Increase heat to medium-high and bring mixture just to a boil. Stir in lentils and apricots; then reduce heat, cover, and simmer until liquid has been absorbed and both rice and lentils are tender to bite (about 25 minutes). If any cooking liquid remains, drain and discard it.

3. While rice mixture is simmering, peel mangoes and slice fruit from pits into a large bowl. Add lime juice and mix gently to coat. Arrange mangoes decoratively around edge of a rimmed platter; cover and set aside.

4. Remove rice mixture from heat; stir in currants and onions. Spoon pilaf into center of platter; sprinkle macadamia nuts over mangoes and pilaf. Garnish with lime wedges. Makes 6 servings.

Per serving: 519 calories (25% calories from fat), 16 g total fat, 3 g saturated fat, 3 mg cholesterol, 745 mg sodium, 91 g carbohydrates, 6 g fiber, 14 g protein, 63 mg calcium, 4 mg iron

---

White rice seasoned with tomatoes and chiles is a superb accompaniment for your favorite Mexican-style entrées.

Mexican Rice

Preparation time: About 10 minutes
Cooking time: About 35 minutes

- 1 large can (about 28 oz./795 g) tomatoes
  About 3 cups (710 ml) low-sodium chicken broth
- 2 teaspoons butter or margarine
- 2 cups (370 g) long-grain white rice
- 1 large onion, chopped
- 2 cloves garlic, minced or pressed
- 2 medium-size fresh green Anaheim or other large mild chiles (about 4 oz./115 g *total*), seeded and chopped; or 1 small can (about 4 oz./115 g) diced green chiles
  Salt and pepper
- ¼ cup (13 g) firmly packed cilantro leaves

1. Drain liquid from tomatoes into a glass measure. Add enough of the broth to make 4 cups (950 ml) liquid. Set tomatoes and broth mixture aside.

2. Melt butter in a 4- to 6-quart (3.8- to 5.7-liter) pan over medium-high heat. Add rice and cook, stirring, until it begins to turn opaque (about 3 minutes). Add onion, garlic, chiles, and ¼ cup (60 ml) water; continue to cook, stirring, for 5 more minutes. Add more water, 1 tablespoon (15 ml) at a time, if pan appears dry.

3. Add tomatoes and broth mixture to pan (break tomatoes up with a spoon). Bring to a boil over medium-high heat; then reduce heat, cover, and simmer until liquid has been absorbed and rice is tender to bite (about 25 minutes).

4. To serve, season to taste with salt and pepper; garnish with cilantro. Makes 10 to 12 servings.

Per serving: 161 calories (10% calories from fat), 2 g total fat, 0.7 g saturated fat, 2 mg cholesterol, 159 mg sodium, 33 g carbohydrates, 1 g fiber, 4 g protein, 39 mg calcium, 2 mg iron

Fruited Basmati Pilaf
(recipe on facing page)

If you can't find small peppers, just cut medium-size ones down: slice the tops off the peppers as directed, then trim the cut edges of both top and bottom pieces so the whole peppers will be just 2 to 3 inches tall when reassembled.

....

10 to 12 very small red, yellow, or orange bell peppers (*each* 2 to 3 inches/5 to 8 cm tall)

1 cup (200 g) short- or medium-grain white rice

4 teaspoons grated lemon peel

8 ounces (230 g) sliced bacon, crisply cooked, drained, and crumbled

¼ cup (43 g) drained capers

¼ cup (60 ml) seasoned rice vinegar

Red Bell Peppers Stuffed with Caper Rice

....

Preparation time: 20 minutes
Cooking time: 35 to 40 minutes

1. Cut off the top third of each pepper. With a small spoon, scoop out seeds and white membranes from pepper bases and tops; rinse and drain both bases and tops. If needed, trim pepper bases (without piercing them) so they will sit steadily.

2. In a 2- to 3-quart (1.9- to 2.8-liter) pan, combine rice, lemon peel, and 2½ cups (590 ml) water. Bring to a boil

over high heat. Reduce heat, cover, and simmer until rice is tender to bite and almost all liquid has been absorbed (about 20 minutes). Remove from heat. With a fork, stir in bacon, capers, and vinegar.

3. Set pepper bases upright, spacing them slightly apart, in a shallow 10- by 15-inch (25- by 38-cm) baking pan. Mound rice mixture equally in pepper bases; set pepper tops in place. Bake in a 450°F (230°C) oven until peppers are blistered and rice mixture is hot in center (8 to 12 minutes). Makes 10 to 12 servings.

....

Per serving: 131 calories (21% calories from fat), 3 g total fat, 1 g saturated fat, 5 mg cholesterol, 263 mg sodium, 22 g carbohydrates, 2 g fiber, 4 g protein, 12 mg calcium, 1 mg iron

---

Green split peas, wholesome brown rice, and vivid fresh spinach team up in this colorful entrée. Serve the dish on a bed of whole spinach leaves, with a garnish of crisp salted almonds.

....

2 cups (370 g) long-grain brown rice

¾ cup (150 g) split peas

4 cups (950 ml) vegetable broth

2½ cups (590 ml) nonfat milk

2 tablespoons drained capers

½ teaspoon ground nutmeg

6 ounces (170 g) fresh spinach, stems and any yellow or wilted leaves discarded, remaining leaves rinsed, drained, and finely chopped

½ cup (40 g) grated Parmesan cheese

⅓ cup (35 g) thinly sliced green onions

Whole fresh spinach leaves, rinsed and crisped

Green & Brown Rice

....

Preparation time: 25 minutes
Cooking time: About 1 hour and 10 minutes

⅓ cup (20 g) finely chopped parsley

½ cup (65 g) salted roasted almonds, chopped

....

1. Spread rice in a shallow 3- to 3½-quart (2.8- to 3.3-liter) casserole, about 9 by 13 inches (23 by 33 cm). Bake in a 350°F (175°C) oven, stirring occasionally, until rice is golden brown (about 25 minutes).

2. Meanwhile, sort through peas, discarding any debris; rinse and drain peas, then set aside.

3. In a 3- to 4-quart (2.8- to 3.8-liter) pan, combine 3½ cups (830 ml) of the

broth, milk, capers, and nutmeg. Bring just to a boil over medium-high heat. Leaving casserole in oven, carefully stir broth mixture and peas into rice. Cover tightly and bake until almost all liquid has been absorbed (about 40 minutes); stir after 20 and 30 minutes, covering casserole tightly again each time.

4. Uncover casserole and stir in remaining ½ cup (120 ml) broth, chopped spinach, cheese, and onions; bake, uncovered, for 5 more minutes.

5. To serve, line 6 individual plates with whole spinach leaves. Stir rice mixture and spoon atop spinach; sprinkle with parsley and almonds. Makes 6 servings.

....

Per serving: 463 calories (24% calories from fat), 13 g total fat, 3 g saturated fat, 7 mg cholesterol, 1,049 mg sodium, 70 g carbohydrates, 6 g fiber, 19 g protein, 309 mg calcium, 3 mg iron

Green Rice with Pistachios

Looking for a new way to serve rice? Try this colorful side dish. Start by oven-toasting the rice; then simmer it in broth with green peppercorns, spinach, and parsley. A sprinkling of pistachios adds a crunchy finishing touch.

Preparation time: About 15 minutes
Cooking time: About 1 hour

2 cups (370 g) long-grain white rice

5½ cups (1.3 liters) low-sodium chicken broth

½ teaspoon ground nutmeg

1½ tablespoons canned green peppercorns in brine, rinsed and drained

12 ounces (340 g) stemmed spinach leaves, rinsed well, drained, and finely chopped (about 3 cups lightly packed)

1 cup (60 g) minced parsley
Salt and pepper

½ cup (60 g) shelled salted roasted pistachio nuts, coarsely chopped

1. Spread rice in a shallow 3- to 3½-quart (2.8- to 3.3-liter) baking dish (about 9 by 13 inches/23 by 33 cm). Bake in a 350°F (175°C) oven, stirring occasionally, until rice is lightly browned (about 35 minutes).

2. In a 2- to 3-quart (1.9- to 2.8-liter) pan, combine 5 cups (1.2 liters) of the broth, nutmeg, and peppercorns. Bring to a boil over high heat. Leaving baking dish on oven rack, carefully stir broth mixture into rice. Cover dish tightly with foil. Continue to bake until liquid has been absorbed and rice is tender to bite (about 20 more minutes). Stir after 10 and 15 minutes, covering dish again after stirring.

3. Uncover baking dish and stir in remaining ½ cup (120 ml) broth, spinach, and ¾ cup (45 g) of the parsley; bake for 5 more minutes. To serve, stir rice and season to taste with salt and pepper. Sprinkle with remaining ¼ cup (15 g) parsley and pistachios. Makes 8 to 10 servings.

Per serving: 222 calories (22% calories from fat), 6 g total fat, 1 g saturated fat, 0 mg cholesterol, 161 mg sodium, 38 g carbohydrates, 3 g fiber, 7 g protein, 77 mg calcium, 4 mg iron

Pork Fried Rice

Fresh ginger, meaty shiitake mushrooms, and bright vegetables give this side dish its savory appeal. For best results, use cooked rice that has been cooled thoroughly.

Preparation time: About 10 minutes
Cooking time: About 10 minutes

1 tablespoon (15 ml) salad oil

1 clove garlic, minced or pressed

½ teaspoon minced fresh ginger

½ cup (50 g) thinly sliced green onions

4 ounces (115 g) lean ground pork

8 fresh shiitake mushrooms (about 2 oz./55 g *total*), stems removed and caps thinly sliced

½ cup (75 g) *each* frozen peas and frozen corn kernels, thawed and drained

½ cup (120 ml) fat-free reduced-sodium chicken broth

2 tablespoons (30 ml) reduced-sodium soy sauce

3 cups (390 g) cooked, cooled long-grain white rice

1. Heat oil in a wide nonstick frying pan or wok over medium-high heat. When oil is hot, add garlic, ginger, and onions; then crumble in pork. Stir-fry until pork is browned (about 5 minutes).

2. Add mushrooms, peas, corn, and ¼ cup (60 ml) of the broth to pan; stir-fry until liquid has evaporated (about 2 minutes). Add remaining ¼ cup (60 ml) broth; then stir in soy sauce and rice. Stir-fry until rice is heated through. Makes 6 servings.

Per serving: 234 calories (26% calories from fat), 7 g total fat, 2 g saturated fat, 14 mg cholesterol, 282 mg sodium, 35 g carbohydrates, 1 g fiber, 8 g protein, 25 mg calcium, 2 mg iron

Quinoa, often called the "super grain" thanks to its high protein content, replaces the traditional arborio rice as the base for this hearty risotto. You'll find quinoa in natural food stores and well-stocked supermarkets; be sure to rinse it thoroughly before cooking to remove the slightly bitter coating.

1½ cups (255 g) quinoa

1 teaspoon butter or margarine

1 large onion, finely chopped

1 cup (240 ml) vegetable broth

¾ cup (180 ml) nonfat milk

1½ teaspoons chopped fresh sage or ½ teaspoon dried rubbed sage

8 ounces (230 g) slender asparagus

¼ cup (30 g) shredded fontina or jack cheese

½ cup (40 g) finely shaved or grated Parmesan cheese

Sage sprigs

Quinoa Risotto

Preparation time: 15 minutes
Cooking time: About 40 minutes

1. Place quinoa in a fine strainer and rinse thoroughly with cool water; drain well. Then place quinoa in a wide nonstick frying pan and cook over medium heat, stirring often, until darker in color (about 8 minutes). Remove from pan and set aside.

2. Increase heat to medium-high. Melt butter in pan and add onion and 2 tablespoons (30 ml) water. Cook, stirring often, until onion is soft (about 5 minutes); add water, 1 tablespoon (15 ml) at a time, if pan appears dry.

3. To pan, add broth, milk, quinoa, and dried sage (or if using fresh sage, add later, as directed). Bring just to a boil, stirring often. Reduce heat and simmer, uncovered, stirring occasionally, until quinoa is almost tender to bite (about 10 minutes). Meanwhile, snap off and

discard tough ends of asparagus; then cut stalks diagonally into 1-inch (2.5-cm) pieces.

4. Add asparagus to quinoa mixture and cook, stirring often, until asparagus is tender when pierced and almost all liquid has been absorbed (about 5 more minutes; reduce heat and stir more often as mixture thickens).

5. Remove pan from heat and gently stir in fontina cheese and chopped fresh sage (if using). Let stand until cheese is melted (about 2 minutes). Transfer to a shallow serving bowl or 4 individual bowls; top with Parmesan cheese and garnish with sage sprigs. Makes 4 servings.

Per serving: 356 calories (23% calories from fat), 9 g total fat, 4 g saturated fat, 17 mg cholesterol, 495 mg sodium, 54 g carbohydrates, 10 g fiber, 17 g protein, 242 mg calcium, 6 mg iron

---

Serve this vegetable-dotted "relish" as you would salsa, as an accent for meats, poultry, or fish. It's based on chewy bulgur; carrots, zucchini, and red bell pepper add bright color and fresh flavor.

2 teaspoons olive oil or salad oil

2 medium-size carrots (about 8 oz./230 g *total*), shredded

2 medium-size zucchini (about 12 oz./340 g *total*), shredded

1 medium-size red or green bell pepper (about 6 oz./170 g), seeded and slivered

3 cloves garlic, minced or pressed

Bulgur Relish

Preparation time: About 15 minutes
Cooking time: About 30 minutes

⅓ cup (51 g) bulgur

2 cups (470 ml) low-sodium chicken broth

2 tablespoons (30 ml) reduced-sodium soy sauce

1. Heat oil in a wide nonstick frying pan over medium-high heat. Add carrots, zucchini, bell pepper, and garlic; cook, stirring, until vegetables are soft (about 5 minutes).

2. Stir in bulgur, broth, and soy sauce. Bring to a boil over high heat; then cover, remove from heat, and let stand until liquid has been absorbed and bulgur is tender to bite (about 20 minutes). Serve warm or at room temperature. If made ahead, cover and refrigerate for up to 2 days. Makes about 10 servings.

Per serving: 50 calories (24% calories from fat), 2 g total fat, 0.3 g saturated fat, 0 mg cholesterol, 153 mg sodium, 9 g carbohydrates, 2 g fiber, 2 g protein, 20 mg calcium, 0.5 mg iron

Universally lauded by nutritionists, broccoli is a popular choice at the dinner table these days. In this quick dish, the bright, tender flowerets are teamed with bell pepper and served over couscous.

Broccoli & Bell Pepper with Couscous

Preparation time: About 15 minutes
Cooking time: About 15 minutes

1½ cups (360 ml) fat-free reduced-sodium chicken broth (or use canned vegetable broth)

¼ to ½ teaspoon dried oregano

1 cup (185 g) couscous

1 tablespoon pine nuts or slivered almonds

4 cups (285 g) broccoli flowerets

1 teaspoon olive oil or salad oil

1 small red bell pepper (about 4 oz./115 g), seeded and cut into thin slivers

2 tablespoons (30 ml) balsamic vinegar

1. In a 3- to 4-quart (2.8- to 3.8-liter) pan, combine broth and oregano. Bring to a boil over high heat; stir in couscous. Cover, remove from heat, and let stand until liquid has been absorbed (about 5 minutes). Transfer couscous to a rimmed platter and keep warm; fluff occasionally with a fork.

2. While couscous is standing, stir pine nuts in a wide nonstick frying pan or wok over medium-low heat until gold-en (2 to 4 minutes). Pour out of pan and set aside.

3. To pan, add broccoli and ¼ cup (60 ml) water. Cover and cook over medium-high heat until broccoli is tender-crisp to bite (about 5 minutes). Uncover and stir-fry until liquid has evaporated. Spoon broccoli over couscous and keep warm.

4. Heat oil in pan. When oil is hot, add bell pepper and stir-fry until just tender-crisp to bite (2 to 3 minutes). Add vinegar to pan and remove from heat; stir to scrape any browned bits free from pan bottom. Immediately pour pepper mixture over broccoli and couscous; sprinkle with pine nuts and serve. Makes 4 servings.

Per serving: 248 calories (10% calories from fat), 3 g total fat, 0.4 g saturated fat, 0 mg cholesterol, 278 mg sodium, 45 g carbohydrates, 7 g fiber, 12 g protein, 72 mg calcium, 2 mg iron

---

Creamy polenta is enhanced by an easy sauce based on fresh tomatoes, yellow bell peppers, and basil.

Polenta with Fresh Tomato Sauce

Preparation time: 25 minutes
Cooking time: About 20 minutes

3 pounds (1.35 kg) pear-shaped (Roma-type) tomatoes, peeled (if desired) and coarsely chopped

2 large yellow bell peppers (about 1 lb./455 g *total*), seeded and chopped

1 cup (40 g) lightly packed slivered fresh basil or ¼ cup (8 g) dried basil

2 cloves garlic, minced

2 cups (470 ml) low-fat (2%) milk

½ cup (120 ml) canned vegetable broth

1 cup (138 g) polenta or yellow cornmeal

1 teaspoon chopped fresh sage or ¼ teaspoon ground sage

½ teaspoon salt

½ cup (40 g) grated Parmesan cheese

Basil sprigs

1. In a 3- to 4-quart (2.8- to 3.8-liter) pan, combine two-thirds each of the tomatoes and bell peppers, half the slivered basil, and all the garlic. Cook over medium-high heat, stirring often, until tomatoes begin to fall apart (15 to 20 minutes).

2. Meanwhile, in a 4- to 5-quart (3.8- to 5-liter) pan, bring milk and broth just to a boil over medium-high heat. Stir in polenta, sage, and salt. Reduce heat and simmer, uncovered, stirring often and scraping bottom of pan with a long-handled spoon (mixture will spatter), until polenta tastes creamy (about 15 minutes). Remove pan from heat; stir in cheese. Keep warm.

3. Working quickly, stir remaining tomatoes, bell peppers, and slivered basil into sauce. Divide polenta equally among deep individual bowls and top with sauce. Garnish with basil sprigs. Makes 4 servings.

Per serving: 346 calories (19% calories from fat), 7 g total fat, 4 g saturated fat, 18 mg cholesterol, 681 mg sodium, 58 g carbohydrates, 8 g fiber, 16 g protein, 414 mg calcium, 5 mg iron

If you're planning a banquet of Asian-inspired offerings, don't leave out this colorful medley of noodles, vegetables, and browned ground turkey. The combination of textures and tastes—soft with crisp, sweet with salty—makes the dish memorable.

12 ounces (340 g) fresh Chinese noodles or linguine

1 teaspoon Oriental sesame oil

1 tablespoon (15 ml) salad oil

1 small onion, thinly sliced lengthwise

2 tablespoons (30 ml) oyster sauce

8 ounces (230 g) ground turkey

1 pound (455 g) napa cabbage, thinly sliced crosswise

4 ounces (115 g) oyster mushrooms, thinly sliced

2 medium-size carrots (about 8 oz./230 g *total*), cut into matchstick strips

Low-fat Lo Mein

Preparation time: About 15 minutes
Cooking time: About 15 minutes

½ cup (120 ml) fat-free reduced-sodium chicken broth

2 tablespoons (30 ml) reduced-sodium soy sauce

1. In a 5- to 6-quart (5- to 6-liter) pan, cook noodles in about 3 quarts (2.8 liters) boiling water until just tender to bite (3 to 5 minutes); or cook according to package directions. Drain well, toss with sesame oil, and keep warm.

2. Heat salad oil in a wide nonstick frying pan or wok over medium-high heat. When oil is hot, add onion and oyster sauce; then crumble in turkey. Stir-fry until onion is soft and turkey is no longer pink (about 3 minutes).

3. Add cabbage, mushrooms, carrots, and broth; cover and cook until carrots are just tender to bite (about 3 minutes). Uncover and continue to cook until liquid has evaporated (1 to 2 more minutes). Stir in soy sauce; add noodles and stir-fry until heated through. Makes 6 servings.

Per serving: 295 calories (23% calories from fat), 7 g total fat, 1 g saturated fat, 69 mg cholesterol, 563 mg sodium, 41 g carbohydrates, 4 g fiber, 16 g protein, 89 mg calcium, 3 mg iron

---

Soft buckwheat noodles tossed with tender-crisp vegetables and topped with roasted cashews make a great complement to grilled pork tenderloin.

Cooking Sauce (recipe follows)

8 ounces (230 g) dried soba noodles or capellini

1 large red or green bell pepper (about 8 oz./230 g), seeded and cut into thin slivers

½ cup (60 g) thinly sliced celery

½ cup (50 g) thinly sliced green onions

½ cup (70 g) salted roasted cashews

1. Prepare Cooking Sauce; set aside.

Vegetable Stir-fry with Soba

Preparation time: About 15 minutes
Cooking time: About 10 minutes

2. In a 4- to 5-quart (3.8- to 5-liter) pan, cook pasta in about 8 cups (1.9 liters) boiling water until just tender to bite (about 5 minutes for soba, about 3 minutes for capellini); or cook according to package directions. Drain well, transfer to a warm wide bowl, and keep warm.

3. In a wide nonstick frying pan or wok, combine bell pepper, celery, and ¼ cup (60 ml) water. Stir-fry over high heat until vegetables are tender-crisp to bite and liquid has evaporated (about 5 minutes).

4. Stir Cooking Sauce and pour into pan; bring just to a boil. Pour vegetable mixture over noodles, then add onions and mix gently but thoroughly. Sprinkle with cashews. Makes 4 servings.

Cooking Sauce. In a small bowl, stir together 2 tablespoons (30 ml) *each* **oyster sauce, reduced-sodium soy sauce,** and **lemon juice.** Stir in 1 teaspoon **Oriental sesame oil.**

Per serving: 329 calories (24% calories from fat), 10 g total fat, 2 g saturated fat, 0 mg cholesterol, 1,225 mg sodium, 54 g carbohydrates, 5 g fiber, 13 g protein, 51 mg calcium, 3 mg iron

For a refreshing side dish, serve this combination of tiny pasta beads, sweet peas, and mint-lemon dressing.

....

2 ounces (55 g) thinly sliced prosciutto or bacon, cut into thin strips

1½ cups (340 g) dried orzo or other tiny rice-shaped pasta

1 package (about 1 lb./455 g) frozen tiny peas

¼ cup (25 g) thinly sliced green onions

¼ cup (10 g) chopped fresh mint

¼ cup (60 ml) olive oil

1 teaspoon finely shredded lemon peel

Pastina with Peas

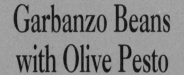

....

Preparation time: 15 minutes
Cooking time: About 20 minutes

2 tablespoons (30 ml) lemon juice

Mint sprigs

Pepper

....

1. In a wide nonstick frying pan, cook prosciutto over medium-high heat, stirring often, just until crisp (about 3 minutes). Remove from pan and set aside.

2. In a 5- to 6-quart (5- to 6-liter) pan, bring about 3 quarts (2.8 liters) water to a boil over medium-high heat; stir in pasta and cook until just tender to bite, about 8 minutes. (Or cook pasta according to package directions.) Drain, rinse with cold water until cool, and drain well again. Pour pasta into a large serving bowl; add peas, onions, and chopped mint. Mix gently.

3. In a small bowl, beat oil, lemon peel, and lemon juice until blended. Add to pasta mixture; mix gently but thoroughly. Sprinkle with prosciutto and garnish with mint sprigs. Season to taste with pepper. Makes 6 servings.

....

Per serving: 364 calories (28% calories from fat), 12 g total fat, 2 g saturated fat, 8 mg cholesterol, 282 mg sodium, 52 g carbohydrates, 4 g fiber, 14 g protein, 29 mg calcium, 3 mg iron

---

Garbanzos in a ripe-olive pesto taste great atop juicy sliced tomatoes.

....

4 slices sourdough sandwich bread (about 4 oz./115 g *total*), cut into ½-inch (1-cm) cubes

5 large tomatoes (about 2½ lbs./ 1.15 kg *total*), thinly sliced

1 cup (113 g) pitted ripe olives, drained

3 tablespoons drained capers

4 teaspoons (20 ml) lemon juice

2 teaspoons *each* Oriental sesame oil and Dijon mustard

1 tablespoon (15 ml) honey (or to taste)

2 or 3 cloves garlic, peeled

¼ cup (10 g) finely chopped fresh basil

Garbanzo Beans with Olive Pesto

....

Preparation time: 15 minutes
Cooking time: 15 to 20 minutes

3 tablespoons grated Parmesan cheese

2 cans (about 15 oz./425 g *each*) garbanzo beans, drained and rinsed

Basil sprigs

....

1. Spread bread cubes in a single layer in a shallow baking pan. Bake in a 325°F (165°C) oven, stirring occasionally, until crisp and lightly browned (15 to 20 minutes). Set aside.

2. Arrange tomato slices, overlapping if necessary, in a large, shallow serving bowl. Set aside.

3. In a food processor or blender, combine olives, capers, lemon juice, oil, mustard, honey, and garlic; whirl until coarsely puréed, scraping sides of container as needed. With a spoon, stir in chopped basil and cheese. Transfer olive pesto to a large bowl; add beans and two-thirds of the croutons. Mix gently but thoroughly.

4. Spoon bean salad over tomatoes; sprinkle with remaining croutons. Garnish with basil sprigs. Makes 4 to 6 servings.

....

Per serving: 286 calories (29% calories from fat), 10 g total fat, 2 g saturated fat, 2 mg cholesterol, 803 mg sodium, 41 g carbohydrates, 9 g fiber, 11 g protein, 147 mg calcium, 5 mg iron

Beautiful, ruffly, bursting with vitamins—once it catches your eye in the produce department, kale can be impossible to resist. But what can you do with it once you've brought it home? We suggest stir-frying the sliced leaves in a small amount of bacon drippings, then serving them with mild cannellini beans to make a robust side dish.

- 1¼ pounds (565 g) kale
- 4 slices bacon, chopped
- 2 large onions, thinly sliced
- 2 cans (about 15 oz./430 g *each*) cannellini (white kidney beans), drained and rinsed
  Salt and pepper

Sautéed Kale with Cannellini

Preparation time: About 10 minutes
Cooking time: About 20 minutes
Pictured on facing page

1. Remove and discard tough stems from kale; then rinse kale, drain, and cut crosswise into ½-inch (1-cm) strips. Set aside.

2. In a wide nonstick frying pan or wok, stir-fry bacon over medium-high heat until crisp (about 3 minutes). Remove from pan with a slotted spoon and set aside.

3. Add onions to drippings in pan and stir-fry until soft (about 5 minutes). Add kale and stir-fry until wilted and bright green (3 to 4 minutes). Transfer to a platter and keep warm.

4. Add beans to pan, reduce heat to medium-low, and stir until heated through (about 4 minutes). Spoon beans over kale; sprinkle beans and kale with bacon. Season to taste with salt and pepper. Makes 6 servings.

Per serving: 190 calories (19% calories from fat), 4 g total fat, 1 g saturated fat, 4 mg cholesterol, 276 mg sodium, 28 g carbohydrates, 11 g fiber, 11 g protein, 125 mg calcium, 3 mg iron

---

Spicy-sweet beans flavored with a hint of beer are just right with your favorite meat or poultry entrées.

- 4 slices bacon, coarsely chopped
- 1 large onion, chopped
- 2 cans (about 15 oz./425 g *each*) pinto beans
- 1 can (about 8 oz./240 ml) tomato sauce
- ½ cup (120 ml) regular or non-alcoholic beer, or to taste
- 3 tablespoons (45 ml) molasses
- 1½ teaspoons dry mustard
- 1½ teaspoons Worcestershire
- ¼ teaspoon pepper
  Salt

Cerveza Beans

Preparation time: About 5 minutes
Cooking time: About 20 minutes

1. In a 3- to 4-quart (2.8- to 3.8-liter) pan, cook bacon and onion over medium heat, stirring often, until browned bits form on pan bottom and onion is soft (8 to 10 minutes). Discard any fat.

2. Drain beans, reserving ¼ cup (60 ml) of the liquid from cans. To pan, add beans and reserved liquid (if using home-cooked beans, use ¼ cup (60 ml) low-sodium chicken broth mixed with ½ teaspoon cornstarch). Then stir in tomato sauce, ¼ cup

(60 ml) of the beer, molasses, mustard, Worcestershire, and pepper. Bring to a boil; then reduce heat so beans boil gently. Cook, stirring occasionally, until flavors are blended—about 10 minutes. (At this point, you may let cool, then cover and refrigerate for up to 2 days; reheat before continuing.)

3. To serve, stir in remaining ¼ cup (60 ml) beer and season to taste with salt. Makes 4 to 6 servings.

Per serving: 220 calories (14% calories from fat), 3 g total fat, 1 g saturated fat, 4 mg cholesterol, 870 mg sodium, 37 g carbohydrates, 7 g fiber, 10 g protein, 92 mg calcium, 3 mg iron

Sautéed Kale with Cannellini
(recipe on facing page)

Pasta Side Dishes

Because it's so versatile, pasta can play a variety of roles in menu planning. Here are several recipes that are ideal accompaniments for unadorned main dishes, such as roast chicken, broiled fish steaks, and grilled meat.

Creamy Pasta Pilaf can be prepared with any small pasta shape, such as rice-shaped pasta (riso or orzo), tiny bows, or whimsical stars. The relish that tops the pancake in Crisp Pasta Pancake with Spicy Pepper Relish must cool slightly before serving; the spicy caramelized peppers get very hot and can burn your mouth. Ravioli with Mushrooms, Carrots & Zucchini is full of fresh vegetables; it's hearty enough to satisfy two as a main course. Offer Spanish-style Linguine with roasted meat or poultry.

Other pasta recipes throughout this book can be adapted to serve as side dishes. Some can be offered just as they are, but in smaller portions. With some others, just eliminate the meat or fish.

Pasta Pilaf

Preparation time: About 15 minutes
Cooking time: About 20 minutes

....

1 tablespoon butter or margarine

1 large onion (about 8 oz./230 g), finely chopped

1 clove garlic, minced or pressed

6 medium-size pear-shaped (Roma-type) tomatoes (about 12 oz./340 g *total*), peeled, seeded, and chopped

1 tablespoon chopped fresh basil or 1 teaspoon dried basil

8 ounces/230 g (about 1 cup) dried riso, stars, or other small pasta shape

¾ cup (110 g) frozen peas

½ cup (120 ml) half-and-half

½ cup (40 g) freshly grated Parmesan cheese

....

1. Melt butter in a wide non-stick frying pan over medium heat. Add onion and garlic. Cook, stirring occasionally, until onion is soft (about 5 minutes).

2. Add tomatoes, basil, and ¼ cup (60 ml) water; reduce heat, cover, and simmer for 10 minutes. Meanwhile, bring 8 cups (1.9 liters) water to a boil in a 4- to 5-quart (3.8- to 5-liter) pan over medium-high heat. Stir in pasta and cook just until tender to bite (8 to 10 minutes); or cook according to package directions. Drain well.

3. Add peas and half-and-half to pan with tomato mixture. Increase heat to high and bring to a boil; stir in pasta. Remove from heat and stir in ¼ cup (20 g) of the cheese. Transfer to a serving dish. Offer remaining ¼ cup (20 g) cheese to add to taste. Makes 4 to 6 servings.

Per serving: 305 calories (25% calories from fat), 9 g total fat, 5 g saturated fat, 21 mg cholesterol, 217 mg sodium, 45 g carbohydrates, 3 g fiber, 12 g protein, 169 mg calcium, 3 mg iron

Crisp Pasta Pancake with Spicy Pepper Relish

Preparation time: About 20 minutes
Cooking time: About 30 minutes

....

2 *each* large red and yellow bell peppers (about 2 lbs./905 g *total*)

8 fresh green or red serrano chiles (about 2 oz./55 g *total*)

1 cup (200 g) sugar

⅔ cup (160 ml) distilled white vinegar

8 ounces (230 g) fresh capellini

1 tablespoon (15 ml) Oriental sesame oil

2 teaspoons salad oil

....

1. Seed bell peppers and chiles; cut into thin strips. Transfer to a large bowl and add sugar and vinegar. Mix well.

2. Spoon pepper mixture into a wide nonstick frying pan. Cook over medium heat, stirring often, until most of the liquid has evaporated (about 30 minutes). Meanwhile, bring 8 cups (1.9 liters) water to a boil in a 4- to 5-quart (3.8- to 5-liter) pan over medium-high heat. Stir in pasta and cook just until tender to bite (about 45 seconds); or cook according to package directions. Drain; transfer to a bowl, sprinkle with sesame oil, and lift with 2 forks to mix. Place a 12-inch (30-cm) pizza pan in oven while it heats to 500°F (260°C). When pan is hot (about 5 minutes), pour in salad oil, tilting pan to coat. Spread pasta in pan and bake on lowest rack until golden (about 20 minutes).

3. Slide pancake onto a platter. Spread pepper mixture on top; cut into wedges. Makes 8 servings.

....

Per serving: 257 calories (12% calories from fat), 3 g total fat, 0.5 g saturated fat, 0 mg cholesterol, 5 mg sodium, 54 g carbohydrates, 2 g fiber, 5 g protein, 15 mg calcium, 2 mg iron

Ravioli with Mushrooms, Carrots & Zucchini

Preparation time: About 15 minutes
Cooking time: About 12 minutes

....

1 tablespoon butter or margarine

8 ounces (230 g) mushrooms, finely chopped

2 large carrots (about 8 oz./230 g *total*), finely shredded

2 medium-size zucchini (about 8 oz./230 g *total*), finely shredded

3 cloves garlic, minced or pressed

1 tablespoon minced fresh basil or 1 teaspoon dried basil

½ cup (105 g) low-fat (1%) cottage cheese

¾ cup (180 ml) nonfat milk

1 package (about 9 oz./255 g) fresh low-fat or regular cheese ravioli

1. Melt butter in a wide nonstick frying pan over medium-high heat. Add mushrooms, carrots, zucchini, garlic, and basil. Cook, stirring often, until liquid has evaporated (about 10 minutes).

2. Place cottage cheese and ¼ cup (60 ml) of the milk in a blender or food processor. Whirl until smooth. Spoon into pan with vegetables and stir in remaining ½ cup (120 ml) milk. Cook over medium heat, stirring often, just until sauce begins to boil (about 2 minutes). Remove from heat and keep warm.

3. Bring 12 cups (2.8 liters) water to a boil in a 5- to 6-quart (5- to 6-liter) pan over medium-high heat. Separating any ravioli that are stuck together, stir in pasta and cook just until tender to bite (4 to 6 minutes); or cook according to package directions. Drain well. Transfer to a large serving bowl. Add sauce and mix thoroughly but gently. Makes 6 servings.

....

Per serving: 188 calories (22% calories from fat), 5 g total fat, 3 g saturated fat, 32 mg cholesterol, 279 mg sodium, 26 g carbohydrates, 3 g fiber, 11 g protein, 146 mg calcium, 2 mg iron

Spanish-style Linguine

Preparation time: About 10 minutes
Cooking time: About 15 minutes

....

8 ounces (230 g) dried linguine

1 jar (about 6 oz./170 g) marinated artichokes, quartered

2 cloves garlic, minced or pressed

1 tablespoon anchovy paste

1 can (about 2¼ oz./65 g) sliced black ripe olives, drained

½ cup (30 g) chopped parsley

Pepper

Freshly grated Parmesan cheese

....

1. Bring 8 cups (1.9 liters) water to a boil in a 4- to 5-quart (3.8- to 5-liter) pan over medium-high heat. Stir in pasta and cook just until tender to bite (8 to 10 minutes); or cook according to package directions. Meanwhile, drain marinade from artichokes into a 1½- to 2-quart (1.4- to 1.9-liter) pan. Place over medium heat. Add garlic and cook, stirring often, until pale golden (about 3 minutes). Add anchovy paste, olives, and artichokes. Cook, stirring gently, until hot (about 2 minutes).

2. Drain pasta well and return to pan. Add artichoke mixture and parsley. Lift with 2 forks to mix. Transfer pasta to a large serving bowl. Offer pepper and cheese to add to taste. Makes 4 to 6 servings.

....

Per serving: 227 calories (20% calories from fat), 5 g total fat, 0.7 g saturated fat, 2 mg cholesterol, 424 mg sodium, 38 g carbohydrates, 3 g fiber, 8 g protein, 45 mg calcium, 3 mg iron

Easy Corn-Cheese Bread
(recipe on page 336)

Breads

There's nothing quite as delightful as the aroma of bread baking in the oven. With the clever use of nonfat and low-fat dairy products, bread lovers can still savor their favorite food and maintain a low-fat cooking style. Serve the slightly crunchy, lively flavored Chili Batter Bread instead of dinner rolls. Or wake up Sunday morning appetites with breakfast specialties like Quick Cinnamon Buns and Ricotta Pancakes with Lemon-Maple Syrup.

This hearty no-knead yeast bread gets its pleasantly moist texture from cottage cheese.

....

- 1 **cup (170 g) fresh-cut yellow or white corn kernels (from 1 large ear corn); or 1 cup (150 g) frozen corn kernels, thawed**
- 1 **cup (240 ml) beer**
- ½ **cup (105 g) lowfat (2%) cottage cheese**
- ¼ **cup (50 g) sugar**
- 1 **package active dry yeast**
- ¼ **cup (20 g) grated Parmesan cheese**
- ½ **teaspoon** *each* **salt and pepper**
  About 3¼ cups (445 g) bread flour or 3¼ cups (405 g) all-purpose flour

....

1. Place corn in a fine wire strainer; press firmly with the back of a spoon to express liquid. Discard liquid; let corn drain well.

Easy Corn-Cheese Bread

....

Preparation time: About 15 minutes
Rising time: About 45 minutes
Baking time: About 45 minutes
Pictured on page 334

2. In a small pan, combine beer and cottage cheese. Heat over low heat until warm (about 110°F/43°C). Add sugar and yeast; let stand until yeast is softened (about 5 minutes).

3. In a food processor (or a large bowl), combine yeast mixture, corn, Parmesan cheese, salt, and pepper. Gradually add 3¼ cups (405 g) of the flour, about 1 cup (125 g) at a time, to make a soft dough; whirl (or beat) to combine after each addition. If needed, stir in more flour, 1 tablespoon at a time. Whirl (or beat) until dough is stretchy (about 3 minutes in a food processor, about 5 minutes by hand).

4. Scrape dough into a greased 6-cup (1.4-liter) soufflé dish or an 8- or 9-inch (20- or 23-cm) cheesecake pan with a removable rim. Cover dish or pan with oiled plastic wrap and let dough rise in a warm place until almost doubled (about 45 minutes).

5. Bake loaf in a 350°F (175°C) oven until golden brown (about 45 minutes). Let cool on a rack for about 15 minutes. Run a knife between bread and sides of dish; then turn bread out of dish onto rack (or remove pan rim and let bread cool on rack). Serve warm or cool. Makes 1 loaf (16 to 20 servings).

....

Per serving: 114 calories (6% calories from fat), 0.8 g total fat, 0.3 g saturated fat, 1 mg cholesterol, 110 mg sodium, 23 g carbohydrates, 1 g fiber, 4 g protein, 25 mg calcium, 1 mg iron

---

Corn muffins take on an interesting new look and flavor when they're made with blue cornmeal.

....

- 1 **cup (138 g) blue cornmeal**
- 1 **cup (125 g) all-purpose flour**
- 2 **tablespoons sugar**
- 1 **tablespoon baking powder**
- ½ **teaspoon salt**
- 4 **large egg whites**
- 1 **cup (240 ml) nonfat milk**
- ⅓ **cup (80 ml) smooth unsweetened applesauce**
- 2 **tablespoons (28 g) butter or margarine, melted**
  Honey
  Butter or margarine (optional)

....

1. In a large bowl, mix cornmeal, flour, sugar, baking powder, and salt. In

Blue Corn Muffins

....

Preparation time: 10 minutes
Cooking time: About 20 minutes

another bowl, beat egg whites, milk, applesauce, and melted butter until blended. Add egg mixture to flour mixture and stir just until dry ingredients are evenly moistened.

2. Spoon batter into 12 paper-lined or greased 2½-inch (6-cm) muffin cups. Bake in a 400°F (205ºC) oven until muffins are browned and a wooden pick inserted in centers comes out clean (about 20 minutes). Serve warm or cool, with honey and, if desired, butter. If made ahead, wrap cooled muffins airtight and store at room temperature until next day (freeze for longer storage). Makes 1 dozen muffins.

....

Per serving: 121 calories (17% calories from fat), 2 g total fat, 1 g saturated fat, 6 mg cholesterol, 262 mg sodium, 21 g carbohydrates, 1 g fiber, 4 g protein, 97 mg calcium, 1 mg iron

Double Corn Biscuits

Preparation time: About 20 minutes
Baking time: About 1¼ hours

Though inspired by Italian biscotti, these twice-baked treats are savory, not sweet. Flavored with Parmesan and cumin, they're delicious with Creamy Guacamole (page 9), fresh fruit, or Corn Salsa (page 21).

- ⅔ cup (85 g) all-purpose flour
- ⅓ cup (27 g) grated Parmesan cheese
- ¼ cup (35 g) yellow cornmeal
- 2 tablespoons sugar
- ½ teaspoon *each* baking powder and salt
- ¼ teaspoon *each* baking soda and ground cumin
- 1 cup (170 g) fresh-cut yellow or white corn kernels (from 1 large ear corn); or 1 cup (150 g) frozen corn kernels, thawed
- 1 large egg
- 1 large egg white

1. In a small bowl, mix flour, cheese, cornmeal, sugar, baking powder, salt, baking soda, and cumin; set aside.

2. In a food processor, whirl corn until coarsely chopped (or chop corn with a knife and place in a large bowl). Add egg and egg white; whirl (or beat) just until blended. Add flour mixture and whirl (or stir) just until dry ingredients are evenly moistened.

3. Scrape dough directly onto a 12- by 15-inch (30- by 38-cm) nonstick (or lightly greased regular) baking sheet. With a spatula or floured fingers, shape dough into a flat loaf about 1½ inches (3.5 cm) thick and 2 inches (5 cm) wide; keep loaf 1 inch (2.5 cm) from ends of baking sheet.

4. Bake loaf in a 325°F (165°C) oven until firm to the touch (about 25 minutes). Remove from oven and let stand until cool enough to touch; then cut loaf crosswise on baking sheet into ½-inch (1-cm) slices. Spread slices apart. Bake in a 300°F (150°C) oven until slices are lightly toasted all over (about 50 minutes). Transfer to racks and let cool. Makes about 2 dozen biscuits.

Per serving: 36 calories (16% calories from fat), 0.7 g total fat, 0.3 g saturated fat, 10 mg cholesterol, 95 mg sodium, 6 g carbohydrates, 0.4 g fiber, 2 g protein, 23 mg calcium, 0.3 mg iron

Orange Polenta Cakes

Preparation time: 20 minutes
Cooking time: About 20 minutes

Fresh orange juice infuses mild polenta with its tartly sweet flavor. Topped with honey yogurt and ripe fruit, these muffin-sized cakes are beautifully tempting brunch entrées.

- ½ teaspoon grated orange peel
- 2½ cups (590 ml) fresh orange juice
- ½ teaspoon salt
- 1 cup (138 g) polenta or yellow cornmeal
- 2 tablespoons (28 g) butter or margarine
  About ¼ cup (60 ml) honey
- ½ cup (60 g) slivered almonds
- 1½ cups (360 ml) plain nonfat yogurt
  About 2 cups (330 g) peeled, sliced fresh fruit, such as oranges, pears, or apricots

1. In a 2- to 2½-quart (1.9- to 2.4-liter) pan, bring orange peel, orange juice, and salt to a boil over medium-high heat. Gradually add polenta, stirring until blended. Reduce heat and boil gently, uncovered, stirring often and scraping bottom of pan with a long-handled spoon (mixture will spatter), until polenta is thick (about 10 minutes). Reduce heat to low; continue to stir until polenta stops flowing after spoon is drawn across pan bottom (3 to 5 more minutes). Stir in butter and ¼ cup (60 ml) of the honey.

2. Divide hot polenta among 4 greased ¾-cup (180-ml) custard cups or decorative molds; with the back of a spoon, press polenta solidly into cups. Let cool for at least 5 minutes or up to 30 minutes.

3. Meanwhile, toast almonds in a wide frying pan over medium heat until golden (about 3 minutes), stirring often. Pour out of pan and set aside. Sweeten yogurt to taste with honey.

4. To serve, run a knife around edge of each cup; invert polenta cakes onto individual plates. Sprinkle cakes with almonds; accompany with sweetened yogurt and fruit. Makes 4 servings.

Per serving: 522 calories (26% calories from fat), 16 g total fat, 5 g saturated fat, 17 mg cholesterol, 402 mg sodium, 87 g carbohydrates, 5 g fiber, 13 g protein, 258 mg calcium, 3 mg iron

Cornmeal gives this quick batter bread a light crunch; green chiles and a touch of chili powder add lively flavor.

Chili Batter Bread

Preparation time: About 10 minutes
Baking time: About 30 minutes
Pictured on facing page

2½ cups (290 g) all-purpose flour
½ cup (69 g) yellow cornmeal
3 tablespoons sugar
1 teaspoon *each* chili powder and baking powder
½ teaspoon baking soda
¼ teaspoon salt
1 cup (240 ml) low-fat buttermilk
1 small can (about 4 oz./115 g) diced green chiles
1 large egg white

1. In a large bowl, mix flour, cornmeal, sugar, chili powder, baking powder, baking soda, and salt. Add buttermilk, chiles, and egg white; beat just until dry ingredients are evenly moistened. Scrape batter into a 10- by 15-inch (25- by 38-cm) nonstick (or lightly greased regular) rimmed baking pan.

With a spatula, spread batter out to a 7-inch (18-cm) round.

2. Bake bread in a 375°F (190°C) oven until golden brown (about 30 minutes). Serve warm or cool, cut into wedges. If made ahead, wrap cooled loaf airtight and store at room temperature until next day (freeze for longer storage). Makes 1 loaf (12 to 14 servings).

Per serving: 132 calories (4% calories from fat), 0.6 g total fat, 0 g saturated fat, 1 mg cholesterol, 207 mg sodium, 27 g carbohydrates, 1 g fiber, 4 g protein, 29 mg calcium, 1 mg iron

---

A perfect accompaniment to spicy Mexican dishes, this mildly sweet yellow cornbread is especially easy to make. If you prefer a nippier flavor, add diced green chiles to the batter.

Cornbread

Preparation time: About 5 minutes
Baking time: About 30 minutes
Pictured on facing page

1 cup (138 g) yellow cornmeal
1 cup (125 g) all-purpose flour
4 teaspoons baking powder
¼ teaspoon salt
1 large egg
2 large egg whites
1 cup (240 ml) low-fat buttermilk
3 tablespoons (45 ml) honey
2 tablespoons (28 g) butter or margarine, melted

1. In a large bowl, mix cornmeal, flour, baking powder, and salt. In a small bowl, beat egg, egg whites, buttermilk, honey, and butter until blended. Add egg mixture to flour mixture and stir just until dry ingredients are evenly moistened.

2. Spread batter in a square 8-inch (20-cm) nonstick (or greased regular) baking pan. Bake in a 375°F (190°C) oven until bread pulls away from sides of pan and a wooden pick inserted in center comes out clean (about 30 min-utes). Cut into 8 pieces (*each* 2 by 4 inches/15 by 10 cm). Makes 8 servings.

Per serving: 200 calories (20% calories from fat), 4 g total fat, 2 g saturated fat, 36 mg cholesterol, 396 mg sodium, 34 g carbohydrates, 1 g fiber, 6 g protein, 148 mg calcium, 2 mg iron

Chile Cornbread

Follow directions for **Cornbread,** but stir 1 large can (about 7 oz./200 g) diced **green chiles** into egg mixture before combining with flour mixture. Makes 8 servings.

Per serving: 206 calories (19% calories from fat), 4 g total fat, 2 g saturated fat, 36 mg cholesterol, 547 mg sodium, 36 g carbohydrates, 2 g fiber, 6 g protein, 150 mg calcium, 2 mg iron

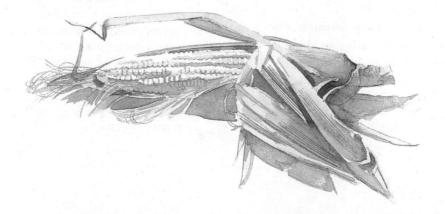

Chili Batter Bread, Cornbread
(recipes on facing page);
Anise Biscuits (recipe on page 343)

Focaccia

Focaccia (foh-Kah-chee-ah) is a marvelous Italian flatbread enjoying a newly discovered popularity in this country.

Focaccia dough is similar to the dough prepared for pizzas but, unlike pizza dough, it rises a second time. Its dimpled surface is most often topped with rosemary or other aromatic herb and drizzled with olive oil for a crispy crust. But the unassertive flavor of the dough is perfect for all types of toppings. Serve focaccia as an appetizer or side dish.

Pear & Pepper Focaccia

Preparation time: 25 minutes
Rising time: 45 to 60 minutes
Cooking time: About 30 minutes

- 1 loaf (about 1 lb./455 g) frozen white bread dough, thawed
- 3 tablespoons (45 ml) lemon juice
- 3 medium-size firm-ripe pears (about 18 oz./510 g *total*)
- 1½ cups (90 g) firmly packed Italian or regular parsley sprigs
- 3 tablespoons (45 ml) olive oil
- 1 tablespoon grated lemon peel
- 2 tablespoons sugar
- ½ to 1 teaspoon coarsely ground pepper
- ⅓ cup (30 g) grated Parmesan cheese

1. Place dough in a nonstick or lightly oiled shallow 10- by 15-inch (25- by 38-cm) baking pan; press and push to cover pan evenly. If dough is too elastic, let it rest for a few minutes, then press again. Cover dough lightly with plastic wrap and let rise in a warm, draft-free place until almost doubled (45 to 60 minutes).

2. Meanwhile, pour lemon juice into a medium-size bowl. Core pears and thinly slice into bowl, turning fruit to coat with juice. Also make parsley pesto: in a blender or food processor, combine parsley sprigs, oil, and lemon peel. Whirl until smoothly puréed, scraping sides of container as needed.

3. With your fingertips, gently press dough down all over, giving surface a dimpled look; also press dough gently into corners of pan. Spread pesto evenly over dough. Arrange pear slices on dough and press in gently. Mix sugar and pepper and sprinkle over pears.

4. Bake in a 400°F (205°C) oven until focaccia is well browned at edges and on bottom (about 30 minutes); after 20 minutes, sprinkle with cheese. If topping is browned before bread is done, cover loosely with foil. Serve hot or warm. Makes 12 servings.

Per serving: 176 calories (30% calories from fat), 6 g total fat, 1 g saturated fat, 4 mg cholesterol, 227 mg sodium, 27 g carbohydrates, 1 g fiber, 4 g protein, 58 mg calcium, 1 mg iron

Grape-studded Focaccia

Preparation time: 25 minutes
Rising time: 1½ to 2 hours
Cooking time: 30 to 35 minutes

- Focaccia Dough (recipe follows); or 2 loaves (about 1 lb./455 g *each*) frozen white bread dough, thawed and kneaded together
- 1 tablespoon (15 ml) olive oil
- 40 to 50 seedless red grapes (6 to 8 oz./170 to 230 g *total*)
- 1 tablespoon chopped fresh rosemary or 1 teaspoon dried rosemary
- Coarse salt and coarsely ground pepper
- 3 ounces (85 g) pancetta or bacon, coarsely chopped

1. Prepare Focaccia Dough. When dough is almost doubled, punch it down, turn out onto a lightly floured board, and knead briefly to release air. Roll dough into a 9- by 12-inch (23- by 30-cm) rectangle about ½ inch (1 cm) thick. Fold rectangle loosely in half; transfer to an oiled shallow 10- by 15-inch (25- by 38-cm) baking pan and unfold. Press and stretch dough to cover pan evenly. If dough is too elastic, let it rest for about 5 minutes, then press again. Cover dough lightly with plastic wrap and let rise in a warm, draft-free place until almost doubled (45 to 60 minutes).

2. Brush oil lightly over dough. With your fingertips, gently press dough down all over, giving surface a dimpled look. Also press dough gently into corners of pan. Press grapes in even rows into dimpled dough, spacing them about 1 inch (2.5 cm) apart. Sprinkle with rosemary, then with salt and pepper.

3. Bake in a 400°F (205°C) oven until focaccia is well browned at edges and on bottom (30 to 35 minutes); after 20 minutes, sprinkle with pancetta. If topping is browned before bread is done, cover loosely with foil. Serve hot or warm. Makes 12 servings.

Focaccia Dough. In a large bowl, sprinkle 1 package **active dry yeast** over 1½ cups (360 ml) **warm water** (about 110°F/ 43°C); let stand until foamy (about 5 minutes). Stir in ½ teaspoon **salt** and 2 tablespoons (30 ml) **olive oil.** Add 2½ cups (310 g) **all-purpose flour;** stir to blend. Beat with an electric mixer on high speed until dough is glossy and stretchy (3 to 5 minutes). Stir in 1⅓ cups (165 g) more **all-purpose flour.**

To knead by hand, scrape dough onto a lightly floured board and knead until smooth and springy (about 10 minutes), adding more flour as needed to prevent sticking.

To knead with a dough hook, beat dough on medium speed

until it pulls cleanly from sides of bowl and is springy (5 to 7 minutes); if dough is sticky, add more flour, 1 tablespoon at a time.

Place dough in a greased bowl and turn over to grease top. Cover bowl with plastic wrap; let dough rise in a warm, draft-free place until almost doubled (45 to 60 minutes). Or let rise in refrigerator until next day.

Eggplant & Onion Focaccia

Preparation time: 30 minutes
Rising time: 1½ to 2 hours
Cooking time: 55 to 60 minutes

Focaccia Dough (recipe left); or 2 loaves (about 1 lb./455 g *each*) frozen white bread dough, thawed and kneaded together

2 **medium-size eggplants (about 2 lbs./905 g *total*), unpeeled, cut into ¾-inch (2-cm) cubes**

1 **small red onion (about 8 oz./230 g), cut into ¾-inch (2-cm) cubes**

2 **tablespoons (30 ml) olive oil**

1½ **cups (about 6 oz./170 g) shredded smoked or plain part-skim mozzarella cheese (or use smoked Gouda cheese)**

2 **tablespoons chopped Italian or regular parsley**

1. Prepare Focaccia Dough. When dough is almost doubled, punch it down, turn out onto a lightly floured board, and knead briefly to release air. Roll dough into a 9- by 12-inch

(23- by 30-cm) rectangle about ½ inch (1 cm) thick. Fold rectangle loosely in half; transfer to an oiled shallow 10- by 15-inch (25- by 38-cm) baking pan and unfold. Press and stretch dough to cover pan evenly. If dough is too elastic, let it rest for about 5 minutes, then press again. Cover dough lightly with plastic wrap and let rise in a warm, draft-free place until almost doubled (45 to 60 minutes).

2. Meanwhile, place eggplant and onion in a large, shallow baking pan. Drizzle with 1 tablespoon (15 ml) of the oil and mix gently; then spread vegetables out evenly. Bake in a 450°F (230°C) oven, stirring occasionally, until eggplant is lightly browned and beginning to soften (about 25 minutes); add water, ¼ cup (60 ml) at a time, if pan appears dry. Remove vegetables from pan and set aside.

3. Brush remaining 1 tablespoon (15 ml) oil lightly over dough. With your fingertips, gently press dough down all over, giving surface a dimpled look. Also press dough gently into corners of pan. Evenly sprinkle cheese over dimpled dough; distribute eggplant mixture over cheese.

4. Bake in a 400°F (205°C) oven until focaccia is well browned at edges and on bottom (30 to 35 minutes). If topping is browned before bread is done, cover loosely with foil. Sprinkle with parsley. Serve hot or warm. Makes 12 servings.

Sopaipillas
(recipe on facing page)

Our tender sopaipillas are as crisp and chewy as the traditional deep-fried breads, but to slim down the recipe, we've changed the cooking technique: the pastries are first boiled, then baked.

Sopaipillas

Preparation time: About 20 minutes
Rising time: 65 to 70 minutes
Cooking time: 50 to 55 minutes
Pictured on facing page

1 package active dry yeast

¼ cup (60 ml) warm water (about 110°F/43°C)

1½ cups (360 ml) nonfat milk

3 tablespoons (38 g) solid vegetable shortening

1 teaspoon salt

3 tablespoons granulated sugar

About 4 cups (500 g) all-purpose flour

Powdered sugar (optional)

Honey or flavored syrups (optional)

1. In a large bowl, combine yeast and warm water; let stand until yeast is softened (about 5 minutes). In a small pan, combine milk, shortening, salt, and 2 tablespoons of the granulated sugar; heat over low heat until warm (about 110°F/43°C), then stir into yeast mixture.

2. *To mix and knead by hand*, beat 4 cups (500 g) of the flour into yeast mixture with a heavy spoon; continue to beat until dough is stretchy (about 5 minutes). Scrape dough out onto a floured board; knead until smooth and satiny (8 to 10 minutes), adding more flour as needed to prevent sticking.

To mix and knead in a food processor, combine yeast mixture and 4 cups (500 g) of the flour in work bowl of a food processor. Whirl for 1 minute; dough should pull from sides of work bowl and no longer feel sticky. If it's still sticky, add more flour, 1 tablespoon at a time, whirling just until incorporated after each addition.

3. Place dough kneaded by either method in an oiled bowl and turn over to grease top. Cover with oiled plastic wrap and let rise in a warm place until almost doubled (about 45 minutes).

4. Punch dough down to release air, turn out onto a lightly floured board, and knead briefly. Divide dough into 4 equal pieces. Roll each piece out to about a 7-inch (18-cm) round. With a floured knife, cut each round into 6 equal pieces. Transfer to lightly floured baking sheets and cover with oiled plastic wrap. Let stand at room temperature until puffy (20 to 25 minutes).

5. Meanwhile, bring 3 quarts (2.8 liters) water and remaining 1 tablespoon granulated sugar to a boil in a large pan over high heat; adjust heat so water boils gently. Also lightly grease two 12- by 15-inch (30- by 38-cm) baking sheets.

6. Transfer puffy dough wedges, up to 5 at a time, to simmering water. Cook, turning often, for 4 minutes. With a slotted spoon, lift each piece from water and drain well. Set on prepared baking sheets. Bake in a 400° (205°C) oven until golden brown (30 to 35 minutes), switching positions of baking sheets halfway through baking. Serve warm (sopaipillas are best eaten when freshly baked). Or, if made ahead, let cool on racks; then wrap airtight and freeze for up to 1 month. Thaw before reheating; reheat just until warm (if overheated, pastries will harden).

7. Dust warm sopaipillas liberally with powdered sugar and serve with honey, if desired. Makes 2 dozen sopaipillas.

Per serving: 107 calories (16% calories from fat), 2 g total fat, 0.4 g saturated fat, 0.3 mg cholesterol, 100 mg sodium, 20 g carbohydrates, 0.6 g fiber, 3 g protein, 23 mg calcium, 1 mg iron

---

Tender, slightly sweet drop biscuits flavored with anise are delicious with jam at breakfast time, and just as good in place of dinner rolls.

Anise Biscuits

Preparation time: About 10 minutes
Baking time: About 20 minutes
Pictured on page 339

1⅓ cups (165 g) all-purpose flour

⅓ cup (46 g) yellow cornmeal

2 tablespoons sugar

1½ teaspoons baking powder

¼ teaspoon salt

½ to ¾ teaspoon anise seeds, crushed

½ cup (120 ml) nonfat milk

2 tablespoons (30 ml) *each* water and salad oil

2 large egg whites

½ teaspoon vanilla

1. In a large bowl, mix flour, cornmeal, sugar, baking powder, salt, and anise seeds (use the ¾-teaspoon amount for a stronger anise flavor). In a small bowl, beat milk, water, oil, egg whites, and vanilla until blended. Add egg mixture to flour mixture; stir just until dry ingredients are evenly moistened.

2. Spoon batter in 14 equal mounds (*each* about 4-teaspoon size) on two 12- by 15-inch (30- by 38-cm) nonstick (or lightly greased regular) baking sheets, spacing mounds 2 inches (5 cm) apart. Bake in a 375°F (190°C) oven until biscuits are firm to the touch and lightly browned (about 20 minutes), switching positions of baking sheets halfway through baking. Serve warm or cool. Makes 14 biscuits.

Per serving: 86 calories (23% calories from fat), 2 g total fat, 0.3 g saturated fat, 0.2 mg cholesterol, 104 mg sodium, 14 g carbohydrates, 0.5 g fiber, 2 g protein, 43 mg calcium, 0.8 mg iron

Crown your table with Three Kings Bread—a fruit-laced yeast bread traditionally served in Mexico on Twelfth Night (January 6). The bread is baked in a ring and royally jeweled with fruits and nuts; a tiny ceramic doll or dried lima bean is baked inside. The guest who discovers the "treasure" is obliged to host a party on February 2, the Feast of Candelaria.

Three Kings Bread

Preparation time: About 25 minutes
Rising time: About 40 minutes
Baking time: 35 to 40 minutes

¼   cup (38 g) raisins

¼   cup (35 g) chopped dried or candied cherries (or use all raisins or all cherries)

¼   cup (31 g) finely chopped walnuts

   About 3 cups (375 g) all-purpose flour

¼   teaspoon salt

1   package active dry yeast

1   cup (240 ml) nonfat milk

¼   cup (60 ml) honey

2   tablespoons (28 g) butter or margarine

1   large egg

1   teaspoon *each* grated lemon peel and grated orange peel

   Sugar Glaze (recipe follows)

   Dried or candied fruits and nuts

1. In a small bowl, combine raisins, cherries, and walnuts; set aside. In a large bowl, mix 1½ cups (185 g) of the flour, salt, and yeast; set aside. In a small pan, heat milk, honey, and butter over medium heat until very warm (120° to 130°F/49° to 54°C).

2. *To mix and knead by hand*, gradually add milk mixture to flour mixture; beat with a heavy spoon until smooth. Add egg, lemon peel, and orange peel; beat until well blended. Add 1½ cups (185 g) more flour and beat until dough is stretchy (about 5 minutes). Scrape dough out onto a lightly floured board and knead until smooth and satiny (8 to 10 minutes), adding more flour as needed to prevent sticking.

To mix and knead in a food processor, combine milk mixture and flour mixture in work bowl of food processor; whirl to combine. Add egg, lemon peel, and orange peel; whirl to blend. Add 1½ cups (185 g) more flour and whirl for 1 minute; dough should pull from sides of work bowl and no longer feel sticky. If it's still sticky, add more flour, 1 tablespoon at a time, whirling just until incorporated after each addition.

3. On lightly floured board, pat dough out to make a 7-inch (18-cm) round. Top dough with raisin-nut mixture, fold up edges, and knead until fruits and nuts are evenly distributed. Then shape dough into a roll 24 inches (61 cm) long (let dough rest for a few minutes between kneading and stretching if it's too elastic to stay in place). Carefully transfer roll to a lightly greased 12- by 15-inch (30- by 38-cm) nonstick baking sheet. Join ends to form a ring; pinch firmly to seal. Cover lightly with oiled plastic wrap and let rise in a warm place until almost doubled (about 40 minutes).

4. Bake in a 350°F (175ºC) oven until bread is golden brown and sounds hollow when tapped on bottom (35 to 40 minutes). Carefully transfer bread from baking sheet to a rack and let cool almost completely. If made ahead, wrap cooled loaf airtight and store at room temperature until next day (freeze for longer storage).

5. To serve, prepare Sugar Glaze and drizzle evenly over loaf. Decorate with fruits and nuts. Makes 1 loaf (14 to 16 servings).

Sugar Glaze. In a bowl, combine 1 cup (100 g) sifted **powdered sugar**, about 4 teaspoons **nonfat milk** (or a little more if needed for desired consistency), and ½ teaspoon **vanilla**. Stir until smooth.

Per serving: 197 calories (17% calories from fat), 4 g total fat, 1 g saturated fat, 190 mg cholesterol, 67 mg sodium, 37 g carbohydrates, 1 g fiber, 4 g protein, 33 mg calcium, 1 mg iron

Mangoes, a favorite Mexican fruit, give this coconut-flecked quick bread its golden color and sweet flavor.

1 cup (240 ml) puréed ripe mango (about a 1-lb./455-g mango)

¾ teaspoon baking soda mixed with 2 teaspoons water

1 cup (200 g) sugar

2 large eggs

½ cup (40 g) sweetened flaked coconut, minced

¼ cup (60 ml) salad oil

2½ cups (310 g) all-purpose flour

1½ teaspoons baking powder

Mango Quick Bread

Preparation time: About 15 minutes
Baking time: 50 to 55 minutes

1. In a large bowl, stir together mango purée and baking soda mixture. Let stand for 5 minutes. Then add sugar, eggs, coconut, and oil; beat until blended. Stir together flour and baking powder; add to mango mixture and beat until very well blended.

2. Pour batter into a 5- by 9-inch (12.5- by 23-cm) nonstick (or lightly greased regular) loaf pan. Bake in a 350°F (175°C) oven until loaf is richly browned, begins to pull away from sides of pan, and springs back when pressed (50 to 55 minutes). Let cool in pan on a rack for about 10 minutes. Run a knife between bread and sides of pan; then turn loaf out of pan onto rack to cool completely. Serve warm or cool. If made ahead, wrap cooled loaf airtight and store at room temperature until next day (freeze for longer storage). Makes 1 loaf (10 to 12 servings).

Per serving: 266 calories (24% calories from fat), 7 g total fat, 2 g saturated fat, 39 mg cholesterol, 174 mg sodium, 47 g carbohydrates, 1 g fiber, 4 g protein, 49 mg calcium, 2 mg iron

---

Breads and other baked goods are a national passion in Mexico. This delicate, slightly sweet raisin loaf offers all the fresh-baked goodness of its traditional counterpart, but it's missing much of the fat.

1 large egg

2 large egg whites

2 tablespoons (30 ml) water

⅔ cup (135 g) sugar

5 tablespoons (71 g) butter or margarine, at room temperature

1 tablespoon grated orange peel

1 cup (240 ml) reduced-fat or regular sour cream (do not use nonfat sour cream)

2 cups (274 g) bread flour or 2 cups (250 g) all-purpose flour

Raisin Batter Bread

Preparation time: About 10 minutes
Baking time: About 1¼ hours
Pictured on page 414

2 teaspoons baking powder

½ teaspoon baking soda

1¼ cups (188 g) raisins

1. In a large bowl, beat egg, egg whites, water, sugar, butter, and orange peel until blended. Stir in sour cream. In a small bowl, mix flour, baking powder, and baking soda; add to egg mixture and beat until blended. Stir in raisins.

2. Scrape batter into a lightly greased 5- by 9-inch (12.5- by 23-cm) nonstick loaf pan. Spread batter to smooth top. Bake in a 325°F (165°C) oven until bread begins to pull away from sides of pan and a wooden pick inserted in center comes out clean (about 1¼ hours). Let cool in pan on a rack for about 15 minutes. Run a knife between bread and sides of pan; then turn loaf out of pan onto rack to cool completely. If made ahead, wrap cooled loaf airtight and store at room temperature for up to 2 days (freeze for longer storage). Makes 1 loaf (10 to 12 servings).

Per serving: 276 calories (29% calories from fat), 9 g total fat, 5 g saturated fat, 41 mg cholesterol, 229 mg sodium, 44 g carbohydrates, 1 g fiber, 6 g protein, 66 mg calcium, 2 mg iron

Tortillas

In Mexican homes, tortillas are enjoyed plain with most meals—sometimes eaten whole, sometimes torn or cut into pieces.

Warm Tortillas

6 corn tortillas (6-inch/15-cm diameter) or flour tortillas (7- to 9-inch/18- to 23-cm diameter)

1. Brush tortillas lightly with hot water; then stack, wrap in foil, and heat in a 350°F (175°C) oven until warm (10 to 12 minutes). Makes 6 tortillas.

Per corn tortilla: 56 calories (10% calories from fat), 0.6 g total fat, 0.1 g saturated fat, 0 mg cholesterol, 40 mg sodium, 12 g carbohydrates, 1 g fiber, 1 g protein, 44 mg calcium, 0.4 mg iron

Per flour tortilla: 114 calories (20% calories from fat), 2 g total fat, 0.4 g saturated fat, 0 mg cholesterol, 167 mg sodium, 19 g carbohydrates, 1 g fiber, 3 g protein, 44 mg calcium, 1 mg iron

Crisp Taco Shells

6 corn tortillas (6-inch/15-cm diameter) or flour tortillas (7- to 9-inch/18- to 23-cm diameter)

Salt (optional)

1. Dip tortillas, one at a time, in hot water; drain briefly. Season to taste with salt, if desired.

2. Arrange tortillas in a single layer on large baking sheets. Do not overlap tortillas. Bake in a 500°F (260°C) oven for 4 minutes. With a metal spatula, turn tortillas over; continue to bake until crisp and browned (about 2 more minutes). If made ahead, let cool; then store airtight at room temperature for up to 5 days. Makes 6 crisp taco shells (unlike commercial curved taco shells, these are flat shells for open-faced tacos).

Per corn taco shell: 56 calories (10% calories from fat), 0.6 g total fat, 0.1 g saturated fat, 0 mg cholesterol, 40 mg sodium, 12 g carbohydrates, 1 g fiber, 1 g protein, 44 mg calcium, 0.4 mg iron

Per flour taco shell: 114 calories (20% calories from fat), 2 g total fat, 0.4 g saturated fat, 0 mg cholesterol, 167 mg sodium, 19 g carbohydrates, 1 g fiber, 3 g protein, 44 mg calcium, 1 mg iron

Water-crisped Tortilla Chips

6 corn tortillas (6-inch/15-cm diameter) or flour tortillas (7- to 9-inch/18- to 23-cm diameter)

Salt (optional)

1. Dip tortillas, one at a time, in hot water; drain briefly. Season tortillas to taste with salt, if desired. Stack tortillas; then cut the stack into 6 to 8 wedges.

2. Arrange wedges in a single layer on large baking sheets. Do not overlap wedges. Bake in a 500°F (260°C) oven for 4 minutes. With a metal spatula, turn wedges over; continue to bake until crisp and browned (about 2 more minutes). If made ahead, let cool; then store airtight at room temperature for up to 5 days. Makes about 4 cups (170 g) corn chips, about 6 cups (255 g) flour chips.

Per serving of corn chips: 83 calories (10% calories from fat), 0.9 g total fat, 0.1 g saturated fat, 0 mg cholesterol, 60 mg sodium, 17 g carbohydrates, 2 g fiber, 2 g protein, 66 mg calcium, 0.5 mg iron

Per serving of flour chips: 114 calories (20% calories from fat), 2 g total fat, 0.4 g saturated fat, 0 mg cholesterol, 168 mg sodium, 19 g carbohydrates, 1 g fiber, 3 g protein, 44 mg calcium, 1 mg iron

Crisp Corn Tortilla Strips

3 corn tortillas (6-inch/15-cm diameter)

Salt (optional)

1. Dip tortillas, one at a time, in hot water; drain briefly. Season to taste with salt, if desired. Stack tortillas; cut stack in half, then cut into strips ¼ inch (6 mm) wide.

2. Arrange strips in a single layer on a large baking sheet. Do not overlap strips. Bake in a 500°F (260°C) oven for 3 minutes. With a metal spatula, turn strips over and continue to bake until crisp and browned (about 1 more minute). If made ahead, let cool; then store airtight at room temperature for up to 5 days. Makes about 1½ cups (64 g).

Per serving: 56 calories (10% calories from fat), 0.6 g total fat, 0.1 g saturated fat, 0 mg cholesterol, 40 mg sodium, 12 g carbohydrates, 1 g fiber, 1 g protein, 44 mg calcium, 0.4 mg iron

Topped with yogurt and sugared berries, puddinglike spoonbread is a delicious breakfast treat.

- 10 cups (1.4 kg) mixed fresh berries, such as blackberries, raspberries, and hulled strawberries
- ⅓ cup (70 g) sugar
- 4 cups (950 ml) low-fat (1%) milk
- ¼ cup (2 oz./55 g) butter or margarine
- 2 tablespoons sugar
- ½ teaspoon salt
- 1⅓ cups (185 g) yellow cornmeal
- 6 large eggs, separated
- 4 teaspoons baking powder
- 1 teaspoon cream of tartar
- 2 cups (470 ml) lemon-flavored nonfat yogurt

1. In a large bowl, combine berries and the ⅓ cup (70 g) sugar. Mix gently; then set aside.

Spoonbread with Berries

Preparation time: About 20 minutes
Cooking time: About 1 hour

2. In a 5- to 6-quart (5- to 6-liter) pan, combine milk, butter, the 2 tablespoons sugar, and salt. Heat over medium-low heat, stirring occasionally, until mixture is just steaming (about 4 minutes). Reduce heat to low and gradually add cornmeal, stirring constantly; cook, stirring, until mixture is thick (about 6 minutes). Remove from heat and let cool slightly. Whisk in egg yolks and baking powder until blended; set aside.

3. In a large bowl, beat egg whites and cream of tartar with an electric mixer on high speed until whites hold stiff peaks. Blend 1 cup (240 ml) of the

beaten egg whites into cornmeal mixture; then gently fold cornmeal mixture into remaining whites. Scrape mixture into a buttered 9- by 13-inch (23- by 33-cm) baking pan. Bake in a 350°F (175°C) oven until top is golden brown and firm to the touch and a wooden pick inserted in center comes out clean (about 45 minutes).

4. Meanwhile, in a medium-size bowl, mix yogurt with 2 cups (290 g) of the sugared berries.

5. Top portions of spoonbread with berry-yogurt mixture; serve remaining berries and their juices alongside. Makes 8 servings.

Per serving: 415 calories (25% calories from fat), 12 g total fat, 6 g saturated fat, 180 mg cholesterol, 577 mg sodium, 65 g carbohydrates, 8 g fiber, 14 g protein, 446 mg calcium, 3 mg iron

---

Though it's made without oil, this quick spoonbread is nonetheless moist and rich-tasting. Fresh corn kernels give it a nice texture and a naturally sweet flavor.

- ½ cup (70 g) blue cornmeal
- ½ cup (60 g) all-purpose flour
- 2 tablespoons sugar
- 1½ teaspoons baking powder
- ½ teaspoon ground coriander
- ¼ teaspoon *each* salt and pepper
- 1 cup (240 ml) nonfat milk
- 1 large egg
- 2 large egg whites
- ⅔ cup (113 g) fresh-cut yellow or white corn kernels (from about 1 medium-size ear corn); or ⅔ cup (100 g) frozen corn kernels, thawed

Blue Corn Spoonbread

Preparation time: 15 minutes
Cooking time: About 20 minutes

1. In a large bowl, mix cornmeal, flour, sugar, baking powder, coriander, salt, and pepper. In a small bowl, beat milk, egg, and egg whites until blended. Add egg mixture and corn to flour mixture and stir just until dry ingredients are evenly moistened.

2. Pour batter into a 9-inch (23-cm) nonstick (or lightly greased regular) pie or cake pan. Bake in a 400°F (205°C) oven until spoonbread is browned on top and a wooden pick

inserted in center comes out clean (about 20 minutes). For best flavor, serve spoonbread freshly baked; spoon out of pan to serve. Makes 8 servings.

Per serving: 108 calories (9% calories from fat), 1 g total fat, 0.3 g saturated fat, 27 mg cholesterol, 199 mg sodium, 20 g carbohydrates, 1 g fiber, 5 g protein, 95 mg calcium, 1 mg iron

What better way to start a wonderful weekend than with the aroma of fresh-brewed coffee and homemade breakfast specialties?

Ricotta Pancakes with Lemon-Maple Syrup

Preparation time: 20 minutes
Cooking time: 10 to 15 minutes

½ cup (120 ml) pure maple syrup

½ teaspoon grated lemon peel

1 teaspoon lemon juice

2 large eggs

⅔ cup (152 g) nonfat ricotta cheese

¼ cup (50 g) sugar

¼ cup (60 ml) half-and-half

1 teaspoon vanilla

½ cup (60 g) all-purpose flour

¼ teaspoon baking powder

2 large egg whites

¼ teaspoon cream of tartar

⅛ teaspoon salt

2 tablespoons (30 ml) salad oil

1. In a small pan, combine syrup, ¼ teaspoon of the lemon peel, and lemon juice. Stir over medium heat until steaming (3 to 5 minutes); keep warm over very low heat.

2. In a food processor or blender, combine eggs, ricotta cheese, 2 tablespoons of the sugar, half-and-half, vanilla, and remaining ¼ teaspoon lemon peel; whirl until smooth. Add flour and baking powder; whirl until flour is evenly moistened. Transfer batter to a medium-size bowl.

3. In a large, deep bowl, beat egg whites and 1 tablespoon (15 ml) water with an electric mixer on high speed until frothy. Beat in cream of tartar and salt. Add remaining 2 tablespoons sugar, 1 tablespoon at a time, beating until mixture holds stiff, moist peaks. Stir about a third of the egg white mixture into batter to lighten it; then fold batter into remaining egg white mixture.

4. Heat 1 tablespoon (15 ml) of the oil on each of 2 nonstick griddles over medium heat (or heat oil in wide nonstick frying pans). For each pancake, measure out ⅓ cup (80 ml) batter, scooping it up from bottom of bowl; pour onto griddle and spread out slightly. Cook until tops of pancakes are bubbly and almost dry (2 to 3 minutes); turn over and cook until browned on bottoms (about 2 more minutes). Serve with warm syrup. Makes about 12 pancakes (4 servings).

Per serving: 379 calories (27% calories from fat), 11 g total fat, 3 g saturated fat, 115 mg cholesterol, 209 mg sodium, 56 g carbohydrates, 0.4 g fiber, 14 g protein, 289 mg calcium, 2 mg iron

Quick Cinnamon Buns

Preparation time: 35 minutes
Cooking time: About 30 minutes

Filling:

½ cup (75 g) raisins

¾ cup (165 g) firmly packed brown sugar

4 ounces (115 g) Neufchâtel cheese, at room temperature

⅓ cup (28 g) graham cracker crumbs

1½ teaspoons ground cinnamon

Buns:

2 cups (274 g) bread flour or 2 cups (250 g) all-purpose flour

1 tablespoon baking powder

¼ teaspoon salt

¾ cup (158 g) low-fat (2%) cottage cheese

⅓ cup (70 g) granulated sugar

⅓ cup (80 ml) nonfat milk

¼ cup (60 ml) salad oil

2 teaspoons vanilla

Glaze:

1 cup (120 g) sifted powdered sugar

¼ to ½ teaspoon vanilla

1. In a small bowl, combine raisins and ½ cup (120 ml) hot water; let stand until raisins are softened (about 10 minutes), stirring occasionally. In another small bowl, mix brown sugar, Neufchâtel cheese, graham cracker crumbs, and cinnamon until mixture resembles coarse, moist crumbs; set aside. In a medium-size bowl, combine flour, baking powder, and salt; set aside.

2. In a food processor or a large bowl, combine cottage cheese, granulated sugar, milk, oil, and the 2 teaspoons vanilla. Whirl or beat with an electric mixer until smoothly puréed. Add flour mixture; whirl or stir to make a soft dough. Transfer dough to a lightly floured board and knead several times, or until dough holds together.

3. With floured fingers, pat dough into a 9- by 14-inch (23- by 35.5-cm) rectangle. Distribute brown sugar mixture evenly over dough to within ½ inch (1 cm) of edge; press mixture gently into dough. Drain raisins well; scatter over sugar mixture and press gently into dough.

4. With floured fingers, snugly roll up dough jelly-roll style, starting with a long edge; pinch ends and seam to seal. Using a serrated knife, cut roll into 12 equal slices; if desired, wipe knife clean between cuts. Place buns, cut side up, in a greased nonstick or regular 10-inch (25-cm) cheesecake pan with a removable rim. Bake in a 400°F (205°C) oven until buns are richly browned (about 30 minutes).

5. Meanwhile, in a small bowl, beat powdered sugar, about 1 tablespoon (15 ml) water, and the ¼ to ½ teaspoon vanilla until smoothly blended. If needed, add more water, ½ teaspoon at a time, to make glaze thin enough to drizzle. Set glaze aside.

6. Remove baked buns from oven and let cool on a rack for 5 minutes. Carefully remove pan rim; stir glaze and drizzle over buns. Serve at once. Makes 12 buns.

Per bun: 301 calories (23% calories from fat), 8 g total fat, 2 g saturated fat, 8 mg cholesterol, 292 mg sodium, 52 g carbohydrates, 1 g fiber, 6 g protein, 114 mg calcium, 2 mg iron

Cheese Blintzes

Preparation time: 30 minutes
Cooking time: About 25 minutes

- 2 large eggs
- ½ cup (60 g) all-purpose flour
- ¾ cup (180 ml) nonfat milk
- About 3 tablespoons (43 g) butter or margarine
- 12 ounces (340 g) farmer's cheese or dry-curd cottage cheese
- 2 to 3 tablespoons sugar
- 1 tablespoon (15 ml) plain non-fat yogurt or nonfat milk
- 2 teaspoons grated lemon peel
- ¾ teaspoon vanilla
- ½ teaspoon ground cinnamon
- Finely shredded lemon peel (optional)
- ¾ cup (180 ml) strawberry preserves
- ¾ cup (180 ml) nonfat sour cream

1. In a blender or a medium-size bowl, combine eggs, flour, and milk. Whirl or beat until smoothly blended.

2. Melt ½ teaspoon of the butter in a small nonstick frying pan over medium heat. Pour about 2 tablespoons (30 ml) of the batter into hot pan; tip and swirl pan to cover bottom evenly with batter. Cook until top of pancake feels dry when lightly touched (about 1 minute). Gently turn pancake over with a wide spatula (be careful not to tear pancake); cook until faintly speckled with brown on bottom. Turn pancake out of pan and lay flat.

3. Repeat to cook remaining pancakes, stirring batter before you make each pancake and adding more butter to pan as needed. Stack pancakes, sepa-rating them with wax paper or plastic wrap; you should have about 12 pancakes.

4. In a food processor or a large bowl, combine farmer's cheese, sugar, yogurt, grated lemon peel, vanilla, and cinnamon; whirl or beat with an electric mixer until well blended.

5. Divide filling into as many portions as you have pancakes. Lay one pancake flat, darker side down. Mound one portion of filling in center. Fold opposite sides of pancake over filling; then fold ends over filling to enclose. Set blintz seam side down and pat gently to make filling evenly thick. Repeat to fill remaining pancakes. (At this point, you may arrange blintzes in a 12- by 15-inch/30- by 38-cm pan, cover tightly, and refrigerate for up to 4 hours.)

6. Melt 2 teaspoons of the butter in a wide nonstick frying pan over medium-high heat. Add about half the blintzes (do not crowd pan); cook until blintzes are golden brown on bottom (about 1 minute). Turn with a wide spatula and cook until browned on other side (1 to 2 more minutes). Repeat to cook remaining blintzes; as blintzes are cooked, transfer them to a platter and keep warm. Garnish with shredded lemon peel, if desired. Offer preserves and sour cream to add to taste. Makes 4 servings.

Per serving: 521 calories (29% calories from fat), 18 g total fat, 4 g saturated fat, 153 mg cholesterol, 446 mg sodium, 75 g carbohydrates, 1 g fiber, 22 g protein, 247 mg calcium, 2 mg iron

Cream Cheese Blond Brownies,
Trail Mix Bars (recipes on page 352);
Cranberry Walnut Bars (recipe on page 353)

Cookies, Bars & Brownies

Rich, fudgy brownies and moist, chewy cookies need not be off-limits to a low-fat diet. Small amounts of butter carry the deep chocolate flavor of unsweetened cocoa without unnecessary fat. And dried cherries and cranberries add interest and flavor to old favorites. Treat yourself to luscious Chocolate Cherry Brownies or sweet-tart Lemon Bars. For a continental delight, relax with coffee and Currant Biscotti— perfect for dunking.

A swirl of cream cheese enriches these golden brownies.

- 1 large package (about 8 oz./ 230 g) nonfat cream cheese, at room temperature
- ½ cup (100 g) granulated sugar
- 2 large egg whites
- ¼ cup (60 ml) nonfat sour cream
- 1 tablespoon all-purpose flour
- 1 teaspoon vanilla
- 1¼ cups (155 g) all-purpose flour
- 1 teaspoon baking powder
- ¼ cup (31 g) chopped walnuts
- ⅓ cup (80 ml) pure maple syrup
- ⅓ cup (73 g) firmly packed brown sugar
- ⅓ cup (76 g) butter or margarine, at room temperature
- 1 large egg
- 2 teaspoons vanilla

Cream Cheese Blond Brownies

Preparation time: 15 minutes
Cooking time: About 25 minutes
Pictured on page 350

1. In a small bowl, combine cream cheese, granulated sugar, egg whites, sour cream, the 1 tablespoon flour, and the 1 teaspoon vanilla. Beat until smooth; set aside. In another small bowl, stir together the 1¼ cups (155 g) flour, baking powder, and walnuts; set aside.

2. In a large bowl, combine syrup, brown sugar, butter, egg, and the 2 teaspoons vanilla. Beat until smooth. Add flour mixture; beat until dry ingredients are evenly moistened.

3. Pour two-thirds of the brownie batter into a lightly greased square 8-inch (20-cm) nonstick or regular baking pan; spread to make level. Pour cheese mixture evenly over batter. Drop remaining batter by spoonfuls over cheese mixture; swirl with a knife to blend batter slightly with cheese mixture.

4. Bake in a 350°F (175°C) oven until a wooden pick inserted in center comes out clean (about 25 minutes; pierce brownie, not cheese mixture). Let cool in pan on a rack, then cut into 2-inch (5-cm) squares. Makes 16 brownies.

Per brownie: 168 calories (30% calories from fat), 6 g total fat, 3 g saturated fat, 25 mg cholesterol, 153 mg sodium, 25 g carbohydrates, 0.4 g fiber, 4 g protein, 76 mg calcium, 0.7 mg iron

---

Just right for taking along on a hiking trip, these tempting blond brownies are chunky with chocolate chips and plenty of dark and golden raisins.

- 1 cup (125 g) all-purpose flour
- 1 teaspoon baking powder
- ¾ cup (110 g) *each* golden and dark raisins
- ½ cup (85 g) semisweet chocolate chips
- ⅓ cup (76 g) butter or margarine, at room temperature
- ½ cup (110 g) firmly packed brown sugar
- ½ cup (120 ml) smooth unsweetened applesauce
- 2 large egg whites
- 2 teaspoons vanilla

Trail Mix Bars

Preparation time: 20 minutes
Cooking time: About 40 minutes
Pictured on page 350

1. In a small bowl, stir together flour, baking powder, raisins, and chocolate chips. In a food processor or a large bowl, combine butter, sugar, applesauce, egg whites, and vanilla; whirl or beat with an electric mixer until smoothly blended. Add flour mixture; whirl or beat until dry ingredients are evenly moistened. Spread batter in a lightly greased square 8-inch (20-cm) nonstick or regular baking pan.

2. Bake in a 325°F (165°C) oven until cookie is golden around edges and a wooden pick inserted in center comes out clean (about 40 minutes; do not pierce chocolate chips). Let cool in pan on a rack. To serve, cut into 2-inch (5-cm) squares. Makes 16 bars.

Per bar: 163 calories (30% calories from fat), 6 g total fat, 3 g saturated fat, 10 mg cholesterol, 81 mg sodium, 28 g carbohydrates, 1 g fiber, 2 g protein, 34 mg calcium, 0.9 mg iron

Both fresh and dried cranberries go into these bars, adding color and bursts of tart flavor.

- 1 cup (90 g) dried cranberries
- 3 tablespoons (45 ml) orange-flavored liqueur or orange juice
- 1¼ cups (155 g) all-purpose flour
- ¼ cup (30 g) powdered sugar
- ⅛ teaspoon salt
- ⅓ cup (76 g) butter or margarine, cut into chunks
- 1 tablespoon (15 ml) apple jelly, melted and cooled slightly
- 1 large egg
- 2 large egg whites
- ⅔ cup (160 ml) light corn syrup
- ⅔ cup (135 g) granulated sugar
- ½ teaspoon vanilla
- 1 cup (95 g) fresh or frozen cranberries, chopped
- ½ cup (63 g) chopped walnuts

1. In a small bowl, combine dried cranberries and liqueur; let stand until

Cranberry Walnut Bars

Preparation time: 20 minutes
Cooking time: About 1 hour
Pictured on page 350

cranberries are softened (about 10 minutes), stirring occasionally.

2. In a food processor or a medium-size bowl, whirl or stir together flour, powdered sugar, and salt. Add butter and jelly; whirl or rub with your fin-gers until mixture resembles coarse crumbs. Press crumbs firmly over bottom and about ½ inch (1 cm) up sides of a lightly greased square 8-inch (20-cm) nonstick or regular baking pan. Prick dough all over with a fork. Bake in a 350°F (175°C) oven until pale golden (about 15 minutes).

3. Meanwhile, in a large bowl, beat whole egg, egg whites, corn syrup, granulated sugar, and vanilla until smoothly blended. Stir in fresh cranberries, dried cranberry–liqueur mixture, and walnuts. Remove hot baked crust from oven; pour filling into crust. Return to oven and bake until filling no longer jiggles in center when pan is gently shaken (35 to 40 minutes; cover edge of crust with foil if it begins to brown excessively). Let cool in pan on a rack. Serve at room temperature or chilled; to serve, cut into 2-inch (5-cm) squares. Makes 16 bars.

Per bar: 218 calories (28% calories from fat), 7 g total fat, 3 g saturated fat, 24 mg cholesterol, 84 mg sodium, 37 g carbohydrates, 1 g fiber, 2 g protein, 9 mg calcium, 0.6 mg iron

Bits of crystallized or candied ginger are a piquant surprise in these dark, moist bars.

- 1 cup (120 g) whole wheat flour
- ¼ cup (50 g) granulated sugar
- ½ teaspoon baking soda
- 3 tablespoons coarsely chopped crystallized or candied ginger
- ¼ cup (60 ml) *each* nonfat milk and molasses
- 2 large egg whites
- About 3 tablespoons powdered sugar (optional)

Ginger Bars

Preparation time: 15 minutes
Cooking time: 20 to 25 minutes

1. In a large bowl, stir together flour, granulated sugar, baking soda, and ginger. Add milk, molasses, and egg whites; beat until smoothly blended.

2. Spread batter evenly in a lightly greased square 8-inch (20-cm) nonstick or regular baking pan. Bake in a 350°F (175°C) oven until center springs back when lightly pressed (20 to 25 minutes). Serve warm or cool; to serve, cut into 2-inch (5-cm) squares and sprinkle with powdered sugar, if desired. These bars are best eaten fresh, so serve them the same day you make them. Makes 16 bars.

Per bar: 67 calories (5% calories from fat), 0.4 g total fat, 0.1 g saturated fat, 0.1 mg cholesterol, 52 mg sodium, 15 g carbohydrates, 0.9 g fiber, 2 g protein, 25 mg calcium, 1 mg iron

Dense and moist, these brownies are a chocoholic's dream come true.

1 package (about 5 oz./140 g) pitted dried cherries, chopped

¼ cup (60 ml) kirsch or berry liqueur

½ cup (4 oz./115 g) butter or margarine, cut into chunks

4 ounces (115 g) unsweetened chocolate, coarsely chopped

2 cups (400 g) sugar

2 teaspoons vanilla

¼ to ½ teaspoon instant espresso or coffee powder

2 large egg whites

2 large eggs

1 cup (125 g) all-purpose flour

½ teaspoon *each* baking powder and salt

¾ to 1 cup (180 to 240 ml) cherry preserves

Chocolate Cherry Brownies

Preparation time: 20 minutes
Cooking time: 45 to 50 minutes
Pictured on facing page

1. In a small bowl, combine dried cherries and liqueur; let stand until cherries are softened (about 15 minutes), stirring occasionally.

2. Meanwhile, melt butter in a 4- to 5-quart (3.8- to 5-liter) pan over medium-low heat. Remove pan from heat, add chocolate, and stir until chocolate is melted and mixture is smooth. Let cool for 10 minutes. Add sugar, vanilla, and instant espresso. Mix well. Beat in egg whites; then add whole eggs, one at a time, beating well after each addi-

tion. Add dried cherry mixture, flour, baking powder, and salt; stir until dry ingredients are evenly moistened.

3. Spoon two-thirds of the batter into a lightly greased and floured 9- by 13-inch (23- by 33-cm) baking pan; spread to make level. Drop preserves by spoonfuls over batter and gently spread out evenly. Drop remaining batter by spoonfuls over preserves; swirl with a knife to blend batter slightly with preserves.

4. Bake in a 350°F (175°C) oven until a wooden pick inserted in center comes out clean (45 to 50 minutes). Let cool in pan on a rack, then cut into about 2-inch (5-cm) squares. Makes 24 brownies.

Per brownie: 200 calories (30% calories from fat), 7 g total fat, 4 g saturated fat, 28 mg cholesterol, 110 mg sodium, 35 g carbohydrates, 1 g fiber, 2 g protein, 16 mg calcium, 0.7 mg iron

---

Here's a cookie version of a popular campfire treat.

1½ cups (128 g) graham cracker crumbs (about twenty square 2-inch/5-cm crackers)

¼ cup (50 g) sugar

¼ cup (2 oz./55 g) butter or margarine, melted

1 jar (about 7 oz./200 g) marshmallow fluff (marshmallow creme)

⅔ cup (115 g) semisweet chocolate chips

½ cup (43 g) unsweetened cocoa powder

1½ cups (69 g) small marshmallows

1. In a food processor or a medium-size bowl, combine graham cracker

One-pan S'mores

Preparation time: 15 minutes
Cooking time: About 20 minutes
Chilling time: At least 1 hour

crumbs, sugar, butter, and 1 tablespoon (15 ml) water. Whirl or stir with a fork until mixture resembles coarse crumbs. Press crumbs firmly over bottom and about ½ inch (1 cm) up sides of a lightly greased square 8-inch (20-cm) nonstick or regular baking pan. Bake in a 350°F (175°C) oven until crust feels firm when pressed (about 15 minutes). Let cool completely in pan on a rack.

2. Meanwhile, in a 1½- to 2-quart (1.4- to 1.9-liter) pan, combine marshmallow fluff and 1 tablespoon (15 ml)

water. Stir constantly over medium-low heat just until fluff is melted and smooth. Remove pan from heat and add chocolate chips; stir constantly until chocolate is melted and mixture is smooth. Add cocoa and stir well. Working quickly, stir in marshmallows just until combined (don't let marshmallows melt). Immediately spoon marshmallow mixture over cooled crust and spread to make level.

3. Cover and refrigerate until firm (at least 1 hour) or for up to 8 hours. To serve, cut into 2-inch (5-cm) squares. Makes 16 bars.

Per bar: 173 calories (30% calories from fat), 6 g total fat, 3 g saturated fat, 8 mg cholesterol, 105 mg sodium, 30 g carbohydrates, 1 g fiber, 2 g protein, 7 mg calcium, 0.8 mg iron

Chocolate Cherry Brownies (recipe on facing page),
Cherry-Vanilla Ice Cream (recipe on page 416)

Here's a low-fat version of an all-time favorite. Oatmeal goes into the crust, providing a chewy, nutty-tasting complement to the sweet-tart custard filling.

- 1 **cup (80 g) regular rolled oats**
- 1¼ **cups (155 g) all-purpose flour**
- ⅓ **cup (40 g) powdered sugar**
- ½ **teaspoon grated lemon peel**
- ¼ **cup (2 oz./55 g) butter or margarine, cut into chunks**
- 2 **tablespoons (30 ml) smooth unsweetened applesauce**
- 1 **large egg**
- 2 **large egg whites**
- 1 **cup (200 g) granulated sugar**
- ½ **to 1 teaspoon grated lemon peel**
- 2 **tablespoons (30 ml) lemon juice**
- 1 **tablespoon all-purpose flour**
- ½ **teaspoon baking powder**
- 3 **tablespoons powdered sugar**
- 4 **thin lemon slices, cut into quarters, seeds discarded**

Lemon Bars

Preparation time: 20 minutes
Cooking time: About 50 minutes

1. In a food processor or blender, whirl oats until finely ground. Distribute evenly over bottom of a lightly greased square 8-inch (20-cm) nonstick or regular baking pan; set aside.

2. In a food processor or large bowl, whirl or stir together the 1¼ cups (155 g) flour, the ⅓ cup (40 g) powdered sugar, and the ½ teaspoon lemon peel. Add butter and applesauce; whirl or rub with your fingers until mixture resembles coarse crumbs. Scatter crumbs evenly over oats in pan; press firmly to make an even layer that covers bottom of pan and extends about ½ inch (1 cm) up sides. Prick dough all over with a fork. Bake in a 325°F (165°C) oven until pale golden (about 20 minutes).

3. Meanwhile, in a small bowl, beat

whole egg and egg whites with an electric mixer on high speed until foamy. Gradually add granulated sugar, beating until mixture is thick and pale in color. Add the ½ to 1 teaspoon lemon peel, lemon juice, the 1 tablespoon flour, and baking powder; beat until smooth.

4. Remove hot baked crust from oven; pour lemon mixture into crust. Return to oven and bake until filling no longer jiggles in center when pan is gently shaken (about 30 minutes). Let cool in pan on a rack. Serve at room temperature or chilled. To serve, cut into 2-inch (5-cm) squares. Just before serving, sprinkle with the 3 tablespoons powdered sugar and garnish with quartered lemon slices. Makes 16 bars.

Per bar: 155 calories (20% calories from fat), 4 g total fat, 2 g saturated fat, 21 mg cholesterol, 56 mg sodium, 29 g carbohydrates, 0.8 g fiber, 3 g protein, 19 mg calcium, 0.8 mg iron

---

Moist and chewy, these wholesome bars get their sweetness from dates and maple syrup.

- ¾ **cup (90 g) whole wheat flour**
- ½ **teaspoon *each* baking powder and baking soda**
- ½ **cup (89 g) chopped pitted dates**
- ½ **cup (120 ml) pure maple syrup**
- 2 **large egg whites**
- ½ **teaspoon vanilla**

Maple Date Bars

Preparation time: 15 minutes
Cooking time: About 20 minutes

1. In a large bowl, stir together flour, baking powder, baking soda, and dates. Add syrup, egg whites, and vanilla; beat until smooth.

2. Spread batter evenly in a lightly greased square 8-inch (20-cm) non-

stick or regular baking pan. Bake in a 350°F (175°C) oven until center springs back when lightly pressed (about 20 minutes). Serve warm or cool; to serve, cut into 2-inch (5-cm) squares. These bars are best eaten fresh, so serve them the same day you make them. Makes 16 bars.

Per bar: 65 calories (5% calories from fat), 0.4 g total fat, 0.1 g saturated fat, 0 mg cholesterol, 62 mg sodium, 15 g carbohydrates, 1 g fiber, 1 g protein, 19 mg calcium, 0.4 mg iron

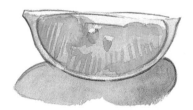

If you love brownies and cheese-cake, you'll find these decadent bars irresistible.

- ½ cup (4 oz./115 g) butter or mar-garine, cut into chunks
- 4 ounces (115 g) unsweetened chocolate, coarsely chopped
- 2 large packages (about 8 oz./ 230 g *each*) nonfat cream cheese, at room temperature
- 3 cups (600 g) sugar
- 4 large egg whites
- ½ cup (120 ml) nonfat sour cream
- 3 tablespoons all-purpose flour
- 4 teaspoons vanilla
- ¼ cup (22 g) unsweetened cocoa powder
- ¼ teaspoon instant espresso or coffee powder
- 2 large egg whites
- 2 large eggs
- 1 cup (125 g) all-purpose flour
- ½ teaspoon *each* baking powder and salt

Chocolate Cheesecake Brownies

Preparation time: 25 minutes
Cooking time: About 45 minutes

1. Melt butter in a 4- to 5-quart (3.8- to 5-liter) pan over medium-low heat. Remove pan from heat, add chocolate, and stir constantly until chocolate is melted and mixture is smooth. Let cool for about 10 minutes.

2. Meanwhile, in a food processor or a large bowl, combine cream cheese, 1 cup (200 g) of the sugar, the 4 egg whites, sour cream, the 3 tablespoons flour, and 2 teaspoons of the vanilla. Whirl or beat with an electric mixer until smooth; set aside.

3. To chocolate mixture, add remaining 2 cups (400 g) sugar, cocoa, remaining

2 teaspoons vanilla, and instant espresso. Mix well. Beat in the 2 egg whites; then add whole eggs, one at a time, beating well after each addition. Add the 1 cup (125 g) flour, baking powder, and salt; stir until dry ingredients are evenly moistened.

4. Spoon two-thirds of the batter into a lightly greased and floured 9- by 13-inch (23- by 33-cm) baking pan; spread to make level. Pour cheese mixture evenly over batter. Drop remaining batter by spoonfuls over cheese mixture; swirl with a knife to blend batter slightly with cheese mixture.

5. Bake in a 350°F (175°C) oven until cheese mixture is golden and a wooden pick inserted in center comes out clean (about 45 minutes; pierce brownie, not cheese mixture). Let cool in pan on a rack, then cut into about 2-inch (5-cm) squares. Makes 24 brownies.

Per brownie: 215 calories (29% calories from fat), 7 g total fat, 4 g saturated fat, 30 mg cholesterol, 208 mg sodium, 34 g carbohydrates, 1 g fiber, 6 g protein, 75 mg calcium, 0.8 mg iron

---

Oatmeal cookies are always a popular choice for the lunchbox.

- 2 cups (250 g) all-purpose flour
- 1 teaspoon *each* baking soda and ground cinnamon
- ½ teaspoon salt
- ¾ cup (6 oz./170 g) butter or margarine, at room temperature
- 1½ cups (330 g) firmly packed brown sugar
- 1 cup (240 ml) nonfat sour cream or plain nonfat yogurt
- 1 teaspoon vanilla
- 3 cups (240 g) regular rolled oats
- 1½ cups (218 g) raisins

Oatmeal Raisin Cookies

Preparation time: 20 minutes
Cooking time: About 15 minutes

1. In a medium-size bowl, stir together flour, baking soda, cinnamon, and salt; set aside.

2. In a food processor or a large bowl, combine butter, sugar, sour cream, and vanilla. Whirl or beat with an electric mixer until well blended. Add flour mixture to butter mixture; whirl or beat until dry ingredients are evenly

moistened. Stir in oats and raisins.

3. Spoon rounded 1-tablespoon (15-ml) portions of dough onto lightly greased large nonstick or regular baking sheets, spacing cookies about 2 inches (5 cm) apart.

4. Bake in a 350°F (175°C) oven until cookies are firm to the touch (about 15 minutes), switching positions of baking sheets halfway through baking. Let cookies cool on baking sheets for about 3 minutes, then transfer to racks to cool completely. Makes about 4½ dozen cookies.

Per cookie: 124 calories (28% calories from fat), 4 g total fat, 2 g saturated fat, 9 mg cholesterol, 97 mg sodium, 21 g carbohydrates, 1 g fiber, 2 g protein, 22 mg calcium, 0.8 mg iron

Cocoa Pepper Cookies, Mexican Wedding
Cookies (recipes on facing page);
Lemon Cookies (recipe on page 360)

A lowfat, more cakelike version of Mexico's famous wedding cookies, these sugar-coated treats will delight guests of all ages.

....

- 1½ cups (185 g) all-purpose flour
- 1 teaspoon baking powder
- ¼ teaspoon salt
- 3 tablespoons (43 g) butter or margarine, at room temperature
- ⅓ cup (80 ml) smooth unsweetened applesauce
- About 1½ cups (180 g) powdered sugar
- 1 large egg
- 1 teaspoon vanilla
- ¼ cup (30 g) chopped pecans

Mexican Wedding Cookies

....

Preparation time: 20 minutes
Cooking time: About 15 minutes
Pictured on facing page

1. In a small bowl, mix flour, baking powder, and salt. In a food processor (or in a large bowl), whirl (or beat) butter and applesauce until well blended. Add ½ cup (60 g) of the sugar, egg, vanilla, and pecans; whirl (or beat) until smooth. Add flour mixture to egg mixture; whirl (or stir) until blended. Dough will be stiff.

2. With lightly floured fingers, shape 2-teaspoon portions of dough into balls; you should have 24. Set balls 1 inch

(2.5 cm) apart on two 12- by 15-inch (30- by 38-cm) nonstick (or lightly greased regular) baking sheets. Bake in a 375°F (190°C) oven until cookies are light golden brown (about 15 minutes), switching positions of baking sheets halfway through baking. Let cool on baking sheets until lukewarm.

3. Sift ½ cup (60 g) of the remaining sugar onto a large sheet of wax paper. Roll each cookie gently in sugar. With your fingers, pack more sugar all over each cookie to a depth of about ⅛ inch (3 mm). Place cookies on a rack over wax paper and dust generously with remaining sugar; let cool completely. Makes 2 dozen cookies.

....

Per cookie: 84 calories (26% calories from fat), 2 g total fat, 1 g saturated fat, 13 mg cholesterol, 60 mg sodium, 14 g carbohydrates, 0.3 g fiber, 1 g protein, 15 mg calcium, 0.4 mg iron

---

If you like spicy flavors, you'll applaud these cookies. Crushed peppercorns add subtle heat and complement the cookies' sweetness.

....

- 1 cup (125 g) all-purpose flour
- 2 tablespoons unsweetened cocoa powder
- 1 teaspoon baking powder
- 1 cup (200 g) sugar
- 1 teaspoon whole black peppercorns, coarsely crushed
- 2 tablespoons (28 g) butter or margarine, melted
- ⅓ cup (80 ml) smooth unsweetened applesauce
- ½ teaspoon vanilla
- Whole black peppercorns (optional)

Cocoa Pepper Cookies

....

Preparation time: 20 minutes
Cooking time: About 20 minutes
Pictured on facing page

1. In a food processor (or in a bowl), combine flour, cocoa, baking powder, ¾ cup (150 g) of the sugar, and crushed peppercorns. Whirl (or stir) until blended. Add butter, applesauce, and vanilla; whirl until dough forms a compact ball. (Or stir in butter, applesauce, and vanilla with a fork, then work dough with your hands to form a smooth-textured ball.)

2. With lightly floured fingers, pinch off 1-inch (2.5-cm) pieces of dough and roll into balls. Arrange balls 2 inches

(5 cm) apart on two 12- by 15-inch (30- by 38-cm) nonstick (or lightly greased regular) baking sheets. Dip bottom of a lightly greased glass into remaining ¼ cup sugar and press each ball gently to a thickness of about ½ inch (1 cm); dip glass again as needed to prevent sticking. If desired, press a whole peppercorn in center of each cookie.

3. Bake in lower third of a 300°F (150°C) oven until cookies are firm to the touch and look dry on top (about 20 minutes), switching positions of baking sheets halfway through baking. Let cookies cool on baking sheets for about 3 minutes; then transfer to racks to cool completely. Makes about 1½ dozen cookies.

....

Per cookie: 84 calories (14% calories from fat), 1 g total fat, 0.8 g saturated fat, 3 mg cholesterol, 41 mg sodium, 18 g carbohydrates, 0.3 g fiber, 0.7 g protein, 17 mg calcium, 0.4 mg iron

Rolled oats give these sweet-tart cookies a chewy texture.

- ½ cup (60 g) all-purpose flour
- ¼ teaspoon *each* baking soda and salt
- ⅛ teaspoon cream of tartar
- 2 tablespoons (28 g) butter or margarine, at room temperature
- 6 tablespoons (75 g) sugar
- 2 teaspoons lemon peel
- ½ teaspoon *each* lemon juice and vanilla
- 1 large egg white
- ½ cup (40 g) regular rolled oats
  Lemon Icing (recipe follows)

1. In a small bowl, mix flour, baking soda, salt, and cream of tartar. In a food processor (or in a large bowl),

Lemon Cookies

Preparation time: 25 minutes
Cooking time: About 15 minutes
Pictured on page 358

whirl (or beat) butter, sugar, lemon peel, lemon juice, vanilla, and egg white until well blended. Add flour mixture to egg mixture; whirl (or stir) until combined. Stir in oats.

2. With floured fingers, divide dough into 1½-teaspoon portions (you should have 18); place mounds of dough 2 inches (5 cm) apart on two 12- by 15-inch (30- by 38-cm) nonstick (or lightly greased regular) baking sheets.

3. Bake in a 350°F (175°C) oven until cookies are light golden and firm to the touch (about 15 minutes), switching

positions of baking sheets halfway through baking. Let cookies cool on baking sheets for about 3 minutes; then transfer to racks to cool completely.

4. Prepare Lemon Icing. Set each rack of cookies over a baking sheet to catch any drips; drizzle icing evenly over cookies. Serve; or let stand until icing hardens (about 2 hours). Makes 1½ dozen cookies.

Lemon Icing. In a small bowl, combine ⅔ cup (67 g) sifted **powdered sugar** and 2 teaspoons *each* **lemon juice** and **water.** Stir until smooth.

Per cookie: 65 calories (20% calories from fat), 1 g total fat, 0.8 g saturated fat, 3 mg cholesterol, 64 mg sodium, 12 g carbohydrates, 0.3 g fiber, 0.9 g protein, 3 mg calcium, 0.3 mg iron

---

To conclude a spicy meal on a sweet note, offer soft cookies filled with orange marmalade and drizzled with a cocoa glaze.

- 1½ cups (185 g) all-purpose flour
- 1 teaspoon baking powder
- ¼ teaspoon salt
- ⅛ teaspoon ground cloves
- 2 tablespoons (28 g) butter or margarine, at room temperature
- ¼ cup (60 ml) smooth unsweetened applesauce
- ½ cup (60 g) powdered sugar
- 1 large egg
- 1 teaspoon vanilla
  About ⅓ cup (80 ml) orange marmalade
  Cocoa Glaze (recipe follows)

1. In a small bowl, mix flour, baking powder, salt, and cloves. In a food processor (or in a large bowl), whirl (or beat) butter and applesauce until well blended. Add sugar, egg, and

Orange & Cocoa Cookies

Preparation time: 30 minutes
Cooking time: About 15 minutes

vanilla; whirl (or beat) until smooth. Add flour mixture to egg mixture and whirl (or stir) until blended. Dough will be stiff.

2. With lightly floured fingers, shape 2-teaspoon portions of dough into balls. Set balls 1 inch (2.5 cm) apart on two 12- by 15-inch (30- by 38-cm) nonstick (or lightly greased regular) baking sheets. With floured thumb, press a well in center of each ball (don't press all the way through to baking sheet). Spoon about ½ teaspoon of the marmalade into each well (marmalade should not flow over rim).

3. Bake cookies in a 400°F (205°C) oven until light golden brown (about

15 minutes), switching positions of baking sheets halfway through baking. Let cookies cool on baking sheets for about 3 minutes; then transfer to racks to cool completely.

4. Prepare Cocoa Glaze. Set each rack of cookies over a baking sheet to catch any drips; drizzle warm glaze evenly over cookies. Serve warm; or let stand until glaze hardens (about 2 hours). Makes about 2 dozen cookies.

Cocoa Glaze. In a 1- to 1½-quart (950-ml to 1.4-liter) pan, combine ¼ cup (60 ml) **light corn syrup** and 1 tablespoon **unsweetened cocoa powder.** Cook over medium heat, stirring, just until mixture comes to a boil. Remove from heat and stir in ½ teaspoon **vanilla.** Use warm. Stir well before using.

Per cookie: 79 calories (14% calories from fat), 1 g total fat, 0.7 g saturated fat, 11 mg cholesterol, 63 mg sodium, 16 g carbohydrates, 0.3 g fiber, 1 g protein, 17 mg calcium, 0.5 mg iron

Chocolate Pistachio Cookies

Preparation time: 20 minutes
Cooking time: About 20 minutes

Nut-topped, chocolaty cookies are pretty on a plate of holiday sweets.

- 1 cup (125 g) all-purpose flour
- 2 tablespoons unsweetened cocoa powder
- 1 teaspoon baking powder
- ¼ teaspoon instant espresso or coffee powder
- 1 cup (200 g) granulated sugar
- 2 tablespoons (28 g) butter or margarine, melted
- ⅓ cup (80 ml) smooth unsweetened applesauce
- ½ teaspoon vanilla
- ¼ cup (30 g) shelled pistachio nuts, chopped
- ½ cup (60 g) powdered sugar

1. In a food processor or a large bowl, whirl or stir together flour, cocoa, baking powder, instant espresso, and ¾ cup (150 g) of the granulated sugar. Add butter, applesauce, and vanilla; whirl until dough forms a compact ball. (Or, if not using a processor, stir in butter, applesauce, and vanilla with a fork, then work dough with your hands to form a smooth-textured ball.)

2. With lightly floured fingers, pinch off about 1-inch (2.5-cm) pieces of dough; roll pieces into balls. Set balls 2 inches (5 cm) apart on lightly greased large nonstick or regular baking sheets.

3. Place remaining ¼ cup (50 g) granulated sugar in a shallow bowl. Dip bottom of a lightly greased glass in sugar; use glass to press each ball of dough gently to a thickness of about ½ inch (1 cm). After flattening each ball, dip glass in sugar again to prevent sticking. Sprinkle cookies evenly with pistachios.

4. Bake in lower third of a 300°F (150°C) oven until cookies are firm to the touch and look dry on top (about 20 minutes), switching positions of baking sheets halfway through baking.

5. Let cookies cool on baking sheets for about 3 minutes, then transfer to racks to cool completely. Meanwhile, in a small bowl, smoothly blend powdered sugar with 1½ to 2 teaspoons water, or enough to make icing easy to drizzle. Drizzle icing over cooled cookies. Makes about 2 dozen cookies.

Per cookie: 83 calories (22% calories from fat), 2 g total fat, 0.8 g saturated fat, 3 mg cholesterol, 31 mg sodium, 16 g carbohydrates, 0.5 g fiber, 0.9 g protein, 15 mg calcium, 0.4 mg iron

Molasses Sugar Cookies

Preparation time: 25 minutes
Cooking time: About 7 minutes

Soft, spicy molasses cookies are favorites with cold milk or cider.

- 2 cups (250 g) all-purpose flour
- 1½ teaspoons baking powder
- 1 teaspoon *each* ground ginger and ground cinnamon
- ½ teaspoon salt
- ¼ teaspoon baking soda
- ½ cup (4 oz./115 g) butter or margarine, at room temperature
- ½ cup (110 g) firmly packed brown sugar
- 2 large egg whites
- ½ cup (120 ml) molasses
- 2 teaspoons instant espresso or coffee powder
  About ⅔ cup (93 g) sugar cubes, coarsely crushed
  About ¼ cup (50 g) granulated sugar

1. In a medium-size bowl, stir together flour, baking powder, ginger, cinnamon, salt, and baking soda; set aside.

2. In a food processor or a large bowl, combine butter, brown sugar, egg whites, molasses, instant espresso, and ½ cup (120 ml) water. Whirl or beat with an electric mixer until smooth. Add flour mixture to butter mixture; whirl or beat until dry ingredients are evenly moistened.

3. Spoon rounded 1-tablespoon (15-ml) portions of dough onto lightly greased large nonstick or regular baking sheets, spacing cookies about 2 inches (5 cm) apart.

4. Bake in a 350°F (175°C) oven for 5 minutes. Remove from oven. Working quickly, sprinkle each cookie with about ¾ teaspoon of the crushed sugar cubes; press in lightly. Return cookies to oven and continue to bake until firm to the touch (about 2 more minutes). Let cookies cool on baking sheets for about 3 minutes. Transfer to racks, sprinkle with granulated sugar, and let cool completely. Makes about 3 dozen cookies.

Per cookie: 93 calories (25% calories from fat), 3 g total fat, 2 g saturated fat, 7 mg cholesterol, 91 mg sodium, 17 g carbohydrates, 0.2 g fiber, 0.9 g protein, 26 mg calcium, 0.6 mg iron

A bit softer than traditional shortbread, these ultra-rich treats feature a dark chocolate cookie layer atop a chocolate graham cracker crust.

- 1 cup (85 g) chocolate graham cracker crumbs (about twelve square 2-inch/5-cm crackers)
- ¾ cup (95 g) all-purpose flour
- ⅔ cup (80 g) powdered sugar
- ½ cup (43 g) unsweetened cocoa powder
- ½ teaspoon instant espresso or coffee powder
- ¼ teaspoon salt
- ¼ cup (2 oz./55 g) butter or margarine, cut into chunks
- ½ cup (60 g) powdered sugar
- 1 tablespoon unsweetened cocoa powder
- ¼ teaspoon vanilla
- 3 to 4 teaspoons (15 to 20 ml) nonfat milk

Chocolate Shortbread

Preparation time: 15 minutes
Cooking time: About 25 minutes
Pictured on facing page

1. In a food processor or a large bowl, whirl or stir together graham cracker crumbs and 1 tablespoon (15 ml) water until crumbs are evenly moistened. Press crumbs evenly over bottom of a lightly greased 9-inch (23-cm) nonstick or regular cheesecake pan with a removable rim; set aside.

2. In food processor or bowl, whirl or stir together flour, the ⅔ cup (80 g) powdered sugar, the ½ cup (43 g) cocoa, 2 teaspoons water, instant espresso, and salt. Add butter; whirl or rub with your fingers until mixture resembles coarse crumbs.

3. Evenly distribute crumbly dough over graham cracker crumbs in pan.

Press out dough firmly to make an even layer that adheres to graham cracker crumbs (if dough is sticky, lightly flour your fingers).

4. Bake in a 325°F (165°C) oven until shortbread smells toasted and feels firm in center when gently pressed (about 25 minutes). Let shortbread cool in pan on a rack for 5 minutes. Then, using a very sharp knife, cut shortbread, still in pan, into 12 equal wedges. Let cool completely in pan on rack.

5. Meanwhile, in a small bowl, combine the ½ cup (60 g) powdered sugar, the 1 tablespoon cocoa, vanilla, and 1 tablespoon (15 ml) of the milk. Beat until smoothly blended; if necessary, add more milk to make glaze easy to drizzle. Remove pan rim from shortbread; drizzle glaze over shortbread. Let stand until glaze is set. Makes 12 pieces.

Per piece: 148 calories (30% calories from fat), 5 g total fat, 3 g saturated fat, 10 mg cholesterol, 137 mg sodium, 25 g carbohydrates, 2 g fiber, 2 g protein, 9 mg calcium, 1 mg iron

---

A touch of olive oil enriches this easy make-ahead dough. Serve the delicate anise-flavored cookies with milk, coffee, or sweet dessert wine.

- About 2 cups (200 g) sifted powdered sugar
- 1 cup (125 g) all-purpose flour
- 1 teaspoon baking powder
- ¼ teaspoon ground cinnamon
- 1 tablespoon (15 ml) olive oil
- 1 large egg, beaten
- 2 tablespoons (30 ml) anisette liqueur; or 1 teaspoon anise extract (or to taste) blended with 5 teaspoons (25 ml) water
- 1 teaspoon vanilla

Anise Poofs

Preparation time: 25 minutes
Standing time: 8 to 24 hours
Cooking time: About 8 minutes

1. In a large bowl, stir together 2 cups (200 g) of the powdered sugar, flour, baking powder, and cinnamon. Add oil, egg, liqueur, and vanilla; stir until well blended. Turn dough out onto a board lightly dusted with powdered sugar; knead until smooth, about 4 turns.

2. Cut dough into 6 pieces. Roll each piece into a rope 20 inches (50 cm) long and about ½ inch (1 cm) wide.

Cut each rope into 2-inch (5-cm) lengths. Place pieces about 1½ inches (3.5 cm) apart on lightly oiled large baking sheets. Let cookies stand, uncovered, for 8 to 24 hours. (Do not omit standing time; if dough does not stand, cookies will not puff.) Then bake in a 325°F (165°C) oven until pale golden (about 8 minutes). Immediately transfer cookies to racks and let cool. Makes 5 dozen cookies.

Per cookie: 27 calories (18% calories from fat), 0.5 g total fat, 0.1 g saturated fat, 4 mg cholesterol, 9 mg sodium, 5 g carbohydrates, 0 g fiber, 0.3 g protein, 5 mg calcium, 0.1 mg iron

Chocolate Shortbread
(recipe on facing page)

Biscotti

These crunchy cookies are perfect for dunking in dessert wine or coffee.

Espresso Biscotti

Preparation time: 35 minutes
Cooking time: About 35 minutes
Pictured on page 366

- ½ cup (68 g) hazelnuts
- 5 tablespoons (71 g) butter or margarine, at room temperature
- ½ cup (100 g) granulated sugar
- 2½ teaspoons instant espresso powder
- 1 large egg
- 2 large egg whites
- 1 teaspoon vanilla
- 2 cups (250 g) all-purpose flour
- 2 teaspoons baking powder
- 1½ cups (150 g) sifted powdered sugar

1. Spread hazelnuts in a single layer in a shallow baking pan. Bake in a 375°F (190°C) oven until nuts are golden beneath skins (about 10 minutes). Let nuts cool slightly; then pour into a towel and rub to remove as much loose skin as possible. Let cool; chop coarsely and set aside. Reduce oven temperature to 350°F (175°C).

2. In a large bowl, beat butter, granulated sugar, and 1½ teaspoons of the instant espresso until well blended. Add egg and egg whites, beating until well blended. Stir in vanilla. In a medium-size bowl, stir together flour and baking powder; add to butter mixture and stir until well blended. Mix in hazelnuts.

3. Divide dough in half. On a lightly floured board, shape each portion into a long roll about 1½ inches (3.5 cm) in diameter. Place rolls on a large nonstick or greased regular baking sheet, 3 inches (8 cm) apart. Flatten rolls to make loaves ½-inch (1-cm) thick. Bake in a 350°F (175°C) oven until loaves feel firm to the touch (about 15 minutes).

4. Remove baking sheet from oven and let loaves cool for 3 to 5 minutes; then cut crosswise into slices about ½ inch (1 cm) thick. Tip slices cut side down on baking sheet (at this point, you may need another sheet to bake biscotti all at once). Return to oven and bake until biscotti look dry and are lightly browned (about 10 minutes); if using 2 baking sheets, switch their positions halfway through baking. Transfer biscotti to racks and let cool.

5. In a small bowl, dissolve remaining 1 teaspoon instant espresso in 4 teaspoons (20 ml) very hot water. Stir in powdered sugar; if needed, add more hot water, 1 teaspoon at a time, to make icing easy to spread.

6. Spread icing over 1 to 1½ inches (2.5 to 3.5 cm) of one end of each cooled cookie. Let stand until icing is firm before serving. Makes about 4 dozen cookies.

Per cookie: 60 calories (30% calories from fat), 2 g total fat, 0.7 g saturated fat, 7 mg cholesterol, 35 mg sodium, 10 g carbohydrates, 0.2 g fiber, 1 g protein, 15 mg calcium, 0.3 mg iron

Anise Biscotti

Preparation time: 25 minutes
Cooking time: About 25 minutes

- 5 tablespoons (71 g) butter or margarine, at room temperature
- 11 tablespoons (132 g) sugar
- 1½ teaspoons anise seeds (or to taste)
- 2 large eggs
- 2 teaspoons vanilla
- 2 cups (250 g) all-purpose flour
- 2 teaspoons baking powder
- 2 large egg whites

1. In a large bowl, beat butter, ½ cup (100 g) of the sugar, and anise seeds until well blended. Add eggs, one at a time, beating well after each addition. Stir in vanilla. In a medium-size bowl, stir together flour and baking powder; add to butter mixture and stir until well blended.

2. Divide dough in half. On a lightly floured board, shape each portion into a long roll about 1½ inches (3.5 cm) in diameter. Place rolls on a large nonstick or greased regular baking sheet, 3 inches (8 cm) apart. Flatten rolls to make loaves ½-inch (1-cm) thick.

3. In a small bowl, whisk egg whites with 1 tablespoon (15 ml) water until blended; brush some of the mixture lightly over loaves. Bake in a 350°F (175°C) oven until loaves feel firm to the touch (about 15 minutes).

4. Remove baking sheet from oven and let loaves cool for 3 to

5 minutes; then cut crosswise into slices about ½ inch (1 cm) thick. Tip slices cut side down on baking sheet (at this point, you may need another sheet to bake biscotti all at once). Brush slices with remaining egg white mixture and sprinkle with remaining 3 tablespoons sugar.

5. Return to oven and bake until biscotti look dry and are lightly browned (about 10 minutes); if using 2 baking sheets, switch positions halfway through baking. Transfer biscotti to racks and cool. Makes about 4 dozen cookies.

Per cookie: 45 calories (29% calories from fat), 1 g total fat, 0.8 g saturated fat, 12 mg cholesterol, 38 mg sodium, 7 g carbohydrates, 0.1 g fiber, 0.9 g protein, 14 mg calcium, 0.3 mg iron

Chocolate Biscotti

Preparation time: 25 minutes
Cooking time: 35 to 40 minutes

¼ cup (2 oz./55 g) butter or margarine, at room temperature

½ cup (100 g) granulated sugar

4 large egg whites

2 cups (250 g) all-purpose flour

⅓ cup (29 g) unsweetened cocoa powder

2 teaspoons baking powder

⅓ cup (33 g) sifted powdered sugar

About 2 teaspoons low-fat (1%) milk

1. In a large bowl, beat butter and granulated sugar until fluffy. Add egg whites and beat until well blended. In a medium bowl, combine flour, cocoa, and baking powder; add to butter mixture and stir until well blended.

2. Turn dough out onto a large nonstick or lightly greased regular baking sheet. Shape dough down length of sheet into a loaf about 2½ inches (6 cm) wide and ⅝ inch (2 cm) thick. Bake in a 350°F (175°C) oven until crusty and firm to the touch (about 20 minutes).

3. Remove baking sheet from oven and let loaf cool for 3 to 5 minutes; then cut diagonally into slices about ½ inch (1 cm) thick. Tip slices cut side down on baking sheet. Return to oven and bake until biscotti feel firm and dry (15 to 20 minutes). Transfer to racks and let cool.

4. In a small bowl, stir together powdered sugar and 2 teaspoons of the milk, or enough to make a pourable icing. Using a spoon, drizzle icing decoratively over biscotti. Let stand until icing is firm before serving. Makes about 1½ dozen cookies.

Per cookie: 112 calories (25% calories from fat), 3 g total fat, 2 g saturated fat, 7 mg cholesterol, 97 mg sodium, 19 g carbohydrates, 0.8 g fiber, 3 g protein, 36 mg calcium, 0.9 mg iron

Currant Biscotti

Preparation time: 15 minutes
Cooking time: About 25 minutes

1 cup (125 g) all-purpose flour

1 teaspoon baking powder

3 tablespoons (43 g) butter or margarine, at room temperature

¼ cup (50 g) granulated sugar

1½ teaspoons grated orange peel

1 large egg

½ teaspoon vanilla

⅓ cup (50 g) dried currants or raisins

1 cup (120 g) powdered sugar

3 to 4 teaspoons (15 to 20 ml) orange juice

1. In a small bowl, stir together flour and baking powder; set aside. In a large bowl, beat butter, granulated sugar, and 1 teaspoon of the orange peel until well blended. Add egg and vanilla and beat well. Add flour mixture to butter mixture and stir to blend thoroughly. Then mix in currants.

2. Shape dough into a long log about 1½ inches (3.5 cm) in diameter. Place log in a lightly greased shallow 10- by 15-inch (30- by 38-cm) nonstick or regular baking pan; then flatten log to make a loaf about ½ inch (1 cm) thick. Bake in a 350°F (175°C) oven for 15 minutes.

3. Remove pan from oven. Let loaf cool slightly in pan. Using a serrated knife, cut loaf crosswise into slices about ½ inch (1 cm) thick. Tip slices cut side down in baking pan; return to oven and bake until cookies look dry and are lightly browned (about 10 more minutes). Transfer cookies to racks to cool.

4. Meanwhile, in a small bowl, smoothly blend powdered sugar, remaining ½ teaspoon orange peel, and 1 tablespoon (15 ml) of the orange juice; if necessary, add more orange juice to make icing easy to spread. Spread icing on about 1 inch (2.5 cm) of one end of each cookie. Before serving, return cookies to racks and let stand until icing is set. Makes about 2 dozen cookies.

Per cookie: 70 calories (24% calories from fat), 2 g total fat, 1 g saturated fat, 13 mg cholesterol, 38 mg sodium, 13 g carbohydrates, 0.2 g fiber, 0.9 g protein, 16 mg calcium, 0.4 mg iron

Espresso Chocolate Cake with Orange Sauce
(recipe on page 368), Espresso Cheesecake (recipe
on page 384), Espresso Biscotti (recipe on page 364)

Cakes, Tortes & Cheesecakes

Can you have your cake and eat it—and still maintain a low-fat cooking style? Yes, indeed. And the outcome will be as scrumptious as any cake you've ever enjoyed. While we reduce fat, we ensure moist, flavorful results with low-fat and nonfat dairy products and fruits—fresh whole fruit, purées, jams, and jellies. Indulge in Chocolate Raspberry Cake or celebrate a special occasion with caramel-amaretto-glazed Amaretto Cheesecake.

Liqueur-laced orange sauce is an ideal accompaniment to this rich, deeply flavored cake.

....

2 tablespoons (28) butter or margarine, at room temperature

1 cup (220 g) firmly packed brown sugar

1 large egg

3 large egg whites

1 cup (240 ml) nonfat sour cream

1 teaspoon vanilla

¾ cup (95 g) all-purpose flour

⅓ cup (29 g) unsweetened cocoa powder

1 tablespoon instant espresso powder

1½ teaspoons baking powder

6 or 7 large oranges (about 8oz./230 g *each*)

6 tablespoons (72 g) granulated sugar

4 teaspoons cornstarch

1½ teaspoons instant espresso powder (or to taste)

1½ cups (360 ml) fresh orange juice

2 tablespoons (30 ml) orange-flavored liqueur (or to taste)

2 tablespoons unsweetened cocoa powder

Mint sprigs

Espresso Chocolate Cake with Orange Sauce

....

Preparation time: 35 minutes
Cooking time: 35 to 40 minutes
Pictured on page 366

1. In a food processor or a large bowl, combine butter and brown sugar; whirl or beat with an electric mixer until well blended. Add egg, egg whites, sour cream, and vanilla; whirl or beat until well blended. Add flour, the ⅓ cup (29 g) cocoa, the 1 tablespoon instant espresso, and baking powder; whirl or beat just until combined. Spread batter in a greased square 8-inch (20-cm) nonstick or regular baking pan. Bake in a 350°F (175°C) oven until cake begins to pull away from pan sides and center springs back when lightly pressed (35 to 40 minutes).

2. While cake is baking, finely shred enough peel (colored part only) from oranges to make 1 to 2 teaspoons for sauce; cover and set aside. Cut off and discard remaining peel and all white membrane from oranges. Cut between membranes to release segments. Cover orange segments and set aside.

3. In a small pan, combine granulated sugar, cornstarch, and the 1½ teaspoons instant espresso. Whisk in orange juice and the reserved shredded orange peel; cook over medium-high heat, stirring constantly, until sauce boils and thickens slightly (about 1 minute). Remove from heat and stir in liqueur.

4. Just before serving, sift the 2 tablespoons cocoa over cake. Cut cake into diamonds, triangles, or squares; transfer to individual plates. Arrange orange segments alongside. Drizzle sauce over oranges. Garnish with mint sprigs. Makes 8 servings.

....

Per serving: 361 calories (12% calories from fat), 5 g total fat, 2 g saturated fat, 34 mg cholesterol, 187 mg sodium, 74 g carbohydrates, 5 g fiber, 8 g protein, 189 mg calcium, 2 mg iron

Filled with smooth, luscious hazelnut spread and topped with chocolate–cream cheese frosting, this fancy dessert gets a quick start with a purchased loaf cake.

- 2 **tablespoons hazelnuts**
- 1 **purchased nonfat chocolate loaf cake (about 15 oz./425 g)**
- ½ **cup (120 ml) purchased hazelnut-cocoa spread**
- 1 **small package (about 6 oz./ 170 g) semisweet chocolate chips**
- 2 **cups (200 g) sifted powdered sugar**
- 1 **large package (about 8 oz./ 230 g) Neufchâtel cheese, cut into chunks**
- ½ **cup (43 g) unsweetened cocoa powder**
- ¼ **cup (60 ml) nonfat sour cream**
- 2 **teaspoons vanilla**

Chocolate Hazelnut Cake

Preparation time: 25 minutes
Cooking time: About 15 minutes
Chilling time: At least 2 hours

1. Toast and coarsely chop hazelnuts as directed for Pear & Hazelnut Upside-down Cake (page 373). Set aside.

2. Cut cake in half horizontally. Set bottom half, cut side up, on a serving plate. Stir hazelnut-cocoa spread to soften, if necessary; then spread evenly over cake to within about ½ inch (1 cm) of edges. Place top half of cake, cut side down, over filling; press lightly.

3. Place chocolate chips in a metal bowl nested over a pan of hot (not boiling) water. Stir often until chocolate is melted and smooth. Remove from heat and transfer to a food processor or blender; let stand for 2 to 3 minutes to cool slightly. Add powdered sugar, Neufchâtel cheese, cocoa, sour cream, and vanilla; whirl until smooth, scraping sides of container often. Let frosting cool slightly; it should be spreadable, but not too soft.

4. Generously spread frosting over sides and top of cake. Cover cake with a cake cover or an inverted bowl (don't let cover touch frosting); refrigerate until cold (at least 2 hours) or until next day. Sprinkle with hazelnuts, pressing them lightly into frosting. Cut into slices to serve. Makes 10 servings.

Per serving: 401 calories (29% calories from fat), 13 g total fat, 6 g saturated fat, 11 mg cholesterol, 324 mg sodium, 67 g carbohydrates, 2 g fiber, 7 g protein, 66 mg calcium, 2 mg iron

---

This rich-tasting cocoa cake features the cinnamon and almond flavors of traditional Mexican chocolate. For an extra treat, top each serving with lean, lightly spiced whipped "cream."

Spiced Cream (optional; page 415)
- 1 **cup (96 g) sifted cake flour**
- ⅓ **cup (29 g) unsweetened cocoa powder**
- 1 **teaspoon *each* baking soda, baking powder, and ground cinnamon**
- 6 **large egg whites**
- 1⅓ **cups (293 g) firmly packed brown sugar**
- 1 **cup (240 ml) plain nonfat yogurt**
- 2 **teaspoons vanilla**

Mexican Cocoa Cake

Preparation time: About 10 minutes
Baking time: 30 to 40 minutes

- ¼ **teaspoon almond extract**
- **Powdered sugar**

1. Prepare Spiced Cream, if desired; refrigerate.

2. In a small bowl, mix flour, cocoa, baking soda, baking powder, and cinnamon. In a large bowl, beat egg whites, brown sugar, yogurt, vanilla, and almond extract until well blended. Stir in flour mixture and beat just until evenly moistened.

3. Pour batter into a square 8-inch (20-cm) nonstick (or greased regular) baking pan. Bake in a 350°F (175°C) oven until center of cake springs back when lightly pressed (30 to 40 minutes). Let cake cool in pan on a rack for 15 minutes; then invert it onto a serving plate. Serve warm or cool. If made ahead, wrap cooled cake airtight and store in a cool place until next day (freeze for longer storage).

4. Just before serving, sift powdered sugar over cake. To serve, cut cake into wedges or rectangles. If desired, sift more powdered sugar over each serving; then top with Spiced Cream, if desired. Makes 8 servings.

Per serving: 226 calories (2% calories from fat), 0.6 g total fat, 0.3 g saturated fat, 0.6 mg cholesterol, 297 mg sodium, 51 g carbohydrates, 1 g fiber, 6 g protein, 133 mg calcium, 2 mg iron

This single-layer cake is flecked with orange peel and soaked with a cinnamon-scented orange-rum syrup. It's a perfect warm-weather dessert—and just as good in any other season, especially after a spicy meal. If you like, garnish the cake with orange segments just before serving.

Spirited Syrup
(recipe follows)
2 large eggs
½ cup (100 g) sugar
¾ cup (95 g) all-purpose flour
1½ teaspoons baking powder
2 tablespoons grated orange peel
¼ cup (2 oz./57 g) butter or margarine, melted
Orange segments (optional)
Mint sprigs

1. Prepare Spirited Syrup; set aside.

Drunken Cake

Preparation time: About 10 minutes
Baking time: About 20 minutes
Pictured on facing page

2. In a food processor (or in a large bowl), whirl (or beat) eggs and sugar until thick and lemon-colored. Add flour, baking powder, orange peel, and butter; whirl (or beat) until well blended. Spread batter in a greased, floured 9-inch (23-cm) cake pan with a removable rim. Bake in a 375°F (190°C) oven until cake just begins to pull away from sides of pan and center springs back when lightly pressed (about 20 minutes).

3. Set warm cake in pan on a rack; set rack over a plate to catch any drips.

Pierce cake all over with a fork. Slowly pour Spirited Syrup over cake; let cool. Just before serving, remove pan rim. Garnish cake with orange segments, if desired, and mint sprigs. Makes 8 servings.

Spirited Syrup. In a small pan, mix ¾ cup (150 g) **sugar**, 1 teaspoon **grated orange peel**, ½ cup (120 ml) **orange juice**, ½ teaspoon **grated lemon peel**, 2 tablespoons (30 ml) **lemon juice**, and ⅛ teaspoon **ground cinnamon**. Bring to a boil over medium-high heat. Boil, stirring, just until sugar is dissolved. Remove from heat and let cool; then stir in 2 to 3 tablespoons **light** or **dark rum** and 1 teaspoon **vanilla.**

Per serving: 259 calories (27% calories from fat), 8 g total fat, 4 g saturated fat, 69 mg cholesterol, 167 mg sodium, 43 g carbohydrates, 0.3 g fiber, 3 g protein, 66 mg calcium, 0.9 mg iron

---

A molasses-accented cream cheese frosting tops this satisfying carrot cake.

½ cup (75 g) raisins
2 tablespoons (30 ml) orange juice
1 teaspoon vanilla
2 cups (250 g) all-purpose flour
2 teaspoons ground cinnamon
1½ teaspoons baking soda
½ teaspoon *each* salt and ground ginger
½ cup (110 g) firmly packed brown sugar
½ cup (120 ml) *each* nonfat sour cream and smooth unsweetened applesauce
¼ cup (60 ml) salad oil
2 large eggs
1½ cups (165 g) grated carrots
1½ cups (180 g) powdered sugar
2 ounces (55 g) nonfat cream cheese, at room temperature

Carrot Cake with Molasses Frosting

Preparation time: 25 minutes
Cooking time: About 1 hour

2 tablespoons (28 g) butter or margarine, at room temperature
1 teaspoon molasses
1 to 3 teaspoons nonfat milk

1. In a small bowl, combine raisins, orange juice, and vanilla. Let stand until raisins are softened (about 10 minutes), stirring occasionally.

2. In a medium-size bowl, stir together flour, cinnamon, baking soda, salt, and ginger; set aside. In a food processor or a large bowl, combine brown sugar, sour cream, applesauce, oil, and eggs. Whirl or beat with an electric mixer until smooth. Add flour mix-

ture, carrots, and raisin mixture; whirl or beat until dry ingredients are evenly moistened.

3. Spoon batter into a greased square 8-inch (20-cm) nonstick or regular baking pan. Bake in a 325°F (165°C) oven until a wooden pick inserted in center of cake comes out clean (about 1 hour). Let cool completely in pan on a rack.

4. Meanwhile, beat powdered sugar, cream cheese, butter, molasses, and 1 teaspoon of the milk until smooth and easy to spread; add more milk, if necessary. Spread frosting over cake. To serve, cut into 2-inch squares. Makes 16 servings.

Per serving: 214 calories (25% calories from fat), 6 g total fat, 2 g saturated fat, 31 mg cholesterol, 244 mg sodium, 37 g carbohydrates, 1 g fiber, 4 g protein, 42 mg calcium, 1 mg iron

Drunken Cake
(recipe on facing page)

Try this spicy, apple-topped cake for a cool-weather brunch treat.

....

- 1 cup (240 ml) dark molasses
- 1 teaspoon baking soda
- 2 cups (250 g) all-purpose flour
- 1 tablespoon baking powder
- 2 teaspoons *each* ground cinnamon and ground ginger
- ¼ teaspoon ground cloves
- 3 tablespoons (43 g) butter or margarine
- 6 cups (660 g) peeled, sliced tart apples such as Granny Smith or Newtown Pippin
- ¼ cup (50 g) granulated sugar
- ¼ cup (60 ml) bourbon or apple juice
- 1 cup (220 g) firmly packed brown sugar
- ½ cup (4 oz./115 g) butter or margarine, at room temperature
- 2 large eggs

....

1. In a 1- to 2-quart (950-ml to 1.9-liter) pan, combine molasses and 1 cup (240

Gingerbread-Apple Cake

....

Preparation time: 20 minutes
Cooking time: About 55 minutes

ml) water. Bring to a boil over medium-high heat. Remove pan from heat and stir in baking soda; let cool completely.

2. In a small bowl, stir together flour, baking powder, cinnamon, ginger, and cloves; set aside.

3. Melt the 3 tablespoons (43 g) butter in a wide nonstick frying pan over medium-high heat. Add apples; cook, turning often with a spatula, until slices are just tender when pierced (about 5 minutes). Stir in granulated sugar and bourbon; continue to cook, stirring occasionally, until liquid has evaporated and apples have begun to brown (about 6 more minutes). Spoon apple mixture into a well-greased 9- by 13-inch (23- by 33-cm) nonstick

or regular baking pan; spread out mixture evenly. Set aside.

4. In a food processor or a large bowl, combine brown sugar, the ½ cup (4 oz./115 g) butter, and eggs. Whirl or beat with an electric mixer until smooth. Alternately add flour mixture and molasses mixture; add about half of each at a time, and whirl or beat until well blended after each addition. Pour batter evenly over apple mixture.

5. Bake in a 350°F (175°C) oven until cake just begins to pull away from sides of pan and center springs back when gently pressed (about 40 minutes). Let cake cool in pan on a rack for 15 minutes. Run a knife around pan sides; then invert pan onto a platter. Lift off pan. If any apple slices remain in pan, remove them and arrange atop cake. Serve warm or cool. To serve, cut into about 2-inch (5-cm) squares. Makes 24 servings.

....

Per serving: 190 calories (28% calories from fat), 6 g total fat, 3 g saturated fat, 32 mg cholesterol, 186 mg sodium, 33 g carbohydrates, 1 g fiber, 2 g protein, 168 mg calcium, 3 mg iron

---

A cross between candy and fruit-cake, panforte ("strong bread") is loaded with fruits and nuts.

....

- 1 cup (130 g) salted roasted almonds, coarsely chopped
- 1 cup (about 5 oz./140 g) dried pitted tart cherries
- 1 cup (185 g) *each* candied orange peel and candied lemon peel, finely chopped
- 1 teaspoon *each* grated lemon peel and ground cinnamon
- ½ teaspoon ground coriander
- ¼ teaspoon *each* ground cloves and ground nutmeg
- ½ cup (60 g) all-purpose flour
- ¾ cup (150 g) granulated sugar
- ¾ cup (180 ml) honey
- 2 tablespoons (28 g) butter or margarine

Panforte

....

Preparation time: 25 minutes
Cooking time: About 1¼ hours

- ½ cup (50 g) sifted powdered sugar

....

1. In a large bowl, combine almonds, cherries, candied orange peel, candied lemon peel, grated lemon peel, cinnamon, coriander, cloves, nutmeg, and flour. Mix until nuts and fruit pieces are thoroughly coated with flour; set aside.

2. In a deep medium-size pan, combine granulated sugar, honey, and butter. Cook over high heat, stirring often, until mixture registers 265°F/129°C (hard-ball stage) on a candy thermometer. Working quickly, pour hot syrup over fruit mixture and mix thor-

oughly. Immediately scrape mixture into a heavily greased, floured 8- to 9-inch (20- to 23-cm) cake pan.

3. Bake in a 300°F (150°C) oven for 1 hour; if cake begins to brown excessively, drape it loosely with foil (don't let foil touch cake). Let cool completely in pan on a rack.

4. Sprinkle a work surface with half the powdered sugar. Using a slender knife and spatula, loosen sides and bottom of cake from pan, then invert cake (prying gently, if needed) onto sugared surface. Sprinkle and pat sugar over entire cake. Then dust cake with remaining powdered sugar to coat completely. Transfer to a platter. To serve, cut into wedges. Makes 12 servings.

....

Per serving: 370 calories (24% calories from fat), 10 g total fat, 2 g saturated fat, 5 mg cholesterol, 131 mg sodium, 71 g carbohydrates, 2 g fiber, 4 g protein, 37 mg calcium, 0.9 mg iron

Toasted hazelnuts and tender pear slices top this liqueur-laced bundt cake.

....

¼ cup (34 g) hazelnuts

½ cup (4 oz./115 g) butter or margarine, melted

⅓ cup (73 g) firmly packed brown sugar

2 medium-size firm-ripe pears (about 12 oz./340 g *total*)

1 tablespoon (15 ml) lemon juice

¼ cup (30 g) all-purpose flour

3 large eggs

2 large egg whites

½ cup (120 ml) smooth unsweetened applesauce

2 tablespoons (30 ml) hazelnut-flavored liqueur

1 cup (200 g) granulated sugar

1½ cups (185 g) all-purpose flour

1 tablespoon baking powder

1 teaspoon ground cinnamon

½ teaspoon ground ginger

½ cup (110 g) firmly packed brown sugar

¼ cup (60 ml) half-and-half

2 tablespoons (30 ml) light corn syrup

1 tablespoon butter or margarine

1 tablespoon cornstarch blended with 2 tablespoons (30 ml) cold water

½ teaspoon grated lemon peel

⅛ teaspoon salt

1½ teaspoons lemon juice

Pear & Hazelnut Upside-down Cake

....

Preparation time: 35 minutes
Cooking time: About 55 minutes
Cooling time: 30 minutes

1. Spread hazelnuts in a single layer in a shallow baking pan. Bake in a 375°F (190°C) oven until nuts are golden beneath skins (about 10 minutes). Let nuts cool slightly; then pour into a towel, fold to enclose, and rub to remove as much of loose skins as possible. Let cool; then coarsely chop and set aside.

2. Pour half the melted butter into a well-greased, floured 3- to 3½-quart (2.8- to 3.3-liter) nonstick or regular fluted tube pan. Sprinkle with the ⅓ cup (73 g) brown sugar; set aside. Core pears and cut into ½-inch (1-cm) slices. Dip slices into the 1 tablespoon (15 ml) lemon juice; then coat slices with the ¼ cup (30 g) flour and arrange decoratively in pan over sugar mixture (overlap slices, if necessary). Set pan aside.

3. In a food processor or a large bowl, combine eggs, egg whites, applesauce,

liqueur, and granulated sugar. Whirl or beat with an electric mixer until mixture is thick and lemon-colored. Add the 1½ cups (185 g) flour, baking powder, cinnamon, ginger, and remaining melted butter; whirl or beat until dry ingredients are evenly moistened. Carefully pour batter over pears.

4. Bake in a 375°F (190°C) oven until cake just begins to pull away from side of pan and a wooden pick inserted in center of cake comes out clean (about 40 minutes). Let cake cool in pan on a rack for 30 minutes.

5. Meanwhile, in a 1- to 1½-quart (950-ml to 1.4-liter) pan, combine the ½ cup (110 g) brown sugar, half-and-half, corn syrup, the 1 tablespoon butter, cornstarch mixture, lemon peel, and salt. Bring to a boil over medium heat. Boil gently, stirring, until slightly thickened (4 to 5 minutes). Remove pan from heat and stir in the 1½ teaspoons lemon juice; let cool for about 4 minutes (glaze continues to thicken as it cools).

6. Invert cake pan onto a serving plate; carefully lift off pan to release cake. If any pears remain in pan, remove them and arrange in their original places atop cake. Drizzle cake with half the warm glaze; then sprinkle with hazelnuts and drizzle with remaining glaze. Makes 16 servings.

....

Per serving: 253 calories (29% calories from fat), 8 g total fat, 4 g saturated fat, 57 mg cholesterol, 199 mg sodium, 42 g carbohydrates, 1 g fiber, 3 g protein, 80 mg calcium, 1 mg iron

Lemon Poppy Seed Cake
(recipe on facing page)

Poppy seeds bring a subtly nutty flavor to a moist lemon layer cake filled with strawberry jam.

....

- 3 large eggs
- 2 large egg whites
- 1 cup (200 g) granulated sugar
- ½ cup (120 ml) smooth unsweetened applesauce
- 1½ cups (185 g) all-purpose flour
- ¼ cup (23 g) poppy seeds
- 1 tablespoon *each* baking powder and grated lemon peel
- ½ cup (4 oz./115 g) butter or margarine, melted
- 3 cups (360 g) powdered sugar
- ½ cup (120 ml) nonfat sour cream
- ⅓ cup (76 g) butter or margarine, at room temperature
- 1 teaspoon grated lemon peel
- ⅔ cup (160 ml) strawberry jam

  Thin strips of lemon peel

  About 8 cups (1.2 kg) fresh strawberries, hulled and halved

Lemon Poppy Seed Cake

....

Preparation time: 30 minutes
Cooking time: 15 to 20 minutes
Pictured on facing page

1. In a food processor or a large bowl, combine eggs, egg whites, granulated sugar, and applesauce; whirl or beat with an electric mixer until mixture is thick and lemon-colored. Add flour, poppy seeds, baking powder, the 1 tablespoon grated lemon peel, and the ½ cup (4 oz./115 g) melted butter; whirl or beat until dry ingredients are evenly moistened. Divide batter equally between 2 greased, floured round 8-inch (20-cm) nonstick or regular baking pans.

2. Bake in a 375°F (190°C) oven until cake layers just begin to pull away from sides of pans and centers spring back when gently pressed (15 to 20 minutes); halfway through baking, gently rotate each pan one-half turn.

Let cakes cool for 10 minutes in pans on racks; then turn out of pans to cool completely.

3. Meanwhile, prepare frosting: In clean food processor or large bowl, combine powdered sugar, sour cream, the ⅓ cup (76 g) butter, and the 1 teaspoon grated lemon peel. Whirl or beat with electric mixer until frosting is smooth and spreadable; cover and refrigerate until ready to use.

4. To assemble cake, brush all loose crumbs from sides and bottom of each cake layer. Center one layer, top side down, on a serving plate. Using a metal spatula, evenly spread jam to within ½ inch (1 cm) of edge. Top with second layer, top side up.

5. Stir frosting and spread over sides and top of cake; arrange strips of lemon peel decoratively atop cake. To serve, cut cake into slices; offer strawberries alongside. Makes 10 to 12 servings.

....

Per serving: 528 calories (30% calories from fat), 18 g total fat, 9 g saturated fat, 95 mg cholesterol, 319 mg sodium, 88 g carbohydrates, 4 g fiber, 6 g protein, 169 mg calcium, 2 mg iron

Sweet-tart raspberries—in the form of whole fresh fruit, jelly, and jam—beautifully complement dark chocolate in this lovely layer cake.

....

- 3 **large eggs**
- 2 **large egg whites**
- ½ **cup (120 ml) raspberry jelly, melted and cooled slightly**
- ¾ **cup (150 g) granulated sugar**
- 1½ **cups (185 g) all-purpose flour**
- ⅓ **cup (29 g) unsweetened cocoa powder**
- 1 **tablespoon baking powder**
- 2 **teaspoons instant espresso or coffee powder**
- 1 **teaspoon vanilla**
- ½ **cup (4 oz./115 g) butter or margarine, melted**
- ⅓ **cup (76 g) butter or margarine, melted**
- 3 **ounces (85 g) bittersweet or semisweet chocolate, melted and cooled slightly**
- 2 **teaspoons vanilla**
- 4 **cups (480 g) powdered sugar**
- ¼ **cup (22 g) unsweetened cocoa powder**
- ½ **cup (120 ml) nonfat sour cream**
- ½ **cup (160 g) raspberry jam**
  About 1¼ cups (154 g) fresh raspberries
  Mint sprigs

Chocolate Raspberry Cake

....

Preparation time: 35 minutes
Cooking time: 15 to 20 minutes

1. In a food processor or a large bowl, combine eggs, egg whites, jelly, and granulated sugar. Whirl or beat with an electric mixer until mixture is thick and fluffy. Add flour, the ⅓ cup (29 g) cocoa, baking powder, instant espresso, the 1 teaspoon vanilla, and the ½ cup (4 oz./115 g) melted butter. Whirl or beat until dry ingredients are evenly moistened. Divide batter equally between 2 greased, floured round 8-inch (20-cm) nonstick or regular baking pans.

2. Bake in a 375°F (190°C) oven until cake layers just begin to pull away from sides of pans and centers spring back when gently pressed (15 to 20 minutes); halfway through baking, gently rotate each pan one-half turn. Let cakes cool for 10 minutes in pans on racks; then turn out of pans to cool completely.

3. Meanwhile, in clean food processor or large bowl, combine the ⅓ cup (76 g) melted butter, chocolate, and the

2 teaspoons vanilla. Whirl or beat with an electric mixer until smooth. Add powdered sugar, the ¼ cup (22 g) cocoa, and sour cream; whirl or beat until frosting is smooth and easy to spread. Cover and refrigerate until ready to use.

4. To assemble cake, brush all loose crumbs from sides and bottom of each cake layer. Center one layer, top side down, on a serving plate. Using a metal spatula, evenly spread jam over cake to within ½ inch (1 cm) of edge; top jam evenly with about 1 cup (123 g) of the raspberries. Place second layer, top side up, atop jam and raspberries. Beat frosting until smooth; then spread over sides and top of cake. Garnish with remaining raspberries and mint sprigs; serve immediately. Makes 10 to 12 servings.

....

Per serving: 582 calories (29% calories from fat), 20 g total fat, 11 g saturated fat, 95 mg cholesterol, 330 mg sodium, 100 g carbohydrates, 3 g fiber, 7 g protein, 119 mg calcium, 2 mg iron

Cornmeal gives this unusual cake its intriguing texture. Soak it with an orange syrup while it's still warm from the oven; then top with blueberries just before serving.

....

1 cup (138 g) yellow cornmeal

½ cup (60 g) all-purpose flour

1½ teaspoons baking powder

½ teaspoon salt

½ cup (4 oz./115 g) butter or margarine, at room temperature

1 cup (200 g) sugar

2 large eggs

2 large egg whites

¾ cup (180 ml) nonfat sour cream

⅓ cup (70 g) sugar

½ teaspoon grated orange peel

¼ cup (60 ml) orange juice

¼ teaspoon grated lemon peel

1 tablespoon (15 ml) lemon juice

2½ cups (363 g) fresh blueberries

¼ cup (60 ml) raspberry jelly, melted and cooled slightly

1 to 2 tablespoons (15 to 30 ml) berry liqueur

Finely shredded orange peel

Cornmeal Cake with Blueberries

....

Preparation time: 25 minutes
Cooking time: About 40 minutes

1. In a small bowl, stir together cornmeal, flour, baking powder, and salt; set aside.

2. In a food processor or a large bowl, combine butter, the 1 cup (200 g) sugar, eggs, egg whites, and sour cream; whirl or beat with an electric mixer until smooth. Add cornmeal mixture; whirl or beat just until dry ingredients are evenly moistened.

3. Pour batter into a lightly greased 9-inch (23-cm) nonstick or regular cheesecake pan with a removable rim. Bake in a 350°F (175°C) oven until cake just begins to pull away from side of pan and a wooden pick inserted in center comes out clean (about 40 minutes).

4. While cake is baking, combine the ⅓ cup (70 g) sugar, grated orange peel, orange juice, lemon peel, and lemon juice in a 1- to 1½-quart (950-ml to 1.4-liter) pan. Bring to a boil over medium-high heat; then boil, stirring, just until sugar is dissolved. Remove from heat and let cool slightly.

5. Set warm cake in pan on a rack; set rack over a plate to catch any drips. Pierce cake all over with a fork. Slowly pour syrup over cake; let cool. Just before serving, in a large bowl, gently combine blueberries, jelly, and liqueur. Working quickly, spoon berry mixture over cake. Remove pan rim; garnish cake with shredded orange peel. Serve immediately. Makes 10 to 12 servings.

....

Per serving: 311 calories (29% calories from fat), 10 g total fat, 6 g saturated fat, 61 mg cholesterol, 293 mg sodium, 50 g carbohydrates, 2 g fiber, 5 g protein, 70 mg calcium, 1 mg iron

Banana Streusel Bundt Cake

Preparation time: 20 minutes
Cooking time: 60 to 70 minutes
Cooling time: 30 minutes
Pictured on facing page

A chewy streusel of rolled oats, chocolate chips, and coconut distinguishes this big, beautiful banana cake.

- ½ cup (60 g) all-purpose flour
- ½ cup (40 g) *each* sweetened shredded coconut and regular rolled oats
- ½ cup (85 g) semisweet chocolate chips
- ¾ cup (165 g) firmly packed brown sugar
- ¼ cup (2 oz./55 g) butter or margarine, cut into chunks
- 1½ cups (338 g) coarsely mashed ripe bananas
- ¾ cup (180 ml) nonfat sour cream
- 3 large eggs
- 2 large egg whites
- 1 cup (200 g) granulated sugar
- 1½ cups (185 g) all-purpose flour
- 1 tablespoon baking powder
- 1 teaspoon *each* ground cinnamon and vanilla
- ⅓ cup (76 g) butter or margarine, melted
- About ¼ cup (30 g) powdered sugar

1. In a medium-size bowl, stir together the ½ cup (60 g) flour, coconut, oats, chocolate chips, and brown sugar. Add the ¼ cup (55 g) butter and 1 tablespoon (15 ml) water; rub with your fingers until mixture is crumbly and well blended. Set aside.

2. In a food processor or a large bowl, combine bananas, sour cream, eggs, egg whites, and granulated sugar. Whirl or beat with an electric mixer until smooth. Add the 1½ cups (185 g) flour, baking powder, cinnamon, vanilla, and the ⅓ cup (76 g) melted butter; whirl or beat until well blended.

3. Sprinkle half the coconut streusel in a well-greased, floured 10-cup (2.4-liter) nonstick or regular fluted tube pan. Pour half the batter over coconut mixture; then sprinkle with remaining coconut streusel. Pour remaining batter over streusel.

4. Bake in a 350°F (175°C) oven until cake just begins to pull away from side of pan and a wooden pick inserted in center comes out clean (60 to 70 minutes). Let cool in pan on a rack for 30 minutes.

5. Invert pan onto a platter; lift off pan to release cake. If any of the streusel topping sticks to pan bottom, gently remove from pan and arrange atop cake. Sprinkle with powdered sugar. Makes 10 to 12 servings.

Per serving: 441 calories (30% calories from fat), 15 g total fat, 9 g saturated fat, 84 mg cholesterol, 286 mg sodium, 71 g carbohydrates, 2 g fiber, 7 g protein, 130 mg calcium, 2 mg iron

Raisin Snack Cake

Preparation time: 20 minutes
Cooking time: About 55 minutes

This spicy sheet cake is dotted with raisins and chunks of apple.

- 3 cups (375 g) all-purpose flour
- 2 cups (400 g) granulated sugar
- 2 teaspoons baking soda
- 1½ teaspoons ground cinnamon
- ½ teaspoon *each* ground nutmeg and salt
- ¼ teaspoon ground cloves
- 1 cup (240 ml) reduced-fat mayonnaise
- ⅓ cup (80 ml) nonfat milk
- 2 large eggs
- 3 large Golden Delicious apples (about 1½ lbs./680 g *total*)
- 1 cup (145 g) *each* golden and dark raisins
- ¼ cup (30 g) powdered sugar

1. In a large bowl, stir together flour, granulated sugar, baking soda, cinnamon, nutmeg, salt, and cloves; set aside.

2. In a food processor or another large bowl, combine mayonnaise, milk, and eggs; whirl or beat with an electric mixer until smooth. Set aside. Peel, core, and coarsely chop apples; stir apples into egg mixture. Then add flour mixture to egg mixture and whirl or beat just until dry ingredients are evenly moistened. Stir in raisins.

3. Spoon batter into a lightly greased 9- by 13-inch (23- by 33-cm) nonstick or regular baking pan; smooth top. Bake in a 350°F (175°C) oven until a wooden pick inserted in center comes out clean (about 55 minutes).

4. Let cake cool completely in pan on a rack. Just before serving, sprinkle with powdered sugar. To serve, cut into about 2-inch (5-cm) squares. Makes 24 servings.

Per serving: 213 calories (12% calories from fat), 3 g total fat, 0.5 g saturated fat, 18 mg cholesterol, 241 mg sodium, 45 g carbohydrates, 2 g fiber, 3 g protein, 18 mg calcium, 1 mg iron

Banana Streusel Bundt Cake
(recipe on facing page)

A special occasion calls for a dessert like this: a grand almond-flavored cheesecake topped with a caramel-amaretto glaze.

- 2 **cups (170 g) graham cracker crumbs (about twenty-four square 2-inch/5-cm crackers)**
- ¼ **cup (2 oz./55 g) butter or margarine, melted**
- ¼ **teaspoon almond extract**
- 2 **tablespoons slivered almonds**
- 4 **large packages (about 8 oz./230 g *each*) nonfat cream cheese, at room temperature**
- 1 **cup (200 g) granulated sugar**
- 3 **large eggs**
- 2 **large egg whites**
- 1 **cup (240 ml) nonfat sour cream**
- 2 **tablespoons (30 ml) almond-flavored liqueur**
- ⅔ **cup (147 g) firmly packed brown sugar**
- 3 **tablespoons (45 ml) each half-and-half and light corn syrup**
- 2 **tablespoons (28 g) butter or margarine**
- 1 **teaspoon almond-flavored liqueur, or to taste**

Amaretto Cheesecake

Preparation time: 20 minutes
Cooking time: About 1½ hours
Cooling & chilling time:
At least 4½ hours

1. In a food processor or a large bowl, whirl or stir together graham cracker crumbs, the ¼ cup (55 g) melted butter, and almond extract just until crumbs are evenly moistened. Press crumbs firmly over bottom of a 9-inch (23-cm) nonstick or regular cheesecake pan with a removable rim. Bake in a 350°F (175°C) oven until crust is slightly darker in color (about 15 minutes).

2. Meanwhile, toast almonds in a small frying pan over medium heat until golden (3 to 5 minutes), stirring often. Transfer almonds to a bowl and set aside. In clean food processor or large bowl, combine cream cheese, granulated sugar, eggs, egg whites, sour cream, and the 2 tablespoons (30 ml) liqueur. Whirl or beat with an electric mixer until smooth.

3. Pour cream cheese filling over baked crust. Return to oven and bake until filling jiggles only slightly in center when pan is gently shaken (about 1 hour and 5 minutes). Let cheesecake cool in pan on a rack for 30 minutes.

4. Meanwhile, in a 1- to 1½-quart (950-ml to 1.4-liter) pan, combine brown sugar, half-and-half, corn syrup, and the 2 tablespoons (28 g) butter. Bring mixture just to a boil over medium heat, stirring constantly. Remove pan from heat and let cool for about 4 minutes; glaze thickens as it cools. Stir in the 1 teaspoon liqueur; set aside.

5. Run a slender knife between cheesecake and pan rim, then remove pan rim. Stir glaze and drizzle over cheesecake; let cool completely. Then lightly cover cooled cheesecake and refrigerate until cold (at least 4 hours) or until next day. Makes 12 to 16 servings.

Per serving: 321 calories (23% calories from fat), 8 g total fat, 4 g saturated fat, 67 mg cholesterol, 505 mg sodium, 47 g carbohydrates, 0.6 g fiber, 14 g protein, 227 mg calcium, 0.8 mg iron

For a new take on an old favorite, try a silky chocolate cheesecake topped with coconut and pecans.

....

1 cup (85 g) chocolate graham cracker crumbs (about twelve square 2-inch/5-cm crackers)

3 tablespoons (45 ml) apple jelly, melted and cooled slightly

3 large packages (about 8 oz./ 230 g *each*) nonfat cream cheese, at room temperature

1 cup (200 g) granulated sugar

¾ cup (65 g) unsweetened cocoa powder

⅓ cup (40 g) all-purpose flour

⅓ cup (55 g) semisweet chocolate chips, melted and cooled slightly

½ cup (120 ml) nonfat milk

2 large eggs

2 large egg whites

2 teaspoons vanilla

⅔ cup (53 g) regular rolled oats

⅓ cup (27 g) sweetened shredded coconut

¼ cup (30 g) finely chopped pecans

⅔ cup (147 g) firmly packed brown sugar

3 tablespoons (45 ml) *each* half-and-half and light corn syrup

2 tablespoons (28 g) butter or margarine

German Chocolate Cheesecake

....

Preparation time: 30 minutes
Cooking time: About 1 hour and 10 minutes
Cooling & chilling time:
At least 4½ hours

1. In a food processor or a large bowl, whirl or stir together graham cracker crumbs and jelly just until crumbs are evenly moistened. Press crumbs firmly over bottom of a 9-inch (23-cm) non-stick or regular cheesecake pan with a removable rim. Bake in a 350°F (175°C) oven until crust is slightly darker in color (about 15 minutes).

2. Meanwhile, in clean food processor or large bowl, combine cream cheese, granulated sugar, cocoa, flour, chocolate, milk, eggs, egg whites, and vanilla. Whirl or beat with an electric mixer until smooth.

3. Pour cream cheese filling over crust. Return to oven and bake until filling jiggles only slightly in center when

pan is gently shaken (about 45 minutes). Remove pan from oven and run a slender knife between cheesecake and pan rim; let cheesecake cool in pan on a rack for 30 minutes.

4. Meanwhile, toast oats in a wide nonstick frying pan over medium heat for 5 minutes, stirring often. Add coconut and pecans; continue to cook, stirring often, until mixture is slightly darker in color (3 to 5 more minutes). Transfer oat mixture to a bowl and let cool. In same pan, combine brown sugar, half-and-half, corn syrup, and butter. Cook over medium heat, stirring, until butter is melted and mixture is smoothly blended. Stir in oat mixture. Remove pan from heat and let mixture cool for 5 minutes.

5. Gently spoon coconut topping over cheesecake; let cool completely. Then cover cooled cheesecake and refrigerate until cold (at least 4 hours) or until next day. Remove pan rim before serving. Makes 12 to 16 servings.

....

Per serving: 300 calories (21% calories from fat), 7 g total fat, 3 g saturated fat, 41 mg cholesterol, 326 mg sodium, 51 g carbohydrates, 2 g fiber, 11 g protein, 176 mg calcium, 2 mg iron

Pumpkin Cheesecake
(recipe on facing page)

Pumpkin cheesecake is almost as popular as pumpkin pie for holiday desserts. This one has a gingersnap crust and a sour cream topping.

- 2 cups (170 g) finely crushed gingersnaps (about thirty-five 2-inch/5-cm cookies)
- ⅔ cup (147 g) firmly packed brown sugar
- 3 tablespoons all-purpose flour
- ¼ cup (2 oz./55 g) butter or margarine, melted
- 2 large packages (about 8 oz./ 230 g *each*) nonfat cream cheese, at room temperature
- 1 can (about 1 lb./455 g) pumpkin
- 2 large eggs
- ¾ cup (150 g) granulated sugar
- 2 tablespoons all-purpose flour
- 1 teaspoon ground cinnamon
- 1 teaspoon vanilla
- ¼ teaspoon *each* ground ginger and ground nutmeg
- 1 cup (240 ml) nonfat sour cream
- 1 tablespoon granulated sugar
- ½ cup (43 g) coarsely crushed gingersnaps (about nine 2-inch/5-cm cookies)

Pumpkin Cheesecake

Preparation time: 25 minutes
Cooking time: About 1 hour
Cooling & chilling time:
At least 4½ hours
Pictured on facing page

1. In a food processor or a large bowl, whirl or stir together the 2 cups (170 g) finely crushed gingersnaps, brown sugar, and the 3 tablespoons flour. Add butter; whirl or rub with your fingers until mixture resembles coarse crumbs. Press crumb mixture firmly over bottom and ½ inch (1 cm) up sides of a 9-inch (23-cm) nonstick or regular cheesecake pan with a removable rim. Bake in a 350°F (175°C) oven until crust smells toasted and feels slightly firmer in center when gently pressed (about 10 minutes).

2. Meanwhile, in clean food processor or large bowl, combine cream cheese, pumpkin, eggs, the ¾ cup (150 g) granulated sugar, the 2 tablespoons flour, cinnamon, vanilla, ginger, and nutmeg. Whirl or beat with an electric mixer until smooth.

3. Pour cream cheese filling into baked crust. Return to oven and bake until filling jiggles only slightly in center when pan is gently shaken (about 50 minutes). Let cool in pan on a rack for 30 minutes. Meanwhile, in a small bowl, gently stir together sour cream and the 1 tablespoon sugar; cover and refrigerate.

4. Spread cooled cheesecake with sour cream topping. Cover and refrigerate until cold (at least 4 hours) or until next day. Just before serving, remove pan rim; sprinkle cheesecake with the ½ cup (43 g) coarsely crushed gingersnaps. Makes 12 servings.

Per serving: 317 calories (20% calories from fat), 7 g total fat, 3 g saturated fat, 50 mg cholesterol, 404 mg sodium, 54 g carbohydrates, 0.8 g fiber, 10 g protein, 179 mg calcium, 3 mg iron

Lime Cheesecake

This easy cheesecake is rich—but refreshing, too, thanks to plenty of tangy fresh lime peel and juice.

Preparation time: 20 minutes
Cooking time: 45 to 55 minutes
Cooling & chilling time: At least 4½ hours

1½ cups (128 g) graham cracker crumbs (about eighteen square 2-inch/5-cm crackers)

1 cup (200 g) plus 1 tablespoon sugar

¼ cup (2 oz./55 g) butter or margarine, at room temperature

2 large packages (about 8 oz./230 g *each*) nonfat cream cheese, at room temperature

2 cups (470 ml) nonfat sour cream

2 large eggs

2 large egg whites

1 tablespoon grated lime peel

¼ cup (60 ml) lime juice

3 tablespoons all-purpose flour
Lime slices

1. In a food processor or a large bowl, whirl or stir together graham cracker crumbs, 2 tablespoons of the sugar, and butter until mixture resembles coarse crumbs. Press mixture firmly over bottom and ½ inch (1 cm) up sides of a 9-inch (23-cm) nonstick or regular cheesecake pan with a removable rim. Bake in a 350°F (175°C) oven until lightly browned (about 10 minutes).

2. Meanwhile, in clean food processor or large bowl, combine ¾ cup plus 2 tablespoons (175 g) of the sugar, cream cheese, 1 cup (240 ml) of the sour cream, eggs, egg whites, lime peel, lime juice, and flour. Whirl or beat with an electric mixer until smooth.

3. Pour cream cheese filling into crust. Return to oven and bake until filling jiggles only slightly in center when pan is gently shaken (35 to 45 minutes). Let cool in pan on a rack for 30 minutes. Meanwhile, in a small bowl, gently stir together remaining 1 cup (240 ml) sour cream and remaining 1 tablespoon sugar; cover and refrigerate.

4. Spread cooled cheesecake with sour cream topping. Cover and refrigerate until cold (at least 4 hours) or until next day. Before serving, remove pan rim and garnish cheesecake with lime slices. Makes 12 to 16 servings.

Per serving: 211 calories (21% calories from fat), 5 g total fat, 2 g saturated fat, 43 mg cholesterol, 305 mg sodium, 31 g carbohydrates, 0.4 g fiber, 9 g protein, 141 mg calcium, 0.5 mg iron

Espresso Cheesecake

A crispy chocolate crust and a flavorful espresso filling create a lavish taste experience.

Preparation time: 25 minutes
Cooking time: 1½ to 1¾ hours
Cooling & chilling time: At least 4½ hours
Pictured on page 366

1 package (about 9 oz./255 g) chocolate wafer cookies

¼ cup (2 oz./55 g) butter or margarine, melted and cooled slightly

1 tablespoon instant espresso powder

½ teaspoon vanilla

4 large packages (about 8 oz./230 g *each*) nonfat cream cheese, at room temperature

1 cup (200 g) sugar

3 large eggs

2 large egg whites

2 cups (470 ml) nonfat sour cream

3 tablespoons (45 ml) coffee-flavored liqueur

1 tablespoon sugar

1 tablespoon unsweetened cocoa powder
Chocolate-covered espresso beans or mocha candy beans

1. In a food processor, whirl cookies to form fine crumbs. Add butter, instant espresso, and vanilla; whirl just until crumbs are evenly moistened. Press crumb mixture firmly over bottom and about 1 inch (2.5 cm) up sides of a greased 9-inch (23-cm) cheesecake pan with a removable rim. Bake in a 350°F (175°C) oven until crust feels slightly firmer when pressed (about 15 minutes).

2. In clean food processor or in a large bowl, combine cream cheese, the 1 cup (200 g) sugar, eggs, egg whites, 1 cup (240 ml) of the sour cream, and liqueur. Whirl or beat with an electric mixer until smooth.

3. Pour cheese filling into baked crust. Return to oven and bake until filling is golden on top and jiggles only slightly in center when pan is gently shaken (1¼ to 1½ hours).

4. Gently run a slender knife between cheesecake and pan rim; then let cheesecake cool in pan on a rack for 30 minutes. Meanwhile, in a small bowl, gently stir together remaining 1 cup (240 ml) sour cream and the 1 tablespoon sugar; cover and refrigerate.

5. Spread cooled cheesecake with sour cream topping. Cover and refrigerate until cold (at least 4 hours) or until next day. Just before serving, sprinkle with cocoa; then remove pan rim. Garnish with chocolate-covered espresso beans. Makes 12 to 16 servings.

Per serving: 276 calories (23% calories from fat), 7 g total fat, 3 g saturated fat, 62 mg cholesterol, 492 mg sodium, 37 g carbohydrates, 0.7 g fiber, 15 g protein, 239 mg calcium, 0.9 mg iron

Striking to look at and quick to prepare, this majestic torte features layers of pound cake and chocolate-flecked cream filling, all cloaked in a mocha-flavored cream cheese frosting.

- 2 tablespoons slivered almonds
- 1 large package (about 8 oz./ 230 g) nonfat cream cheese, at room temperature
- ¼ cup (30 g) powdered sugar
- ½ teaspoon vanilla
- 1 cup (240 ml) frozen reduced-fat whipped topping, thawed
- 1 ounce (30 g) semisweet chocolate, coarsely grated
- 1 loaf (about 13.6 oz./386 g) purchased nonfat chocolate or regular pound cake, thawed if frozen
- 1½ cups (180 g) powdered sugar
- 2 ounces (55 g) nonfat cream cheese, at room temperature
- 2 tablespoons (28 g) butter or margarine, at room temperature
- ½ teaspoon instant espresso or coffee powder
- 1 to 3 teaspoons nonfat milk

Mocha Almond Fudge Torte

Preparation time: 30 minutes
Cooking time: 3 to 5 minutes

1. Toast almonds in a small nonstick frying pan over medium heat until golden (3 to 5 minutes), stirring often. Transfer almonds to a bowl and set aside.

2. In a food processor or a large bowl, combine the 8-ounce (230-g) package cream cheese, the ¼ cup (30 g) powdered sugar, and vanilla. Whirl or beat with an electric mixer until smooth and fluffy; then gently fold in whipped topping and chocolate. Cover and refrigerate until ready to use.

3. With a serrated knife, cut pound cake horizontally into 3 equal layers. Place top cake layer, cut side up, on a rack set over a sheet of wax paper; spread with half the cream cheese filling. Add middle layer and spread with remaining filling; top with remaining cake layer, cut side down.

4. In clean food processor or large bowl, combine the 1½ cups (180 g) powdered sugar, the 2 ounces (55 g) cream cheese, butter, instant espresso, and 1 teaspoon of the milk. Whirl or beat until smooth and easy to spread; add more milk, if necessary. Frosting will be soft.

5. Spread frosting over top of cake; some of it will flow down to cover sides of cake. Sprinkle top of cake with almonds; scrape up frosting that has dripped onto wax paper and spread it gently on sides of cake. With wide spatulas, carefully transfer cake to a platter. Serve; or cover lightly and refrigerate until ready to serve. Makes 14 servings.

Per serving: 194 calories (16% calories from fat), 3 g total fat, 2 g saturated fat, 7 mg cholesterol, 257 mg sodium, 36 g carbohydrates, 0.6 g fiber, 5 g protein, 63 mg calcium, 0.7 mg iron

Tender almond-flavored cake studded with sliced fresh apricots makes a pretty company dessert. Serve it with a silky, orange-accented apricot sauce.

....

1   tablespoon (15 ml) lemon juice

5   medium-size apricots (about 1 lb./455 g *total*)

¼   cup (30 g) slivered almonds

2   large eggs

1   cup (200 g) sugar

4   to 5 tablespoons (60 to 75 ml) almond-flavored liqueur

½   teaspoon almond extract

¾   cup (95 g) all-purpose flour

2   teaspoons baking powder

⅛   teaspoon salt

¼   cup (2 oz./55 g) butter or margarine, melted and cooled slightly

4   teaspoons cornstarch

1   cup (240 ml) apricot nectar

½   cup (120 ml) fresh orange juice

½   teaspoon vanilla

Apricot-Amaretto Torte

....

Preparation time: 25 minutes
Cooking time: About 25 minutes
Pictured on facing page

1. Pour lemon juice into a medium-size bowl. Quarter and pit apricots; add to bowl and turn to coat with juice. Set aside.

2. In a food processor, whirl almonds until finely ground. (Or finely chop almonds with a knife, then place in a large bowl.) To almonds, add eggs, ½ cup (100 g) of the sugar, 1 table-spoon (15 ml) of the liqueur, and almond extract; whirl or beat with an electric mixer until thick and well blended. Add flour, baking powder, salt, and butter; whirl or beat until well blended. Spread batter in a greased, floured 9-inch (23-cm) cake pan with a removable rim. Decoratively arrange apricots in batter, over-lapping as needed; press fruit lightly into batter.

3. Bake in a 375°F (190°C) oven until cake just begins to pull away from side of pan and a wooden pick inserted in center comes out clean (about 25 minutes; pierce cake, not fruit). Let cool slightly on a rack.

4. While cake is cooling, stir together cornstarch and 6 tablespoons (72 g) of the remaining sugar in a small pan. Whisk in apricot nectar and orange juice; cook over medium-high heat, whisking constantly, until mixture boils and thickens slightly (about 2 minutes). Remove from heat and stir in vanilla and remaining 3 to 4 tablespoons (45 to 60 ml) liqueur; keep warm.

5. Sprinkle cake with remaining 2 tablespoons sugar. Remove pan rim and cut cake into wedges; serve with apricot-orange sauce. Makes 8 servings.

....

Per serving: 340 calories (28% calories from fat), 10 g total fat, 4 g saturated fat, 69 mg cholesterol, 240 mg sodium, 54 g carbohydrates, 1 g fiber, 5 g protein, 100 mg calcium, 1 mg iron

Apricot-Amaretto Torte
(recipe on facing page)

Candies & Confections

Perfect for lunch-box surprises or for those occasions when cake or another dessert is just "too much," our candies and confections are scrumptiously low in fat. Delectably creamy Peppermint Fudge is a perfect gift for chocolate-loving friends, or satisfy your own sweet tooth with chewy Apricot Slims. While these treats are low in fat, they are not necessarily low-calorie. So indulge with moderation.

Peppermint Fudge

Preparation time: 10 minutes
Cooking time: About 10 minutes
Chilling time: At least 2 hours

½ cup (120 ml) evaporated skim milk

1¼ cups (250 g) sugar

¼ teaspoon salt

¼ cup (2 oz./55 g) butter or margarine

1 package (about 6 oz./170 g) semisweet chocolate chips

¾ cup (180 ml) marshmallow fluff (marshmallow creme)

1 teaspoon vanilla

½ cup (85 g) crushed hard peppermint candy

1. In a heavy 2½- to 3-quart (2.4- to 2.8-liter) pan, combine milk, sugar, salt, and butter. Bring to a rolling boil over medium-low heat, stirring; then boil for 5 minutes, stirring constantly and reducing heat as needed to prevent scorching.

2. Remove pan from heat; add chocolate chips and stir until melted. Quickly stir in marshmallow fluff and vanilla; then mix in peppermint candy until blended. Pour into a buttered square 8-inch (20-cm) baking pan; spread to make an even layer. Let cool, then cover and refrigerate until firm (at least 2 hours). To serve, cut into 1-inch (2.5-cm) squares. If made ahead, wrap airtight and refrigerate for up to 2 weeks. Makes 64 pieces (about 1½ lbs./680 g *total*).

Per piece: 45 calories (30% calories from fat), 2 g total fat, 1 g saturated fat, 2 mg cholesterol, 21 mg sodium, 8 g carbohydrates, 0 g fiber, 0.3 g protein, 7 mg calcium, 0.1 mg iron

Apricot Slims

Preparation time: 15 minutes
Chilling time: At least 30 minutes

1 package (about 6 oz./ 170 g) dried apricots

¼ cup (20 g) sweetened shredded or flaked coconut

1 tablespoon (15 ml) orange juice

2 tablespoons finely chopped almonds

3 tablespoons powdered sugar

1. If apricots are not moist, place them in a wire strainer and steam over simmering water for 5 minutes.

2. In a food processor, combine apricots, coconut, and orange juice. Whirl until mixture begins to hold together in a ball, about 1 minute. (Or put apricots through a food chopper fitted with a fine blade; add coconut and put through food chopper again, then stir in orange juice and mix well.)

3. Divide apricot mixture into 4 equal portions and wrap each in plastic wrap. Refrigerate until cold and easy to handle (at least 30 minutes).

4. In a small bowl, mix almonds and powdered sugar. Sprinkle a fourth of the almond mixture on a board. Place one portion of the apricot mixture atop almond mixture; roll apricot mixture back and forth with your palms to form a 16-inch (40-cm) rope. Repeat to make 3 more ropes, using remaining almond and apricot mixtures. To serve, cut ropes diagonally into 2-inch (5-cm) pieces. Makes 32 pieces.

Per piece: 20 calories (14% calories from fat), 0.3 g total fat, 0.2 g saturated fat, 0 mg cholesterol, 2 mg sodium, 4 g carbohydrates, 0.5 g fiber, 0.3 g protein, 3 mg calcium, 0.3 mg iron

Pear Slims: Follow directions for **Apricot Slims,** but substitute 6 ounces (170 g) **moist-pack dried pears** for apricots; remove any bits of stem or core from pears. Instead of orange juice, use 1 tablespoon (15 ml) **lemon juice. Makes 32 pieces.**

Per piece: 22 calories (17% calories from fat), 0.5 g total fat, 0.2 g saturated fat, 0 mg cholesterol, 2 mg sodium, 5 g carbohydrates, 0.1 g fiber, 0.2 g protein, 3 mg calcium, 0.1 mg iron

Do-It-Yourself Chocolate Date Bars

Preparation time: 10 minutes
Cooking time: 2½ to 3 minutes
Chilling time: About 30 minutes

1 **package (about 6 oz./170 g) semisweet chocolate chips**

1 **cup (178 g) chopped pitted dates**

¼ **cup (60 ml) light corn syrup**

½ **cup (75 g) raisins**

1½ **cups (45 g) oven-toasted rice cereal**

1. In a large microwave-safe bowl, combine chocolate chips, dates, and corn syrup. Microwave on HIGH (100%) for 1½ minutes; stir. Then microwave again on HIGH (100%) for 1 to 1½ more minutes or until chocolate is melted and smooth and dates are soft. Stir in raisins and cereal.

2. Line a flat tray with wax paper. Working quickly, spoon chocolate mixture onto paper into 8 bars, each about 1 inch (2.5 cm) wide and 5 inches (12.5 cm) long; smooth with 2 spoons. Refrigerate until firm to the touch (about 30 minutes). If made ahead, wrap bars individually in plastic wrap and refrigerate for up to 2 weeks. Makes 8 bars.

Per bar: 220 calories (22% calories from fat), 6 g total fat, 3 g saturated fat, 0.2 mg cholesterol, 62 mg sodium, 46 g carbohydrates, 2 g fiber, 2 g protein, 16 mg calcium, 1 mg iron

Chocolate Taffies

Preparation time: 15 minutes
Cooking time: 5 to 8 minutes

1 **can (about 14 oz./400 g) sweetened condensed milk**

1 **cup (86 g) unsweetened cocoa powder**

About 1 tablespoon butter or margarine

3½ **ounces (100 g) chocolate sprinkles (about ½ cup)**

1. In a 2- to 3-quart (1.9- to 2.8-liter) pan, combine milk, cocoa, and butter. Place over medium-low heat; cook, stirring, until mixture begins to bubble. Then continue to stir until mixture holds together as a soft mass when pushed to side of pan (3 to 5 minutes). Remove from heat and let stand until cool enough to touch.

2. Spread chocolate sprinkles on a plate. With lightly buttered hands, shape cocoa mixture into 1-inch (2.5-cm) balls. Roll balls, 4 or 5 at a time, in sprinkles to coat. If desired, place each candy in a small paper or foil bonbon cup. Serve at room temperature. If made ahead, cover airtight and refrigerate for up to 1 week; freeze for longer storage. Makes about 34 candies.

Per candy: 59 calories (26% calories from fat), 2 g total fat, 1 g saturated fat, 5 mg cholesterol, 21 mg sodium, 11 g carbohydrates, 0.8 g fiber, 1 g protein, 37 mg calcium, 0.4 mg iron

Oat, Coconut & Cocoa Drops

Preparation time: 15 minutes
Cooking time: 2 to 3 minutes
Standing time: 40 minutes to 1 hour

½ **cup (120 ml) light corn syrup**

¼ **cup (50 g) granulated sugar**

¼ **cup (2 oz./55 g) butter or margarine**

¼ **cup (60 ml) milk**

2 **tablespoons unsweetened cocoa powder**

2⅓ **cups (190 g) regular rolled oats**

½ **cup (40 g) sweetened shredded coconut**

About ¼ cup (30 g) powdered sugar

1. In a 2-quart (1.9-liter) glass measuring cup or microwave-safe bowl, combine corn syrup, granulated sugar, butter, and milk. Microwave on HIGH (100%) for 2 minutes; then stir until butter is melted. Microwave on HIGH (100%) again for 30 seconds to 1 minute or until mixture bubbles; then microwave for 30 more seconds. Remove from microwave. Stir in cocoa until well blended; then stir in oats and coconut. Set mixture aside and let cool slightly.

2. To shape candies, roll 1-tablespoon (15-ml) portions of oat mixture into balls. Roll balls in powdered sugar to coat, then place slightly apart on a plate. Let stand or refrigerate until firm (40 minutes to 1 hour). If made ahead, wrap airtight and refrigerate for up to 4 days. Makes 24 candies.

Per candy: 89 calories (29% calories from fat), 3 g total fat, 2 g saturated fat, 6 mg cholesterol, 333 mg sodium, 15 g carbohydrates, 1 g fiber, 1 g protein, 9 mg calcium, 0.4 mg iron

Fresh Strawberry Pie
(recipe on page 392)

Pies, Tarts & Cobblers

While pies and tarts can be sweet or savory, our luscious collection takes advantage of the naturally low-fat fruits of the garden and orchard as well as the rich, deep chocolate flavor of cocoa for trim, mouth-watering treats. Warm up a crisp autumn afternoon with coffee and a slice of Caramel Apple Pie studded with pecans or make any occasion special with a beautiful Maple & Raspberry Tart. And silky smooth Chocolate Cream Pie will delight any chocolate lover.

Glazed whole strawberries glisten like jewels in this springtime favorite.

Pie Pastry:

- 1 **cup plus 2 tablespoons (141 g) all-purpose flour**
- ¼ **teaspoon salt**
- 6 **tablespoons (75 g) solid vegetable shortening; or 6 tablespoons (85 g) butter or margarine, cut into chunks**

Filling:

- ¾ **cup (150 g) sugar**
- 3 **tablespoons cornstarch**
- 1 **teaspoon grated orange peel**
- 7 **cups (1 kg) fresh strawberries, hulled**
- 2 **tablespoons (30 ml) orange-flavored liqueur or orange juice (or to taste)**

Topping:

- 3 **large oranges (about 1½ lbs./ 680 g *total*)**
- ¼ **cup (50 g) sugar**

1. To prepare pastry, stir together flour and salt in a medium-size bowl. Using a pastry blender or your fingers, cut or rub in shortening until mixture resembles fine crumbs. Sprinkle with 2 to 3 tablespoons (30 to 45 ml) cold water, stirring with a fork until pastry holds together. On a lightly floured board, pat pastry into a flat, smooth round.

Fresh Strawberry Pie

Preparation time: 35 minutes
Cooking time: About 30 minutes
Chilling time: At least 1 hour
Pictured on page 390

Then roll pastry into a 12-inch (30-cm) circle; ease into a lightly greased 9-inch (23-cm) nonstick or regular pie pan. Fold edge of pastry under; flute rim decoratively. Prick pastry all over with a fork to prevent puffing.

2. Bake pastry shell on lowest rack of a 425°F (220°C) oven until golden (12 to 15 minutes). Let cool completely on a rack.

3. Meanwhile, in a small pan, stir together the ¾ cup (150 g) sugar, cornstarch, and orange peel. In a blender or food processor, combine 2 cups (298 g) of the least perfect strawberries and 6 tablespoons (90 ml) water; whirl until smoothly puréed. Pour purée into pan with sugar mixture and stir well. Then cook over medium-high heat, stirring often, until mixture comes to a full boil and thickens slightly (about 4 minutes). Remove pan from heat and stir in liqueur.

4. Working quickly, arrange remaining strawberries, tips up, in pastry shell; evenly spoon hot glaze over berries, covering them completely. Refrigerate, uncovered, until glaze is cool and set (at least 1 hour); then cover and refrigerate until ready to serve or until next day.

5. While pie is chilling, make topping. Cut peel (colored part only) from oranges; cut peel into thin slivers. Squeeze oranges to extract juice; set juice aside. Place slivered peel in a small pan and add enough water to cover; bring to a boil. Drain, then cover with water and bring to a boil again. Drain well; add orange juice and the ¼ cup (50 g) sugar. Bring to a boil over high heat; boil, stirring often and watching closely to prevent scorching, until almost all liquid has evaporated and syrup forms big bubbles (about 10 minutes). Remove from heat; let cool, stirring occasionally to separate slivers of peel. If made ahead, cover and refrigerate until next day.

6. Just before serving, sprinkle about a third of the candied orange peel over pie. Offer additional candied peel to accompany individual servings. Makes 8 servings.

Per serving: 337 calories (27% calories from fat), 10 g total fat, 2 g saturated fat, 0 mg cholesterol, 70 mg sodium, 58 g carbohydrates, 4 g fiber, 3 g protein, 35 mg calcium, 1 mg iron

Enjoy a sweet summer harvest of blueberries and nectarines in this tempting pie.

....

Pie Pastry (facing page)

1   cup (240 ml) nonfat sour cream

1   teaspoon cornstarch

2   cups (290 g) fresh blueberries

4   cups (680 g) peeled, sliced firm-ripe nectarines

1   teaspoon vanilla

½   cup (100 g) granulated sugar

3   tablespoons quick-cooking tapioca

½   cup (110 g) firmly packed brown sugar

⅔   cup (85 g) all-purpose flour

3   tablespoons (43 g) butter or margarine, melted and cooled slightly

2   tablespoons (30 ml) smooth unsweetened applesauce

....

1. Prepare Pie Pastry and line pie pan as directed for Fresh Strawberry Pie on

Nectarine- Blueberry Cream Pie

....

Preparation time: 35 minutes, plus 15 minutes for filling to stand
Cooking time: About 1¼ hours

facing page, but *do not* prick pastry after lining pan. Bake pastry shell on lowest rack of a 425°F (220°C) oven until golden (12 to 15 minutes; pastry may puff, but filling will press it down again). Remove from oven and place on a rack. Reduce oven temperature to 350°F (175°C).

2. While pastry is baking, in a large bowl, beat sour cream and cornstarch until smoothly blended. Stir in blueberries, nectarines, and vanilla. Stir together granulated sugar and tapioca;

add to fruit mixture and mix gently. Let stand for 15 minutes to soften tapioca, stirring occasionally. Then pour filling into warm pastry shell and set aside.

3. In a small bowl, combine brown sugar, flour, butter, and applesauce. Stir until mixture is evenly moistened. With your fingers, squeeze mixture to form large lumps; then crumble evenly over filling.

4. Set pie pan in a larger baking pan to catch any drips. Bake pie on lowest oven rack until filling is bubbly in center and topping is well browned (about 1 hour); if crust or topping begins to darken excessively, cover it with foil. Let cool on a rack before serving; serve warm. Makes 8 to 10 servings.

....

Per serving: 390 calories (30% calories from fat), 13 g total fat, 5 g saturated fat, 10 mg cholesterol, 139 mg sodium, 64 g carbohydrates, 3 g fiber, 6 g protein, 57 mg calcium, 2 mg iron

---

Traditional for autumn, this caramel, apple, and pecan pie is just as welcome at any other time of year.

....

Pie Pastry (facing page)

3   large Red Delicious apples (about 1½ lbs./680 g *total*), cored and cut into ½-inch (1-cm) chunks

1   tablespoon (15 ml) lemon juice

½   cup (60 g) all-purpose flour

1   cup (240 ml) purchased nonfat caramel topping

⅔   cup (180 ml) apple butter

½   cup (59 g) coarsely chopped pecans

Caramel Apple Pie

....

Preparation time: 20 minutes
Cooking time: About 55 minutes

1. Prepare Pie Pastry and line pie pan as directed for Fresh Strawberry Pie on facing page, but *do not* prick pastry after lining pan. Set aside.

2. In a large bowl, combine apples and lemon juice. Sprinkle with flour, then add caramel topping and apple butter;

mix well. Pour mixture into pastry shell and sprinkle chopped pecans evenly over top.

3. Set pie pan in a larger baking pan to catch any drips. Bake pie on lowest rack of a 350°F (175°C) oven until crust is deep golden and apples are tender when pierced (about 55 minutes); cover pie loosely with foil if nuts begin to brown excessively. Let cool on a rack before serving; serve warm. Makes 8 to 10 servings.

....

Per serving: 401 calories (30% calories from fat), 14 g total fat, 3 g saturated fat, 0 mg cholesterol, 110 mg sodium, 67 g carbohydrates, 3 g fiber, 4 g protein, 12 mg calcium, 1 mg iron

Fresh and dried cherries, spiked with brandy and lightly flavored with almond, fill this flaky-crusted pie.

1⅔ cups (233 g) pitted dried cherries

3 tablespoons (45 ml) brandy or orange juice

6 cups (870 g) pitted fresh Bing or other dark sweet cherries

1 tablespoon (15 ml) lemon juice

¼ teaspoon almond extract

⅔ cup (135 g) granulated sugar

3 tablespoons cornstarch

1½ recipes of Pie Pastry (page 392)

2 to 3 tablespoons powdered sugar

1. In a small bowl, combine dried cherries and brandy. Let stand until cherries are softened (about 10 minutes), stirring occasionally. Meanwhile, in a large bowl, combine fresh cherries, lemon juice, and almond extract. Stir

Cherry Brandy Pie

Preparation time: 30 minutes
Cooking time: About 50 minutes

together granulated sugar and cornstarch; stir into fresh cherry mixture. Add dried cherry–brandy mixture; mix gently to combine thoroughly. Set aside.

2. Prepare 1½ recipes of Pie Pastry as directed for Fresh Strawberry Pie on page 392, using 1½ cups plus 3 tablespoons (208 g) flour, ¼ teaspoon salt, 9 tablespoons (113 g) shortening, and 3 to 5 tablespoons (45 to 75 ml) cold water. Cut off a third of the pastry; on a lightly floured board, pat into a flat, smooth round. Cover and set aside. On floured board, pat remaining pastry into a round; then roll into a 12-inch (30-cm) circle and ease into a lightly

greased 9-inch (23-cm) nonstick or regular pie pan. Fold edge under; flute rim decoratively. Fill pastry with cherry mixture.

3. On floured board, roll reserved portion of pastry into a 9-inch (23-cm) circle. Trim edge evenly; then cut circle into quarters. Fold back inside corner of each quarter about ¾ inch (2 cm). Lift quarters and carefully place atop pie.

4. Set pie pan in a larger baking pan to catch any drips. Bake pie on lowest rack of a 400°F (205°C) oven until filling is bubbly in center and crust is golden brown (about 50 minutes); if crust begins to darken excessively, cover it with foil.

5. Serve pie warm or at room temperature. Just before serving, sprinkle with powdered sugar. Makes 8 to 10 servings.

Per serving: 426 calories (30% calories from fat), 14 g total fat, 4 g saturated fat, 0 mg cholesterol, 62 mg sodium, 71 g carbohydrates, 2 g fiber, 4 g protein, 19 mg calcium, 1 mg iron

A touch of brandy flavors a creamy, streusel-topped pie filled with pear slices and raisins.

- ¾ cup (110 g) raisins
- 3 tablespoons (45 ml) brandy or orange juice
  Pie Pastry (page 392)
- 1 cup (240 ml) nonfat sour cream
- 1 large egg
- 1 large egg white
- ½ cup (100 g) granulated sugar
- 2 tablespoons all-purpose flour
- 1 teaspoon vanilla
- ½ teaspoon ground cinnamon
- ¼ teaspoon ground nutmeg
- ½ cup (110 g) firmly packed brown sugar
- ⅔ cup (85 g) all-purpose flour
- 3 tablespoons (43 g) butter or margarine, melted and cooled slightly
- 2 tablespoons (30 ml) smooth unsweetened applesauce
- 4 large firm-ripe D'Anjou or Bartlett pears (about 2 lbs./ 905 g *total*)

Pears & Cream Pie

Preparation time: 35 minutes
Cooking time: About 1 hour

1. In a large bowl, combine raisins and brandy. Let stand until raisins are softened (about 10 minutes), stirring occasionally.

2. Meanwhile, prepare Pie Pastry and line pie pan as directed for Fresh Strawberry Pie on page 392, but *do not* prick pastry after lining pan. Cover and refrigerate.

3. In a small bowl, combine sour cream, egg, egg white, granulated sugar, the 2 tablespoons flour, vanilla, cinnamon, and nutmeg. Beat until smoothly blended; set aside. In another small bowl, combine brown sugar, the ⅔ cup (85 g) flour, butter, and applesauce. Stir until mixture is evenly moistened. Then, with your fingers, squeeze mixture to form large lumps; set aside.

4. Peel and core pears; cut into slices about ½ inch (1 cm) thick. As pears are sliced, add to bowl with raisin mixture and turn to coat with brandy. Add sour cream mixture to pear mixture; mix gently to coat fruit evenly. Spoon pear filling into pastry shell. Crumble brown sugar mixture evenly over filling.

5. Set pie pan in a larger baking pan to catch any drips. Bake pie on lowest rack of a 375°F (190°C) oven until filling is bubbly in center and topping is browned (about 1 hour); if crust or topping begins to darken excessively, cover it with foil. Let cool on a rack before serving; serve warm. Makes 8 to 10 servings.

Per serving: 435 calories (29% calories from fat), 14 g total fat, 5 g saturated fat, 34 mg cholesterol, 137 mg sodium, 70 g carbohydrates, 4 g fiber, 6 g protein, 70 mg calcium, 2 mg iron

The classic combination of peanut butter and chocolate makes this cool and creamy pie irresistible.

- 2 cups (170 g) chocolate or honey graham cracker crumbs (about twenty-four square 2-inch/ 5-cm crackers)
- 2 tablespoons granulated sugar
- 1 tablespoon all-purpose flour
- ½ cup (120 ml) apple jelly, melted and cooled slightly
- 1 envelope unflavored gelatin
- ½ cup (120 ml) nonfat milk
- 1 large package (about 8 oz./ 230 g) nonfat cream cheese, at room temperature
- 1 jar (about 7 oz./200 g) marsh-mallow fluff (marshmallow creme)
- ¼ cup (30 g) powdered sugar
- ¼ cup (60 ml) reduced-fat or regular creamy peanut butter
- 1 teaspoon vanilla
- ¼ to ½ teaspoon Oriental sesame oil
- ½ cup (120 ml) half-and-half
- 2 cups (480 ml) frozen reduced-calorie whipped topping, thawed
- ¼ cup (36 g) chopped salted roasted peanuts

Peanut Butter Chocolate Pie

Preparation time: 25 minutes
Cooking time: About 25 minutes
Chilling time: At least 4 hours

1. In a food processor or a large bowl, whirl or stir together graham cracker crumbs, granulated sugar, and flour. Add jelly; whirl or stir until mixture is evenly moistened. Press mixture firmly over bottom and ½ inch (1 cm) up sides of a lightly greased 9-inch (23-cm) non-stick or regular pie pan. Bake in a 350°F (175°C) oven until crust turns a slightly darker brown (about 15 minutes). Let cool completely on a rack.

2. Meanwhile, in a small bowl, sprinkle gelatin over milk; let stand for about 5 minutes to soften gelatin. In clean food processor or large bowl, combine cream cheese, marshmallow fluff, powdered sugar, peanut butter, vanilla, and oil. Whirl or beat with an electric mixer until smooth; set aside.

3. In a 1- to 1½-quart (950-ml to 1.4-liter) pan, bring half-and-half to a boil over medium heat. Add gelatin mixture; reduce heat to low and stir until gelatin is dissolved (about 5 minutes).

4. With food processor running, slowly pour gelatin mixture into cream cheese mixture; whirl until smooth. (Or beat with electric mixer until smooth.) With a spatula, gently fold in whipped topping. Pour filling into cooled crust; smooth top. Cover pie, making sure cover does not touch filling (hold a "tent" of plastic wrap above pie with wooden picks, or cover pie with a cake cover). Refrigerate until filling is firm (at least 4 hours) or for up to 8 hours.

5. Just before serving, sprinkle peanuts around edge of pie. Makes 8 to 10 servings.

Per serving: 426 calories (30% calories from fat), 14 g total fat, 3 g saturated fat, 8 mg cholesterol, 244 mg sodium, 64 g carbohydrates, 0.6 g fiber, 10 g protein, 107 mg calcium, 1 mg iron

Silky chocolate mousse fills a rich chocolate crust in this chocolate-lover's special.

....

- 2½ cups (213 g) chocolate or honey graham cracker crumbs (about thirty square 2-inch/5-cm crackers)
- 2 tablespoons granulated sugar
- 1 tablespoon all-purpose flour
- ½ to 1 teaspoon instant espresso or coffee powder
- ½ cup (120 ml) apple jelly, melted and cooled slightly
- 1 envelope unflavored gelatin
- ½ cup (120 ml) nonfat milk
- 1 large package (about 8 oz./ 230 g) nonfat cream cheese, at room temperature
- 1 jar (about 7 oz./200 g) marshmallow fluff (marshmallow creme)
- ½ cup (43 g) unsweetened cocoa powder
- ¼ cup (30 g) powdered sugar
- 1 teaspoon vanilla
- ½ cup (120 ml) half-and-half
- ¼ cup (43 g) semisweet chocolate chips
- 2 cups (470 ml) frozen reduced-fat whipped topping, thawed

Chocolate Cream Pie

....

Preparation time: 30 minutes
Cooking time: About 25 minutes
Chilling time: At least 4 hours

1. In a food processor or a large bowl, whirl or stir together 2 cups (170 g) of the graham cracker crumbs, granulated sugar, flour, and ¼ to ½ teaspoon of the instant espresso. Add jelly; whirl or stir until mixture is evenly moistened. Press mixture firmly over bottom and ½ inch (1 cm) up sides of a lightly greased 10-inch (25-cm) nonstick or regular pie pan. Bake in a 350°F (175°C) oven until crust turns a slightly darker brown (about 15 minutes). Let cool completely on a rack.

2. Meanwhile, in a small bowl, sprinkle gelatin over milk; let stand for about 5 minutes to soften gelatin. In clean food processor or large bowl, combine cream cheese, marshmallow fluff, cocoa, powdered sugar, vanilla, and remaining ¼ to ½ teaspoon instant espresso. Whirl or beat with an electric mixer until smooth; set aside.

3. In a 1- to 1½-quart (950-ml to 1.4-liter) pan, bring half-and-half to a boil over medium heat. Add gelatin mixture; reduce heat to low and stir until gelatin is dissolved (about 5 minutes). Remove pan from heat, add chocolate chips, and stir until melted and smooth.

4. With food processor running, slowly pour gelatin mixture into cream cheese mixture; whirl until smooth. (Or beat with electric mixer until smooth.) With a spatula, gently fold in whipped topping. Pour filling into cooled crust; smooth top. Cover pie, making sure cover does not touch filling (hold a "tent" of plastic wrap above pie with wooden picks, or cover pie with a cake cover). Refrigerate until filling is firm (at least 4 hours) or for up to 8 hours.

5. Just before serving, sprinkle remaining ½ cup (43 g) graham cracker crumbs around edge of pie. Makes 8 to 10 servings.

....

Per serving: 365 calories (19% calories from fat), 8 g total fat, 4 g saturated fat, 8 mg cholesterol, 311 mg sodium, 68 g carbohydrates, 2 g fiber, 8 g protein, 112 mg calcium, 2 mg iron

Chocolate Hazelnut Tart
(recipe on facing page)

Whole toasted hazelnuts adorn a dense, fudgy tart with a dark chocolate crust.

- ½ cup (68 g) hazelnuts
- 2 cups (170 g) chocolate or honey graham cracker crumbs (about twenty-four square 2-inch/5-cm crackers)
- 2 tablespoons granulated sugar
- 1 tablespoon all-purpose flour
- ½ cup (120 ml) apple jelly, melted and cooled slightly
- ⅔ cup (135 g) granulated sugar
- ⅔ cup (147 g) firmly packed brown sugar
- ½ cup (43 g) unsweetened cocoa powder
- ½ cup (120 ml) *each* smooth unsweetened applesauce and light corn syrup
- 2 tablespoons (30 ml) *each* hazelnut-flavored liqueur and light molasses
- 4 large egg whites
- 1 large egg
- ¼ cup (43 g) semisweet chocolate chips

Chocolate Hazelnut Tart

Preparation time: 25 minutes
Cooking time: About 1 hour and 5 minutes
Pictured on facing page

1. Spread hazelnuts in a single layer in a shallow baking pan. Bake in a 350°F (175°C) oven until nuts are golden beneath skins (about 10 minutes). Let nuts cool slightly; then pour into a towel, fold to enclose, and gently rub to remove as much of loose skins as possible. Set aside.

2. In a food processor or a large bowl, whirl or stir together graham cracker crumbs, the 2 tablespoons granulated sugar, and flour. Add jelly; whirl or stir until mixture is evenly moistened. Press mixture firmly over bottom and ½ inch (1 cm) up sides of a 10-inch (25-cm) nonstick or regular tart pan with a removable rim. Bake in a 350°F (175°C) oven until crust turns a slightly darker brown (about 15 minutes). Let cool on a rack for 10 minutes.

3. Meanwhile, in clean food processor or large bowl, combine the ⅔ cup (135 g) granulated sugar, brown sugar, cocoa, applesauce, corn syrup, liqueur, and molasses. Whirl or beat with an electric mixer until smooth. Whirl or beat in egg whites; then add egg and whirl or beat until well blended. Stir in chocolate chips. Pour filling into baked crust. Arrange hazelnuts decoratively atop filling, then push them down gently to cover with filling.

4. Set tart pan in a larger baking pan to catch any drips. Return to oven and bake until edge of filling is set but center still jiggles slightly when tart pan is gently shaken (about 40 minutes). Let cool on a rack before serving; serve warm. If made ahead, let cool completely; then cover and refrigerate until next day. Remove pan rim before serving. Makes 10 to 12 servings.

Per serving: 387 calories (23% calories from fat), 10 g total fat, 1 g saturated fat, 19 mg cholesterol, 108 mg sodium, 72 g carbohydrates, 2 g fiber, 5 g protein, 40 mg calcium, 2 mg iron

Luscious to eat and beautiful to look at, this tart features a dense maple filling topped with fresh raspberries and a lime-accented berry glaze.

....

- 2 cups (170 g) graham cracker crumbs (about twenty-four square 2-inch/5-cm crackers)
- 2 tablespoons granulated sugar
- 1 tablespoon all-purpose flour
- ⅓ cup (76 g) butter or margarine, melted
- ½ cup (60 g) all-purpose flour
- ½ cup (110 g) firmly packed brown sugar
- ½ cup (120 ml) pure maple syrup
- 3 tablespoons (43 g) butter or margarine, cut into chunks
- ½ cup (120 ml) raspberry jelly, melted and cooled slightly
- ½ teaspoon grated lime peel
- 1½ teaspoons lime juice
- 4 cups (492 g) fresh raspberries or other fresh berries
  Mint sprigs

Maple & Raspberry Tart

....

Preparation time: 20 minutes
Cooking time: About 35 minutes

1. In a food processor or a large bowl, whirl or stir together graham cracker crumbs, granulated sugar, and the 1 tablespoon flour. Add melted butter; whirl or stir until mixture resembles coarse crumbs. Press mixture firmly over bottom and ½ inch (1 cm) up sides of a lightly greased, floured 9-inch (23-cm) nonstick or regular tart pan with a removable rim.

2. Bake in a 325°F (165°C) oven for 10 minutes. Remove pan from oven and place in a larger baking pan to catch any drips; set aside. Increase oven temperature to 375°F (190°C).

3. In a small bowl, stir together the ½ cup (60 g) flour and brown sugar; set aside. In a 1- to 1½-quart (950-ml to 1.4-liter) pan, bring syrup to a boil

over high heat. Remove pan from heat, add butter, and whisk until butter is melted. Then whisk in brown sugar mixture. Pour hot filling into crust; spread to cover bottom of crust.

4. Return tart to oven and bake until filling is covered with large, shiny bubbles and crust is a deep golden brown (about 25 minutes); if crust begins to darken excessively, cover it with foil. Let cool on a rack for 10 minutes, then carefully remove pan rim. Slide a thin knife between crust and pan bottom to free crust (if not loosened in this way, crust will stick fast to pan once it's cool). Leave tart on pan bottom. Let cool completely.

5. Just before serving, in a small bowl, stir together jelly, lime peel, and lime juice. Top tart evenly with raspberries; brush berries with jelly glaze. Garnish with mint sprigs and serve immediately. Makes 8 to 10 servings.

....

Per serving: 379 calories (30% calories from fat), 13 g total fat, 7 g saturated fat, 29 mg cholesterol, 224 mg sodium, 65 g carbohydrates, 3 g fiber, 3 g protein, 44 mg calcium, 2 mg iron

---

Whole wheat bread crumbs sweetened with brown sugar serve as both a thickener and a crunchy topping for this traditional dessert.

....

- 2 cups (90 g) soft whole wheat bread crumbs
- 3 tablespoons (43 g) butter or margarine, melted
- ¼ cup (55 g) firmly packed brown sugar
- ¼ cup (50 g) granulated sugar
- ½ teaspoon ground cinnamon
- ⅛ teaspoon ground nutmeg
- 4 cups (440 g) peeled, sliced tart apples
- ½ cup (89 g) coarsely chopped pitted dates
- 1 tablespoon (15 ml) lemon juice

Apple & Date Betty

....

Preparation time: 20 minutes
Cooking time: 50 to 55 minutes

1. In a medium-size bowl, lightly mix bread crumbs, butter, and brown sugar. Sprinkle half the mixture over bottom of a shallow 2-quart (1.9-liter) casserole; set aside remaining mixture.

2. In a large bowl, stir together granulated sugar, cinnamon, and nutmeg. Add apples and dates; mix gently to coat fruit with sugar mixture. Drizzle fruit mixture with lemon juice, then spoon evenly over crumb mixture in

casserole. Sprinkle with 2 tablespoons (30 ml) water; cover evenly with remaining crumb mixture.

3. Set casserole in a larger baking pan to catch any drips. Cover and bake in a 375°F (190°C) oven for 30 minutes. Then uncover and continue to bake until filling is bubbly in center, apples are very tender when pierced, and topping is crisp (20 to 25 more minutes). Serve hot or warm; to serve, spoon into bowls. Makes 6 servings.

....

Per serving: 242 calories (24% calories from fat), 7 g total fat, 4 g saturated fat, 16 mg cholesterol, 151 mg sodium, 47 g carbohydrates, 3 g fiber, 2 g protein, 32 mg calcium, 1 mg iron

Jumbleberry Crumble

Preparation time: 15 minutes, plus 15 minutes for filling to stand
Cooking time: 50 to 60 minutes

Three kinds of fresh berries bake together beneath a cinnamon-spiced oatmeal topping to make a luscious summer dessert.

- ⅔ cup (135 g) granulated sugar
- 3 tablespoons quick-cooking tapioca
- 1½ cups (218 g) fresh blueberries
- 1½ cups (185 g) fresh raspberries
- 3 cups (447 g) hulled, halved strawberries
- ½ cup (40 g) quick-cooking rolled oats
- ½ cup (110 g) firmly packed brown sugar
- ½ cup (60 g) all-purpose flour
- 1 teaspoon ground cinnamon
- ⅓ cup (76 g) butter or margarine, melted

1. In a shallow 2-quart (1.9-liter) casserole, stir together granulated sugar and tapioca. Add blueberries, raspberries, and strawberries; mix gently to coat fruit with sugar mixture. Let stand for 15 minutes to soften tapioca, stirring occasionally; then spread out fruit mixture in an even layer.

2. In a small bowl, combine oats, brown sugar, flour, and cinnamon. Add butter and stir with a fork until mixture is crumbly. Sprinkle topping evenly over fruit mixture.

3. Set casserole in a larger baking pan to catch any drips. Bake in a 350°F (175°C) oven until fruit mixture is bubbly in center and topping is crisp and brown (50 to 60 minutes); if topping begins to darken excessively, cover it with foil. Serve hot, warm, or at room temperature; to serve, spoon into bowls. Makes 6 to 8 servings.

Per serving: 330 calories (25% calories from fat), 10 g total fat, 5 g saturated fat, 23 mg cholesterol, 117 mg sodium, 61 g carbohydrates, 4 g fiber, 3 g protein, 41 mg calcium, 2 mg iron

Cherry-Blueberry Crisp

Preparation time: 30 minutes
Cooking time: 35 to 40 minutes

For an indulgent finishing touch, top this warm fruit treat with scoops of vanilla frozen yogurt.

- ⅓ cup (73 g) firmly packed brown sugar
- 2 tablespoons all-purpose flour
- ½ teaspoon ground cinnamon
- 3 cups (435 g) pitted fresh Bing or other dark sweet cherries
- 2 cups (290 g) fresh blueberries
- 1 tablespoon (15 ml) lemon juice
- 1 cup (80 g) quick-cooking rolled oats
- ¼ cup (55 g) firmly packed brown sugar
- ¼ teaspoon *each* ground cinnamon and ground ginger
- 3 tablespoons (43 g) butter or margarine, melted

1. In a shallow 2-quart (1.9-liter) casserole, stir together the ⅓ cup sugar, flour, and cinnamon. Add cherries, blueberries, and lemon juice; mix gently to coat fruit with sugar mixture. Spread out fruit mixture in an even layer.

2. In a small bowl, combine oats, the ¼ cup sugar, cinnamon, and ginger; add butter and stir with a fork until mixture is crumbly. Sprinkle mixture evenly over fruit.

3. Set casserole in a larger baking pan to catch any drips. Bake in a 350°F (175°C) oven until fruit mixture is bubbly in center and topping is golden brown (35 to 40 minutes); if topping begins to darken excessively, cover it with foil. Serve hot, warm, or at room temperature. To serve, spoon into bowls. Makes 6 servings.

Per serving: 273 calories (24% calories from fat), 7 g total fat, 4 g saturated fat, 16 mg cholesterol, 71 mg sodium, 51 g carbohydrates, 3 g fiber, 4 g protein, 45 mg calcium, 2 mg iron

Fresh pears mingle with maple syrup and lime in a tempting autumn cobbler with a gingersnap cookie crust.

- 6 large firm-ripe D'Anjou pears (about 3 lbs./1.35 kg *total*), peeled, cored, and thinly sliced
- 2 tablespoons (30 ml) lime juice
- ¼ cup (60 ml) pure maple syrup
- 2 cups (170 g) finely crushed gingersnaps (about thirty-five 2-inch/5-cm cookies)
- ⅔ cup (147 g) firmly packed brown sugar
- 3 tablespoons all-purpose flour
- ¼ cup (2 oz./55 g) butter or margarine, melted
- 1 teaspoon vanilla

Pear Cobbler with Ginger Crust

Preparation time: 20 minutes
Cooking time: 25 to 35 minutes
Pictured on facing page

1. In a shallow 1½- to 2-quart (1.4- to 1.9-liter) casserole, combine pears and lime juice. Add syrup; mix gently to coat fruit evenly. Spread out fruit in an even layer; set aside.

2. In a food processor or a medium-size bowl, whirl or stir together crushed gingersnaps, sugar, and flour. Add butter and vanilla; whirl or stir until mixture resembles coarse crumbs. With your fingers, squeeze mixture to form large lumps; then crumble evenly over pear mixture.

3. Set casserole in a larger baking pan to catch any drips. Bake in a 325°F (165°C) oven until fruit is tender when pierced and topping feels firm when gently pressed (25 to 35 minutes); if topping begins to darken excessively, cover it with foil. Serve warm; to serve, spoon into bowls. Makes 8 servings.

Per serving: 370 calories (22% calories from fat), 9 g total fat, 4 g saturated fat, 16 mg cholesterol, 253 mg sodium, 73 g carbohydrates, 4 g fiber, 3 g protein, 64 mg calcium, 3 mg iron

---

A crunchy crust reminiscent of oatmeal–chocolate chip cookies bakes atop tender sliced apples to make this wonderful dessert.

- 5 tablespoons (71 g) butter or margarine, at room temperature
- 1 cup (200 g) sugar
- 1 large egg white
- 1 teaspoon vanilla
- ¾ teaspoon ground cardamom or ground cinnamon
- 1 cup (125 g) all-purpose flour
- ¾ cup (60 g) regular rolled oats
- ½ cup (85 g) semisweet chocolate chips
- 10 large tart apples such as Granny Smith or Gravenstein (about 5 lbs./2.3 kg *each*)
- ¾ cup (150 g) sugar
- 1 tablespoon cornstarch
- 1½ teaspoons ground cinnamon
- ½ teaspoon ground allspice

Apple Cobbler with Oatmeal-Chocolate Cookie Crust

Preparation time: 20 minutes
Cooking time: About 1 hour

1. In a food processor or a large bowl, combine butter and the 1 cup (200 g) sugar; whirl or beat with an electric mixer until smooth. Add egg white, vanilla, and cardamom; whirl or beat until blended. Stir in flour, oats, and chocolate chips; set aside. (At this point, you may wrap crust mixture airtight and refrigerate until next day.)

2. Peel, core, and slice apples; arrange in a shallow 3- to 3½-quart (2.8- to 3.3-liter) casserole. Sprinkle with the ¾ cup (150 g) sugar, cornstarch, cinnamon, and allspice; mix gently to coat fruit with sugar mixture, then spread out fruit mixture in an even layer. Crumble oat mixture over fruit mixture.

3. Set casserole in a larger baking pan to catch any drips. Bake in a 350°F (175°C) oven until fruit mixture is bubbly in center and topping is richly browned (about 1 hour). Serve warm or at room temperature; to serve, spoon into bowls. Makes 8 servings.

Per serving: 516 calories (19% calories from fat), 11 g total fat, 6 g saturated fat, 19 mg cholesterol, 82 mg sodium, 105 g carbohydrates, 6 g fiber, 4 g protein, 29 mg calcium, 2 mg iron

Pear Cobbler with Ginger Crust
(recipe on facing page)

The best-known pairing of peaches and raspberries is doubtless found in a classic Peach Melba—but the combination is equally wonderful in this easy crumb-topped dessert.

....

1 tablespoon cornstarch

½ teaspoon ground nutmeg

⅓ cup (70 g) sugar

4 cups (680 g) peeled, sliced peaches

1 cup (123 g) fresh raspberries

1½ cups (192 g) coarsely crushed crisp almond macaroons (about thirty 1¾-inch/3.5-cm cookies)

Amaretti-topped Raspberry-Peach Bake

....

Preparation time: 20 minutes
Cooking time: 40 to 45 minutes

1. In a shallow 1½- to 2-quart (1.4- to 1.9-liter) casserole, stir together cornstarch, nutmeg, and sugar. Add peaches and raspberries; mix gently to coat fruit with sugar mixture. Spread out fruit mixture in an even layer; then sprinkle evenly with crushed macaroons.

2. Bake in a 375°F (190°C) oven until fruit mixture is bubbly in center (40 to 45 minutes); cover with foil during last 10 to 12 minutes of baking if topping begins to darken excessively. Serve warm or at room temperature; to serve, spoon into bowls. Makes 6 servings.

....

Per serving: 159 calories (15% calories from fat), 3 g total fat, 0.03 g saturated fat, 0 mg cholesterol, 9 mg sodium, 32 g carbohydrates, 3 g fiber, 3 g protein, 32 mg calcium, 0.6 mg iron

---

Crisp strips of fila bake separately to form the lattice crust that tops this sweet plum cobbler.

....

8 sheets fila pastry (each about 12 by 16 inches/30 by 40 cm), about 5 ounces (140 g) *total*

3 tablespoons (43 g) butter or margarine, melted

About 1 cup (200 g) sugar

3 tablespoons plus 1 teaspoon quick-cooking tapioca

2 tablespoons grated orange peel

½ teaspoon ground cinnamon

About 3 pounds (1.35 kg) firm-ripe plums

....

1. Lightly butter and flour a 12- by 15-inch (30- by 38-cm) baking sheet. Place a shallow 3- to 3½-quart (2.8- to 3.3-liter) casserole upside down on baking sheet. With the handle of a spoon, trace around casserole sides. Lift off casserole.

2. Lay one sheet of fila flat on a work surface, keeping remaining fila covered with plastic wrap to prevent drying. Brush fila sparingly with butter. Top with a second fila sheet. Brush with

Plum Orange Cobbler with Fila Lattice

....

Preparation time: 35 minutes, plus 15 minutes for filling to stand
Cooking time: About 1 hour

more butter, then top with another fila sheet. Repeat to use remaining fila sheets; brush top layer of fila stack with all but 2 teaspoons of the remaining butter.

3. Cut fila stack crosswise into strips 1 inch (2.5 cm) wide. Lay about half the strips diagonally across outline traced on baking sheet, spacing strips 1 inch (2.5 cm) apart. Trim ends of strips so they are about ⅓ inch (8 mm) inside tracing. Lay remaining fila strips at an angle on top of the first layer, again spacing them 1 inch (2.5 cm) apart and trimming ends so they are about ⅓ inch (8 mm) inside tracing. Sprinkle lattice with 2 tablespoons of the sugar.

4. Bake fila lattice in a 350°F (175°C) oven until golden brown (15 to 20 minutes). Let cool on baking sheet on a rack. If made ahead, let lattice cool completely; then cover airtight and hold at room temperature until next day.

5. In the 3- to 3½-quart (2.8- to 3.3-liter) casserole, stir together ¾ cup plus 2 tablespoons (174 g) of the sugar, tapioca, orange peel, and cinnamon. Pit and thinly slice plums; add to sugar mixture and mix gently to coat fruit evenly. Let stand for 15 minutes to soften tapioca, stirring occasionally. Spread out fruit mixture in an even layer.

6. Set casserole in a larger baking pan to catch any drips. Bake in a 350°F (175°C) oven until fruit mixture is bubbly in center (35 to 45 minutes), stirring occasionally. Serve hot, warm, or at room temperature. Just before serving, carefully lift fila lattice from baking sheet, using 2 spatulas; set atop fruit mixture. Serve at once; to serve, spoon into bowls. Makes 8 servings.

....

Per serving: 300 calories (20% calories from fat), 7 g total fat, 3 g saturated fat, 13 mg cholesterol, 154 mg sodium, 60 g carbohydrates, 3 g fiber, 3 g protein, 14 mg calcium, 0.8 mg iron

Juicy, sweet peaches baked under a crunchy almond topping make a winning summertime treat.

Peach Cobbler with Almond Topping

Preparation time: 20 minutes
Cooking time: 45 to 50 minutes

1 cup (about 7 oz./200 g) almond paste

½ cup (100 g) sugar

¼ cup (32 g) cornstarch

9 medium-size firm-ripe peaches (about 3 lbs./1.35 kg *total*)

2 tablespoons sugar

2 tablespoons (30 ml) lemon juice

1. Crumble almond paste into a medium-size bowl. Add the ½ cup (100 g) sugar and 2 tablespoons of the cornstarch. Rub together with your fingers until well blended. With your fingers, squeeze mixture to form large lumps; set aside.

2. Peel and pit peaches; then slice them into a shallow 1½- to 2-quart (1.4- to 1.9-liter) casserole. Add the 2 tablespoons sugar, lemon juice, and remaining 2 tablespoons cornstarch; mix gently. Spread out fruit mixture in an even layer; then crumble almond topping over top.

3. Set casserole in a larger baking pan to catch any drips. Bake in a 350°F (175°C) oven until fruit mixture is bubbly in center and topping is browned (45 to 50 minutes); if topping begins to darken excessively, cover it with foil. Let cool slightly; spoon into bowls. Makes 6 to 8 servings.

Per serving: 277 calories (24% calories from fat), 8 g total fat, 0.7 g saturated fat, 0 mg cholesterol, 4 mg sodium, 51 g carbohydrates, 2 g fiber, 4 g protein, 73 mg calcium, 1 mg iron

---

A dark chocolate topping covers bananas and raisins baked in a spiced rum sauce.

Chocolate Banana Cobbler

Preparation time: 25 minutes
Cooking time: About 35 minutes

¾ cup (110 g) raisins

2 tablespoons (30 ml) light or dark rum

½ cup (110 g) firmly packed brown sugar

¼ cup (60 ml) half-and-half

2 tablespoons (30 ml) light corn syrup

⅛ teaspoon salt

2 tablespoons (30 ml) lemon juice

1 tablespoon cornstarch

5 large bananas (about 2½ lbs./ 1.15 kg *total*), cut into slanting slices ½ inch (1 cm) thick

¾ cup (95 g) all-purpose flour

½ cup (100 g) granulated sugar

½ cup (43 g) unsweetened cocoa powder

¼ teaspoon salt

¼ teaspoon instant espresso or coffee powder

⅛ teaspoon ground ginger

⅓ cup (76 g) butter or margarine, cut into chunks

1. In a small bowl, combine raisins and rum. Let stand until raisins are softened (about 10 minutes), stirring occasionally. Meanwhile, in another small bowl, mix brown sugar, half-and-half, corn syrup, and the ⅛ teaspoon salt.

2. In a shallow 1½- to 2-quart (1.4- to 1.9-liter) casserole, blend lemon juice, cornstarch, and 2 tablespoons (30 ml) water; gently mix in bananas. Add brown sugar mixture and raisin mixture; stir gently to coat fruit. Spread out fruit mixture in an even layer; set aside.

3. In a food processor or a medium-size bowl, whirl or stir together flour, granulated sugar, cocoa, the ¼ teaspoon salt, instant espresso, and ginger. Add butter; whirl or rub with your fingers until mixture resembles fine crumbs. With your fingers, squeeze mixture to form large lumps; then crumble over banana mixture.

4. Set casserole in a larger baking pan to catch any drips. Bake in a 375°F (190°C) oven until fruit mixture is bubbly in center and topping feels firm when gently pressed (about 35 minutes). Let cool slightly; spoon into bowls. Makes 8 servings.

Per serving: 385 calories (22% calories from fat), 10 g total fat, 6 g saturated fat, 23 mg cholesterol, 199 mg sodium, 76 g carbohydrates, 4 g fiber, 4 g protein, 44 mg calcium, 2 mg iron

Rum Raisin Crème Brûlée
(recipe on page 408)

Desserts

For velvety puddings and custards, smooth ice creams, refreshing sherbet, and light soufflés we substitute low-fat and nonfat dairy products and use lots of fluffy egg whites with delectable low-fat results. Enjoy Raisin Rice Pudding or discover the intriguing delights of Tropical Sherbert, a creamy banana-mango confection. And Amaretto Soufflé is an elegant finale to any dinner menu.

When you're in the mood for a truly indulgent dessert, choose these luxurious custards, flavored with maple syrup–soaked raisins and topped with crunchy broiled sugar.

- 2 **teaspoons butter or margarine, at room temperature**
- ½ **cup (110 g) firmly packed light or dark brown sugar**
- 1 **cup (145 g) raisins**
- ½ **cup (120 ml) pure maple syrup**
- ¼ **cup (55 g) firmly packed light or dark brown sugar**
- ¾ **cup (180 ml) nonfat milk**
- ⅔ **cup (160 ml) half-and-half**
- 2 **large eggs**
- 2 **large egg yolks**
- 2 **tablespoons cornstarch blended with 2 tablespoons (30 ml) cold water**

  About 2 teaspoons light or dark rum

1. Cover a rimless 12- by 15-inch (30- by 38-cm) baking sheet with foil. Set a 1-cup (240-ml) custard cup upright on foil and gently trace around its base with a pencil, taking care not to tear foil. Repeat to make 3 more impressions. Coat the area with-

Rum Raisin Crème Brûlée

Preparation time: 25 minutes
Cooking time: About 1¼ hours
Pictured on page 406

in each outline with butter. Rub the ½ cup (110 g) sugar through a fine strainer to coat buttered areas evenly. Gently press sugar to make a firm, even layer that adheres to foil.

2. Bake in a 500°F (260°C) oven until sugar begins to melt and bubble (2 to 4 minutes), rotating baking sheet to melt sugar evenly. Check to see if sugar has run outside impressions; if it has, immediately scrape it gently back into place with a metal spoon. Let sugar crusts cool completely; then slide a slender spatula under them to release from foil. Trim sugar crusts with a sharp knife to even out, if needed. Set aside in a cool, dry place.

3. In a small bowl, combine raisins and syrup; let stand until raisins are softened (about 10 minutes), stirring occasionally.

4. Divide the ¼ cup (55 g) sugar evenly among four 1-cup (240-ml) custard cups; place cups in a large baking pan. With a slotted spoon, lift raisins from syrup; drain well (reserve syrup), then divide equally among cups.

5. Pour syrup into a food processor or blender. Add milk, half-and-half, eggs, egg yolks, cornstarch mixture, and 2 teaspoons of the rum. Whirl until smooth; quickly pour over raisins in cups.

6. Set pan on center rack of a 350°F (175°C) oven. Pour boiling water into pan around cups up to level of custard. Bake until custard jiggles only slightly in center when cups are gently shaken (about 1 hour and 10 minutes).

7. Lift cups from pan. Let stand for about 10 minutes; then top each custard with a sugar crust and serve immediately. Offer additional rum to add to custards to taste. Makes 4 servings.

Per serving: 540 calories (19% calories from fat), 12 g total fat, 6 g saturated fat, 234 mg cholesterol, 119 mg sodium, 103 g carbohydrates, 2 g fiber, 8 g protein, 202 mg calcium, 3 mg iron

Warm raisin-rich bread pudding served with a velvety smooth pumpkin custard spiced with nutmeg is a comforting winter dessert.

Cinnamon Bread Pudding with Pumpkin Custard

Preparation time: 20 minutes
Cooking time: About 30 minutes

¾ cup (110 g) raisins

8 to 10 ounces (230 to 280 g) unsliced day-old crusty sourdough bread

¼ cup (2 oz./55 g) butter or margarine, melted

¾ cup (150 g) sugar

2 teaspoons ground cinnamon

3 large eggs

2¾ cups (650 ml) low-fat (2%) milk

1 can (about 1 lb./455 g) pumpkin

½ teaspoon ground nutmeg

1 teaspoon vanilla

1. In a small bowl, combine raisins and ¾ cup (180 ml) hot water; let stand until raisins are softened (about 10 minutes), stirring occasionally.

2. Meanwhile, tear bread into about 1-inch (2.5-cm) chunks; you should have about 6 cups. Place bread in a large bowl and mix in butter. In a small bowl, combine ¼ cup (50 g) of the sugar with cinnamon; sprinkle over bread, then mix gently but thoroughly. In another small bowl, beat one of the eggs with ¾ cup (180 ml) of the milk until blended; gently mix into bread mixture. Drain raisins well; add to bread mixture and mix just until evenly distributed.

3. Spoon bread mixture into a greased shallow 1½- to 2-quart (1.4- to 1.9-liter) baking dish. Bake in a 375°F (190°C) oven until crisp and deep brown (about 30 minutes).

4. Meanwhile, in the top of a 2- to 3-quart (1.9- to 2.8-liter) double boiler, combine remaining ½ cup (100 g) sugar, remaining 2 eggs, remaining 2 cups (470 ml) milk, pumpkin, nutmeg, and vanilla. Beat until blended. Then set over simmering water and cook, stirring often, until custard is steaming and thickly coats a metal spoon (about 12 minutes). Keep warm.

5. To serve, pour custard into individual bowls; spoon warm bread pudding on top. Makes 6 servings.

Per serving: 466 calories (28% calories from fat), 15 g total fat, 7 g saturated fat, 136 mg cholesterol, 431 mg sodium, 74 g carbohydrates, 3 g fiber, 12 g protein, 221 mg calcium, 3 mg iron

---

Low-fat dairy products streamline this lovely summer pudding flavored with cinnamon and abundant with fresh ripe nectarines.

Nectarine Pudding

Preparation time: 20 minutes
Cooking time: About 45 minutes

6 medium-size nectarines (about 1½ lbs./680 g total), pitted and quartered

1 tablespoon (15 ml) lemon juice

1 cup (240 g) low-fat (2%) cottage cheese

⅓ cup (80 ml) half-and-half

1 cup (240 g) low-fat (2%) milk

½ cup (100 g) sugar

1 large egg

2 large egg whites

1 teaspoon vanilla

½ cup (60 g) all-purpose flour

1 teaspoon ground cinnamon

1 cup (240 ml) pure maple syrup

1 teaspoon finely shredded lemon peel

1. In a large bowl, combine nectarines and lemon juice; turn fruit to coat with juice. Arrange nectarines attractively in a greased shallow 2½-quart (2.4-liter) casserole; set aside.

2. In a food processor or blender, whirl cottage cheese and half-and-half until smoothly puréed. Add milk, sugar, egg, egg whites, and vanilla. Whirl until smooth. Add flour and cinnamon; whirl just until evenly combined.

3. Carefully pour batter over nectarines. Bake in the top third of a 425°F (220°C) oven until top of pudding is golden brown and center jiggles only slightly when casserole is gently shaken (about 45 minutes). Let stand for about 5 minutes before serving.

4. Meanwhile, in a 1- to 1½-quart (950-ml to 1.4-liter) pan, combine syrup and lemon peel. Cook over medium heat, stirring, just until hot. To serve, spoon pudding into bowls and top with hot maple sauce. Makes 6 servings.

Per serving: 384 calories (10% calories from fat), 5 g total fat, 2 g saturated fat, 47 mg cholesterol, 213 mg sodium, 77 g carbohydrates, 2 g fiber, 11 g protein, 141 mg calcium, 2 mg iron

Two fruit purées—one vibrant magenta, the other pale yellow—are poured side by side into each individual bowl to create this dramatic, delectable dessert. The fruit of a native Mexican cactus, prickly pears (also called cactus pears or tunas) are available in the United States in Mexican markets and some well-stocked supermarkets from August through December. If you can't find them, substitute fresh or frozen raspberries.

Red Prickly Pear Purée or
Raspberry Purée
(recipes follow)

Tree Pear Purée
(recipe follows)

6 to 8 star anise (optional)

Mint sprigs (optional)

1. Prepare Red Prickly Pear Purée and Tree Pear Purée; pour each into a small pitcher.

2. With a pitcher in each hand, simultaneously and gently pour purées into an individual 1½- to 2-cup (360- to 470-ml) soup bowl (wide bowls create the most dramatic effect). Repeat to fill 5 to 7 more bowls, allowing a total of 1 to 1¼ cups (240 to 300 ml) purée for each serving. Garnish each serving with a star anise and mint sprigs, if desired. Makes 6 to 8 servings.

Cactus Pear & Tree Pear Soup

Preparation time: About 30 minutes
Cooking time: About 15 minutes
Pictured on facing page

Red Prickly Pear Purée. Wearing rubber gloves to protect your hands from hidden needles, cut about 5 pounds (2.3 kg) despined **red prickly pears** (also called **cactus pears** or **tunas**) into halves lengthwise. Using a small knife, pull off and discard outer layer (including peel) from fruit; this layer will separate easily. Place fruit in a food processor (do not use a blender, which will pulverize seeds). Whirl until smoothly puréed, then pour into a fine strainer set over a bowl. Firmly rub purée through strainer into bowl; discard seeds. (Or rub purée through a food mill; discard seeds.) To purée, add ⅓ cup (80 ml) **lemon juice** and 2 tablespoons **sugar.** If made ahead, cover and refrigerate until next day; stir before using.

Raspberry Purée. In a food processor, whirl 4 cups (492 g) fresh or frozen unsweetened **raspberries** until smoothly puréed (do not use a blender, which will pulverize seeds). Pour purée into a fine strainer set over a bowl. Firmly rub purée through strainer into bowl; discard seeds. (Or rub purée through a food mill; discard seeds.) To purée, add 1 cup (240 ml) **orange juice,** ⅓ cup (80 ml) **lemon juice** and ⅓ cup (70 g) **sugar.** If made ahead, cover and refrigerate until next day; stir before using.

Tree Pear Purée. Drain 2 cans (about 1 lb. 455 g *each*) **pears in extra-light syrup;** reserve 1½ cups (360 ml) of the syrup and discard remainder. In a small pan, combine reserved syrup and 1 **star anise** or 1 teaspoon anise seeds. Bring syrup to a boil over high heat; then reduce heat, cover, and simmer very gently until flavors are blended (about 10 minutes). Pour syrup through a fine strainer set over a bowl; discard star anise or seeds. In a food processor or blender, whirl pears until smoothly puréed; then add syrup (if using a blender, add syrup while you are puréeing pears). Stir in ¼ cup (60 ml) **lemon juice** and 1 tablespoon **sugar.** If made ahead, cover and refrigerate until next day; stir before using.

Per serving: 187 calories (6% calories from fat), 1 g total fat, 0 g saturated fat, 0 mg cholesterol, 19 mg sodium, 46 g carbohydrates, 0 g fiber, 2 g protein, 150 mg calcium, 1 mg iron

Cactus Pear & Tree Pear Soup
(recipe on facing page); Sparkling Jewels
Fruit Soup (recipe on page 415)

Creamy rice pudding flavored with cinnamon and vanilla is a favorite Mexican dessert. Serve it warm or chilled; it's delicious either way.

....

3½ cups (830 ml) nonfat milk

½ cup (100 g) short- or medium-grain rice

¼ teaspoon salt

3 large eggs

¼ cup (50 g) sugar

2 teaspoons vanilla

About ¼ teaspoon ground cinnamon

¼ cup (36 g) golden or dark raisins

1 tablespoon (15 ml) honey

Raisin Rice Pudding

....

Preparation time: About 5 minutes
Cooking time: 50 to 65 minutes

1. In a 1½- to 2-quart (1.4- to 1.9-liter) pan (preferably nonstick), combine 3 cups (710 ml) of the milk, rice, and salt. Bring just to a very gentle boil over medium heat, stirring. Reduce heat to low, cover, and simmer, stirring occasionally, until mixture is reduced to 2¾ cups (650 ml) (45 minutes to 1 hour).

2. In a bowl, beat eggs, sugar, remaining ½ cup (120 ml) milk, vanilla, and ¼ teaspoon of the cinnamon until blended. Stir in raisins.

3. Stir egg mixture into rice mixture. Bring just to a boil, then reduce heat and simmer, uncovered, until thickened (about 5 minutes). Stir in honey. Serve warm or chilled. Sprinkle with additional cinnamon just before serving. Makes 6 servings.

....

Per serving: 213 calories (12% calories from fat), 3 g total fat, 1 g saturated fat, 109 mg cholesterol, 197 mg sodium, 37 g carbohydrates, 0.5 g fiber, 9 g protein, 194 mg calcium, 1 mg iron

---

Low-fat cottage cheese trims the fat from this classic dessert, delicately sweetened with peach nectar and smooth applesauce.

....

Crunch Topping (recipe follows)

5 ounces/140 g (about 4 cups) dried wide egg noodles

1 cup (240 ml) peach or apricot nectar

½ cup (122 g) smooth applesauce

½ cup (105 g) low-fat (1%) cottage cheese

3 tablespoons sugar

2 large egg whites

1 teaspoon cornstarch mixed with 1 tablespoon water

½ cup (75 g) raisins

Noodle Pudding

....

Preparation time: About 15 minutes
Cooking time: About 1 hour

1. Prepare Crunch Topping; set aside.

2. Bring 8 cups (1.9 liters) water to a boil in a 4- to 5-quart (3.8- to 5-liter) pan over medium-high heat. Stir in pasta and cook just until tender to bite (8 to 10 minutes); or cook according to package directions. Meanwhile, combine nectar, applesauce, cheese, sugar, and egg whites in a blender or food processor. Stir cornstarch mixture and add to blender. Whirl until smooth.

3. Drain pasta well and transfer to a nonstick or lightly oiled square 8-inch (20-cm) baking pan. Stir in raisins and cheese mixture. Crumble topping over pudding. Bake in a 350°F (175°C) oven until a knife inserted in center comes out clean and top is golden (about 50 minutes). Makes 8 servings.

....

Crunch Topping. In a food processor or bowl, combine ⅓ cup (70 g) **sugar,** ¼ cup (60 g) **butter** or margarine, and ½ teaspoon **ground cinnamon.** Whirl or beat well. Add 1½ cups (40 g) **corn flake cereal.** Mix gently. Press into lumps.

....

Per serving: 257 calories (23% calories from fat), 7 g total fat, 4 g saturated fat, 33 mg cholesterol, 190 mg sodium, 45 g carbohydrates, 1 g fiber, 6 g protein, 25 mg calcium, 1 mg iron

Here's a lovely autumn dessert: poached whole pears served in a glistening port-citrus syrup spiced with nutmeg.

....

- 2 cups (470 ml) port
- ½ cup (100 g) sugar
- 1 tablespoon shredded orange peel
- ¼ teaspoon ground nutmeg
- 4 large firm-ripe pears (about 2 lbs./905 g *total*)
- 1 tablespoon (15 ml) lemon juice
- 2 teaspoons finely shredded orange peel

....

1. In a 3- to 4-quart (2.8- to 3.8-liter) pan, combine port, sugar, the 1 table-

Poached Pears with Ruby Citrus Syrup

....
Preparation time: 15 minutes
Cooking time: 30 to 45 minutes

spoon orange peel, and nutmeg. Stir over medium heat until sugar is dissolved; then bring to a boil, stirring often.

2. Add whole pears to hot syrup. Reduce heat, cover, and simmer until pears are very tender when pierced

(20 to 30 minutes), turning fruit over a few times. With a slotted spoon, transfer pears to a wide bowl or rimmed platter; set aside.

3. Bring cooking liquid to a boil over high heat; then boil, uncovered, until liquid is thickened and reduced to about ½ cup (120 ml), 10 to 12 minutes. Stir in lemon juice; then pour syrup over pears. Garnish with the 2 teaspoons orange peel. Serve warm or at room temperature. Makes 4 servings.

....

Per serving: 282 calories (3% calories from fat), 0.9 g total fat, 0.1 g saturated fat, 0 mg cholesterol, 12 mg sodium, 72 g carbohydrates, 5 g fiber, 1 g protein, 38 mg calcium, 0.8 mg iron

---

For a luxurious dessert, stir a hot froth of Marsala wine, sugar, and egg yolks into whipped topping; then spoon over poached dried fruits.

....

- 1 package (about 12 oz./340 g) mixed dried fruit (whole or halved fruits, not dried fruit bits)
- 1½ cups (360 ml) white grape juice
- ¼ to ½ teaspoon ground cinnamon
- 3 whole cloves
- 6 large egg yolks
- 3 tablespoons sugar
- ½ cup (120 ml) Marsala
- 2 cups (470 ml) frozen reduced-calorie whipped topping, thawed

....

1. Cut large pieces of fruit into bite-size chunks; set fruit aside. In a medium-

Zabaglione Cream over Warm Fruit Compote

....
Preparation time: 15 minutes
Cooking time: About 40 minutes

size pan, combine grape juice, cinnamon, and cloves; bring to a boil over high heat. Stir in fruit; then reduce heat, cover, and simmer until fruit is plump and tender when pierced (about 30 minutes). Remove from heat and keep warm.

2. In the top of a double boiler, combine egg yolks and sugar. Beat with an electric mixer on high speed or with a

whisk until thick and lemon-colored. Beat in Marsala. Set double boiler over (not in) gently simmering water; beat mixture constantly just until it is thick enough to retain a slight peak briefly when beater or whisk is withdrawn (3 to 6 minutes).

3. Working quickly, pour warm egg mixture into a large bowl. Fold in about a third of the whipped topping to lighten egg mixture; then fold in remaining whipped topping. Serve immediately.

4. To serve, lift fruit from pan with a slotted spoon and divide among six 8-ounce (240-ml) stemmed glasses; discard cooking liquid or reserve for other uses. Top with zabaglione cream. Makes 6 servings.

....

Per serving: 346 calories (22% calories from fat), 8 g total fat, 4 g saturated fat, 213 mg cholesterol, 24 mg sodium, 61 g carbohydrates, 3 g fiber, 4 g protein, 48 mg calcium, 2 mg iron

Oranges with Rum Syrup & Spiced
Cream (recipe on facing page), Raisin
Batter Bread (recipe on page 345)

A sweet rum syrup infused with cloves is served over orange slices for a refreshing dessert. Garnish each serving with a dollop of whipped "cream."

Oranges with Rum Syrup & Spiced Cream

Preparation time: About 15 minutes
Cooking time: About 20 minutes
Freezing & chilling time:
45 minutes to 1 hour
Pictured on facing page

Spiced Cream
(recipe follows)
½ cup (100 g) sugar
1½ cups (360 ml) water
2 teaspoons whole cloves
2 tablespoons (30 ml) light rum
4 large oranges
(about 3 lbs./1.35 kg *total*)

1. Prepare Spiced Cream; refrigerate.

2. In a small pan, combine sugar, water, and cloves. Bring to a boil over high heat; then boil until reduced to ¾ cup (180 ml) (about 20 minutes). Remove from heat, stir in rum, and let cool. (At this point, you may cover and refrigerate for up to 5 days.)

3. With a sharp knife, cut peel and all white membrane from oranges. Slice fruit into 6 dessert bowls, dividing equally. Add rum syrup and Spiced Cream to taste. Makes 6 servings.

Spiced Cream. Pour ¼ cup (60 ml) **nonfat milk** into small bowl of an electric mixer. Cover bowl; then freeze mixer beaters and bowl of milk until milk is slushy (30 to 45 minutes). In a small pan, sprinkle ½ teaspoon

unflavored gelatin over ¼ cup (60 ml) **cold water;** let stand until gelatin is softened (about 3 minutes). Then stir mixture over low heat just until gelatin is dissolved. Remove from heat.

To slushy milk, add gelatin, ⅔ cup (80 g) **instant nonfat dry milk,** 2 tablespoons **sugar,** 1 teaspoon **vanilla,** and ½ teaspoon **ground cinnamon.** Beat on high speed until mixture holds soft peaks (5 to 10 minutes). Cover and refrigerate for at least 15 minutes or for up to 2 days. If needed, whisk or beat again before serving until cream holds soft peaks. Serve cold. Makes about 2 cups (470 ml).

Per serving of oranges: 153 calories (2% calories from fat),0.4 g total fat, 0.1 g saturated fat, 0 mg cholesterol, 0.6 mg sodium, 36 g carbohydrates, 4 g fiber, 1 g protein, 74 mg calcium, 0.2 mg iron

Per tablespoon of Spiced Cream: 9 calories (1% calories from fat),0 g total fat, 0 g saturated fat, 0.3 mg cholesterol, 9 mg sodium, 2 g carbohydrates, 0 g fiber, 0.6 g protein, 20 mg calcium, 0 mg iron

---

This beautiful summertime dessert is easy to make: just float your choice of colorful fresh fruit in a clear, slightly sweet "broth" of white grape juice spiked with crystallized ginger.

Sparkling Jewels Fruit Soup

Preparation time: About 10 minutes
Cooking time: About 5 minutes
Pictured on Page 411

Mixed Fruit
(suggestions follow)
2 tablespoons (30 ml) lemon juice
2 cups (470 ml) white grape juice
2 tablespoons minced crystallized ginger
3 tablespoons (45 ml) orange-flavored liqueur
Mint sprigs (optional)

1. Prepare fruit of your choice. Place fruit in a large bowl and mix gently with lemon juice. (At this point, you may cover and refrigerate for up to 2 hours.)

2. In a small pan, bring grape juice and ginger to a boil over high heat. Stir in liqueur; pour over fruit. Ladle soup

into bowls; garnish with mint sprigs, if desired. Makes 4 to 6 servings.

Mixed Fruit. You need 2½ cups (360 g) **fruit** *total.* We suggest using 1 large firm-ripe **kiwi fruit** (about 4 oz./ 115 g), peeled and thinly sliced; ½ cup (85 g) diced firm-ripe **nectarine** or peeled peach; ⅓ cup (48 g) fresh or frozen unsweetened **blueberries;** ⅓ cup (85 g) thinly sliced hulled **strawberries;** and ⅓ cup (55 g) very thinly sliced firm-ripe **plum.**

Per serving: 145 calories (2% calories from fat),0.3 g total fat, 0 g saturated fat, 0 mg cholesterol, 15 mg sodium, 33 g carbohydrates, 2 g fiber, 0.5 g protein, 24 mg calcium, 1 mg iron

Smooth, creamy, and studded with pistachios, this easy ice cream is sure to be a family favorite.

....

- 2 jars (about 7 oz./200 g *each*) marshmallow fluff (marshmallow creme)
- 1 large package (about 8 oz./ 230 g) Neufchâtel cheese, at room temperature
- ½ cup (120 ml) low-fat buttermilk
- 2 teaspoons vanilla
- 1 large carton (about 1 lb./ 455 g) nonfat sour cream
- ½ cup (60 g) shelled salted roasted pistachio nuts

Pistachio Ice Cream

....

Preparation time: 15 minutes
Chilling time: About 1 hour
Freezing time:
Depends on ice cream machine

1. In a food processor or blender, combine marshmallow fluff, Neufchâtel cheese, buttermilk, and vanilla. Whirl until smooth. Stir in sour cream.

2. Transfer mixture to a large bowl; cover and refrigerate until cold (about 1 hour) or until next day. Stir in pistachios.

3. Transfer mixture to container of a self-refrigerated ice cream machine and freeze according to manufacturer's instructions. Makes about 12 servings.

....

Per serving: 217 calories (30% calories from fat), 7 g total fat, 3 g saturated fat, 15 mg cholesterol, 146 mg sodium, 32 g carbohydrates, 0 g fiber, 7 g protein, 85 mg calcium, 0.5 mg iron

Rich and sweet, this ice cream is the perfect partner for our Chocolate Cherry Brownies (page 354).

....

- 2 jars (about 7 oz./200 g *each*) marshmallow fluff (marshmallow creme)
- 2 cups (470 ml) nonfat sour cream
- 1 large package (about 8 oz./ 230 g) nonfat cream cheese, at room temperature
- 1 cup (240 ml) low-fat (2%) milk
- 2 teaspoons vanilla
  About ¾ cup (180 ml) cherry preserves

Cherry-Vanilla Ice Cream

....

Preparation time: 10 minutes
Chilling time: At least 2 hours
Freezing time: Varies, depending on ice cream freezer used
Pictured on page 355

1. In a food processor or blender, combine about half each of the marshmallow fluff, sour cream, cream cheese, milk, and vanilla. Whirl until smooth, scraping sides of container often (some lumps of marshmallow fluff may remain, but they'll dissolve during freezing). Scrape into a large bowl.

Repeat to purée remaining marshmallow fluff, sour cream, cream cheese, milk, and vanilla; scrape into bowl.

2. Cover and refrigerate until cold (at least 2 hours) or until next day. Scrape mixture into an electric or ice- and salt-cooled ice cream maker; freeze according to manufacturer's instructions or until dasher is hard to crank.

3. Spoon preserves, a portion at a time, over ice cream; stir gently to swirl preserves into ice cream. Serve ice cream; or, if made ahead, pack into a container, cover, and freeze for up to 1 week. Makes about 8 servings.

....

Per serving: 310 calories (2% calories from fat), 0.7 g total fat, 0.4 g saturated fat, 5 mg cholesterol, 225 mg sodium, 67 g carbohydrates, 0.4 g fiber, 10 g protein, 200 mg calcium, 0.2 mg iron

For a cooling conclusion to a special meal, serve a simple, vividly colored ice made from a blend of port wine, orange juice, and aromatic bitters.

Port Ice

Preparation time: 10 minutes
Cooking time: About 5 minutes
Chilling & freezing time: About 5 hours

½ cup (100 g) sugar

1 cup (240 ml) port or cream sherry

¼ cup (60 ml) fresh orange juice

1 teaspoon aromatic bitters

1. In a 1- to 2-quart (950-ml to 1.9-liter) pan, combine sugar and 1½ cups (360 ml) water. Bring to a boil over high heat, stirring until sugar is dissolved. Remove from heat and let cool; then stir in port, orange juice, and bitters. Cover and refrigerate until cold (about 1 hour).

2. Pour port mixture into a metal pan 8 to 9 inches (20 to 23 cm) square; cover and freeze until solid (about 4 hours) or for up to 3 days.

3. To serve, break mixture into chunks with a heavy spoon, transfer to a blender or food processor, and whirl until slushy; then spoon into bowls and serve at once. (Or pour cold port mixture into container of a self-refrigerated ice cream machine and freeze according to manufacturer's instructions.) Makes 6 to 8 servings.

Per serving: 114 calories (0% calories from fat), 0 g total fat, 0 g saturated fat, 0 mg cholesterol, 3 mg sodium, 19 g carbohydrates, 0 g fiber, 0.1 g protein, 4 mg calcium, 0.1 mg iron

---

This refreshing ice of sweet vermouth and astringent Campari is a welcome hot-weather dessert—or an unusual starter for a special meal.

Campari Ice

Preparation time: 10 minutes
Cooking time: About 5 minutes
Chilling & freezing time: About 5 hours

½ cup (100 g) sugar

1 cup (240 ml) sweet vermouth or fresh orange juice

2 tablespoons (30 ml) Campari or 2 teaspoons aromatic bitters

1 tablespoon (15 ml) lime juice
Thin lime slices

1. In a 1- to 2-quart (950-ml to 1.9-liter) pan, combine sugar and 1½ cups (360 ml) water. Bring to a boil over high heat, stirring until sugar is dissolved. Remove from heat and let cool; then stir in vermouth, Campari, and lime juice. Cover mixture and refrigerate until cold (about 1 hour).

2. Pour mixture into a metal pan 8 to 9 inches (20 to 23 cm) square; cover and freeze until solid (about 4 hours) or for up to 3 days.

3. To serve, break mixture into chunks with a heavy spoon, transfer to a blender or food processor, and whirl until slushy; then spoon into bowls and serve at once. (Or pour cold port mixture into container of a self-refrigerated ice cream machine and freeze according to manufacturer's instructions.) Garnish individual servings with lime slices. Makes 6 to 8 servings.

Per serving: 120 calories (0% calories from fat), 0 g total fat, 0 g saturated fat, 0 mg cholesterol, 4 mg sodium, 20 g carbohydrates, 0 g fiber, 0 g protein, 3 mg calcium, 0.1 mg iron

For a pretty presentation, serve this creamy banana-mango sherbet in Frozen Citrus Bowls and accompany it with golden mango slices.

Frozen Citrus Bowls
(recipe follows)

5 or 6 medium-size firm-ripe mangoes (2½ to 3 lbs./1.15 to 1.35 kg *total*)

6 tablespoons (90 ml) lime juice

1 can (about 14 oz./400 g) mango nectar

1 jar (about 7 oz./200 g) marshmallow fluff (marshmallow creme)

2 medium-size ripe bananas (about 10 oz./285 g *total*)

½ cup (120 ml) low-fat (2%) milk

Mint sprigs (optional)

1. Prepare Frozen Citrus Bowls; keep frozen.

2. Peel 1 mango; thinly slice fruit from pit into a food processor or blender. Add 2 tablespoons (30 ml) of the lime juice. Then add half each of the mango nectar, marshmallow fluff, bananas, and milk. Whirl until smooth, scraping sides of container often; transfer to a bowl. Smoothly purée remaining mango nectar, marshmallow fluff, bananas, and milk; pour into bowl.

Tropical Sherbet

Preparation time: 1 hour
Cooking time: About 10 minutes
Chilling time: About 2 hours
(for Frozen Citrus Bowls)
Freezing time: About 2½ hours for Frozen Citrus Bowls, about 3 hours for sherbet
Pictured on facing page

3. Pour fruit mixture into a metal pan, 8 or 9 inches (20 or 23 cm) square. Cover and freeze until solid (about 3 hours) or for up to 1 week. Break into small chunks with a heavy spoon; whirl in a food processor or beat with an electric mixer until smooth. Serve; or, for firmer sherbet, freeze for up to 1 more hour. If made ahead, pack into containers, cover, and freeze for up to 1 week; before serving, whirl or beat until soft enough to scoop.

4. Just before serving, peel remaining 4 or 5 mangoes; thinly slice fruit from pits into a large bowl. Add remaining ¼ cup (60 ml) lime juice; mix gently to coat.

5. Serve sherbet in Frozen Citrus Bowls; garnish with mint sprigs, if desired. Drain mangoes and serve alongside. Makes 6 servings.

Per serving: 392 calories (3% calories from fat), 1 g total fat, 0.4 g saturated fat, 2 mg cholesterol, 39 mg sodium, 108 g carbohydrates, 2 g fiber, 4 g protein, 146 mg calcium, 2 mg iron

Frozen Citrus Bowls

In a 1- to 2-quart (950-ml to 1.9-liter) pan, combine ½ cup (100 g) **sugar** and ½ cup (120 ml) **water**. Bring to a boil over high heat, stirring occasionally. Remove from heat and let cool; then refrigerate until very cold (about 2 hours).

Meanwhile, with a sharp knife, cut 2 *each* **lemons, limes, and oranges** (or use all one kind of fruit) into even, paper-thin slices, ⅟16 to ⅛ inch (1.5 to 3 mm) thick. Line six 1½- to 2-cup (360- to 470-ml) bowls (2 to 2½ inches/5 to 6 cm deep) with plastic wrap. Selecting the prettiest citrus slices, dip them in cold sugar syrup; lift out slices and drain briefly, then use to line bottoms and sides of bowls snugly, overlapping as needed. Reserve any leftover syrup and citrus slices for other uses.

Wrap bowls airtight and freeze until fruit is firm (about 2½ hours) or for up to 1 week. To use, gently lift frozen citrus bowls from molds. Working quickly, peel off plastic wrap, place each bowl on a dessert plate, and fill with sherbet. Serve filled bowls immediately (they keep their shape for only about 15 minutes); or return to freezer for up to 1 hour, then serve. Makes 6 bowls.

Tropical Sherbet
(recipe on facing page)

Dips & Fondues

Dessert dips and fondues are sweet renditions of the more familiar savory variety. As ideal complements to fresh fruit, they are wonderful enticements to enjoy nature's own sweets.

Nonfat and low-fat dairy products lend a delectably creamy quality to our dips, while unsweetened cocoa powder delivers the impact of chocolate without the fat. Choose an array of unblemished, fully ripe fruits for a pretty and tempting display.

Lemon Curd Dip

Preparation time: 5 to 10 minutes

2 cups (470 ml) vanilla nonfat or low-fat yogurt

⅓ cup (80 ml) purchased lemon curd

1 teaspoon grated lemon peel

Large whole strawberries, preferably with stems

1. In a medium-size bowl, combine yogurt, lemon curd, and lemon peel; stir until well blended. If made ahead, cover and refrigerate until next day. To serve, transfer dip to a serving bowl; place on a tray and surround with strawberries for dipping. Makes about 2⅓ cups (550 ml), 6 to 8 servings.

Per serving: 106 calories (21% calories from fat), 2 g total fat, 1 g saturated fat, 21 mg cholesterol, 72 mg sodium, 17 g carbohydrates, 0 g fiber, 4 g protein, 98 mg calcium, 0.1 mg iron

Caramel Dip

Preparation time: 5 to 10 minutes

2 cups (470 ml) nonfat, reduced-fat, or regular sour cream

⅓ cup (80 ml) purchased caramel topping

1 tablespoon minced fresh ginger

Crisp apple or pear wedges

1. In a medium-size bowl, combine sour cream, caramel topping, and ginger; stir until well blended. If made ahead, cover and refrigerate until next day. To serve, transfer to a serving bowl; place on a tray and surround with apple wedges for dipping. Makes about 2⅓ cups (550 ml), 6 to 8 servings.

Per serving: 85 calories (0.1% calories from fat), 0.01 g total fat, 0.01 g saturated fat, 0 mg cholesterol, 100 mg sodium, 15 g carbohydrates, 0 g fiber, 5 g protein, 95 mg calcium, 0 mg iron

Hot Cocoa-Mocha Fondue

Preparation time: 10 minutes
Cooking time: About 5 minutes

1 cup (220 g) firmly packed brown sugar

½ cup (43 g) unsweetened cocoa powder

2 tablespoons cornstarch

1 teaspoon instant coffee powder

¼ cup (60 ml) light corn syrup

1 teaspoon vanilla

2 tablespoons (30 ml) crème de cacao (optional)

Angel food cake cubes, tangerine segments, banana slices, pear wedges, whole strawberries, and/or sweet cherries with stems

1. In a 1½-quart (1.4-liter) pan, combine sugar, cocoa, cornstarch, and instant coffee; stir to blend well. Gradually blend in corn syrup and 1 cup (240 ml) water, stirring until smooth. Then cook over medium-high heat, stirring constantly, until mixture boils and thickens (about 5 minutes).

2. Remove pan from heat and stir in vanilla and, if desired, crème de cacao. Pour fondue into a heatproof serving bowl over a candle warmer or into a small electric slow cooker. Spear cubes of cake and fruits with fondue forks or bamboo skewers and dip into warm fondue; stir fondue occasionally. Makes about 2 cups (470 ml), 8 servings.

Per serving: 154 calories (4% calories from fat), 0.7 g total fat, 0.4 g saturated fat, 0 mg cholesterol, 24 mg sodium, 40 g carbohydrates, 2 g fiber, 1 g protein, 31 mg calcium, 1 mg iron

Creamy Gingered Cheese Dip

Preparation time: 5 minutes

....

1½ cups (315 g) low-fat (2%) cottage cheese

¼ cup (30 g) powdered sugar

1 tablespoon (15 ml) lemon juice

1 teaspoon vanilla

2 tablespoons chopped preserved ginger in syrup

2 tablespoons (30 ml) nonfat milk

Large whole strawberries, preferably with stems

....

1. In a food processor or blender, combine cottage cheese, sugar, lemon juice, vanilla, ginger, and milk. Whirl until smooth; scrape down sides of container occasionally

2. Transfer dip to a serving bowl. If made ahead, cover and refrigerate until next day. To serve, place bowl of dip on a tray and surround with strawberries for dipping. Makes about 1¾ cups (420 ml), 6 to 8 servings.

Per serving: 80 calories (11% calories from fat), 0.9 g total fat, 0.6 g saturated fat, 4 mg cholesterol, 202 mg sodium, 11 g carbohydrates, 0 g fiber, 7 g protein, 49 mg calcium, 1 mg iron

Hot Cranberry Fondue

Preparation time: 10 minutes
Cooking time: About 15 minutes

....

1 cup (90 g) dried cranberries

1 cup (240 ml) ruby port

⅔ cup (133 g) sugar

1 cinnamon stick (about 3 inches/8 cm long)

1 tablespoon grated orange peel

2 tablespoons (30 ml) orange-flavored liqueur (optional)

Crisp tart apple wedges

....

1. In a 1½- to 2-quart (1.4- to 1.9-liter) pan, combine cranberries, port, ½ cup (120 ml) water, sugar, cinnamon stick, and orange peel. Bring to a boil over medium-high heat, stirring until sugar is dissolved. Then continue to cook until mixture is reduced to about 1½ cups (360 ml), about 15 minutes; stir occasionally at first, more often as mixture thickens toward end of cooking time.

2. Remove from heat and stir in liqueur, if desired. Remove and discard cinnamon stick. Transfer mixture to a blender or food processor and whirl until coarsely puréed. Pour fondue into a heatproof serving bowl over a candle warmer or into a small electric slow cooker. Pick up apple wedges with your fingers (or spear them with fondue forks or bamboo skewers) and dip into warm fondue. Makes about 1½ cups (360 ml), 6 servings.

Per serving: 209 calories (1% calories from fat), 0.3 g total fat, 0 g saturated fat, 0 mg cholesterol, 4 mg sodium, 42 g carbohydrates, 1 g fiber, 0.01 g protein, 7 mg calcium, 0.2 mg iron

Chocolate Soufflés
(recipe on facing page)

Top off a cold-weather meal with these fudgy individual soufflés.

··

- ⅔ cup (57 g) unsweetened cocoa powder

  About ¾ cup (150 g) granulated sugar

- 4 teaspoons cornstarch

- 1 teaspoon instant espresso or coffee powder

- 1 cup (240 ml) low-fat (2%) milk

- 2 ounces (55 g) bittersweet or semisweet chocolate, finely chopped

- 2 teaspoons vanilla

- 7 large egg whites, at room temperature

- ¼ teaspoon cream of tartar

- ¹⁄₁₆ to ⅛ teaspoon salt

  About 2 tablespoons powdered sugar

Chocolate Soufflés

··

Preparation time: 20 minutes
Cooking time: About 30 minutes
Pictured on facing page

1. In a 1½- to 2-quart (1.4- to 1.9-liter) pan, stir together cocoa, ¼ cup (50 g) of the granulated sugar, cornstarch, and instant espresso. Whisk in milk. Cook over medium heat, whisking constantly, until mixture boils and thickens slightly (about 1 minute). Remove from heat and add chocolate and vanilla; whisk until chocolate is melted and mixture is smooth. Let cool completely.

2. While mixture cools, lightly grease six 1½-cup (360-ml) custard cups; sprinkle each lightly with granulated sugar to coat bottom. Place cups in a large baking pan and set aside.

3. In a deep bowl, beat egg whites with an electric mixer on high speed until frothy. Add cream of tartar, salt, and ½ cup (100 g) of the granulated sugar, 1 tablespoon at a time; beat until whites hold firm, moist peaks. Stir about a third of the whites into cooled chocolate mixture; then fold chocolate mixture into remaining whites.

4. Gently fill custard cups equally with batter. Position oven rack in bottom third of a 350°F (175°C) oven; set baking pan on rack. Pour boiling water into pan around cups up to level of batter. Bake until soufflés are puffy and feel firm when gently pressed (about 25 minutes). Carefully lift cups from pan and sprinkle soufflés with powdered sugar. Serve immediately. Makes 6 servings.

··

Per serving: 238 calories (23% calories from fat), 7 g total fat, 3 g saturated fat, 3 mg cholesterol, 122 mg sodium, 42 g carbohydrates, 3 g fiber, 8 g protein, 69 mg calcium, 2 mg iron

---

This soufflé owes its intense almond flavor to crushed amaretti cookies, amaretto liqueur, and almond extract.

··

- ½ cup (64 g) coarsely crushed amaretti cookies (about ten 1½-inch/4-cm cookies)

- ¾ cup (180 ml) low-fat (2%) milk

- 3 large egg yolks

- 6 tablespoons (72 g) granulated sugar

- ¼ cup (30 g) all-purpose flour

- ¼ cup (60 ml) almond-flavored or other nut-flavored liqueur

- ⅛ teaspoon almond extract

- 5 large egg whites

- ½ teaspoon cream of tartar

- ⅛ teaspoon salt

  About 1 tablespoon sifted powdered sugar

··

1. Sprinkle crushed cookies over bottom of a greased 1½- to 1¾-quart (1.4- to 1.7-liter) soufflé dish. Place dish in

Amaretto Soufflé

··

Preparation time: 25 minutes
Cooking time: About 35 minutes

a larger pan (at least 2 inches/5 cm deep); set aside.

2. Bring milk to a boil in a medium-size nonstick pan over medium heat (about 5 minutes), stirring often. Remove from heat and let cool slightly.

3. In a large bowl, whisk egg yolks and 3 tablespoons of the granulated sugar until thick and lemon-colored. Add flour and whisk until smoothly blended. Whisk in a little of the warm milk, then whisk egg yolk mixture back into warm milk in pan. Return to heat and stir constantly (be careful not to scratch pan) just until mixture boils and thickens slightly. Return to large bowl and whisk in liqueur and almond extract; let cool completely.

4. In a clean large, deep bowl, beat egg whites and 1 tablespoon (15 ml) water with an electric mixer on high speed until frothy. Beat in cream of tartar and salt. Then beat in remaining 3 tablespoons granulated sugar, 1 tablespoon at a time; continue to beat until mixture holds stiff, moist peaks. Stir about a third of the egg white mixture into yolk mixture; then fold all of yolk mixture into egg white mixture.

5. Gently spoon soufflé batter into prepared dish. Set pan with dish on middle rack of a 350°F (175°C) oven. Pour boiling water into larger pan up to level of soufflé batter. Bake until soufflé is richly browned and center jiggles only slightly when dish is gently shaken (about 25 minutes); if top begins to brown excessively, carefully cover dish with foil. As soon as soufflé is done, sprinkle it with powdered sugar and serve immediately. Makes 6 servings.

··

Per serving: 198 calories (21% calories from fat), 4 g total fat, 1 g saturated fat, 109 mg cholesterol, 115 mg sodium, 29 g carbohydrates, 0.1 g fiber, 6 g protein, 51 mg calcium, 0.5 mg iron

A perfect partner for hot coffee at any time of day, popular tiramisu features a filling of sweet, creamy cheese spooned over ladyfingers soaked in brandy and espresso. Garnish the dessert with chocolate curls and a dusting of cocoa before serving.

....

- 20 **ladyfingers (about 5 oz./ 140 g *total*)**
- ⅔ **cup (67 g) sifted powdered sugar**
- 6 **ounces (170 g) nonfat cream cheese, at room temperature**
- 2 **ounces (55 g) mascarpone cheese, at room temperature**
- 2 **cups (470 ml) frozen reduced-calorie whipped topping, thawed**
- 9 **tablespoons (108 g) granulated sugar**
- 3 **large egg whites**
- ¼ **teaspoon cream of tartar**
- 1 **tablespoon instant espresso powder**
- 2 **tablespoons (30 ml) brandy, coffee-flavored liqueur, or orange juice**

    About 2 tablespoons unsweetened cocoa powder

    Semisweet chocolate curls

Tiramisu

....

Preparation time: 25 minutes
Cooking time: About 5 minutes
Chilling time: At least 3 hours

1. Split ladyfingers into halves. Arrange half the ladyfinger halves, cut side up, over bottom of a square 8-inch (20-cm) dish or pan; overlap ladyfingers as needed to fit. Set aside.

2. In a food processor or a large bowl, combine powdered sugar, cream cheese, and mascarpone cheese. Whirl or beat with an electric mixer until smooth. Gently fold in 1 cup (240 ml) of the whipped topping; cover and refrigerate.

3. In a large metal bowl, combine ½ cup (100 g) of the granulated sugar, ¼ cup (60 ml) water, egg whites, and cream of tartar. Beat with an electric mixer on low speed until foamy. Nest bowl over a pan of simmering water (do not let bowl touch water) and beat on high speed until mixture holds stiff peaks. Lift bowl from pan; stir about a fourth of the egg white mixture into cheese mixture to lighten it, then gently but thoroughly fold in remaining egg white mixture. Set aside.

4. Working quickly, stir together ½ cup (120 ml) hot water, remaining 1 tablespoon sugar, instant espresso, and brandy in a small bowl. Drizzle half the hot espresso mixture evenly over ladyfingers in dish. Top with half the cheese mixture, spreading mixture level. Top with remaining ladyfinger halves (cut side up), espresso mixture, and cheese mixture. Cover with remaining 1 cup (240 ml) whipped topping and smooth top.

5. Cover dessert airtight (do not let cover touch topping) and refrigerate until cold (at least 3 hours) or until next day. Spoon out of dish or cut to serve. Sift cocoa over individual servings and garnish with chocolate curls. Makes 8 servings.

....

Per serving: 261 calories (25% calories from fat), 7 g total fat, 3 g saturated fat, 77 mg cholesterol, 153 mg sodium, 40 g carbohydrates, 0.3 g fiber, 7 g protein, 71 mg calcium, 0.8 mg iron

Index

426 Index

Index 431